# MANAGERIAL ACCOUNTING

Costing, Decision-making
and Control

# MANAGERIAL ACCOUNTING

## Costing, Decision-making and Control

2nd Edition

By

## Peter Clarke

Chartered Accountants Ireland

Published by
Chartered Accountants Ireland
Chartered Accountants House
47-49 Pearse Street
Dublin 2
www.charteredaccountants.ie

ISBN: 978-1-907214-24-0

Typeset by Datapage
Printed by ColourBooks

# Contents

# Preface

The essence of management is decision-making and the making of good decisions requires relevant and understandable information. Management accounting exists in order to influence managerial decision-making. Throughout this book, two important themes are stressed. The first theme is concerned with the type of information that is required by managers. This is a technical matter and the type of information required will vary with the nature of the decision and who has decision responsibility. The second theme is concerned with the response by managers to that information. This is a behavioural issue. Thus, good management accounting information should be technically correct and generate the appropriate response from managers.

## Aims

This book aims to meet the needs of students of management accounting and it can be used for those preparing for professional accountancy examination or those studying managerial accounting at undergraduate or postgraduate levels. Practising business managers may also find this book useful. It attempts to explain the conceptual basis of management accounting and covers the key areas in suitable depth. It describes the variety of techniques available to provide relevant information to managers. Each chapter contains illustrations of these techniques.

## Contents

The contents of this book can be loosely divided into three sections. The first section deals with various aspects of costing. Initially, **Chapter 1** provides an introduction to accounting information and decision-making. **Chapters 2**, **3** and **4** provide an overview of what can be referred to as traditional cost accumulation systems. **Chapter 2** examines the general principles by which costs are accumulated and classified within an organisation including the technique of overhead absorption. **Chapters 3** and **4** outline two specific cost accumulation techniques, namely, job-costing and process-costing systems respectively. In recent times, these traditional product-costing systems have been the subject of much criticism. Specifically, it is argued that the traditional method of absorbing overheads into products should be replaced by an Activity-Based Costing (ABC) system. The topic of ABC is discussed in **Chapter 5**, as is the relevance of Activity-Based Cost Management (ABCM). **Chapter 6** reviews certain refinements to cost accumulation systems arising from adopting a World-Class Manufacturing (WCM) philosophy.

Section 2 consists of **Chapters 7** to **13** (inclusive) and these are concerned with specific aspects of managerial decision-making. Initially, **Chapter 7** looks at the importance of strategy in decision-making and its relevance to management accounting and **Chapter 8** deals with the strategy-related topic of performance measurement and management. **Chapters 9**, **10** and **11** deal with profit planning, together with a variety of decision-making situations including pricing and decision-making with scarce resources. **Chapter 12** covers the area of decision-making under risk and uncertainty and **Chapter 13** discusses the long term nature and techniques of capital expenditure proposals.

The third section of the book is represented by the final three chapters dealing with different aspects of performance evaluation and control. **Chapter 14** discusses the issue of control with the emphasis on budgetary control and flexible budgeting. **Chapter 15** is devoted to standard costing systems and shows how important cost variances can be computed. Variances represent important signals that require managerial attention and action. Finally, **Chapter 16** investigates how organisations can be viewed as a collection of different responsibility centres, each of which requires to be evaluated with reference to appropriate performance metrics.

## Acknowledgements

This book could not have been completed without the help and encouragement of many individuals who need to be acknowledged. Generations of UCD students have contributed, unconsciously, to this publication. Michael Diviney provided support and encouragement. Pat Bond of Thomson Learning kindly agreed to allow me to revise and include here some material previously used in *Accounting Information for Managers*.

Finally, this book is dedicated to Kieran Lyons without whose vision, encouragement and commitment it would never have been written. He is sorely missed by many but not forgotten. This text memorialises his significant contribution to accounting education in Ireland.

**Peter Clarke**
**Dublin**
**September 2010**

# Managerial Decision-making and Accounting Information

When you have completed studying this chapter you should be able to:

1. Define the role of the management accountant in organisations
2. Distinguish between managerial and financial accounting
3. Outline the evolution of managerial accounting as a practical and academic discipline
4. Describe current developments in managerial accounting
5. Write a properly formatted memorandum

## 1.1 Introduction to Accounting Information

It may come as a surprise to readers that the discipline and role of accounting has been defined in many ways during the years. However, it is now recognised that the task of accounting is to record, report and interpret information (mainly financial) about a business entity, which is considered relevant to various interested parties (i.e. users) in order to influence their decisions. Thus, the purpose of all accounting information is to help someone make decisions about a business entity or a segment of that entity. This focus was given significant impetus by the American Accounting Association's 1966 publication that defined accounting as the:

"process of identifying, measuring and communicating economic information to permit informed judgements and decisions by the users of the information".

Some recent definitions of accounting have expanded the attributes of 'economic information' to include non-financial information. At this stage it is worthwhile to briefly highlight two points. First, there are many sources and types of information available to decision-makers, of which accounting information is but one. Secondly, we can make a distinction between **information** and **data**, even though we use the terms interchangeably.

**Data** can be defined in terms of the raw material to be organised for subsequent analysis and relates to facts, events and transactions. Data can be classified as either quantitative or qualitative. **Quantitative data** consists of numbers representing measurements, e.g. hours required to produce one unit of output. Much quantitative data within an accounting system will be expressed in financial terms, e.g. cost per unit. In contrast, **qualitative data** describes in a subjective manner, rather than measures, certain characteristics, e.g. staff morale.

**Information** can be defined as 'data that has been processed in such a way that it is meaningful to the end user'.

In summary, data represent mere facts gathered on a particular phenomenon and will include financial statistics such as cost per unit and non-financial measures such as hours worked. Information, on the other hand, represents data that has a surprise effect on the user and has decision relevance. Thus, given a decision to make, one gathers the data and organises it into information. In other words, it is this human intervention that translates data into information. If the result is something that can affect user's decisions, then we have created information out of data. For accounting information to have any utility to the modern business world, it must be decision-orientated, i.e. it must influence users' decisions regarding a business entity, or a segment of that entity, for which the information is being reported.

This orientation of accounting information poses the question: who are the users of accounting information? The answer to this question is explored in the section below.


## Users of Accounting Information

Users of accounting information are usually classified by groups, and the main user groups or stakeholders are presented in **Exhibit 1.1** below. The purpose of this exhibit is to argue that business entities do not exist in a vacuum – rather they are resource dependent and can only exist provided they receive an adequate contribution (or input) from each user group. In return, user groups expect to receive something from the firm in the future. The decision by individual users to contribute to the firm, or not, will be influenced, to a large extent, by relevant accounting information relating to the business. However, it should be acknowledged that other types of information may also influence the decisions of various stakeholders.

The relationship between each user group and the firm will now be discussed in turn. This relationship is facilitated by the discipline of financial accounting or financial reporting.

EXHIBIT 1.1: USERS OF ACCOUNTING INFORMATION

| Providers of finance | |
|---|---|
| Shareholders | Loan Creditors |

| Providers of labour | |
|---|---|
| Employees | Trade Unions |

Managers of the firm

| Providers of goods | |
|---|---|
| Trade creditors (suppliers) | |

| Providers of demand | |
|---|---|
| Trade debtors (customers) | |

### Providers of finance: Shareholders

Shareholders provide share capital to the business in the form of cash. They will be interested in the financial benefit that they expect to receive in the future. These benefits may be in the form of cash dividends and/or increase in the market value of the business. In evaluating investment opportunities, shareholders will be interested in the earnings stream of the company and the portion paid out to shareholders by way of dividend. In addition, they will be concerned with the current and future market value of their shares in the company. They will also be interested in the performance of other companies who are offering greater or lesser returns.

Based on past performance shareholders may make estimates of likely future profits of the company and the dividends that can be paid out of such profits. Information on the firm's future cash inflows and future cash outflows would also be relevant to shareholders. Without adequate cash flows, a firm cannot survive in the long term – no matter how skilled the managers and employees.

### Providers of finance: Loan Creditors

Loan creditors are those individuals or institutions that provide (repayable) finance by way of cash loans to the company. The concern of the loan creditor is twofold. First, they are concerned whether future interest payments can be made by the firm and secondly, whether the loan can be repaid on maturity. Loan creditors will be interested in the company's profitability and cash flow. They will also be interested in the availability of security for their loans and whether the company has any other loans due to be repaid.

### Providers of finance: Trade Creditors

Trade creditors supply goods and services to the company and they are interested in the ability of the company to pay the amount owing to them without delay. Consequently, trade creditors will focus on the future cash flows of the firm. The excess of cash or near cash assets compared with the immediate obligations of the firm provides an indication of the liquidity of the company. They will also be interested in the time taken by the company to pay its bills and whether this credit period is static, increasing or decreasing compared with previous accounting periods.

### Providers of labour: Employees

It is natural that employees, and their trade union representatives, should want information about the cost structures, salaries, bonuses and profitability of their companies, together with comparative information about other companies. This information is, for example, essential to wage negotiation. However, employees are also concerned with matters other than monetary gain. They are interested in challenge, reward for and recognition of their services, together with job security.

### Providers of demand: Customers

Not all customers are interested in accounting information about the firm before buying goods. For example, we purchase our daily newspaper without asking to see financial information about the vendor! However, some customers may be interested in the analysis and interpretation of the financial reports produced by companies from whom they are intending to purchase goods or services. Usually their interest will be to establish the overall profitability of the supplier, as this may provide some indication of pricing practices and, perhaps, previous overcharging by the supplier. Also, customers may be interested in knowing whether the company will continue to operate in future years as this would indicate whether a back-up service, together with replacement goods, will be available from that company. Furthermore, some customers may be interested in obtaining information on the company's social responsibility (CSR) and whether it is paying adequate prices to its third-world suppliers and employees.

### Managers of the firm

In the middle of **Exhibit 1.1** (see above) are the managers of the firm. Managers are very important users of accounting information; their information needs and their decision-making is the focus of this book, and this represents the discipline of managerial accounting. The decisions that business managers make have enormous significance for the business entity itself, for its shareholders, creditors, employees, and for customers. Though the key element in their decision-making process is information, it should also be acknowledged that some managerial decisions are made purely on the basis of intuition or inspiration.

The likelihood of making a good decision is increased by using available accounting information. Nevertheless, one should appreciate that accounting information has its limitations, e.g. information about future demand for a company's products will always be subject to an element of unreliability because the future itself is uncertain. In addition, product cost information, as we shall see throughout this book, may be calculated in different ways.

It is important to stress that the distinction between financial and management accounting is sometimes made for teaching convenience. The reality is sometimes different. A manager is interested in financial accounting reports, e.g. the overall financial position of his company. Also, a potential financier may be interested in a specific piece of information, e.g. the break-even point of a particular proposal for funding. In other words, **all accounting information may be relevant to managers**. The relevance of the information will be determined by the decision being made.

Nevertheless, there are a number of distinguishing features between financial and management accounting and these are highlighted below in **Exhibit 1.2**. However, it is the intended users of accounting information that primarily distinguish between the separate disciplines of financial and management accounting.

Much of its financial and management accounting information is derived from the same accounting system within an organisation. Essentially, it is the way that the accounting information is presented to different users, and the circulation or availability of that information that distinguishes financial from management accounting.

Thus, management accounting information is presented by way of an internal document that is primarily intended for managerial, i.e. internal, use only. Financial accounting information is usually presented in a document that is primarily intended to be circulated outside the firm, i.e. for external use. Nevertheless, one must expect that accounting information would be of interest to many users. For example, internal sales reports may be shared with people external to the business for a variety of reasons. Similarly, annual financial statements are of immediate relevance to managers. Furthermore, while financial accounting reports are required by law for most business entities, management accounting information is discretionary. In other words, management accounting information is not mandatory: rather, managerial accounting exists because the information it provides is considered useful by managers.

EXHIBIT 1.2: DIFFERENCE BETWEEN FINANCIAL AND MANAGEMENT ACCOUNTING

| Source of difference | Financial | Management |
|---|---|---|
| Primary users of accounting information | External to company, e.g. shareholders | Internal users, i.e. managers |
| Type of information | Financial summaries, i.e.<br>• Balance sheet<br>• Income statement<br>• Cash flow | Very detailed and includes both financial and non-financial information |
| Reporting period | Typically an annual basis | As required by managers, e.g. daily if necessary |
| Time orientation of information | Historical orientation | Both historical and future orientation |
| Format of reports | Regulated by legislation and increasingly by International Financial Reporting Standards (IFRS) | Not regulated by legislation or IFRS |

## 1.2  The Role of the Management Accountant

In the previous section we discussed the different user groups, i.e. shareholders, creditors, employees, and customers, and we described them as being **external** to the organisation in the sense that they take no active part in the day-to-day management of the firm. Their information needs should be satisfied by annual financial accounting reports which would enable participants to decide whether to continue or terminate their involvement with the firm.

The three principal statements of the financial accounting process are the income statement, the cash flow statement and the balance sheet (statement of financial position). The income statement (or profit and loss account) reports the performance of a business in relation to its expenses and sales revenues and profit (or loss) over a period of time. The cash flow statement reports the inflow and outflow of cash funds during an accounting period. All outflows, whether of a capital (e.g. purchase of fixed assets) or revenue (e.g. payment of wages) nature are reported. The balance sheet reports the financial position of an organisation at the year-end, i.e. the resources that are controlled by the organisation (assets) and how those assets have been financed by either equity or liabilities.

Conversely, the final group of users, i.e. managers, are **internal** to the organisation in the sense that they are responsible for the day-to-day functioning of the company. Thus, information will be reported to managers more frequently and regularly than to any of the other user groups.

Managers need information for a variety of decisions and the formal provision of this information represents the discipline of managerial accounting. This information set comprises both financial and non-financial data. Thus, management accounting is, essentially, a practical discipline and it has evolved over the decades as a subject in its own right (and as a professional accountancy qualification) simply because of its utilitarian nature. It is also a very broad discipline, with undefined borders due to the different types of managers within organisations with a range of different responsibilities, and also because of the different decisions that they are required to make. In addition, these decisions can have either short-term or long-term consequences.

Managers of the business enterprise will analyse and interpret accounting information for the purpose of planning and controlling the performance of the company. We will use the terms 'planning' and 'control' extensively throughout this textbook. In brief, planning is the process of deciding on goals and objectives and how to achieve them. Controlling is the process of monitoring results against targets and deciding on suitable corrective action, if appropriate. The use of accounting information by managers to plan and control the activities of a business comprises Management or Managerial Accounting. It is crucial to stress that one can only attempt to control a phenomenon or event either before it has happened or while it is in the process of happening. Once an event has happened it cannot be controlled. Thus, reporting actual performance after the expiry of the accounting period cannot facilitate the control process for that accounting period; the information is too late for the current period but it could be used in formulating plans and actions for future periods.

At a basic level, the difference between management planning and management control decisions can be appreciated from the following simple questions presented in **Exhibit 1.3** below.

EXHIBIT 1.3: BASIC DIFFERENCES BETWEEN PLANNING AND CONTROL DECISIONS

| Planning decisions | Control decisions |
|---|---|
| What will be the cost of offering a new course for the University? | Is the cost of the new course in line with projections? |
| What selling price should be charged for a new product? | Why was the actual selling price, on average, less than budget? |
| How many meals must the restaurant serve to break-even? | Why was the number of meals sold less than expected? |

To summarise: managerial accounting is concerned with providing information to managers in order to help them in planning and controlling the operations of the company. In reality, management planning and control decisions should be viewed as a continuum and are very much interrelated. Planning occurs before control since, in the absence of objectives and plans, control is meaningless. Moreover, setting easy plans would ensure that the performance of the organisation will always be deemed to be 'in control'. Furthermore, it makes little sense for an organisation to spend time and money in preparing plans for the future if it does not monitor progress towards them.

### Characteristics of Good Management Accounting Information

In order to be useful for decision-making, management accounting information must possess at least five characteristics as follows:

- **Relevant** This means that accounting information must relate to the decision being considered. Thus, information may be relevant to one particular decision but not to another. Likewise, information may be relevant to one user group but not to another. It goes without saying that information should be communicated to the right person within the organisation. The user and the decision being taken ultimately determines relevance. Information has the quality of relevance when it influences the economic decisions of the users by helping them evaluate past, present or future events.
- **Understandable** Managers can only use information to good effect if they understand its message. If managers do not understand accounting information then it is of little use to them. It is important to present accounting information in such a way that it is comprehensible to the less informed user without omitting information which would be of value to the informed user. Thus, the level and skill of the receiving manager is an important consideration.

- **Accurate** If accounting information is not accurate then misinformed decisions by the user will inevitably result. To be accurate, the accounting information must represent fairly the effect of the transactions it reports and the information must be complete. However, since a great amount of management accounting information deals with future estimates, its accuracy can always be questioned. Also, there is an inevitable trade-off between timely and accurate information – to get information that is entirely accurate may impose unacceptable time delays.
- **Timely** For effective decisions to be taken, information needs to be reported to management on a timely basis. Accounting information that is not up to date is of little use for decision-making. For example, a budgetary control or standard costing report containing adverse variances would need to be timely for managers to take immediate corrective action. Likewise, if a favourable position was reported 'late', the reward and recognition to employees may be delayed and thereby affect morale. However, as noted above, the need to ensure accuracy of accounting information may impact on the timeliness of its reporting to managers. Thankfully, modern computer technology enables real-time information to be available to managers.
- **Consistent in preparation and format** If management accounting reports are not prepared on a consistent basis, then meaningful comparisons between performance in different time periods is virtually impossible. This characteristic also implies that business segments of the same entity should adopt similar accounting practices. In addition, this characteristic requires that any change in the measurement and presentation of accounting information should be properly disclosed.

## 1.3 Evolution of Management Accounting

Before we discuss the main information required by managers for decision-making, and various managerial accounting techniques and systems, it is worthwhile to briefly describe how the discipline of management accounting developed. While the origin of financial accounting can be traced back over a thousand years, the origin of management accounting is relatively more recent.

Many, but not all accounting historians, consider the development of management accounting as one of the many consequences of the Industrial Revolution. The main reason for its development was the change in the way that economic activity was organised around that time. Prior to the Industrial Revolution there was no incentive to produce goods other than those that could be easily distributed using existing, primitive methods of transport. The period of canal construction and the subsequent railway boom greatly improved transportation systems and encouraged small manufacturers to increase production levels. Improved transport systems coincided with improved methods and volumes of production.

The manufacturing firms of the Industrial Revolution – especially in the textile industry – were among the first in history to centralise, into a single location, the conversion of raw materials into finished goods. Prior to the Industrial Revolution, an entrepreneur bought raw materials, such as cotton, on the open market and he provided these materials to independent household artisans. Using equipment they owned or rented, the artisans transformed the raw goods into finished yarn or fabric. The merchant would then compensate the artisan according to market-determined piece rates, and he sold the finished goods on the open market. Market-based prices supplied all the information required for managerial decision-making.

With the advent of mass production, accurate internal conversion cost information needed to be determined and this laid the foundation for what is often referred to as 'cost accounting'. The managers of large-scale production enterprises were concerned with the efficiency and productivity of employees, since many, if not all, were paid on a piece-rate basis. By the late 1800s, iron and steel, chemical and machinery manufacturing became vastly more complex and capital intensive. This fuelled the need for additional cost information both for managerial decision-making and also stock valuation purposes, since unsold stock at the end of the accounting period was required for financial reporting purposes and was usually valued at cost of production. Despite this, however, the widespread adoption of cost accounting techniques in the late 1800s was still slow. There are a number of possible explanations for this:

- Cost accountants were inclined to keep their costing methods secret so that competitors could not adopt them. This attitude obviously prevented the spread of new ideas.
- Books and journal articles on this emerging topic were comparatively rare and this prevented the discussion and diffusion of internal accounting ideas and techniques.
- The absence of cost accounting societies or professional organisations further restricted publicity and debate. Even when these professional accountancy bodies – mainly the Institutes of Chartered Accountants – were formed in the late Nineteenth Century, it would take a number of years for the subject of cost or managerial accounting to be formally included in their curricula and examined.

The First World War, however, ensured that cost accounting was a subject to be taken more seriously. There were vast amounts of profits to be earned from securing government contracts. This obviously required realistic and competitive pricing. War was a costly business and governments disliked cost overruns. Therefore, cost accumulation techniques and cost control within munitions firms became crucial. At the end of the War, cost accountants had reached sufficient stature within their organisations to form their own professional bodies. In the UK, the Institute of Cost and Works Accountants was formed in 1919 and is now referred to as the Chartered Institute of Management Accountants. In the same year, its American equivalent – the National Association of Cost Accountants – was also formed. Both professional bodies gradually promoted developments in cost accountancy. (At time of writing, the major professional organisations for management accounting in the world are the Chartered Institute of Management Accountants in the UK, the Institute of Management Accountants in the US and the Society of Management Accountants in Canada, and all have worldwide membership.)

## Management Accounting

The application of economic thinking to accounting also began to change cost accounting during the 1930s, mainly due to the work of academics. *Studies in the Economics of Overhead Costs* (University of Chicago Press, 1923) by American economist, **John Maurice Clark**, was a particularly important contribution. Clark extensively discussed the nature of overhead costs and their use in managerial decisions. He pointed out that overhead costs – defined as 'costs that cannot be traced to particular units of output' – are all-pervasive and he predicted that overheads were likely to continue to grow in importance. In relation to the analysis of costs he coined the phrase 'different costs for different purposes' which could be reworded to suggest that managers need different information for different purposes. Clark was calling attention to the fact that historical cost information must, necessarily, be revised and amended to make it suitable for decision-making. He argued that cost calculation depends on the particular purpose for which it is required, and pointed out that:

> "If cost accounting sets out, determined to discover what the cost of everything is and convinced in advance that there is one figure which can be found and which will furnish exactly the information which is required for every possible purpose, it will necessarily fail, because there is no such figure. If it finds a figure which is right for some purpose, it must necessarily be wrong for others."

From the 1930s onwards, businesses paid increased attention to using cost information in assisting managerial decision-making. In addition to refining existing cost accounting systems, firms began to introduce budgetary control systems together with standard costing systems. Profit planning, based on the simple concept of cost behaviour relative to volume changes, was increasingly applied and gave rise to the 'absorption v. direct' controversy, which still remains in management accounting. In addition, prompted by the writings of **Dean** in the 1950s, discounted cash flow techniques were being adopted by firms when making capital expenditure decisions.

There were other considerations also emerging. One such consideration was the acknowledgement that management accounting systems were costly to develop and maintain. Organisations worldwide increasingly devote resources to their accounting and information systems. Nevertheless, accounting information should be viewed as an economic good, which is obtainable at a cost and different amounts of information are available at different costs. Thus, the cost of information must be related to its value. Information can only have value if it influences human behaviour to make better decisions. On the other hand, if accounting information does not influence behaviour, then it has no value.

Secondly, from the 1950s onwards, and arising from the work of **Argyris**, the behavioural dimension of management accounting information was increasingly noted. For example, it was accepted that budgeting within organisations was not just a technical exercise; it also had important behavioural implications. Thus, anyone studying the discipline of management accounting must be aware of its potential and actual behavioural consequences. This influence may be positive in the sense that it encourages people to make decisions to achieve the goals of the organisation. This phenomenon is often referred to as 'goal congruence'. However, accounting systems can also have negative, adverse or dysfunctional consequences such as creating tension and anxiety among employees. Also, inappropriate behaviour can result by placing too much reliance on budgets, such as reducing the marketing spend to achieve short-term profit targets. In such a case, it is possible that the short-term profit target has been achieved at the expense of the long-term strategic position of the firm. Thus, the discipline of management accounting should not be viewed as a purely technical phenomenon but in the context of group and individual goals and the complex workings of modern organisations.

During the 1960s these developments received even wider exposure with the publication of two important management accounting texts written by American academics – **Gordon Shillinglaw** (1961) and **Charles Horngren** (1962). The availability of such textbooks facilitated the development and expansion of cost and management accounting courses both at university and at professional accountancy levels. Another influential book appeared in 1965 – *Management Control Systems* by **Robert Anthony** – which focused on the implementation and monitoring of strategy within organisations. The behavioural dimension together with issues of performance measurement, evaluation and managerial compensation, were also addressed.

In the 1980s, however, the traditional practice of management accounting was severely criticised by **Thomas Johnson** and **Robert Kaplan**, who argued that:

"management accounting information, driven by the procedures and cycle of the organisation's financial reporting system, is too late, too aggregated, and too distorted to be relevant for managers' planning and control decisions".
(*Relevance Lost: The Rise and Fall of Management Accounting*, 1987)

Johnson and Kaplan argued that management accounting practice had lost much of its relevance in the modern business environment and, while many other authors have since then criticised traditional management accounting practice, it is fair to argue that Johnson and Kaplan's book has stimulated more debate in this area than any other publication.

## 1.4  Current Developments in Management Accounting

Reflecting recent developments in the broad discipline of managerial accounting, new titles for courses and textbooks have appeared. These new titles usually include words such as "Strategic or Strategy", "Cost Management", "Cost Reduction", "Performance Measurement" or "Value". While these terms have different meanings, it is realistic to suggest that they share common implications for the discipline of management accounting. Specifically, they all require the broadening of the type of information that is presented by the management accountant to managers for decision-making, including strategy formulation and monitoring of its implementation. Moreover, as business practices grow in volume and complexity, so will the discipline of management accounting evolve and develop. Currently, there are a number of themes and developments, which in addition to traditional management accounting material, will be covered in this text. Some of these **evolving management accounting themes** are as follows:

## Shift towards the Service Economy

Over the past 20 years or so there has been a significant shift, worldwide, from manufacturing to the service-based economy. Recent figures published by *The Economist* (2009), presented in **Exhibit 1.4** below, show that nearly two-thirds of all employment in developed countries now occurs in the service sector which also contributes substantially to overall gross domestic product (GDP):

EXHIBIT 1.4: IMPORTANCE OF SERVICE SECTOR IN SELECTED ECONOMIES

|  | Ireland | United States | Euro area |
|---|---|---|---|
| Employment: % services | 65% | 76% | 64% |
| GDP: % services | 50% | 80% | 71% |

Source: Pocket World in Figures, *The Economist* (2009)

The management of service companies differs in many ways from manufacturing concerns. For example, most service firms are labour intensive and the costs of many service firms are essentially fixed in relation to volume changes. In contrast, manufacturing firms incur a variety of non-pay costs, e.g. material and equipment-running costs, many of which are considered to be variable with respect to changes in the level of output. Also, manufacturing firms must invest heavily in tangible fixed assets – as much as 50% of total assets for some manufacturing companies – whereas service firms will have relatively few such assets but may possess a great deal of 'intellectual property' which is extremely difficult to measure for financial reporting purposes.

Furthermore, in manufacturing companies, unused products are placed into closing stock and this requires inventory valuation calculations. Also, goods can be inspected for quality before delivery to customers. In contrast, with service firms, the service can only be inspected after delivery. In addition, there is little closing stock; thus, the valuation of closing inventory (except in the case of work-in-progress of some professional services firms) is not required. The differences between manufacturing and service firms are noted in **Exhibit 1.5** below.

EXHIBIT 1.5: DIFFERENCES BETWEEN MANUFACTURING AND SERVICE FIRMS

|  | Manufacturing firm | Service firm |
|---|---|---|
| **Composition of assets** | Tangible fixed assets can represent 50% of total assets | Few tangible fixed assets; emphasis on intellectual property |
| **Timing of production and sales** | Unsold products can be placed in inventory in times of excess demand and will generate future revenues | Unused services cannot be stored, therefore, unused capacity must be minimised to prevent wastage |
| **Inspection of quality** | Products can be inspected before delivery to prevent inferior quality | Quality control is more difficult, since services are produced and consumed simultaneously |

## Customer Focus And Quality

Increasingly, organisations are proclaiming themselves to be 'customer driven', and the shift towards customer satisfaction is understandable in the context of corporate strategy. Without customer satisfaction and resulting loyalty, financial performance will be disappointing in the long run. Some implications from happy and unhappy customers can be gleaned from the following rules of thumb used by some marketers:

- Only about 5% of unhappy customers will complain directly to the organisation involved.
- On average, a customer with a complaint relating to an organisation will tell 10 other people.
- Customers who have complaints satisfactorily resolved only tell five other people.
- It costs approximately five times as much to gain new customers than to retain existing customers. Thus, customer retention and loyalty are crucial issues in determining the long-term success of any organisation.

An important element in determining customer satisfaction is that of quality. 'Quality' is a term that we all use fairly loosely, partly reflecting the fact that there are different dimensions to quality, which include reliability, performance, appearance and special features. However, the important thing to note is that it is the customer who is the final judge of a firm's quality performance. Customers, and competitors, are now driving the quality dimension of production or services provided and it is now acknowledged that quality is an important source of competitive advantage for many firms.

## Strategy and Strategic Management Accounting

An interesting way to highlight the notion of strategy is to compare the difference between, say, planning our personal finances and planning for a football match. The former has many similarities with traditional management accounting practices; the latter is concerned with competition, group performance and highlights the need for strategic thinking. Strategic thinking provides the answer to three fundamental questions:

1. Where are we now? What are our current strengths and weakness, together with the threats and opportunities facing the organisation?
2. Where do we want to be at some future date?
3. How will we get there (which may include a consideration of new products and new inputs)?

Within the discipline of management accounting an external (in addition to an internal) focus is emerging and can be referred to as strategic management accounting. **Strategic management accounting** is concerned with issues such as market growth and market share, competitor's products, prices and cost structure, changing customer preferences, spending on research and training, workforce attitude, relative levels of technology and manufacturing efficiency. It is only with this wider set of information that management can know their true competitive position and appreciate both the threats and opportunities facing the organisation. Traditional management accounting practice has focused on internal performance against an historically set budget. Strategic management accounting looks continually at the future, the firm's external environment and the organisation's capability to successfully compete in chosen markets.

## Critical Success Factors and Non-Financial Indicators (NFIs)

Traditionally, management accounting reports were mainly concerned with the financial consequences of the decisions and activities within an organisation during an accounting period. However, managers need to know not only the end result, but also the *determinants* of those results. In the context of management accounting these determinants are referred to as critical success factors. In brief, **critical success factors** are the limited number of key areas in which superior performance is required for a business to be successful. They represent critical areas to be monitored on a regular basis since an unfavourable change in them indicates the need for prompt action.

Information relating to critical success factors tends to be predominantly of a non-financial nature. Because of this they have been described as **non-financial indicators** (NFIs) or **performance measures** and an important task for management accountants is to develop a range of performance measures which relate to these critical success factors. Typical non-financial performance priorities will include:

- producing consistently low defect rates
- delivering goods on time
- providing reliable and durable products
- customising products and services to customer needs
- providing effective after sales service.

It should be noted, however, that the generation of non-financial measures is not the exclusive province of accounting. On the contrary, such performance measures are often collected by the function to which they directly relate or else by IT specialists. The accounting function has some expertise in data collection and reporting, and could, therefore, be encouraged to become more involved in collecting and reporting this information to set it alongside the accounting reports that are currently produced.

## Cost Management

The internal cost accumulation system and the reporting of such costs will also have to change. Costs have always been an important consideration for businesses and it is likely that, with increased competition and globalisation, the cost issue, and particularly the issue of cost reduction, will become important in the future. In simple terms, if costs are too high, the business is likely to be uncompetitive and unprofitable. Traditionally, management accountants were concerned with 'counting the costs' for product costing purposes. Counting costs is not the same as cost reduction. (It is intuitive to say that weighing yourself 10 times a day will not, in itself, take off excess weight.) Cost management is about ways of transforming a firm's cost base through the identification those activities which cause costs to be incurred. It is rather simplistic to note that organisations consist of a myriad of activities. The important thing about activities is to determine whether these activities are necessary in the first place.

One way to answer this question is to segregate activities into value-added or non-value-added activities. The feature of a **value-added activity** is that a customer is prepared to pay for it; however, a customer will only pay for an activity if it provides him with value and satisfaction. If organisations undertake even a crude inventory of activities they will discover many activities that do not add value to customers. In essence, they are wasteful and should be reduced or eliminated.

In **summary**, the evolving themes and developments of management accounting highlight the need to broaden the range of information relevant to managerial decision-making. This information can be classified as either financial or non-financial. In turn, this information can be either historical or projected and, furthermore, can relate to the firm itself or its environment. These types of information are displayed in the matrix presented in **Exhibit 1.6**.

EXHIBIT 1.6: THREE-WAY CLASSIFICATION OF MANAGEMENT ACCOUNTING
INFORMATION

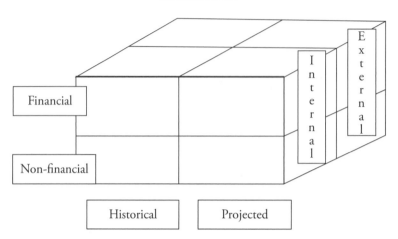

Typical information, relating to this three-way classification, would be as follows:

| Financial/<br>Non-financial | Internal/<br>External | Historical/<br>Projected | Information |
|---|---|---|---|
| Financial | Internal | Historical | Actual unit cost |
| Non-financial | Internal | Historical | On time delivery % (quality) |
| Financial | External | Historical | Competitor's actual price |
| Non-financial | External | Historical | Customer satisfaction index |
| Financial | Internal | Projected | Standard unit cost |
| Non-financial | Internal | Projected | No. of expected new products |
| Financial | External | Projected | Expected price of competitor |
| Non-financial | External | Projected | Predicted market share |

The above classification of managerial accounting information captures the emerging issues in management accounting such as customer satisfaction, quality, strategic thinking, information on competitors and critical success factors, and these issues will be dealt with in the remainder of this textbook.

## 1.5  Ethics and Management Accounting

There is also an ethical dimension to management accounting and, indeed, to accounting in general. In recent years, these ethical considerations have received much greater attention due, partly, to the adverse and sensational news headlines associated with financial scandals such as those involving Anglo Irish Bank, Lehman Brothers, Enron and Parmalat. (Actually, if history teaches us anything it is that financial scandals will never be eliminated, largely because of unethical behaviour.) Therefore, it is worthwhile briefly discussing the ethical dimensions associated with the practice of management accounting within organisations.

Ethics is concerned with what we should do in a decision situation. It is concerned with the appropriateness of a particular course of action and often differs from what we can do or what we want to do. Ethical conflict arises whenever we face a decision whereby what we either *can or want to do* is not consistent with what we *should* do. Ethical behaviour goes beyond legality – which relates to what is permitted by law – and focuses on the moral aspects of a situation. Major ethical dilemmas often evolve from a series of small compromises, none of which appears serious enough to warrant taking a stand on ethical grounds. Unfortunately, these small compromises establish a pattern of behaviour that is increasingly difficult to reverse. Some examples, drawn from the practice of management accounting, are as follows and refer to a financial year ending on 31 December:

1. No provision for accrued expenses is made at financial year end in order to boost profitability.
2. Deferring essential monthly maintenance in December on production equipment by an independent contractor until January of the following year, in an attempt to reduce reported costs for the current period.
3. Altering dates of delivery dockets and supporting invoices of next January's sales to record them as revenue in December of the current year.
4. Writing back to the income statement a large provision account, on the grounds that the provision was not utilised this year.
5. The company includes the full amount of royalty income received in the income statement as a revenue item in the year of receipt rather than over the life of the agreement.
6. Inflating closing stock valuation in order to improve current profitability.
7. Preparing a budget based on an easy-to-achieve target.

Many other items could be cited. It is useful to divide the **motives** for the above behaviour into three categories:

(a) **Management Incentives** The organisation may have a financial incentive scheme for its managers based on the achievement of single-year profit targets. In such a situation, there is an incentive for managers to engage in earnings management techniques either by boosting current sales revenue or transferring current costs to the subsequent accounting period. Clearly, the above actions may simply transfer profits from the next accounting period to the current accounting period and, therefore, the company is no better or worse off in terms of overall cash flow over the two-year period. However, managers may prefer to believe that events will improve 'next year' or they simply may not care about next year because the problem will then belong to somebody else. In some cases the action taken may disadvantage the firm in the long term, e.g. deferring essential machine maintenance.

(b) **Promotion Opportunities** Managers who can deliver on profit targets are more likely to have better job promotion prospects either within the firm or by being recruited by other firms to a better position. In contrast, managers who do not meet profit targets may be viewed in a negative manner.

(c) **Avoid Scrutiny** Managers are evaluated with reference to various budgeted performance measures, both financial and non-financial. In subsequent sections of this book we shall refer to '**control by comparison**' whereby budgeted performance is compared with reference to actual performance to determine either favourable or unfavourable variances. If these variances are *not* deemed to be significant or material, then the manager usually avoids detailed scrutiny. In contrast, significant and adverse performance is much more likely to attract more top management scrutiny and supervision.

## Codes of Conduct

Not surprisingly, many firms have established codes of ethics or codes of conduct for their employees. They are intended to inform and direct employee behaviour and can be a useful defence against alleged wrongdoing, i.e. it may be a legitimate defence that an employee complied with his company's code of conduct. Alternatively, unethical behaviour may lead to legal penalties, a damaged reputation or, in extreme cases, termination of employment. In other words, unethical behaviour is generally costly in the long term. Moreover, such codes may be useful in helping to attract new employees. However, more important than a published code of ethics or code of conduct is the ethical 'tone at the top', i.e. norms of behaviour set by top management. If employees perceive top management as being involved in unethical decisions, they will be less inclined to maintain ethical standards. In addition to codes of conduct in specific firms, professionally qualified management accountants must also comply with codes of their respective professional accountancy body.

All professional accountancy bodies have a Code of Ethics for their members which are based on the Code of Ethics for Professional Accountants prepared by the International Federation of Accountants (IFAC). This Code (revised July 2009) applies to all professional accountants, whether working in public practice or in business/ industry. **Four important principles** can be identified from the various professional accountancy codes as follows:

### *Integrity*

The principle of integrity imposes an obligation on all professional accountants to be straightforward and honest in all professional and business relationships and this implies fair dealing and truthfulness. It follows that a professional accountant's advice and work must be uncorrupted by self-interest and not influenced by the interests of other parties. Therefore, professional accountants should, for example:

• Not be associated with reports or information where they believe that the information contains a materially false or misleading statement, or omits information where such omission would be misleading.

- Refrain from engaging in any activity that would prejudice one's ability to carry out his or her duties ethically.
- Refuse any gift or preferential treatment that would or would appear to influence one's actions.
- Communicate unfavourable as well as favourable information.

### Objectivity

This principle requires the need for impartial judgement with regard to all considerations relating to the task in hand and this principle can be compromised (as can integrity) due to bias, conflict of interest or the undue influence of others. Therefore, professional accountants should, for example:

- avoid situations that may compromise their professional judgement because of bias, conflict of interest or the undue influence of others; and
- communicate information fairly and objectively.

### Professional Competence

This principle is concerned with exercising due care, skill and diligence, and avoiding any action that would discredit the profession. Therefore, professional accountants should, for example:

- Maintain an appropriate level of professional knowledge and skill to ensure competent performance in accordance with laws, regulations and applicable technical standards.
- Act in accordance with the requirements of the assignment, carefully, thoroughly and on a timely basis.
- Prepare clear reports and recommendations after appropriate analysis of the relevant information.
- Be prepared to take legal advice or, in extreme situations, resign from the organisation if they believe that unethical behaviour or actions by others will continue to occur within the employing organisation.

### Confidentiality

The principle of confidentiality is concerned with respecting and protecting the privacy of information and not disclosing any such information to third parties without proper and specific authority. Therefore, professional management accountants should, for example:

- Refrain from disclosing confidential information to third parties without proper and specific authority, unless there is a legal or professional right or duty to do so.
- Inform subordinates as appropriate regarding the confidentiality of information acquired in the course of the work and monitor their activities to assure the maintenance of that confidentiality.
- Refrain from using confidential information acquired in the course of the work for personal advantage or for the advantage of third parties.

### Resolution of Ethical Conflict

In applying the principles of ethical conduct, professional management accountants may encounter problems in resolving ethical conflict and should follow the recognised policies of the firm bearing on the resolution of such conflict. If these policies do not resolve the ethical conflict, the professional accountant should consider the following sequence:

- Discuss such problems with the immediate superior except when it appears that the superior is part of the situation, in which case the problem should be presented initially to the person with the next higher level of responsibility. If a satisfactory resolution cannot be achieved when the problem is initially presented, submit the issues to the next higher managerial level.
- If the immediate superior is the managing director or equivalent, the acceptable reviewing authority may be a group such as the board of directors. However, direct contact with levels above the immediate superior should be initiated only with the superior's knowledge, assuming the superior is not involved. Except where legally prescribed, communication of such problems to authorities or individuals outside the organisation is not considered appropriate.
- Clarify relevant ethical issues through confidential discussion with an objective advisor (e.g. professional accountancy body) to obtain a better understanding of possible courses of action and be prepared to take legal advice regarding obligations and rights concerning the ethical conflict.
- If the ethical conflict still exists after exhausting all levels of internal review, there may be no recourse other than to withdraw from the assignment team or specific assignment or to resign from the organisation and to submit an informative memorandum to the appropriate representative of the organisation. After resignation, depending on the nature of the ethical conflict, it may be appropriate to notify appropriate regulatory authorities.

In summary, many ethical dilemmas involve actions that are perceived to have desirable short-run consequences and highly probable undesirable long-term consequences. Thus, a general rule once quoted to me was that individuals should never do anything that they would not like reported on the front page of the national newspapers. Solid advice!

## 1.6 Communicating Information to Managers

The majority of information provided by the management accountant to managers is likely to be in written form, e.g. by letter, memorandum or report. In turn, this may be either by way of hard copy or e-mail. In recent decades, management accounting educators have been called upon to enhance the communication skills of their students. One such method is to require students to write a short 'memorandum' to a specified person, regarding a specific matter under consideration. The following section provides some general guidance to students in writing a memorandum (usually shortened to 'memo').

A memo can be described as a short report (usually about 1 to 2 pages) in a specific format for which the following suggestions are made:

- **Title format**: Each memo should have a basic format indicating the matter of the communication (i.e. Memo); the name (and possibly the position) of the intended recipient; the author (i.e. yourself); a date and, finally, a subject title. A typical memo is presented below in **Exhibit 1.7**.
- **Introductory paragraph**: Your memo should start with a short introductory paragraph explaining to the intended reader why the memo is being sent and indicate, briefly, its main points or key recommendations. The suggested memo in **Exhibit 1.7** is presented in response to a request to recommend a minimum selling price for goods to be manufactured and delivered to a new overseas customer, together with some non-financial factors to be considered before a final decision is made.
- The main points of your memo can now be made and explained in some detail, but keep them brief. Remember, the longer your memo is, the less likely it is to be fully read by busy executives. If you want to make some detailed points, possibly backed up with lengthy calculations, then these should be added as an appendix to the memo.
- Finish your memo with a closing paragraph where, if you have not already done so, acknowledge the limitations of your work. An obvious limitation could refer to the shortage of time available to you. It is usual to finish a memo with an ending sentence such as 'please do not hesitate to contact me should you have any queries'. The reader is now aware of your availability to answer additional questions that s/he may have. A memo does not have a formal ending as in a letter e.g. *yours sincerely* or *yours faithfully*. A memo is not signed but, in practice, it is sometimes useful to initial the memo to indicate that you have approved it before it was sent.

EXHIBIT 1.7: SUGGESTED FORMAT OF A MEMO

## MEMO

To:      A. N. Other (Managing Director)
From:   A. Count (Management Accountant)
Re:      Recommended selling price to Ms Buy
Date     15 July 2010

I refer to your e-mail (dated 13 July) requesting a recommended selling price for the manufacture and delivery of goods, following an enquiry from Ms Buy who is a potential new customer. You will recall that her enquiry related to a small customisation of our basic product. My calculations suggest that our minimum price request (in total) should be €100,000 but this assumes that we can use some of our current spare capacity and that we are prepared to simply 'break-even' for this order. I can provide you with my detailed calculations.

Before a final price is determined for this potential new customer there are a number of important factors that should be taken into consideration. The most important of these are as follows:

1. The customer has requested that our price is specified in dollars rather than in Euro. Essentially, this request transfers any foreign exchange (FX) risk on this transaction to us. Based on recent currency fluctuations, this FX risk could be as high as 15% of the contract price.

2. Since Ms Buy is a potential new customer, we will need to assess her creditworthiness to ensure guarantee of payment within our normal credit terms.

3. My recommended price is based on using some of our current spare capacity. In reality, the validity of this assumption may not be correct as additional orders may be generated by contacts made elsewhere by yourself during your participation in a recent trade mission to Asia.

4. While a low quotation price may attract additional orders from this client, one must be conscious that additional orders may require the application of our normal pricing procedures. Thus a significant price increase may be required for subsequent orders.

Please contact me if you require additional information or clarification.

## SUMMARY OF LEARNING OBJECTIVES

**Learning Objective 1:** Define the role of the management accountant in organisations.

The primary role of the management accountant within organisations is to provide relevant information to facilitate managerial planning and control decisions.

**Learning Objective 2:** Distinguish between managerial and financial accounting.

Financial accounting provides historical information to users who are external to the firm and this information is regulated by, e.g. International Financial Reporting Standards (IFRS). Managerial accounting information may be historical or future-orientated and is for internal use, nor is it regulated in format or content.

**Learning Objective 3:** Outline the evolution of managerial accounting as a practical and academic discipline.

The Industrial Revolution heralded the need for accurate product costing in manufacturing firms. In the early 1930s, economists began to illustrate the wider use of cost information, and techniques such as budgetary control, profit planning and net present values became an integral part of the discipline. By the early 1960s the discipline of managerial accounting had evolved to a position whereby it was recognised in its own right.

**Learning Objective 4:** Describe current developments in managerial accounting.

During the 1980s, criticisms of managerial accounting practice emerged and these have resulted in the use of activity-based costing and activity-based cost management techniques and the greater emphasis on performance measurement in general. In addition, there are calls for a greater external focus for the discipline especially in the formation and implementation of strategy.

**Learning Objective 5:** Write a properly formatted memorandum.

Management accounting information must be presented in an easy-to-understand manner if it is to be used in managerial decision-making. Therefore, it is essential that accounting students are well versed in preparing a properly formatted memo.

## Questions

### Review Questions

(See Appendix One for Solutions to Review Questions **1.1** and **1.2**)

### Question 1.1 (Descriptions of Financial or Managerial accounting)

In relation to each of the descriptions contained below, indicate whether they relate more to financial or managerial accounting.

| | | | |
|---|---|---|---|
| (a) | Accuracy | (n) | Key performance indicators (KPIs) |
| (b) | Annually | | |
| (c) | Assets and liabilities | (o) | Market share |
| (d) | Audited | (p) | Non-financial performance measures |
| (e) | Budgets | | |
| (f) | Cost per unit | (q) | Objectivity |
| (g) | Critical success factors (CSF) | (r) | On-time delivery of products |
| | | (s) | Regulated |
| (h) | Detailed information | (t) | Reports on customer loyalty |
| (i) | External users | (u) | Shareholders |
| (j) | External information | (v) | Strategy |
| (k) | Future orientated | (w) | Subjective |
| (l) | Internal users | (x) | Summarised information |
| (m) | International Financial Reporting Standards | (y) | Threats and opportunities |
| | | (z) | Vision |

### Question 1.2 (Profit v. Performance Measures)

Many articles in management accounting journals, especially during the past decade, have suggested that the provision of a broad range of performance indicators (or performance measures) represents more relevant information to managers than simply financial information with its focus on profit.

**Requirements:** Explain:

(a) the arguments for using the amount of profit generated as the measure of the performance of a business;

(b) the limitations of using profit only as a measure of performance within commercial entities.

(**Note:** Because of the introductory nature of this chapter, the questions are not graded between Intermediate and Advanced levels. They are in all other chapters.)

*Question 1.3 (Information Needs of Managers)*

You have just qualified as an accountant, and you have set up your own management consultancy business. During the first week you have been engaged for a short assignment. Your client is a recently established coffee shop which specialises in freshly brewed coffee and assorted snacks and is open for business from mid-morning to late at night. It occupies an area of about 2,000 sq. feet (including kitchen) and is located directly opposite the well-known *Starbucks* coffee chain. The owner does not take any active part in the overall management of the shop.

The coffee shop is run by a manager – with a background in the sector – but who is not well-versed in accounting matters. He supervises 10 employees, of which seven work on a part-time basis. You understand that there is no formal management accounting information available and you have been engaged, for a suitable fee, by the owner to provide assistance in this regard.

The mission statement of the coffee shop requires it to:

*"Sell the finest-quality coffee and assorted snacks in a comfortable surrounding to clients, so that the company will operate on a sound financial basis."*

**Requirement:** The relevant information needs of managers are sometimes categorised between historical or future orientated; financial or non-financial; and internal or external. (This gives us eight unique combinations of information classification.)

Using the above mission statement and your own knowledge of this sector, you are required to suggest information that could be included in the following eight headings:

| Financial/<br>non-financial | Internal/<br>external | Historical/<br>projected | Information |
|---|---|---|---|
| Financial | Internal | Historical | |
| Non-financial | Internal | Historical | |
| Financial | External | Historical | |
| Non-financial | External | Historical | |
| Financial | Internal | Projected | |
| Non-financial | Internal | Projected | |
| Financial | External | Projected | |
| Non-financial | External | Projected | |

*Question 1.4 (Current Developments)*

Write brief notes on each of the following:

(a) The distinction between a value-added cost and a non-value added cost.
(b) 'Short-termism'.
(c) Traditional (i.e. incremental) budgeting practices.

## Question 1.5 (Current Developments)

Write brief notes on each of the following:

(a) Activity-based costing.
(b) Strategic management accounting.

## Question 1.6 (The Differences between Financial and Managerial Accounting)

Within large organisations the accounting function may be divided into two broad classes of activity which are referred to as 'financial accounting' and 'managerial accounting' respectively.

**Requirement:** Explain the role of and main differences between these two functions on the basis of users, timeliness, frequency of reporting, orientation towards the past or future and format.

## Question 1.7 (Financial and Managerial Accounting Statements)

Outline the major differences that exist between the published financial statements available to the shareholders of a limited company and the internal management accounting reports to managers of that company.

## Question 1.8 (Identifying Non-financial Performance Indicators)

For each of the entities outlined below, specify two non-financial indicators that would be appropriate to monitor progress towards agreed goals. Also, propose how targets and rewards can be integrated into your suggestions:

(a) A business school wants to measure the success of its recent MBA class
(b) A courier company wants to measure its promise to customers for on-time delivery
(c) A hotel wants to measure the performance of its central reservations system
(d) A public hospital wants to measure the success of its accident and emergency department
(e) A service firm wants to measure the 'quality' of its workforce.

## Question 1.9 (Information Needs of Managers)

The recently appointed Dean of the GIM Business School is concerned with the school's future. The GIM offers a MBA degree and this degree is highly respected in the locality. However, the GIM MBA degree is not listed in the *International Times* rankings of MBA programmes. It is argued that such an omission creates difficulties in recruiting international students. The formal mission statement for the GIM Business School reads:

> "To be and be seen to be among the leaders in business education in Europe by aiming for the highest international standards in our research and scholarly publications and by the communication of that knowledge to successive generations through excellence in teaching and learning."

The MBA rankings, computed annually, are currently determined by four major factors, each factor is weighted to provide an overall score. These factors are as follows:

---

1.  Increase in salary of graduates as measured by salary before admission and salary three years after graduation
2.  Index of student satisfaction with MBA programme
3.  % of women faculty in the Business School
4.  % of woman students in programme

---

**Requirement:** Suggest ways in which overall scores in each of the above factors could be manipulated and suggest whether this manipulation would be a positive or negative development in ensuring the long-term success of the GIM Business School.

## Question 1.10 (The Relevance of Historical Accounting Information)

"Accounting reports are generally backward looking and therefore have no role to play in managerial decision-making."

**Requirement:** Draft a 1-page memorandum to your lecturer, critically evaluating the above statement.

## Question 1.11 (Management Accounting and Ethics)

Mr E. Thic, a non-accountant, is the chief executive of the ROC Water company – a subsidiary of an Irish multinational group – which has reported 10% growth in sales and profits during the past decade of the Celtic Tiger. Thic and other senior managers earn a significant bonus if they achieve previously agreed profit targets. However, towards the end of the current year, the company was not performing well due to the prevailing economic climate and it is likely that the firm will not achieve its profit targets. In a private discussion with you – as management accountant – Thic politely makes the following suggestions with respect to the current accounting year ending 31 December:

*   Postponing the purchase of new equipment, scheduled for December, until January of next year.
*   Changing the date of shipment of next January's sales to record them as sales in December of the current year. The goods will still be delivered to customers in January.
*   Moving closing stock around different locations so that the auditors will count it "twice". Thus, closing stock valuation will be inflated and reported profits increased.
*   Writing back to the income statement a large amount of the bad debts provision, on the grounds that such a provision is no longer required.
*   The firm is in receipt of a considerable amount of rebate income from various retail outlets. To date ROC has recognised this revenue over the life of the agreement,

but Thic suggests that the total expected amount of the rebate be now included in this year's income statement.
- No provision for accrued wages based on overtime worked in the days before Christmas.

**Requirements:**

1. Why might Thic want to distort this year's income statement?
2. From an ethical point of view, and as the management accountant of the firm, how would you react, assuming each of the above items was significant?

*Question 1.12 (The Role of the Management Accountant in a Manufacturing Firm)*

Draft a memorandum to the senior manager which outlines *briefly* the activities of a management accountant in a manufacturing company with regard to the following functions:

- stock valuation
- planning decisions
- control decisions.

# Terms and Concepts of Cost Accumulation

LEARNING OBJECTIVES

When you have completed studying this chapter you should be able to:

1. Describe the three main reasons for providing cost information about cost objects.
2. Distinguish between fixed and variable costs, and between direct and overhead costs.
3. Prepare summary cost statements for manufacturing, retail and service firms.
4. Calculate the profit impact of using absorption versus variable (direct) costing.
5. Assign costs using and distinguishing between cost apportionment and cost allocation.
6. Explain the technique of overhead absorption rates (OHARs) using cost drivers.
7. Outline the benefits and limitations associated with using departmental or plant-wide, budgeted or actual and annual or seasonal OHARs.
8. Illustrate the alternative accounting treatments of joint and by-products.
9. Calculate OHARs with service department apportionments.

## 2.1 Introduction to Cost Accumulation

This chapter explains how costs can be accumulated within organisations and used to identify, for example, the costs of running a department or the cost of providing a unit of output or the cost of performing a specific activity. It should be remembered that in the previous chapter we mentioned that American economist, John Maurice Clark, who coined the famous phrase "different costs for different purposes" (*Studies in the Economics of Overhead Costs* (1923). This simply means that no single cost figure will be correct for all purposes. Rather, cost calculations are conditional on the purpose for which the cost information is required. The following (hypothetical) story is indicative.

One day a farmer was out working in his field. He was disturbed by a car horn. Soon a stranger appeared and asked: "Do you own the cow walking down the road over there, and if so, well, how much did it cost?"

The farmer paused to reflect on this unusual question from the stranger. "It all depends", the farmer replied and asked: "Are you from the tax authorities, or do you want to buy it, or did you just hit it but are covered by insurance?"

The term 'cost' is defined in terms of resources consumed and/or foregone in order to achieve a particular objective. The resources consumed are generally equal to the amount of expenditure. However, there may also be benefits foregone or sacrifices involved and we shall subsequently refer to this as an **opportunity cost**. The cost calculation can be done on an *ex post* basis, i.e. identifying the historical costs incurred, or on an *ex ante* basis, i.e. identifying costs before they are incurred. Managers need to know the cost of products they make or services they provide for the following reasons:

1. **Stock valuation** At the end of the accounting period, any unsold stock of a manufacturing or retail firm must be valued at cost in accordance with International Financial Reporting Standards (IFRS). The cost figure represents the historical cost incurred but, for manufacturing firms, will include only costs associated with the production process.
2. **Planning** In many situations, selling prices must be determined and agreed with the customer before the work commences. This is particularly the case with special order quotations. If the quoted selling price cannot be subsequently changed, overall company profitability will depend crucially on the ability to accurately predict costs. It is likely that cost determination for the purpose of setting selling prices would include, for manufacturing firms, both production and non-production costs.
3. **Control** Actual costs can be compared with planned costs and variances identified. These cost variances can be adverse or favourable, significant or insignificant. The benefit of reporting cost variances is that they increase management's knowledge of current operating conditions and they can be used to increase the accuracy of future cost projections.

## 2.2 Cost Classification and Cost Statements

In order to accumulate and summarise cost data in an orderly manner, a cost classification system is needed. **Cost classification** involves systematically grouping costs together according to their common characteristics and this will facilitate the cost accumulation process. Without a cost classification system it is difficult to accumulate costs in a meaningful manner and difficult to plan and control the operations of a business. There are different cost classification systems used by management accountants. They all serve a useful purpose and they are often used simultaneously. The main cost classification systems are:

1. cost classification by nature
2. cost classification by behaviour

3. cost classification by traceability
4. cost classification by function.

## 1. Cost Classification by Nature

Cost classification by nature is a classification system which indicates *what* resources have been consumed and includes basic cost categories such as materials, wages, light and heat, advertising, etc. This classification system is used extensively in recording transactions for financial accounting purposes and is the classification system with which most people are familiar from previous accounting courses. Its main advantage is that it facilitates the auditing and verification process as usually each transaction under this heading is related to a supplier invoice or some form of receipt. This classification system is used within managerial accounting in the area of planning and budgeting, especially when different cost increases are expected for different expense items, e.g. wages may increase by 5% due to a national wage agreement but raw material costs may decrease because of falling prices.

## 2. Cost Classification by Behaviour

This classification system allows us to identify fixed and variable costs within the overall cost structure of the firm. It is based on how costs behave in response to changes in the level of an organisation's activities and it is usual to refer to these activities as cost drivers. A **cost driver** is any factor that affects costs in a significant way.

Thus, in a university, the number of students is a significant cost driver – the greater the number of students, the higher will be the overall cost level. But, there are also other cost drivers in a university, e.g. the amount of floor space occupied may be a significant driver of cleaning costs and light and heat. Traditionally, in management accounting cost behaviour was defined in relation to a single cost driver, i.e. volume of output. However, it must be stressed that, while volume (or output) may be a significant cost driver in many businesses today, it is not the only cost driver. Nevertheless, unless otherwise stated in this text, we shall assume that volume is the dominant cost driver in the organisation.

A **fixed cost** can be defined as a cost that is unchanged, in total, in response to changes in the level of related cost driver. Typical examples of fixed costs include rent, insurance and administration salaries. This definition does not suggest, however, that fixed costs do not change. It is important to note that all costs change due to a number of factors such as inflation and seasonality. However, the important characteristic of a fixed cost is its unresponsive behaviour, in total, with respect to output or volume changes, over a range of activity. (We shall discuss this relevant range of activity later in this chapter.)

A **variable cost** is a cost that changes, in total, in response to changes in the level of the related cost driver. Typical variable costs include raw materials and power for machines. Thus, as volume increases, so will the total amount of variable costs.

There are only two cost elements that can be definitely considered a variable cost in the modern environment: raw materials and sales commission paid on a per unit basis. Many management accounting texts assume that **labour** is also a variable cost. However, the reader should be aware of several valid arguments suggesting that labour should no longer be considered a variable cost.

First, in some countries, employees have a certain degree of job protection and it may be difficult for them to be laid off in times of falling demand and output.

Secondly, in times of rising output, some employers may postpone the recruitment of staff since they fear a subsequent downturn which would result in idle staff.

Thirdly, some employers may be reluctant to lay off some of their staff in time of falling demand due to the difficulty in recruiting new staff in the future, if needs be.

Thus, it may be more appropriate to consider labour as being a mixed cost – comprising elements of both fixed and variable costs.

Both fixed and variable costs can be graphed as shown in **Exhibit 2.1**. The vertical axis of the graph represents the total amount of the cost whereas the horizontal axis represents output or volume, i.e. the assumed cost driver.

In order to highlight overall cost behaviour, both fixed and variable costs can be combined on the same graph. We depict total costs on the vertical axis and the cost driver (e.g. volume) is presented on the horizontal axis. The graph for total costs is shown below in **Exhibit 2.2**.

EXHIBIT 2.1: GRAPH OF FIXED AND VARIABLE COSTS

EXHIBIT 2.2: GRAPH OF TOTAL COSTS

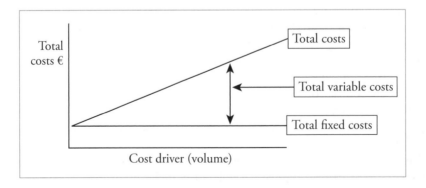

The distinction between fixed and variable costs is extremely useful in routine profit planning, including calculation of break-even point, and decision-making. A key term used in this context is that of unit contribution. **Unit contribution** represents the unit selling price (SPu) minus unit variable cost (VCu). It represents the amount remaining from the selling price after all variable expenses have been deducted. In turn, **total contribution** for a given level of activity can be calculated by multiplying unit contribution by the total number of units sold. Total contribution represents the amount available to cover all fixed costs and then provide a profit (or loss) for the period.

The distinction between fixed and variable costs will allow us to generate meaningful accounting reports to management that are based on cost behaviour rather than being prepared according to a natural classification. The natural classification can often include both fixed and variable costs under the same heading, e.g. some wages may be considered fixed whereas some may be considered variable with respect of output or volume changes.

A recent criticism of the fixed/variable cost classification system is that many costs in contemporary organisations relate to non-volume related activities and reflect the growing complexities of modern business. In many modern businesses, there are quality control costs, set-up costs, purchasing costs, etc., which are not volume driven. In other words, it is argued that the traditional assumption that output is the most significant factor affecting costs is rather simplistic.

We have defined both fixed and variable costs in relation to how the total of such costs behave relative to changes in the related cost driver levels. However, both fixed and variable costs can be defined in terms of *average* cost per unit rather than in terms of total cost. Thus, the average variable cost (per unit) will remain constant (e.g. each unit of output will require a constant input of raw materials) over a relevant range of activity. On the other hand, as output changes, the average fixed cost per unit will also change (in the opposite direction). **Exhibit 2.3** below indicates the two ways of describing both fixed and variable costs and it is important to be comfortable with both types of definitions.

**Exhibit 2.3** makes reference to the 'relevant range' of activity which is the range of activity within which the assumption about fixed and variable cost behaviour,

EXHIBIT 2.3: DIFFERENT DEFINITIONS OF FIXED AND VARIABLE COSTS

|  | Fixed costs | Variable costs |
|---|---|---|
| Total costs over a relevant range of activity | Do **not** change with changes in volume | Do change with changes in volume |
| Average cost per unit over a relevant range of activity | Do change with changes in volume | Do **not** change with changes in volume |

with reference to volume changes, remains valid. Within this range of activity total fixed costs remain constant and average variable *unit* costs also remain constant. In some circumstances, fixed costs may behave in a step function, i.e. they are constant within a narrow range of activity, but shift to a higher level with an increased range of activity. Step costs reflect the fact that fixed costs are subject to managerial decisions and will rarely remain constant in the long term. Therefore, as output increases, additional supervisors or storage space may be required, so that fixed costs will increase in a step-like manner as volume expands. Likewise, the assumption of a constant average variable cost will not be valid where, for example, quantity discounts on material purchases are available for large orders or where operatives become more efficient as output expands. Such factors do not invalidate the classification of fixed and variable costs as long as we focus on the range of activity within which a particular cost/volume relationship remains valid. In any event, it is plausible at this introductory stage to assume that the change in cost behaviour caused by such events is too small to be significant and therefore can be usefully ignored.

The preference in this textbook is to define fixed and variable costs in relation to how they respond, in total, to changes in the related cost driver, e.g. the volume of output. This approach should reduce the possibility of making errors in decision-making. For example, the average fixed costs per mile of a taxi driver, e.g. insurance cost per mile, will decrease as the number of miles driven increases. However, it does not make sense for the owner just to drive his taxi around his neighbourhood in order to reduce his average fixed cost per mile driven!

## 3. Cost Classification by Traceability

Classifying costs according to traceability allows us to identify direct and indirect costs. (The more common expression for an indirect cost is that of overhead and this latter term will be used extensively from now on in this text.)

First we need to briefly introduce the term **'cost objective'**. Simply, a cost objective is any object or activity relating to the organisation for which we require cost data. In a manufacturing firm, this could be a product, a machine or a department. It could also represent an activity such as the cost of setting up machines or the cost of making a cheque payment.

Once a cost objective has been identified, we need to assign or trace costs to it. *Traceability* is the essence of this direct/overhead cost classification system. A direct cost is a cost that can be identified specifically with, or traced to, a given cost objective in an economically feasible way. In other words, there is an easy to identify cause-and-effect relationship between the cost objective and the cost itself, e.g. direct materials can be easily traced and identified to a specific product. The two main direct costs that will be frequently mentioned in this textbook are:

• Direct Materials  Materials that are part of the product being produced, e.g. wood for tables, cotton and wool in clothes, etc.

- **Direct Labour** Work performed on the product itself (or service) – one can observe the work being done in producing the unit or providing the service.

In addition, there may be **additional direct costs**, depending on the particular context. For example, a manufacturing firm may have to hire special machinery in order to complete a specific job for a client. This is an additional direct cost of this specific job since it can be traced, unambiguously, to the job in question. Also, a professional accountancy firm may incur hotel and travel expenses on behalf of a client and these, too, are direct costs of the work performed, since they can be traced directly to the specific client.

In contrast, an **overhead** or **indirect cost** is a cost that is shared in an arbitrary manner between two or more cost objectives. The practical implication of this is that all costs, with the exception of direct materials, direct labour and other direct costs, are often grouped as overhead costs. Thus, typical overhead costs include, for example, factory rent and insurance, machine depreciation, selling and administration costs and salary costs of supervisors.

It is important to note that a cost objective may be very broad, e.g. the entire firm, or it can be narrow, e.g. a unit of output. Thus, a cost may be 'direct' for one cost objective but an 'overhead' for another cost objective. For example, a manager's salary may be direct in terms of ascertaining the total cost of running his department but his salary would be classified as an overhead if the cost objective was a unit of output.

Because the internal costing system is required to provide information for stock (inventory) valuation at the end of the accounting period for financial reporting purposes, it is traditionally assumed that the main cost objective within the firm is that of unit cost. As a result, and for convenience, it is often implicitly assumed that anything other than direct materials and direct labour can be classified as 'overhead'. This assumption is technically correct if the cost per unit is the stated cost objective. However, it must be remembered that there are many other cost objectives about which managers will require accurate cost information and thus we should be especially careful in our use of the word 'overhead'.

It should also be noted that some direct costs may be classified as overhead/direct, because they are insignificant in relation to overall costs. In addition, some direct costs cannot be traced to a cost objective in an economically feasible way and, therefore, the cost of detailed record-keeping outweighs any benefit for decision-making purposes. An example here would be thread in a shirt. Technically, material thread is a direct cost of each shirt produced. However, its overall insignificance in the context of total unit cost and, indeed, the cost of tracing the cost of threads to individual shirts results in it being treated as a production overhead.

In contrast, some overheads, e.g. general factory power, can be identified as direct costs for a specific machine by installing recording meters for each machine. In this case, power becomes a direct cost of each machine but would still remain an overhead in relation to a unit of output.

The classification of direct/overhead cost can also be used in the context of a service industry. For example, an airline would probably want to accumulate and segregate its costs according to the various routes flown. **Exhibit 2.4** below is a useful summary of a typical direct/overhead cost classification system for an airline that flies to only three destinations, namely the United States, France and Italy. Note that the direct costs can be traced in an objective manner to the three different cost objectives. In contrast, the overheads incurred (advertising, maintenance, insurance and salaries of head office personnel) represent common costs of all three locations and will have to be shared between all three cost objectives.

EXHIBIT 2.4: DIRECT/OVERHEAD COST CLASSIFICATION SYSTEM FOR AIRLINES

| Cost objective | Direct costs | | Overheads |
|---|---|---|---|
| | Direct materials | Direct labour | |
| Route to US | Fuel; Food/beverages; Landing charges | Salary costs of pilots and crew | Advertising; Salaries of check-in desk; General insurance; |
| Route to France | Fuel; Food/beverages; Landing charges | Salary costs of pilots and crew | Salaries of head office; Directors' fees; Audit fees |
| Route to Italy | Fuel; Food/beverages; Landing charges | Salary costs of pilots and crew | |

Associated with the classification of direct and overhead costs are the important terms 'cost allocation' and 'cost apportionment', though sometimes this distinction is not made. **Cost allocation** represents the assignment of an entire cost to a single cost objective. Only direct costs, by definition, are allocated. **Cost apportionment**, on the other hand, represents the assignment of overhead costs between two or more cost objectives. Cost apportionment is a much more subjective and arbitrary process. For example, using the airline example above, how could one apportion advertising costs between the various routes? Several alternatives can be suggested and this issue will be discussed in **Section 2.4**.

Generally speaking, overhead costs are common costs associated with the many different aspects of business operations and cannot be objectively traced to individual cost objectives. We shall see later that overheads are assigned to products (as cost objectives in their own right) using (subjective) overhead absorption rates.

## 4. Cost Classification by Function

Costs may also be classified by their function within the organisation. The main functions in a manufacturing enterprise are:

- production of finished goods
- selling and distribution
- administration

The functional classification system is primarily used for stock valuation purposes and our discussion in this section will relate, mainly, to a manufacturing firm. Under International Financial Reporting Standards (IFRS) the cost of manufactured goods, which remain unsold at the end of the accounting period, should be determined with reference to production cost only. Production costs (or simply, product costs) will typically include:

- Direct Materials A manufacturer buys raw materials and converts them into finished goods. These materials can be physically and easily traced to the product, e.g. flour in a loaf of bread.
- Direct Labour In converting raw materials into finished goods, a manufacturer incurs direct labour costs, representing the wages paid to factory employees who work directly on the products being manufactured. Direct labour costs include the cost of machine operators, assembly line workers and others who work on the goods by hand or with tools.
- Production Overhead All manufacturing costs other than direct material and direct production labour (and other direct costs if any) may be classified as production overheads. Expenditure on such overheads is necessary to engage in production but overhead costs, by their nature, cannot be traced to an individual product (in a multi-product firm). Rather, they must be shared, in some equitable manner, among the various products. It is easier for the management accountant to include all these costs under a single overhead cost heading. Typical production overheads include salaries of supervisors and maintenance personnel, depreciation and insurance of factory, and power for machinery.

Non-production overheads typically comprise selling, distribution costs and administration expenses but also finance costs should also be included although this issue is rarely mentioned in managerial accounting texts. Selling and distribution costs represent the costs of creating and stimulating demand for the company's products and also the costs of getting the goods to the customers. Examples of selling and distribution costs include advertising, salaries paid to members of the sales force, including commission and travel expenses, as well as bad debts associated with credit sales.

Administration costs are the costs associated with the various support functions within the firm and are typically associated with accounting, personnel and various executive functions. Examples of administration costs include all administrative salaries, telephone costs and depreciation of administrative equipment. It should be noted that selling, distribution and administration costs do not relate to the production process. They are sometimes described as 'period' rather than 'product costs' since they should never be included in the calculation of production costs. Certain costs, such as insurance, may be applicable in part to factory operations and in part to administration. In such cases, these costs should be shared, in some equitable manner, between production overheads and non-production (or period) costs. (We will discuss the important topic of closing stock valuation in the next section.)

## Cost Statements

We now turn our attention to **cost statements** and **cost structures** of different types of enterprise, i.e. manufacturer, retailer and service provider and we will use, as far as practicable, the same figures for illustration purposes.

Why are we concerned with overall cost statements and cost structures? A number of reasons can be offered. First, for all firms, overall cost structure will be a major determinant of profitability and operating cash flow. It will also indicate whether a cost leadership strategy is, in fact, feasible. **Cost leadership** is a strategy whereby a firm outperforms its competitors by producing products or services at the lowest cost. Secondly, overall cost structure can reveal scope for cost reduction based on external benchmarking – i.e. comparison with similar firms in the industry – provided comparative data is available. Thirdly, it can highlight the dangers of external cost pressures as, e.g. where airline profitability is heavily impacted on by rising fuel prices. Fourthly, for manufacturing firms, overall cost structure facilitates the 'make v. buy' decision. And, finally, overall cost structure may provide evidence in anti-dumping allegations made by the EU and other international organisations.

A typical cost statement and income summary for a manufacturing company would appear as in **Exhibit 2.5** below. Costs are classified with reference to function, traceability and nature. A typical cost statement (with revenue figures) for both a retail and service firms is presented in **Exhibits 2.6** and **2.7** respectively.

The reader will notice that both the manufacturer and retailer generate the same amount of profit for the year. This is because the manufacturer has incurred total

EXHIBIT 2.5: COST STATEMENT AND INCOME SUMMARY FOR A MANUFACTURER
FOR YEAR ENDED 31 DECEMBER 20X8

|  | € | € |
|---|---|---|
| Production costs: |  |  |
| (a) Direct materials consumed: |  |  |
| Opening inventory of raw materials | 20,000 |  |
| Add: Purchases of raw materials | 150,000 |  |
| Less: Closing inventory of raw materials | (30,000) |  |
| Cost of raw materials consumed |  | 140,000 |
| (b) Direct labour |  | 400,000 |
| (c) Production overhead: |  |  |
| Salaries of factory managers | 100,000 |  |
| Depreciation of production equipment | 20,000 |  |
| Depreciation of factory building | 10,000 | 130,000 |
| = Cost of finished goods manufactured |  | 670,000 |

**Income summary for year ended 31 Dec. 20x8**

| | | |
|---|---:|---:|
| Sales | | 1,200,000 |
| Less: Cost of goods sold: | | |
| Opening inventory of finished goods | 100,000 | |
| Add: Cost of finished goods manufactured (above) | 670,000 | |
| Less: Closing inventory of finished goods | (120,000) | (650,000) |
| = Gross profit | | 550,000 |
| Less: Selling and distribution costs | | (200,000) |
| Less: Administration costs | | (100,000) |
| Profit before interest and tax | | 250,000 |

EXHIBIT 2.6: COST STATEMENT AND INCOME SUMMARY FOR A RETAILER
FOR YEAR ENDED 31 DECEMBER 20X8

| | € | € |
|---|---:|---:|
| Sales | | 1,200,000 |
| Less: Cost of goods sold: | | |
| Opening inventory of goods for resale | 100,000 | |
| Add: Purchases of finished goods | 670,000 | |
| Less: Closing inventory of goods for resale | (120,000) | (650,000) |
| Gross profit | | 550,000 |
| Less: Selling and distribution costs | | (200,000) |
| Less: Administration costs | | (100,000) |
| Profit before interest and tax | | 250,000 |

EXHIBIT 2.7: COST STATEMENT AND INCOME SUMMARY FOR A SERVICE
FIRM FOR YEAR ENDED 31 DECEMBER 20X8

| | € |
|---|---:|
| Sales | 1,200,000 |
| Less: Cost of goods sold: | N/A |
| Less: Selling and distribution costs | (200,000) |
| Less: Administration costs | (100,000) |
| Profit before interest and tax | 900,000 |

expenses of €650,000, after adjusting for changes in inventory levels, in manufacturing the goods. The retailer has also spent €650,000, after adjusting for changes in stock levels. However, the retailer has incurred these costs in purchasing the finished goods from suppliers. The cost statement of the service provider is altogether much more straightforward. There are no production costs and no issues regarding inventory valuation. The overall cost structure is dominated by selling, distribution and administration costs.

In the next section we shall look at how inventory valuation is computed for a manufacturing firm, based on product costing principles. We shall stress, again, the fact that cost information is used for various purposes, of which inventory valuation for financial reporting purposes is but one. Product-costing systems have been heavily influenced by the requirements of financial reporting.

## 2.3 Stock Valuation: Absorption v. Direct (Variable) Costing

In **Section 2.2** we discussed four cost classification methods. In this section we shall focus on cost information for inventory valuation purposes (in a manufacturing firm) and, in particular, we shall discuss two costing methods, namely, absorption costing and variable (or direct) costing. Both methods will provide different cost figures, and in many cases different profit figures will be reported for the accounting period under review.

For inventory valuation purposes, the total cost structure of a manufacturing firm can be classified as either production costs or non-production costs and this is highlighted below in **Exhibit 2.8**.

It is important to stress that, for inventory valuation purposes in a manufacturing business, only production costs can be used. This is because the production costs have

EXHIBIT 2.8: COST STRUCTURE AND INVENTORY CALCULATION

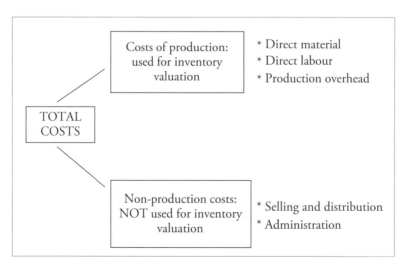

already been incurred in bringing the product to its present state and condition. Sometimes, we describe these costs as product costs. In contrast, costs not associated with production should **never** be assigned to closing inventory, e.g. selling, distribution and administration costs. Sometimes, we refer to such costs as 'period costs' – they are written off entirely to the income statement in the accounting period in which they are incurred. The reason for not including non-production costs in closing inventory valuation is that they have not been incurred in bringing the product to its present state and condition.

### The Difference between Absorption and Direct (or Variable) Costing

While there is general agreement that only production costs should be included in inventory calculations, there is less agreement on which production costs should be taken into consideration. Within the discipline of management accounting there are two schools of thought relating to the valuation of closing inventory – namely those who favour **absorption costing** and those who favour **direct costing** (alternatively referred to as **variable costing**). It should be stressed that the debate is concerned *only* with the valuation of inventory for management accounting purposes and focuses only on the accounting treatment of *fixed* production overhead. (Variable production costs will always be included in stock valuation computations.)

The absorption school argues that fixed production overheads should be included in inventory valuation since they have been incurred in bringing the product to its present location and condition. Thus, you cannot manufacture the goods without incurring fixed production overheads.

In contrast, the direct (or variable) costing school argues that these fixed production overheads are associated with providing production capacity as distinct from using it for manufacturing purposes. Thus, fixed production overheads would be incurred regardless of the level of output and, therefore, it is argued, they should not be included in inventory valuation but written off immediately and in total to the income statement. Actually, it is not conceptually correct to use the terms 'direct' or 'variable' costing in relation to this inventory valuation! The term 'direct' costing is not appropriate since variable production overheads are included in inventory valuation. Likewise, the term 'variable' is not appropriate since variable, non-production costs are specifically excluded from inventory valuation. Really, the term '**variable production costing**' would be preferable instead of the terms 'direct' or 'variable' costing.

For financial reporting purposes the 'absorption v. direct' debate is irrelevant. This is because International Financial Reporting Standards (IFRS) require the use only of absorption costing for inventory valuation. However, it must be stressed that, for management accounting, i.e. internal reporting to managers, the company may use whatever inventory valuation method it prefers. Finally, it must be recalled that the distinction between absorption and variable (direct) costing is determined with reference only to the accounting treatment of fixed production overheads. The main accounting differences between these two methods are as follows:

| Direct costing | Absorption costing |
|---|---|
| Cost behaviour analysis is required to calculate variable production overhead (in addition to direct materials and direct labour) | Total production cost identified (without classification between fixed and variable production overhead) |
| Variable production costs are the only overheads included in inventory valuation | Total production costs are included in inventory valuation |
| All fixed costs (production and non-production) are written off entirely to the income statement when incurred | Non-production fixed overheads are written off entirely to the income statement when incurred |

## ILLUSTRATION: ABSORPTION V. DIRECT COSTING FOR INVENTORY VALUATION

A firm plans to manufacture a new product for which the following data is provided over the next three months and, for convenience, direct materials, direct labour and variable manufacturing overheads have been included under the single heading of variable manufacturing costs:

| | |
|---|---|
| Selling price per unit | €8 |
| Variable manufacturing costs per unit | €2 |
| Fixed production overheads | €10,000 per month |
| Fixed administration costs | €5,000 per month |

Units produced and unit sales are expected as follows:

| | Jan. | Feb. | Mar. | Total |
|---|---|---|---|---|
| Production (units) | 5,000 | 5,000 | 5,000 | 15,000 |
| Sales (units) | 4,000 | 5,000 | 6,000 | 15,000 |

**Requirements:**

1. You are required to indicate the closing inventory valuations for each month under absorption costing and prepare a forecast income statement for the above three months using normal production levels as a denominator for your fixed production overhead per unit calculation.

2. You are required to indicate the closing inventory valuations for each month under direct (variable) costing and prepare a forecast income statement for the above three months under direct costing.

**Solution and Analysis:** The respective calculations under (i) absorption and (ii) direct (variable) costing are presented below. Initially, we compute the valuation of closing inventory and then proceed with the presentation of the income summary for the respective three months.

**Under absorption costing, inventory is valued as follows:**

| | |
|---|---|
| Variable production costs (given) | 2.00 |
| Fixed production overhead (€10,000/5,000) | 2.00 |
| | 4.00 |

| SUMMARISED INCOME STATEMENTS | | | |
|---|---|---|---|
| Income statements – absorption costing | | | |
| | Jan. | Feb. | Mar. |
| Total sales revenue | €32,000 | €40,000 | €48,000 |
| Opening inventory (1,000 units @ €4) | – | 4,000 | 4,000 |
| Variable production costs incurred | 10,000 | 10,000 | 10,000 |
| Fixed production overheads | 10,000 | 10,000 | 10,000 |
| Less: Closing inventory (1,000 units @ €4) | (4,000) | (4,000) | — |
| Cost of sales | 16,000 | 20,000 | 24,000 |
| Gross profit | 16,000 | 20,000 | 24,000 |
| Administration costs | (5,000) | (5,000) | (5,000) |
| Net profit | 11,000 | 15,000 | 19,000 |
| Total profit (three months) | €45,000 | | |

**Under direct (or variable) costing, inventory is valued as follows:**

| | |
|---|---|
| Variable manufacturing costs (given) | 2.00 |
| Fixed production overhead | Nil |
| | 2.00 |

| SUMMARISED INCOME STATEMENTS | | | |
|---|---|---|---|
| Income Statements – Direct Costing | | | |
| | Jan. | Feb. | Mar. |
| Total sales revenue | €32,000 | €40,000 | €48,000 |
| Opening inventory (1,000 units @ €2) | – | 2,000 | 2,000 |
| Variable manufacturing costs incurred | 10,000 | 10,000 | 10,000 |
| Fixed production costs | 10,000 | 10,000 | 10,000 |
| Less: Closing inventory (1,000 units @ €2) | (2,000) | (2,000) | — |
| Cost of sales | 18,000 | 20,000 | 22,000 |
| Gross profit | 14,000 | 20,000 | 26,000 |
| Administration costs | (5,000) | (5,000) | (5,000) |
| Net profit | 9,000 | 15,000 | 21,000 |
| Total profit (three months) | €45,000 | | |

**Profit Reconciliation:**
The reported profit figures for the two costing methods for inventory valuation are significantly different for two of the above months (January and March) but exactly similar for the month of February. Using the notation below, these differences can be calculated:

F   =  € fixed production overheads
O   =  € other fixed (non-production) overheads
C   =  € contribution margin per unit
Y   =  actual sales volume (units)
X   =  actual production volume (units)
N   =  normal production volume (units)
PA  =  € net profit under absorption costing
PD  =  € net profit under variable costing calculated by: $PD = C \times Y - [F+O]$

Thus, reported profit under variable (direct) costing for January can be calculated as follows, based on a unit contribution of (€8−€2) = €6.

$$PD = €6 \times 4{,}000 \text{ units} - (€10{,}000 + €5{,}000) = €9{,}000 \text{ profit.}$$

The difference between the two profit figures is entirely attributable to the accounting treatment of fixed production overhead for inventory valuation purposes, adjusted for the change in inventory levels during the period. This can be written as:

$$PD - PA = \frac{F(Y-X)}{N}$$

Thus, in January, the profit difference is $= \frac{€10,000 \times (4,000 - 5,000)}{5,000 \text{ units}} = (€2,000)$

For January, a profit of €11,000 under absorption costing was reported compared with a profit of €9,000 under direct costing. This is explained by the different accounting treatment of fixed production overheads. The fixed overhead per unit is €2 (i.e. €10,000/5,000 units). During the month of January, an additional 1,000 units were placed in inventory. Thus, under absorption costing, inventory will be valued at €2,000 more than under direct costing and this provides the higher reported profit for that month.

## General Comments

The differences in reported profit between variable and absorption costing methods can be significant. Generally, absorption costing will provide less volatile profit figures relative to variable costing. Basically, there are only three possible situations in relation to changes in inventory levels during the accounting period:

1. When production equals sales, then both methods will provide the same profit figures.
2. When production exceeds sales (i.e. inventory build-up), then absorption costing provides the relatively higher profit figures. This is because a portion of the fixed production overhead incurred will be included in the closing inventory valuation figure and, therefore, transferred to the closing balance sheet rather than being written off immediately to the income statement. The essence of absorption costing is that an enterprise could, in theory, boost its reported profit performance by engaging in an inventory build up at the end of an accounting period.
3. When sales exceed production (i.e. inventory run down), then variable costing will provide the relatively higher profit figure. This is because under variable costing only the fixed overheads applicable to the period in question are being written off to the income statement. Under an absorption costing system, the fixed production overheads for the period in question are being written off (since sales volume exceed production volume) in addition to a portion of the previous period's fixed production overheads which were included in the valuation of opening inventory.

## Arguments in Favour of Variable (Direct) Costing

Management accounting reports (including inventory valuation methods) are not constrained by International Financial Reporting Standards. Thus, management have the discretion to value inventory using either absorption or direct costing methods. Accordingly, it is useful to review some of the main arguments in favour of both costing systems. The advocates of **direct costing** argue as follows:

(a) Fixed production overhead costs are incurred whether production takes place or not. Fixed production overheads, they argue, are costs associated with providing capacity rather than using that capacity and are not, therefore, product costs in the strict definition of the term.

(b) The use of direct costing avoids the variation of unit cost with every change in the level of output as illustrated below:

|  | 100 units<br>€ | 200 units<br>€ | 300 units<br>€ |
|---|---|---|---|
| Total fixed production overheads | 1,000 | 1,000 | 1,000 |
| Total variable production cost | 500 | 1,000 | 1,500 |
| Total production cost (F + V) | 1,500 | 2,000 | 2,500 |
| Total production cost per unit | 15.00 | 10.00 | 8.33 |

It should be noted that under direct (or variable) costing, the variable production cost is constant at €5 per unit whereas the total production cost per unit fluctuates with volume changes.

(c) The use of variable costing will assist pricing policy when considering the use of spare capacity for special order decisions. In such situations, variable cost will be an important consideration.

## Arguments against Direct Costing

The main argument against variable costing is that it cannot be used for external reporting purposes. Therefore, the use of variable costing for management accounting purposes would probably require the maintenance of two separate inventory valuation systems – one for financial reporting and one for management accounting purposes. The availability of two reported profit figures for the same period would probably cause confusion. As a result, most companies use absorption costing for both financial and management accounting purposes.

### Arguments in Favour of Absorption Costing

On the other hand, those who favour **absorption costing** put forward the following arguments:

(a) Production cannot take place without incurring a certain level of fixed production overheads. Therefore, it is correct to include such costs in inventory valuation.
(b) Over the long term, prices cannot be set without regard to total cost, which includes an element of fixed production overheads. If a large proportion of sales volume is priced by reference to the variable cost only, then the overall contribution generated may not be sufficient to meet fixed costs.
(c) It is not always easy to segregate fixed and variable overheads – with absorption costing any such difficulty is not necessary since the focus is on total production costs.

### Arguments against Absorption Costing

The main argument against absorption costing is that managers have the incentive to build up year-end inventory levels in order to increase profits. This is because, under absorption costing, profits are heavily influenced by levels of production rather than the level of sales. The scope and potential for profit manipulation is therefore evident from the following scenarios:

(a) Production managers may defer routine maintenance work to increase production levels.
(b) Production managers may produce goods for which definite orders have not been received.

The second disadvantage of absorption costing lies in the area of routine profit planning, which usually starts with the identification of contribution per unit and then the calculation of break-even point. Since absorption costing automatically includes a portion of fixed production overhead in calculating unit cost (for inventory valuation purposes), the calculation of break-even point is more complicated when compared with variable (direct) costing. (This complication is not explored in this text.)

## 2.4 Disaggregation of Cost Structure: Allocation and Apportionment

In **Section 2.2** we looked at overall cost statements and cost structures of manufacturing, retail and service companies. We now turn our attention to a segment of those businesses and we shall focus on various cost objectives.

In simple terms, a cost objective is an object or activity relating to the organisation for which we require cost data. Clearly, there are a large variety of cost objectives within an organisation. For example, in the context of a university, the cost objective may be relatively broad, e.g. to ascertain the costs of running the business school; on the other hand, it may be very narrow, e.g. to ascertain the cost per student in a particular academic department. Information on cost per student could be used for planning purposes, e.g. setting future fee levels. Alternatively, the information could be used for control and evaluation purposes, i.e. how well does actual cost per student compare with budget?

This section looks at how costs may be ascertained for a cost objective and this, in the author's opinion, represents the kernel of managerial accounting – **the disaggregation of cost data**.

Before discussing the issue of assigning costs to cost objectives, it may be useful to review a previous distinction between cost allocation and cost apportionment. *Cost allocation* represents the assignment of cost to a single cost objective, for example, the costs of a specific product line. Cost allocation means that there is no requirement to share the cost between different cost objectives. On the other hand, *cost apportionment* involves sharing a cost between two or more cost objectives, for example, advertising costs may have to be shared between two or more product lines. **Indirect (overhead) costs are apportioned, in contrast to direct costs which are allocated** and this distinction is highlighted below in **Exhibit 2.9.**

Many management textbooks do not make this subtle but important distinction between cost allocation and cost apportionment but, rather, use the words interchangeably. To avoid ambiguity, it is preferable to use these terms in their appropriate context. However, the term 'cost assignment' can be used as the generic term.

It is important to note that cost apportionment is very much an arbitrary task – there is no such thing as a single, best method of apportioning costs. Cost apportionment is ultimately a matter of opinion and different methods of apportionment will give different results. Consequently, cost apportionment can mislead users of management accounting information because users do not often appreciate the arbitrary nature of cost apportionment. To complicate matters, a cost may be direct for one purpose (and therefore is allocated) and an overhead for another (and therefore apportioned). For example, the production manager's salary is a direct cost of the manufacturing

EXHIBIT 2.9: COST ALLOCATION AND COST APPORTIONMENT

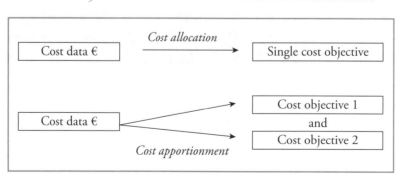

department (and thus allocated), while it would be classified as an overhead in ascertaining the production cost per unit of output from that department. The **general principle** is **that the larger the cost objective, the more costs that can be allocated to it; the smaller the cost objective, the more costs that are apportioned to it** and this is presented in **Exhibit 2.10** in relation to a retail store:

EXHIBIT 2.10 COST OBJECTIVE, COST ALLOCATION AND APPORTIONMENT IN A RETAIL STORE

| Cost objective | How many cost objectives are there in the store? | Comment re direct and overhead costs |
| --- | --- | --- |
| The (entire) store | One store only, i.e. the location | All costs are direct of the 'store' |
| An individual department | 75 departments in store | Mixture of direct and overhead costs |
| A specific product line | 2,000 brands in store | Some direct costs but many overhead costs |
| An item for sale | 3 million different items for sale | Purchase cost is direct; the rest are overheads |

Usually, costs are assigned to cost objectives using the **benefit principle**. This means that costs are assigned to cost objectives based on the perceived benefit that they generate. In other words, we try to identify a cause and effect relationship, though this may be a difficult task. The following methods of cost apportionment for different costs are commonly used within organisations:

| Costs to be apportioned | Method of apportionment | Type of firm |
| --- | --- | --- |
| Rent and rates | Area occupied | All firms |
| Light and heat | Area occupied | All firms |
| Power for machines | Machine running hours | Manufacturer |
| Machine maintenance | Machine running hours | Manufacturer |
| Administration costs | Number of employees | All firms |
| Canteen costs | Number of employees | All firms |
| Advertising costs | Sales revenue | All firms |
| Exam costs | Student numbers | University |

Alternatively, some costs are apportioned among various cost objectives according to agreed percentages, reflecting the arbitrary nature of cost apportionment and to facilitate clerical convenience.

The illustration below is set in a retail context and the selected cost objectives are three different product lines offered by the company. We are starting with a product line because it is easy to envisage, as we are all familiar with various product lines of consumer products. Why might we want to ascertain the costs of a product line? A reasonable answer is that we want to find out whether a specific product line is profitable or otherwise as we might want to either promote it or withdraw it. Also, we may want to know whether the profitability is increasing or decreasing. In turn, each product line may have a manager that is responsible and part of his remuneration could be linked to its profitability.

## ILLUSTRATION OF COST ALLOCATION AND APPORTIONMENT

Dublin Fashions is a small family-owned retail company which sells three different product lines, namely men's, women's and children's clothes. During its most recent financial year the company made an operating profit of €30,000 as disclosed in the summarised income statement below:

### SUMMARISED INCOME AND COST STATEMENT FOR YEAR ENDED 31 DECEMBER 20XI

| | € | € |
|---|---|---|
| **Sales** | | |
| Men's clothes | 50,000 | |
| Women's clothes | 30,000 | |
| Children's clothes | 20,000 | 100,000 |
| **Less: Costs:** | | |
| Cost of men's clothes | 20,000 | |
| Cost of women's clothes | 10,000 | |
| Cost of children's clothes | 15,000 | |
| Advertising costs (fixed cost) | 10,000 | |
| Rent and rates (fixed cost) | 5,000 | |
| Wages (fixed cost) | 10,000 | 70,000 |
| Operating profit for year | | 30,000 |

**Requirement:** Based on the above data, prepare an accounting statement showing the profitability of each of the three product lines in a manner suitable for managerial decision-making and which distinguishes between fixed and variable costs.

Advertising costs should be apportioned to each product line on the basis of sales turnover; rent and rates should be apportioned on the basis of square footage occupied (1/2, 1/4 and 1/4 respectively); and wages should be apportioned on the basis of numbers of employees engaged in each product line (2, 2 and 1 employees respectively). You may assume that fixed overheads will continue to be incurred. Based on your calculations, should any of the product lines be discontinued? Give your reasons.

**Solution and Analysis:** Since the information to be generated will be used in decision-making, it is useful to prepare the statement in a contribution-based format and therefore report fixed and variable costs separately. (The term '**contribution**' refers to the surplus of sales revenue over total variable costs and this surplus, if any, is available to pay total fixed costs.) The respective cost of clothes is a direct cost for each product line and can be allocated directly to a specific product line. All other costs must be apportioned, in order to provide an overall cost picture for each product line. The contribution format statement is presented below.

## Dublin Fashions

CONTRIBUTION FORMAT INCOME STATEMENT FOR YEAR
ENDED 31 DECEMBER 20X1

|  | Men's € | Women's € | Children's € | Total € |
|---|---|---|---|---|
| Total Sales | 50,000 | 30,000 | 20,000 | 100,000 |
| Variable costs: |  |  |  |  |
| Men's clothes | 20,000 | – | – | 20,000 |
| Women's clothes | – | 10,000 | – | 10,000 |
| Children's clothes | = | = | 15,000 | 15,000 |
| Total variable cost | 20,000 | 10,000 | 15,000 | 45,000 |
| Total contribution | 30,000 | 20,000 | 5,000 | 55,000 |
| Fixed costs: |  |  |  |  |
| Advertising | (5,000) | (3,000) | (2,000) | (10,000) |
| Rent and rates | (2,500) | (1,250) | (1,250) | (5,000) |
| Wages | (4,000) | (4,000) | (2,000) | (10,000) |
| Total fixed costs | 11,500 | 8,250 | 5,250 | 25,000 |
| Product profit (loss) | 18,500 | 11,750 | (250) | 30,000 |

Although children's clothes show a small loss of €250 during the period, we would recommend its retention in the product line, in the absence of a specified alternative. The reason for this recommendation is that this product line generates an overall contribution of €5,000 towards fixed costs. The apportioned fixed costs, amounting to €5,250, will be incurred whether this product line is continued or not – at least based on the limited information available. Thus, the notion of contribution, rather than profit, is important in decision-making.

There are also non-quantifiable factors involved in the above analysis. In this case, the continued availability of children's clothes might create long-term customers, as children grow into adults. Also, parents, looking for clothes for their children, may identify some clothes for themselves. Both of these factors are relevant to the decision to close down, for example, the children's product line but they are not easily quantified. Thus, we should always remember that managerial decisions are influenced by quantitative and also qualitative considerations.

## 2.5  Assigning Overheads to Units Using Overhead Absorption Rates

In the previous section we defined a cost objective as an object or activity relating to the organisation for which we require cost data. Clearly, there are a large variety of cost objectives within an organisation. Some are very broad, e.g. a product line (as discussed in the previous section) or very narrow, e.g. the cost of a unit of output. The purpose of this section is to establish the unit cost of a manufactured product. We have already suggested that **unit cost information is necessary for three purposes**:

1.  In the context of pricing a product or service, we have to know how much it costs. Unless the selling price covers the cost, no profit can be earned on the transaction. When we talk about 'cost' here for the purposes of selling price determination, we focus on all costs – both production and non-production costs. However, it must be acknowledged that sometimes selling prices are deliberately set below cost in order to attract new customers. Also, selling prices are established taking into account a number of factors, of which cost is only one.
2.  Unit costs must also be ascertained in order to control operations. For example, managers want to know whether planned costs are being adhered to as otherwise profit targets may not be achieved. However, managers may learn from cost overruns and use this information in planning for the future.
3.  Any unsold goods at the end of the accounting period must be valued, in accordance with IFRS, at production cost (or net realisable value, if this is lower than cost). Production costs comprise three elements: direct materials, direct labour and

production overheads; and we shall concentrate on these three elements for the time being. (It should be remembered that non-production costs are not considered as 'product' costs for stock valuation purposes and are ignored in this section.)

There should be little difficulty in tracing direct material cost to manufactured units as most manufacturing enterprises control direct material movements by way of a goods requisition docket which indicates the type and quantity of each material issued to production. They are normally pre-printed for convenience and numbered to identify if some documents have been misplaced. Direct labour is usually traced to the product by way of job cards, or time sheets in the case of a service business. Such a record reveals the time spent by an employee on a specific manufacturing operation (or for a client in the context of a service firm). The relevant hours worked by employees multiplied by the appropriate pay rate, represents the labour cost involved.

### Assigning Production Overheads

The third category of cost – overhead – is more problematic, because there is no single, correct method of assigning overhead costs (which are incurred for all products) into a unit of output.

To complicate the issue, production overhead is becoming increasingly important in manufacturing cost structures due to increased automation. Automation generally increases production overheads due to increased machine maintenance, insurance and depreciation. The gradual switch towards increased automation in many firms is likely to continue in the future so that direct labour will become relatively unimportant and production overheads will become increasingly significant in the overall cost structure. In some manufacturing firms, direct labour can be as low as 10% of total costs, whereas production overhead can be as high as 30% or 40% of total cost.

A simple method of assigning production overheads to units of output is to divide total production overhead by the number of units produced during the accounting period. For example, this might be done in a university to calculate the overhead cost per student since students can be considered reasonably similar in their consumption of the university's resources (ignoring the difference between undergraduate and postgraduate students). Likewise, this could be done in a single-product manufacturing firm since all units of output are similar and hence consume an equal amount of overhead. However, this simple approach of dividing overheads by total units produced is not appropriate in a multi-product firm because the various products consume different amounts of overhead costs. This overhead cost-assignment problem is solved by the technique of calculating an overhead absorption rate (OHAR). **Overhead absorption** is a technique used to assign overhead costs to units of output and requires a cost driver. (A **cost driver** is any factor that significantly affects cost behaviour and some measure of volume of output is often regarded as the most significant cost driver.) The three steps needed to calculate overhead absorption rates (OHARs) are as follows:

1. Estimate total production overheads to be incurred during the forthcoming period (the numerator).

2. Identify an appropriate cost driver and estimate the level of this cost driver for the period (the denominator).
3. Divide (1) by (2) to arrive at an OHAR i.e.

$$\text{OHAR} = \frac{\text{Estimated total production overhead}}{\text{Estimated level of cost driver}}$$

Typical cost drivers used in manufacturing firms for the purpose of calculating overhead absorption rates (OHARs) are machine running hours or direct labour hours. However, a cost item may have different cost drivers in different settings. For example, in a manufacturing company, electricity costs would be driven by the number of machine hours or possibly the number of units manufactured. In a retail firm, the cost of electricity would be driven by the number of hours the retail store was open for business. If an inappropriate cost driver is used to calculate overhead absorption rates, then the costing result will be inaccurate product costs.

For example, if direct labour hours is used to assign overheads, but in reality production overhead has little relationship with direct labour hours, then products with high direct labour hour requirements will be assigned an unrealistic amount of overhead and will be overcosted.

**Overhead absorption** represents the third 'A' of cost accounting. The other two 'As' are represented by **cost allocation** and **cost apportionment**, which we have discussed in **Section 2.4**. Overhead absorption is the assignment of overhead costs to units of output. In contrast, both cost allocation and cost apportionment represent assigning costs to broad cost objectives, e.g product lines or departments. Therefore, assigning overhead costs to units of output can be described as a two-stage process and this is depicted in **Exhibit 2.11** below. Initially, overhead costs are assigned to departments. As work is performed, the products are assigned direct material and direct labour costs. Also, production overhead is added using overhead absorption rates (OHARs) in order to provide a total production cost per unit figure.

EXHIBIT 2.11: ASSIGNING PRODUCTION OVERHEAD COSTS TO COST UNITS

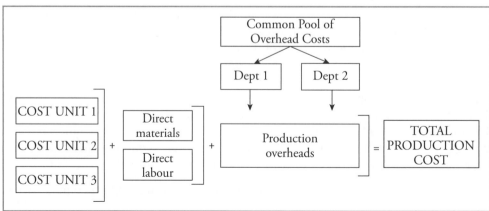

## ILLUSTRATION OF OHAR CALCULATION

For illustration purposes, we shall assume that a manufacturing firm expects to incur production overheads of €200,000 per annum and considers that direct labour hours (DLH) is the appropriate cost driver. It is anticipated that 20,000 direct labour hours will be worked during the forthcoming year. The overhead absorption rate (OHAR) is calculated as:

$$\text{OHAR} = \frac{\text{Total production overhead}}{\text{Direct labour hours}} = \frac{€200,000}{20,000} = €10 \text{ per DLH}$$

This OHAR means that €10 overheads will be added to each unit of output for every direct labour hour worked on that particular unit. If a certain unit (or job) required five hours of direct labour, the overheads assigned (in addition to direct labour and material costs) to this product would be €50 (5 hours × €10).

Readers will appreciate that OHAR is a very simple concept and technique. However, it was developed a long time ago when direct labour cost was a significant cost element in the overall cost structure of manufacturing firms and production overheads were, correspondingly, much smaller than they are in today's environment. (We shall return to this point later and especially in **Chapter 5**.)

It should be remembered that we are using OHARs to estimate production overhead cost to be included in a calculation of total production cost (under absorption costing). This cost figure is required for a number of purposes. For example, the cost figure will be used for stock valuation. It may also be used in a decision whether to subcontract or continue with existing production. However, this figure should not be confused with 'total cost', which will include both production and non-production cost. Obviously, many selling price decisions will be based on total cost considerations and such pricing decisions will be discussed in **Chapter 3, Section 3.2**.

### Additional Considerations for OHAR

Establishing OHARs requires four additional factors to be considered. Each factor represents a choice that must be made and each will now be addressed in turn:

- Should we use departmental or plant-wide rates?
- What cost driver should be used?
- Should we use annual or seasonal rates?
- Should we use predetermined or actual rates?

## Departmental or Plant-wide Rates?

In terms of calculating OHARs, management accountants must make a choice between departmental and plant-wide rates. The former represents calculating an OHAR for each individual department in the production process. The latter involves a single calculation for the plant (i.e. factory) as a whole.

## Illustration of Departmental and Plant-wide OHARS

The Cork Company normally manufactures two different products – Products A and B – in two different manufacturing departments. The total budgeted production overhead and estimated direct labour hours are shown below for the forthcoming period:

|  | Budgeted Overhead € | Budgeted Hours |
|---|---|---|
| Department 1 | 400,000 | 100,000 |
| Department 2 | 200,000 | 200,000 |
| Total | 600,000 | 300,000 |

The amount of labour hours required to manufacture each product is:

|  | Product A | Product B |
|---|---|---|
| In Department 1 | 4 hours | 1 hour |
| In Department 2 | 1 hour | 4 hours |
| Total | 5 hours | 5 hours |

**Requirements:**

1. Calculate departmental overhead absorption rates (OHARs) for Departments 1 and 2 using direct labour hours (DLH) and indicate the overheads assigned to a unit of Product A and B based on your calculations.
2. Calculate a plant-wide overhead absorption rate using direct labour hours (DLH) and indicate the overheads assigned to a unit of Product A and B.

**Solution and Analysis:**

1. The departmental production overhead absorption rates are computed as follows:

Dept 1 €400,000/100,000 = €4 per DLH. This means that for every direct labour worked on a product in Department 1, the product will receive €4 of production overhead, in addition to its direct costs.

Dept 2 €200,000/200,000 = €1 per DLH. This means that for every direct labour hour worked in Department 2, the product will receive €1 of production overhead, in addition to its direct costs.

2. Therefore, the amount of overhead assigned to a unit of product A and B using departmental OHARs is as follows:

|  | Product A | Product B |
|---|---|---|
| Department 1 | €16 (4 hours × €4) | €4 (1 hour × €4) |
| Department 2 | € 1 (1 hour × €1) | €4 (4 hours × €1) |
| Overhead per unit | €17 | €8 |

3. Using a single plant-wide overhead absorption rate, only one computation is required since we are looking at the plant in its entirety. The computation of OHAR is as follows:

$$\frac{\text{Production Overheads}}{\text{Cost driver i.e. DLH}} = \frac{€600,000}{300,000} = €2 \text{ per DLH}$$

This means that for every direct labour hour work on a product, regardless of whether it is done in Department 1 or Department 2, the product will receive €2 of production overheads, in addition to its direct costs. Using this plant–wide OHAR, the overhead assigned to products is as follows:

|  | Product A | Product B |
|---|---|---|
| Overhead per unit | 5 hours at €2 each = €10 | 5 hours at €2 each = €10 |

Using a plant-wide absorption rate, the overhead assigned to each product is the same because they both require the same amount of labour hours. However, this ignores the fact that Department 1 is relatively more expensive to operate. Also, there is an unequal amount of labour performed on each product in each department. It is generally considered that the use of department overhead absorption rates is preferable to a single, plant-wide rate because:

• Departmental overhead absorption rates allow the use of different cost drivers in the separate departments. Thus, in one department, overhead costs may be absorbed into units on the basis of direct labour hours and, in another department, on the basis of machine hours.

- The relative efficiency of different operating departments can be monitored by identifying the amount of production overhead absorbed at the end of the accounting period. A department with levels of output below budget may not be able to absorb all its production overheads. In turn, responsible managers can be held accountable for their operations.
- In a multi-product firm, it is likely that some units will pass through some departments but not others. Therefore, using departmental absorption rates, overhead costs will be assigned to units only if work is performed in a specific department and this should provide more accurate costing figures.

## What Cost Driver to Use?

The choice of appropriate cost driver to use in calculating OHARs is by no means an easy task. With traditional cost accumulation systems, three cost drivers are commonly used:

1. **Direct labour hours** Many production overhead costs are time-related or associated with the amount of labour input. Thus, production overheads are commonly absorbed on the basis of direct labour hours. In many professional service firms, overheads are absorbed (and charged out to clients) on the basis of professional labour hours worked. However, this cost driver assumes that all labour hours utilise the same proportion of overheads. Since this is not a valid assumption, firms sometimes calculate overhead absorption rates for different categories of staff.

2. **Direct labour cost** This cost driver can also be used. However, if employees are paid at different rates, overheads charged to units of output by higher-paid employees will be greater than those charged to output involving lower-paid employees. Having said that, in some service businesses, overheads are charged out on the basis of direct labour cost because the more expensive labour (senior staff) consume more overheads (larger offices, secretarial assistance, etc.) than junior staff. Furthermore, direct labour cost is a simpler system to operate than having different absorption rates for different grades of labour. The advantage lies in its simplicity and convenience.

3. **Machine running hours** Many production overheads, especially in an automated plant, are related to machine capacity and utilisation, e.g. depreciation and maintenance of machinery. In such cases, it is logical to use machine running hours as the cost driver. However, small manufacturing firms, with primitive accounting systems, may have difficulty in obtaining accurate readings of machine running hours for various items of work. Thus, machine running hours is not widely used in small manufacturing firms because of the added clerical time involved in their calculation.

## Annual or Seasonal Rates?

Another decision in setting OHARs is the choice between annual or seasonal rates. 'Annual rates', as the term implies, involves establishing an OHAR rate for the year. In contrast, seasonal rates involve setting OHARs for each quarter or season. It is considered that annual rates are preferable since they automatically eliminate distortions due to, say, quarterly fluctuations in the amount of production overhead costs incurred (the numerator) or the level of cost driver (the denominator).

If quarterly/seasonal rates are used, for example, the following distortion could arise where there is a quarterly fluctuation in the level of cost driver (direct labour hours), but where production overheads remain unchanged.

|  | Quarter 1 | Quarter 2 | Quarter 3 | Quarter 4 | Total |
|---|---|---|---|---|---|
| Fixed overheads | €12,000 | €12,000 | €12,000 | €12,000 | €48,000 |
| Cost driver (DLhours) | 2,000 | 3,000 | 4,000 | 6,000 | 15,000 |
| OHAR per DLH | €6.00 | €4.00 | €3.00 | €2.00 | €3.20 |

From the above, it can be seen that the OHAR calculated on a quarterly basis changes due to different levels of cost driver in each quarter. (Fluctuations would also occur where there were changes in the amount of overheads incurred in each quarter.) To avoid these distortions, and therefore distorted product costs, it is preferable to calculate OHARs on an annual basis. In the illustration above an OHAR of €3.20 per DLH (€38,000 /15,000 DLHs) is calculated and this will be used for the full year.

## Budget (Predetermined) or Actual Rates?

The final choice facing management accountants is to calculate OHARs using either actual or budgeted information. (It should be remembered that in the above discussion we have recommended the use of annual rather than seasonal rates.) If actual data (i.e. actual overhead cost and actual cost driver level) is used in computing OHARs then product costs (including production overhead) cannot be determined until the end of the accounting year. While this may have the advantage of accuracy – both the numerator and denominator are known with certainty – it is of little use in trying to calculate product cost for units that were produced early during the accounting period. Therefore, it would be difficult to establish selling prices in the absence of timely cost information if actual and annual OHARs were used. Also, since annual OHARs are being used, it would not be possible to prepare quarterly profit reports due to the absence of inventory valuation figures.

To overcome this problem an OHAR is calculated on a budgeted or predetermined (and annual) basis. The official term given to this approach is 'normal' costing. Thus, for product costing purposes, the only difference between actual and normal costing is that actual costing uses actual overheads (and actual overhead absorption rates) whereas normal costing uses predetermined or budgeted overheads (and predetermined overhead rates). The advantage of normal costing is that it allows an estimated amount of production overhead to be applied to a unit of output at any stage during the accounting year, rather than waiting for financial year end to determine 'actual' overhead absorption rates. Thus, a manufacturing firm that uses normal costing will calculate its production cost as consisting of:

- actual direct material used
- actual direct labour used
- estimated amount of production overhead, based on predetermined OHARs.

The choice of annual and budgeted OHARs creates an additional problem which we shall briefly discuss. The problem is what annual volume level should be used? There are three alternatives: expected, normal and maximum capacity; and each will have an impact on the OHAR which, in turn, impacts on the calculation of production cost per unit. These three alternatives are briefly discussed below.

- Expected production volume, which represents the expected production volume for the coming year. The reason for this, in addition to the forecasting problems with estimating other volume levels, is the idea that the accounting period for financial reports is one year and that each year must stand alone. Therefore, the expected fixed overhead costs for each year should be assigned to the production for that year. Most of the illustrations in this book, that require OHARs use expected annual production volume as the denominator in the calculation of the predetermined overhead absorption rate. In other words, we base our calculations on estimates for the forthcoming year only. However, in addition to expected annual production volume there are two possible other production volumes that we need to consider:
- Maximum production volume, which represents the maximum production volume that can be attained, giving consideration to uncontrollable machine breakdowns, delays in material delivery, and other factors that could cause a reduction in production volume.
- Normal production volume, which represents the average production volume that will satisfy the average demand on the production facility for a particular time span. The time span is usually three to five years, enough to smooth out cyclical and trend factors in demand. The concept behind normal volume is that the fixed costs of the manufacturing facility are to be 'recovered' over a long period of time. The constant fixed cost per unit resulting from normal volume is effectively spreading the fixed cost for, say, a five-year period, over the production for all those five years. When it is feasible to develop accurate forecasts over a five-year period, normal volume provides a 'fair' measure for calculating the overhead cost per unit. The major reason many companies do not use normal levels of activity is due to the difficulties involved in forecasting the production volume and fixed costs over a period of several years into the future.

Therefore, for both theory and exam purposes, it is important to identify what is the 'level' of cost driver being used, i.e. expected, normal or maximum capacity.

One final point to keep in mind is that if total production volume does not change greatly from year to year then normal volume and expected volume will be about the same. Like many techniques in managerial accounting, the choice between the three different measures of annual volume depends on the judgement of managers and management accountants. Also, it should be obvious that the level of production volume chosen will have an impact on the OHAR and, therefore, the unit overhead cost.

Because overhead absorption rates are predetermined, they can only be 'best' estimates of production overhead costs to be assigned to units of output. Consequently, if actual activity or expenditure on production overheads is different from the expected activity or expected spending on such costs, there will be an under-over-absorption of production overheads. This under/over absorption of production overheads should be seen as an inevitable consequence of using predetermined OHARs. They represent the amount of prediction error associated with estimating a year in advance both the level of overhead costs and the level of cost driver activity. These prediction errors can be favourable or adverse and are formally referred to as over-absorption and under-absorption of production overhead respectively.

**Under-absorption of production overhead**, effectively, represents an additional cost to the company and is usually written off immediately to the income statement. In contrast, **over-absorption of production overhead** represents an additional gain and is usually credited as miscellaneous revenue in the income statement. However, technically, it means that customers are being overcharged due to the inflated cost of the product, which could have long-term, adverse, consequences for the business.

## ILLUSTRATION OF UNDER-ABSORBED PRODUCTION OVERHEAD

The Wicklow Manufacturing company predicted the following amounts for the forthcoming year for its two production departments. We shall focus only on production overheads (and ignore non-production overheads) since the emphasis of our calculations is to provide cost figures for stock valuation purposes.

|  | Machining department | Assembly department |
| --- | --- | --- |
| Direct labour (hours) per annum | 10,000 | 6,000 |
| Production overhead per annum | €50,000 | €24,000 |
| Machine running hours per annum | 5,000 | 4,000 |

All production costs other than direct materials and direct labour are included in production overheads. Production overheads are all fixed in nature. The company calculates an overhead absorption rate at the beginning of each year in order to estimate the production cost of its production. The company calculates its OHARs on a departmental basis with machine-hours being used as the cost driver in the machining department and direct labour hours being used as the cost driver in the assembly department.

At the end of the year, the following information was reported (for all operations):

|  | Machining department | Assembly department |
|---|---|---|
| Direct labour hours worked | 8,000 | 5,000 |
| Actual production overhead | €45,000 | €18,000 |
| Actual machine running hours | 4,000 | 3,000 |

**Requirement:** Calculate the amount of under-absorption of production overhead, based on the above information, using normal costing principles.

**Solution and Analysis:** The first step is to calculate an OHAR for each production department, using predetermined (or budgeted) annual figures. The departmental overhead absorption rates are calculated as follows:

|  | Machining department | Assembly department |
|---|---|---|
| Estimated amount of production overheads | €50,000 | €24,000 |
| Cost driver | 5,000 machine hours | 6,000 direct labour hours |
| OHAR | €10 per machine hour | €4 per labour hour |

The total amount of production overheads absorbed during the year, together with the under-absorption of production overheads, can now be calculated. The production overhead absorbed amounts to €40,000 (€10 × 4,000 machine hours) and €20,000 (€4 × 5,000 direct labour hours) respectively for both departments.

| | Machining department | Assembly department |
|---|---|---|
| OHAR (above) | €10 per machine hour | €4 per labour hour |
| Machine running hours (actual) | 4,000 | N/A |
| Direct labour hours (actual) | N/A | 5,000 |
| Overhead absorbed | €40,000 | €20,000 |
| Actual overhead incurred | €45,000 | €18,000 |
| Under–absorbed overhead | (€5,000) Adv | |
| Over–absorbed overhead | | €2,000 Fav |

The total amount of under/over absorbed production overhead can be subdivided into two categories that are of interest to management. These categories are a spending (or budget) variance and a volume variance. The spending variance, which can be favourable (F) or adverse (A), indicates whether spending was higher or lower than anticipated and is calculated by subtracting the budgeted expenditure from the actual expenditure. This variance is as likely to be caused by an incorrect budget estimate as it is by revised spending decisions made during the budget period. Accordingly, spending variances should be closely scrutinised to determine whether the corrective action is to improve the accuracy of the budgeting process or to modify future expenditure.

The volume variance, which can also be favourable (F) or adverse (A), reflects under/over utilisation of capacity and is calculated by subtracting the overheads absorbed from the budgeted amount. The reason why budget figures are used is because the OHAR is based on budget figures. Some people argue that the volume variance is purely a book-keeping variance and that it can be attributed to incorrect sales and marketing projections more than anything else. In which case, the production manager should not be held responsible for this. The detailed calculations are as follows:

| | Machining department | Assembly department |
|---|---|---|
| **Spending variance:** | | |
| Budgeted overheads | €50,000 | €24,000 |
| Actual overheads | €45,000 | €18,000 |
| | (€5,000) Fav | (€6,000) Fav |

| Volume variance: | | |
|---|---|---|
| Budgeted overheads | €50,000 | €24,000 |
| Absorbed overheads | €40,000 | €20,000 |
| | €10,000 Adv* | €4,000 Adv** |
| **Total variance** | €5,000 Adv | €2,000 Fav |

\* Or, (5,000 – 4,000 machine hours) × €10 = €10,000 A
\*\* Or, (6,000 – 5,000 labour hours) × €4 = €4,000 A

Another explanation is that, in the machining department, the firm operated at 20% less (i.e. 1,000 machine hours less than the budgeted 5,000 machine hours) than anticipated. Therefore, there was no production to absorb €10,000 (20% × €50,000) of production overhead that was expected to occur. In the assembly department, the firm operated at 16.6% (1,000 labour hours less than the budgeted 6,000 labour hours) less than anticipated. Therefore, there was no production to absorb €4,000 (16.6% × €24,000) of production overhead that was expected to occur.

## 2.6  Costing of Joint and By-Products

In this section we initially turn our attention to 'joint products' or 'joint product costing' and we shall finish the section with a consideration of 'by products'. Throughout this section we shall learn that there are 'different costs for different purposes' and the two main purposes for cost ascertainment in this section will be:

1. to value closing stock for financial reporting purposes, and
2. to provide information for decision-making. We shall also review aspects of cost apportionment, i.e. how to share costs between two or more cost objectives, where the cost objectives will be units of output.

Not surprisingly, we shall discover that there are different methods to apportion cost and different methods will give us different cost figures.

**Joint product costing** represents a situation where an input of resources to a process yields two or more products simultaneously. Such a situation is more common than we might think. For example, in the poultry industry, a chicken carcass will produce chicken breasts and chicken legs which represent different products to be sold at different prices. In the dairy industry, milk can be processed to produce cream and butter. In the petroleum industry the processing of crude oil can yield petrol, gas oil and lubricating oil. The feature of joint product processing is that it is not possible to produce a product in isolation. Rather, a joint process will result in the simultaneous output of two or more products. In turn, it may well be that the separate outputs can either be then sold or further processed. Such decisions should be made on the basis of incremental costs and incremental revenues and, in many cases, the relevant cost figures will be unrelated to the figures used for stock valuation purposes.

**Joint product costing** has its own set of terminology that is discussed below and refers to **Exhibit 2.12**. In this exhibit, a joint process results in the production of an intermediate product (product 1) and a final product (product 2). Product 1 can be sold immediately at the split-off point or can be further processed to make a new product. Product 2 is in its final form and can be sold.

The specific TERMINOLOGY relating to **joint products** is explained as follows:

**Split-off point** This is the stage of production when the joint products assume separate identities for the first time and it represents the end of the processing of the joint products *per se*. Some products may have an immediate sales value at split-off point. Other products have no value at that stage and may be abandoned, sometimes with disposal costs. Other joint products are further processed to enhance their value. It is important that the cost accounting system provides management with the information required to make the correct decision at split-off point. Like all decision situations, the decision to sell a product at split-off point or to further process should be based on incremental revenues and incremental, out of pocket, cash costs. We will see that the joint processing costs represent sunk or historical costs and they are not relevant to the further processing decision. Joint costs are only required for inventory valuation and financial reporting purposes. Therefore, we need to be very clear why the cost information is required – is it for stock valuation/financial reporting purposes or, alternatively, decision-making purposes? Remember, there are different costs for different purposes!

**Specific Costs** These are all the costs incurred ***after*** split-off point and are sometimes referred to as separable costs. Such specific costs may either be additional processing costs or additional selling and distribution costs and they can usually be easily traced to the specific products or processes.

EXHIBIT 2.12: JOINT PRODUCT COSTING

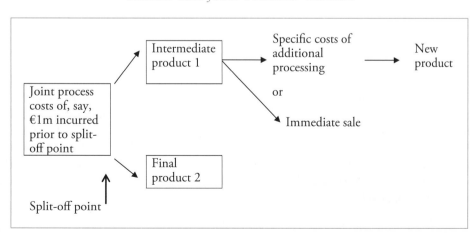

**Net Realisable Value** The difference between a joint product's sales revenue and further processing costs is referred to as Net Realisable Value (NRV).

**Joint Costs** These are the costs of the various inputs (materials, labour and overheads) which are incurred in producing all the joint products simultaneously, i.e. as a group. They are sometimes referred to as 'common' costs. By definition, joint costs are always incurred PRIOR to split-off point. The technical problem is, therefore, how to assign these joint (or common) costs between the various joint products? Such cost information will be required for stock valuation purposes in order to satisfy financial reporting requirements and three methods of assigning joint product costs to units of output can be used. Because we are dealing with the arbitrary nature of cost apportionment, it will come as no surprise that different methods will give us different figures and, therefore, different unit cost figures. Furthermore, the product profitability will also differ. There are three methods of assigning joint costs:

## 1. Physical Unit of Output

This is the simplest method to use. The total physical output is counted and the joint processing costs are assigned on the basis of the physical units of output. However, this method will result in the unit cost of all the joint products being equal. As a result, many people would criticise this method since costs are incurred to generate value. Therefore, it would be more appropriate, it is argued, to assign joint costs based on some consideration of value obtained.

## 2. Market Value at Split-off Point

Using this method, the joint processing costs are assigned on the basis of their share of market value at split-off point. The problem with this approach is that some products have a zero or very low market value at split-off point. Other joint products may have a small market value at split-off point but may be very valuable when fully processed and, in such a case, the market value at split-off will be significantly below its future value.

## 3. Net Realisable Value

Using this method the joint product costs are assigned on the basis of net realisable value of the individual products. Net realisable value (NRV) is the difference between the final selling price less any specific costs (processing and non-processing costs) incurred *after* split-off point. This concept is equivalent to the concept of net realisable value used in IFRS dealing with inventory valuation. The use of NRV has two major advantages over the other two methods mentioned. Firstly, an estimate of NRV is readily available in most cases. Secondly, it is more realistic since it assigns joint costs in relation to final value.

## ILLUSTRATION: ASSIGNING JOINT PRODUCT COSTS

The Monivea Chemical Company has a joint production process which produces three products referred to as A, B and C. The joint costs of processing prior to split-off point for a typical month are:

| Direct materials 100,000 pounds | €20,000 |
| Direct labour | €30,000 |
| Production overhead | €40,000 |
| | €90,000 |

The joint process products have the following physical quantities and their estimated sales value at split-off point:

A 50,000 pounds with an estimated (immediate) sales value of €40,000
B 20,000 pounds with an estimated (immediate) sales value of €30,000
C 30,000 pounds with an estimated (immediate) sales value of €30,000
  100,000 pounds

However, after split-off point, all three products are currently further processed and refined before being sold as final products. These additional specific, processing costs are presented below:

| Additional costs: | Product A | Product B | Product C |
|---|---|---|---|
| Direct material | €3,000 | €2,000 | €4,000 |
| Direct labour | €2,000 | €2,000 | €1,000 |
| Production overhead | €2,000 | €2,000 | €3,000 |
| Total specific costs | €7,000 | €6,000 | €8,000 |

During the month all units produced were sold to generate the following sales revenue:

|   |   |
|---|---|
| A | € 75,000 |
| B | € 45,000 |
| C | € 32,000 |
|   | €152,000 |

**Requirement:**

1. Apportion the joint costs using the physical method of apportionment and prepare a product line income statement.

2. Apportion the joint costs on the basis of net realisable value and prepare a product line income statement.
3. Apportion the joint costs on the basis of sales value at split-off point and prepare a product line income statement.
4. Comment on which products should be further processed and which should be sold (immediately) at split-off point.

## Solution and analysis:

1. The apportionment of joint costs (€90,000) is based on the physical output (100,000 lbs) and the apportionment is as follows:

|  | Physical output (lbs) | % of output | Joint cost assigned | Joint cost per unit |
|---|---|---|---|---|
| Product A | 50,000 | 50% | €45,000 | 90c |
| Product B | 20,000 | 20% | €18,000 | 90c |
| Product C | 30,000 | 30% | €27,000 | 90c |
|  | 100,000 |  | €90,000 |  |

Each joint product has the same unit cost (90c) and this figure would be used for end of period inventory valuation purposes. However, in this illustration all the products have been sold. Therefore, the summarised income statement for each product for the period, using the physical units as the basis of joint product cost apportionment, is as follows:

|  | Product A | Product B | Product C | Total |
|---|---|---|---|---|
| Sales revenue | €75,000 | €45,000 | €32,000 | €152,000 |
| Joint costs apportioned | (€45,000) | (€18,000) | (€27,000) | (€90,000) |
| Specific costs (given) | (€7,000) | (€6,000) | (€ 8,000) | (€21,000) |
| Net profit | €23,000 | €21,000 | (€3,000) | €41,000 |

As can be seen, products A and B are reported as being profitable and product C is reported as a loss-maker.

2. The apportionment of joint costs (€90,000) on the basis of NRV is illustrated below (using rounded figures for convenience):

|  | Final sales value | Additional processing costs | Net realisable value | % of NRV | Joint cost assigned | Joint cost per unit |
|---|---|---|---|---|---|---|
| Product A | €75,000 | (€7,000) | €68,000 | 52% | €46,800 | 93.6c |
| Product B | €45,000 | (€6,000) | €39,000 | 30% | €27,000 | 135c |
| Product C | €32,000 | (€8,000) | €24,000 | 18% | €16,200 | 54c |
|  |  |  | €131,000 |  | €90,000 |  |

Using this method, the unit cost of the joint products are 93.6c, 135c and 54c for Products A, B and C respectively. These figures would be used for end of period inventory valuation purposes. However, in this illustration all products have been sold. Therefore, the summarised income statement for the period, using NRV as the basis of joint product cost apportionment, is as follows:

|  | Product A | Product B | Product C | Total |
|---|---|---|---|---|
| Sales revenue | €75,000 | €45,000 | €32,000 | €152,000 |
| Joint costs apportioned | (€46,800) | (€27,000) | (€16,200) | (€90,000) |
| Specific costs (given) | (€7,000) | (€6,000) | (€8,000) | (€21,000) |
| Net profit | €21,200 | €12,000 | € 7,800 | €41,000 |

As can be seen from the above presentation, all three products are now reported as being profitable.

3. The apportionment of joint costs (€90,000) on the basis of sales value at split-off point is illustrated below:

|  | Sales value at split-off point | % of sales value at split-off point | Joint cost assigned | Joint cost per unit |
|---|---|---|---|---|
| Product A | €40,000 | 40% | €36,000 | 72c |
| Product B | €30,000 | 30% | €27,000 | 135c |
| Product C | €30,000 | 30% | €27,000 | 90c |
|  | €100,000 | 100% | €90,000 |  |

Using this method, the unit cost of the joint products is 72c, 135c and 90c for Products A, B and C respectively and these are the figures which would be used for end of period inventory valuation. However, in this illustration all products have been sold. Therefore, the summarised income statement for the period, using sales value at split-off point as the basis of joint product cost apportionment, is as follows:

|  | Product A | Product B | Product C | Total |
|---|---|---|---|---|
| Sales revenue | €75,000 | €45,000 | €32,000 | €152,000 |
| Joint costs apportioned | (€36,000) | (€27,000) | (€27,000) | (€90,000) |
| Specific costs (given) | (€7,000) | (€6,000) | (€8,000) | (€21,000) |
| Net profit | €32,000 | €12,000 | (€3,000) | €41,000 |

It can be seen from the above presentation, both products A and B are reported as being profitable but Product C is a loss-maker.

However, it would be wrong to draw conclusions on the viability or otherwise of Product C from the above three presentations – only one of which reported it as being profitable. This is because the net profit or loss attributable to a specific product will always be influenced by how the common joint processing costs are assigned to the three products. In addition, this share of joint processing costs represents a sunk or historical cost. Simply, the cost has already been incurred and therefore it cannot be influenced in any way by future decisions.

The decision which sometimes is made in relation to Product C (and other products) is whether the product should be sold immediately at split-off point or whether the product should be further processed. In relation to Product C (only) the relevant figures are as follows:

| Product C | € |
|---|---|
| (i)  Sales value at split-off point (given) | 30,000 |
| (ii) Incremental cash flows of further processing | |
| Final sales value (given) | 32,000 |
| Less: additional costs | (8,000) |
| = Incremental cash flows | 24,000 |

Thus, further processing of Product C generates a contribution of €24,000. However, the preferred alternative is to sell the product at split-off point since it generates a cash contribution of €30,000. The share of joint product costs is irrelevant in this decision since they will not change in relation to the alternatives being considered.

## By-Products

A working definition of a by-product is a joint product whose sales value is not significant compared with the total market value of all the joint products. Thus, the distinction between joint and by-products can be a little unclear. However, as a rough guide, 5% of total sales value would be the approximate threshold for determining significance. The main method of accounting for by-products is to deduct the sales proceeds of the by-products from the joint processing costs to be assigned. The remaining joint costs are then assigned to the remaining joint products using an appropriate method, e.g. net realisable value. This is the simplest and most practical approach of accounting for by-products. It recognises that by-products reduce the cost of the remaining joint products and, therefore, it does not require costly or complex accounting calculations.

However, by-product revenues can be recognised at either production or sale. Deferring until point of sale has the advantage that the sale proceeds are known and there is no need to estimate them. Thus, unsold by-products would be valued (for stock valuation purpose) at zero. Alternatively, it would be possible to account for the value of by-products at time of production rather than at time of sale. This method will provide different figures but it should be remembered that, by definition, the overall sales proceeds of by-products are deemed to be insignificant.

## ILLUSTRATION OF A BY-PRODUCT

The Nenagh Company produces two products (hereafter referred to as X and Y) in a single joint process. The total cost incurred prior to the split-off point is €800,000 a month. Monthly production is 2.1 million gallons of X and 250,000 gallons of Y.

In turn, X is further processed, without any physical loss, to make the company's branded product, Z. The final sales price of Z is 50c per gallon which is generated after incurring further (specific) processing costs amounting to €100,000. The average selling price of Y, which is not further processed, is 20c per gallon and this is sold at split-off point.

**Requirements:**

1. Compute the total cost and unit cost of X on the assumption that Y is a joint product, using the NRV method.
2. Compute the total cost and unit cost of X on the assumption that Y is a by-product, using the NRV method.
3. Would you classify product Y as a by-product or as a joint product? Defend your recommendation and accounting treatment.

**Solution and Analysis:** The situation can be depicted as follows and, based on the limited information provided, Product Y can be considered either as a by-product or a joint product.

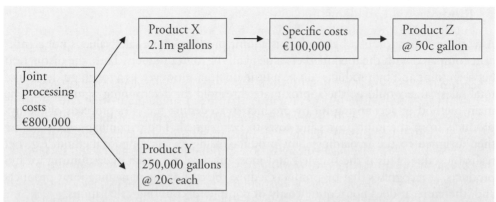

1. If we assume that product Y is a joint product, then the relevant calculations are as follows, apportioning joint costs (€800,000) on the basis of net realisable values.

|  | Final sales value | Additional processing costs | Net realisable value | % of NRV | Joint cost assigned |
|---|---|---|---|---|---|
| Product X | €1,050,000 | (€100,000) | €950,000 | 95% | €760,000 |
| Product Y | €50,000 | Nil | €50,000 | 5% | €40,000 |
|  |  |  | €1,000,000 |  | €800,000 |

The joint product costs of X is 36c per gallon (€760,000/2,100,000) and Y is 16c per gallon (€40,000/250,000).

2. If we assume that product Y is a by-product, then the relevant calculations are presented below. The sales revenue from the by-product is simply deducted from the joint costs to be apportioned. In this case the remaining joint costs are assigned to product X.

| | |
|---|---|
| Total joint costs | €800,000 |
| Less: sales proceeds of by-product (250,000 @ 20c each) | (€50,000) |
| Remaining joint costs | €750,000 |
| | |
| Joint cost per unit of X (€750,000/2,100,000) = | 35.7c |

3. Comment: Given the above information, it can be seen that the total market value of product Y is small, representing 5% of the total net realisable value generated from the joint process. In such circumstances it is likely that managerial decisions will focus on the profitability or otherwise of product X. For this reason, the calculations would have more managerial relevance if product Y is treated as a by-product. This confirms the view that product Y is not material in terms of either physical or monetary considerations.

## 2.7 Incorporating Service Costs in Predetermined Overhead Rates

In **Section 2.5** we introduced and favoured the idea of using departmental overhead rates to absorb production overheads rather than use a single plant-wide rate. Within departments, some costs will be *allocated* directly and examples of such costs include the salary of the department manager or insurance costs of department equipment. Other costs will be *apportioned* among various production departments and such costs include rent, lighting and factory maintenance.

This section is concerned with a particular type of overhead cost, i.e. the costs of running a service or support department. Service departments provide support services to other departments in the organisation and will include services such as machine maintenance, security and other services. In a university context, administration and library are good examples of support departments. In contrast, production departments (or operating departments in a non-manufacturing environment) are the departments within an organisation that manufacture goods or provide services to external customers or clients. Alternatively stated, production (operating) departments ultimately generate revenue for the organisation. Support departments simply provide a service internally. **Exhibit 2.13** provides examples of operating (or production) and service (or support) departments for different types of firm.

EXHIBIT 2.13: PRODUCTION AND SERVICE DEPARTMENTS (VARIOUS FIRMS)

| Type of firm | Production/operating departments | Service departments |
|---|---|---|
| Clothes manufacturer | Cutting department | Product design |
|  | Machining department | Maintenance |
| Retail firm | Toys department | Accounting and payroll |
|  | Confectionery department | Customer service |
| Service firm (accounting) | Audit department | Secretarial |
|  | Tax department | Library |

Support department costs are initially assigned to each service department, in keeping with the concept of responsibility accounting. This allows managers to assess whether a responsible individual is keeping authorised spending under control. However, for costing purposes, service department costs will, in turn, be reapportioned to production departments for three reasons. The first reason involves motivation – to provide an incentive for the appropriate use of support services. It is plausible to argue that if production departments were not 'charged' for using support services then these services would be over-consumed by users for the simple reason that free services tend to be abused and overused. Moreover, we can identify whether the support service is being used internally and this can give an indication of its commitment to quality of service.

The second reason for service department reapportionment concerns financial reporting and inventory valuation. In accordance with generally accepted accounting principles, closing inventory must be valued at cost of production and this will include any service costs that support the production process. Thirdly, service department costs are reapportioned to facilitate a range of decisions by management including pricing and whether to continue with current use of existing facilities or to outsource. Failure to reapportion service department costs to production departments will result in setting overhead absorption rates too low to absorb all production overhead costs in the organisation.

There are three methods by which service department costs can be reapportioned to production departments. These are the direct method, the step-down method, and the reciprocal method. The direct method involves assigning service department costs only to production departments and not to other service departments. Thus, this method ignores services provided or interactions between service departments and is displayed in **Exhibit 2.14**.

EXHIBIT 2.14: DIRECT METHOD OF SUPPORT DEPARTMENT APPORTIONMENT

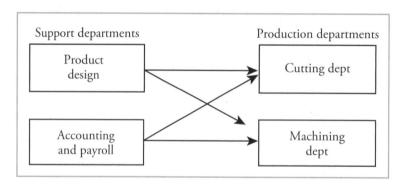

The sequential (or step-down) method allows for partial recognition of services rendered by a service department to other service departments. This method assigns support department costs, one department at a time, to remaining support and production departments in a cascading manner until all support departments have been assigned.

However, when a service department's costs have been apportioned, it does not receive back any costs from other service departments. Consequently, overall cost figures can vary depending on which service department is first selected. The apportionment sequence usually starts with the service department that provides the highest percentage of its total services to other service departments.

An alternative, but similar approach, is to start with the service department that renders the highest monetary amount of services to other service departments. Either way, we start the process with the largest provider of interdepartmental services first with the smallest provider of interdepartmental services being apportioned last in the sequence. Any production overheads apportioned to a service department in this process are added to that department's costs to be subsequently apportioned to remaining

EXHIBIT 2.15: STEP DOWN METHOD OF SUPPORT DEPARTMENT APPORTIONMENT

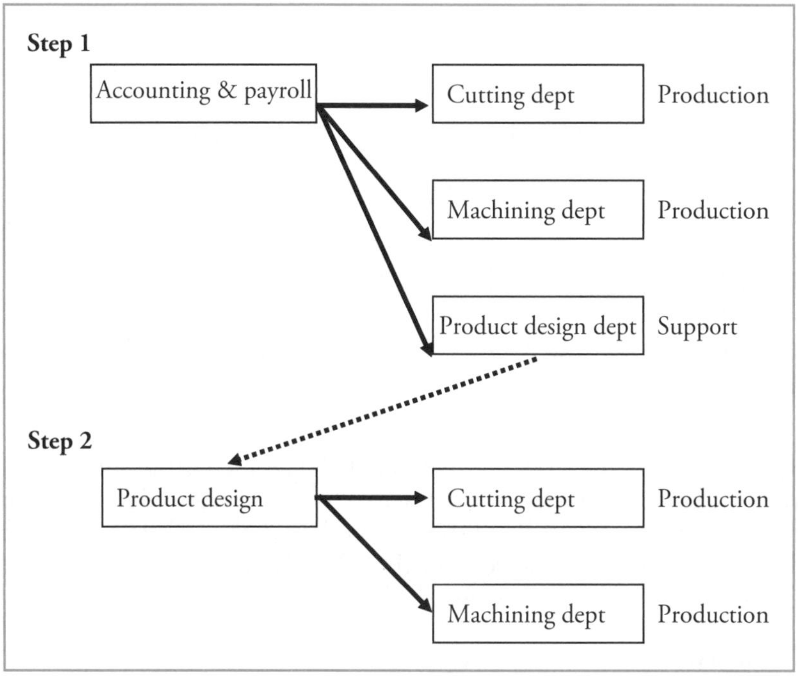

departments. The sequence is depicted in **Exhibit 2.15** and, since there are two service departments in this exhibit, there are two 'steps' involved and it is assumed that it is appropriate to start with the accounting and payroll department.

Regardless of the method used, there are three basic steps involved. First we need to identify the production and support departments for which costs should be assigned. Secondly, for each support department we need to select an appropriate method to use in cost reapportionment. Thirdly, we assign costs from service departments to operating departments, using the selected method of reapportionment. Initially, we shall concentrate on the direct and step-down methods of service department cost reapportionment.

ILLUSTRATION OF SERVICE DEPARTMENT REAPPORTIONMENT

Wexford Fabrics has two production departments (cutting and assembly) and two service departments (maintenance and administration). Each year, the company develops predetermined departmental overhead rates on a full costing basis for the cutting and assembly departments. Costs and other data at normal volume are budgeted at the following levels:

| | Service departments | | Production depts | |
| --- | --- | --- | --- | --- |
| | Maintenance | Admin. | Cutting | Assembly |
| Factory over-head costs | €30,000 | €60,000 | €300,000 | €200,000 |
| Direct labour hours | – | – | 15,000 | 10,000 |
| Number of employees | 2 | 5 | 6 | 6 |
| Square feet occupied | 3,000 | 4,000 | 14,000 | 16,000 |
| Machine hours | – | – | 20,000 | 40,000 |

The company wants to select the most appropriate method of assigning service department costs to production departments. It has been agreed that maintenance department costs should be reapportioned on the number of square feet occupied in each department, while the costs of the administration department should be reapportioned on the basis of the number of employees.

**Requirements:**

1. You are required to reapportion service department costs to production departments using the direct method, and develop overhead absorption rates for each production department on the following basis:

   - Cutting – machine hours
   - Assembly – labour hours.

2. You are required to reapportion service department costs to production departments using the sequential method and develop overhead absorption rates for each production department on the following basis:

   - Cutting – machine hours
   - Assembly – labour hours.

**Solution and Analysis:**

**1. Direct method of service department apportionment:** The reapportionment of service department costs to production departments is relatively straightforward. First, both service departments have been assigned overheads (€30,000 and €60,000) in keeping with the concept of responsibility accounting. These overheads must then be reapportioned to production departments in order to establish production OHAR. Because we are using the direct method of service department apportionment it does not matter with which department we start. Service maintenance costs are assigned (reapportioned) using square feet occupied by both production departments. (Under the direct method service department costs are not assigned to other service departments.) In turn, the administration costs are assigned to both cutting and assembly departments using the number of employees as the basis of apportionment.

| | Service departments | | Production departments | |
|---|---|---|---|---|
| | Maint. | Admin. | Cutting | Assembly |
| Total overheads | €30,000 | €60,000 | €300,000 | €200,000 |
| Apportionment of: | | | | |
| Maintenance (sq. ft) | (30,000) | – | €14,000 | €16,000 |
| Admin. (Employees) | Nil | €(60,000) | €30,000 | €30,000 |
| Revised Overheads | Nil | Nil | €344,000 | €246,000 |
| Estimated M/hrs | | | 20,000 | |
| Estimated DLHs | | | | 10,000 |
| OHAR | | | €17.20 per machine hour | €24.60 per DLH |

Having assigned the service departments costs, we are left with production overhead costs only in the two production departments (€344,000 in cutting and €246,000 in assembly). Finally, OHARs for the two production departments can be calculated by dividing overheads to be absorbed by the level of cost driver. This provides us with an OHAR of €17.20 per machine hour for the cutting department, and €24.60 per direct labour hour for the assembly department.

**2. Sequential (or step-down) method of service department apportionment:** Using the sequential method, we must make an initial decision as to what service department to start the cost reapportionment process with. The general rule is to start with the department that provides the greatest amount of service to other service departments. Based on the data provided, maintenance provides a service to 34,000 square feet (4,000 + 14,000 + 16,000) to other departments, of which 4,000 is to administration i.e. about 12% of its services. Alternatively, administration provides service to 14 employees (2 + 6 + 6) in other departments, of which 2 employees work in maintenance i.e. about 14% of its services. Thus we start the process with the administration department and we acknowledge its support to the maintenance, cutting and assembly departments. When these costs have been apportioned, it cannot receive any other costs. Thereafter, we assign maintenance department costs only to the two production departments i.e. cutting and assembly.

| | Service departments | | Production departments | |
|---|---|---|---|---|
| | Maint. | Admin. | Cutting | Assembly |
| Total overheads | €30,000 | €60,000 | €300,000 | €200,000 |
| Apportionment of: | | | | |
| Administration (2:6:6) | 8,572 | (60,000) | €25,714 | €25,714 |
| Maintenance (14:16) | (38,572) | – | €18,000 | €20,572 |
| Revised overheads | Nil | Nil | €343,714 | €246,286 |
| Estimated M/hrs | | | 20,000 | |
| Estimated DLHs | | | | 10,000 |
| OHAR | | | €17.18 per machine hour | €24.63 per DLH |

Having assigned the service departments costs, we are left with production overhead costs only in the two production departments (€343,714 in cutting and €246,286 in assembly). Finally, OHARs for the two production departments can be calculated by dividing overheads to be absorbed by the level of cost driver. This provides us with an OHAR of €17.18 per machine hour for the cutting department, and €24.63 per direct labour hour for assembly. In this illustration the figures are remarkably similar to the direct method.

The above illustration highlights the fact that different methods of support department apportionment result in different figures. These differences can be increased or decreased when different cost pools and bases of cost apportionment are used.

## ILLUSTRATION OF THE RECIPROCAL METHOD

**3. The reciprocal method:** There is a third method of apportioning a service department's costs, although this is rarely examined. It is called the reciprocal method and it is, conceptually, the most correct of all methods because it acknowledges the interdependency of all departments i.e. where service departments can carry out work for other service departments. The reciprocal method of apportioning a service department's costs enables us to incorporate interdepartmental relationships *fully* into service department apportionments. It is a little more complex, in the sense that it uses simultaneous equations. It is unlikely to be used if it does not provide significantly different figures than the other two methods.

A manufacturer has two service departments ($S_1$ and $S_2$) and three production departments ($P_1$, $P_2$ and $P_3$). An overhead absorption rate is now required. The company makes the reapportionment of overhead from service departments to production departments on a reciprocal basis, recognising the fact that services of one service department are utilised by another. The percentage utilisation of such services is summarised in the percentages below:

| | $S_1$ | $S_2$ | $P_1$ | $P_2$ | $P_3$ |
|---|---|---|---|---|---|
| **S1** | 0% | 10% | 20% | 40% | 30% |
| **S2** | 20% | 0% | 50% | 10% | 20% |
| **Production overheads** | | | | | |
| Overheads | €98,000 | €117,600 | €1,400,000 | €2,100,000 | €640,000 |

**Requirement:** Use the reciprocal method to calculate the total overhead cost of each production department for the purposes of calculating overhead absorption rates. Show the OHAR assuming that the appropriate cost driver is labour hours of which 10,000, 20,000 and 30,000 hours are expected in $P_1$, $P_2$ and $P_3$ respectively.

**Solution and Analysis:** We first need to identify the overheads to be assigned from each service department, recognising fully interdependency between the service departments. Thus, our calculations are:

$S_1 = €98,000 + 20\% \times S_2$

$S_2 = €117,600 + 10\% \times S_1$

Therefore:

$S_1 \quad = €98,000 + 20\% (€117,600 + 10\% S_1)$

$S_1 \quad = €98,000 + €23,520 + 2\% S_1$

$98\% S_1 = €121,520$

$S_1 \quad = €124,000$

$S_2 \quad = €117,600 + 10\% \times (€124,000)$

$S_2 \quad = €130,000$

Thus, the schedule of service department cost apportionment can be summarised as follows:

| | S₁ | S₂ | P₁ | P₂ | P₃ |
|---|---|---|---|---|---|
| Overhead incurred | €98,000 | €117,600 | €1,400,000 | €2,100,000 | €640,000 |
| Apportionment of S₁ | €(124,000) | €12,400 | €24,800 | €49,600 | €37,200 |
| Apportionment of S₂ | €26,000 | €(130,000) | €65,000 | €13,000 | €26,000 |
| Revised overheads | Nil | Nil | €1,489,800 | €2,162,600 | €703,200 |
| DLHs | | | 10,000 | 20,000 | 30,000 |
| OHAR | | | €148.98 per DLH | €108.13 per DLH | €23.44 per DLH |

In conclusion, we have covered a great deal of basic material in this chapter, especially in relation to product costing, and outlined how management accountants disaggregate the overall cost structure using cost allocation and cost apportionment. In the next two chapters we outline two specific cost accumulation systems which operate within certain types of enterprises, namely, a job costing system (**Chapter 3**) and a process costing system (**Chapter 4**).

## SUMMARY OF LEARNING OBJECTIVES

**Learning Objective 1**: Describe the three main reasons for providing cost information about cost objects.

Cost information is required for end of period stock (inventory) valuation. More importantly, cost information is required for both planning and control decisions by managers.

**Learning Objective 2**: Distinguish between fixed and variable costs and between direct and overhead costs.

A fixed cost is a cost whose total amount does not respond to changes in the cost driver (usually assumed to be volume of output). A variable cost is a cost whose total does respond to changes in the cost driver. A direct cost can be traced entirely to a single cost objective whereas an overhead cost is a common cost, and must be shared between cost objectives.

**Learning Objective 3**: Prepare summary cost statements for manufacturing, retail and service firms.

Summary cost statements were presented in various exhibits and illustrations in this chapter.

**Learning Objective 4**: Calculate the profit impact of using absorption versus variable (direct) costing.

The essential difference between absorption and variable (direct) costing is the accounting treatment of fixed production overheads. As a result, exhibits and illustrations in this chapter showed how the reported profit figure for an accounting period differs when stock levels either increase or decrease.

**Learning Objective 5**: Assign costs using and distinguishing between cost apportionment and cost allocation.

In order to generate detailed information, total costs need to be assigned between different cost objectives. Cost allocation is associated with direct costs which can be traced, in entirety, to a single cost objective. In contrast, overheads, being common costs, must be apportioned among two or more cost objectives making apportionment a much more subjective task.

**Learning Objective 6**. Explain the technique of overhead absorption rates (OHARs) using cost drivers.

Accurate product costing requires the tracing of direct materials, direct labour and overheads. Because overheads are common costs they are 'absorbed' into product costs using predetermined overhead absorption rates, based on a suitable cost driver.

**Learning Objective 7**. Outline the benefits and limitations associated with using departmental or plant-wide, budgeted or actual and annual or seasonal OHARs.

Departmental OHARs are more accurate than plant-wide but they require accurate apportionment of costs. Budgeted OHARs allow an estimated amount of overhead to be assigned but will, inevitably, contain prediction errors. Annual rates automatically eliminate possible distortions associated with seasonal variation of costs.

**Learning Objective 8**. Illustrate the alternative accounting treatments of joint and by-products.

Joint costs are (common) costs incurred prior to split-off point in a production process and they must be apportioned using either physical units, market value at split-off point, or net realisable value. These different methods were demonstrated in the exhibits and illustrations in this chapter. Any revenue from the sale of by-products can be deducted from joint costs, since overall revenue is usually insignificant.

**Learning Objective 9**. Calculate OHARs with service department apportionments.

Service department overheads are also part of overall product cost. Otherwise product costs will be underestimated. The three methods of service department apportionment, namely, direct, step-down and reciprocal were illustrated in the exhibits and illustrations in this chapter.

## Questions

### Review Questions

(See Appendix One for Solutions to Review Questions **2.1** and **2.2**)

*Question 2.1 (Absorption v. Variable (Direct) Costing)*

You are the management accountant in a newly established manufacturing company. At present, production levels exceed sales levels, as the company is building up stock levels. The company uses absorption costing. The Managing Director has approached you for advice regarding the introduction of variable (direct) costing, as he is concerned that absorption costing may be leading to the overstatement of profits.

**Requirement:** Prepare a memorandum for the Managing Director in which you should:

  (i)  Distinguish between absorption costing and variable (direct) costing.
 (ii)  List the arguments put forward in respect of absorption costing and variable (direct) costing respectively.
(iii)  Explain the potential impact on profits of using absorption costing as opposed to variable (direct) costing.

*Question 2.2 (Calculation of Unit Cost Data for Pricing Decisions)*

Due to the arrival of a new managing director, **CORTEC,** a computer parts manufacturer, has decided to review its basis for pricing some of its products. Currently, the company produces three separate chips – the ZC100, the ZC150 and the ZC200 – as part of its product portfolio. The costing cards for these products are summarised below:

| Per Unit of Production | ZC100 | ZC150 | ZC200 |
| --- | --- | --- | --- |
| | € | € | € |
| Direct materials | 8.50 | 10.25 | 12.75 |
| Direct labour | 8.00 | 9.00 | 9.50 |
| Variable overheads | 2.50 | 2.80 | 2.50 |
| Assigned fixed overheads (based on units produced) | 5.00 | 5.00 | 5.00 |
| Total cost per unit | 24.00 | 27.05 | 29.75 |
| Selling price per unit | 30.00 | 33.81 | 37.19 |
| Total units produced in a year are as follows: | 95,000 | 105,000 | 150,000 |

All production staff are paid a standard wage of €8 per hour (with no overtime being worked). Also, company policy has always been to price all products at a set mark-up of 25% on total costs.

In addition, the following information has come to light:

- The company has located a new foreign supplier for the materials being used to produce ZC200. The existing supplier is locally based. The new supplier is willing to supply at €11.00 per unit. The managing director is keen to agree this contract. The price will be guaranteed for 1 year. The Quality Department has tested a small sample of the new proposed supplier's material and has found some faults in the sample.
- A time and motion study was conducted on one specific Monday morning where it was noted that the ZC150 actually took 1.5 hours of labour to produce 1 unit, while the ZC100 and ZC200 required 1.25 hours each per unit. You have been instructed to make this change.
- Because of an error in the previous costing exercise prepared by a trainee cost accountant, €0.40 of the variable overhead allocated to the ZC100 actually relates to the ZC200. The work of junior accountants is not reviewed by any senior accountants. It was agreed to correct the costing error noted.
- On reviewing the allocation of fixed overheads it was observed that one machine – the X430 – (which accounted for €350,000 of the annual fixed overhead charge) was used to produce the ZC100 and ZC150. The previous costing exercise had, in error, shown this machine as being used for all three chips. Again, it was agreed to correct this. (All other fixed overheads are regarded as general in nature.)

**Requirements:**

1. Calculate the revised net profit of CORTEC, by product and in total, based on the information given above **after** the review of costs. State the new unit selling price of each product (to the nearest cent) based on company policy.
2. Analyse critically the logic behind the revisions proposed and discuss briefly the impact that these may have on CORTEC's overall profitability. You should also assess whether you consider the review as complete.

Source: Chartered Accountants Ireland, Management Accounting and Business Finance, Paper 3, Autumn 2004

### Intermediate Questions

*Question 2.3 (Mini Case Regarding Cost Classification and Stock Valuation)*

In the end, the decision by Bob Anthony to resign from his €30,000 a year job as a tax lecturer was taken with relative ease. Anthony had been lecturing for the past 10 years. While working as a lecturer, he developed an excellent set of teaching notes and illustrative problems and realised he could make more money in the long run (and hopefully achieve a better quality of life) by focusing his energies and technical ability on writing and publishing study manuals for professional accountancy exams. He commissioned a market research exercise, at a cost of €1,000, which confirmed a huge demand for professionally written taxation manuals. This demand was due to the significant growth in professional accountancy students and the existing lack of suitably priced but comprehensive study material. Future demand would be enhanced by the virtual zero resale value of his manuals, since the taxation legislation changed each year.

After the passing of the annual Finance Act, Anthony anticipated spending three or four months updating and improving his material, which would be available for sale in early September – the start of the academic year. Using soft covers and good reproduction techniques, he expected his tax manuals to be much cheaper (and earlier to market) than existing hardcover texts. For the time being, Anthony intended to concentrate on a single taxation study manual.

Bob Anthony resigned his job and immediately became self-employed on 1 January 20x8, trading under the name 'Financial Training Ltd', which had a share capital of €10,000. He worked from his home. The only fixed assets acquired were a new computer, printer, desks and chairs. The total cost was €3,000, and Bob expected them to last about three years before they would need to be replaced. He paid himself a salary of €22,000 per annum. Being single, he felt that he could adequately cope with the reduction in personal income. He hired a part-time secretary to handle the day-to-day administration of the office, which included telephone and customer orders.

In his first year as an author, Anthony produced 1,000 copies of his taxation study manual for the tax year 20x8. The 'production' process involved writing/updating his study manual, inputting the material into the computer, then copying and binding it within a soft cover. He did all this production work himself. All administration was the responsibility of the part-time secretary. He sold 900 study manuals at €50 each; of which €10,000 remain unpaid at the year end. (Anthony is confident of their eventual collection.) He is also confident that the unsold manuals will be disposed of since his recent expenditure on advertising (€2,000) generated a number of enquiries about his new business.

Mr Anthony has asked your assistance in preparing financial statements, which he will use in making decisions about his business, and which will also be shown and used by the taxation authorities and his bank manager. He provides you with the following list of expense payments for the past year. For your information he has classified these cash expense payments, as best as possible, between fixed and variable in relation to volume changes, i.e. the volume of taxation manuals produced and sold:

|  | Total € | Fixed € | Variable € |
| --- | --- | --- | --- |
| Paper | 5,000 | Nil | 5,000 |
| Photocopying charges including rental | 6,000 | 3,500 | 2,500 |
| Secretarial wages | 3,000 | 3,000 | Nil |

| | Total € | Fixed € | Variable € |
|---|---|---|---|
| Insurance | 2,000 | 2,000 | Nil |
| Personal Salary | 22,000 | 22,000 | Nil |
| Advertising | 2,000 | 2,000 | Nil |
| Postage, telephone & stationery | 2,000 | 1,100 | 900 |
| Audit fee | 500 | 500 | Nil |
| Market Research | 1,000 | 1,000 | Nil |
| | 43,500 | 35,100 | 8,400 |

Mr Anthony now requires financial statements and an analysis of current operations for his first year of trading (year ended 31 December 20x8) and has asked your assistance and advice on what could be done to improve his company's financial situation.

**Requirements:**

1. Prepare a Statement of Cash Flows, an Income Statement and Balance Sheet for Mr Anthony for his first year of trading:
   (a) assuming closing inventory is valued using variable costing principles; and
   (b) assuming closing inventory is valued using full absorption costing principles.

   **Note**: For convenience, we shall assume the only production costs to consist of raw materials (paper), Mr Anthony's production salary and photocopying charges. You can also ignore the possibility that the net realisable value of manuals at year end is lower than cost.

2. Why is there a difference between the profit figures in the income statements?
3. Identify the following costs for the year ended 31 December 20x8:
   (a) Total material costs.
   (b) Total labour/wages costs.
   (c) Total fixed costs and total variable costs.
   (d) Total production costs incurred and total non-production (period) costs.
4. Calculate the total variable cost and contribution per unit.
5. What is the total cost per unit for year ended 31 December 20x8?
6. Calculate the break-even point (in units) for the year under variable costing.
7. What is the required volume of units to generate a profit of €3,000 for 20x8, under variable costing?
8. What is Bob Anthony's opportunity cost of becoming self-employed?

*Question 2.4 (Cost Allocation, Cost Apportionment and Product Line Profitability)*

Rialto is a small family-owned shop which occupies the ground floor of a recently constructed apartment block. The shop sells three different product lines, i.e. fish, chips and chocolate confectionery. The following summarised income statement has been prepared for a recent accounting period:

| SUMMARISED INCOME STATEMENT FOR YEAR ENDED 31 DECEMBER 20XI | | |
| --- | --- | --- |
| | € | € |
| **Sales:** | | |
| Fried fish | 40,000 | |
| Chips | 50,000 | |
| Confectionery | 10,000 | 100,000 |
| **Less: Expenses:** | | |
| Cost of fish | 28,000 | |
| Cost of potatoes | 9,000 | |
| Cost of confectionery | 8,000 | |
| Frying oil used | 8,100 | |
| Depreciation of cash register* | 5,000 | |
| Rent and rates* | 6,600 | |
| General wages* | 9,000 | 73,700 |
| **Net Profit** | | 26,300 |

\* For the purposes of this illustration, depreciation, rent and rates and wages are classified as fixed costs and you may assume that there were no opening or closing stocks.

**Requirements:**

1. Explain your understanding of the term 'contribution' and its relevance to managerial decision-making in the context of dropping a loss-making product line.
2. Prepare a product profitability report in contribution-based format for the above three product lines. For the sake of convenience, all overhead costs should be apportioned on the basis of sales turnover.
3. Should sales of confectionery be discontinued? Explain why or why not. It is not necessary to reapportion the cost data in making your recommendation.
4. What is the amount of additional profit if sales of fish **only** increase by 10% in volume terms? (This will not impact on cost apportionment.)
5. What is the annual break-even point of the shop in terms of sales revenue?

*Question 2.5 (Cost Allocation, Apportionment and Overhead Absorption)*

Paragon Limited is a family-owned manufacturing company. The company has four production departments through which manufactured parts must pass before completion. The following details, together with the amount of overheads incurred in each department, are available for 12 months of operations:

|  | Dept A | Dept B | Dept C | Dept D | Total |
|---|---|---|---|---|---|
| Production overheads | €35,000 | €20,000 | €80,000 | €18,000 | €153,000 |
| Staff employed (numbers) | 10 | 15 | 5 | 10 | 40 |
| Machine hours (hours) | 5,000 | 7,000 | 5,000 | 8,000 | 25,000 |
| Kilowatts used (watts) | 50,000 | 30,000 | 90,000 | 30,000 | 200,000 |
| Spare parts used (parts) | 10 | 10 | 15 | 15 | 50 |
| Space required (Sq. m) | 900 | 750 | 750 | 600 | 3,000 |

In addition, the company incurs general overheads which require to be apportioned to the four departments in an equitable manner, in order to establish production overhead absorption rates. The total of these general overheads to be apportioned are estimated as follows for the year:

|  | € |
|---|---|
| Electricity costs | 5,000 |
| Rent and rates | 6,000 |
| Canteen costs | 6,000 |
| Machine maintenance (materials) | 7,000 |
|  | 24,000 |

**Requirements:**

1. Calculate an overhead absorption rate (OHAR) for each of the production departments A, B, C and D on the basis of machine running hours, having assigned all overhead costs to the production departments using the most appropriate basis. Explain briefly your choice of basis and please appreciate that there are several different but acceptable answers that can be presented.
2. Calculate a plant-wide OHAR, using machine running hours.
3. Briefly describe the advantages and disadvantages associated with both departmental and plant-wide OHARs.

Source: Chartered Accountants Ireland, Management Accounting and Business Finance, Paper 3, Summer 2003 (adapted)

*Question 2.6 (Costing of Joint and By-products)*

The Kingdom Company grows, processes, packages, and sells three joint products, manufactured from apples. The products are referred to as: (a) sliced apples that are used in frozen pies (b) apple sauce, and (c) apple juice. Kingdom Company uses the estimated **Net Realisable Value (NRV)** method to allocate costs of the joint process to its joint products.

In addition, there is a by-product which represents the outside skin of the apple which is processed as animal feed. The estimated NRV (i.e. sales price less separable costs) of this by-product is used to reduce the amount of joint production costs to be assigned to the three main products.

Details of Kingdom Company's manufacturing process are as follows:

- Initially, the apples are washed and the outside skin is removed in the Cutting Department. The core of the apple is then removed. Any bruised or discoloured apple parts are also removed. At the end of this cutting process, the three joint products and the by-product are recognisable. Each product is then transferred to a separate department for final processing.
- The apples are forwarded to the Slicing Department, where they are sliced and frozen.
- The pieces of bruised apple and other trimmings (excluding the apple cores) are processed into apple sauce in the Crushing Department. The juice generated during this operation is used in producing the apple sauce.
- The apple cores, transferred from the Cutting Department, are pulverised into a liquid in the Juicing Department. There is a loss equal to 8% of the weight of the ***good*** output produced in this department.
- The outside skin is processed into animal feed and packaged in the Feed Department. It can be kept in cold storage until needed.

The production process is outlined below, showing the three joint products and the single by-product (animal feed).

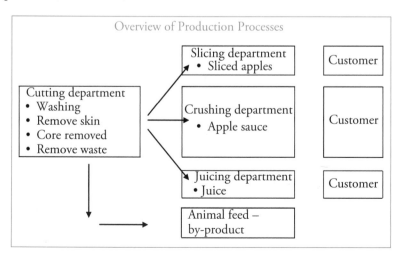

A total of 270,000 pounds of apples entered the Cutting Department during November. The following schedule shows the costs incurred in each department, the proportion by weight transferred to the four final processing departments, and the selling price of each end product.

| Processing Data and Costs – November 20x7 | | | |
|---|---|---|---|
| Department | Costs incurred | Proportion of product by weight transferred to Depts | Selling price per lb of final product |
| Cutting | €60,000 | | |
| Slicing | 11,280 | 33% | €0.80 |
| Crushing | 8,550 | 30 | 0.55 |
| Juicing | 3,000 | 27 | 0.40 |
| Feed | 700 | 10 | 0.10 |
| Total | €83,530 | 100% | |

**Requirements:**

1. The Kingdom Company uses the estimated NRV method to determine the cost of its joint products. For the month of November 20x7, calculate the gross profit margin of each of the three joint products, using the NRV method. Your workings should be clearly shown.
2. Comment on the significance to management of the gross-margin dollar information by joint product for decision-making purposes.

*Question 2.7 (OHAR and Cost-plus pricing)*

Headover Limited is preparing its production overhead budgets for the year ending 31 December 20x1. It has Machining and Assembly departments which process the raw materials into finished goods. In addition, there is a repairs department which provides a service to the two production (operating) departments but does not produce output in its own right. It is company policy to apportion and allocate all overhead costs to each of the three responsibility centres. The following budgeted cost information has been presented to you:

| Department | Machining | Assembly | Repairs | Total |
|---|---|---|---|---|
| General overheads (€) | 51,000 | 34,000 | 91,000 | 176,000 |
| Rent and rates (€) | ?? | ?? | ?? | 36,000 |
| Machine power (€) | ?? | ?? | ?? | 20,000 |

| Department | Machining | Assembly | Repairs | Total |
|---|---|---|---|---|
| Heat and light (€) | ?? | ?? | ?? | 10,000 |
| Depreciation (S/line (€)) | ?? | ?? | ?? | 8,000 |
| | | | | 250,000 |

Other information is provided for the forthcoming year as follows:

| Department | Machining | Assembly | Repairs | Total |
|---|---|---|---|---|
| Area (sq. metres) | 2,000 | 3,000 | 1,000 | 6,000 |
| Machinery cost (€) | 40,000 | 30,000 | 10,000 | 80,000 |
| Power usage (%) | 60% | 40% | – | 100% |
| Direct labour hours | n/a | 5,000 | – | 5,000 |
| Machine usage hours | 2,000 | n/a | – | 2,000 |

**Requirement**: Determine budgeted overhead absorption rates for each of the two production departments, having apportioned and allocated the above costs. You are informed that you should use machine usage hours as the cost driver in the machining department and direct labour hours in the Assembly department.

**Note:** In order to calculate OHARs for both production departments, the overhead costs of the repairs (support) department should be reapportioned to the two production departments based on an agreed split of 60% : 40%.

## Advanced Questions

*Question 2.8 (Cost Classification and Different Costs for Different Purposes)*

Due to the illness of her father, Sarah Mulligan took up an appointment with her family company, the Shanghai Clothing Company, a manufacturer of quality overcoats. This was also an opportunity for Sarah to test her managerial skills in her new position as General Manager.

The Shanghai Clothing Company has been under the conservative leadership of Jimmy Mulligan for 50 years. While maintaining a reputation for high quality craftsmanship, the Shanghai Clothing Company was never particularly innovative in the styles it put out. During the last three years, the company has experienced a steady decline in sales due to a shrinking consumer demand for its overcoats.

Reduced to only one product line, the company produced 7,000 overcoats last year, but sold 6,500 coats at an average price of €150 each. At this level of output, the company is currently operating at near full capacity. At the end of her first year (20x1) in charge of the company, Sarah was given an analysis of last year's costs (**Exhibit 1**):

| Exhibit 1: Costs incurred in 20x1 | € |
|---|---|
| **Cost item:** | |
| (a)  Fabric used for coats | 140,000 |
| (b)  Factory rent | 12,000 |

| | |
|---|---:|
| (c) Labour – cutting and stitching (variable) | 420,000 |
| (d) Production supervisor's salary | 15,000 |
| (e) Maintenance – equipment (fixed) | 1,000 |
| (f) Utilities – factory (fixed) | 6,000 |
| (g) General Manager's salary (Sarah Mulligan) | 28,000 |
| (h) Sales commission to agents (variable) | 9,750 |
| (i) Shipping costs (variable) | 6,500 |
| (j) Miscellaneous administration costs (fixed) | 17,500 |
| (k) Depreciation (straight line) – cutting equipment | 1,000 |
| (l) Coat lining, hoods, buttons etc. | 70,000 |
| (m) Advertising (fixed) | 3,250 |

In addition, in a recent conversation with the company's administrator, Sarah discovered that the Shanghai Clothing Company had conducted very favourable marketing tests on a new coat. Sarah believed that the company could introduce the new product line this Spring, and predicted that they could expect to sell 4,000 coats (i.e. units) per annum. Since the Company was operating at near capacity, the production of this new product line would involve employees working overtime. Sarah recognised the sales potential in this new coat, which differed radically from the traditional coat in its overall style and lightness. It was 'trendy' without sacrificing the quality and comfort of the existing coat.

The cost accountant supplied Sarah with the following facts and figures (**Exhibit 2**), which he had prepared on full costing principles:

| Exhibit 2: Anticipated costs of new product range (4,000 coats) | € |
|---|---:|
| Fabric including coat lining etc. | 100,000 |
| Labour – cutting and stitching | 280,000 |
| General fixed manufacturing overhead costs (apportioned) | 5,000 |
| Shipping costs (variable) | 5,200 |
| Sales commission to agents | 6,000 |
| Share of general administration costs (apportioned) | 10,000 |
| Development work (already carried out) | 5,000 |

Having been presented with this information Sarah realised that she needed to analyse current operations and come up with a strategy to reverse the company's fortunes.

**Requirements:**

1. Prepare a schedule of 'manufacturing costs incurred' during the past year. Why is this schedule important in valuing closing stock and why have you omitted some costs and included others? What was the average unit cost of last year's inventory under full absorption costing?

2. Prepare an overall cost statement for the past year and show the amount of net profit generated. Then calculate the following information:
   (a) Unit direct material costs.
   (b) Unit direct labour costs.
   (c) Unit variable manufacturing overhead.
   (d) Total fixed manufacturing overhead.
   (e) Unit variable selling, distribution and administration costs.
   (f) Total fixed selling, distribution and administration costs.
3. Calculate the company's annual break-even point (in units), but ignoring the possible impact of the additional 4,000 coats.
4. If the company wishes to produce an additional 4,000 new coats, list the relevant, incremental cash costs.

## Question 2.9 (Direct and Sequential Method of Service Cost Apportionment)

Nobes Limited has two production departments (cutting and assembly) and two service departments (maintenance and administration). Each year Nobes Limited develops predetermined departmental overhead rates on a full costing basis for the cutting and assembly departments. Costs and other data at normal volume are budgeted at the following levels:

|  | Service: Main. | Service: Admin. | Production: Cutting | Production: Assembly |
|---|---|---|---|---|
| Factory overhead cost | €94,000 | €48,000 | €188,000 | €49,200 |
| Direct labour hours | – | – | 15,000 | 10,000 |
| Number of employees | 5 | 20 | 9 | 36 |
| Square feet occupied | 10,000 | 20,000 | 30,000 | 30,000 |
| Machine hours | – | – | 20,000 | 40,000 |

Nobes Limited is now deciding on the most appropriate method of assigning service department costs to individual job orders. It has been agreed that maintenance department costs be apportioned on the number of square feet occupied in each department, while the costs of the administration department would be apportioned on the basis of the number of employees.

**Requirements:** You are required to apportion service department costs to production departments using the following two methods:

(a) Direct Method
(b) Step or sequential method

and calculate overhead absorption rates for each production department on the following basis:

- Cutting department – machine hours
- Assembly department – labour hours

### Question 2.10 (Cost Apportionment, Overall Profitability and Profit Planning)

The Nicosia Institute of Management (NIM) was founded in the late 1980s to service the needs of middle managers that did not have a formal academic education. Initially, the Institute offered only one course, a one-year advanced diploma in management, which was accredited by the National Authority. Demand for similar courses increased, and within two years NIM was offering two more courses, both advanced diplomas – one in shipping and the other in finance.

NIM rents purpose-built premises and is equipped with a well-stocked library, up-to-the-minute IT facilities and a sizeable restaurant. A full-time director with assistance from an administrator and an office secretary run the Institute. A part-time library assistant is also employed. The following summarised, projected income statement was circulated in relation to the forthcoming academic year:

| Summarised Income Statement for the Forthcoming Year | |
|---|---:|
| Income: | |
| Student fees (note 1) | 535,000 |
| Rental for canteen facility (note 2) | 3,000 |
| | 538,000 |
| | |
| Costs: | |
| Student teaching materials (note 3) | 30,000 |
| Exam corrections (note 4) | 7,500 |
| Lecturers' salaries (note 5) | 54,000 |
| Administration costs | 450,000 |
| | 541,500 |
| Projected deficit for year | (3,500) |

The projected deficit – the first ever – came as a surprise to the Director of the Institute. As a matter of urgency, he wants to know which programmes were or were not generating a surplus. The following is the specific data for the forthcoming academic year (20x6–x7):

1. **Student enrolment and fees**
   | | |
   |---|---|
   | Diploma in Management | 60 students @ €4,000 each |
   | Diploma in Shipping | 50 students @ €3,500 each |
   | Diploma in Finance | 40 students @ €3,000 each |
2. **Canteen rental income** An external catering company pays NIM a rental per annum to run the catering facility in the Institute, based on the number of registered students. This sum is negotiated each year. Profits (or losses) generated by the canteen belong to the catering company and are not shared with the School.

3. **Student materials** At the start of each academic year students are presented with specially printed folders containing all the required teaching material. The cost of providing folders is estimated at €20 per student. In addition, photocopying costs are estimated at €180 per student per annum. Any required textbooks must be purchased by the students themselves from a local bookshop of their choice.
4. **Exam correction costs** The exam correction costs are €50 per student for the academic year 20x6–x7.
5. **Lecturing hours and costs** Each course runs for 150 hours per semester. There are two semesters per academic year. All the lecturing is provided by local academics that are recruited specially for each course and they are paid at a rate of €60 per hour.

**Requirements:**

1. Prepare a financial analysis for each of the three academic programmes for the academic year 20x6–x7, which can be used to highlight the financial impact of (a) increasing/decreasing students, and (b) the financial impact of closing down a programme. Your figures should be consistent with the summarised Income Statement for the forthcoming year. (**For convenience, please use 'student numbers' as the basis of apportioning all costs that require apportionment.**)
2. Calculate the number of students required to break even in 20x6–x7.
3. If an additional 10 students were recruited for the finance programme from a leading international bank, what would be the financial impact? (The additional payment will be received from the catering company for these students.) What non-quantifiable (or qualitative) factors are relevant to this decision?
4. Assume that NIM decides to reduce all its course fees by 10% with the expected student enrolment unchanged. What impact will this have on the overall profitability?
5. The mission of the Institute is to be a centre of excellence in business education in Europe by achieving highest international standards in its research publications and by communication of that knowledge through excellence in learning. Specify 10 critical success factors (CSFs) that will, in your opinion, be important in achieving the Institute's mission. In addition, what related performance measures should be used to articulate these CSFs? What problems, if any, do you anticipate in gathering and implementing your suggested performance measurement system?

*Question 2.11 (Mini Case Involving Cost Apportionment in a Retail Firm)*

As a recently appointed management accountant of **Moscow Stores**, a large retail facility, you have been asked to evaluate the trading performance of its newly opened department store, which occupies 40,000 square feet near the centre of Moscow. The store is considered to be a profit centre and the manager is responsible for generating adequate profitability. The following summarised income statement was provided to you for the most recent financial year and shows an overall operating deficit of €32,000.

| INCOME STATEMENT FOR YEAR ENDED 31 DECEMBER 20x1 | |
|---|---:|
| | €000 |
| Sales (see note 1) | 1,685 |
| Cost of sales (see note 1) | (874) |
| Gross profit (see note 1) | 811 |
| Commission to staff (see note 3) | (37) |
| Theft of goods (see note 3) | (71) |
| Salaries of department managers (see note 2) | (60) |
| Salaries of sales employees (see note 2) | (160) |
| Light and heat etc. of store (see notes 1 and 3) | (200) |
| Advertising (see note 3) | (315) |
| Operating deficit for year | (32) |

The following notes and detailed information are provided to you in order to assist with your financial analysis:

1. **Operating data for each department**: The store is divided into several product lines and you have been provided with the following in respect of the most recent accounting year:

| | A Clothes | B Furniture | C Food | D Toys | E Electrical |
|---|---|---|---|---|---|
| Sales (in €000s) | €600 | €125 | €400 | €240 | €320 |
| Mark-up % on cost | 33⅓% | 25% | 100% | 300% | 400% |
| Floor space % | 10% | 25% | 25% | 10% | 30% |

2. **Salaries and wages**: One manager is employed in each department at an inclusive cost of €12,000 per annum. In addition it is company policy to employ one sales assistant for every 2,000 (or part of) square feet of floor space at an annual salary of €8,000. Because of the unique selling skills of each product line it is not considered feasible to move employees between product lines.

3. **Other costs**: The department store incurs a number of other costs which are to be apportioned as follows:

| Item | Amount | Basis of apportionment |
|---|---|---|
| Light, heating, etc. | €200,000 | Floor space |
| Advertising | €315,000 | Sales |
| Sales commission | ?? | Provided at 4% of sales on product B, and 10% on product E |
| Theft of goods | ?? | Estimated 10% of cost of sales on lines A, C and D only |

## Requirements:

1. The management of the department store are concerned with the operating loss of €32,000 reported for the recent financial year. Prepare a revised statement identifying the product line contribution and product line profit/loss using the bases of apportionment as indicated above. Comment on your calculations.
2. Calculate the overall BEP (in sales revenue) of the department store.
3. Indicate the overall financial impact if an advertising campaign was launched at a cost of €50,000, and which increased overall sales by 10%.
4. You are required to undertake a basic benchmarking exercise. Comparable figures for the store's main competitor for a recent accounting period are provided below. Comment on the store's comparative performance in relation to these metrics:

|  | Competitor |
|---|---|
| Sales (excluding taxes) | €3,960,000 |
| Operating profit | €56,000 |
| Retail footage | 50,000 sq. feet |
| Staffing (full-time equivalents) | 41 |

5. In determining selling prices, critically evaluate the roles of both variable and full costs, especially in relation to the retail sector.
6. What do you consider to be the critical success factors (financial and non-financial) of this store and how would you measure them? Be specific and justify your choice.

*Question 2.12 (Service Department Cost Apportionments)*

The ALLTHREE Company manufactures a number of products in its modern production facility consisting of two production departments (Machining and Assembly). The Machining department is machine-intensive whereas the Assembly is labour intensive. There are two production support departments (Maintenance and Production scheduling). The production scheduling department is mainly responsible for scheduling various production runs. The maintenance department provides support services to both machining and assembly departments and also to carry out necessary maintenance costs for production scheduling. The maintenance costs are to be reapportioned on the basis of its support work provided to other departments as measured by the amount of hours provided to the other departments. The scheduling costs are to be re-apportioned on the basis of scheduling hours provided to other departments. Based on past performance and experience, the following interdepartmental relationships and estimated overhead costs are given below:

|  | Machining | Assembly | Maintenance | Scheduling |
|---|---|---|---|---|
| Overheads for year | €400,000 | €200,000 | €600,000 | €116,000 |
| Machine running hours | 20,000 | 30,000 | Nil | Nil |

|  | Machining | Assembly | Maintenance | Scheduling |
|---|---|---|---|---|
| Number of inspections | 560 | 300 | N/A | N/A |
| Space occupied (footage) | 200,000 | 100,000 | 85,000 | 50,000 |
| Direct labour hours | 30,000 | 30,000 | Nil | Nil |
| Support work provided by Maintenance dept: (hours) | 2,400 | 4,000 | N/A | 1,600 |
| Support work provided by Scheduling dept: (hours) | 1,600 | 200 | 200 | N/A |

**Requirements:**

1. Calculate a plant-wide overhead absorption rate using direct labour hours as the only cost driver. Also, you should briefly highlight the arguments both for and against the use of plant-wide overhead absorption rates.
2. Calculate the production overhead absorption rate for both the Machine and Assembly departments, reapportioning service department overheads using
   (a) the direct method;
   (b) the step-down/sequential method;
   (c) the reciprocal (cross) method.

You should use machine hours as the cost driver in the Machining department and direct labour hours in the Assembly department.

3. Briefly indicate whether firms should use plant-wide or departmental OHARs.
4. The allocation (apportionment) of service department costs serves no useful purpose. Comment critically on this statement.
5. Should support-department costs be apportioned on a budget or actual basis? Support your reasoning.

# 3

# Job Costing Systems

LEARNING OBJECTIVES

When you have completed studying this chapter you should be able to:

1. Describe job costing systems under a traditional cost accounting system.
2. Apply cost plus pricing techniques in a service firm.
3. Record cost flows in a manufacturing firm.
4. Explain how direct materials and direct labour are assigned to jobs.

## 3.1 Job Costing Systems

Broadly speaking, there are two different types of cost accumulation system which can be used by manufacturing or service firms – a job costing system or a process costing system. This chapter will focus on job costing systems and the next chapter will describe process costing systems. Both systems have a common objective – the identification of accurate product costs. However, the method of cost accumulation on which each system is based is different and reflects the manufacturing process or, for service companies, the duration involved in providing services to customers.

A job cost accumulation system is usually operated in a business that undertakes different types of orders for clients rather than mass-producing a single product. Typically, in a job costing system, work is carried out on a 'once-off' basis as in the case of a special order. In this section, we shall provide an overview of the system and in subsequent sections we will describe the range of information and transactions that are recorded, with emphasis on recording through ledger accounts. We can define a job costing system as that which involves the manufacture of customised products (or delivery of services) for specific customers and in accordance with a customer's specification. The main features of a job costing system are:

1. Each job originates against a specific order (and should be given a specific job number to distinguish it from all other jobs). Therefore, each job has a separate job card, on which the required activities to be performed are written and on which all

the data is collected. Thus, at any time, it should be possible to see the stage of completion of the job, simply by looking at the job card. As the job is being completed, various cost details will be added. Job costing systems are usually found in:

- the construction industry
- printing companies
- professional service firms, e.g. accountancy firms
- car service/car repair firms.

2. Each job is *different,* especially in terms of resources (materials and labour) consumed. As a result, each job should be costed separately. In this chapter we shall concentrate initially on how to compute 'production' cost, since this is the amount that would be used for end of period inventory valuation. However, it must be noted that a total cost figure (which includes an element of non-production cost) may be required for selling price determination.

It will be recalled from **Chapter 2** that the production cost of each job comprises direct materials, direct labour and an appropriate share of production overheads. The direct materials assigned to the job are based on materials requisition dockets, since direct materials should only be released from the stock room on foot of a properly completed materials requisition docket. Direct labour hours are assigned as job costs on the basis of clock cards or time sheets, with the relevant number of hours worked being multiplied by the appropriate wage rate per hour. Again, it should be relatively easy to trace the amount of hours worked by employees on specific jobs.

In addition to the direct costs of each job, each job should receive a share of production overheads from each department through which it passes. (This assumes that the company is absorbing production overheads on the basis of several departments rather than a single plant-wide, production overhead absorption rate.) It will be recalled that, under normal costing procedures, the production OHAR will be predetermined at the start of the year, based on the following formula:

$$\text{OHAR} = \frac{\text{Estimated total production overhead } €}{\text{Estimated cost driver level}}$$

Therefore, the production cost of any job can be summarised as follows:

SUMMARISED JOB COSTING CARD (NORMAL COSTING)

| Cost item | Information used |
|---|---|
| Direct materials | Quantity and type of materials used multiplied by unit cost, based on materials requisition dockets |
| Direct labour | Actual hours worked on job, based on clock cards or time sheets, multiplied by rate per hour |
| Production overhead | Predetermined OHAR multiplied by actual DLH (or machine hours, as appropriate) |
| = Total production cost | |

## ILLUSTRATION: JOB COSTING

Galway Toys Limited manufactures a range of wooden toys according to the specifications of their large department store customers. It operates a normal job costing system. The toys are produced in two different departments: Department A is labour-intensive and Department B is machine-intensive. Total costs and operating data for the forthcoming year (20x1) are budgeted as follows:

| | Department A | Department B | Total |
|---|---|---|---|
| Direct materials | €100,000 | €90,000 | €190,000 |
| Direct labour hours | 15,000 | 23,000 | |
| Direct labour cost | €150,000 | €230,000 | €380,000 |
| Machine running hours | 7,500 | 4,500 | |
| Production overhead | €150,000 | €180,000 | €330,000 |
| Total budget production cost | | | €900,000 |

During January 20x1, the firm completed only two orders for specific clients. Actual costs and other data pertinent to these jobs are given below and you may assume that direct labour is paid at the rate of €10 per hour.

| | Job J1 | Job J2 |
|---|---|---|
| **Direct materials cost:** | | |
| Department A | €6,000 | €5,000 |
| Department B | €4,000 | €3,000 |
| **Direct labour hours worked:** | | |
| Department A @ €10 | 600 hours | 650 hours |
| Department B @ €10 | 800 hours | 1,200 hours |
| **Machine running hours:** | | |
| Department A | 300 hours | 325 hours |
| Department B | 150 hours | 250 hours |

### Requirements:

1. Compute predetermined production overhead absorption rates for the two departments, using direct labour hours for Department A and machine hours for Department B as the appropriate cost drivers.
2. Calculate the total (production) costs of both jobs, given the information provided.

## Solution and Analysis:

1. Since the company operates a normal job costing system, the first calculation required is that of the production OHAR, based on budgeted information. This must be calculated for both departments, using direct labour hours and machine hours as the cost driver for department A and B respectively. The budgeted (or predetermined) production OHAR for each department is as follows:

|  | Department A | Department B |
|---|---|---|
| Overheads € | €150,000 | €180,000 |
| Cost driver | 15,000 | 4,500 |
| OHAR = | €10 per labour hour | €40 per machine hour |

2. The production cost for each job is computed as follows and it should be remembered that production overheads are absorbed on the basis of direct labour hours in Department A and on the basis of machine running hours for Department B:

|  | Job J1 € | Job J2 € |  |
|---|---|---|---|
| Direct material cost: |  |  |  |
| Department A (given) | 6,000 | 5,000 |  |
| Department B (given) | 4,000 | 3,000 |  |
| Direct labour cost: |  |  |  |
| Department A (hours × rate) | 6,000 | 6,500 |  |
| Department B (hours × rate) | 8,000 | 12,000 |  |
| Production overhead |  |  |  |
| Department A (€10 × 600) | 6,000 | 6,500 | (€10 × 650) |
| Department B (€40 × 150) | 6,000 | 10,000 | (€40 × 250) |
| Total production cost | 36,000 | 43,000 |  |

The total production cost figures indicated above for both jobs would be used in inventory calculation if the goods were unsold at the end of the accounting period. The above figures are based on normal costing whereby actual direct materials used, actual direct labour cost incurred and an estimated amount of production overhead is used to determine production cost. Total production cost may also be required for certain decisions, e.g. the decision to cease production of a particular product or to outsource production to another location or company. (It is likely that the production cost calculations will have to be amended to reflect the important differences between fixed and variable costs.) Thus, knowledge of production cost will always be required within any manufacturing firm.

However, an estimate of total costs, i.e. production and non-production costs, may also be required. For example, in determining selling prices, the calculation of total cost will be important and the use of cost plus pricing will be discussed, separately, in the next section.

## 3.2 An Introduction to Cost Plus Pricing

Pricing decisions made by management have wide-ranging implications both for the firm itself and for the environment in which it operates. Pricing (and related volume levels) is a major determinant of both the profitability and cash flow of a business. If prices are too low, costs will not be covered and the firm incurs a loss. Alternatively, if prices are too high, then demand may be restricted and total sales revenue may be insufficient to cover costs. Prices can be used to generate additional market share, in which case they will impact on the performance of competitors. In addition, prices may have an impact on the national and international economy. This is particularly true for key raw materials such as oil, gas and food prices in general.

Cost plus pricing, as the name suggests, is an approach to setting selling prices based on cost and consists of three separate stages:

1. Determine Unit Cost These costs can either be the 'marginal' or 'full-costs' and both alternatives will give a different cost figure. The marginal cost represents the change in total costs associated with the production of one additional unit. In many cases it should approximate, closely, the calculation of variable cost, though it should be remembered that the calculation of variable cost is based on the 'relevant range' assumption. The use of marginal costing is particularly suited to once-off pricing decisions, especially pricing in the context of utilising spare capacity situations.

    Alternatively, unit cost can be based on full-cost calculations which, in addition to all the relevant variable costs, take into consideration the fixed costs – both production and non-production. Therefore, we need to include the large proportion of administration and marketing costs in addition to fixed manufacturing overheads. However, there is a paradox with this approach in that, in order to calculate unit fixed costs, you need to first know the total units to be sold. Dividing total fixed costs by total units to be sold provides a figure for fixed cost per unit. However, the paradox with this method of price determination is that we use (future) sales volume to determine unit fixed costs which, in turn, determines unit selling price. This approach is in contrast with basic economics, which argues that selling price determines sales volume, and NOT that sales volume determines selling price!

Full cost calculations include both production and non-production overheads. To avoid possible confusion, we shall refer to the 'recovery' of non-production overheads in the context of selling price determination in contrast to the 'absorption' of production overheads for stock valuation purposes. Non-production overheads are usually recovered using some cost base, e.g. total production cost, a logical calculation being as follows, with the amount of non-production overhead to be recovered expressed as a percentage of total production cost:

$$\text{Recovery of non-production overhead} = \frac{\text{Total non-production overhead} \; € \times 100}{\text{Total production cost}} = X\%$$

The above percentage indicates the estimated amount of non-production overhead to be included in our estimate of total cost for selling price decisions.

It is important to note that neither marginal nor full cost pricing guarantees a profit at the end of the accounting period. This is because, with marginal costing, our volume may not be high enough to cover all fixed costs (which have been omitted from our calculations). With full cost pricing, there is no guarantee that customers will pay the price that we have determined by way of a cost plus formula, and so there will be a shortfall in relation to demand – referred to as an adverse volume variance. (It is also possible that customers would have paid higher prices in specific circumstances, in which case we could have earned additional profits.)

2. **Mark-up on Cost** The second stage in cost-plus pricing is to determine an appropriate mark-up for profit. This mark-up can be related to a profit margin on sales or a return on shareholders' funds. Where a profit margin on sales is required, it is important to note that there is a difference between mark-up on cost and a profit margin on sales. For example, if the mark-up on cost is 25%, then this is equivalent to a 20% margin on sales. It is always useful to prepare a simple schedule and work with '100' as your base figure. If the margin is based on sales, then the sales figure is equivalent to '100'. If the margin is based on cost, then cost is equivalent to '100' as follows:

| | |
|---|---|
| Cost of goods | 100 |
| Mark-up on cost (given as 25% on cost) | 25 |
| Therefore, sales price must be | 125 |
| | |
| Profit margin on sales (25/125) × 100 | 20% |

The above calculation is particularly important in cost plus pricing. Sometimes, and especially in examinations, you are provided with the required profit margin on sales and requested to ascertain the required selling price. The only known financial item is the cost to which the mark-up on cost must be added – in the above case the mark up on cost is 25%, whereas the margin on sales is 20%. However, both methods will give the same amount of profit per unit if applied correctly.

3. **Market Adjustment** The final stage in cost-plus pricing is that of market adjustment. The cost-plus price is rarely the final price since an adjustment is usually made for psychological purposes. For example, a computed price of €5.02 would probably be rounded down to €4.99.

As well as a price of €4.99 being perceived as cheaper than €5.02, these '99' prices serve another purpose. A price of, say, €4.99 became an important internal control mechanism to prevent employee fraud. Where a customer tendered a €5 note, the sales assistant would be forced to register the sale in order to provide the correct amount of change. If the price was exactly €5, no change would be required and it would be possible for the sales assistant to pocket the money without registering the transaction. In addition to psychological considerations, market adjustment may be due to the existence of actual or potential competitors, or the price may be adjusted to what the customer is prepared to pay. Alternatively, the price may be reduced in order to entice new customers. Thus cost plus pricing in reality represents an initial price to be considered and discussed.

We shall now illustrate cost-plus pricing in the context of a professional services firm that operates a job costing system. We introduce a service firm to reduce the emphasis on inventory valuation issues. Because the focus of our decision is selling price determination based on cost plus principles, all costs need to be included and there is no need to distinguish between production and non-production costs. In addition, we shall see that cost-plus pricing does not necessarily guarantee a profit and this occurs whenever there is an adverse volume variance, i.e. we overestimate potential demand. (We shall conveniently ignore the additional possibility that costs exceed budget.)

## ILLUSTRATION: COST-PLUS PRICING UNDER JOB COSTING SYSTEMS (SERVICE FIRM)

Fairyhouse Associates is a management consulting firm in which all professional staff are employed at the same staff grade and all receive the same annual salary. The professional staff are contracted to work for a fixed number of hours per annum. Fairyhouse Associates uses a job costing system to identify the costs of each engagement (job). For cost accumulation purposes, there are three categories of cost, i.e. salary cost of professional (direct) labour, secretarial salaries and, finally, office costs. (In theory, we could refer to the first category as production direct labour and the other categories as non-production overheads.)

The firm provides a range of consulting services to clients and the fee is determined by the number of chargeable professional hours, multiplied by the 'billing rate' per hour. The billing (or chargeout) rate for professional staff is determined at the start of each year and is intended to cover all costs and provide a margin of profit. Budgeted chargeable, professional hours and budgeted costs for the year are as follows:

| Annual budget for year .... | Chargeable hours | € |
|---|---|---|
| Salary cost of professional staff | 25,000 | 300,000 |
| Salary cost of secretarial staff | | 80,000 |
| Office costs including telephone, postage | | 200,000 |
| Budgeted total costs for year | | 580,000 |
| Budgeted net profit | | 120,000 |
| Budgeted fee income | | 700,000 |

Based on your preliminary analysis, all costs are considered fixed in relation to changes in the level of cost driver, i.e. professional hours charged to clients.

### Requirements:

1. Calculate the 'billing rate' (charge-out rate) for professional hours to cover all costs and to provide a required profit target of €120,000 for the year, assuming a total of 25,000 chargeable hours are worked in total during the year. Based on your calculation indicate what is the amount of the fee note (invoice) for a specific client for whom 70 professional hours are recorded.
2. Assume that the charge-out rate to clients is €28 per professional hour and that all budgeted costs were incurred during the year as anticipated. Calculate the overall profit or loss for the year if only 20,000 hours were billed to clients.

### Solution and analysis:

1. The 'billing rate' represents the selling price of an hour of professional labour. In this case, the selling price is intended to cover all costs and also generate a satisfactory profit. Because we are making a selling price decision, as distinct from, say, valuing work-in-progress at the end of the financial year, all costs should be included in our calculation. Also, because we need to set the sales price in advance, we use forecast data.

   It should be noted that, based on a preliminary analysis, all costs are considered fixed in relation to the volume of chargeable hours within a relevant range of activity. In order to calculate the cost per hour we need to first decide on the number of chargeable hours that will be worked (25,000 hours) by professional staff. The calculation of the billing rate is as follows (including required profit per hour). These figures are obtained from the firm's budget.

   'Billing rate' per hour:
   Total costs and profit    = €700,000
   Total hours worked       = 25,000 hours
   Billing rate per hour    = €28 per hour

   This means that Fairyhouse Associates will charge clients a standard rate of €28 per hour for each hour worked and this billing rate includes both costs and profit margin. However, the paradox of this calculation is that there is no guarantee that clients will be prepared to pay €28 per hour! They may consider this rate excessive and decline the offer of work. Alternatively, clients may be prepared to pay more than €28 per hour.

Under a job costing system, we note the individual hours (because this is a service firm) worked on behalf of specific clients. Each client will require different amounts of professional service and they will be charged accordingly. Thus, the proposed fee note for the specific client for whom 70 hours is worked is:

$$€28 \times 70 \text{ hours} = €1,960$$

2. In this illustration selling prices per hour are set in advance using estimates of future costs and future activity (hours) levels. Of course, these estimates may not materialise. We need to be particularly concerned with an adverse volume variance, i.e. when our forecast of chargeable hours (25,000 hours) does not materialise. At the end of the year it was discovered that only 20,000 chargeable hours were worked on behalf of clients. The financial consequences can be presented in a summarised income statement as follows, where all costs incurred exactly match those budgeted:

|  | € |
| --- | --- |
| Actual sales revenue (20,000 chargeable hours × €28 per hour) | 560,000 |
| Salaries of professional staff (as per budget) | (300,000) |
| Salaries of secretarial staff (as per budget) | ( 80,000) |
| Office costs (as per budget) | (200,000) |
| Net loss for year | (20,000) |
| Budgeted profit for year (given) | 120,000 |
| Total reduction in profitability | (140,000) |

The above calculation highlights a dramatic reduction in profit – an overall decline of €140,000 between budget and actual outturn. This figure is easily proved. Since all the costs are considered fixed, then the contribution per hour is equivalent to the selling price per hour (€28). The firm 'sold' 5,000 hours less than anticipated. Therefore, the overall reduction in profit is:

Reduction of 5,000 hours × €28 per hour = (€140,000).

The profit decline is entirely due to the fact that our volume forecast did not materialise. Furthermore, in the above illustration actual costs were exactly in line with budget. Therefore, there was no spending variance. In reality, there is likely to be either a favourable or adverse spending variance in conjunction with either an adverse or favourable volume variance.

## 3.3  Recording Cost Flows in Job Costing Systems

Thus far in this chapter we have described the nature of cost accumulation and also described job costing systems. We have also outlined 'normal' costing systems, whereby actual material and actual labour costs are identified for a particular job, in addition to an estimated amount of production overheads. In this section, we illustrate the recording of such cost flows, by way of double-entry ledger accounts and we shall focus on manufacturing operations. (It is assumed that the reader is familiar with double-entry book-keeping.)

### Recording Direct Material Cost Flows

Direct material represents the material that is built into the product and can be visually seen in the product. For a manufacturer of, say, televisions, this includes the various components that are necessary for the television to function. For a printing company, this represents the different types and quality of paper used. The recording of direct material cost flows involves two related elements as follows:

• knowing the recording process in terms of debit/credit convention; and
• knowing the documents and vouchers that 'trigger' the recording process and the related controls.

The key point to note in recording cost flows is that **the recording process in ledger accounts follows the sequence of production**. In reality there are four stages of cost flows for recording purposes:

1. **The acquisition of resources**, i.e. purchase of material:
      Dr. Direct materials (or purchases) account
      Cr. Creditors (or bank) account

   The source document for recording the above transaction is the approved purchase invoice backed by a properly authorised goods received note. Both of these documents prove the receipt of the required goods from the supplier or approved vendor, at the appropriate price. If goods are returned, then the above transaction can, simply, be reversed.

2. **The issue and usage of resources**, i.e. transfer of materials to production:
      Dr. Work in progress (or job) account
      Cr. Direct materials (or purchases) account

   The source document for the above transaction is the (internal) materials requisitions docket, which indicates the type and quantity of material required and the specific job for which it is required. The unit price and total cost of the requested materials will, eventually, be included by the store manager before sending this docket to the management accountant for recording.

3. **Completion of work-in-progress and recognition of finished goods:**
      Dr. Finished goods account
      Cr. Work-in-progress account

The source document for this transaction is the end of period production report from the production manager, to which the management accountant adds the appropriate cost figures.

4. Sale of finished good, i.e. recording cost of goods sold:
   Dr. Cost of sales account
   Cr. Finished goods account

The source document for this transaction is the delivery docket signed by the customer as proof of delivery. This is proof that revenue has been generated and the cost of goods sold can be recognised within the accounting system.

### Recording Direct Labour Cost Flows

The recording of direct labour cost flows is similar to materials, but with an added distinction being made between direct and indirect labour costs. (Labour costs include any employer's social welfare and pension contributions.) Direct labour represents the work performed on the product itself. In contrast, indirect labour represents the work of supervisors and managers, together with support services such as maintenance and cleaning. Indirect labour costs will be recorded as part of production overhead.

To assist the assignment of **direct** labour costs, some companies require their employees to complete some type of clock cards indicating the amount of work performed on each job. The clock card system will have to be supplemented by a job or time ticket since the former only indicates the amount of hours worked and not on what job the work was performed. Thus, an employee will have to complete one clock card a week but probably several job tickets. The total hours figure on both should be equal. (In professional service firms, employees are required to complete time sheets, usually on a weekly basis.)

Direct labour cost flows are recorded when the work is performed. Two ledger entries could be recorded as follows:

| Clock card summary: | Dr. Wages control account<br>Cr. Bank account (the payment of wages) |
| --- | --- |

However, the total wages payment will have to be assigned to the various jobs worked on during the week. The entry will be:

| Job card summary: | Dr. Work-in-progress account<br>Cr. Wages control account |
| --- | --- |

It should be noted that if any balance remains on the wages control account, i.e. amounts not transferred to specific jobs, this constitutes idle time and can be reported separately on the cost statement – depending on its significance.

### Labour and Overtime Premium

It is common for direct employees to work overtime and this is usually paid at a premium. How does one record such premiums? Overtime premiums are considered direct costs if they are due to the customer rather than a lack of capacity. In other words, the overtime premium is a direct cost of a particular job if it is generated by the demands of the customer, e.g. special order situations with special delivery terms. In other situations, e.g. where the overtime is caused by general lack of capacity, then the premium involved should be classified as indirect labour and recorded as part of manufacturing overhead. This treatment recognises that overtime, in this case, is caused by excess aggregate demand in relation to the availability of production facilities. In which case, all production generated during the period should share such overtime premium.

### Recording Production Overhead Cost Flows

The recording of production overhead cost flows are more problematic since, by definition, they are not directly traceable to a specific job. The amount of overheads incurred is determined by invoices received for, say, factory rent, insurance, together with indirect labour costs (e.g. supervisors) and perhaps some indirect materials. Initially, the expenditure on production overheads is generally recorded as follows:

Dr. Production overhead control account

Cr. Accounts payable (or bank account or aggregate depreciation account)

Secondly, it is necessary for costing purposes to transfer these production overheads to work-in-progress (WIP). Here, we must remember that most manufacturing firms will use a 'normal' costing system. It will be recalled that, under a normal costing system, the production overhead is assigned to work-in-progress by way of a predetermined overhead rate (OHAR), which is based on budgeted data. The overhead absorption rate is calculated as follows:

$$OHAR = \frac{€ \text{ Estimated total production overhead}}{\text{Estimated level of cost driver e.g. DL hours}}$$

Using this OHAR, production overhead is assigned to production completed during the period as follows:

Dr. WIP account

Cr. Production overhead control account

The overhead assigned to production during the accounting period will rarely correspond to actual production overheads incurred. This gives rise to either under- or over-absorbed production overhead at the year end and which results from either incorrectly estimating overheads to be incurred (the numerator) and/or incorrectly estimating the level of cost driver (the denominator).

Most firms will write off such under/over-absorbed production overhead to the cost statement as a separate line item. This is the simplest accounting treatment. There is an alternative and more complicated method which prorates the amount of under/over-absorbed production overhead to work-in-progress, finished goods and cost of sales accounts (but never raw materials) based on the percentage of applied overhead in each account. The simpler of the two methods is recommended here.

A summarized job cost sheet appears in **Exhibit 3.1**, for 3,000 units of Job 101, which required 3,000 shell casings and 6,000 other components, skilled direct labour and where production overhead is absorbed on the basis of direct labour hours.

EXHIBIT 3.1: JOB COST SHEET

| Description | Job 101 | | |
|---|---|---|---|
| Date ordered | 11 May 2009 | Date completed | 24 May 2009 |
| Quantity ordered | 3,000 units | | |
| Materials costs: | | | € |
| Casings (specified) | 3,000 units | €1.50 | 4,500 |
| Component (specified) | 6,000 units | €4.00 | 24,000 |
| Labour costs: | | | 28,500 |
| Skilled labour | 250 hours | €30.00 | 7,500 |
| Production overhead costs: | | | |
| OHAR × DLH | 250 hours | €12.00 | 3,000 |
| = Total production costs | | | 39,000 |

## Recording Non-production Overheads

Manufacturing firms will incur expenditure on non-production overheads such as advertising, administrative and sales personnel, cleaning of office accommodation, lighting, heating and telephone. All such expenditures are classified as non-production overheads and can be generally recorded as follows:

      Dr. Non-production overhead control account
      Cr. Accounts payable (or bank account)

Production and non-production overheads are usually recorded separately, simply because of the financial reporting requirement that unsold inventory should only be valued at production cost.

ILLUSTRATION OF RECORDING COST FLOWS UNDER NORMAL<br/>JOB COSTING SYSTEMS

We shall now illustrate the recording of cost flows in a job costing manufacturer, using normal job costing principles. For ease of presentation, we shall assume that only two jobs (101 and 102) were worked on and are completed during the year and both of these were delivered to the respective customers. In addition, one completed job (100) was in stock on 1 January 20x7 and was sold during the year. There was no opening or closing stock of work-in-progress.

You are provided with the following information relating to the year ended 31 December 20x7, which you may assume to be accurate:

| | |
|---|---:|
| Raw materials in stock at 1 January | 3,000 |
| Finished goods at cost at 1 January | 8,000 |
| Direct material purchases during the year | 26,000 |
| Analysis of Material Requisition notes for year: | |
|   For production (Job 101) | 17,000 |
|   For production (Job 102) | 7,000 |
| Wages paid (by cheque) | 49,000 |
| Time Sheets and other labour records indicate the following: | |
|   For production (Job 101: 1,100 hours) | 11,000 |
|   For production (Job 102: 900 hours) | 9,000 |
|   Factory supervision | 10,000 |
|   Administration salaries | 8,000 |
|   Selling salaries | 9,000 |
| Production overheads (non-salary) incurred and paid | 10,000 |
| Administration overheads (non-salary) incurred and paid | 7,000 |
| Selling overheads (non-salary) incurred and paid | 16,000 |
| Sales revenue for period (all cash sales) | |
| Job 100 | 20,000 |
| Job 101 | 100,000 |
| Job 102 | 60,000 |

**Notes:**

1. After stocktaking, it was agreed that there was €2,000 of direct materials in stock at the end of the period. Any discrepancy in the raw materials account should be treated as wastage. Any discrepancy in the wages control account should be treated as idle time of production employees.
2. Production overhead was absorbed at €12 per direct labour hour.

**Requirement:** Record the above information in the appropriate ledger accounts and prepare an overall cost summary at financial year end.

**Solution and Analysis:** For presentation purposes, we shall first note the transactions by way of journal entries and then record them in the appropriate ledger accounts in the same sequence.

| | | Dr. | Cr. |
|---|---|---:|---:|
| **1.** | Record opening balances (memorandum entry): | | |
| | a. Direct materials control a/c | 3,000 | |
| | b. Finished goods (Job 100) a/c | 8,000 | |

**2.** Purchase of direct materials:

| | | |
|---|---|---|
| Direct materials control a/c | 26,000 | |
| Creditors a/c | | 26,000 |

**3.** Issue of direct materials to production:

| | | |
|---|---|---|
| WIP (Job 101) a/c | 17,000 | |
| WIP (Job 102) a/c | 7,000 | |
| Direct materials control a/c | | 24,000 |

**4.** Payment of wages:

| | | |
|---|---|---|
| Wages control a/c | 49,000 | |
| Bank a/c | | 49,000 |

**5.** Assigning labour costs:

| | | |
|---|---|---|
| WIP (Job 101) a/c | 11,000 | |
| WIP (Job 102) a/c | 9,000 | |
| Production overhead control a/c | 10,000 | |
| Administration overhead a/c | 8,000 | |
| Selling overhead a/c | 9,000 | |
| Wages control a/c | | 47,000 |

**6.** Overheads incurred:

| | | |
|---|---|---|
| Production overhead control a/c | 10,000 | |
| Administration overhead a/c | 7,000 | |
| Selling overhead a/c | 16,000 | |
| Bank a/c | | 33,000 |

**7.** Absorption of production overhead costs:

| | | |
|---|---|---|
| WIP a/c (Job 101: 1,100 DLH × €12 per hour) | 13,200 | |
| WIP a/c (Job 102: 900 DLH × €12 per hour) | 10,800 | |
| Production overhead control a/c | | 24,000 |

**8.** Sales revenue (Cash sales):

| | | |
|---|---|---|
| Bank a/c | 180,000 | |
| Sales a/c (Job 100) | | 20,000 |

|  | | |
|---|---|---|
| Sales a/c (Job 101) | | 100,000 |
| Sales a/c (Job 102) | | 60,000 |

**9.** Recording closing balances (memorandum entry):

|  | | |
|---|---|---|
| Direct materials control a/c (given) | | 2,000 |
| Finished goods control a/c | | Nil |

**10.** Noting and recording direct material wastage:

|  | | |
|---|---|---|
| Material wastage a/c | 3,000 | |
| Direct materials control a/c | | 3,000 |

**11.** Recording cost of production completion:

|  | | |
|---|---|---|
| Finished goods control (Job 101) a/c | 41,200 | |
| Finished goods control (Job 102) a/c | 26,800 | |
| WIP a/c (Job 101) | | 41,200 |
| WIP a/c (Job 102) | | 26,800 |

**12.** Noting and recording labour idle time:

|  | | |
|---|---|---|
| Idle time a/c | 2,000 | |
| Wages control a/c | | 2,000 |

**13.** Noting and recording of over-absorbed overhead:

|  | | |
|---|---|---|
| Production overhead control a/c | 4,000 | |
| Over-absorbed overheads a/c | | 4,000 |

**14.** Recording cost of sales of Jobs

|  | | |
|---|---|---|
| Cost of sales a/c | 76,000 | |
| Finished goods a/c (Jobs 100, 101 & 102) | | 76,000 |

The appropriate ledger entries can now be recorded, based on the above sequence.

### Direct materials control a/c

|  | € |  | € |
|---|---|---|---|
| 1a Balance (1 Jan) | 3,000 | 3. WIP (Jobs 101 & 102) | 24,000 |
| 2. Creditors control a/c | 26,000 | 10. Wastage (unexplained) | 3,000 |
|  |  | 9. Balance (given) | 2,000 |
|  | 29,000 |  | 29,000 |

## Job 101 – Work-in-progress control a/c

| | | € | | € |
|---|---|---|---|---|
| 3. | Direct materials | 17,000 | 11. Finished goods | 41,200 |
| 5. | Wages | 11,000 | control | 41,200 |
| 7. | Production overhead | 13,200 | | |
| | | 41,200 | | |

## Job 102 – Work-in-progress control a/c

| | | € | | € |
|---|---|---|---|---|
| 3. | Direct materials | 7,000 | 11. Finished goods | 26,200 |
| 5. | Wages | 9,000 | control | 26,200 |
| 7. | Production overhead | 10,800 | | |
| | | 26,800 | | |

## Wages control a/c

| | | € | | € |
|---|---|---|---|---|
| 4. | Bank | 49,000 | 5. Transfer to other accounts | 47,000 |
| | | | 12. Idle time | 2,000 |
| | | 49,000 | | 49,000 |

## Production overhead control a/c

| | | € | | € |
|---|---|---|---|---|
| 5. | Wages | 10,000 | | |
| 6. | Bank | 10,000 | 7. WIP (Job 101 & 102) | 24,000 |
| 13. | Over-absorption of overhead | 4,000 | | 24,000 |
| | | 24,000 | | |

## Administration overhead a/c

| | | € | | € |
|---|---|---|---|---|
| 5. | Wages | 8,000 | | |
| 6. | Bank | 7,000 | | |

## Selling overhead a/c

| | | € | | € |
|---|---|---|---|---|
| 5. | Wages | 9,000 | | |
| 6. | Bank | 16,000 | | |

## Sales a/c

| | € | | € |
|---|---|---|---|
| | | 8. Bank (Job 100) | 20,000 |
| | | 8. Bank (Job 101) | 100,000 |
| | | 8. Bank (Job 102) | 60,000 |

### Finished goods a/c

| | € | | € |
|---|---|---|---|
| 1b Balance (1 Jan<br>Job 100) | 8,000 | 14. Cost of sales | 76,000 |
| 11. WIP (Job 101) | 41,200 | | |
| 11. WIP (Job 102) | 26,800 | | |
| | 76,000 | | 76,000 |

### Cost of sales a/c

| | € | | € |
|---|---|---|---|
| 14. Finished goods | 76,000 | | |

### Creditors control a/c

| | € | | € |
|---|---|---|---|
| | | 2. Direct materials | 26,000 |

### Bank a/c

| | € | | € |
|---|---|---|---|
| 8. Sales | 180,000 | 4. Wages | 49,000 |
| | | 6. Overheads (total) | 33,000 |

### Material wastage a/c

| | € | | € |
|---|---|---|---|
| 10. Direct materials<br>control | 3,000 | | |

### Idle time a/c

| | € | | € |
|---|---|---|---|
| 12. Labour control a/c | 2,000 | | |

### Over-absorbed production overhead a/c

| | € | | € |
|---|---|---|---|
| | | 13. Production<br>overhead | 4,000 |

The summarised cost and income statement for year ended 31 December 20x7 can be presented as follows:

| | Job 100 € | Job 101 € | Job 102 € | Total € |
|---|---|---|---|---|
| Sales | 20,000 | 100,000 | 60,000 | 180,000 |
| Cost of sales | (8,000) | (41,200) | (26,800) | (76,000) |
| Gross profit | 12,000 | 58,800 | 33,200 | 104,000 |
| Less: Materials wastage | | | | (3,000) |
| Labour idle time | | | | (2,000) |
| Add: Production overhead over-absorbed | | | | 4,000 |

|  | Job 100 € | Job 101 € | Job 102 € | Total € |
|---|---|---|---|---|
| = Production margin |  |  |  | 103,000 |
| Less: Administration overheads |  |  |  | (15,000) |
| Less: Selling overheads |  |  |  | (25,000) |
| Profit before interest and tax |  |  |  | 63,000 |

## 3.4   Direct Materials Recording Procedure

The nature of a manufacturing process suggests that direct material expense will be a dominant element in the overall cost structure. Therefore, proper procedures should be put in place to minimise loss and wastage of materials.

Earlier in this chapter, we saw that direct materials should only be issued to production on receipt of a materials requisition docket, which indicates the type and quantity of materials required and the work or job reference number. In turn, such material issues should be recorded on a stock record card. If all issues (and receipts) are recorded accurately on the appropriate stock record card (this system is often maintained electronically), then the balance of any stock item can be ascertained immediately from that stock card. This system is referred to as a perpetual inventory system. Under a perpetual inventory system, the physical amount of inventory on hand will be kept continuously up-to-date. Traditionally, perpetual inventory systems are used by companies selling high unit value items. Such businesses have relatively few business transactions each day in these items and thus keeping up-to-date records is relatively easy – and important!

A perpetual inventory system is the opposite of a periodic inventory system. Under a periodic inventory system, the amount of inventory is only determined at the end of each accounting period by way of a physical count. A periodic inventory system is widely used by businesses that sell products of relatively low unit value.

However, inventory valuation requires cost figures and this, in reality, causes some problems, especially where unit purchases are similar. In other words, there is no economically feasible way that one product can be identified separately from another. Yet, the identical products may have been purchased at different times and at different prices. A good example is that of a coal merchant who buys bulk coal at different times during the year. Each purchase of coal is added to a large fuel bunker and so it is not practical to try to separate the different purchases. The main difficulty with inventory in this case is to determine 'cost' for any unused stock at the end of the accounting period.

It is usual, therefore, to determine cost by any one of three methods:

- First In First Out (FIFO),
- Last In First Out (LIFO), or
- Average Cost.

## First In First Out (FIFO)

The most common method is the First In First Out (FIFO), which assumes that the first unit purchased (i.e. the first unit 'in') is assumed to be the first unit issued to production (i.e. the first unit 'out'). Thus, the valuation of closing inventory will be based on the relatively recent purchases. FIFO's common usage among manufacturing and retail firms is due to its acceptability for both financial accounting and taxation purposes.

## Last In First Out (LIFO)

The Last In First Out (LIFO) method assumes that the last unit purchased (i.e. the last unit 'in') is assumed to be the first unit issued to production (i.e. the first unit 'out'). Closing inventory valuation will therefore be based on the relatively older purchases during the accounting period. During times of rising prices, LIFO will provide the lower stock valuation and, therefore, lower reported profits and lower taxation liabilities. (It should perhaps be noted that, in Ireland, LIFO is rarely, if ever, used, since this method is not acceptable as a basis for taxation computations.)

## Average Cost Basis

The third method is referred to as the average cost basis. This involves computing the average cost of units purchased during the accounting period (together with any opening stock) and this average figure is used for cost of sales and closing inventory valuation purposes.

Consider the following example, using the purchase and sale of identical articles. (The units involved are finished goods but the principle equally applies to the purchase of raw materials and their issue to production.)

## ILLUSTRATION: FIFO, LIFO AND AVERAGE COST METHODS OF INVENTORY VALUATION

| Date | Units purchased | Unit cost price |
|---|---|---|
| 5 January | 10 | €6 |
| 14 January | 8 | €7 |
| 25 January | 12 | €8 |
| | 30 | — |

During the period, 25 units were sold, which generated €250 in sales revenue. There were five units unsold and on hand at the end of the period.

**Requirement:** Identify the gross profit, cost of goods sold, and value of closing inventory under FIFO, LIFO and Average Cost assumptions.

**Solution and Analysis:** The FIFO Method: Closing inventory is valued at the cost of the most recent goods purchased. The total value of purchases during the period is €212 as indicated below.

| Purchases | € |
|---|---|
| 10 × €6 = | 60 |
| 8 × €7 = | 56 |
| 12 × €8 = | 96 |
| | 212 |

Closing inventory is determined by considering the cost of the most recent purchases. Hence, closing stock is valued at (5 units at €8 each) = €40.

LIFO Method: Closing inventory is valued with reference to the oldest goods purchased. From the information above, the closing stock of five units would be valued at (5 units at €6 each) = €30.

Average Cost Method: Under this method, the average cost of all purchases during the accounting period, together with the opening inventory, is calculated and the cost of sales and closing inventory are based on that figure. (In some cases, the purchases during the period may be weighted.) Based on the information provided, the average cost method would provide a unit cost of (€212/30) = €7 (rounded). Closing inventory would be valued at (5 units at €7 each) = €35.

The varying results arising from using these three methods can be seen in the following summary:

| | Purchases € | Less: Closing stock € | = Cost of sales € | Gross profit € | Sales € |
|---|---|---|---|---|---|
| **FIFO** | 212 | (40) | 172 | 78 | 250 |
| **LIFO** | 212 | (30) | 182 | 68 | 250 |
| **Average Cost** | 212 | (35) | 177 | 73 | 250 |

Using the above figures, the different results arising from choosing one inventory valuation method and not another is insignificant. However, with inventory of, say, €50 million a significant difference would appear under each of these methods. Which method should be used? The choice is that of the directors of the business but the concept of consistency applies most forcefully in this instance. Any change in the method of stock valuation must be disclosed in the published financial statements and an indication given of the financial impact of such a change.

## Internal Controls and Procedures for Direct Materials

Internal controls represent the whole system of operating and financial controls, established by management in order to carry on business in an orderly manner, safeguard its assets and secure, as far as is possible, the accuracy of its accounting records. Such procedures relating to materials might be:

### Receipt and Checking of Goods

1. All goods should be checked on receipt for quantity and quality, and agreed with the original purchase order.
2. On receipt, a goods received note should be raised indicating the quantity and quality of goods received, the purchase order number and the supplier's name. One copy should be retained in the store area. A second copy should be linked with the purchase order in the accounts department awaiting receipt of the invoice.
3. When received, the supplier invoice should be matched with the corresponding purchase order/goods received note before being authorised for payment.
4. The supplier invoice should be checked to ensure that it is arithmetically correct and that all discounts and VAT calculations have been made correctly.

### Material Issues to Production Departments

1. Issues of materials should only to be made on foot of a properly authorised requisition note which identifies the job or cost centre code.
2. Issues of materials should only be made by properly authorised personnel.
3. Excess issues of materials should be returned immediately to store. This avoids unnecessary losses through excess materials simply being left to one side in the production process.

In conclusion, in this chapter we applied some basic cost accumulation principles to the specific context of job costing. Direct materials and direct labour are traced to various jobs with relative ease.

Production overhead is assigned to each job with reference to an appropriate cost driver, and many firms will use direct labour hours as a typical cost driver. In turn, we recorded the various accounting entries by way of ledger accounts and also discussed a recording process for direct materials. In the next chapter, we look at an alternative cost accumulation system, namely, process costing, which is concerned with mass production of a similar product.

## SUMMARY OF LEARNING OBJECTIVES

**Learning Objective 1:** Describe job costing systems under a traditional cost accounting system.

The distinguishing feature of a job costing system is that all work is completed on behalf of a specific client and, as a result, each job must be separately costed.

**Learning Objective 2:** Apply cost plus pricing techniques in a service firm.

Cost plus pricing is an approach to pricing that computes materials, labour and overheads attributable to the job in question, to which a profit margin is added to determine selling price. Essentially, cost plus pricing is an internally orientated calculation and is only one factor influencing pricing policy.

**Learning Objective 3:** Record cost flows in a manufacturing firm.

Cost flows for material, labour and overheads were recorded through ledger accounts. It is usual that overheads are assigned to jobs using a predetermined OHAR and this may result in either under- or over-absorbed production overhead at the end of the accounting period.

**Learning Objective 4:** Explain how direct materials and direct labour are assigned to jobs.

Specific procedures were outlined in respect to recording the flow of direct materials into and out of the storeroom. Labour costs are usually applied to jobs with reference to time sheets or clock cards.

## Questions

### Review Questions

(See Appendix One for Solutions to Review Questions **3.1** and **3.2**)

*Question 3.1 (Recording Cost Flows under a Job Costing System)*

Commerce Contractors Limited operates a job cost system. The following limited information is available in respect of a recent accounting period:

1. Opening ledger balances:

| | |
|---|---|
| Creditors Control account | €10,000 |
| Direct materials control account | €20,000 |
| Work-in-progress control account | Nil |
| Finished goods control account | €40,000* |

| * Consisting of: | |
|---|---|
| Direct materials | €18,400 |
| Direct Labour | €12,000 |
| Production overheads | €9,600 |

2. Payments to suppliers of direct materials amounted to €50,000 while trade creditors at the end of the month amounted to €20,000.
3. Actual production overheads incurred amounted to €19,000.
4. Administration overheads incurred amounted to €20,000.
5. During August the following jobs were commenced and the costs incurred as indicated below. Jobs 81, 82 and 83 were completed during the period.

| Job Ref. | No. of units | Material € | Labour hours | Labour cost € |
|---|---|---|---|---|
| 81 | 100 | 10,000 | 800 | 4,000 |
| 82 | 200 | 15,000 | 1,800 | 8,500 |
| 83 | 100 | 12,000 | 1,200 | 6,000 |
| 84 | 400 | 16,000 | 800 | 4,200 |
| | | 53,000 | 4,600 | 22,700 |

6. Production overhead is absorbed at €4 per direct labour hour.
7. During the accounting period, Jobs 81, 82 and 83 were completed. However, Job 84 is still in progress.
8. During the period, half of the opening stock of finished goods, all of Job 81, half of Job 82 and one quarter of Job 83 were sold.

**Requirements:**

1. Write up the appropriate accounts in the company's ledger. It is company policy to write-off any under- or over-applied overhead to Cost of Goods Sold in the period in which it arises.
2. Prepare a schedule of:
   (a) Closing work-in-progress.
   (b) Closing stock of finished goods.
   (c) Cost of sales.

*Question 3.2 (Job Costing and Pricing in a Manufacturing Company)*

The Timmons Company manufactures wooden furniture to order, for a variety of customers. It operates a job costing system and, for accounting purposes, all overheads are assigned to any one of three departments: Manufacturing, Polishing and Packing. Expensive machines mainly do the manufacturing work whereas both the polishing and packing processes are labour intensive. For the year 20x2 the following information is presented to you:

| | Total € | Manufacturing € | Polishing € | Packing € |
|---|---|---|---|---|
| Supervisory Labour | 420,000 | 230,000 | 110,000 | 80,000 |
| Light and heat | 48,000 | ?? | ?? | ?? |
| Rent and rates | 27,000 | ?? | ?? | ?? |
| Machine maintenance | 16,000 | ?? | ?? | ?? |
| Machine depreciation (S/line) | 80,000 | ?? | ?? | ?? |
| Factory canteen | 35,000 | ?? | ?? | ?? |

The following information relates to the 3 departments.

| | | | | |
|---|---|---|---|---|
| Floor space in square metres | 9,000 | 4,000 | 3,000 | 2,000 |
| Machine cost € | 400,000 | 240,000 | 100,000 | 60,000 |
| Machine hours | 60,000 | 30,000 | 15,000 | 15,000 |
| Number of employees | 70 | 30 | 30 | 10 |
| Labour hours | 160,000 | 80,000 | 60,000 | 20,000 |

A specific job (Job No 999) has just been completed and a calculation of product cost and selling price is now required. You are provided with the following information:

| | Direct materials | Direct labour cost | Machine hours | Labour hours |
|---|---|---|---|---|
| Manufacturing department | €7,500 | €850 | 50 | 20 |
| Polishing department | €2,800 | €3,900 | 15 | 90 |
| Packing department | Nil | €1,500 | 6 | 25 |

**Requirements:**

1. Apportion the above costs to the three operating departments. State clearly the basis of apportionment used. Calculate the production overhead absorption rate for each department using machine hours for the manufacturing department and direct labour hours for both the Polishing and Packing departments.
2 Compute the selling price of Job No 999, assuming that the company budgets for a 20% profit margin on selling price for all its products.

Intermediate Questions

*Question 3.3 (Job Costing)*

A manufacturing firm uses a job costing system and all manufacturing is carried out in a single location. The following information has been collected for Job 786, Job 800, Job 805 and Job 808 over a two-month period for the purpose of quoting the price to a customer:

Month 1: Total production costs (materials, labour and production overhead) incurred:

|                          | Job 786 | Job 800 | Job 805 | Job 808 |
|--------------------------|---------|---------|---------|---------|
| Total costs (incurred)   | €1,000  | €1,200  | €6,400  | €3,600  |

Month 2: in addition, the following direct materials were added during month 2:

| Stores requisition No | Job No | Cost (€) |
|-----------------------|--------|----------|
| 11 | 786 | 750 |
| 12 | 786 | 900 |
| 13 | 800 | 1,100 |
| 14 | 805 | 1,200 |
| 15 | 805 | 300 |
| 16 | 808 | 200 |

Also during Month 2, in addition to direct material costs (above), direct labour is paid at the rate of €50 per hour and production overhead is absorbed at the rate of €20 per machine hour. The direct labour and machine hours used in Month 2 are summarised below:

| Job No | Labour (hours) | Machine (hours) |
|--------|----------------|-----------------|
| 786 | 25 | 25 |
| 800 | 80 | 30 |
| 805 | 70 | 10 |
| 808 | 60 | 5 |

During Month 2, Job numbers 786, 800, 805 and 808 were completed.

For selling price determination, management estimate that the administration and selling overheads are 10% of the production cost and the management's target is to add a profit margin of 20% on to total cost.

**Requirements:**

1. Determine the production cost of Job numbers 786, 800, 805 and 808 which would be used for stock (inventory) valuation purposes.
2. Compute the normal selling price of Job numbers 786, 800, 805 and 808.
3. Briefly discuss the major features of a job costing system.

*Question 3.4 (Job Costing and Pricing Decisions)*

Speciality Printers Limited is a small printing company, and carries out specialised printing jobs for a variety of clients. It operates a cost-plus pricing system. The initial part of this system is concerned with the computation of overhead absorption rates (OHARs) for the forthcoming year ended 31 December 20x1. It absorbs overheads on a departmental basis with overheads in Department A being absorbed on the basis of direct labour hours since this is a labour intensive department. Department B is machine intensive and production overheads are absorbed on the basis of machine hours.

The total production overheads for the year, which are assumed to be entirely fixed in relation to volume changes within a relevant range of activity, and other data are estimated to be as follows:

|  | Dept A | Dept B |
|---|---|---|
| Total production overhead (fixed) | €450,000 | €415,000 |
| Direct labour hours (variable cost) | 150,000 | 25,000 |
| Machine hours | 100,000 | 415,000 |

During January 20x1, the firm completed only *two* orders, details of which and other data pertinent to these orders are given below:

| Cost item and Department | Job 101 | Job 102 |
|---|---|---|
| Total cost of direct materials consumed | €1,000 | €800 |
| Total costs of direct labour | €2,500 | €2,800 |
| Direct labour hours worked: |  |  |
| In Department A | 1,600 hours | 2,000 hours |
| In Department B | 1,000 hours | 1,300 hours |
| Machine running hours for jobs: |  |  |
| In Department A | 800 m/hours | 600 m/hours |
| In Department B | 2,000 m/hours | 2,500 m/hours |

**Requirements:**

1. Compute overhead absorption rates for the two departments, using direct labour hours for Department A and machine hours for Department B.
2. What is the normal selling price for Job 101 and Job 102, assuming selling prices are required to provide a profit margin on sales price of 20%?
3. Assume that the only variable costs are direct materials and direct labour, indicate the 'marginal' cost for both jobs, based on the information available.
4. List three disadvantages of using 'marginal' costing for pricing decisions.

*Question 3.5 (Job Costing, Pricing and Under-absorbed (under-applied) Overhead)*

Murray Printers Limited is a small printing firm and operates a job costing system. For costing purposes, the company uses a plant-wide overhead absorption rate due to the small size of the business and also because most overheads associated with the printing process are performed in a single department. You are also informed that it is company (and industry) policy to assign overhead costs to jobs on the basis of direct material costs. In addition, a profit margin is added, based on total cost, in order to determine normal selling price. Indeed, most firms in the printing industry use a full-cost pricing policy. Direct labour is considered a fixed cost because all printers are employed on a fixed contract.

You also learn that planning and budgeting process is very elementary and the actual out-turn of last year becomes the budget for the forthcoming year! The summarised budget for 20x5 is presented below:

| Summarised income statement for 20x5 | € |
|---|---|
| Direct materials (variable) | 38,000 |
| Labour (fixed in relation to volume changes) | 32,000 |
| Total overheads (fixed) | 76,000 |
| Budgeted profit | 43,800 |
| Sales (billings to customers) | 189,800 |

A potential customer has asked the manager of Murray Printers to provide a quotation price for a special order (Job 101) to be completed during the forthcoming months of the year 20x5. A first estimate of the direct costs for Job 101 is shown below:

| | |
|---|---|
| Direct materials | €4,000 |
| Direct labour | €3,600 |

**Requirements:**

1. Comment on the validity of using last year's data as the budget for next year.
2. Based on the summarised budget for 20x5, calculate the predetermined (budgeted) overhead absorption rate (based on material cost) and indicate the profit margin (mark-up) on cost to be used in setting normal selling prices for 20x5.
3. Prepare a recommended selling price for Job 101 based on the information provided and your calculations in (2) above, and explain your method.
4. A rival (competitor) printing firm is prepared to quote €10,000 for the same job. What is the minimum selling price you could accept, assuming that you do not want overall profitability to decline? Explain your reasoning.
5. Assume that during the year in question (20x5), this printing firm experienced a fall in anticipated demand and operated only at 70% of its projected volume. Actual sales for the year amounted to €132,860 and no special price reductions were offered to customers. For example, raw material used in all jobs amounted to €26,600. In addition, actual direct labour cost incurred was as budgeted and actual overheads incurred amounted to €80,000 for the year. Calculate the overall profit or loss for the actual year and explain how this came about. (The actual sales of €132,860 represent 70% of the planned sales of €189,800.)
6. Suggest some critical success factors and related performance measures for this printing firm and indicate how they could be incorporated within the firm's performance measurement system.

*Question 3.6 (Cost flows under Job Costing)*

The Flow Company's financial year runs from 1 July to the following 30 June. The company uses a normal job order costing system for its production costs. The company would typically only have a few job orders (production runs) each month with only one or two of these being finished each month. Thus, the calculation and valuation of closing work-in-progress (WIP) is an important task for the cost accountant. A predetermined overhead rate based upon direct labour hours is used to absorb overhead to individual jobs. A budget of (production) overhead costs was prepared for the financial year as follows for different levels of activity:

| | Direct Labour Hours | | |
| --- | --- | --- | --- |
| | 100,000 | 120,000 | 140,000 |
| Variable overhead costs | €325,000 | €390,000 | €455,000 |
| Fixed overhead costs | 216,000 | 216,000 | 216,000 |
| Total overhead | €541,000 | €606,000 | €671,000 |

The normal capacity for the year is 120,000 direct labour hours. The following information relates to the month of November when Job 87-50 was completed and sold. During the previous month (October) this same job (Job 87-50) incurred €20,850 in direct materials and 3,000 direct labour hours, costing €18,000.

Inventories: 1 November:
  Raw materials and supplies                                     €10,500
  WIP (Job 87-50)                                                54,000
  Finished goods                                                112,500

Purchases of raw materials and supplies:
  Raw materials                                                € 150,000

Materials and supplies requisitioned for production:
  Job 87-50                                                      €45,000
  Job 87-51                                                      37,500
  Job 87-52                                                      25,500
  Supplies (used for production overheads)                       12,000
                                                                €120,000

Direct labour hours:
  Job 87-50                                                      3,500 hours
  Job 87-51                                                      3,000 hours
  Job 87-52                                                      2,000 hours
                                                                 8,500 hours

Labour costs:

| | |
|---|---:|
| Direct labour wages | €51,000 |
| Supervisory salaries | 21,000 |
| | €72,000 |

Building occupancy costs (heat, light, depreciation, etc.):

| | |
|---|---:|
| Factory facilities | €6,500 |
| Sales and administrative offices | 2,500 |
| | €9,000 |

Factory equipment costs:

| | |
|---|---:|
| Power | €4,000 |
| Repairs and maintenance | 2,500 |
| Depreciation | 1,500 |
| | €8,000 |

## Requirements:

1. What is the predetermined overhead absorption rate to be used in applying production overhead to individual jobs during the financial year?
2. Prepare all ledger/journal entries based on the transactions during the month.
3. Prepare a work-in-progress inventory and job cost schedule for November.

*Question 3.7 (Job Costing in a Service Company)*

John Chart is an architect who intends to set up his own practice. He is independently wealthy, having inherited Stock Exchange investments from a rich aunt. His wife also has a full-time job teaching. From previous experience he realises that the key to profitability is to accurately estimate costs for fixed price quotations for potential clients. Consequently, it is essential that he has the ability to predict the time required for the various subtasks on the job.

For the first year of business he will operate with himself and with two seniors. Because it is his first year of business, he intends to break-even only. He prepares the following budget for his first year of trading for himself (J. Chart) together with two senior managers (seniors) and related administration costs:

| | | |
|---|---|---:|
| Salary: Chart | @ €20,000 per annum | €20,000 |
| Seniors (x 2) | @ €16,000 per annum each | €32,000 |
| General office overheads including secretarial costs | | €44,000 |
| Total budgeted costs | | €96,000 |

In addition, he budgets for the following 'chargeable' hours for the next year, based on a 35-hour week:

| Staff members | Holidays | Average hours chargeable |
|---|---|---|
| J. Chart | 4 weeks | 70% |
| Seniors | 3 weeks | 90% |

In terms of absorbing (or recovering overheads), the office overheads together with secretarial costs are apportioned to each grade of labour, based on the total number of chargeable hours of that grade. The total number of chargeable hours is then used to determine the total cost per labour hour. Each professional staff member must submit a weekly time report (time sheet), which is used for charging hours to a client. This is also used for measuring the profitability of various jobs and for providing an 'experience base for improving predictions on future jobs'.

For a prospective job (Job ABC), the following summarised time sheet has been proposed:

| Staff member | Total chargeable hours required |
|---|---|
| J. Chart | 35 hours |
| Seniors | 80 hours |

## Requirements:

1. Calculate appropriate charge-out or billing rates (to the nearest €) for both categories of staff assuming a desired break-even situation for the first year of trading.
2. Prepare a full quotation (or fee note) for Job ABC, assuming the charge out rate is calculated separately for both categories of staff, and it is the intention to only operate at break-even point for the year.
3. What is the minimum price for Job ABC that Chart could accept in order not to incur losses on it? What assumptions have you made and what factors should be considered before a final decision is made?
4. Calculate the profit or loss for the year assuming all costs were incurred as budgeted and the following total hours were charged to clients for the year under review:

    J. Chart . . . . . 1,000 hours
    Seniors . . . . . . 3,000 hours

Explain why this profit shortfall occurred.

## Advanced Questions

### Question 3.8 (Job Costing in a Service Firm)

William ('Bill') Vickers, a newly qualified accountant, has just opened an accountancy practice and plans to sell his professional services to individuals and small companies. He anticipates that individuals will avail of his accounts preparation and taxation services, while his corporate clients will require audit services. As a result, he has divided his accountancy practice into two client divisions, namely, accounts preparation and audit. He will take overall day-to-day responsibility for running the accounts preparation division while his partner, Ivan Tott, will look after the auditing division. Both will be paid reasonable, but not excessive, salaries and these are included in the number of staff and average salary per person shown below.

One of Bill's early tasks is to establish appropriate 'charge out' or 'billing' rates for his two client departments. These charge-out rates are intended to cover all labour and office overhead costs. However, he intends to break-even for the first year so no allowance is made for a profit margin. Other costs, such as hotel and travel expenses, will be charged separately and directly to clients.

As part of his budgeting activities, the following figures have been predicted for the year beginning 1 January 20x1. All the costs identified below can be considered fixed and committed for the forthcoming year:

|  | Accounts Preparation Dept | Audit Department | Administration Department |
| --- | --- | --- | --- |
| No. of staff employed | 4 | 6 | 3 |
| Annual salary per person | €30,000 | €35,000 | €20,000 |
| Total work hours per week | 35 | 35 | 35 |
| Annual holiday time | 4 weeks | 4 weeks | 2 weeks |
| % productive (chargeable) time at work | 80% | 70% | N/A |
| Other specific costs per annum | €25,000 | €25,000 | €10,000 |

In addition, there are general office costs amounting to €60,000 per annum, consisting of rent, insurance, etc. In order to calculate charge out rates for his professional staff, Bill has decided to assign these general office costs to all three departments on an equal basis. Thereafter, all administration costs should be assigned to the accounts preparation and audit departments on the basis of numbers of staff employed in those departments.

In early January 20x1, Bill Vickers receives an enquiry from a potential client, which concerns the provision of both accounts preparation and audit services. Bill was interested in this enquiry even though, as an out-of-town assignment, it required some travel. He estimated the following for this potential job:

|  | Accounts Preparation Dept | Audit Department |
| --- | --- | --- |
| No. of professional hours required | 200 hours | 100 hours |
| Total travel costs for engagement | €3,600 | €2,700 |

**Requirements:**

1. Prepare a summarised and budgeted cost statement for the forthcoming year, on a departmental basis and for the business as a whole, based on the information provided (but excluding the special enquiry received in January). You should clearly identify the service department apportionment and the appropriate 'charge-out' rates for both the Accounts Preparation and Audit Departments.
2. Calculate the normal selling price for the recent enquiry received.
3. Assume that for 20x1 spending on all fixed costs were as anticipated but that, due to lack of demand, professional hours worked were only 80% of what was originally budgeted. However, no employees were released, as the fall in demand was considered temporary. Calculate the level of sales and overall profit or loss incurred during the 20x1 year (excluding the special order). Briefly comment on your findings and include recommendations to the company for next year.
4. Suggest FIVE non-financial measures of performance that Bill Vickers might use in evaluating the performance of his accountancy practice.

*Question 3.9 (Mini Case regarding Job Costing and Cost Flows)*

It was not the type of assignment for which Kevin Fox would have volunteered had he been given the choice. However, he felt obliged to help out his old school pal, John Davis, who was the owner-manager of New Home Furniture. Since leaving school, the two pals had lost contact with each other. Kevin concentrated on his accounting studies and had since qualified as an accountant.

John Davis pursued a career in art and design and had spent several years acquiring expertise in the design of quality home furniture. Thereafter, he set up a small manufacturing operation. From modest beginnings, the company had grown to a size where several production personnel were employed together with a small administrative staff. Unfortunately, New Home Furniture did not have the services of a full-time accountant. The end result, admitted Davis, was that the accounting records were in a 'frightful mess'. After further discussion, Fox promised to pay a visit to the factory the following Saturday.

Fox arrived at the prearranged time. After exchanging pleasantries, Davis said: 'Probably the best place for you to start is with some basic information' and pointed to a large file on the edge of the desk. The front page represented the company's opening trial balance with an accompanying note (see **Exhibit 1**).

EXHIBIT 1: TRIAL BALANCE AT 1 JANUARY 20X1

|  | Debit | Credit |
|---|---|---|
| Net Fixed assets (for production) | 20,000 | |
| Raw materials control | 25,000 | |
| Work-in-progress (see note 1 below) | 15,480 | |
| Share capital | | 24,000 |

| | | | | |
|---|---|---|---|---|
| Retained earnings | | | | 10,080 |
| Bank overdraft | | | | 29,000 |
| Trade Debtors | | | 20,600 | |
| Trade Creditors | | | | 18,000 |
| | | | 81,080 | 81,080 |

NOTE 1: Analysis of work-in-progress

| Job No. | Materials € | Labour € | Overhead € | Total € |
|---|---|---|---|---|
| 92 | 1,000 | 3,400 | 1,020 | 5,420 |
| 97 | 2,000 | 6,200 | 1,860 | 10,060 |
| | 3,000 | 9,600 | 2,880 | 15,480 |

Davis explained that the company made several varieties of quality home furniture to order, including tables, chairs and bookshelves. The orders came mainly from large department stores. Earlier this year New Home Furniture had entered into a number of large contracts with several department stores requiring the production of different units with an agreed production quota per month. Typically, the buyer from a department store would visit Davis in his office and discuss an order, its feasibility and delivery dates. Once broad agreement was reached on these issues a detailed quotation was sought. Davis would estimate the type and specific amount of materials required for each job. The material estimating process was relatively simple. This was because if a client wanted, say, a bookshelf, the required amount of wood could be estimated accurately and wastage was negligible due to the skill of the workforce. Likewise labour hour requirements were fairly easily calculated since most of the work involved could be estimated from previous orders. Labour was paid at the rate of €10 per hour and no overtime was worked. In turn, production overhead was absorbed at the rate of €3 per direct labour hour worked on each job.

Fox requested sight of any other documents or information, especially in relation to cash movements, goods purchased and sold and Davis produced a summary for the past six months (**Exhibit 2**).

In addition, Fox reviewed the file and discovered a summary of agreed sales price, the amount of materials requisitioned and labour hours worked on each job during the past six months (**Exhibit 3**).

After discussion, Fox discovered that the direct materials figure had been obtained from requisitions dockets which had to be completed before material was issued for production. These dockets showed the amount and cost of direct materials required for each job. The labour hours worked was obtained from job cards, which all production employees were obliged to complete each week and which recorded the amount of time *worked* on each job. Fox wondered how this matched up with the actual hours paid for since he realised, from previous experience, that idle time could be significant in some instances. It was obvious that New Home Furniture operated a *normal* costing system whereby each job was costed for actual materials and direct labour consumed together with an appropriate amount of production overhead absorbed using predetermined overhead rates.

EXHIBIT 2: SUMMARY OF TRANSACTIONS DURING SIX MONTHS
ENDING 30 JUNE 20XI

| | |
|---|---|
| Raw material purchase invoices | €35,000 |
| Invoices received for production overhead | €38,000 |
| Invoices received for administration expenses | €46,000 |
| Payments to trade creditors for materials invoiced | €16,000 |
| Payments for production and administration expenses | €84,000 |
| Wages paid (11,000 hours) | €110,000 |
| Receipts from debtors | €200,000 |

EXHIBIT 3: USAGE OF MATERIALS AND LABOUR FOR SIX MONTHS
ENDING 30 JUNE 20XI

| Quotation price | Job No. | Materials € | Labour hours |
|---|---|---|---|
| €10,000 | 92 | Nil | 100 |
| €15,000 | 97 | Nil | 60 |
| €25,000 | 98 – 1 | 3,500 | 1,000 |
| €32,000 | 98 – 2 | 5,400 | 1,400 |
| €20,000 | 98 – 3 | 2,500 | 700 |
| €35,000 | 98 – 4 | 4,250 | 1,500 |
| €55,000 | 98 – 5 | 6,400 | 2,600 |
| €60,000 | Various | 7,000 | 2,700 |
| €252,000 | | €29,050 | 10,060 |

Davis indicated that all work performed during the six months had been completed with the exception of job No. 98 - 5 which was still in progress. The completed work had been delivered to customers and invoiced although payments from some customers were outstanding. There was no closing stock of finished goods. Also, amounts prepaid or accrued in respect of operating expenses were negligible but depreciation should be recorded at the rate of 20% per annum on opening book amount.

Davis concluded: 'I hope you have enough information to build up a financial picture of the company for the past six months. Your observations of what we're doing wrong in financial terms would be appreciated. I'll leave you alone, now,' and he departed from the office and quietly closed the door.

A quick review by Fox confirmed that he had sufficient information, admittedly not verified by him, to prepare draft financial statements for the six-month period and extract some basic management accounting information. The first thing he noticed was that the firm's bank overdraft amounted to €39,000 at the end of the period and, perhaps, this was indicative of the general state of the company. Fox realised that Davis would require not alone provisional figures for the recent six months but also recommendations as well.

**Requirements:**

1. Record the above information in the ledger of New Home Furniture.
2. Prepare an income statement for the *six* months ended 30 June 20x1 – separately disclosing both idle labour time and under-absorbed production overhead – and a balance sheet as at 30 June 20x1.
3. With hindsight, what predetermined production overhead absorption rate (OHAR) should Davis have used during the six-month period? Why?
4. Prepare a schedule comparing the quotation price of **each job** with the actual production cost incurred. The schedule should clearly indicate sales price, material cost, labour cost and production overhead absorbed. What do your figures reveal?
5. What general or specific recommendations would you make to Davis?

*Question 3.10 (Mini Case involving Job Costing with recommendations)*

In two weeks, Tony Ryan is due to join Medal Printers Ltd as company accountant with both financial and management accounting responsibilities. The managing director, Paddy Phelan, has asked him to visit the factory for a preliminary briefing on the company's situation. The company is a quality printer of a wide range of products including books, diaries, instruction leaflets, cards, invitations, etc. The company has enjoyed rapid expansion of turnover and recently it acquired clients in the UK. The company employs about 50 persons. The factory is located in the suburbs of Dublin, on a relatively new industrial estate and Tony has no difficulty finding a parking space near the reception area. Within minutes he is being shown into Paddy Phelan's plush office and, after preliminary greetings and a reference to the weekend's rugby results, Paddy gets down to business.

**Paddy Phelan**: "I asked you here today, Tony, to introduce you to the rest of the management team. As you probably know we print a wide range of products. In addition, all the design work and typesetting is done internally. Quality, both in terms of complying with customer specifications and delivery time, is of the utmost importance. If customers are not satisfied, we don't make money."

**Tony**: "How do the customers specify exactly what they want?"

**Paddy**: "Let me run you through a typical scenario of a customer tender. It all starts with a potential client who indicates what he wants. The bigger clients produce layout, drawings with specifications, which are sent out to companies like ours with a request for a quotation. Smaller clients sometimes ask us to do some preliminary design work. Eventually, for pricing purposes, our production manager, Tom Devlin, determines direct costs (materials and labour) for all printing jobs for which we are asked to tender. He then adds a 10% margin to cover production and other overheads and then a further 15% is added to total cost as a profit margin. These figures are then discussed with Frank Bradley, our sales manager, who has the authority to reduce them before forwarding them to the client as a quotation. Subsequently, there is always a bit of 'horse-trading' before a final price is agreed and sometimes we have to 'compromise' on the VAT figure. Anyway, if our tender is successful, we receive a fixed price order with required delivery within a specified time. The estimating is crucial, as we must stick to our estimate once given. Likewise, quality is all-important. If the printed product does not match up to what the customer requires, it is returned and scrapped. Defective printing work is useless."

**Tony**: "How do the estimates match up with actual costs?"

**Paddy**: "Ah, that's an area I'd like you to look into closely. When we arrived into this new building 18 months ago we wanted to introduce a better accounting system. Our problem appears to be that we operate a job costing system, since each job must be costed separately. Obviously, there are different design specifications for each job and this affects labour/production time and material costs. As you will appreciate one of the principal problems associated with estimating is identifying how long a job will take to pass through a work centre. You must appreciate that it is also difficult to anticipate the time taken in proof-reading and correction work. We hired an account-ant of sorts, but things didn't work out. When we discovered recently that we had incurred a loss in the region of €90,000 for the first nine months of this year, we agreed to part company. Losses are bad at any time but we operate an informal profit sharing scheme with senior managers. This is normally paid 'under the counter', so my colleagues are not happy with the current situation."

Tony was also told that, when tenders were accepted, the printing components required for each job (Bill of Materials) and a description of the work to be performed (Routing Slip) were prepared by Tom Devlin. This formed the basis of the production schedule for the next week.

Phelan continued: "You will find out more about that later. Come with me and I will introduce you to the rest of the team. I've asked each of them to spend some time with you discussing their own areas. I believe in everyone knowing what everyone else is doing. It helps communications and improves efficiency."

At this point they left the office to meet Tony's future colleagues.

Tom Devlin, the production manager, gave Tony a tour of the shop floor. They strolled along the central aisle as Tom described the various processes involved in printing operations. Tony couldn't help notice the cluttered conditions in some work areas. When he enquired about this Tom told him "stores are sometimes short of specific paper". Devlin continued: "Another problem is Frank Bradley, our sales man-ager. He's forever charging down here and rushing through his priority orders. This leaves other work by the wayside." Tony wondered how this fitted into production scheduling, as he knew it. His thoughts were interrupted by the appearance of a casually dressed Frank Bradley. (He was usually referred to as "The Brad", but not to his face!)

**Frank Bradley said**: "Welcome to Medal Printers, Tony. Now, what can I tell you?"

**Tony**: "How about filling me in on the customer profile?"

**Frank**: "Customers, yes, we supply to a huge range of customers. No job is too small or too big. The market is competitive and we must therefore keep our prices keen and our performance high. Also, we have a few big clients in the UK and there is always a problem with the Euro/Sterling differential. However, I leave that problem to you accountants."

**Tony**: "How are we doing in regard to sales?"

**Frank**: "Up to six months ago I would have said fine. Now, I'm not so sure. Our delivery record has been getting worse and our customers are beginning to complain about our quality and refuse to accept delivery. We've lost a few key customers recently! What's more, Tom Devlin, who does the initial estimates, doesn't seem to realise how competitive the market is."

Bradley indicated that he nearly always has to reduce Tom's figures before making a final quotation to a potential customer. Frank went on to draw a picture of potential disaster in the near future and complained about production being inefficient and disorganised, subcontracted work being slow and stores nearly always being short of printing material.

As Tony left Frank's office he was wondering what he was letting himself in for!

It was harder to get time with John Byrne, the purchasing manager. John was also responsible for dealing with subcontract work. He was making phone calls to a bookbinder. After Tony had been standing around for about five minutes John put the phone down.

**John**: "Sorry to keep you waiting Tony." The phone rang AGAIN but was ignored. "Let's go to the canteen for a cup of coffee and a chat. If we stay here we'll get no peace. Everybody wants things yesterday!"

In the canteen John outlined the nature of his work. "I'm responsible for purchasing and maintaining stores and any subcontract work. I'm also responsible for delivery to customers. In terms of stores control we operate a general coding system as follows:

- Paper (with sub codes for different sizes and quality)
- Packing materials including boxes
- Subcontracted services
- Miscellaneous."

**Byrne continued**: "We keep all materials at the far end of the factory. Our stock records are kept on a cardex system. However because of the nature of our business and occasional lack of 'communication', production staff are constantly coming into the stores area and taking paper for production without signing for it. This makes the maintenance of accurate records very difficult."

**Tony**: "What processes are subcontracted?"

**John**: "Binding. We don't have full binding facilities and some job orders, for example, require special binding. The binding of books (and other heavy materials) requires a special 'spine' and stitching. Otherwise, with use, the cover detaches itself from the pages. We send out all this special binding work to Bookbinders Limited. They are usually very quick and good, but over the past few months they obtained a few big jobs from other clients and their delivery lead-time to us is suffering. It's just another hassle factor."

Before leaving, Ryan paid a courtesy visit to Paddy Phelan. Both agreed that there was much need and scope for improvement in the company's accounting and information system.

Phelan: "I think you should have a pretty good overview of what's happening here. We consider ourselves to be an enlightened company and the Board recently approved a vision statement for the company that I shall give you later. I'd like you to draw up a provisional check-list for Board presentation and discussion, based on your initial observations as to how things can and should change. Be brief and succinct – a sort of mini action plan. Since you will be part of the management team, feel free to raise any matter." As the meeting concluded, Tony was given the following documents:

1. Current organisation structure (**Exhibit 1**)
2. Invoicing and accounting procedure (**Exhibit 2**)
3. Summarised accounting data (**Exhibit 3**)
4. Vision statement (**Exhibit 4**)

**Requirements:** As Tony Ryan, you are required to prepare a memorandum to the Managing Director to include:

1. a profit statement for the year ended 31 December, 20x1 and for the nine months ended 30 September, 20x2 from the information provided in **Exhibit 3**, together with balance sheets as at 31 December, 20x1 and at 30 September, 20x2.
2. the main weaknesses/deficiencies which you observed within the organisation, especially in regard to the management accounting and information system, and the main improvements which you suggest, particularly the information necessary to correct the deficiencies which you have identified.
3. a range of performance measures to assist the communication of the firm's Vision statement and monitoring progress towards this goal.
4. a brief discussion of both the ethical and strategic management accounting issues raised in this case and any other issues which you consider important.

Source: Chartered Accountants Ireland (adapted)

EXHIBIT 1: CURRENT ORGANISATION STRUCTURE

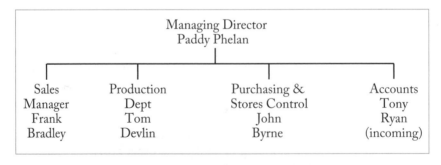

EXHIBIT 2: INVOICING AND ACCOUNTING PROCEDURE

* Completed job comes into stores from the shop floor with a jobcard. The job number and actual labour hours recorded will have been handwritten on the job card.
* Stores prepare the job for delivery and a three-part docket is raised by stores regarding each job as follows:
   Copy 1 filed in stores for permanent record.

Copy 2 represents proof of delivery to customer. Goes with delivery where customer signs it and it is then returned to the stores for filing.

Copy 3 to accounts section: This copy is used to 'trigger' the preparation of an invoice and match jobs completed with job orders. For invoicing, the cost of materials issued is notified to accounts section by stores personnel from their records. Thereafter, the accounts section adds special charges such as transport and an invoice is raised based on the original job order and quotation price. The copy docket is subsequently filed and referred to again only in the event of a customer query.

Problems: Several problems arise in relation to invoicing:

1. Wrong job numbers appear on documents raised by stores so wrong quotation prices are given on invoices, resulting in excessive credit notes being issued to clients.
2. Invoices include incorrect tots and incorrect recording of VAT, including the wrong rate and/or VAT not being charged due to prior agreement. In addition, trade discounts are sometimes deducted without prior approval by an authorised person.

### Sources of error:

1. Incorrect job numbers and material codes appear on job cards. This is as a result of cards being lost on the shop floor and operatives filling in new cards incorrectly since stores will not accept jobs without completed job cards. Operatives must identify material codes if stores personnel are not present when goods are being withdrawn.
2. Recording of labour hours for each job is the sole responsibility of each operative. Some hours are not recorded due to negligence or genuine error.
3. Typing errors on invoices since no cross-checking takes place in accounts department before invoices go out.

EXHIBIT 3: SUMMARISED ACCOUNTING DATA

|  | Year ending 31 Dec 20x1 | 9 months to 30 Sept 20x2 |
| --- | --- | --- |
|  | €000s | €000s |
| Closing debtors | 650 | 900 |
| Closing creditors | 550 | 450 |
| Closing bank loans | 2,500 | 2,726 |
| Opening shareholders' funds | 2,805 | ?? |
| Closing stock of finished goods | 460 | 370 |
| Closing stock of raw materials | 30 | 50 |

|  | Year ending 31 Dec 20x1 | 9 months to 30 Sept 20x2 |
|---|---|---|
| Closing work-in-progress | 100 | 150 |
| Opening stock of finished goods | 430 | 460 |
| Direct material purchased | 2,200 | 1,800 |
| Closing fixed assets (net) | 4,800 | 4,600 |
| Direct manufacturing labour | 850 | 700 |
| Production overheads (including depreciation) | 300 | 330 |
| Opening stock of work-in-progress | 50 | 100 |
| Sales | 3,900 | 3,150 |
| Loan interest paid | 100 | 80 |
| Opening stock of raw materials | 30 | 30 |
| Selling and distribution expenses | 185 | 166 |
| Administration expenses | 160 | 150 |

EXHIBIT 4: VISION STATEMENT

We are bound together in these common beliefs and values. We must...

**For the Customer**

- Have a total quality commitment to consistently meet the product, delivery and service expectations of all customers.

**For the Employee**

- Reward teamwork, trust, honesty, openness and performance.
- Ensure a safe and clean workplace.

**For the Company**

- Continuously invest in new technology and equipment.
- Manage our financial resources for long-term profitability.

**For the Community**

- Commit to environmental responsibility and fulfil our responsibility to enhance the quality of community life.

*Question 3.11 (Recording Cost Flows)*

CALCANO Limited manufactures garden statues to customer order. The company operates a job-order costing system and, at the beginning of the financial year on 1 January 20x3, the following balances were included in the accounts:

|  | € |
|---|---|
| Finished goods | 330,000 |
| Work-in-progress | 360,000 |
| Raw materials | 225,000 |

During the year to 31 December 20x3 the following transactions and activities occurred:

1. Raw materials were purchased at a cost of €1,050,000. Returns of faulty materials to suppliers amounted to €33,000.
2. Issues of raw materials from stores to production amounted to €950,000 for direct materials and €75,000 for indirect materials. However, €10,000 worth of direct materials was returned from production to stores.
3. Direct manufacturing employees earned a total of €1,600,000 but 30% of the gross wage cost of direct manufacturing employees is classified as a production overhead for costing purposes. Production supervisors earned €480,000.
4. Manufacturing overhead is absorbed to jobs using a predetermined machine-based rate of €35 per machine hour. In addition to indirect materials and indirect labour, other manufacturing overheads amounted to €1,200,000 and a total of 60,000 machine hours were worked. Non-manufacturing costs amounted to €760,000.
5. There were no losses of any stocks during the year. At 31 December 20x3 finished goods were valued at €450,000 and work-in-progress was valued at €290,000.
6. Sales revenue for the year was €6,300,000.

**Requirements:**

1. Prepare the following accounts for the year ended 31 December 20x3:

   - Raw materials control account
   - Labour control account
   - Manufacturing overhead control account
   - Work-in-progress control account
   - Finished goods control account

2. Prepare a profit statement for CALCANO for the year ended 31 December 20x3.
3. Explain briefly what distinguishes job costing from process costing.

Source: Chartered Accountants Ireland, PE2 (Autumn 2004)

*Question 3.12 (Recording Cost Flows)*

Violin Limited is a manufacturing company and commenced to trade on 1 February 20x2 with an issued share capital of €700,000, plant and machinery costing €200,000, buildings costing €350,000 and cash at bank of €150,000. During the four-week period to 28 February 20x2 the following transactions occurred:

1. Purchases of raw materials on credit: 50,000 units of raw materials were purchased on 7 February at a price of €3 per unit.

2. Usage of raw materials: on 10 February, 25,000 units of material were issued to production. On 15 February, 8,000 units of material were issued to activities classified as production overheads.
3. Direct workers: 15 direct workers were employed at a rate of €10 per hour for a 35-hour week throughout the four-week period. In addition, 100 hours of overtime were worked during February in order to meet general production requirements. Overtime was paid at a premium of 20% over the basic rate. Fifty of the direct labour hours constituted unproductive time and are to be treated as a production overhead. Wages were paid on 27 February.
4. Production supervisory workers: 5 supervisors were employed at a rate of €7 per hour, for a 35-hour week, throughout February. Supervisors were also paid on 27 February.
5. Production overheads: €5,000 in expenses classified as production overheads were paid by cheque on 16 February. Production overheads of €35,000 were absorbed using a predetermined overhead absorption rate.
6. Depreciation: depreciation of productive plant and equipment was €4,000. Depreciation in respect of motor vehicles was €2,000.
7. Selling and administrative expenses: selling and administrative expenses of €6,000 were incurred and paid for during the period.
8. Finished goods: stock valued at €110,000 was transferred from work-in-progress to finished goods during the period. At the close of business on 28 February the value of finished goods in stock was €10,000.

**Requirements:**
Write up the following accounts for the period:

1. Raw materials stores account
2. Work-in-progress account
3. Finished goods account
4. Production overhead account
5. Wages control account

Source: Chartered Accountants Ireland, PE2 (Summer 2002)

# Process Costing Systems

When you have completed studying this chapter you should be able to:

1. Describe process costing systems.
2. Record cost flows in a process costing system.
3. Discuss the concept of an equivalent unit and calculate the cost per equivalent unit.
4. Apply both average and FIFO costing methods.
5. Report costs of normal and abnormal spoilage.

## 4.1 Introduction to Process Costing

In the previous chapter we discussed 'job costing' systems which are used in firms that produce customised products or offer customised services to their clients. Examples of job costing systems are to be found in, for example, construction companies, printing firms, professional service firms and even private healthcare institutions. Job costing is a method of accumulating costs so that the costs of specific jobs can be accurately identified. In this chapter we discuss an alternative cost accumulation system that is used by companies that produce large volumes of similar products in a continuous flow process. This system is referred to as 'process costing'.

It is important to stress that the selection of either a job or process costing system often depends on whether the internal conversion operation is carried out under instructions mainly to a particular customer's specification, or whether there is a continuous, mass production process. The former lends itself to a job costing system; the latter lends itself to a process costing system. Process costing represents the manufacture of similar products (or services) on a mass and continuous basis. Under process costing, costs are accumulated for each clearly identifiable process, whereby a process represents a set of related activities intended to achieve a common purpose. The costs identified are divided by the output or amount of work done during the accounting period, to provide average unit cost. Thus, an added requirement of process costing is to collect accurate output (or physical) statistics so that a reliable unit cost can be calculated.

A process costing system is relatively easy to understand. Initially, resources are input into the process and these typically consist of direct materials and direct labour. In addition, production overhead is assigned to each process using either actual or normal costing described in **Chapter 3**. Thus, we build up a total cost picture for each separate process. Secondly, we need to identify the output that was achieved with these cost inputs. The outputs are identified in physical terms and the obvious output consists of a number of identical finished goods and some amount of work-in-progress at the end of the period. (Some spoilage may be anticipated and this will be explained below.)

Based on the data obtained, and on the assumption that the units of output are homogeneous, we obtain an average cost per unit by dividing the total cost of the input resources by the total (physical) number of units of output. Perhaps the simplest example to illustrate process costing is in relation to a university. If the running costs of, say, a department is €1 million per annum, and the department has 2,000 students (all at the same level), then the annual cost is €500 per student, on the assumption that all students are similar.

In the examples below, however, we shall focus on manufacturing firms. Thus, if total costs of €7,000 are traced to a particular manufacturing process, with an output of 1,000 (identical) units, then, in the absence of either opening or closing work-in-progress, all units of output are valued at the average cost of €7 per unit. The key items are the total cost inputs and the physical outputs for a given accounting period.

## 4.2  Recording Cost Flows in Process Costing

It is relatively easy to understand process costing systems with reference to the underlying cost flows and related information, and this is illustrated below. We shall use the double-entry system outlined in the previous chapter. It will be recalled that the debit side of the T account represents the costs assigned to the process. The credit side of the T account shows how the costs have been assigned to units of output.

### ILLUSTRATION: PROCESS COSTING SYSTEM

The Cork Company operates a process costing system for one of its manufacturing operations. During the recent period, 1,000 units of material were introduced into this process and 1,000 completed units were produced. Cost of the raw materials added to the process was €3,000. In addition, direct labour amounting to €2,000 was incurred and production overhead amounted to €3,000. Calculate the average cost per unit and prepare the process account.

**Solution and Analysis:** In this example, the data is presented by way of a T account with physical units as well as monetary values to be shown on both sides of the process account. The first step is to record both the physical and monetary inputs. Thus, we debit the process account with 1,000 units and total costs (itemised) amounting to €8,000.

PROCESS ACCOUNT

|  | Units | € |  | Units | € |
|---|---|---|---|---|---|
| Material control a/c | 1,000 | 3,000 | Finished goods | 1,000 | 8,000 |
| Labour control a/c | Nil | 2,000 | | | |
| Overhead control a/c | Nil | 3,000 | | | |
| | 1,000 | 8,000 | | 1,000 | 8,000 |

The second stage is to calculate the cost of finished goods (together with unit costs). This is done by equating the costs to be assigned (€8,000) with the output (1,000 units). The unit cost is calculated by dividing the total monetary inputs (€8,000) by the number of units of finished goods (€8,000 ÷ 1,000 = €8 per unit).

It is important to understand that the above is a very straightforward example. In reality (and in examination questions) complications do arise. Some of the complications may be summarised as follows (and will be dealt with in subsequent sections of this chapter):

1. There may be some work-in-progress at the end of a period, so some of the costs incurred during the period must be assigned to 'closing work-in-progress'. This introduces the concept of equivalent units.

2. There may be sequential processes. Thus, the output of one process becomes the input of the next and so forth.

3. When there is closing work-in-progress, this must be recorded as 'opening work-in-progress' at the start of the subsequent period. In turn, this opening work-in-progress will be completed during the period and so costs will have to be assigned to it. However, it is virtually inevitable that the cost per unit of opening work-in-progress will be different from the unit cost of work performed during the current period. In other words, unit cost of equivalent units can be expected to change between periods for a variety of reasons. Unless this difference is specifically taken into our calculations, there will be a discrepancy in the process cost account. This discrepancy is automatically adjusted for by using either the FIFO method or AVERAGE method of process costing. (This is discussed in **Section 4.3**.)

4. The output may not equal the sum of all the inputs, so there may be 'normal loss' to account for. In addition, 'abnormal losses' (or abnormal gains) may need to be accounted for. (This topic is illustrated in **Section 4.4**.)

5. Spoiled items may be saleable as 'scrap' and this is discussed in **Section 4.5**.

Each of the above calculations will now be discussed.

## Closing Work-in-Progress and Equivalent Units

At the end of the accounting period, there may be some unfinished work in the process and, therefore, some of the input resources must be assigned to this 'closing work-in-progress'. This introduces the concept of equivalent units and is illustrated below:

### Illustration: Equivalent Units

The Kerry Company operates a process costing system. During the recent accounting period, 1,000 units were introduced into a process costing €1,600 to which other conversion costs of €4,000 were added. During the period, 600 finished units were produced. The remaining 400 units held in work-in-progress were 50% complete as regards all cost elements. Calculate the average cost per unit and prepare the process account.

It is recommended to adopt a particular sequence in solving any process costing question. The first sequence is always to record both the physical and monetary inputs, in this case 1,000 units and €5,600 (itemised) respectively, on the debit side of the process account.

#### Process Account

|  | Units | € | | Units | € |
|---|---|---|---|---|---|
| Material control a/c | 1,000 | 1,600 | | | |
| Conversion costs a/c | | 4,000 | | | |
| | 1,000 | 5,600 | | | |

The second stage is to record the output of the process for the period, in this case 600 completed units and 400 units in work-in-progress. Since we have now reconciled the physical inputs and outputs, we can conclude there are no losses or gains arising in this process during this accounting period.

#### Process Account

|  | Units | € | | Units | € |
|---|---|---|---|---|---|
| Material control a/c | 1,000 | 1,600 | Finished goods | 600 | ? |
| Conversion costs a/c | | 4,000 | Balance (WIP) | 400 | ? |
| | 1,000 | 5,600 | | 1,000 | 5,600 |

The third stage is to assign monetary values to both finished goods and closing work-in-progress. In this illustration, 1,000 units were started in the period at a total cost of €5,600. We obviously cannot divide €5,600 by 1,000 because 600 of the units are complete but the remaining 400 are not. Therefore, we must express the unfinished units, or closing work-in-progress, in terms of 'equivalent units'. In this case, 400 half-finished units are assumed to have consumed the same quantity of resources as 200 fully finished units. They are, therefore, regarded as *equivalent* to 200 completed units and these 200 *equivalent* units can now be added to the number of units finished to give the equivalent total output for the period. Finally, we divide the total costs for the period by the equivalent units. Thus, assigning costs can be done as follows:

|  | Material costs | Conversion costs |
|---|---|---|
| **(a) Costs to be assigned** | | |
| Cost inputs during period | €1,600 | €4,000 |
| **(b) Equivalent units** | | |
| Finished goods | 600 | 600 |
| Closing WIP (50% × 400) | 200 | 200 |
| | 800 | 800 |
| **Cost per equivalent unit (a/b)** | €2 | €5 |

The above calculation is used to assign costs to both finished goods and closing work-in-progress. The 400 half-finished units are equivalent to 200 completed units, with an average cost of €7 per unit, giving a closing WIP valuation of €1,400. The cost of finished goods amounts to €4,200 (600 units × €7). The completed process account now appears as follows.

PROCESS ACCOUNT

|  | Units | € |  | Units | € |
|---|---|---|---|---|---|
| Material control a/c | 1,000 | 1,600 | Finished goods | 600 | 4,200 |
| Conversion costs a/c | ___ | 4,000 | Balance (WIP) | 400 | 1,400 |
| | 1,000 | 5,600 | | 1,000 | 5,600 |

## Work-in-Progress with Cost Elements at Different Stages of Completion

In the above illustration we have assumed that closing work-in-progress was exactly 50% complete with respect to all cost elements. In manufacturing operations, this is not often the case. Rather, it is likely that direct materials may be introduced at the beginning of the process and labour and production overhead costs are added gradually during the process. We now introduce an illustration whereby various cost elements accumulate at different rates during the process. Therefore, we will have closing work-in-progress at different stages of completion as regards each cost element. The implication of this is that the equivalent units will be different for each cost element.

## ILLUSTRATION: EQUIVALENT UNITS FOR VARIOUS ELEMENTS

The Sligo Company operates a process costing system. During the most recent accounting period, 1,000 units were introduced into a process and 600 finished units were produced. The remaining 400 units in work-in-progress were 75% completed as regards material, 50% completed as regards labour and 25% completed as regards overhead. Cost of the material assigned to this process amounted to €2,700, labour amounted to €2,000 and overheads amounted to €2,450. Calculate the average cost per unit and prepare the process account for the above accounting period.

Much of the process account can be prepared from the data provided, with the only figures that cannot be entered into the process account at this stage being the values for the output and work-in-progress; for this we need to complete the detailed workings.

### PROCESS ACCOUNT

| | Units | € | | Units | € |
|---|---|---|---|---|---|
| Material control a/c | 1,000 | 2,700 | Finished goods | 600 | ? |
| Labour control a/c | | 2,000 | Balance (WIP) | 400 | ? |
| Overhead control a/c | | 2,450 | | | |
| | 1,000 | 7,150 | | 1,000 | 7,150 |

The calculation of cost per equivalent unit, which provides monetary amounts for both finished goods and closing work-in-progress, can now be computed. The following presentation is strongly recommended for all process costing questions. Such workings are presented in a columnar set of workings.

| | Materials | Labour | Overheads |
|---|---|---|---|
| **(a) Cost to be assigned:** | | | |
| Costs added (a) | €2,700 | €2,000 | €2,450 |
| **(b) Equivalent units:** | | | |
| Finished goods | 600 | 600 | 600 |
| Closing WIP (400 units) | 300 | 200 | 100 |

|  |  |  |  |
|---|---|---|---|
| = Total equivalent output (b) | 900 | 800 | 700 |
| Cost per equivalent unit (c = a/b) | €3.00 | €2.50 | €3.50 |
| **Total cost per equivalent unit =** | | €9.00 | |

The process account can now be completed as follows:

PROCESS ACCOUNT

|  | Units | € |  | Units | € |
|---|---|---|---|---|---|
| Material control a/c | 1,000 | 2,700 | Finished goods (W1) | 600 | 5,400 |
| Labour control a/c | | 2,000 | Balance (WIP) (W2) | 400 | 1,750 |
| Overhead control a/c | | 2,450 | | | |
| | 1,000 | 7,150 | | 1,000 | 7,150 |

W1. Valuation of finished goods transferred

| | |
|---|---|
| 600 units × €9 each = | €5,400 |

W2. Valuation of closing WIP

| | |
|---|---|
| 400 × 75% × €3.00 = | 900 |
| 400 × 50% × €2.50 = | 500 |
| 400 × 25% × €3.50 = | 350 |
| | 1,750 |

## Sequential Processing/Prior Department/Process Work

Within manufacturing operations there can be a number of separate processes. **Exhibit 4.1** shows a manufacturing plant with three production processes, producing a single product. At the start of the production process, unprocessed materials are introduced and worked on in Department A so that other processing costs are added. The output of Department A becomes the input of Department B, which also incurs additional processing costs. Eventually, a large volume of homogeneous products are completed after processing in Department C.

Each process may need to be costed separately but much will depend on our ability to accurately assign costs to a particular process, together with the overall significance of such costs in the overall cost structure and the cost of collection involved. Thus, we now discuss the situation where one department transfers its output to another process, i.e. the output from process A becomes the input to Process B. In computing costs of Process B, we can refer to costs incurred in Process A as 'prior department' (prior process)

| Input of unpro-cessed materials | ⇨ | Dept A | ⇨ | Dept B | ⇨ | Dept C | = | Finished Product |
|---|---|---|---|---|---|---|---|---|
| | | + | | + | | + | | |
| | | Processing costs added | | Processing costs added | | Processing costs added | = | Total Cost |

costs and it is recommended to separate 'prior department' costs from other costs added this period. Obviously, prior department costs must always be 100% complete and this should be kept in mind when computing equivalent units.

## ILLUSTRATION OF SEQUENTIAL PROCESSING

The Leitrim Company operates a process costing system whereby materials are passed through two consecutive processes. 1,000 units of material were introduced into Process A during a period and 1,000 completed units were transferred to process B. Total costs incurred in Process A amounted to €7,000 (consisting of materials, €3,000, labour €2,000, and overheads, €2,000). Process B incurred labour costs of €5,000 and overheads of €3,000.

**Requirement:** Calculate the average cost per unit in each process and prepare the process accounts.

**Solution and analysis:** The debit side of the Process A account is reasonably straightforward and the initial entries appear below:

### PROCESS A ACCOUNT

| | Units | € | | Units | € |
|---|---|---|---|---|---|
| Material control a/c | 1,000 | 3,000 | Process B a/c | 1,000 | ? |
| Labour control a/c | | 2,000 | | | |
| Overhead control a/c | | 2,000 | | | |
| | 1,000 | 7,000 | | 1,000 | 7,000 |

The second stage involves the calculation of cost per equivalent unit. This can be done using the following presentation:

|  | Materials | Labour | Overheads |
|---|---|---|---|
| **(a) Costs to be assigned:** | | | |
| Costs added | €3,000 | €2,000 | €2,000 |
| **(b) Equivalent units:** | | | |
| Finished goods | 1,000 | 1,000 | 1,000 |
| Closing WIP | Nil | Nil | Nil |
| = Total equivalent units | 1,000 | 1,000 | 1,000 |
| Cost per equivalent unit (c = a/b) | €3 | €2 | €2 |
| **Total cost per unit** | €7 | | |

The completed Process A account is as follows, with the appropriate figure inserted for the cost of goods completed and transferred to Process B during the period.

PROCESS A ACCOUNT

|  | Units | € |  | Units | € |
|---|---|---|---|---|---|
| Material control a/c | 1,000 | 3,000 | Process B a/c | 1,000 | 7,000 |
| Labour control a/c |  | 2,000 |  |  |  |
| Overhead control a/c |  | 2,000 |  |  |  |
|  | 1,000 | 7,000 |  | 1,000 | 7,000 |

The initial entries in the Process B account are reasonably straightforward and readers should notice the debit entry representing the cost of goods transferred from Process A. The (incomplete) Process B account appears as follows:

PROCESS B ACCOUNT

|  | Units | € |  | Units | € |
|---|---|---|---|---|---|
| Process A a/c | 1,000 | 7,000 | Process B a/c | 1,000 | ? |
| Labour control a/c |  | 5,000 |  |  |  |
| Overhead control a/c |  | 3,000 |  |  |  |
|  | 1,000 | 15,000 |  | 1,000 | 15,000 |

The cost per equivalent unit can be computed by the following presentation:

|  | Prior costs | Labour | Overheads |
|---|---|---|---|
| **(a) Costs to be assigned:** | | | |
| Costs added (a) | €7,000 | €5,000 | €3,000 |
| **(b) Equivalent units:** | | | |
| Finished goods | 1,000 | 1,000 | 1,000 |
| Closing WIP | Nil | Nil | Nil |
| = Total equivalent units | 1,000 | 1,000 | 1,000 |
| | | | |
| Cost per equivalent unit (c = a/b) | €7 | €5 | €3 |
| **Total cost per unit** | | €15 | |

The completed Process B account is as follows, with the appropriate figure inserted for the cost of goods completed during the period.

PROCESS B ACCOUNT

|  | Units | € |  | Units | € |
|---|---|---|---|---|---|
| Process A a/c | 1,000 | 7,000 | Finished goods | 1,000 | 15,000 |
| Labour control a/c | | 5,000 | @ €15 each | | |
| Overhead control a/c | ____ | 3,000 | | ____ | ____ |
| | 1,000 | 15,000 | | 1,000 | 15,000 |

We shall now introduce an example which revises the basic principles of process costing that we have outlined to date. Specifically, we focus on prior department costs and WIP at different stages of completion. This is a fairly typical examination question.

ILLUSTRATION: PRIOR DEPARTMENTS AND WORK-IN-PROGRESS AT DIFFERENT STAGES OF COMPLETION

During the month of February 1,200 units were transferred from Process A to Process B at a total cost of €4,800. Process B added further materials at a cost of €2,320 and incurred conversion costs of €5,500. At the end of February 1,000 units had been transferred to Process C, and the remaining work-in-progress was 80% completed as regards Process B materials, and 50% as regards conversion costs. There was no opening work-in-progress and no process losses.

**Requirement:** Calculate the average cost per unit and prepare the Process B account.

**Solution and analysis:** The initial entries in the T account for Process B are reasonably straightforward and readers should notice the debit entry representing the cost of goods transferred from Process A. Notice how, by identifying the physical units in Process B, we can establish the number of units in closing work-in-progress. We are not given this information directly, but as there are no process losses the balance of units must be closing work-in-progress.

The (incomplete) Process B account appears as follows:

PROCESS B ACCOUNT

| | Units | € | | Units | € |
|---|---|---|---|---|---|
| Process A a/c | 1,200 | 4,800 | Finished goods | 1,000 | ?? |
| Materials control a/c | | 2,320 | | | |
| Conversion costs a/c | | 5,500 | Balance (WIP) | 200 | ?? |
| | 1,200 | 12,620 | | 1,200 | 12,620 |

Secondly, the cost per equivalent unit can be computed by the following presentation:

| | Prior cost | Materials | Conversion |
|---|---|---|---|
| **(a) Costs to be assigned:** | | | |
| Costs added | €4,800 | €2,320 | €5,500 |
| **(b) Equivalent units:** | | | |
| Finished goods | 1,000 | 1,000 | 1,000 |
| Closing WIP | 200 | 160 | 100 |
| Total Equivalent units | 1,200 | 1,160 | 1,100 |
| Cost per Equivalent unit (c = a/b) | €4 | €2 | €5 |
| **Total cost per unit** | | €11 | |

The completed Process B account is as follows, with the appropriate figure inserted for the cost of goods completed during the period:

PROCESS B ACCOUNT

| | Units | € | | Units | € |
|---|---|---|---|---|---|
| Process A a/c | 1,200 | 4,800 | Finished goods (W1) | 1,000 | 11,000 |
| Materials control a/c | | 2,320 | | | |

| Conversion costs a/c | | 5,500 | Balance (WIP) (W2) | | |
|---|---|---|---|---|---|
| | | | | 200 | 1,620 |
| | 1,200 | 12,620 | | 1,200 | 12,620 |

| | €|
|---|---|
| W1. Valuation of finished goods | |
| 1,000 units × €11 each = | 11,000 |
| W2. Valuation of closing WIP | |
| 200 × 100% × €4 (Process A) = | 800 |
| 200 × 80% × €2 (Materials) = | 320 |
| 200 × 50% × €5 (Conversion) = | 500 |
| | 1,620 |

Remember that closing work-in-progress must always be 100% complete with respect to prior department costs. If work-in-progress was not 100% complete with regard to Process A costs, then the goods would still be in Process A.

## 4.3 Average and FIFO Methods

So far we have discussed two problem areas within process costing. The first was the existence of closing work-in-progress (WIP) at different stages of completion with respect to different cost elements. This problem was solved with reference to the concept of equivalent units. The second issue concerned 'prior department' costs, which should always be treated separately.

We now introduce a third complication, which sometimes arises, namely the existence of opening WIP. Clearly, if there is no opening WIP, this complication will not arise! But, if opening WIP exists and its unit costs are different to unit costs incurred in the process during the current period, there will be a monetary discrepancy in the process account. It must be stressed that this discrepancy will only occur when the cost per equivalent unit differs between accounting periods. To eliminate this discrepancy, we must use either the (weighted) Average or FIFO method of process costing. (In the absence of opening WIP, both Average and FIFO will provide the same figures.) The difference between these two methods rests on a rather crucial assumption. The FIFO method assumes that the first work done during the current period is the completion of opening work-in-progress. In contrast, the Average does NOT make the assumption regarding the first work done in the period. We must keep this distinction in mind when computing costs per equivalent unit.

The FIFO method is initially concerned with calculating the cost per equivalent unit of work done this period. Under the Average method, we do NOT make the assumption regarding the first work done during the period. Thus, our calculation of cost per equivalent unit will be different. Using the Average method, the total costs incurred to date (including opening WIP) form a common pool. The equivalent units represent the total work done to date (in contrast to work done this period under FIFO). It is best to illustrate this by way of an example; however, **Exhibit 4.2** is also a useful summary of the key aspects involved in FIFO and the Average methods.

EXHIBIT 4.2: COST PER EQUIVALENT UNIT UNDER FIFO AND AVERAGE

|  | FIFO method | Average method |
|---|---|---|
| Costs to be assigned | Costs added this period only | Costs added to date and opening WIP |
| Equivalent units | Work done this period only | Total work performed to date |

ILLUSTRATION: FIFO AND AVERAGE METHODS OF PROCESS COSTING

Meath Company has two processing departments. Material is introduced at the beginning of the process in Department A, and additional material is added at the end of the process in Department B. Conversion costs are applied uniformly throughout both processes. Data for the month of March 20×8 includes the following:

|  | Dept A | Dept B |
|---|---|---|
| Opening work-in-progress (units) | Nil | 12,000 |
| Units put into process | 50,000 | Transferred from A |
| Units completed during March | 48,000 | 44,000 |
| Closing work-in-progress (units) | 2,000 | 16,000 |
| Material costs added for 50,000 units | €22,000 | N/A |
| Material costs added during March | N/A | €13,200 |
| Conversion costs added during March | €19,600 | €63,000 |

In Department A, there was no opening WIP. Closing stock was 50% complete and there were no gains or losses during the month.

In Department B, opening work-in-progress was 50% complete and valued at €21,000 (comprising prior department costs, €9,800 and conversion costs, €11,200). Closing stock was 25% complete and there were no gains or losses during the period.

**Requirement:** Compute the amount and cost of goods transferred from each department and closing WIP valuations under both (1) FIFO and (2) Average process costing systems.

**Solution and Analysis (FIFO):** The debit side of the Process A account is reasonably straightforward and the initial entries are presented below. There is no physical discrepancy, since the number of units traced to this process (50,000) matches the output i.e. 48,000 completed and 2,000 units in closing WIP.

PROCESS A ACCOUNT (FIFO METHOD)

| | Units | € | | Units | € |
|---|---|---|---|---|---|
| Opening WIP | Nil | Nil | | | |
| Material control a/c | 50,000 | 22,000 | Process B a/c | 48,000 | ? |
| Conversion costs a/c | | 19,600 | Closing WIP | 2,000 | ? |
| | 50,000 | 41,600 | | 50,000 | 41,600 |

The basic question is how are we going to assign total costs of €41,600 between 50,000 units of output, some of which are not fully completed? This is done by computing the cost per equivalent unit for each cost element. This will allow us to assign costs to the completed units (48,000) and also closing WIP – which are 50% complete. Under the FIFO assumption, we need to identify the costs added this month only, together with work done **this month only**. The cost per equivalent unit can be computed by the following presentation:

| | Materials | Conversion |
|---|---|---|
| **(a) Costs to be assigned:** | | |
| Costs added this month | €22,000 | €19,600 |
| **(b) Equivalent units:** | | |
| Finished goods during month | 48,000 | 48,000 |
| Add: Closing WIP | 2,000 | 1,000 (50%) |
| Less: Opening WIP | (Nil) | (Nil) |
| = Total equivalent units | 50,000 | 49,000 |
| Cost per equivalent unit (c = a/b) | 44c | 40c |
| **Total cost per unit** | | 84c |

The completed Process A account is presented below, with the appropriate figures inserted for the cost of goods completed and transferred to Process B during the period. Since there is no opening WIP, the 48,000 units completed must have been started AND finished during the period, so that the cost of work transferred to Process B amounts to €40,320 (48,000 units @ 84c). Secondly, the valuation of closing WIP is now relatively easy, based on our calculation of cost per equivalent unit:

PROCESS A ACCOUNT (FIFO METHOD)

| | Units | € | | Units | € |
|---|---|---|---|---|---|
| Opening WIP | Nil | Nil | | | |
| Material control a/c | 50,000 | 22,000 | Process B (W1) | 48,000 | 40,320 |
| Conversion costs a/c | | 19,600 | Closing WIP (W2) | 2,000 | 1,280 |
| | 50,000 | 41,600 | | 50,000 | 41,600 |

| | € |
|---|---|
| W1. Valuation of finished goods transferred to Process B: | |
| Opening WIP (given) | Nil |
| Add: Completion of opening WIP | N/A |
| Add: Work started and finished during month: | |
| 48,000 units × 84c = | 40,320 |
| | 40,320 |
| W2. Valuation of closing WIP | |
| 2,000 × 100% × 44c (Materials)  = | 880 |
| 2,000 × 50% × 40c (Conversion) = | 400 |
| | 1,280 |

The initial entries in the Process B account are straightforward and readers should notice the debit entry representing the cost of goods transferred from Process A. The (incomplete) Process B account appears below. There is no physical discrepancy, since the number of units traced to this process (60,000) matches the output i.e. 44,000 completed and 16,000 units in closing WIP.

### Process B account (FIFO method)

| | Units | € | | Units | € |
|---|---|---|---|---|---|
| Opening WIP | 12,000 | 21,000 | | | |
| Process A a/c | 48,000 | 40,320 | | | |
| Material control a/c | | 13,200 | Finished goods | 44,000 | ? |
| Conversion costs a/c | | 63,000 | Closing WIP | 16,000 | ? |
| | 60,000 | 137,520 | | 60,000 | 137,520 |

The second stage in the calculation is to compute cost per equivalent unit for each cost element. This will allow us to assign costs to the units completed (44,000) during the period and also closing WIP – which are 25% complete. Under the FIFO assumption we need to calculate the cost based on costs added this month only, together with work done this month only. The cost per equivalent unit can be computed by the following presentation:

| | Prior Dept | Materials | Conversion |
|---|---|---|---|
| **(a) Costs to be assigned** | | | |
| Costs added this month | €40,320 | €13,200 | €63,000 |
| **(b) Equivalent units (work done this month)** | | | |
| Finished this month | 44,000 | 44,000 | 44,000 |
| Add: Closing WIP | 16,000 | Nil | 4,000 (25%) |
| Less: Opening WIP | (12,000) | Nil | (6,000) (50%) |
| = Total equivalent units | 48,000 | 44,000 | 42,000 |
| Costs equivalent unit (c = a/b) | 84c | 30c | 150c |
| **Total costs per equivalent unit** | | 264c | |

The completed Process B account is as follows, with the appropriate figure inserted for the cost of goods completed and transferred to finished goods during the period. We initially start with the cost of finished goods. This comprises the opening WIP that needs to be finished, i.e. 12,000 units with respect to both materials (added at the end of the process) and conversion costs. In addition, 32,000 (44,000-12,000) units must have been started **and** finished during the month.

As detailed below, the total cost of work transferred to finished goods amounts to €118,080. Secondly, the valuation of closing WIP is now relatively easy, based on our calculation of cost per equivalent unit.

### PROCESS B ACCOUNT (FIFO METHOD)

| | Units | € | | Units | € |
|---|---|---|---|---|---|
| Opening WIP | 12,000 | 21,000 | | | |
| Process A | 48,000 | 40,320 | Finished goods (W1) | 44,000 | 118,080 |
| Materials a/c | | 13,200 | | | |
| Conversion a/c | | 63,000 | Closing WIP (W2) | 16,000 | 19,440 |
| | 60,000 | 137,520 | | 60,000 | 137,520 |

| W1. Valuation of finished goods transferred to Process B | € |
|---|---|
| Opening WIP (given) | 21,000 |
| Add: Completion of opening WIP: | |
| Materials (12,000 × 100% × 30c) = | 3,600 |
| Conversion (12,000 × 50% × 150c) | 9,000 |
| Add: Work started and finished during month | |
| (i.e. 32,000 units × 264c) = | 84,480 |
| | 118,080 |

| W2. Valuation of closing WIP | |
|---|---|
| 16,000 × 100% × 84c (Prior department) = | 13,440 |
| 16,000 × Nil × 30c (Materials) = | Nil |
| 16,000 × 25% × 150c (Conversion) = | 6,000 |
| | 19,440 |

**Solution and Analysis (Average Method):** Using the above illustration, we now turn our attention to the Average method. Clearly, the costs incurred in the respective process will be identical. However, it is the method with which such costs are assigned to the output for the period that differs. The method depends on a simple assumption. Using the Average method, we do not assume that the completion of opening work-in-progress is the first work to be completed during the period. Thus, we base our calculations on the total costs incurred to date (including opening WIP) and also the total work done to date, regardless of whether some of this related to an earlier accounting period. Actually, the underlying calculations are relatively easier than the FIFO method.

The debit side of the Process A account is straightforward and the initial entries are presented below. There is no physical discrepancy, since the number of units traced to this process (50,000) matches the output, i.e. 48,000 completed and 2,000 units in closing WIP.

### PROCESS A ACCOUNT (AVERAGE METHOD)

|  | Units | € |  | Units | € |
|---|---|---|---|---|---|
| Opening WIP | Nil | Nil |  |  |  |
| Material control a/c | 50,000 | 22,000 | Process B a/c | 48,000 | ? |
| Conversion costs a/c |  | 19,600 | Closing WIP | 2,000 | ? |
|  | 50,000 | 41,600 |  | 50,000 | 41,600 |

The basic question is how are we going to assign total costs of €41,600 between 50,000 units of output, some of which are not fully complete? Thus, we compute the cost per equivalent units for each cost element as this will allow us to assign costs to the units completed during the period (48,000) and also closing WIP – which are 50% complete. Under the Average method we need to calculate the costs incurred to date (including opening WIP) together with work done *to date*. The cost per equivalent unit can be computed by the following presentation.

|  | Materials | Conversion |
|---|---|---|
| **(a) Costs to be assigned:** |  |  |
| Opening WIP | Nil | Nil |
| Costs added this month | €22,000 | €19,600 |
| Total costs to be assigned | €22,000 | €19,600 |
| **(b) Equivalent units:** |  |  |
| Finished goods during month | 48,000 | 48,000 |
| Add: Closing WIP | 2,000 | 1,000 (50%) |
| = Total equivalent units | 50,000 | 49,000 |
| Cost per equivalent unit (c = a/b) | 44c | 40c |
| **Total cost per unit** | | 84c |

The completed Process A account is presented below, with the appropriate figure inserted for the cost of goods completed and transferred to Process B during the period. We initially start with the cost of finished goods and our calculation is simply computed at €40,320 (48,000 units × 84c). Secondly, the valuation of closing WIP is based on our calculation of cost per equivalent unit. (**Note:** due to the absence of opening stock, the calculations are identical under FIFO and Average methods.)

### PROCESS A ACCOUNT (AVERAGE METHOD)

|  | Units | € |  | Units | € |
|---|---|---|---|---|---|
| Opening WIP | Nil | Nil |  |  |  |
| Material control a/c | 50,000 | 22,000 | Process B a/c (W1) | 48,000 | 40,320 |
| Conversion costs a/c |  | 19,600 | Closing WIP (W2) | 2,000 | 1,280 |
|  | 50,000 | 41,600 |  | 50,000 | 41,600 |

| | |
|---|---|
| W1. Valuation of finished goods transferred to Process A (48,000 units × 84c) = | 40,320 |
| W2. Valuation of closing WIP | |
| 2,000 × 100% × 44c (Materials)  = | 880 |
| 2,000 × 50% × 40c (Conversion) = | 400 |
| | 1,280 |

The initial entries for the Process B account are straightforward and readers should notice the debit entry representing the cost of goods transferred from Process A. The (incomplete) Process B account appears below. There is no physical discrepancy, since the number of units traced to this process (60,000) matches the output, i.e. 44,000 completed and 16,000 units in closing WIP.

### PROCESS B ACCOUNT (AVERAGE METHOD)

|  | Units | € |  | Units | € |
|---|---|---|---|---|---|
| Opening WIP | 12,000 | 21,000 |  |  |  |
| Process A a/c | 48,000 | 40,320 |  |  |  |
| Material control a/c |  | 13,200 | Finished goods | 44,000 | ? |
| Conversion costs a/c |  | 63,000 | Closing WIP | 16,000 | ? |
|  | 60,000 | 137,520 |  | 60,000 | 137,520 |

The second stage in the calculation is to compute the cost per equivalent unit for each cost element. This will allow us to assign costs to the units completed (44,000) during the period and also closing WIP – which are 25% complete. Under the Average method we need to calculate the cost based on total costs incurred to date (including opening WIP), together with total work done to date, regardless of whether it was done in the previous accounting period. The cost per equivalent unit can be computed by the following presentation:

|  | Prior Dept | Materials | Conversion |
|---|---|---|---|
| **(a) Costs to be assigned:** | | | |
| Opening WIP (given) | €9,800 | Nil | €11,200 |
| Costs added this month | €40,320 | €13,200 | €63,000 |
| Total costs to be assigned | €50,120 | €13,200 | €74,200 |
| **(b) Equivalent units (work done to date):** | | | |
| Finished this month | 44,000 | 44,000 | 44,000 |
| Add: Closing WIP (16,000 units) | 16,000 | Nil | 4,000 (25%) |
| Total equivalent units | 60,000 | 44,000 | 48,000 |
| Cost per equivalent unit (c = a/b) | 83.5c | 30c | 154.6c |
| **Total cost per unit** | | 268c (R) | |

The completed Process B account is as follows, with the appropriate figures inserted for the cost of goods completed and transferred to finished goods during the period. As detailed below, the total cost of work transferred to finished goods amounts to €117,920 (44,000 units at 268c each). Secondly, the valuation of closing WIP is now relatively easy, based on our calculation of cost per equivalent unit. (There is an inevitable small rounding error.)

PROCESS B ACCOUNT (AVERAGE METHOD)

| | Units | € | | Units | € |
|---|---|---|---|---|---|
| Opening WIP | 12,000 | 21,000 | | | |
| Process A | 48,000 | 40,320 | Finished goods (W1) | 44,000 | 117,920 |
| Materials a/c | | 13,200 | Rounding difference | | 60 |
| Conversion costs a/c | | 63,000 | Closing WIP (W2) | 16,000 | 19,540 |
| | 60,000 | 137,520 | | 60,000 | 137,520 |

W1. Valuation of finished goods              €
(44,000 units × 268c) =                                       117,920

W2. Valuation of closing WIP
16,000 × 100% × 83.5 (Prior) =                        13,360
16,000 × Nil% × 30c (Materials) =                     Nil
16,000 × 25% × 154.5c (Conversion) =                 6,180
                                                         19,540

### Which Method to Use – FIFO or Average?

The FIFO method is theoretically more accurate because it separates prior period costs from current period costs. In contrast, the Average method mixes prior period and current period costs. Thus, if the average costs per unit in the previous period were significantly different to the current period's costs, then it could be argued that our closing work-in-progress valuation was incorrect. However, the average method is undoubtedly simpler to operate and, given a choice in an exam, this is the method that should be adopted. In any event, the overall difference between the two methods is unlikely to be very different.

## 4.4 Reporting Spoilage (Normal and Abnormal) of Processes

In any production process, some kind of wastage or spoilage will occur. In some instances it may be technically possible to eliminate spoilage altogether, but it may be uneconomical to do so since the costs of prevention would be greater than the existing loss due to spoilage. There are two main issues associated with spoilage, which are interrelated:

1. there are different types of spoilage – normal and abnormal – which should be separately identified; and
2. how to account for normal and abnormal spoilage.

### Different Types of Spoilage and Identifying the Amount of Normal Spoilage

Spoilage represents the physical amount of defective goods produced by a manufacturing process during the accounting period. Normal spoilage is an inherent result of a particular production process and represents a rate of physical loss that is expected in the manufacturing process. On the other hand, abnormal spoilage is spoilage that is not expected to arise under efficient operating conditions. In other words, abnormal spoilage is not an anticipated feature of the production process and represents the amount of physical loss that occurs in a manufacturing process, over and above that which is normally expected.

In identifying the physical amount of normal spoilage, it is theoretically preferable to calculate this based on GOOD output, as distinct from the total ACTUAL units started. This is because actual units started include any abnormal spoilage in addition to normal spoilage. However, in reality, normal spoilage is often calculated as a percentage of units started and the difference between the two approaches is seldom significant. (Nevertheless, it is important to read the question carefully and identify how normal spoilage is to be calculated.)

## Accounting for Spoilage

Accounting for spoilage depends on whether it is normal or abnormal. The easier one to deal with is abnormal spoilage since abnormal spoilage should always be costed separately and will always figure in the calculation of cost per equivalent unit. In turn, it should be written off and highlighted separately on the income statement. It should not be regarded as a cost of 'good' production.

Regarding the costs of normal spoilage, there are two viewpoints. The modern approach, in keeping with the increased focus on quality and waste elimination, makes the costs of normal spoilage visible by reporting it as a separate cost item in the income statement. This has the advantage of bringing such costs to the attention of management.

The alternative, more traditional, approach is to view the costs of normal spoilage as a cost of good production (for product costing purposes) since obtaining good units simultaneously produces spoiled units. Where normal costs of spoilage are added to the cost of goods completed, this raises an additional question: should normal spoilage cost be assigned to both completed goods and closing work-in-progress? The usual assumption here is that normal spoilage is detected only when the goods have been inspected. In turn, it is assumed that only completed goods are inspected. Thus:

1. If spoilage is detected by inspection on completion of production, then normal spoilage should not be assigned to closing work-in-progress since spoiled units relate solely to goods that have passed the inspection point and, therefore, must be in a finished stage. This means that normal spoilage must be included in the computation of equivalent units and then added only to cost of goods completed. This is the most common method used.

2. If spoilage is detected uniformly throughout the production cycle, then the cost of normal spoilage should be allocated both to good production and closing work-in-progress. In such circumstances, normal units spoiled will not enter the calculation of equivalent units. In this way, the cost of normal spoilage is automatically assigned to both completed goods and closing WIP.

In summary, normal spoilage is detected at a specific point in the production process. These costs, therefore, should be allocated only to those units which had passed this inspection point. Where spoilage is detected upon completion, no cost of normal spoilage is allocated to closing work-in-progress.

## ILLUSTRATION: NORMAL AND ABNORMAL SPOILAGE

The Longford Company accumulates the cost of producing one of its products on a process-cost basis. Materials for this product are added at the start of the production cycle whereas conversion costs are assumed to be incurred evenly over the cycle. Inspection of finished goods indicates that spoiled units are normally one-tenth of the good output.

The following information was provided for the month of January. At 1 January, opening work-in-progress was 80% completed and valued at €29,600 represented by 2,000kgs of materials (€15,000) and conversion costs (€14,600). During January 8,000kgs of materials were placed in production at a cost of €61,000. Conversion costs amounted to €80,400 for the month. Closing work-in-progress consisted of 1,500kgs two-thirds completed.

During the month, 7,200kgs of good product were transferred to finished goods after inspection.

**Requirement:** Using the Average costing method, show the process ledger account (and your calculations) for the month of January. Clearly highlight your calculation in relation to both normal and abnormal spoilage.

**Solution and Analysis:** Since there is opening WIP, one should select either the FIFO or the Average method. However, in this case, we are required to use the Average method – which is the less tedious of the two methods. In this illustration the spoilage is detected at inspection of finished goods. Thus, the cost of normal spoilage should be charged only to goods completed. This is achieved by including normal spoilage as part of equivalent units, thus costing it separately. However, this separate costing is charged, in turn, entirely to the cost of finished goods.

The preliminary calculations relating to the process account can be recorded as shown below. Normal spoilage is calculated as 10% of good output. The discrepancy remaining in relation to the physical quantities must represent abnormal spoilage of 580 kgs.

### PROCESS ACCOUNT (AVERAGE METHOD)

| | Kgs | € | | Kgs | € |
|---|---|---|---|---|---|
| Opening WIP | 2,000 | 29,600 | | | |
| | | | Finished goods | 7,200 | |
| | | | Normal spoilage | 720 | |
| Materials a/c | 8,000 | 61,000 | Abnormal spoilage | 580 | |
| Conversion costs a/c | | 80,400 | Closing WIP | 1,500 | |
| | 10,000 | 171,000 | | 10,000 | 171,000 |

The next stage is to compute the cost per equivalent unit for each cost element. This will allow us to assign costs to the kgs completed (7,200) during the period, to normal and abnormal spoilage and also to closing WIP – which is two-thirds completed. Under the average method we need to calculate the cost based on total costs incurred to date (including opening WIP), together with total work done to date, regardless of whether it was done in the previous accounting period. The cost per equivalent unit can be computed by the following presentation, including both normal and abnormal spoilage during the period:

|  | Materials | Conversion |
|---|---|---|
| **(a) Costs to be assigned:** | | |
| Opening WIP (given) | €15,000 | €14,600 |
| Costs added this month | €61,000 | €80,400 |
| Total costs to be assigned | €76,000 | €95,000 |
| **(b) Equivalent units (work done to date)** | | |
| Finished this month | 7,200 | 7,200 |
| Normal spoilage | 720 | 720 |
| Abnormal spoilage | 580 | 580 |
| Add: Closing WIP | 1,500 | 1,000 (2/3rds) |
| Total equivalent units | 10,000 | 9,500 |
| Cost per equivalent unit (Rounded) (c = a/b) | €7.60 | €10.00 |
| **Total cost per unit** | €17.60 | |

The completed process account is produced below. Since spoilage is detected at final inspection, the total cost of normal spoilage is included in the cost of good output. Abnormal spoilage is always shown separately.

PROCESS ACCOUNT (AVERAGE METHOD)

| | Kgs | € | | Kgs | € |
|---|---|---|---|---|---|
| Opening WIP | 2,000 | 29,600 | | | |
| | | | Finished goods (W1) | 7,200 | 139,392 |
| Materials a/c | 8,000 | 61,000 | Normal spoilage (W1) | 720 | N/a |
| | | | Ab. spoilage (W2) | 580 | 10,208 |
| Conversion costs a/c | | 80,400 | Closing WIP (W3) | 1,500 | 21,400 |
| | 10,000 | 171,000 | | 10,000 | 171,000 |

W1. Finished goods
Completed units (7,200 × €17.60)                                         126,720
Normal spoilage (720 × €17.60)                                          <u>12,672</u>
                                                                        <u>139,392</u>

W2. Abnormal spoilage
    (580 × €17.60)                                                      <u>10,208</u>

W3. Closing WIP
Materials (1,500 × 100% × €7.60)                                         11,400
Conversion costs
    (1,500 × 2/3rds × €10.00)                                          <u>10,000</u>
                                                                        <u>21,400</u>

## 4.5 Accounting for Proceeds of Scrap

Related to the issue of spoilage is that of 'scrap'. **Scrap** is, essentially, defective production that is sold for a minimal value. In theory, the question of scrap raises two issues:

1. when is this miscellaneous revenue recognised; and
2. how do you account for such scrap value?

**Recognising Scrap Revenue** In theory this can be done either at the production stage or when the goods are sold. To recognise scrap at the production stage introduces an element of uncertainty into the calculations as one must estimate the possible scrap value. Alternatively, it makes more sense to recognise scrap value only when the sale is made. This is in conformance with the usual accounting concept of conservatism. It should be appreciated that, since we are dealing with small amounts, by definition, the difference in methods should be rather small.

**Accounting for Scrap** It is usual to credit the revenue received from scrap to the relevant process account and this, therefore, becomes a deduction from the operating costs.

### ILLUSTRATION: ACCOUNTING FOR SCRAP

Mayo Company processes a single product. At the start of January, there was no WIP. It received 2,400 unprocessed products, costing €19,200. In addition, during the month it incurred €28,560 on conversion costs in the process, which were added, gradually, during the process.

The department completed work on 1,800 products during the month. However, another 200 (completed) units were ruined due to a severe malfunctioning of machines and this was considered to be abnormal spoilage. The ruined products were sold immediately for scrap at a price of €1 each. The department had 400 half-processed products in process at the end of the month.

**Requirement:** Prepare a process cost account to reflect the above information. Comment on your figures, especially with regard to using full cost figures for calculating spoilage.

**Solution and Analysis:** In the absence of opening WIP, it does not matter whether we use the FIFO or Average methods. However, since the average method is computationally easier to use, we shall present the calculations in that format. The preliminary figures can be identified as follows:

PROCESS ACCOUNT (AVERAGE METHOD)

| | Units | € | | Units | € |
|---|---|---|---|---|---|
| Opening WIP | Nil | Nil | Finished goods | 1,800 | ? |
| | | | Abnormal spoilage | 200 | ? |
| Materials a/c | 2,400 | 19,200 | Cash received | N/A | 200 |
| Conversion costs a/c | | 28,560 | Closing WIP | 400 | ? |
| | 2,400 | 47,760 | | 2,400 | 47,760 |

The next stage is to compute the cost per equivalent unit for each cost element which will allow us to assign costs to the work completed during the period (1,800 units), to abnormal spoilage and also to closing WIP – which are 50% complete. Under the Average method we need to identify the total costs incurred to date (including opening WIP), together with total work done to date, regardless of whether it was done in the previous accounting period or not. The cost per equivalent unit can be computed by the following presentation, including both normal and abnormal spoilage during the period.

| | Materials | Conversion |
|---|---|---|
| **(a) Costs to be assigned:** | | |
| Costs added this month | €19,200 | €28,560 |
| Less: cash received (assigned to either) | | (200) |
| Total costs to be assigned | €19,200 | €28,360 |
| **(b) Equivalent units (work done to date)** | | |
| Finished this month | 1,800 | 1,800 |
| Abnormal spoilage | 200 | 200 |
| Add: Closing WIP | 400 | 200 (50%) |
| Total equivalent units | 2,400 | 2,200 |
| Cost per equivalent unit (c = a/b) | €8.00 | €12.89 |
| **Total cost per unit** | | €20.89 |

The completed process account is produced below. Since spoilage is detected at final inspection, the total cost of normal spoilage is included in the cost of good output. Abnormal spoilage is always shown separately.

### PROCESS ACCOUNT (AVERAGE METHOD)

|  | Units | € |  | Units | € |
|---|---|---|---|---|---|
| Opening WIP | Nil | Nil | Finished goods (W1) | 1,800 | 37,602 |
|  |  |  | Abnormal spoilage (W2) | 200 | 4,178 |
| Materials a/c | 2,400 | 19,200 | Cash received | N/A | 200 |
| Conversion costs a/c |  | 28,560 | Closing WIP (W3) | 400 | 5,780 |
|  | 2,400 | 47,760 |  | 2,400 | 47,760 |

W1. Finished goods
  Completed units (1,800 × €20.89)                                    37,602

W2. Abnormal spoilage (200 × €20.89)                                  4,178

W3. Closing WIP
  Materials (400 × 100% × €8.00) =     3,200
  Conversion costs (400 × 50% × €12.89) = 2,580 (rounded)            5,780

## Additional Comments on Spoilage/Scrap

It is important to highlight the financial implications associated with spoilage and scrap. We shall return to this issue when discussing **Cost of Quality (CoQ)** reports. However, at this stage, one should also note the benefit of reporting **non-financial measures of performance** in this area. Such measures include:

- Reject rate, i.e. rejects as a percentage of items inspected or completed. Rejected goods can be very expensive since the material used, and other costs incurred, are now worthless. To overcome this problem, inspection is sometimes carried out at an early stage in the production process and this should reduce overall losses. However, there is an interesting behavioural dimension. There is a practice in many companies that rejected or spoiled units are sold to staff, usually at discount prices. It has been discovered, in a minority of situations, that production operatives have a tendency to classify items as defective in order to avail of such cheap goods!

- While most of the discussion has applied to the production process, it should be noted that the same principles apply to both service and retail sectors. In retail sectors, spoilage also includes statistics on theft. It is commonly suggested that, for example, theft can amount to over 5% of turnover for retail concerns in busy city centre locations. Not surprisingly, retail companies have the incentive to increase overall security levels, while being conscious of maintaining an appropriate ambience for its shopping clientele.
- In service companies, the concept of 'first time fix' is growing in popularity. This means that the service is provided correctly the first time, e.g. electrical maintenance work.
- Finally, absolute performance in relation to such metrics is not very important. It is the relative performance against internal comparatives, say, over different time periods or against preset targets, or external comparisons, that provides relevant information to managers.

## Conclusion

Over the past two chapters we have looked at two different cost accumulation systems, namely job costing and process costing systems. It is common to find that both systems use a predetermined overhead absorption rate, using direct labour hours as the cost driver. The use of direct labour hours (or other volume-based cost drivers) is frequently referred to as **traditional cost accounting (TCA)**. In the next chapter, **Chapter 5**, we shall see that this traditional cost accounting can provide misleading product costs and we explain an alternative costing system – **Activity-based costing (ABC)**.

## SUMMARY OF LEARNING OBJECTIVES

**Learning Objective 1**: Describe process costing systems.

A process costing system is appropriate when units produced are identical and mass-produced. Unit costs can be computed by dividing the total process costs by the number of units produced.

**Learning Objective 2**: Record cost flows in a process costing system.

Under a process costing system, costs are recorded in ledger process accounts, with emphasis being placed on the flows of materials, labour and overheads. It is usual to record both the physical and financial flows.

**Learning Objective 3**: Discuss the concept of an equivalent unit and calculate the cost per equivalent unit.

By definition, closing work-in-progress cannot be complete with regard to all cost elements. Therefore, the notion of an equivalent unit is used so that, say, 200 half-finished goods are equivalent to 100 completed units.

**Learning Objective 4**: Apply both Average and FIFO costing methods.

The average method of process costing calculates the cost per equivalent unit with reference to the total costs added to date including opening WIP, divided by the total equivalent units completed to date. In contrast, FIFO calculates the cost per equivalent with reference to costs added this period only, divided by the work done this period. In the absence of opening WIP, both methods will provide identical results.

**Learning Objective 5**: Report costs of normal and abnormal spoilage.

Normal wastage or spoilage represents the amount of physical wastage or loss that management expect and tolerate within a manufacturing process. It is usually included as a normal cost of good output. In contrast, abnormal loss is unexpected wastage or loss. Because of this it is usually reported as a separate cost element.

## Questions

### Review Questions

(See Appendix One for Solutions to Review Questions **4.1** and **4.2**)

*Question 4.1 (Process Costing with Equivalent Units – Single Process)*

The Alpha company manufactures identical components and operates a process costing system. During the most recent accounting period, 1,000 units were introduced into a process during a period and 600 finished units were produced. The remaining 400 units work-in-process were 75% complete as regards material, 50% complete as regards labour and 25% complete as regards overhead. Cost of the material was €2,700, labour was €2,000 and overhead €2,450.

**Requirement:** Calculate the average cost per unit and prepare the process ledger account.

*Question 4.2 (Multi-choice Questions on Process Costing and Spoilage)*

1. Which of the following is not an issue for quality control?
   (a) What does it cost to detect defective units?
   (b) What happens to the defective units?

(c)  What is the cost of spoilage?

(d)  How can defective units be prevented?

2. If spoilage is to be reported separately in the management accounts, the journal entry to record such spoilage, amounting to €2,500, is as follows:

|  | Dr. | Cr. |
|---|---|---|
| (a)  Finished Goods | 2,500 | |
|        Work-in-Process | | 2,500 |
| (b)  Production Overhead Control | 2,500 | |
|        Work-in-Process | | 2,500 |
| (c)  Loss from Spoilage | 2,500 | |
|        Work-in-Process | | 2,500 |
| (d)  Materials Control | 2,500 | |
|        Work-in-Process | | 2,500 |

3. In a process costing system, the cost of the spoilage could be added to the cost of the good units produced if the spoilage is:

|  | **Normal** | **Abnormal** |
|---|---|---|
| (a) | No | No |
| (b) | No | Yes |
| (c) | Yes | Yes |
| (d) | Yes | No |

4. The sale of scrap from a manufacturing process usually would be recorded as a:

(a)  decrease in process costs.

(b)  increase in process costs.

(c)  decrease in finished goods control.

(d)  increase in finished goods control.

5. Gold Company manufactures electric drills to the exacting specifications of various customers. During April 20x9, Job 246 for the production of 3,300 drills was completed at the following costs per unit:

| Direct materials | €10 |
|---|---|
| Direct manufacturing labour | 8 |
| Allocated manufacturing overhead | 12 |
| | €30 |

Final inspection of Job 246 disclosed 150 defective units and 300 spoiled units. The defective drills were reworked at a total cost of €1,500, and the spoiled drills were sold for €4,500. What would be the unit cost of the good units produced on Job 246?

(a)  €33

(b)  €32

(c)  €30

(d)  €29

6. In manufacturing its products for the month of March 20x9, Bull Company incurred normal spoilage of €5,000 and abnormal spoilage of €9,000. How much spoilage cost should Bull Company recognise for stock valuation for the month of March 20x9?

(a) €14,000
(b) €9,000
(c) €5,000
(d) €0

7. During February 20x9, Harry Company incurred the following costs on Job 901 for the manufacture of 400 motors:

| | |
|---|---|
| Direct materials | €1,320 |
| Direct manufacturing labour | €1,600 |
| Factory overhead (150% of direct manufacturing labour) | €2,400 |
| | €5,320 |

Direct costs of reworked 20 units:

| | |
|---|---|
| Direct materials | € 200 |
| Direct manufacturing labour | 320 |
| Production overhead | 480 |
| | €1,000 |

The rework costs were attributable to the exacting specifications of Job 901. The cost per finished unit of Job 901 was:

(a) €14.60
(b) €15.80
(c) €14.00
(d) €13.30

8. The Defect Company has noticed that defective units occur in their manufacturing more on Monday than on any other day of the operating week. The high occurrence of defects on Monday indicates:

(a) a measure of the extent to which the day of the week accounts for the variability in the defective units.
(b) a measure of the extent to which the spoiled units account for the variability in the day of the week.
(c) that one variable is the cause of the other.
(d) all of the above.

9. Right Ltd installed a new process in October. During October, 10,000 units were started in Department A. Of the units started, 1,000 were rejected on completion, 7,000 were transferred to Department B and 2,000 remained as work-in-progress at the end of October. The work-in-progress at 31 October was 100% complete as to material cost and 50% complete as to conversion costs. Material costs of €27,000 and conversion costs of €40,000 were charged to Department A in

October. The cost of spoiled units is to be allocated to finished goods only. What are the total costs transferred to Department B?

(a) €46,900
(b) €51,600
(c) €59,000
(d) €57,120 (rounded)

10. The Wrong Company accumulates the cost of producing one of its products on a process cost basis. Materials for this product are added at the start of the production cycle; conversion costs are assumed to be incurred evenly over the cycle. Inspection of finished product indicates that spoiled units are normally one-tenth of the good output. At January 1, opening work-in-progress was 80% complete and valued at €29,600, represented by 2,000lbs of materials (€15,000) and conversion costs (€14,600). During January, 8,000lbs of materials were placed in production at a cost of €61,000. Conversion costs amounted to €80,400 for the month. Closing work-in-progress consisted of 1,500lbs two-thirds completed.

During the month, 7,200lbs of good product were transferred to finished goods after inspection. Using the weighted average cost method, the cost of normal and abnormal spoilage is:

|     | Normal | Abnormal |
| --- | --- | --- |
| (a) | €11,400 | €10,000 |
| (b) | €11,400 | €15,000 |
| (c) | €12,672 | €10,208 |
| (d) | €12,817 | €10,325 |

## Intermediate Questions

*Question 4.3 (Process Costing with Equivalent Units)*

The Easy Company manufactures identical components and operates a process costing system. During the recent accounting period, 1,000 units were introduced into a process costing €1,600 to which labour costs of €2,000 and overhead costs of €2,800 were added. During the period 600 finished units were produced. The remaining 400 units work-in-progress were 50% complete as regards all cost elements.

**Requirement:** Calculate the average cost per unit and prepare the process account.

*Question 4.4 (Process Costing with Equivalent Units)*

Hardy Limited is a manufacturing firm and its identical products undergo an assembly process. Data for the most recent month for this Assembly department is summarised as follows:

| | Physical units | Material costs € | Conversion costs € |
|---|---|---|---|
| Opening WIP | 5,000 | 4,800 | 3,750 |
| Added during month | 45,000 | 52,800 | 53,750 |
| Units completed | 42,000 | | |
| Closing WIP | 8,000 | | |

The opening WIP was 80% complete as to materials and 60% complete as to conversion costs. The closing WIP was 75% complete as to materials and 50% complete as regards conversions costs. The company operates a weighted average method of process costing.

**Requirement:** Calculate the average cost per unit and prepare the process account.

## Question 4.5 (Process Costing with Normal Spoilage)

The Pack Company Limited operates a process costing system and data for the most recent month are as follows:

| | |
|---|---|
| Opening WIP | Nil |
| Units input and started | 10,000 |
| Material costs added during period | €38,880 |
| Conversion costs added during period | €50,337 |
| Units completed and transferred to finished goods | 7,500 |
| Closing work-in-progress (units) | 1,500 |

The closing work-in-progress was 100% complete regarding material and 60% complete regarding conversions costs. Normal loss is 10% of input. The company calculates a cost of its normal loss each month which, in turn, is assigned only to cost of goods completed, since loss is only detected on final inspection.

**Requirement:** Calculate the average cost per unit and prepare the process ledger account.

## Question 4.6 (Process Costing with Prior Department Costs)

The production costs of the manufacturing operations of the Dot Company Limited are accumulated by way of a process costing system. There are two distinct but consecutive processes with the output of Process 1 being transferred to Process 2 for final assembly.

During the most recent accounting period, 2,000 units of material were introduced into Process 1 and 2,000 completed units were transferred to Process B. Total costs incurred in Process 1 consisted of materials, €3,000, and conversion costs of €4,000.

Process 2 incurred conversion costs amounting to €8,000 during the same accounting period. There was no work-in-progress at the end of the accounting period.

**Requirement:** Calculate the average cost per unit in each process and prepare the process accounts.

### Question 4.7 (Process Costing with Prior Department Costs)

The production costs for the manufacturing operations of the Stop Company Limited are accumulated by way of a process costing system. There are two distinct but consecutive processes with the output of Process 1 being transferred to Process 2 for final assembly.

At the start of the accounting period, there was no opening work-in-progress. During the accounting period, 1,200 units were transferred from Process 1 to Process 2 at a total cost of €4,800. Further processing took place in Process 2 with additional materials being added, amounting to €2,320 and conversion costs amounting to €4,840. At the end of the month, 1,000 completed units had been transferred to Finished Goods. The remaining units were still in process and were considered 80% complete as regards Process 2 materials and 50% complete regarding conversion costs.

**Requirement:** Calculate the average cost per unit and prepare the Process B account assuming there were no losses or gains in Process 2.

### Advanced Questions

### Question 4.8 (Process Costing involving FIFO and Average Costing)

Leo Company Limited has two departmental processes. Material is introduced at the beginning of the process in Department A, and additional material is added at the end of the process in Department B. Conversion costs are applied uniformly throughout both processes. Data for the month of March 20x8 include the following:

|  | Department A | Department B |
|---|---|---|
| Units completed during March | 48,000 | 44,000 |
| Material costs added for 40,000 units | €22,000 | — |
| Material costs added (Dept B) | — | €13,200 |
| Conversion costs added during March | €18,000 | €63,000 |
| Opening work-in-progress (units) | 10,000 | 12,000 |
| Closing work-in-progress (units) | 2,000 | 16,000 |

In Department A, opening work-in-progress was 40% complete and valued at €7,500 (comprising materials, €6,000 and conversion costs €1,500). Closing stock was 50% complete.

In Department B, opening work-in-progress was 66.67% complete and valued at €21,000 (comprising prior department costs, €9,800 and conversion costs, €11,200). Closing stock was 37.5% converted.

**Requirement:** Compute cost of goods transferred from each department and closing stock valuations under:

(a) FIFO product costing, and
(b) weighted average product costing.

## Question 4.9 (Process Costing, Prior Departments and FIFO)

The production costs for the manufacturing operations of the Sam Company Limited are accumulated by way of a process costing system. There are two distinct but consecutive processes with the output of Process 1 being transferred to Process 2 for final assembly.

For the recent accounting period, Process 2 had opening work-in-progress of 200 units, valued at €1,660, comprising €900 for Process 1 costs, €320 for Process 2 materials and €440 for Process 2 conversion costs. These 200 units were 80% complete regarding Process B materials and 50% complete regarding conversion costs.

During the month a further 1,500 units were transferred from Process A at a cost of €6,750. In addition, Process B materials were added at a cost of €2,800 together with conversion costs amounting to €6,116. At the end of the month 1,350 units had been completed and were transferred to finished goods account but 350 units remained in process. The closing work-in-progress was 60% complete as regards Process B materials, 40% as regards conversion costs.

**Requirement:** Using the First-In-First-Out (FIFO) method calculate the average cost per unit and prepare the Process 2 account.

## Question 4.10 (Process Costing, Prior Departments and Average Method)

The production costs for the manufacturing operations of the Sam Company Limited are accumulated by way of a process costing system. There are two distinct but consecutive processes with the output of Process 1 being transferred to Process 2 for final assembly.

For the recent accounting period, Process 2 had opening work-in-progress of 200 units, valued at €1,660, comprising €900 for Process 1 costs, €320 for Process 2 materials and €440 for Process 2 conversion costs. These 200 units were 80% complete regarding Process B materials and 50% complete regarding conversion costs.

During the month a further 1,500 units were transferred from Process A at a cost of €6,750. In addition, Process B materials were added at a cost of €2,800 together with conversion costs amounting to €6,116. At the end of the month 1,350 units had been completed and were transferred to finished goods account but 350 units remained in process. The closing work-in-progress was 60% complete as regards Process B materials, 40% as regards conversion costs.

**Requirement:** Using the (weighted) Average method calculate the average cost per unit and prepare the Process 2 account.

## Question 4.11 (Process Costing with Abnormal Spoilage)

The Erin Company Limited is a manufacturer of a single product and operates a process costing system. Material X is introduced at the start of production while Material Y is introduced when the production process is 70% complete. Conversion costs comprise labour and overheads and are added continuously during the production process.

The opening work-in-progress for the most recent accounting period consisted of 2,000 units which were 20% complete and valued overall at €14,260, representing €11,518 for material X, Nil for material Y and €2,742 for conversion costs. During the period, 15,000 units were started and the following costs were incurred:

| | |
|---|---|
| Material X | €87,600 |
| Material Y | €26,100 |
| Conversion costs | €111,060 |

The number of products produced during the period was 14,000 and the ending work-in-progress consisted of 1,000 products which were 60% complete. Normal spoilage, equivalent to 3.333% of units started during the period, is detected by inspection when production is complete.

**Requirement:** Prepare the process account for the period and show your calculations of the cost per unit for the period, the value of ending work-in-progress and the cost of finished goods produced. Use the weighed average method.

## Question 4.12 Process Costing with Normal and Abnormal Spoilage

The Paddy Company Limited manufactures a single product and accumulates production costs using a process costing system. The following are details of the finishing process for a recent accounting period:

There was no opening work-in-progress.

During the period, 3,900 units were transferred from a prior process and these units were valued at €19,500. In addition, during the period, additional costs were incurred:

| | |
|---|---|
| Materials | €3,510 |
| Conversion costs | €21,000 |

Normal loss during the month was 400 units. Abnormal loss during the month was 200 units. The company transferred 2,500 units from the finishing process to the finished goods store.

At the end of the period, 800 units were in closing work-in-progress with the following degrees of completion:

> 100% re materials
> 50% re conversion costs

There is a quality inspection in the finishing process which is undertaken when the goods are completed. All normal and abnormal losses occur at this quality inspection.

**Requirement:** Prepare the finishing process account for the recent accounting period, using the (weighted) Average method.

# Activity-based Costing Systems

## LEARNING OBJECTIVES

When you have completed studying this chapter you should be able to:

1. Present the limitations of traditional cost accounting systems.
2. Contrast and compare activity-based costing and traditional cost accounting systems.
3. Calculate product costs using ABC.
4. Describe the nature of activity-based cost management.
5. Prepare customer profitability calculations.
6. Describe the limitations of ABC.

## 5.1 Limitations of Traditional Costing Systems

Traditional cost accounting (TCA) systems have been discussed in the three previous chapters. In summary, traditional cost accounting assigns production overheads to products using volume-based cost drivers, e.g. direct labour hours. This means that production overhead costs are assigned to cost units in proportion to volume. This system has **three major limitations**:

1. Some manufacturing companies, e.g. electronics and pharmaceutical, have a very low direct labour content, perhaps as low as 10% of total product cost and the term 'direct labour cost' has little relevance in such industries. This is especially the case in a highly automated plant. Coupled with the decline in direct labour costs is a dramatic increase in production overhead costs resulting from the purchase of expensive machinery and technology. The impact of this explosion of overhead costs is twofold:

   (a) as firms increase the pace of automation, production overhead grows in percentage terms as direct labour costs fall; and

   (b) overheads grow in real terms because of the increased support costs associated with maintaining and running automated equipment.

2. Increasingly, production overheads are transaction-driven rather than volume-driven. By transactions, we mean the vast range of internal activities that are associated with processing orders, facilitating production, storage and delivery of goods. These transactions or activities involve exchanges of materials and/or information necessary to move production along but do not directly result in physical products.

3. Also, overheads relate to the complexity of business operations because, in the modern competitive environment, companies must become more responsive to customer needs. This involves rapid development of new products with enhanced product characteristics, a wider range of product choice and quicker response to customer needs. Meeting these needs has created a growing demand for support functions such as engineering and product development, quality control and staff training. Such costs are largely independent of the number of units produced. In addition, non-production overheads have significantly increased as a proportion of the total cost structure of firms due to increased attention on post-sales service, advertising and administration. Until recently, these non-production costs did not receive the attention they deserved from management accountants, who were more preoccupied with costs of production.

To address these limitations, an alternative product costing system has been suggested – Activity-based Costing (ABC). ABC is based on a fundamental concept: **products consume activities and activities consume overhead resources**.

For example, when a machine's specifications are recalibrated in order to produce a different product, resources are consumed by the set-up requirements involved and this consumption of resources is independent of the number of units produced in that particular batch.

It is argued that, for example, low-volume products create more transactions per unit manufactured than their high-volume counterparts. Consequently, the transaction cost per unit will be higher for the low-volume products relative to volume products. Therefore, the traditional cost accounting system, which absorbs production overhead based on volume-only considerations, may distort product costs.

After installing ABC systems, managers have frequently found that the low-volume products should be assigned more overheads since they consume more overhead resources.

## 5.2 The Nature and Technique of Activity-based Costing

Activity-based costing (ABC) focuses on activities that cause costs to be incurred. Essentially, it divides activities into a three-category hierarchy though other textbooks use a four or even a five-category hierarchy.

1. Unit level activities, which are performed each time a unit is produced (e.g. machine power or machine depreciation based on running hours).
2. Transaction-related activities, which are performed each time a transaction (internal or external) takes place. For example, this would include first-item inspection, machine set-up and materials' movement. These transactions do not directly result in physical products.

3. **Plant level** activities, which include costs that are common to a variety of products and can only be assigned to products in an arbitrary manner (e.g. rent of factory or factory maintenance).

The major difference between the traditional product costing systems and ABC lies in the way in which transaction-related costs are assigned to cost units. Traditionally, companies use a two-stage approach to the assignment of production overhead costs to units of output:

1. initially, overheads are assigned to production departments, and
2. then the overheads are absorbed as product costs using volume-related absorption bases such as direct labour hours.

Activity-based costing, on the other hand, **involves the following three steps:**

1. **Identify the cost pools** A cost pool is any area that performs a significant activity and for which costs can be accumulated. (Some textbooks refer to them as cost 'buckets'.) For example, the machine set-up pool would include all costs that relate to setting up machines for production runs. Under ABC, cost pools may cover more than one department. For example, the decision to raise a purchase requisition may result in costs being incurred in purchasing, materials handling and accounts payable. All these costs may be included in the same cost pool under ABC.
2. **Identify the appropriate cost driver for each cost pool** Cost drivers represent those activities or factors that affect costs in a significant way. There are two types of cost drivers under ABC:

    (a) **Volume-based cost drivers:** These include volume-based measures such as direct labour hours and machine running hours. These cost drivers are the primary determinants of conventionally defined variable costs. Such overheads should be traced to products using volume-related cost drivers and they correspond to traditional OHARs. Some examples of activity cost pools and volume-based cost drivers are:

| Activity Cost Pool | Specimen Cost Driver |
| --- | --- |
| Machine maintenance | Amount of machine running hours |
| Product packaging | Volume of production (units) |

    (b) **Transaction-based cost drivers:** These include activities such as materials purchasing, quality control and setting-up machines for production. In addition, ABC assigns non-production costs to products since the objective is to more accurately estimate product costs to be used for managerial decision-making as distinct from stock valuation. Therefore, under ABC, all costs are considered as 'product' costs. In contrast, under TCA, management accountants have focused on production costs in order to value closing stock for financial reporting purposes. This should not be a source of confusion; rather it confirms that 'there are different costs for different purposes'.

Below is a sample of production and non-production cost pools and related cost drivers. It should be noted that there are different cost drivers that could be used in relation to any activity cost pool.

| Activity cost pool | Specimen cost driver |
|---|---|
| Materials purchasing | Number of purchase orders |
| Quality control | Number of inspections |
| Machine set-up | Number of set-ups |
| Material handling | Number of material movements |
| Training and staff development | Number of people trained |
| Personnel services | Number of employees |

3. The third and final stage of ABC is to assign activity costs to products using appropriate cost driver rates, in much the same way as we have previously used overhead absorption rates (OHARs) (**Chapter 2**, Section 2.5). For example, if the total cost of quality control is €240,000 and 600 inspections are carried out during the accounting period, then the cost driver rate is €400 per inspection. In turn, inspection costs will be assigned to products by multiplying the cost driver rate by the number of inspections performed on that product. However, there will be plant level cost pools, which would include, for example, rent of premises. The choice of cost driver for plant level cost pools is arbitrary.

The overall ABC process is depicted in **Exhibit 5.1** and we focus only on production overheads for simplicity. There are plant level overheads such as rent of premises and they will continue to be absorbed into products using arbitrary OHARs. There are unit level overheads, e.g. power for machines and they will continue to be absorbed in products using volume-based OHARs, e.g. machine running hours. There are transaction-related overheads and we focus on only three activity cost pools (machine set up, quality control and material handling) and the related cost drivers are the number of machine set ups, the number of inspections and the number of material movements.

The dramatic difference in *unit* product costs between traditional and ABC systems is illustrated in the Kildare Company illustration below. This involves three processes:

1. machine processing,
2. machine set-up, and
3. inspection.

One should note that the ***total*** costs of the organisation do not change under ABC. Instead, individual product costs change due to the way that overheads are assigned to products. This confirms that ABC is an alternative, and conceptually better, method of assigning overhead costs to units of output.

EXHIBIT 5.1: SCHEME OF ACTIVITY-BASED COSTING

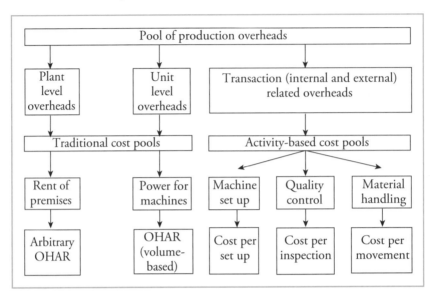

## ILLUSTRATION: ACTIVITY-BASED COSTING V TRADITIONAL COST ACCOUNTING

The Kildare Company produces two different office chairs, referred to as product X and Y, which are sold for €70 and €100 respectively. For convenience purposes production takes place within a single department and production overheads amount to €1,000,000. (We shall ignore non-production overhead costs for illustration purposes.) We shall initially assume that the company uses a traditional cost accounting system whereby production overheads are absorbed on the basis of direct labour hours. You are provided with the following information:

|  | Product X | Product Y | Total |
|---|---|---|---|
| Production and sales (units) | 25,000 units | 5,000 units | 30,000 units |
| Direct materials cost per unit | €25 | €20 | |
| Direct labour hours required per unit and total | 15 hours | 5 hours | 400,000 hours |
| Labour rate per hour | €1 | €1 | |
| Total production overhead costs | | | €1,000,000 |

**Requirement:** Calculate the unit cost for each product using the traditional method of overhead absorption, i.e. based entirely on direct labour hours, using a single plant-wide rate. What are your initial conclusions if the respective selling prices are €70 for X and €100 for Y?

**Solution and Analysis (TCA):** In this example (for convenience purposes) the traditional product costing method accumulates all production overhead costs into a single cost pool and these are absorbed into products on the basis of direct labour hours as follows:

$$\text{OHAR} = \frac{\text{Overhead} \in}{\text{Direct Labour hours}} = \frac{\text{€1,000,000}}{400,000} = \text{€2.50 per DLH}$$

Since all production overheads (machine processing, machine set-ups and inspection) are included in a single cost pool, and absorbed on the basis of direct labour hours, the unit costs of products X and Y are:

|  | Product X | Product Y |
|---|---|---|
|  | € | € |
| Direct materials (given) | 25.00 | 20.00 |
| Direct labour (given) | 15.00 | 5.00 |
| Overhead (€2.50 per DLH) | <u>37.50</u> | <u>12.50</u> |
| Total cost | <u>77.50</u> | <u>37.50</u> |

Based only on the above information, and ignoring other considerations, product X generates a loss of €7.50 (€70.00 – €77.50). In such circumstances managers may decide, for example, to delete this product or increase its selling price. (In competitive situations, increasing selling prices may not be an appropriate option.) In contrast, product Y generates a profit of €62.50 per unit (€100.00 – €37.50) and managers would be anxious to retain this product, given the information provided.

However, there is additional information available relating to significant activities within the firm. Three cost pools and relevant cost drivers have been identified as follows:

| Cost pools | Overheads | Cost drivers |
|---|---|---|
| Machine processing | €700,000 | No. of machine running hours |

| | | |
|---|---|---|
| Machine set-up | €120,000 | No. of machine set-ups |
| Inspection | €180,000 | No. of inspections |
| Total overhead costs | €1,000,000 | |

| Other operating data: | Product X | Product Y | Total |
|---|---|---|---|
| Machine running hours (per unit of X and Y and total) | 1 hour | 2 hours | 35,000 machine hours |
| Number of machine set-ups (per product line and total) | 4 set-ups | 20 set-ups | 24 set-ups |
| Number of inspections (per product line and total) | 40 inspections | 80 inspections | 120 inspections |

**Solution and Analysis (ABC):** Three separate ABC cost pools have been identified, namely:

1. machine processing,
2. machine set-up, and
3. inspection.

The cost drivers and cost driver levels have been provided as follows:

| Cost pool | Cost driver | Cost driver level |
|---|---|---|
| Machine processing | Number of machine hours | 35,000 machine hours |
| Machine set-up | Number of machine set-ups | 24 machine set-ups |
| Inspection | Number of inspections | 120 inspections |

Based on the above cost pools and cost driver levels, cost driver rates can now be calculated for each of the three activity cost pools.

The cost driver rate for machine processing overhead costs is as follows:

$$\text{OHAR} = \frac{\text{Overhead } \euro}{\text{No. of machine hours}} = \frac{\euro 700,000}{35,000} = \euro 20 \text{ per machine hour}$$

The cost driver rate for machine set-up overhead costs is as follows:

$$OHAR = \frac{Overhead \, €}{No. \, of \, machine \, set\text{-}ups} = \frac{€120,000}{24} = €5,000 \, per \, set\text{-}up$$

The cost driver rate for inspection overhead costs is as follows:

$$OHAR = \frac{Overhead \, €}{No. \, of \, inspections} = \frac{€180,000}{120} = €1,500 \, per \, inspection$$

The final part of the ABC process is to use the cost driver rates to assign overhead costs to each of the two products. The treatment of direct costs (materials and labour) is identical to the traditional cost accounting method since, by definition, a direct cost is one that can be traced unambiguously and in entirety to a single cost objective. The significant difference between traditional cost accounting (TCA) and Activity-based Costing (ABC) is the method of assigning overheads to different products. TCA uses an OHAR based on direct labour hours. In contrast, ABC uses three OHARs, based on different activities performed in the production process. Product costs under ABC are as follows:

| ABC Product cost | Product X | Product Y |
|---|---|---|
| Direct materials (given) | 25.00 | 20.00 |
| Direct labour (given) | 15.00 | 5.00 |
| Machine processing costs (i) | 20.00 | 40.00 |
| Set-up costs (ii) | 0.80 | 20.00 |
| Inspection costs (iii) | 2.40 | 24.00 |
| | 63.20 | 109.00 |

Based on the above cost figures, and given the respective selling prices it now appears that Product X is actually profitable, whereas Product Y is a loss maker! We received entirely different signals under traditional cost accounting:

1. X = €20 x 1 machine hour = €20
   Y = €20 x 2 machine hours = €40
2. X = (€5,000 x 4 set-ups)/25,000 units = €0.80
   Y = (€5,000 x 20 set-ups)/5,000 units = €20
3. X = (€1,500 x 40 inspections)/25,000 units = €2.40;
   Y = (€1,500 x 80 inspections)/5,000 units = €24.

The comparison of unit costs under the two systems is highlighted below:

|  | Product X € | Product Y € |
|---|---|---|
| Traditional approach | 77.50 | 37.50 |
| Activity-Based Costing | 63.20 | 109.00 |
| Sales price (given) | 70.00 | 100.00 |

The difference in unit costs is explained by the different demands each product places on the resources of the company and how these overhead resources are assigned. Traditional cost accounting systems, which use volume-based overhead absorption rates, tend to over-cost high-volume products and to under-cost low-volume products. ABC, on the other hand, is based on the fundamental concept that products consume activities and activities consume overhead resources. Typically, low-volume products create more transactions per manufactured unit than their high-volume counterparts. Consequently, these transaction costs per unit will be higher for the low-volume products relative to high-volume products.

The selection of cost driver pools and related cost drivers is an important decision to be made in implementing an ABC system. It requires an understanding of all the activities required to make the product (or provide services to customers). In identifying cost drivers, a sensible starting point is to consult departmental managers and supervisors and ask them what activities cause costs to be incurred in their departments. In other words, ask them what actually happens in their departments.

Two points are worth stressing at this stage regarding such leading questions: First, if respondents perceive that possible redundancies may take place in the future as a result of the implementation of ABC, uncooperative behaviour and general resistance can be expected from them. Secondly, it is important that management accountants react with patience to a likely initial response that your request is too complex. Ask the manager how much of his time has been devoted to a particular task over the past six months on average? Is it 10% or is it 90%? In this way, some progress will be made as options can be narrowed down.

## 5.3 Activity-based Cost Management

Initially, ABC systems were designed to more accurately assign overhead costs (production and non-production) to units of output. However, it was quickly realised that ABC systems could also be used by managers in the context of cost management practices.

The fundamental aspects of the relationship between ABC and **ABC Management (ABCM)** are shown below in **Exhibit 5.2**, which is based on the 1991 *CAM-I Glossary of Activity-Based Management.* In brief, ABC information (shown running from top to bottom) seeks to provide more accurate information for product costing. On the other hand, ABCM (shown running from left to right) is concerned with managing costs rather than simply counting them.

One of the lessons of ABC is that costs are incurred both due to volume of output and the complexity of operations. To understand the role of **complexity,** consider two separate manufacturing companies, each of which produces 1 million pens. In the first company, only blue pens are produced for a single customer and delivered in one consignment. In the second company, 900,000 blue pens are produced in a single batch, 80,000 black pens are produced in a few batches, and 20,000 green pens are produced in many small batches. Although both plants have the same volume of output, it is clear that overall costs in Plant 2 will be relatively higher because it has a more complicated system of dealing with customer orders and incurs significantly more set-up costs. Furthermore, in Plant 2 if each pen uses the same number of hours (labour or machine), the traditional costing system assigns the same amount of overhead to each unit. This does not seem to be intuitively correct since the three different types of pens are likely to place different demands on the company's resources.

Two areas of ABCM will now be briefly outlined:

1. cost management through the identification of non-value added activities; and
2. assessing employee productivity.

EXHIBIT 5.2: ACTIVITY-BASED COSTING AND ACTIVITY-BASED COSTING MANAGEMENT

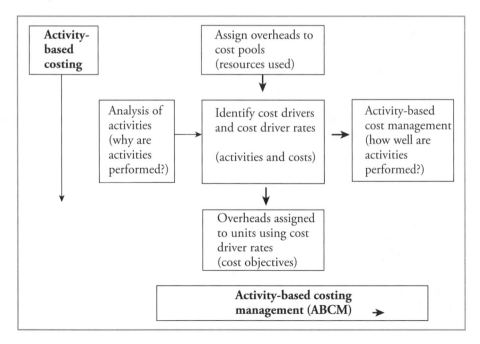

A more important application of ABCM is in the area of customer profitability analysis and this is covered in **Section 5.4**.

## 1. Cost Management by Identifying Non-value Added Activities

Costs have always been an important consideration for businesses. Indeed, it is likely that with increased competition and globalisation, the cost issue will become more dominant during the coming decade.

In simple terms, if costs are too high, a business is likely to be uncompetitive and unprofitable. Traditionally, cost accountants were mainly concerned with 'counting costs' for product costing purposes. In such an environment, it is possible that companies found it difficult to control costs or to implement successful cost reduction schemes. A number of reasons explain why cost reduction initiatives may not be entirely successful within organisations.

First, the annual budgeting exercise within companies is likely to represent an **incremental** process, whereby targets for the forthcoming accounting period are based on agreed percentage changes applied to the previous period's budget or actual expenditure in the previous year. If last year's actual expenditure is used, then managers have the incentive to always overspend in a given year. Unspent budgets represent targets for budget cuts in the following year! Therefore, the only budget items that receive scrutiny are those that are 'incremental' to last year, either in the form of increases for inflation or new spending proposals. In this way, it is likely that a significant amount of the annual budget escapes serious scrutiny.

Secondly, the emphasis on 'counting costs' frequently meant that cost accountants were at a loss to explain **why** the costs were incurred. (Keeping the score in a match does not explain why the goals were scored!) This is particularly relevant in the case of overhead costs. Overheads refer to common costs that are not directly traceable to any individual product and can typically comprise as much as 50% of the overall cost structure in a manufacturing company.

It became clear some years ago that merely 'counting' costs would not provide sufficient information to managers to enable them to make important strategic and operating decisions. The discipline of cost management emerged, and this differs from the traditional cost accumulation in a number of ways.

### Cost Management

First, the accountant does not monopolise cost management. Successful cost management is everyone's responsibility, and is an interdisciplinary and multifunctional activity. Certainly, the accountant will be involved but he will be influenced by the insights of production managers and engineers, design experts and others. The management accountant will act more like a facilitator rather than a leader or source of inspiration. The management accountant will be part of a cost management project team which should identify and influence those factors that can radically affect costs.

Secondly, cost management does not accept that the cost structure in an organisation is an inflexible baseline. Rather, managers and employees are encouraged and expected to manage costs in a proactive way. Cost management is about ways of transforming costs. Indeed, formal staff suggestion scheme programmes can be useful in this regard.

Thirdly, there is an external focus in the sense that it is acknowledged that costs should be incurred within organisations in order to provide customer value and satisfaction. Therefore, it is important to identify which costs add value to customers and which do not.

Finally, there is a growing awareness that a significant proportion of costs are determined at the design rather than the production stage of manufacturing. For example, the number of features included in a new product together with the type of material used will significantly impact on the overall cost of that product. The design of the manufacturing process also impacts on costs. Some Japanese manufacturers operate on the principle that over 70% of their production cost is determined at the design stage. As a result, Japanese firms prefer to spend a great deal of time getting the design stage right and spend considerably less time trying to control or reduce costs at the production stage.

ABC information focuses attention on the things that matter – activities and their related costs. Because ABC focuses attention on the cost of activities, it allows managers to ask whether they can perform an activity more efficiently by changing the process. For example, the range of aircraft used by a carrier significantly impacts on the number of spare parts required and the amount of training required by mechanics. If the range of aircraft used is reduced, then obvious cost reductions can be effected.

Alternatively, managers can ask whether an activity adds value to the customer. **Non-value added activities** are those activities that could be eliminated without reducing product quality, performance or value. In contrast, the feature of a **value added activity** is that a customer is prepared to pay for it, but a customer will only pay for an activity if it provides him with value and satisfaction. If an organisation undertakes even a crude inventory of its activities, it will discover that many activities do not add value to customers. In essence, these are wasteful and should be reduced or eliminated. When action is taken to reduce what causes the activities that consume resources, a lasting reduction in costs takes place.

## ILLUSTRATION OF VALUE ADDED AND NON-VALUE ADDED ACTIVITIES

The following major activities (numbered 1–8) have been identified in the manufacture of a standard consumer product.

1. Quality inspection of materials on arrival
2. Storage of material in warehouse
3. Machining of raw materials in Process 1
4. Moving work-in-progress from Process 1 to Process 2
5. Staff idle time waiting for work to start in Process 2
6. Machining of work-in-progress in Process 2

7. Inspection of finished goods
8. Packaging of goods with instruction leaflet

**Requirement:** Identify the value added and non-value added activities and comment generally on your observations.

**Solution and Analysis:** Value-added activities are those activities that the customer is prepared to pay for. If activities do not add value then they can be considered as wasteful expenditure and should be reduced or eliminated. The only activities which add value are:

3. Machining of raw materials in Process 1
6. Machining of work-in-progress in Process 2
8. Packaging of goods with instruction leaflet

### Non-Value Added Activities

Within organisations, the following types of activities are candidates for elimination because they do not add value to the product:

1. **Storage** Storage of raw materials and finished goods is an obvious non-value added activity. Many companies are turning to the Just in Time (JIT) philosophy for both their purchasing and production needs. A JIT system arranges the delivery of raw materials when they are needed for production and also arranges the production of finished goods only when required by customers. Therefore, one impact of a JIT system is to reduce or eliminate storage of both raw materials and finished goods. (There are also savings in various accounting entries.)
2. **Moving Items** Moving materials around the factory floor is another activity that does not add value to the end product. Redesigning the production process can reduce the amount of materials' movement within the factory.
3. **Waiting for Work** Idle time does not add value. Reducing the amount of time that workers wait on work reduces the overall cost of idle time. Better planning and co-ordination of production can achieve this.
4. **Inspection** It is debatable whether inspection of incoming materials and inspection of finished goods adds value to products. It is realistic to argue that some degree of inspection is necessary and appreciated by customers. However, adding more inspections to a product will not increase the price that customers are prepared to pay for it. In addition, a large amount of inspection costs are incurred due to faulty production, which may be partly due to inferior raw materials. Clearly, it is appropriate to eliminate such wasteful practices which do not add value to the customer.

In conclusion, many companies are using ABC information and techniques to help them 're-engineer' or 'reprocess' the organisation. This means that all the activities and processes in the organisation are analysed – for example, purchasing, production, inspection, distribution, etc. – to identify the extent to which they are necessary and how they can be made more efficient. Processes should be simplified and restructured with non-value added activities targeted for future elimination. Failure to do so is clearly a missed opportunity for cost management.

*Cost Management – Low-Fare Airlines*

It is worthwhile reflecting at this stage on cost management practices within low-cost or low-fare airlines. The idea of a low-cost (and therefore a low-fare) airline was the brainchild of Herb Kelleher and Rollin King when they formed Southwest Airlines in the US in the early 1970s.  Their key business principle was:

> "If you get your passengers to their destinations when they want to get there, on time, at the lowest possible fares, and make darn sure that they have a good time doing it, people will fly your airline." (www.southwest.com)

The idea worked and some other airlines now follow this successful business model with its emphasis on the aggressive management of the overall cost base. Typical business practices include:

- Low-fare airlines buy their aircraft in bulk, and from a single supplier, to save money and it is estimated that discounts of about 30% can be obtained in this manner.
- Passengers book their flights over the Internet, eliminating a standard payment of 15% to travel agents. Appropriate software for booking flights is now relatively cheap and is programmed to deal with different capacity levels, i.e. ticket prices can easily be increased or decreased, depending on available capacity or when extra demand is anticipated, e.g. on the occasion of a major sporting event. In addition, such Websites generate additional advertising revenue.
- Snacks and refreshments are available during flights, so that passengers become an additional source of revenue. Other items are also sold, from watches to scratch cards. In addition, other ancillary services are sold, e.g. car hire, hotels and insurance for which the airline receives a commission.
- Passengers who miss flights do not, generally, receive rebates of either the ticket price or tax paid.
- Such airlines operate a standard fleet, which reduces the cost of pilot training, the number and range of spare parts held in stock, and also maintenance costs.
- Staff costs are kept as low as possible by insisting on flexible work practices. Generally, there is no demarcation and all staff members are expected to help out when required.
- The elimination of business or executive class increases the number of seats in the flight deck, so that more passengers can be accommodated. Also, costs are reduced since first-class passengers require separate check-in facilities, and additional staff is required on board the aircraft.
- Low-cost airlines use secondary airports, having negotiated competitive long-term deals, e.g. cheaper landing and handling charges. This also allows quick turnaround times which results in extra flights per day. Such performance is not possible in large, congested airports.

- Reclining seats are eliminated to reduce maintenance costs and seat pouches have been removed to speed up cleaning of the airplanes.

## 2. Assessing Employee Productivity

Though productivity has been a topic of considerable discussion for a number of years in the fields of general management and economics, readers may be surprised that it is now surfacing in a textbook on managerial accounting. This illustrates how the boundaries of managerial accounting are no longer clearly defined.

What is 'productivity' and why is it considered important? In a general sense, productivity is an economic measure of efficiency, based on what was produced during a period (output) relative to the resources consumed (input). It is usual to calculate productivity at a national level and, in this context, the noted commentator Paul Krugman, in his book *The Age of Diminished Expectations* 3rd Edition (MIT Press, 1997), said: "productivity isn't everything, but in the long run it is almost everything". At a national level, the more productive an economy is – the more effectively it uses capital and labour – the greater its prosperity.

Productivity can also be calculated at a company level or at the level of an individual employee. At a company and individual level, productivity is important for three reasons:

1. Since productivity reflects the relationship between outputs and inputs, it is the primary determinant of a firm's overall profitability and, ultimately, its ability to compete and survive. If a firm is more productive than its competitors it means that it has produced more goods (or services) and these have the potential to generate additional profits for shareholders and reinvestment.
2. Productive employees are more likely to be rewarded for their performance and this requires a transparent incentive system to be in operation within the firm.
3. Efforts to improve productivity in organisations will require the involvement and agreement of workers and often involves staff training. Without prior agreement, there may be employee resistance because they perceive that the introduction of a productivity programme threatens their job security.

Some commentators make a subtle distinction between efficiency and productivity. Efficiency is calculated using the financial amount of inputs and, therefore, a typical efficiency measure would be the cost per unit, which could also be referred to as **financial productivity**. Productivity, on the other hand, is measured by physical inputs. Thus, a typical productivity measure would be the number of units produced per hour and this could be referred to as **operational productivity**.

ABC information can be used in assessing employee productivity since it focuses on various activities performed by employees and it is especially applicable where these activities are repetitive. Productivity targets can be based on the previous year's performance or set with reference to the performance of another unit within the organisation. Alternatively, there is no reason why productivity of different firms cannot be compared provided the data collection process is similar.

## ILLUSTRATION OF ASSESSING EMPLOYEE PRODUCTIVITY

The Monivea Bank wishes to compare the productivity of teller clerks in two of its branches that are adjacent to each other. For comparison purposes, it uses an overall productivity measure for each branch, as defined by the percentage ratio of the standard workload hours for work completed to total actual teller hours worked during the week. Each teller works a 40-hour week. The standard workload (in number of minutes) is determined based on the following work model which uses only three activities, i.e. cash withdrawals, cash lodgements and FX transactions, and the estimated time (minutes) taken per activity is as follows:

Standard workload (minutes) = (2 × Cash withdrawal + 3 × Cash deposit + 4 × FX transaction)

The above work standards automatically include rest and inactive time and are based on actual workload completed and reported by each teller. The following information was reported by the teller clerks for a recent week of operations for the two branches:

| Branch | No. of tellers | No. of withdrawals | No. of lodgements | FX transactions |
|---|---|---|---|---|
| 1 | 6 | 1,000 | 1,600 | 800 |
| 2 | 12 | 2,400 | 2,200 | 1,200 |

**Requirement:** Calculate (using minutes) the productivity ratio for both branches for the week.

**Solution and Analysis:**

| | Cash withdrawals | Cash lodgements | FX transactions | Total minutes required | Total minutes available | Productivity % |
|---|---|---|---|---|---|---|
| **Branch 1** | 1,000 | 1,600 | 800 | | | |
| Standard | 2 mins | 3 mins | 4 mins | | | |
| Minutes | 2,000 | 4,800 | 3,200 | 10,000 | 14,400 | 69% |
| | | | | | (6×40×60) | |

| Branch 2 | 2,400 | 2,200 | 1,200 | | | |
| Standard | 2 mins | 3 mins | 4 mins | | | |
| Minutes | 4,800 | 6,600 | 4,800 | 16,200 | 28,800 (12×40×60) | 56% |

Based on the agreed productivity ratio, i.e. standard workload hours for work completed time as a percentage of actual hours worked, Branch 1 is more productive than Branch 2. The causes of this discrepancy need to be investigated and management should also be aware of the underlying trend in both productivity ratios. In addition, it would be appropriate if teller clerks were evaluated with reference to suitable non-financial measures of performance. (We shall discuss this in greater depth in **Chapter 8, Sections 8.2** and **8.3**.) For the time being, the following non-financial measures of performance could be used in assessing the overall performance of its teller clerks:

- Customer satisfaction index
- Queuing time in bank
- Number of lost customers (which could reflect poor customer satisfaction)
- Bad debts (non-performing loans)

## 5.4 Customer Profitability Analysis

The dynamic and competitive business environment in recent decades has led organisations to respond to competition, for example by increasing the level of customer service and promoting greater customer satisfaction. Organisations recognise that, if they do not respond effectively to the changes in the business environment, problems will occur which may be reflected in lost revenue opportunities or increased levels of customer dissatisfaction relative to the competition. This phenomenon highlights a contradiction of modern management – companies proclaim that they are 'customer focused', but their management accounting systems are not. Specifically, it is argued that many companies fail to correctly measure the overall profitability of different segments of its customer base. However, it is interesting to note that the concept of Customer Profitability Analysis is not new. For example, Magee (1933) argued that:

> "...the total expense for which each product is responsible is determined by a variety of considerations and not by its selling price, and it will be readily appreciated that wide variations in the ratio of expense to selling price, and therefore in the final margin of net profit, may easily occur (and) one product may be sold with a minimum of advertising and sales effort and another may

require constant stimulation...a manufacturer should ask where should I sell and to whom?" ("The Practical Control of Selling Expense: An Examination of Distribution Accounting", *The Accountant*, 7 and 14 October 1933, p.582)

Since no two customers are the same, even when they are in receipt of an identical product, the starting point is to separate customers with reference to their overall profitability, i.e. revenue less cost. Cost is made up of its two key elements:

- cost-to-serve (how much it normally costs to provide the customer with the product and service) and
- risk-to-serve (covering a menu of activities such as potential bad debts, returned products, service call-outs, calls to help lines, repairs against warranty and so on).

## ILLUSTRATION OF CUSTOMER PROFITABILITY ANALYSIS

The Waterpark Bank has experienced a reduction in overall profitability in recent years. It has been suggested that an activity-based costing (ABC) system may help in analyzing customer profitability. A task force examined the customer services section activities and related costs which is responsible for five major activities, namely: (1) processing lodgements, (2) processing cheques, (3) processing cash withdrawals, (4) servicing customer enquiries, together with account maintenance, and (5) opening new accounts. The task force has identified the following information regarding customer service support costs and activities for a recent month:

| Support Activity | Estimated cost € | Activity cost driver | Monthly level |
|---|---|---|---|
| Processing lodgements | 60,000 | No. of lodgements processed | 15,000 |
| Processing cheques | 35,000 | No. of cheques processed | 70,000 |
| Processing cash withdrawals | 28,000 | No. of withdrawals processed | 14,000 |
| Servicing customer enquiries | 20,000 | No. of customer enquiries | 10,000 |
| Opening new accounts | 7,000 150,000 | No. of accounts opened | 500 |

The task force has developed the following inventory of activities for two typical groups of customers: (a) a retired customer, and (b) a business client. Each customer requires, on average, the following:

| Support activity | Average monthly volume | |
|---|---|---|
| | Retired person | Business client |
| Processing lodgements | 2 lodgements | 24 lodgements |
| Processing cheques | 10 cheques | 150 cheques |
| Processing cash withdrawals | 6 withdrawals | 4 withdrawals |
| Servicing customer enquiries | 2 enquiries | 14 enquiries |
| Opening new accounts | ½ per month | 2 per month |

**Requirement:** Using the above information obtained as part of the pilot study, present calculations relating to customer profitability for both groups of clients. The monthly fees charged amount to €10 for a retired customer and €200 for a business client. Comment on both the methodology and implications of your figures for managerial decision-making.

**Solution and Analysis:** The first step is to calculate the cost driver rate for each of the five activities. This is done by dividing the estimated costs by the estimated costs driver level. Thus, for processing lodgements, the estimated monthly cost is €60,000, which is divided by 15,000 transactions to provide the cost driver rate of €4 per transaction processed. The individual calculations are presented below:

| Computation of Cost Driver Rate | | | | |
|---|---|---|---|---|
| Activity | Estimated costs € | Activity cost drivers | Cost driver level | Cost driver rate |
| Processing lodgements | 60,000 | No. of lodgements processed | 15,000 | €4.00 |
| Processing cheques | 35,000 | No. of cheques processed | 70,000 | €0.50 |
| Processing withdrawals | 28,000 | No. of withdrawals processed | 14,000 | €2.00 |
| Servicing enquiries | 20,000 | No. of enquiries | 10,000 | €2.00 |
| Opening new accounts | <u>7,000</u><br>150,000 | No. of accounts opened | 500 | €14.00 |

The second step is to assign the various activity costs to each customer segment, based on their estimated usage of those activities. Thus, a retired person makes, on average, two lodgements per month. Since each lodgement costs €4 to process, the total cost of this activity is €8 for this customer. The costs of each of the five activities for retired clients are provided below. When compared with the monthly fee of €10, then this (retired) customer segment shows a loss of €26 per customer.

| Monthly Profitability (Loss) of a Retired Customer | | | |
|---|---|---|---|
| Activity | Average monthly volume | Activity cost driver rate € | Total support costs for retired customer € |
| Process lodgements | 2 | €4.00 | 8 |
| Process cheques | 10 | €0.50 | 5 |
| Process withdrawals | 6 | €2.00 | 12 |
| Servicing enquiries | 2 | €2.00 | 4 |
| Open new account | ½ | €14.00 | 7 |
| Total costs | | | 36 |
| Total fee per month | | | 10 |
| Profit (Loss) per month | | | (26) |

The same process applies to ascertaining the profitability, or otherwise, of business clients. Since business clients make, on average, 24 lodgements per month and each lodgement costs €4 to process, the total cost of this activity is €96 for business clients. The cost of each of the five activities for business clients are provided below. When compared with the monthly fee of €200, then this customer segment shows a loss, on average of €35 per customer.

This pilot study reveals that both customer segments are loss-makers. However, this conclusion depends entirely on the accuracy of the figures used together with the validity of using monthly data. There is a strong argument that the time horizon should be broadened. It could be argued that the customer segmentation is too small, i.e. only two customer groups. Additional segments could be added. Also, it should be recognised that, treated as a separate section, customer support services would generally be a loss-maker in its own right. Therefore, it may be appropriate to include other revenue items such as interest received from loans advanced. It should be noted that, inevitably, the issue of cost apportionment is always present in ABC. For example, many customers would simultaneously engage in two or more transactions, e.g. making of lodgements and withdrawing cash.

| Monthly Profitability (Loss) of a Business Customer | | | |
|---|---|---|---|
| Activity | Average monthly volume | Activity cost driver rate € | Total support costs for business client € |
| Process lodgements | 24 | €4.00 | 96 |
| Process cheques | 150 | €0.50 | 75 |
| Process withdrawals | 4 | €2.00 | 8 |
| Servicing enquiries | 14 | €2.00 | 28 |
| Open new account | 2 | €14.00 | 28 |
| Total costs | | | 235 |
| Total fee per month | | | 200 |
| Profit (Loss) per month | | | (35) |

The above analysis confirms that an ABC system is feasible but the current proposal needs to be refined. While the figures in this illustration are contrived it highlights that the most expensive activity is that of opening a new account. In order to facilitate cost reduction, managers will need to determine why it is so expensive to open new accounts. For example, it may be due to the time involved in opening a new account, e.g. formalities to be completed, and this has the potential to impact significantly on potential customers.

### Benefits and Problems of Customer Profitability Analysis

Customer profitability analysis (CPA) information can facilitate decision-making within an organisation by distinguishing between profitable and unprofitable customers.

Obviously, unprofitable customers could be deleted from the customer line with immediate effect. However, care is required in responding to CPA information. Some customers may be currently unprofitable, yet have the potential to generate profits in the future by increasing, for example, the number of units requested.

In addition, it may be feasible to charge unprofitable customers for some of the services that they require. In many cases, when it is pointed out to customers that such services (activities) are costly, they are prepared to pay extra for those services, or, are willing to curtail their demand for those services, e.g. special delivery times.

Alternatively, it may be possible to deliver low costs methods of dealing with unprofitable customers. For example, it is much more cost effective for banks to process transactions using ATMs rather than providing a personal service from bank tellers. Therefore, if a customer wants a personalised teller service, he will have to travel to his branch where he may encounter a long queue in front of the only teller. This sends a strong signal to customers to transact electronically, not personally.

Finally, some companies will retain unprofitable customers due to the prestige involved, e.g. providing free jewellery or clothes to famous fashion models.

## Difficulties with Customer Profitability Analysis

The difficulties and challenges that are associated with undertaking customer profitability analysis should also be noted. These include the difficulties of obtaining reliable and accurate cost and revenue data in order to carry out CPA. These problems arise from the fact that many organisations have a dispersed customer base that uses different distribution channels and purchasing locations.

An added complication is that there are at least **three ways to analyse customer profitability**:

1. The first approach is to base calculations on a transaction by transaction basis, i.e. the difference between revenue generated by the transaction less costs incurred in supplying the customer. However, the vast number of transactions virtually precludes this method of analysis. In any event, the focus of the analysis is too narrow as a customer may be deemed profitable on one transaction but not another. For example, immediately after a product has been sold, but before a warranty claim, a customer may look profitable. Then, if one isolates a second transaction involving a subsequent warranty claim, the customer would be unprofitable! Another problem with this approach is that the customer may be going through a lifestyle change so that successive transactions are either increasingly more profitable or less profitable.

2. The second approach to customer profitability analysis groups all transactions during the current accounting period. This has the advantage of using a longer time frame and therefore captures the full revenue stream, less related costs, during the accounting period. However, being based on historical data, it ignores the future spending patterns of identified customers.

3. The third approach is based on 'expected' or 'lifetime' profitability — the profitability of the customer over the expected lifetime of the relationship. However, this is very difficult to estimate since it depends on several unknown factors, such as the likelihood of the customer's failure or switching to a competitor. This simply confirms that future income and costs are difficult to predict, especially in the context of customer profitability analysis.

In summary, customer profitability analysis is being increasingly viewed as a highly beneficial activity within businesses. It is a powerful analytical tool that puts the customer at the centre of managerial attention. It recognises that no two customers are the same even if they are in receipt of an identical product or service. However, a key difficulty in applying CPA is that today's unprofitable customer may be tomorrow's profitable customer. And, the reverse may also be true.

## 5.5 Limitations of Activity-based Costing

ABC is not without its critics, who point to its limitations, and a few of these can be mentioned here:

1. Identifying suitable cost pools can be problematic since the number of activities performed within a business is typically vast. Ordinarily, many tasks must be aggregated into a small number of specific activity pools. Unfortunately, as more and more tasks are aggregated into an activity, the ability of a cost driver to trace accurately the resources consumed by products decreases. Furthermore, in many cases there can be two or more cost drivers of which one must be selected. For example, machine set-up costs may be driven either by the number of set-ups or the duration of individual set-ups.

2. ABC does not eliminate the arbitrary apportionment problem in cost accounting – for example, a single purchase order may contain items used on several different products.

3. The implementation of ABC systems may create adverse behavioural and organisational consequences. For example, where a manager reduces the number of set-ups because of their costly nature, the effect is to produce more units per batch and thereby increase stock levels with related costs. In addition, the new product information associated with ABC may sometimes meet resistance within the organisation, e.g. the sales department of the company may not be happy with the new ABC cost figures, which suggest eliminating some products. Furthermore, employees may perceive the introduction of ABC as part of a process to justify subsequent redundancies. In such circumstances, employees may feel threatened and may be reluctant to co-operate and provide the initial information on which the operation of the ABC system will be based. The behavioural dimension is important as ABC requires a willingness by all participants to accept new ideas and practices.

4. Some management accountants are reluctant to change the internal accounting system with which they are familiar. This is particularly the case in the context of financial reporting. For financial reporting purposes, stocks must be valued at 'cost', which comprises material costs, direct conversion costs, production overheads and any other overheads in bringing the product to its present location and condition. On the other hand, ABC considers all costs (production and non-production) as being part of product costs. Non-production costs cannot be used for stock valuation purposes in accordance with accounting standards. Thus, it is

unlikely that (unadjusted) ABC product costs would be acceptable for stock valuation purposes in financial reporting. Finally, most ABC information will be historically based. While this information has an important role in cost control and cost management it may require suitable adjustment for use in decision-making.

However, the main disadvantage of ABC is the cost of establishing such a system. An ABC system is more expensive to set up and maintain than a traditional costing system because an organization has first to consider all of its overhead costs (production and non-production) and try to align the main activities with suitable cost pools and cost drivers. There are no standard rules as to what these major activities should be and they will differ in each organisation.

Implementation of ABC is a very time-consuming process. Furthermore, organisations may lack in-house expertise with ABC and would therefore need to hire external consultants to assist with the design and implementation. In addition, having implemented ABC, a significant cost is incurred in maintaining the ABC system as activities have to be regularly reviewed to ensure that there is a continuing relationship between overheads, cost pools and cost drivers. Therefore, the introduction of a new system must be evaluated in the context of cost/benefit analysis. There are many reasons why ABC systems might not provide net benefits for some companies due to, for example, the cost of implementation, small company size, low amount of overheads or a single product company.

Given the work and time required to establish an ABC system, it would be inappropriate to expect all companies to adopt it. However, it should be noted that an ABC system could be used in parallel with the regular accounting system by loading the relevant data into appropriate computer software every quarter. In this situation, the ABC data can be manipulated in a spreadsheet format, viewed and arranged to provide relevant information to managers.

## Conclusion

In summary, this chapter has highlighted the technique of ABC which is an alternative costing system and differs from traditional cost accounting in the way that overheads are assigned to units of output. It is argued that ABC provides more accurate product costs. In addition, it facilitates cost management practices within firms and provides a solid basis for improved customer profitability analysis. In the next three chapters we will continue our discussion on some of the developments taking place within the discipline of management accounting. First, we discuss the changes fashioned by the World Class Manufacturing (WCM) philosophy and this is followed by a discussion on Strategy (**Chapter 7**) and Performance Measurement (**Chapter 8**).

## SUMMARY OF LEARNING OBJECTIVES

**Learning Objective 1:** Present the limitations of traditional cost accounting systems.

Traditional cost accounting (TCA) assumes that all overheads are volume related and are best assigned to products using a cost driver such as direct labour hours. However, in some industries direct labour is a relatively small cost element. Furthermore, overheads are caused by complexity and are driven by 'transactions', such as machine set up, which are often independent of volume of output.

**Learning Objective 2**: Contrast and compare activity-based costing and traditional cost accounting systems.

TCA initially traces overheads to departments and then absorbs them using volume based cost drivers such as direct labour hours. In contrast, ABC recognises the existence of several activity cost pools and assigns overhead to products using activity-based cost drivers. However, the objective of both systems are the same – to trace overhead cost to units of output.

**Learning Objective 3**: Calculate product costs using ABC.

Product costs, using several activity cost pools and activity-based cost drivers were presented in the exhibits and illustrations in this chapter.

**Learning Objective 4**: Describe the nature of activity-based cost management.

Activity-based cost management (ABCM) focuses on various activities within the firm and identifies if they are value-adding or non-value adding activities. In addition, activities are scrutinised to see whether they can be performed in a different or in a more economical way.

**Learning Objective 5**: Prepare customer profitability calculations.

Customer profitability calculations, based on ABC information, were presented in the exhibits and illustrations in this chapter. However, unprofitable customers should not be deleted without first identifying the cause, relevance and future potential of such customer groups.

**Learning Objective 6**: Describe the limitations of ABC.

While conceptually better than TCA, ABC suffers from the limitation of being complex, costly and time-consumings to implement and operate. Furthermore, in situations such as single product firms with low overheads, ABC and TCA figures may be similar.

## Questions

### Review Questions

(See Appendix One for Solutions to Review Questions **5.1** and **5.2**)

### Question 5.1 (*Limitations of TCA and advantages of ABC*)

Suggest why companies might decide to introduce an ABC system and indicate what difficulties companies might experience with trying to implement it.

### Question 5.2 (*Traditional Cost Accounting v. Activity-based Costing*)

(**Note:** this question is divided into two parts.)

### Part 1

The Alpha Company produces two different executive office chairs, namely Product X and Y, which are sold for €70 and €100 respectively. For convenience purposes production takes place within a single department and we shall *ignore non-production costs*. Production overheads amount to €1,000,000. For illustration purposes we shall initially assume that the company uses a traditional cost accounting system whereby production overheads are absorbed on the basis of direct labour hours. You are provided with the following information:

|  | Product X | Product Y | Total |
|---|---|---|---|
| Production and sales (units) | 25,000 units | 5,000 units | 30,000 units |
| Direct materials cost per unit | €25 | €20 |  |
| Total direct materials cost | — | — | €725,000 |
| Direct labour hours per unit | 15 hours | 5 hours |  |
| Direct labour cost per unit | €15 | €5 |  |
| Total direct labour hours | — | — | 400,000 |
| Total direct labour cost | — | — | €400,000 |
| Total production overhead costs | — | — | €1,000,000 |

**Requirements:**

1. Prepare a summary of the overall cost structure (with %), based on the above information. What comments are obvious? Please note that only the total for each cost

element (i.e. direct materials, direct labour and production overhead) needs to be calculated.
2. Calculate the plant-wide overhead absorption rate (OHAR) using direct labour hours as the cost driver and calculate the unit cost for each product. What are your initial conclusions in terms of each product's profitability, if the selling prices are €70 for X and €100 for Y?

## Part 2

The Managing Director of Alpha Company has recently attended a seminar on Activity-based Costing (ABC). During the seminar he was impressed at the quality of arguments made by the various speakers that traditional cost accounting systems can distort product costs by using volume-based overhead cost drivers.

He obtained information from his management accountant on Alpha's overhead costs, which were divided into three categories. The first, and largest, was the cost of material ordering. This was because Alpha only use quality raw materials and these were difficult to obtain from reliable suppliers. As a result, one full-time employee was required to travel the world, at regular intervals, to source raw materials. The second and third cost pools were self-explanatory and related to the cost of setting up machines for production runs and, finally, inspection of finished goods, as part of the firm's quality initiative.

The following data pertains to overhead costs and related information:

| Cost pools | Overheads € | Cost drivers |
|---|---|---|
| Materials ordering | €700,000 | Number of orders |
| Machine set-up | €120,000 | Number of machine set-ups |
| Inspections | €180,000 | Number of inspections |
| Total production overhead costs | €1,000,000 | |

| Other operating data: | Product X | Product Y | Total |
|---|---|---|---|
| Materials ordering (per product line and total) | 25 orders | 10 orders | 35 orders |
| Number of machine set-ups (per product line and total) | 40 set-ups | 200 set-ups | 240 set-ups |
| Number of inspections (per product line and total) | 400 inspections | 800 inspections | 1,200 inspections |
| Product and sales (units) | 25,000 units | 5,000 units | 30,000 units |

## Requirement:

3. Calculate the unit cost for each product under Activity-based Costing, based on the above information.

## Intermediate Level Questions

### Question 5.3 (Traditional Cost Accounting v Activity-based Cost Accounting)

(**Note**: this question is divided into two parts.)

## Part 1

The Beta Company produces two metal products, X and Y, to be used in machine making and assembly. The products are produced for a variety of customers at different times of the year and in different quantities. The company uses a traditional cost accounting system whereby overheads are absorbed into products using direct labour hours.

The manager of the company has provided you with the following information relating to a recent accounting year:

|  |  | Product X | Product Y | Total |
|---|---|---|---|---|
| Production and sales | units | 20,000 | 10,000 | 30,000 |
| Unit data |  |  |  |  |
| Unit selling price | € | €60 | €40 | — |
| Direct material cost | € | €20 | €10 | — |
| Total material costs | € | — | — | €500,000 |
| Direct labour hours | Hours | 1 | 0.5 | 25,000 hours |
| Direct labour costs | € | €10 | €5 | €250,000 |
| Overheads | € | ?? | ?? | €800,000 |

## Requirements:

1. Prepare a summarised income statement for the above accounting period. It is not necessary to assign costs to individual products.
2. Calculate the overhead absorption rate, based on direct labour hours and calculate the unit cost of each product.

## Part 2

The managing director of Beta Company has recently attended a seminar on activity-based costing (ABC). During the seminar he was impressed at the quality of arguments made by the various speakers that traditional cost accounting systems have the ability to distort product costs by using volume-based overhead cost drivers. The following information was relevant for unit costing purposes and relates to a recent accounting year:

|  |  | Product X | Product Y | Total |
|---|---|---|---|---|
| Production and sales |  | 20,000 | 10,000 | 30,000 |
| Unit data |  |  |  |  |
| Unit selling price | € | €60 | €40 | — |
| Direct material cost | € | €20 | €10 | — |
| Direct labour costs | € | €10 | €5 | €250,000 |
| Machine hours | Hours | 1 m/hr | 2 m/hrs | 40,000 m/hours |
| Overheads | € | — | — | €800,000 |

In addition, the manager obtained information from his management accountant on Beta's overhead costs which were divided into three categories. The first, and largest, was the cost of machine processing the two products. In fact, both products required extensive machine operations with minimal direct labour content. The second and third cost pools were self-explanatory and related to the cost of setting up machines for different production runs and, finally, inspection of finished goods, as part of the firm's quality initiative.

The following information concerns overhead costs and related information:

| Activity cost pool | Overhead € | Product X | Product Y | Total |
|---|---|---|---|---|
| Machining | 500,000 | 20,000 m/hours | 20,000 m/hours | 40,000 m/hours |
| Set-up | 100,000 | 5 set ups | 20 set ups | 25 set ups |
| Inspection | 200,000 | 10 inspections | 40 inspections | 50 inspections |
| Total overhead | 800,000 |  |  |  |

**Requirements:**

3. Calculate the cost driver rates for each of the above activity cost pools and use this information to calculate unit product costs under ABC.
4. Calculate the total costs incurred (direct and overhead) during the year using: (a) TCA and (b) ABC, assuming sales of X and Y amounted to 20,000 and 10,000 units respectively. Why are the total costs the same under both alternatives?

5. What are your objections to or observations of using the 'number of inspections' as the cost driver for inspection costs?
6. Briefly suggest how the above ABC information could be used to ascertain the profitability of different customers.

## Question 5.4 (Product Line Profitability under Traditional Cost Accounting and Activity-Based Cost Accounting)

Cappa Company manufactures three soft drink products for the consumer market. The products are manufactured in different quantities, at different times during the year, for different customers. There are two separate processes involved in the manufacture of these drinks. The first process is labour intensive as it involves mixing and testing the various ingredients. The second process is machine intensive and involves filling, sealing and stamping the bottles with the various liquids. The two processes are referred to as mixing and filling respectively. However, for convenience purposes, the company absorbs all its production overheads on the basis of direct labour hours (DLH). The selling and distribution costs are the responsibility of the administration department.

The manager has recently attended a seminar detailing some of the recent developments in management accounting. One development that caught his attention was that of activity-based costing as he could see its potential in terms of the quality of financial data within his company. He asks for your assistance and has provided you with the following information relating to the most recent financial year:

|  | A | B | C | Total |
|---|---|---|---|---|
| Production and sales (units) | 50,000 | 35,000 | 5,000 | |
| Selling price per unit (€) | €25 | €30 | €35 | |
| Direct materials (€) | €3 | €2 | €1 | |
| Direct labour (€) | €6 | €8 | €4 | |
| DLH per unit | 1.5 hours | 2 hours | 1 hours | 150,000 hours |
| Machine hours per unit | 4 hours | 2 hours | 10 hours | 320,000 hours |
| No. of Production runs | 5 runs | 10 runs | 13 runs | 28 runs |
| No. of Deliveries | 2 deliveries | 13 deliveries | 25 deliveries | 40 deliveries |

| | A | B | C | Total |
|---|---|---|---|---|
| **Overhead costs** | | | | € |
| Set-up overhead costs | | | | 140,000 |
| Mixing overhead costs | | | | 600,000 |
| Filling overhead costs | | | | 160,000 |
| SDA overhead costs | | | | 500,000 |

**Requirements:**

1. Calculate the unit cost of each product under the traditional approach to product costing, with emphasis on financial reporting purposes, i.e. that all production overheads are absorbed on the basis of direct labour hours. Prepare a product line profitability statement in terms of total revenue and total attributable costs, apportioning selling and administration costs on the basis of sales revenue.
2. Calculate the unit cost of each product under activity-based costing (ABC), using the above four cost pools (set-up, mixing, filling and SDA) and selecting the appropriate cost drivers. Prepare a product line profitability statement in terms of total revenues and total attributable costs for each of the three product lines.

*Question 5.5 (Traditional Cost Accounting v Activity-Based Cost Accounting)*

(**Note:** this question is in two parts.)

**Part 1**

The New Daley Company is a manufacturer of electrical components that are used by computer manufacturers overseas. The company manufactures to order and, when each job is finished (and inspected), it is dispatched by special courier to the customer. The current costing system of New Daley Company has two direct cost categories, namely direct materials and direct labour, with direct labour being paid at the rate of €25 per hour.

In addition, production overhead is absorbed into products using a single overhead absorption rate based on direct labour hours. The total overheads for the year amount to €880,000 and the estimated amount of direct labour hours is 8,000 hours giving an OHAR of €110 per direct labour hour, based on annual and budgeted information. The manager of the company wants you to cost two jobs that the company is producing and the following information is provided to you:

|  | Job order 410 | Job order 411 |
|---|---|---|
| Direct material cost | €9,700 | €59,900 |
| Direct labour cost | €750 | €11,250 |
| Direct labour hours required | 25 | 375 |

**Requirement:**

1. Compute the cost of each job under the existing (traditional) costing system, i.e. using direct labour hours as the only cost driver for the plant.

**Part 2**

The New Daley Company is a machine precision manufacturer of metal components that are used by computer manufacturers overseas. The company manufactures to order and, when each job is finished (and inspected), it is dispatched by special courier. The current costing system of New Daley Products has two direct cost categories, namely direct materials and direct labour, with direct labour being paid at the rate of €25 per hour. In addition, the total overheads for the year amount to €880,000.

The manager of the company wants you to cost two jobs that the company is producing and the following information is provided to you:

|  | Job order 410 | Job order 411 |
|---|---|---|
| Direct material cost | €9,700 | €59,900 |
| Direct labour cost | €750 | €11,250 |

Recently, the managing director attended a management seminar and, as a result, he is considering implementing an ABC system based on the following cost pools and cost drivers:

| Cost pool | Overhead costs | Cost driver | Cost driver level |
|---|---|---|---|
| Material handling | € 50,000 | No. of parts | 40,000 |
| Lathe work | € 20,000 | No. of turns | 100,000 |
| Inspection | €360,000 | No. of inspections | 18,000 |
| Dispatch | €450,000 | No. of shipments | 300 |
|  | €880,000 |  |  |

Information technology has advanced to the point where all the necessary data for budgeting in these four activity areas are automatically collected. By way of testing the overall accuracy and usefulness of the proposed new system, the following information was obtained for two job orders completed during a recent period, in addition to the direct cost information already provided:

|  | Job order 410 | Job order 411 |
| --- | --- | --- |
| No. of component parts per job | 500 | 2,000 |
| No. of lathe turns per job | 20,000 | 60,000 |
| No. of inspections | 15 | 100 |
| No. of shipments | 1 | 1 |

**Requirements:**

2. Assume the company adopts an activity-based accounting system based on the four activity cost pools provided. Calculate the cost driver rate for each of the four cost pools and compute the cost of each job under the activity-based accounting system.
3. Briefly explain why TCA figures can vary from ABC product cost figures.

*Question 5.6    (Activity-based Costing)*

The Cheesecake Shop is a national bakery that produces different kinds of cheesecake. The company operates a traditional cost accounting system whereby production overheads are absorbed on the basis of direct labour hours. For the accounting period under review, total overheads are budgeted at €335,000, together with direct labour hours of 15,000.

One of its famous products is called the Strawberry Cheesecake for which the following information is available:

| Annual production | 40,000 units |
| --- | --- |
| Direct materials per unit | €5 |
| Direct labour cost per unit | €1 (6 minutes per cheesecake) |

However, the managing director of the firm recently attended a seminar on ABC and has asked your assistance in applying ABC principles to the Strawberry Cheesecake, for which he has presented you with the following information:

| Cost pool | Cost | Cost driver |
| --- | --- | --- |
| Materials ordering | € 60,000 | Number of purchase orders |
| Materials inspection | € 80,000 | Number of receiving reports |
| Equipment set up | €75,000 | Number of set ups |
| Quality control | €45,000 | Number of final inspections |
| Other | €75,000 | Direct labour hours |
| Total | €335,000 | |

Annual activity information related to cost drivers:

| Cost pool | All products | Strawberry cheesecake |
|---|---|---|
| Materials ordering | 7,500 orders | 2,000 |
| Materials inspection | 400 receiving reports | 50 |
| Equipment set up | 2,000 set ups | 20 |
| Quality control | 2,000 final inspections | 100 |
| Miscellaneous | 15,000 direct labour hours | 4,000 |

**Requirements:**

1. Using traditional cost accounting i.e. a single plant-wide rate based on DLH, determine the OHAR per DLH and calculate the total unit cost for the Strawberry Cheesecake.
2. Using ABC, calculate the total unit cost (direct cost and overhead cost) for the Strawberry Cheesecake.
3. Discuss the general difference between TCA and ABC methodologies.

*Question 5.7 (Activity Analysis and Employee Productivity)*

The Broke Bank has a number of retail branches in the Dublin area and uses activity analysis to assess the productivity of its cash tellers on a weekly basis. Employee productivity is measured by the ratio of output i.e. total activities performed by branch tellers during the accounting period, multiplied by the agreed standard time allowance for each activity, divided by the total time worked in that branch for the reporting week. For example, if a branch processes 1,000 cash withdrawals during the week, and each cash withdrawal has a standard time allowance of 3 minutes, then the outputs for that week is equivalent to 3,000 minutes. The employee productivity formula used, and which has been agreed by union representatives, is as follows:

$$\text{Employee productivity} = \frac{\text{Total activities multiplied by standard time allowance}}{\text{Total time available during week}} \times 100 = \%$$

Essentially, three activities have been identified for each cash teller, i.e. processing a cash withdrawal, making an account deposit and, finally, transferring funds between accounts, e.g. from a deposit account to a current account, on behalf of the client.

The standard time allowance for processing each cash withdrawal is three minutes, for each account deposit it is two minutes and, for each transfer of funds between accounts, the standard time allowance is 1 minute. Total workload (in minutes) for each branch is estimated based on the following equation:

$$\text{Workload} = (3 \times \text{Withdrawal}) + (2 \times \text{Deposit}) + (1 \times \text{Account Transfer})$$

Management are concerned about the productivity of a particular branch, which employs eight cash tellers. Each teller works (and is paid for) a 40-hour week, with four weeks per month. Reported teller transactions for a particular month are as follows:

| Week | Cash Withdrawals | Deposits | Account Transfers |
|------|------------------|----------|-------------------|
| 1 | 1,450 | 1,900 | 650 |
| 2 | 1,600 | 2,000 | 700 |
| 3 | 1,550 | 1,800 | 650 |
| 4 | 1,650 | 1,900 | 650 |

**Requirements:**

1. For the above branch, calculate overall productivity ratio for each week using the formula provided and agreed.
2. What comments would you make on the employee productivity system as it is outlined above?

## Advanced Level Questions

*Question 5.8 (Traditional Cost Accounting v. Activity-based Cost Accounting)*

Astra limited produces three products by similar processes on the same processing machinery which is a machine intensive process due to the acquisition of new technology.

Product L is a low volume product:       1,000 units
Product M is a medium volume product:       5,000 units
Product H is a high volume product:       10,000 units

The company uses a traditional cost accounting (TCA) system in that production overheads are absorbed on the basis of direct labour hours. The total production overhead cost of the three products in the six-month budget period is €480,000; an analysis shows that 50% of the total overhead cost is related to the machine processing, 20% is related to purchasing of direct materials and 30% relates to the set-up of production machines.

The company is currently considering changing to an activity-based cost system of absorption of overheads and the output details for the six-month period are as follows:

| Product | Machine hours per unit | DL Hours per unit | Total machine hours | Total labour hours | No. of purchase orders | No. of set ups |
|---------|------------------------|-------------------|---------------------|--------------------|------------------------|----------------|
| Low | 1 | 2 | 1,000 | 2,000 | 180 | 40 |
| Medium | 1 | 2 | 5,000 | 10,000 | 300 | 100 |
| High | 1 | 2 | 10,000 | 20,000 | 480 | 160 |

**Requirements:**

1. Calculate the overhead recovery rate per unit using the existing direct labour hour method.
2. Calculate the overhead recovery rates per unit for each of the three products if an activity-based costing system were adopted.
3. Compare the unit overhead recovery rates per unit for Products Low and High under the methods utilised in (1) and (2). Discuss the factors causing the difference in the unit overhead rates, and comment on the implications for product profitability.

Source: Chartered Accountants Ireland, Management Accounting and Business Finance, Paper 3,
Summer 1999 (adapted)

*Question 5.9 (Activity-based Costing in a Hospital)*

The Emly Hospital is a small hospital with limited facilities. It operates in the public healthcare sector and, in accordance with recent government directives, it is required to cover its day-to-day operating costs from revenue generated from patients. It is not allowed to borrow money but its capital costs for new equipment are provided directly by the Health Service Executive (HSE).

The newly-appointed manager of the Emly hospital has invited you to discuss their existing costing system and to suggest how activity-based costing could assist in the better management of the hospital. She asks you as a starting point to review the costing system in the Radiology (X-ray) department. She states:

> "We currently work out a cost per X-ray for which we bill the patient. I'm not happy that our approach reflects the complexity of the X-ray department activities. Could you review our calculations and figures and make some preliminary suggestions?"

You are provided with the following six cost elements for the Radiology Department and other operating data for the most recent financial year (20x5):

| Costs of Radiology Department | Costs 20x5 € |
|---|---|
| Wages of machine operator (for taking X-rays) | 25,000 |
| Wage costs for film processing (for processing X-rays) | 20,000 |
| Depreciation of X-ray equipment | 57,400 |
| Cost of X-ray film (1,000 metres @ €40/metre) | 40,000 |
| Cost of processing chemicals for X-rays (1,000 kgs @ €15/kg) | 15,000 |
| Electricity costs | 21,600 |
| Total radiology costs per annum | 179,000 |
| Total number of X-ray images performed | 1,900 X-rays |
| Average cost per X-ray | €95 (rounded) |

On checking the Website, you discover that the mission of the Radiology Department is to provide "doctors with information to allow them to diagnose and offer appropriate treatment for illnesses as speedily and safely as possible". You also discover that there are three types of service offered by the department: (ordinary) X-rays; Magnetic Resonance Imaging (MRI); and Positron Emission Tomography (PET) scans. During the year (20x5) a total of 600 (ordinary) X-rays, 500 MRI scans and 800 PET scans were performed by the Radiology Department.

Your discussion with the staff in the Radiology Department generated the following information and confirmed that the activities in the department are more complicated than you imagined. These activities are divided into two phases: taking the X-rays, and processing the X-rays.

The first phase involves taking the image of each patient. The duration (i.e. minutes) of each image varies. For example, ordinary X-rays last 15 minutes on average, MRI scans typically last 30 minutes and PET scans last 60 minutes. Cost elements, such as wages of the machine operator, depreciation of X-ray equipment together with electricity costs are generally determined by the duration (i.e. minutes) of each type of image taken. In addition, each type of image uses a different length of film: ordinary X-rays use 0.2 metres on average; the MRI scan uses 1 metre and the PET scan uses 0.5 metres.

The second phase represents the processing of the X-ray image. When each X-ray image has been taken, the film is then sent for processing and processing time becomes an important driver. For example, the length of time the film processor employee takes to process the film and the chemicals used in processing are both directly related to the size of film being processed.

Thus, you decide to experiment with two cost drivers: the amount of time taken and overall size of X-ray, to better trace the six categories of operating costs to the three different types of X-ray performed by the Radiology Department.

**Requirements:**

1. Using the above information determine what you consider to be a more appropriate cost per unit (and therefore selling price) for each of the three types of X-ray images for the Radiography Department.
2. How would activity-based cost management assist in the management of an organisation such as Emly Hospital?
3. Suggest a range of appropriate performance measures for this Radiography Department related to its stated mission statement. Justify your choice.

*Question 5.10 (Activity-based Costing and Customer Profitability Analysis)*

John Holly is the owner and manager of Holly Distribution, a company specialising in the distribution of pharmaceutical products to a variety of clients in Ireland. The company buys from pharmaceutical manufacturing companies and resells to each of three different retail outlets:

1. national supermarket chains
2. wholesale pharmaceutical companies
3. single-shop pharmacies.

The management accountant reported the following data for the financial year (20x4) for the company:

|  | Supermarkets | Wholesalers | Single Pharmacies |
|---|---|---|---|
| Total sales revenue | €3,708,000 | €3,150,000 | €1,980,000 |
| Gross profit (to sales) % | 30% | 40% | 50% |

Annual operating costs, amounting to €2,615,000, need to be deducted from gross profit to determine net profit for the year. These operating costs are assigned to the three different retail outlets on the basis of sales turnover. In turn, John has used the net profit to sales percentage to evaluate the relative profitability of the three different types of retail outlets.

John recently attended a seminar on activity-based costing and decides to consider applying it to the analysis of operating costs in his company. Having discussed the matter with colleagues, there is general agreement that the three main operating activities in the company, and their related cost drivers, are as follows:

| Cost Pool/Activity Area | Cost Driver |
|---|---|
| 1.  Order processing | Number of orders |
| 2.  Store delivery | Number of store deliveries |
| 3.  Shelf stacking at customer store | Number of hours of shelf stacking |

Each order received from the various retail outlets consists of one or more product line items and each store order requires delivery of one or more cartons of products. Delivery staff are required to stack cartons directly onto display shelves in each retail outlet.

The three cost pools, together with cost drivers and cost driver levels for the financial year ending December 20x4 are as follows:

| Cost Pool | Total Costs (20x4) | Cost driver levels (20x4) |
|---|---|---|
| 1. Order processing | €800,000 | 2,000 orders |
| 2. Store deliveries | 1,207,000 | 1,420 store deliveries |
| 3. Shelf stacking | 608,000 | 640 hours |
|  | €2,615,000 |  |

| Other data for the financial year ending December 20x4 are: | | | |
|---|---|---|---|
|  | Supermarkets | Wholesalers | Single Pharmacies |
| Total number of orders | 140 | 360 | 1,500 |
| Total number of store deliveries | 120 | 300 | 1,000 |
| Avg hours of stacking per delivery | 3 hours | 0.6 hours | 0.1 hours |

## Requirements:

1. Explain your understanding of the term 'cost driver'.
2. Compute the operating profit for the financial year (20x4) for the three different retail outlets using the traditional approach of cost apportionment, i.e. operating costs are assigned on the basis of sales revenue.
3. Compute the operating profit of each distribution outlet for the year ended December 20x4 using the activity-based costing information. Comment on the results. What new insights are available with the activity-based information?
4. Describe challenging problems John Holly would face in designing and implementing an ABC system.

## Question 5.11 (Customer Profitability)

The Master Card of the NAMA Bank is a credit card that competes with national credit cards, such as Visa. Michael Morrison is the manager of the Master Card division of NAMA Bank in Dublin and has been reading about credit card trends. Ireland, though a small country, is one of the most profitable markets in Europe for credit card issuers. One factor contributing to this profitability is that 45-50% of all credit card holders roll over their balance from month to month, thereby incurring interest charges, making the issuance of credit cards a lucrative business. This high profitability has been achieved despite increased competition. For example, the large supermarkets have also issued their own cards which have attracted large numbers of customers.

The NAMA bank has invested heavily in designing an activity-based costing system and Morrison is aware that such information can be applied to identify customer profitability. The credit card customers of NAMA bank are divided into four different segments:

- Customer A is typically a senior professional person who uses his or her credit card for virtually all his/her transactions. S/he is usually of mature age.
- Customer B is a relatively young professional person, typically just qualified with good earning potential.
- Customer C is a student and the average transaction amount is rather small.
- Customer D is a retired person.

The following data applies to the financial year 20x7:

## Income (revenue) to bank:

- An annual membership fee is paid to the bank by its customers as follows:
  - Senior professional: €50
  - Young professional: €50
  - Student: Nil and
  - Retired person: Nil.

This annual fee covers all Card services.

- The NAMA Bank receives a commission of 2% of the purchase amount when the Master Card is used. The average annual purchases per customer are as follows:

| | Senior professional | Young professional | Student | Retired |
|---|---|---|---|---|
| Annual purchases per customer | €20,000 | €16,000 | €4,000 | €8,000 |

- The NAMA Bank had a (net) interest spread of 9% for the financial year 20x7 on the average outstanding balances on which its credit card holders pay interest. An interest spread is the difference between what NAMA Bank receives from card-holders on outstanding balances and what it pays to obtain the funds used and is equivalent to *net interest received.* The average annual unpaid balance on credit card per customer is as follows:

| | Senior professional | Young professional | Student | Retired |
|---|---|---|---|---|
| Average annual unpaid balance on credit card on which interest is due, per customer | €6,000 | €2,000 | €200 | €Nil |

**Costs to bank:** The NAMA Bank has an activity-based costing system and the following information on cost pools, cost drivers and cost driver levels apply for the financial year 20x7:

| Cost pool | € Amount | Cost driver |
|---|---|---|
| Account maintenance | 2,160,000 | Total no. of accounts |
| Transaction processing | 660,000 | Total no. of transactions |
| Customer service | 100,000 | Total no. of enquiries |
| Lost cards | 100,000 | Total no. of replacements |

| Cost driver level | Senior professional | Junior professional | Student | Retired | Total |
|---|---|---|---|---|---|
| Total no. of accounts | 12,000 | 5,000 | 1,000 | 2,000 | 20,000 |
| Total no. of card transactions | 250,000 | 50,000 | 25,000 | 5,000 | 330,000 |
| Total no. of customer enquiries | 8,000 | 12,000 | 4,000 | 1,000 | 25,000 |
| Total no. of card replacements | 200 | 300 | 400 | 100 | 1,000 |

## Requirements:

1. Compute the average cost of each of the cost drivers (activities) that give rise to resource consumption.
2. Compute the total and average profitability of each of the four categories of credit card customers of the Master Card.
3. The level of credit card fraud is of concern to the Bank's management. At the moment, all costs of Card fraud are included in 'account maintenance'. Argue why a separate cost pool should be maintained for this cost base. Specify some cost drivers that could be used for this cost pool.

*Question 5.12 (Activity-based Costing)*

The Alpha Bank is located in Nicosia, Cyprus. In recent years overall profitability, as measured by return on total assets, has declined. Management believes that this is as a result of increasing competition in the market place – partly due to admission to the EU and Euro Zone, but also because some of its activities are wasteful. However, it has, until now, been unable to identify what activities should be eliminated or re-engineered. It has been suggested to management that some form of an ABC system should be introduced.

An ABC task force was recently set up and, as a pilot study, the customer support section within the bank was examined. This customer support section was responsible for a variety of activities and the pilot study initially identified **five** different activities that comprise customer support services:

(1) process deposits,
(2) process cheques,
(3) process cash withdrawals,
(4) answer and service customer enquiries and account maintenance, and
(5) open new accounts.

The task force has identified the following information regarding customer support costs and activities for a recent month:

| Support Activity | Estimated Cost € | Activity Cost Driver | Monthly Level |
|---|---|---|---|
| 1. Process deposits | 60,000 | Number of deposits processed | 15,000 |
| 2. Process cheques | 35,000 | Number of cheques processed | 70,000 |
| 3. Process cash withdrawals | 28,000 | Number of withdrawals processed | 14,000 |
| 4. Answer customer enquiries | 20,000 | Number of customer enquiries | 10,000 |
| 5. Open new accounts | 7,000 | Number of accounts opened | 500 |
| | 150,000 | | |

**Requirements:**

1. Calculate the unit cost of each of the five identified activities.

2. During the pilot phase, the task force has developed the following list of activities for two typical groups of customers: (a) current account marketed to retired persons, and (b) current account for a business client. The monthly fees charged to these customers amount to €10 for the retired customer and €21 for the business client. Each customer requires, on average, the following per month:

| Support Activity | Average Monthly Volume | |
|---|---|---|
| | Retired person | Business client |
| Process deposits/lodgements | 2 deposits | 24 deposits |
| Process cheques | 10 cheques | 150 cheques |
| Process cash withdrawals | 6 withdrawals | 4 withdrawals |
| Answer customer enquiries | 2 enquiries | 14 enquiries |
| Open new account | ½ per month | 2 per month |

Estimate the total monthly support costs for both groups of customer and indicate the resulting profit or loss.

3. Comment on both the methodology and implications of your figures for managerial decision-making.

# 6

# Developments in Cost Accumulation Systems

LEARNING OBJECTIVES

When you have completed studying this chapter you should be able to:

1. Describe the philosophy of World Class Manufacturing.
2. Prepare cost of quality reports.
3. Explain just in time systems.
4. Record accounting entries in a backflush accounting system.
5. Calculate economic order quantities.

## 6.1 World Class Manufacturing (WCM)

Many developments have occurred recently in the practice of management accounting, although it is fair to comment that these developments are more prevalent in large, multinational firms than in small, indigenous businesses. This chapter reviews some of these developments, which can be grouped into three broad areas as follows:

- A new system of product costing, i.e. ABC has been developed and this technique was discussed in **Chapter 5**. The development of ABC had its origin in the perception that, under traditional cost accounting systems, product costs in multi-product firms were inaccurate due to the method of overhead absorption used, which was mainly based on direct labour hours.
- The emphasis on World Class Manufacturing has placed increased attention on the issue of quality in the management of all resources and relationships within the organisation. This theme is the focus of this chapter.
- The need to broaden the orientation of accounting information to include both financial and non-financial information that facilitates strategic decision-making and performance evaluation by managers. These issues will be discussed in **Chapters** 7 (Strategy) and **8** (Performance Measurement).

World Class Manufacturing (WCM) can be defined as the manufacture of high quality products reaching customers quickly (or the delivery of a prompt and quality service) at a low cost to provide high customer satisfaction and loyalty. The emphasis on WCM can be traced back, in English-speaking countries, to the mid-1980s when many US companies began to rigorously investigate the reasons why they were not competitive, particularly when compared to Japanese manufacturers who were taking a significant share of the US market. After investigating this phenomenon, American firms found that continuous improvement in four critical areas was the key:

1. being competitive on unit cost
2. providing consistent quality
3. providing a reliable delivery
4. being responsive to customers' needs.

Until the mid-1980s, most US firms had always regarded the relationship among these four areas as a trade-off. For example, a manufacturer who wanted the lowest unit cost, it was assumed, would have to compromise on quality. In contrast, Japanese manufacturers believed and showed that simultaneous improvement in these four areas was possible and that one factor need not be sacrificed for another.

It is interesting to note that, following the Second World War, the Japanese employed several American consultants to help them rebuild the industrial sector of their economy. The most notable consultant was W. Edwards Deming who is considered by many to be the father of World Class Manufacturing. Deming introduced the concept to Japan that an improved focus on quality performance drives profits *up* rather than *down*. (The Deming Prize, a prestigious award, honours people for their contributions in the field of quality improvement.)

It became obvious to American firms that, in order to survive, they would need to eliminate waste in all parts of production and production support, increase worker involvement in day-to-day operations, improve management practices and become more responsive to customers' needs; in other words, they would need to embrace the World Class Manufacturing philosophy.

Evidence of the financial benefits of the adoption of WCM principles (and its related elements) is readily available from a variety of sources. These benefits include (not listed in order of importance):

- improved quality of products with increased customer satisfaction
- lower warranty claims
- reduced scrap and rework
- reduced inventory with related cost savings
- more economical use of factory space
- reduced set-up time for preparing machines for an assigned task
- reduced labour costs and lower rates of absenteeism.

There are a number of components of World Class Manufacturing performance. Initially, we shall focus on two components, namely Advanced Manufacturing Technology and Just in Time systems. The relationship between these components and the role of management accounting is presented in **Exhibit 6.1**.

EXHIBIT 6.1: WCM SYSTEMS AND MANAGEMENT ACCOUNTING

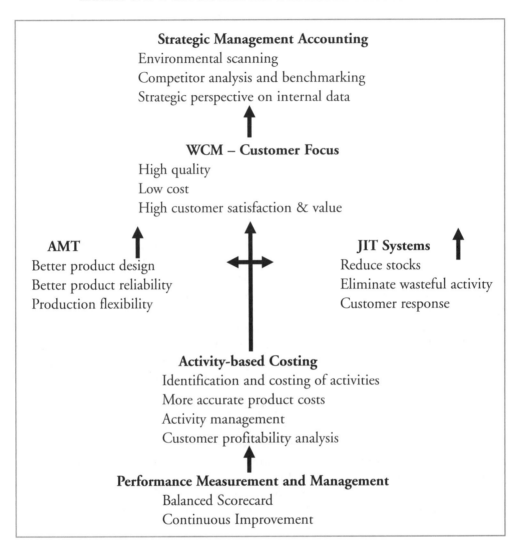

## Advanced Manufacturing Technology (AMT)

In an attempt to achieve WCM performance, some companies have invested heavily in Advanced Manufacturing Technology (AMT). The impact of this new technology is better product design, greater product reliability and improved production flexibility with quicker response time for customer orders.

One should note that the shift towards technology and automation results in a greater proportion of overhead costs in manufacturing companies and a relative decline in direct labour to less than 10% of total costs. In such circumstances labour accounting will become less important. In addition, labour costs will be largely fixed, and with multi-skilled and 'empowered' employees it may not be necessary or cost-effective to record labour time in detail. There will also be a change in emphasis from the control of costs at the operations stage to the control of costs at the design stage of the product and the design of the production process.

## Just in Time (JIT)

Just in time (JIT) systems are also part of the process leading to World Class Manufacturing. As will be explained in **Section 6.3**, a JIT system does not involve running a production facility with fewer inventories, as it is sometimes described. Rather, it is a way of working that reduces or eliminates activities and practices that do not add value to the product.

Non-value-added activities can be reduced or eliminated without decreasing the enterprise's ability to compete and meet customer demands. For example, inspection of incoming raw materials is a non-value-added activity that can be eliminated without diminishing the value received by the enterprise or its customers. If a vendor of raw materials commits to supplying high quality materials, then inspection of incoming components and other testing procedures should be no longer required.

## Other Elements

Underlying the relationship between WCM, AMT and JIT is the management accounting and information system. In the previous chapter we discussed the importance of ABC, which provides more accurate product costs and also facilitates cost management practices. However, to successfully implement a World Class Manufacturing philosophy a broader range of information is required by managers. This orientation is often reflected in the use of a Balanced Scorecard within firms and this topic will be covered in **Chapter 8.**

**Exhibit 6.1** above graphically represents the emerging discipline of strategic management accounting. This topic will be covered in **Chapter 7** but, by way of brief introduction, it refers to the externally orientated information required by managers who must be increasingly aware of what competitors are doing and what customers want. After all, there is not much benefit in having a good product if your competitor has a better one, and especially if you do not know about it! Likewise, there is little consolation in having zero defects in the manufacture of black and white TVs when customers prefer to purchase colour sets.

In summary, if management accountants are to remain as the information specialists within the organisation, they must first realise what they are supposed to measure. It is important to stress that financial performance is the result of operational actions, and financial success should be the logical consequence of doing the fundamentals well. Thus, management accountants need to be concerned both with financial and other objectives and the means by which these objectives are to be achieved.

In addition, the management accounting system must focus on the goal of continuous improvement. Indeed, WCM is based on the principle that there is no limit to improvement. Furthermore, it recognizes that it is the employees involved in work practices and procedures who are in the best position to suggest opportunities for improvement.

## 6.2 Accounting for Quality and Cost of Quality (CoQ) Reports

It is now generally accepted that quality of output is a critical success factor for those firms who want to differentiate themselves from competitors. (It can also be a very good defence against potential litigation.) However, no matter what individuals within the organisation do or say, it will always be the customer who is the ultimate judge of quality. A defective product, even though replaced, or a defective service subsequently rectified, leaves the customer with an unpleasant experience. Such customer experiences (and perceptions) will influence whether people become new and/or remain loyal customers.

Total Quality Management is the process of focusing on quality in the management of all resources and relationships within the organisation and is based on two fundamental principles:

1.  Getting things right first time This acknowledges that the cost of correcting mistakes is greater than the cost of preventing them from happening in the first place.
2.  Continuous improvement The assumption is that it is always possible to improve, no matter how high the quality may already be.

The issue of quality should be discussed in the broad context of World Class Manufacturing. It will be recalled that 'WCM' is a convenient label to describe the manufacture of high quality products reaching customers quickly (or delivery of a prompt and quality service) at a low cost to provide high customer satisfaction and loyalty. It is a customer-orientated philosophy and recognises that modern consumers, faced with a greater range of choices, have requirements other than just a low price. For example, one rarely chooses a restaurant on the basis of menu prices only or an airline on the basis of ticket prices. Rather, a product (and many services) can be considered as a bundle of characteristics and, if a company is to be successful in the market place, then it must match its competitors in each of the relevant product characteristics, which includes quality. We shall now discuss the issue of quality and its measurement in greater detail.

### What is Quality?

Quality is a term that we all use fairly loosely, partly reflecting the fact that there are different dimensions to it. The International Organisation for Standardisation (ISO) defines 'quality' as "the total features and characteristics of a product or service that provide its ability to satisfy stated or implicit needs". Obviously, quality has many dimensions which include the following characteristics:

- Performance – operating ability
- Reliability – dependability
- Durability – operating life
- Serviceability – speed and ease of repair
- Appeal – appearance, taste, etc.

The recent emphasis on quality placed by the WCM philosophy is at variance with traditional views on quality and these different views are highlighted in **Exhibit 6.2**.

EXHIBIT 6.2: DIFFERENT VIEWS ON QUALITY

| Traditional Management View | WCM Philosophy |
|---|---|
| • Improving quality increases costs<br>• Some defects are acceptable<br>• Quality must be inspected into the product | • Improving quality reduces costs<br>• The objective is zero defects<br>• Quality should be designed into the product |

**Exhibit 6.2** indicates that the traditional management view of quality accepted that there was a trade-off between improving quality and incurring higher costs. For many firms, a production process was judged to be satisfactory as long as the number of defective products did not exceed an agreed level. However, this approach acknowledged that some defective units would be delivered to customers. Companies, accordingly, established expensive field service operations and provided generous warranty cover. If failures or defects occurred, they could be replaced or repaired by field personnel.

And there were other consequences. Typically, companies would keep large amounts of both finished goods and raw materials in stock incurring costs in storage, handling, insurance, breakages and pilferage. Rework (or scrap) costs were high and, occasionally, production schedules were changed to facilitate rework. However, all these costs were included, as appropriate, in cost of goods manufactured, wages and salaries, travel expenses, technical services, and so forth. They were not reported separately.

For many enterprises, one of the greatest opportunities for effective cost management and profit improvement lies in better reporting and, therefore, better management of quality. As part of this cost reduction programme there must be an emphasis on zero defects. Zero defects means that there are no rejected materials, parts, or finished products, and no rework. It is a state of perfection. While zero defects may seem an unattainable objective, it is important to believe that this level of quality can and will be achieved, no matter how difficult. The orientation of WCM is to design and build quality in, rather than trying to inspect and repair quality into products. This is not a subtle point: **quality *does* cost less because you design it in rather than inspect it into the product**. Therefore, it is incorrect to believe that quality costs more. What actually costs money is the lack of quality.

## Measuring the Performance of Quality

As companies embrace the quality revolution, they will need to devise and report measures to monitor progress towards specific quality objectives. Management accountants, as information specialists, are ideally placed to make a positive contribution in this regard. Reporting performance in relation to quality can be done in either of two ways:

1. Reporting a range of non-financial measures (or indicators) only in relation to quality (and these can be included as part of a Balanced Scorecard – see **Chapter 8, Sections 8.2** and **8.3**)
2. Reporting the financial consequences of quality in the form of a Cost of Quality (CoQ) report.

### 1. Reporting Non-financial Measures

There is no definitive list of non-financial measures of performance relating to quality. Rather, a representative range of measures is provided in **Exhibit 6.3** and these focus on the quality performance of suppliers of materials, internal performance during the production process, customer satisfaction and loyalty. For each measure, the target metric can be reported alongside actual performance for the relevant period. Unacceptable variations can then be investigated.

### 2. Cost of Quality (CoQ) Report

For maximum impact on managers, it is often suggested to highlight the financial impact associated with quality in a Cost of Quality (CoQ) report. The CoQ report attempts to compute a single aggregate measure of all explicit costs attributable to preventing and correcting defective products. CoQ reports aggregate all the costs of reporting, evaluating and managing costs of quality into four major categories as follows:

- prevention costs
- appraisal costs
- internal failure costs
- external failure costs.

Prevention costs are those costs incurred by actions to reduce or prevent poor quality products or services from being produced in the first place. They include:

- product design work which ensures specifications for existing and new products meet customer needs;
- design, development, maintenance and calibration/set-up of all quality control equipment;
- training of quality control personnel;
- all costs associated with quality planning.

EXHIBIT 6.3: NON-FINANCIAL MEASURES OF QUALITY

| | Target | Actual |
|---|---|---|
| **Suppliers:** | | |
| Number of defective units delivered | | |
| Number of late deliveries | | |
| **Internal production process:** | | |
| First-pass rates (% completed without any rework) | | |
| Scrap and rework costs including overtime | | |
| Number and % of delivery times not adhered to | | |
| Number of accidents in premises | | |
| **Customer satisfaction:** | | |
| Customer complaints (per 1,000 customers) | | |
| Warranty claims (or amounts) | | |
| Customer satisfaction questionnaires/surveys | | |
| % of repeat business as % of total sales | | |
| Rate of billing/invoice errors (e.g. credit notes issued) | | |
| Customer retention rate (%) | | |

Appraisal costs are incurred in discovering the condition of products and raw materials and include actual testing procedures to ensure quality specifications are met. Appraisal costs include the following activities:

- inspection and testing of incoming materials and goods;
- inspection of finished goods;
- supervision;
- gathering accounting information including analysis, reporting and audit.

Internal failure costs If preventive and appraisal techniques do not work adequately, the company will incur internal failure costs. Internal failure costs are those costs incurred when products or services fail to meet quality standards, and the defects are identified after the products or services are produced but before they are delivered to the external customer. They include the following:

- reprocessing, rectifying, re-inspection and re-testing of sub-standard products including any overtime costs;
- costs of scrapping products;

- losses arising from temporary shut-downs of production equipment;
- revenue losses from price reductions of sub-standard products.

External failure costs These costs are potentially the most expensive because they are pertinent to the only reason the company is in business – the customer. External failure costs are incurred because poor quality products or services are delivered to customers. External failure costs are associated with the following:

- customer complaints department;
- sales returns or allowances and replacements, warranties and repairs;
- recall of defective products including related advertising;
- product liability insurance.

A typical Cost of Quality report is presented in **Exhibit 6.4**, with **F** indicating a favourable variance and **A** indicating an unfavourable or adverse variance. Prevention and appraisal costs are sometimes called costs of conformance (i.e. adherence to quality standards). Internal failure and external failure costs are sometimes referred to as costs of non-conformance. This distinction is important since it can be considered that prevention and appraisal costs are voluntary in the sense that these costs do not have to be incurred. In contrast, internal failure and external failure costs are involuntary, because they are costs that the company must incur when bad quality occurs.

### Opportunity Cost of Bad Quality

Most, if not all, of the costs in **Exhibit 6.4** are easy to identify. However, there is one cost that is difficult to assign a monetary value to – the opportunity cost of bad quality, which is part of the external failure classification and represents lost future sales and deteriorating reputation. In many cases, dissatisfied customers do not complain directly to the company. Rather, they take their business elsewhere and tell others about their unsatisfactory experience.

### Advantages of Cost of Quality Reports

Two advantages of Cost of Quality reports may be cited:

1. CoQ reports represent a financial summary of the entire quality programme within organizations and therefore they are an ideal way of getting managerial attention. While non-financial indicators relating to quality can be more important, because they signal future financial consequences, managers often pay more attention to accounting reports. In turn, the total quality spend is usually expressed as, say, a percentage of sales revenue. The financial performance can be compared with predetermined targets including what was achieved in the previous period. Also, this generally accepted classification of quality costs facilitates external benchmarking with other similar organisations. Most companies are surprised to learn that spending on quality-related costs can amount to 15%–30% of sales revenue. Such information can be used as a driver to get top management's attention and create a greater awareness and commitment to quality issues. Literature on the topic of quality performance

EXHIBIT 6.4: COST OF QUALITY REPORT FOR ...

| Cost category | Actual € | Budget € | Variance € |
|---|---|---|---|
| Prevention costs: | | | |
|    Employee training | 6,000 | 8,000 | 2,000 F |
|    Design department | 15,000 | 10,000 | (5,000) A |
| = Total prevention costs | 21,000 | 18,000 | (3,000) A |
| Appraisal costs: | | | |
|    Inspection of raw materials | 5,000 | 10,000 | 5,000 F |
|    Salary of inspection supervisors | 7,000 | 5,000 | (2,000) A |
| = Total appraisal costs | 12,000 | 15,000 | 3,000 F |
| Internal failure costs: | | | |
|    Cost of scrap | 50,000 | 45,000 | (5,000) A |
|    Price reductions | 10,000 | 12,000 | 2,000 F |
| = Total internal failure costs | 60,000 | 57,000 | (3,000) A |
| External failure costs: | | | |
|    Customer complaints department | 10,000 | 25,000 | 15,000 F |
|    Warranties and repairs | 20,000 | 45,000 | 25,000 F |
| = Total external failure costs | 30,000 | 70,000 | 40,000 F |
| Total costs of quality | 123,000 | 160,000 | 37,000 F |
| Sales revenue for period | 615,000 | 640,000 | N/A |
| CoQ as % of sales | 20% | 25% | N/A |

suggests that well-run manufacturing companies, with a commitment to quality, can limit their overall quality costs to between 5–10 % of sales revenue.

2. The CoQ report is logical and sequential in that it portrays the four main elements of quality programmes, i.e. prevention, appraisal, internal and external failure. On the other hand, a listing of several non-financial indicators is more random. Also, based on a CoQ report, managers can appreciate the priorities and trade-offs associated with quality programmes. For example, it is normally desirable to spend additional resources on conformance activities rather than on non-conformance activities.

The focus of quality as a key performance area for all organisations is stressed in all management literature in recent years. Companies are emphasising quality in a number of ways. First, they are planning quality into products at the design stage rather than focusing on quality at the inspection stage. After all, quality has to be built into one's products and services, not inspected into them. Secondly, companies are working closely with suppliers in order to ensure that high quality components are received into the factory. Thirdly, companies are increasing the time and resources spent on staff training and development and actively seek suggestions from employees.

The major benefits of a total quality management (TQM) programme need to be stressed and repeated.

- TQM is a way of operating that requires total organisational commitment to continuous quality improvement. The emphasis on quality becomes part of the culture of the organisation and everyone works with quality in mind. The focus on quality improvement is not on correcting defects but on identifying the underlying causes of poor quality and subjecting these to real corrective action. If this attitude and commitment can be achieved it will give the company a clear focus which will result in greater customer satisfaction, loyalty and increased profitability.
- TQM is a source of competitive advantage and often customers are prepared to pay extra for a product that they know meets their quality expectations.
- TQM should reduce the number of defective products, therefore saving costs on rework and warranty claims. Furthermore, if the product is delivered to the customer without any defects then customer support costs are greatly reduced.

However, TQM is a difficult system to implement since it requires both cultural and physical changes (factory layouts, machines, production scheduling). It requires full participation from all levels within the organization. Furthermore, the company may not have the expertise in-house to implement such a system and this may result in the hiring of outside consultants, which is costly.

## 6.3 JIT Systems and Backflush Accounting

A JIT system refers to either a purchasing or production system whereby goods arrive at a particular destination *exactly* when they are needed. However, JIT is not just about running a production facility with fewer inventories. It is a way of working that reduces or eliminates activities and practices that do not add value to the product and is closely linked to Total Quality Management. Such non-value-adding items include warehousing and stock movement within the factory, testing for quality control, running production machinery merely to accumulate large stocks.

### Just in Time Purchasing

JIT purchasing involves matching the receipt of raw material closely with their usage so that raw material stocks are reduced to near zero. Supplies are delivered on a long-term contract basis as they are needed, but in small quantities. Thus, the costs of space for holding stock and costs such as damage or deterioration in store, stores' administration and security are minimised. In particular, the interest expense associated with large inventories is avoided. JIT requires the quality of materials delivered to be guaranteed by suppliers and the effect of this is to reduce the costs of wastage, returns and reworking. 'Stock-outs' should not occur in theory but, if they do occur, there can be quite significant knock-on costs through idle production facilities and loss of customer goodwill.

## Just in Time Production

There are four main features of a JIT production system:

### 1. Manufacturing Cells

The production function is organised into manufacturing cells, which represent a group of multi-skilled persons, who perform a number of related tasks. In theory, staff morale should be improved due to the multi-tasks being performed rather than a highly specialised task associated with traditional production systems. Also, team work is encouraged and expected. Furthermore, there may be increased levels of motivation due to higher pay in the form of bonuses.

### 2. Quality Production

There is an increased emphasis on quality production and each worker is responsible for finding and correcting his or her own errors before passing the product on to the next stage. If a defect is detected, a worker has the authority to stop the entire production line until the problem causing the defect is corrected. Since production line stoppages are very disruptive, the emphasis is on preventing problems from occurring, instead of trying to correct a problem after it occurs.

### 3. Strong Supplier Relationships

JIT companies expect suppliers to provide high quality goods and make frequent deliveries of the exact quantities specified and at agreed times. In theory, the receiving company places incoming goods immediately into production. This procedure eliminates the non-value-added activities (and related costs) of incoming inspection, storage and material handling. It is usual that cost savings are shared with the supplier in the form of longer contracts and at higher prices. Therefore, a strong, long-term buyer-supplier relationship develops.

### 4. Time

Time, in terms of customer response time, is also an important variable under a JIT system. **Customer response time** is the amount of time between placing an order for a product (or requesting a service) and the delivery of the product. Total response time can be divided into four parts, namely:

**1.** Order time +    **2.** Set-up time +    **3.** Processing time +    **4.** Delivery time

1. **Order Time** This time is external to the company and represents the length of time it takes the customer to place an order. Order time is being continually reduced by using electronic data interchange (EDI) ordering systems, e.g. integrated barcodes. Also the use of EDI reduces the possibility of human error and can also reduce overall staff numbers employed in processing customer orders.
2. **Set-up Time** This represents the time between the order being processed and the start of production. This time lag may be due to: (a) lack of materials, (b) set-up time involved, or (c) the machines are busy either due to lack of capacity or poor production scheduling.
3. **Processing Time** This represents the total time taken to produce the product and it is the main activity that adds value to the product. Short processing times provide flexibility to respond to customer demands.
4. **Delivery Time** This is the time the completed order takes to be delivered to the customer.

## Vendor (Supplier) Performance Measurements

Suppliers to JIT firms must meet standards relating to quality, price and delivery time. A vendor certification programme selects vendors that can meet these standards and an *illustrative* scale to assess a vendor's performance measurement is presented in **Exhibit 6.5**. It rates the vendor's performance on the basis of points

EXHIBIT 6.5: VENDOR PERFORMANCE SCALE AND SCORING

| Quality (40 points) | Scoring points |
| --- | --- |
| Zero rejections | 40 points |
| One rejection | 30 points |
| Two rejections | 20 points |
| Three rejections | 0 points |
| More than three rejections | −40 points |
| **Price (20 points)** | |
| Better price than similar vendors | 20 points |
| Same price as similar vendors | 10 points |
| Higher price than similar vendors | −10 points |
| **On-time delivery (40 points)** | |
| 100% on time | 40 points |
| Each % point below | −2 points |

**Bonus rating (20 points)**

| | |
|---|---|
| Superior performance | 20 points |
| Exceeds goals | 10 points |
| Acceptable | 0 points |
| Needs improvement | −10 points |
| Unacceptable | −20 points |

for quality, price and on-time delivery, with bonus points available for superior performance.

The goal is for each vendor to receive 100 or more points during the reporting period. A score between 95 and 99 points is acceptable but indicates a need for improvement. A score of less than 95 points indicates that performance is unacceptable and is likely to put the vendor on probation with a notification that corrective action is required, otherwise the relationship will be discontinued. What World Class Manufacturers want are a few vendors on whom they can rely for quality, on-time delivery, competitive prices and general performance.

## ILLUSTRATION: JIT AND FINANCIAL IMPLICATIONS

The Moy Company manufactures components for a variety of customers and they have recently implemented a JIT system. At the end of the year it is decided to review the financial consequences of the programme and the following information is provided:

1. Average inventory declined from €550,000 to €150,000. This inventory has been financed by way of a 15% bank loan.
2. Annual insurance costs of €80,000 declined by 60% owing to the lower average inventory.
3. A leased 8,000-square-foot warehouse, previously used for materials storage, was not used by the company during the year even though an annual rent of €11,200 was paid. However, being surplus to requirements, Moy sublet the building to several tenants and received rent of €15,000.
4. The services of two warehouse employees were no longer needed and they were transferred to other duties within the company. This enabled the company to postpone hiring two similar employees at the same wage rate, which it otherwise would have done. The annual salary costs for the two employees amounted to €35,000 in total, i.e. €17,500 each.
5. As a result of switching to JIT, additional overtime was required to manufacture 7,500 spare parts. The relevant cost for this activity amounted to €5.60

per part manufactured. The use of overtime to fill orders was immaterial prior to this time.

**Requirement:** Calculate the cash savings (loss) that resulted from the adoption of its JIT system (Source: CMA, heavily adapted).

**Solution and Analysis:** The financial implications of the JIT system are presented below, but different presentations are acceptable. **Column 1** indicates the cash flows associated with continuing operations without the JIT system, i.e. the current purchasing policy. **Column 3** indicates the cash flows associated with the JIT policy. Therefore, **Column 2** indicates the incremental financial consequences, being the difference between **Columns 1** and **3**. **Column 2** highlights the fact that the introduction of a JIT system provided an incremental cash inflow of €116,000 for the year.

| | 1. Cash flows under current purchasing policy | 2. Incremental cash flows | 3. Cash flows under JIT purchasing policy |
|---|---|---|---|
| | € | € | € |
| 1. Interest on stock holding (15% × €550,000) (15% × €150,000) | (82,500) | +60,000 | (22,500) |
| 2. Annual insurance costs | (80,000) | +48,000 | (32,000)[a] |
| 3a. Warehouse rent paid | (11,200) | Nil | (11,200) |
| 3b. Warehouse rent received | Nil | +15,000 | +15,000 |
| 4a. Salary costs (existing) | (35,000) | Nil | (35,000) |
| 4b. Salary costs (new) | (35,000) | +35,000 | Nil |
| 5. Overtime costs: | | | |
| No overtime | Nil | Nil | Nil |
| Overtime premium (€5.60 × 7,500 units) | Nil | (42,000) | (42,000) |
| Total cash flows incurred | (243,700) | +€116,000 | (127,700) |

[a] €80,000 × (1 − 0.60) = €32,000

The above illustration helps to highlight the general financial benefits of a JIT system which are as follows:

1. Significant cost savings associated with reduced stocks, e.g. storage, handling, and insurance. If a high degree of trust has developed between the manufacturer and supplier, then inspection and the goods receiving process is eliminated. Indeed, if goods were paid for when they are received, then the creditors (accounts payable) ledger is virtually eliminated!
2. The risk of obsolete finished goods is reduced since goods are produced only when demanded.
3. Improved quality results in savings due to reduction of waste and spoilage. This increased quality can be a source of competitive advantage. Also, there are the benefits of greater customer satisfaction associated with an overall reduction in customer response time.
4. Lower investment in stocks has important accounting implications. Since stocks are minimised under JIT, the need for detailed accounting for inventories of raw materials, work-in-progress and finished goods is reduced. Inventory valuation becomes a less important issue and stock valuation figures should be more quickly and accurately obtained. In addition, traditional administrative systems for stock control may become unnecessary. However, additional emphasis will be required to ensure on-time delivery of incoming goods.

## Other Implications of JIT Systems

Some other implications of JIT systems should be briefly noted.

### 1. Employee Involvement in Data Collection

With a JIT system, one change will be that personal observation and, therefore, reaction by production line workers will play an increasing role in cost control. Greater emphasis is placed on in-process control mechanisms, which require operating personnel to isolate a quality problem, stop production and remedy the situation before it results in significant scrap, rework or other effects of poor quality.

In addition, when decision-making responsibility lies with workers, better and quicker decisions are (usually) made. There are a number of reasons for greater employee involvement. First, the dramatic reduction in production cycle time due to small batches means that, for example, monthly cost control reports arrive too late to be of value in controlling production operations except as a guide to identify trends that are not apparent on the spot. Secondly, production employees directly observe non-financial variables such as quality on the factory floor. These non-financial variables are intuitive, easily understood and more relevant to factory personnel. Moreover, many managers believe that, when workers acquire decision-making authority, their overall commitment to the organisation is increased.

## 2. Disruption

Under JIT, both suppliers and employees have greater power to cause disruption to the daily and regular functioning of the business.

## 3. Macroeconomic Consequences

JIT is a demand-orientated system, i.e. goods are not produced until needed. However, the large scale adoption of JIT systems could pose considerable 'demand management' problems for the economy as a whole due to the multiplier effect. For example, a small reduction in aggregate consumer demand could result, dramatically, in manufacturing job layoffs as production output is reduced among JIT firms. In turn, this could lead faster to an economic recession, as aggregate demand is further reduced by lower purchasing power of consumers in the economy.

Other macroeconomic consequences include industrial concentration as economic development becomes regionalised because suppliers will be located close to their manufacturing customers in order to facilitate on-time and frequent deliveries. In turn, other potential impacts, such as road congestion caused by delivery vehicles, could also appear.

In conclusion, implementing a JIT system can present problems for companies not prepared for the complexities inherent in such a system. Implementing JIT systems requires the highly efficient co-ordination of purchasing and production processes. Companies that have consistent problems in either of these areas should not implement JIT until they have resolved these problems.

## Backflush Accounting

A JIT system offers the opportunity to simplify the recording of manufacturing cost flows. First, given low stock levels under a JIT system, it may not be desirable to spend resources assigning costs between cost of goods sold and inventory. Secondly, since budgeted production costs should approximate actual costs, there is little point in laboriously tracking actual cost data. Recognising both these aspects leads to a simplified approach to accounting for manufacturing *cost flows* and is referred to as backflush accounting. Its purpose is to eliminate accounting transactions and does this by, first, focusing on output and then working backwards in assigning costs between cost of goods sold account and closing inventory account. The work-in-progress (WIP) account is not separately accounted for – generally there is an absence of WIP (or it is so small that it can be considered insignificant in terms of overall costs).

A backflush accounting system is really a standard costing system that records input acquisitions at actual costs and outputs at standard cost. Generally, there are only two categories of costs: materials, and conversion costs. Costs are recorded in these accounts and subsequently transferred to either a cost of goods sold account or finished inventory account. There are a number of variants of backflush costing, which have different 'trigger' points for recording cost flows. (Revenue flows will be recorded as normal.)

*Trigger Points*

A **trigger point** is an event that prompts the accounting recognition of certain manufacturing costs. Typical trigger points can be identified as follows:

1. All variants of backflush accounting (and this is similar to traditional cost flow systems) have a common, first trigger point, i.e. record costs when they are actually incurred. These inputs are recorded at actual cost and, for example, the purchase of raw materials would be recorded by the following journal entry:

> Dr:   Raw materials and in process account
> Cr:   Bank (or accounts payable) account

**Note**: under backflush accounting, we use the term 'Raw Materials and In Process' (RIP) account. The unique feature of a backflush accounting system is the absence of a WIP account. Effectively, when raw materials are received, they are put into 'process' in keeping with a JIT philosophy. In addition, direct labour and production overhead costs are combined in a Conversion Costs Account, and posted to this account when incurred.

2. The second trigger point is usually when the goods are completed. (However, another variant is to record the cost flows only when the goods are sold.) Thus, costs are not taken out of the two above mentioned expense accounts until the product is completed. The appropriate journal entry on completion of production, based on a *standard cost calculation*, is:

> Dr:   Finished goods account
> Cr.   Raw materials and in process account
> Cr.   Conversion costs account

The use of direct materials and conversion costs is recorded at standard cost. In this way, costs are flushed out of the general ledger when production is completed. Remaining balances are written off, particularly since they should be insignificant.

## ILLUSTRATION: BACKFLUSH ACCOUNTING

The Jordanstown Company has a plant that manufactures solvents in one litre containers. The production time is a few minutes per unit. There is only one direct manufacturing cost category (direct materials) and one production overhead cost category (conversion costs). Each unit of finished product requires one litre of input. The company operates a JIT production system and uses a backflush costing system with two trigger points for recording accounting cost entries, namely:

- purchase of direct materials
- completion of goods.

The standard cost per unit is €12 (comprising €8 for materials and €4 per conversion costs). The following data relates to a recent accounting period in which 1 million litres of solvent was produced and 950,000 litres were sold:

Direct materials purchased          €8,800,000
Conversion costs incurred (actual)  €4,100,000

Because of the operation of the JIT system, there are no opening stocks. There was no closing stock of unused raw materials, but 50,000 litres of finished product remained in closing stock.

**Requirement:** Record the above entries in appropriate cost accounts, using backflush costing, i.e. Raw Materials and In Process Control, Conversion Costs Control and Cost of Goods Sold.

**Solution and Analysis:** The following transactions can be recorded using the two trigger points stated:

| | | € | € |
|---|---|---|---|
| **1.** | **Actual costs incurred:** | | |
| | Dr. Raw materials and In process a/c | 8,800,000 | |
| | Cr. Accounts payable a/c | | 8,800,000 |
| | (Direct materials purchased) | | |
| | Dr. Conversion costs a/c | 4,100,000 | |
| | Cr. Accounts payable a/c | | 4,100,000 |
| | (Actual conversion costs incurred) | | |
| **2.** | **Completion of goods (1,000,000 litres):** | | |
| | Dr. Finished goods a/c | 12,000,000 | |
| | Cr. Raw materials and In process a/c | | 8,000,000 |
| | Cr. Conversion costs a/c | | 4,000,000 |
| | (Standard cost of goods produced) | | |
| **3.** | **Sale of goods (950,000 litres):** | | |
| | Dr. Cost of goods sold a/c | 11,400,000 | |
| | Cr. Finished goods a/c | | 11,400,000 |
| | (Standard cost of goods sold at €12) | | |

| 4. | End of period write off: | | |
|---|---|---|---|
| | Dr. Cost of goods sold a/c | 100,000 | |
| | Cr. Conversion costs a/c | | 100,000 |
| | (Writing off conversion costs) | | |
| | Dr. Cost of goods sold a/c | 800,000 | |
| | Cr. Raw materials and In process a/c | | 800,000 |
| | (Writing off balancing item in account) | | |

The elimination of WIP account in the above process reduces the amount of detail in the accounting system. The difference on the conversion costs account (€100,000) is written off to the cost of goods sold account. Since there was no closing stock of unused raw materials, the balance on the Raw Materials and In Process account (€800,000) is also transferred to the Cost of Goods Sold account. However, the balance of the finished goods account (€600,000) is recognized and the completed ledger entries are as follows:

**Raw Materials and In-Process account**

| | € | | € |
|---|---|---|---|
| (1) | 8,800,000 | (2) | 8,000,000 |
| | | (4) | 800,000 |

**Conversion Costs Control account**

| | € | | € |
|---|---|---|---|
| (1) | 4,100,000 | (2) | 4,000,000 |
| | | (4) | 100,000 |

**Cost of Goods Sold account**

| | € | | € |
|---|---|---|---|
| (3) | 11,400,000 | | |
| (4) | 100,000 | | |
| (4) | 800,000 | | |

**Finished Goods Control account**

| | € | | | € |
|---|---|---|---|---|
| (2) | 12,000,000 | | (3) | 11,400,000 |
| | _____ | Balance | | 600,000 |
| | 12,000,000 | | | 12,000,000 |
| Balance | 600,000 * | | | |

* 50,000 litres @ €12 each

## Summary

In summary, backflush accounting is a simplified standard costing system that focuses on the output of an organisation and then works backwards, allocating costs, typically, between finished goods account and the cost of goods sold account. It eliminates detailed accounting transactions and this is facilitated by the absence of a work-in-progress account. Apart from its simplicity, other advantages include the reduction in accounting entries, supporting vouchers and documents.

## 6.4 Stock Management and Economic Order Quantity

In the previous section we argued that carrying inventory was a non-value-added activity and should be eliminated where feasible. However, in some situations, the elimination of all stock holding may not be feasible or considered by managers as desirable. For example, having some stock of raw materials might avoid a shutdown in manufacturing due to non-delivery of goods caused by strikes or various types of disruption. For a retail company, the availability of stock is often required to inform customers and complete a sale. Yet, we know from the previous section that holding of stock is expensive and this includes costs of clerical administration, storage, insurance, possible breakages and pilferage, interest paid on loans to acquire the stock and obsolescence among others. Where stock holding is considered necessary, two basic decisions that need to be taken are:

1. How many units of stock should be ordered?
2. How often should a firm place an order for goods?

The literature on management accounting and operations research frequently make reference to an **Economic Order Quantity (EOQ)**. This is a mathematical model that enables us to provide answers to the above two questions. The model is based on two types of cost involved, namely, the carrying cost of stock and the order costs. The **carrying cost (Kc)**, represents the cost of holding one unit in inventory for the period under consideration. These carrying costs include insurance, administration costs and any interest paid on loans for inventory. The **order cost (Ko)**, represents the cost of placing an order. Order costs include all receiving costs including inspection and the cost of processing orders. However, the EOQ model should only include cost items that vary with the level of stock holding. Costs that are not affected by stock holding are not considered incremental costs and therefore should be excluded from the analysis. Thus, salary costs may be very often irrelevant since they are in the nature of fixed costs.

The EOQ model is based on common sense, which suggests that the total cost of holding stock is the aggregate of carrying costs and order costs and this can be formally expressed as:

| Total cost of stock holding per period | = | Total carrying costs per period | + | Total order costs per period |
|---|---|---|---|---|
| TC | = | $Kc \times \dfrac{EOQ}{2}$ | + | $Ko \times \dfrac{D}{EOQ}$ |

where EOQ = the optimal number of items in an order, and D = the demand during the period. Readers should notice that, in terms of calculating the carrying costs per period, EOQ is divided by '2' in the above equation. This is to highlight the average stock holding for the period. Thus, if a firm places only one order during a period for, say, 10,000 units, it will have on average 5,000 units in inventory during the year, which is multiplied by the carrying cost per unit (Kc) to provide the total carrying cost. (However, this approach does not take into account seasonal factors and this may invalidate the calculations.) The demand (D) for the period is divided by the EOQ to provide the optimal number of orders, which is multiplied by the cost per order (Ko) to provide total order cost.

Using differential calculus we can solve for EOQ. There is no need to do this here and there is no need to memorise the formula since it is provided with the exam paper. All that is required is to correctly apply the following EOQ formula:

$$EOQ = \sqrt{\frac{2 \times Ko \times D}{Kc}}$$

The EOQ is a deterministic model in that the answer is automatically generated by the values assigned to the different variables. Therefore, the answer provided will only be as good as the information used. However, the benefit of the model is that it focuses attention on costs associated with stocks that, sometimes, do not receive the scrutiny that they deserve.

## ILLUSTRATION: ECONOMIC ORDER QUANTITY

The Clontarf Company carries stock and provides you with the following information for an accounting period:

> D = demand (in units) for the period, 5,000 units
> Ko = the cost of placing an order, €100
> Kc = the carrying cost of a unit of inventory, €0.50 per unit

$$EOQ = \sqrt{\frac{2 \times €100 \times 5,000}{€0.50}}$$

EOQ = 1,414 units

(Note: be careful to work in either € or cent)

In turn, we can calculate the optimal number of orders for the period. This must be the total demand for the period (D) divided by the EOQ (1,414 units, as per above) and is calculated as:

$$\textbf{No.} = \frac{\textbf{D}}{\textbf{EOQ}} = \frac{5,000}{1,414} = 4 \text{ (rounded) orders per period.}$$

Finally, it is worth noting that order costs and carrying costs are not the only type of costs involved in having stock. There are always the potential costs of *not* having sufficient stock and this includes not only additional cash costs which may include working overtime to regain lost production but also the opportunity cost of lost sales, which is very difficult to measure with any degree of accuracy.

## Materials Requirement Planning (MRP)

EOQ is one technique that can be used for stock management purposes and is based on a mathematical formula that we have presented above. However, during the 1960s, 'Materials Requirement Planning' (MRP1) developed as a computerised approach for the management of materials and stocks. The objective of MRP1 is to ensure that the right materials are on hand, in the right quantities, and at the right time to support the production budget. Clearly, the first element in this computation is an estimate of the quantity and timing of finished goods demanded, i.e. a master production schedule. This information is then used to determine the requirements for raw material components at each stage of production.

A MRP1 system recognises that each basic component is combined with other stock items in the manufacture of products and therefore the ordering of stock items should be linked to the demand for the products for which they are part. Computer technology aids the operation of a MRP system in that the required records and details can be maintained in an integrated fashion in computer files. The computer technology enhances the accuracy of the necessary data and improves the speed of processing the data and therefore improves the timeliness of the information. In addition, presentation of relevant information for management may be improved though the use of spreadsheet and graphic packages. Furthermore, the computer maintained data may be pre-programmed to generate specific, additional information to management.

Gradually, after its introduction, MRP was extended to the management of all manufacturing resources. In particular it focuses on machine capacity planning and labour scheduling as well as materials requirement planning. This extended system is known as 'Manufacturing Resources Planning' or MRP2. Thus, the term MRP1 is used to describe only materials requirement planning. In contrast, MRP2 is an integrated planning approach to the management of all manufacturing resources (materials, labour and machine capacity). The essential features of a MRP2 system are as follows and these are an integral part of any piece of standard computer software:

**Materials** – the management of raw materials is done by incorporating the MRP1 system.

**Labour** – Careful attention is given to ensure the availability of direct labour, together with its scheduling to ensure efficient utilisation.

**Machine capacity** – Planning and monitoring of machine capacity is central to the MRP2 system, to ensure flexibility and efficiency.

In brief, an MRP2 system is an overall planning work flow system that brings together the various resources used in the manufacturing process so that there is an efficient, low-cost, high quality product output system with the minimum of bottlenecks and work-in-progress.

## Conclusion

In summary, we have covered a lot of ground in this chapter, with most of the emphasis on developments that are taking place within the discipline of management accounting. We initially discussed the philosophy of World Class Manufacturing and we also discussed Cost of Quality reports. Thereafter, we discussed JIT systems and a logical implication of JIT is the adoption of backflush accounting which simplifies the internal cost recording system. Finally, for those companies that require the holding of inventory, stock holding costs can be minimised using the EOQ model, but it should be acknowledged that the EOQ model is not a new development but was logical to include when discussing inventory and JIT systems. In the next chapter we shall look at the issue of strategy since management accountants are now being called upon to play a much more important role in strategic decision-making within the organisation.

## SUMMARY OF LEARNING OBJECTIVES

**Learning Objective 1:** Describe the philosophy of World Class Manufacturing.

World Class Manufacturing (WCM) is a management philosophy that embraces the increased use of automation within manufacturing operations but also emphasises an increased focus on better product design and production flexibility, commitment to quality and customer satisfaction.

**Learning Objective 2:** Prepare cost of quality reports.

Cost of quality reports are divided into four cost sections namely, prevention, appraisal, internal and external costs. The preparation of cost of quality reports was highlighted using exhibits and illustrations in this chapter.

**Learning Objective 3:** Explain just in time systems.

Modern manufacturing firms are, increasingly, using just in time purchasing and/or just in time production systems. These systems place increased emphasis on reduced inventory holdings but also the elimination of all wasteful activities by promoting quality and continuous improvement.

**Learning Objective 4:** Record accounting entries in a backflush accounting system.

A logical implication of JIT, with its emphasis on holding lower amounts of inventory, is the adoption of backflush accounting. This system, based on a reduced number of internal transactions, simplifies the internal cost recording system. Effectively, internal cost transfers are recorded by way of a standard cost.

**Learning Objective 5:** Calculate economic order quantities.

For those companies that require the holding of stock – for whatever reason – stock holding costs can be minimised using the EOQ (Economic Order Quantity) model. The EOQ model is a deterministic model, based on the total carrying costs of stock and the total order costs of stock.

## Questions

### Review Questions

(See Appendix One for Solutions to Review Questions **6.1** and **6.2**)

### Question 6.1 (Quality Costs)

The list provided below contains 23 items which would routinely appear in a cost of quality report.

**Requirements:**

1. Outline the four-way cost/activity classification system involved in preparing cost of quality reports.
2. Classify the 23 items associated with quality into their appropriate classification.

| List of costs/activities | P Prevention | A Appraisal | IF Int. failure | EF Ex. failure |
|---|---|---|---|---|
| 1. Final inspection | | | | |
| 2. Warranty repairs | | | | |
| 3. Goods returned and scrapped | | | | |
| 4. Quality training | | | | |
| 5. Settlement of product liability action | | | | |
| 6. Field service personnel | | | | |
| 7. Packaging inspection | | | | |
| 8. Complaint department | | | | |
| 9. Rework units from work-in-progress | | | | |

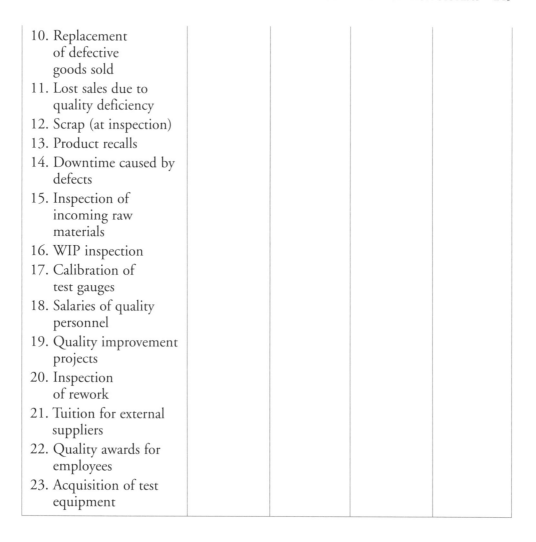

| | | | | |
|---|---|---|---|---|
| 10. Replacement of defective goods sold | | | | |
| 11. Lost sales due to quality deficiency | | | | |
| 12. Scrap (at inspection) | | | | |
| 13. Product recalls | | | | |
| 14. Downtime caused by defects | | | | |
| 15. Inspection of incoming raw materials | | | | |
| 16. WIP inspection | | | | |
| 17. Calibration of test gauges | | | | |
| 18. Salaries of quality personnel | | | | |
| 19. Quality improvement projects | | | | |
| 20. Inspection of rework | | | | |
| 21. Tuition for external suppliers | | | | |
| 22. Quality awards for employees | | | | |
| 23. Acquisition of test equipment | | | | |

### Question 6.2 (JIT Systems and Value Adding Activities)

VA Limited is a subsidiary of a large multinational company. It produces a single product and has one customer to which it sells 100,000 units per annum. The current production management system has operated for a number of years and there are two processing activities involved, referred to as Processing 1 and Processing 2. When the direct materials are received from suppliers in the storehouses, they are immediately inspected. If passed, they are retained and transferred to storage until needed in production. When required for production they are moved by fork lift truck to the Processing 1 area. When Processing 1 is complete they are inspected and, if satisfactory, they are moved to Processing 2 area. After Processing 2 is complete they are again inspected and subsequently sent to the packaging department. When packed they are returned to stores to await distribution to the client.

The following cost estimates have been produced by the cost accountant for the above activities:

The company is considering a move towards a full JIT production (and direct material purchasing) system. It is anticipated that all wasteful activities can be eliminated which will involve working closely with suppliers since they can virtually guarantee delivery to the production lines as needed, with 100% quality, thus eliminating the requirement to inspect incoming raw materials. Also, with the additional emphasis on quality production, production inspection in both processes will be eliminated. Furthermore, the movement of goods in the factory will be reduced and this should generate cost savings of €28,000. Finished goods will be immediately dispatched to customers. However, some additional costs will be incurred. For example, prepaid delivery to customers, on completion of production, will increase delivery cost by €20,000 and a staff and vendor training programme will be initiated costing €50,000 per annum, on an ongoing basis.

| | |
|---|---|
| Materials inspections | €40,000 |
| Materials storage | €70,000 |
| Materials movement to Process 1 and 2 | €40,000 |
| Cost of raw materials | €200,000 |
| Process 1 and 2 costs | €150,000 |
| Inspection – Process 1 work | €50,000 |
| Inspection – Process 2 work | €10,000 |
| Packaging of completed goods | €50,000 |
| Final storage (awaiting distribution to customer) | €10,000 |
| Delivery to customers | €80,000 |

**Requirement:** Based on the information provided and your knowledge of JIT systems in general, prepare a schedule of cost both under the current (traditional) production system and under the proposed JIT system. Highlight the cost savings and comment on your calculations.


Intermediate Questions

*Question 6.3 (New Developments in Managerial Accounting)*

**Requirements:**

1. Write brief notes on the following:
   (a) Just in Time (JIT) and managerial accounting.
   (b) World Class Manufacturing (WCM).

2. Outline the essential features of a Materials Requirement Planning (MRP (I)) system and a Manufacturing Resources Planning (MRP (II)) system and discuss the role of computer technology.

Source: Chartered Accountants Ireland, Management Accounting and Business Finance, Paper 3, various paper (adapted)

## Question 6.4 (Developments in Managerial Accounting)

You are approached by a colleague who is aware that you are studying managerial accounting. He is anxious to discuss some terms with you that he has recently heard but with which he is not familiar. The terms are:

(a) 'customer profitability analysis'
(b) 'value added activities'.

**Requirement:** Briefly explain these terms and outline their role within a management accounting system.

## Question 6.5 (Quality Initiatives and CoQ reports)

You have recently joined a manufacturing firm whose managing director is interested in introducing a quality initiative. He would like you to brief him as he is a little unsure as to what is involved.

**Requirement:** Draft a short memorandum (properly formatted) to the managing director outlining the benefits of a quality initiative and how costs of quality reports might be presented.

## Question 6.6 (Benefits of JIT Purchasing Systems)

The Stout Company is a food processor and carries a large amount of wheat due to the seasonality of the harvest months. Typical average wheat inventory amounts to €4 million which is purchased from a number of vendors. The investment in inventory is financed by way of a 10% bank overdraft. The costs of holding such inventory are large and the company is interested in switching to a JIT system and has located a single supplier who is willing to supply the necessary quantities, as requested. Should the Stout Company switch to a JIT system, the following changes are anticipated:

- Insurance and security costs totalling €350,000 per year would be eliminated.
- Two warehouses presently used for wheat storage would no longer be needed. The company rents one warehouse under a cancellable rental arrangement at an annual cost of €600,000. The other warehouse, consisting of 100,000 square feet, is owned by the company and three-quarters of the space in the owned warehouse could be rented for €10 per square foot per year.
- Additional costs, amount to €100,000 per annum, will be incurred in providing supplier training and assessment programmes.

- The supplier will receive an additional €80,000 per annum for his obligation for regular and frequent deliveries. In addition he will receive a price increase of 5%. The current level of purchases is expected to remain at €20,000,000 per annum (which does not include the additional price payable).

**Requirements:**

1. List and briefly explain the non-quantifiable factors that should be considered by the Stout Company before it switches to a JIT system.
2. Calculate the estimated financial benefit (or otherwise) (loss) for the Stout Company that would result from the adoption of a JIT system.

### Question 6.7 (Backflush Costing and JIT production)

The Liffey Water Company manufactures orange juice in one litre bottles from imported orange concentrate and the production time takes only a few minutes per unit. There is only one direct production cost category (direct materials, i.e. orange concentrate) and one production overhead cost category (conversion costs). The company operates a Just in Time production system and uses a backflush costing system with two trigger points for recording accounting entries:

- purchase of direct (raw) materials
- completion of good finished units of product.

The standard cost per unit is €1 (comprising 30c for materials and 70c for conversion costs). Because of the operation of the JIT system, there are no opening stocks.

The following data pertain to December:

1 million bottles of orange juice were produced and 900,000 litres were sold:

| | |
|---|---|
| Direct materials purchased | €350,000 |
| Conversion costs incurred (actual) | €750,000 |

There was no closing stock of unused raw materials.

**Requirement:** Record the above entries in appropriate cost accounts, using backflush costing, i.e. Raw Material and In Process Control, Conversion Costs Control and Cost of Goods Sold.

### Advanced Questions

### Question 6.8 (Cost of Quality Reports)

The following information has been extracted from the quality records of Bad Limited for the current (20x6) and previous (20x5) accounting years. A quality initiative was formally introduced at the start of 20x6 whereas no quality initiatives were undertaken in previous years.

|  | 20x6 €| 20x5 €|
|---|---|---|
| WIP written off due to faulty work | 45,000 | 50,000 |
| Inspection of raw materials | 15,000 | 27,000 |
| Servicing of customer complaints | 10,000 | 25,000 |
| Vendor (supplier) liaison re quality inputs | 25,000 | Nil |
| Employee training | 6,000 | 1,000 |
| Inspection of finished goods | 5,000 | 10,000 |
| Cost of replacement goods to customers | 20,000 | 45,000 |
| Preventive maintenance | 7,000 | 5,000 |
| Product liability insurance | 26,000 | 34,000 |
| Quality design department | 15,000 | 10,000 |
| Machine breakdowns due to faulty parts | 10,000 | 12,000 |

**Requirement:** Prepare a detailed cost of quality report for the financial year 20x6, showing comparative figures and cost variances.

## Question 6.9 (Backflush Costing and JIT Production)

The Sexton Company Limited manufactures a single electrical component and operates a JIT production system and, at the start of a recent accounting period, there was no opening inventory of raw materials, WIP or finished goods. The Sexton Company uses a backflush costing system with two trigger points for making entries in the accounting system:

- purchase of direct materials
- completion of goods finished units.

The standard cost per unit produced amounts to €50, comprising direct materials of €30 and conversion costs of €20. The following information relates to the recent accounting period:

| | |
|---|---|
| (a)  Direct (raw) materials purchased | €650,000 |
| (b)  Conversion costs incurred (actual) | €430,000 |
| (c)  Number of finished units manufactured | 21,000 (units) |
| (d)  Number of finished units sold | 20,000 (units) |

At the end of the month, there were no closing stocks of raw materials.

**Requirement:** You are required to record the above entries in the appropriate ledger accounts using backflush costing.

*Question 6.10 (New developments/Activity-based Costing)*

An ABC system is justified whenever the costs of installing and operating the new system are more than offset by the long-term benefits that would be derived from the new ABC system.

**Requirement:** Discuss briefly the philosophy underpinning ABC together with its main benefits. Also, suggest reasons why companies may be reluctant to implement a system of ABC.

Source: Chartered Accountants Ireland, Management Accounting and Business Finance,
various exams

*Question 6.11 (Quality)*

You have recently started a new job as a business consultant in a large professional accountancy practice and have just been handed the brief for your first client.

Your client (Company X) is a small indigenous manufacturing company, with less than 50 employees. It is located in Dublin and exports the majority of its engineering product to the UK. The company has been experiencing financial difficulties for the last 18 months due to a reduction in demand for its main product. Company X has reduced its selling prices but this has had little impact in terms of stimulating overall demand. As a result, the company is experiencing both a decline in profitability and a decrease in liquidity.

The Finance Director feels that the company does not pay sufficient attention to the quality of its production and believes that the company needs an improved product offering. However, he has not kept up to date with management ideas and has asked your advice regarding the possible implementation of a Total Quality Management (TQM) system, which would boost demand for the company's product and generate some cost savings.

**Requirement:** Based on the facts presented, prepare a memorandum to the Finance Director outlining the potential benefits and drawbacks of implementing a system of Total Quality Management (TQM) in this company.

Source: Chartered Accountants Ireland, Management Accounting and Business Finance, Paper 3,
Summer 2007 (adapted)

*Question 6.12 (Decision to Introduce a JIT System)*

Tracker Limited engraves expensive gold coins to customer order for commemorative occasions and major sporting events. Recently, the company's management has observed a number of competitors implementing Just in Time (JIT) purchasing systems in their operations. Data has been compiled for Tracker and you, as management accountant, have been asked to recommend whether, based on costings, Tracker should move to a JIT purchasing system.

Currently, Tracker deals with two suppliers. In order to maintain good relations with both suppliers, who are long established and the sole market providers, Tracker purchases 50% of its overall requirements of gold medals to be engraved from each supplier.

(The operatives of Tracker engrave the medal for specific customers which could involve adding a particular logo. On average, engraving costs amount to €50 per medal.)

Supplier A delivers orders received two days later at a unit price of €200 per medal. However, in recent months, Supplier A has been having quality problems and Tracker has had to inspect all medals received. Unfortunately, 5% of these have been discarded by Tracker due to imperfections. Because of the signed contract, Tracker has no recourse to the supplier and this problem is expected to continue. Management have discussed the issue and will tolerate the situation, as it is better for security of supply to deal with two rather than one supplier.

Supplier B, who supplies 50% of Tracker's requirements, will only deliver medals in packs of 200 at a price of €190 per medal. As a consequence, Tracker has to rent additional security storage at an annual cost of €150,000 solely to store unused medals. Supplier B gives a discount of 9% on all items purchased when the overall order size exceeds 70,000 units per annum.

A third supplier (Supplier C) has recently approached Tracker with a view to supplying all of Tracker's medals at €205 per unit. Supplier C is a new company located 50 kilometres from Tracker and operates a TQM system, whereby it guarantees all medals it sells are free of any faults and that all orders will be delivered next day. This means that Tracker could operate on the basis of zero inventory and this would eliminate current rental costs. However, in order to deal with Supplier C, Tracker will have to spend €15,000 on a one-off basis, to acquire a software licence in order to facilitate online ordering and invoicing (Supplier C only accepts orders and issues invoices in an electronic form). The enhanced quality of the medals supplied will also see the cost of engraving fall by 20% on average.

The production manager is keen to place all of Tracker's business with Supplier C and has received a favourable reference about Supplier C from a friend of his who has been dealing with them for the past six months. He also estimates that, if a change is made, four of Tracker's quality controllers can be let go and each receives an annual salary of €35,000. He has remarked that "no checking of incoming medals will be needed with the guarantee given".

Tracker's demand for medal engraving for next year has yet to be finalised. The view of management is that demand will either be 100,000 or 150,000 medals, but they will not know this before signing a contract. Engraved medals sell for €350 per medal.

## Requirements:

1. Based on the information provided, prepare costings for the two alternatives. Your costings should indicate whether Tracker should continue dealing jointly with Suppliers A and B, or switch to Supplier C. You should prepare calculations on the basis of either 100,000 or 150,000 units per annum and no other volume should be considered.
2. Outline briefly other factors that should be considered before a final decision is made.

Source: Chartered Accountants Ireland, Management Accounting and Business Finance, Autumn 2006 (adapted)

# Strategy and Managerial Accounting

Learning Objectives

When you have completed studying this chapter you should be able to:

1. Describe the nature of strategic thinking.
2. Explain the relevance of PEST factors to strategic analysis.
3. Outline the process of industry analysis.
4. Articulate the difference between cost leadership and product differentiation strategies.
5. Describe the nature of strategic management accounting.
6. Discuss the benchmarking process.

## 7.1 Introduction to Strategic Management

In the introductory chapter of this book, although in reality the dividing line between them is blurred, we identified three different types of managerial decisions: strategic, management planning, and management control. In this chapter, we will focus exclusively on strategic decisions and the emerging discipline of strategic management accounting.

Until relatively recently, many managerial accounting textbooks, course syllabi and examination papers concentrated on historical, internal and financial information about a business entity. Admittedly, this information is important in the context of day-to-day operations. However, if this is the only information that is produced, managers will tend to concentrate on operational issues rather than on the overall purpose and direction of the organisation.

Advocates of change suggest that managerial accounting should broaden the range of information it provides to managers, which should include data on the environment in which the company operates, including competitors. In many ways, this new focus is intuitive. Writers on corporate strategy stress that increased global competition favours pre-emptive strategic planning over management by reaction. To survive, companies must have the capability to anticipate and respond to changes in the market place. In order to do this, firms must scan their environment, analyse their strengths and weaknesses and position themselves so as to minimise threats and maximise their ability to take advantage of opportunities. All this highlights the need for strategic thinking.

## What is Strategy?

The term 'strategy' comes from the Greek *strategia* which means the 'art or science of being a general'. This military context required that each battle fought must serve the strategic purpose of ultimately winning the war. In modern business, strategy represents the shared understanding of how the vision of the organisation is to be achieved, given the organisational strengths and weaknesses, together with the environmental opportunities and threats.

It is important to note that not only does strategy indicate what should be done but it also indicates what should *not* be done. It is also important to note that in strategic thinking we should differentiate between the 'end' and the 'means'. Thus, many firms have an objective of, say, generating a required profit target. This profit target is achieved as a result of the firm's various activities during the accounting period. But a profit figure tells us little about the 'means' by which this profit performance was generated.

In some companies management do not bother or are unable to develop a strategic plan for their business. The consequences of not having an agreed strategy within an organisation will probably be reflected in a 'drifting' performance, highlighted by:

- A lack of clarity about direction and priorities and no acknowledgement of and attention to the critical success factors of the business. (Critical success factors are those key activities or areas in which company performance must excel in order to be successful.)
- Many decisions made in reaction to a 'crisis' and on the basis of intuition. Because of the urgency of the situation, managers are unable to identify and/or consider all the possible alternatives available and often a short-term solution is found to a long-term problem. In many cases, the symptoms are resolved but the underlying causes remain, in which case, the problem will reoccur. Because of the demands on managerial time, there is even less time devoted to any form of strategic thinking
- Expansion of sales volume without regard to the financial consequences, such as additional cash required to fund increased working capital requirements and the acquisition of fixed assets.
- Poor knowledge of customer needs and little understanding of why performance of competitors may be superior.
- The firm having too many products and too many customers – due to the inability to identify and eliminate unprofitable products and customers.

Inevitably, the financial performance of these 'drifting' companies is unsatisfactory. Nobody within the organisation seems to understand what the real causes of this low profitability are. As the financial crisis deepens, a typical managerial reaction is to reduce spending on staff training, advertising and customer service. In other words, they often fail to invest in the future of the firm. Of course, the immediate impact of reducing this expenditure on such discretionary items will be positive in terms of short-term profit performance. However, in terms of creating long-term value for the business and its owners, the impact could be extremely negative – skilled employees and important customers could be lost. Indeed, the cost-cutting measures may reflect internal 'politics' whereby spending cuts in certain areas are avoided by well-connected managers.

It is not uncommon for an overall salary cap or limit to be imposed together with a ban on any new staff appointments. The inevitable outcome is decreased employee motivation, high staff turnover and reduced job satisfaction for those employees that stay. This continuous, downward cycle is depicted in **Exhibit 7.1**.

*Strategic Thinking*

In order to reduce the possibility of 'drift', some form of strategic thinking is required. In essence, strategic thinking should provide the answer to three fundamental questions:

1. **Where are we now?** This represents an analysis of the business and its competitive/market situation. It identifies the firm's current strengths and weaknesses, together with the threats and opportunities posed by the market place and the firm's competitors (actual and potential). We can refer to this phase as **strategic analysis.** It will be discussed in **Section 7.2** below.
2. **Where do we want to be at some future date and how will the firm get there?** This phase can be referred to as **strategic choice** and requires agreement on a vision or mission statement for the firm, which gives it a long-term direction. Strategic choice also involves the generation of strategic options, the evaluation of these options and the selection of an appropriate strategy, based on proper financial evaluation, taking into consideration the likely risks involved. An important aspect of strategic choice is about being different! This means performing *different* activities

EXHIBIT 7.1: IMPACT OF LACK OF STRATEGIC THINKING

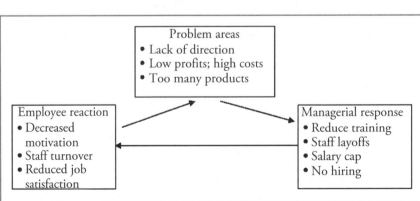

from competitors or performing similar activities to rivals in *different ways*. This topic will be covered in **Section 7.3**.

3. **How well is strategy being translated into action, i.e. to what extent is strategy being implemented?** (This topic is covered in subsequent chapters of this book, especially **Chapters 14, 15** and **16.**)

## 7.2 Strategic Analysis

The first step in strategic thinking involves evaluating the current position of the organisation by analysing the environment in which it operates (environmental analysis) and also the organisation itself (internal analysis). A firm that is insensitive to future changes in its external environment will not maximise its potential and may jeopardise its survival. For example, introducing a new product that requires considerable investment may be an appropriate strategy if the economy is growing and the organisation's financial position is strong. This choice is likely to be a much riskier strategy if the economy is in deep economic recession and the organisation's financial position is precarious. Strategic analysis can be performed at three different levels:

1. at a macro level,
2. at industry level, and
3. at the firm level.

Each of these will now be discussed in turn.

### 1. Macro Analysis

This involves looking at the general business environment. This is sometimes referred to as **PEST analysis** since the political, economic, social and technological factors are considered. (Some writers refer to PESTEL, representing the political, economic, social, technological, ecological and legal factors.) The following aspects could be pertinent and some of the considerations below may be linked.

*Political Factors*

The political (and legal) environment, together with government action, can have a profound impact on organisations. For example, some industries are being increasingly regulated, e.g. health, safety or environment concerns. In contrast, other industries have been deregulated, e.g. the airline industry. In some countries, there are changes in government procurement policies, including increasing emphasis on Public Private Partnerships (PPPs). One should also note changing patterns of government expenditure in areas such as health, education and general infrastructure. More specific aspects of government intervention include corporation tax rules and rates, waste disposal matters, employee legislation including the termination of employee contracts and, in many countries, the ban on smoking in work areas including places of entertainment.

One important aspect of this political dimension is reflected in the exchequer returns which are published on a monthly basis and typically within one week of the month end. The exchequer returns indicate the total tax receipts and also the total expenditure made by central government with the balance being represented by additional borrowing and, therefore, an increase in the national debt, or an exchequer surplus.

The main tax receipts consist of VAT and income tax and both of these reflect on the general condition of the national economy. VAT provides an indication of overall consumer spending and, in some economies, consumer spending can represent about 70% of GDP. Income tax receipts provide an indication of the strength of the labour market and overall income. Government expenditure is listed under a number of departments and headings and expenditure on key areas such as health and education should be closely watched.

### Economic Factors

Corporate success and profitability is often strongly linked to national and international economic conditions. Therefore, the following are some relevant considerations:

- **Growth of national economy as measured by Gross Domestic Product** (Some commentators argue that gross national product is a better measure of total economic performance.) Not only is the growth in the national economy important, but most countries are impacted by the growth in the US economy. The US economy is the world's biggest economy and accounts for, in excess of, 25% of the world's GDP and is a massive source of foreign direct investment (FDI). For example, it has been estimated that a 1% change in US GDP per annum would have approximately a 2% impact on the Irish economy.
- **Retail Sales** Monthly retail sales figures are also produced. Because retail sales are an important element in economic growth, any downturn could be a sign that the economy is heading for an economic recession.
- **Live Register/Unemployment** The Live Register is the timeliest monthly release by the Central Statistics Office (CSO) and many economists consider that this is the most accurate indicator of unemployment levels. However, the Central Statistics Office (CSO) do NOT consider it an unemployment count because it includes part-time workers and also those signing on for benefits and credits at family and social welfare offices all over the country. In addition to the numbers on the Live Register it is important to note the age and gender of those involved.
- **Inflation** The CSO also publishes the Consumer Price Index (CPI) on a monthly basis. The rate of inflation has important implications for personal disposable incomes and, therefore, may impact on pay restraint and wage bargaining. Price reductions are a positive sign they should improve national competitiveness. Furthermore, interest rates are used by the European Central Bank (ECB) to control inflation and they have little hesitation in increasing interest rates whenever they perceive that there are inflationary pressures within the Eurozone.

- **Future Foreign Exchange Rates** Over the past few years, the Euro has appreciated significantly against the US dollar and UK sterling. Thus, Euro competitiveness is being eroded in both manufactured goods and tourism. However, the Euro can also depreciate.
- **Expected demand levels for major products and growth in major markets** At time of writing, GDP growth in the Eurozone countries is extremely low compared to growth rates of about 7% per annum for the BRIC (Brazil, Russia, India and China) economies.
- **Availability and Prices for Key Raw Materials** This is evidenced, for example, by the price of crude oil. In simple terms, many commentators argue that we have reached the level of 'peak oil' whereby the world is consuming more oil than it is discovering. The growth in consumption is partly due to the emerging economies of China and India and current world oil consumption is expected to double within a few decades.

*Social Factors*

Social and demographic considerations will also have a dramatic impact on most organisations and many consider that the key to successful strategy and marketing is to monitor the demographics of the market place. Therefore, it is important to monitor the following:

- **Demographic trends, in terms of population growth** For example, in Western economies the number of older (and retired) people will increase from about 10% to about 20% of the total population over the next 20 years. Also, the life expectancy of both males and females are expected to lengthen considerably. Such a trend will have enormous impact on the demand for consumer goods, and on social security and pension payments. Indeed, it may be inevitable that the retirement age will be extended beyond 65 years.
- **Changes in social fashions, attitudes, habits and trends** For example, in terms of alcohol consumption, there is a significant trend towards drinking 'at home', partly due to the ban on cigarette smoking in places of entertainment but also because of drink-driving laws. In addition, younger drinkers prefer to drink cocktails and wine. These trends are expected to continue.

*Technological Factors*

Technology affects not only the products themselves but also methods of production, design and distribution. If a company is involved in an industry with rapidly changing technology, and if it does not invest as much and as rapidly as its competitors, it runs the risk of going out of business. Thus, the following issues should be considered by managers:

- trends in technology
- improvements in communication and transport
- legal protection of patents together with intellectual property rights.

## 2. Industry Analysis

Organisations prefer to operate in an industry or market where there are weak competitive forces. In such an environment, it will be easier to dominate and increase sales and overall profitability. If the competitive forces are strong it will be much more difficult for the firm to be successful. **Industry analysis** involves looking at the industry in which the firm operates (or might operate in the future) and assessing how attractive it is. **Michael Porter** (in his 1980 book entitled **Competitive Strategy**) presented his **'Five Forces' model** and argued that the overall profitability of the industry is determined by five potential sources of competition:

(a) the rivalry among existing firms,
(b) the threat of new entrants to market, and
(c) the threat of substitute products or services, together with
(d) the bargaining power of customers, and
(e) the bargaining power of suppliers.

It is important that the potential impact of each of these five forces on the firm's sales prices, volume, costs and required level of investment is clarified and agreed. Also, it is important to be aware of entry and exit barriers. **Entry barriers** prevent a new firm entering a market. Exit barriers prevent an existing firm leaving the market due to, e.g. high redundancy costs. Each of the five forces in an industry is presented in **Exhibit 7.2** and will be discussed in turn.

### (a) Rivalry among Existing Firms

At the most basic level, the profits of the industry are a function of the maximum price that customers are willing to pay for the industry's product or service. One of the key

EXHIBIT 7.2: INDUSTRY STRUCTURE AND PROFITABILITY

| Degree of actual and potential competition | | |
|---|---|---|
| **Rivalry among existing firms** | **Threat of new entrants** | **Threat of substitute products** |
| *Industry growth rate* *Concentration* *Excess capacity* *Scale/learning economies* | *Capital intensity* *Distribution access* *Legal barriers* | *Willingness of buyers to switch* |

**INDUSTRY PROFITABILITY**

| **Bargaining power of customers** | **Bargaining power of suppliers** |
|---|---|
| *Customers' price sensitivity* *Relative bargaining power* | *Customers' price sensitivity* *Relative bargaining power* |

**Relative bargaining power of customers and suppliers**

determinants of selling price is whether there is competition between providers of the same or similar products. At one extreme, if there is a state of perfect competition in the industry, economic theory predicts that prices will be equal to marginal (variable) cost and there will be few opportunities to earn super-normal profits. At the other extreme, if a single firm dominates the industry, there will be potential to earn excess profits. In reality, the degree of competition in most industries is somewhere in between perfect competition and monopoly – a situation that economists refer to as an oligopoly. In an **oligopoly**, businesses are mutually dependent: they feel the effects of each other's actions and are prone to react to them.

Several factors determine the intensity of competition between existing firms in an industry:

- **Industry Growth Rate** If an industry is growing very rapidly, existing firms need not take market share from each other to grow. In contrast, if there is slow industry growth the only way existing firms can grow is by taking market share away from competitors and, in this situation, one can expect frequent price wars among firms in the industry.
- **Excess Capacity** If capacity in an industry is larger than customer demand, there is a strong incentive for firms to cut prices to fill capacity. This aspect may also depend on the distinction of fixed/variable costs and assumes that volume is the significant cost driver for firms.
- **Scale/Learning Economies** If there are scale economies in an industry, size becomes an important factor. In such situations, there are incentives to engage in aggressive behaviour in order to increase market share.

### (b) Threat of New Entrants

New entrants bring new capacity, desire for market share and, in some cases, substantial resources. Therefore, the threat of new firms entering an industry potentially constrains the pricing policy of existing firms and is a key determinant of current profitability. The threat of new entrants can be influenced by:

- **Capital intensity, i.e. large capital requirements** This could represent a situation where new entrants face the prospect of investing heavily in large capacity which might not be utilised right away. Thus, new entrants will suffer from a cost disadvantage in competing with existing firms. Capital intensity may be also due to large investments in research and development (e.g. the pharmaceutical industry) or in brand advertising (e.g. alcohol) or in physical plant and equipment (e.g. telecommunications industry).
- **Distribution Access** Access to channels of distribution is important in most industries. Thus, lack of access to existing channels or the high costs of developing new channels can act as a powerful barrier to entry. For example, new consumer goods manufacturers may find it difficult to get shelf space in supermarkets or other retail outlets.
- **Legal Barriers** There are many industries in which legal barriers, such as patents, copyrights and trademarks limit entry. However, trademark protection is only

valid in the country where people or a company applies for a trademark. Thus, a registered trademark in, say, Switzerland does not affect China. Similarly, licensing regulations limit entry into sectors such as taxi services, broadcasting and telecommunications industries.

### (c) Threat of Substitute Products

The third source of (actual and potential) competition in an industry is the threat of substitute products or services. Relevant substitutes are not necessarily those that have the same form as the existing products but those that perform the same function. For example, trains, buses and car rentals may be substitutes for each other when it comes to travel over distances.

Customers' willingness to substitute products is often the critical factor in a competitive situation. For example, even when tap water and bottled water serve the same function, many customers may be unwilling to substitute the former for the latter, enabling the manufacturers of bottled water to charge a premium price. Similarly, designer label clothing commands a premium price even though it may not be generally superior in terms of basic functionality, because customers place a value on the image offered by designer labels.

In some cases, threat of substitution comes not from customers' switching to another product, but from utilising technologies that allow them to do without, or use less of, the existing product. For example, energy-conserving technologies allow customers to reduce their consumption of electricity and coal/turf etc.

### (d) Bargaining Power of Customers

Two factors determine the power of customers: price sensitivity and relative bargaining power. **Price sensitivity** determines the extent to which buyers are willing to bargain on price; **relative bargaining power** determines the extent to which they will succeed in forcing the price down.

**Price Sensitivity**  Buyers are more price sensitive when the product is undifferentiated and there are few switching costs. The sensitivity of buyers to price also depends on the importance of the product to their own price structure. When the product represents a large fraction of the buyer's costs the buyer is likely to shop around for a lower cost alternative. In contrast, if the product is a small fraction of the buyer's cost it may not pay to spend resources to search for lower cost alternatives.

**Relative Bargaining Power**  Even if buyers are price sensitive, they may not have a strong bargaining position. The customer's bargaining power is determined by the number of buyers relative to the number of suppliers, the volume of purchases by a single buyer, the number of alternative products available to the buyer and the buyer's costs of switching from one product to another. For example, in the car industry, car manufacturers have considerable power over component manufacturers because car manufacturers are large buyers, with several alternative suppliers to choose from, and switching costs are relatively low.

## (e) Bargaining Power of Suppliers

The analysis of the bargaining power of suppliers is a mirror image of the analysis of the buyer's power in an industry.

Suppliers are powerful when there are only a few companies and there are few substitutes available to their customers, or if the buyer has to incur high switching costs in moving to another product. For example, in the soft drinks industry, both Coca-Cola and Pepsi are very powerful relative to their bottlers. In contrast, a company is more likely to be in a weak bargaining position relative to suppliers when suppliers are dominated by a few firms. Suppliers can also exert power over buyers when a supplier's product or service is critical to the buyer's business.

## 3. Firm Analysis

Analysis of the firm is the third and final stage in the strategic analysis process. It involves looking at the firm from an internal perspective (internal analysis) and also its competitive position (competitive analysis), i.e. how the company compares with actual or potential competitors in terms of products, quality, cost and customer service. It has been said that, while industry analysis determines whether the race is worth winning, firm analysis determines who will win the race.

### Internal Analysis

The assessment of the internal environment involves determining the current position of the organisation and acts as a reality check for all in the organisation. This internal appraisal will normally involve all the major functional areas of the business. **A sample set of questions that can be asked during this internal analysis is listed below**. (It is important to note that such questioning should be to prompt thinking about future improvements.)

### Overall Organisational and Internal Communication

- Is there a company mission/vision and strategy and how well is it communicated?
- How appropriate is the overall responsibility structure?
- Who are the dominant decision-makers?
- Is the style of management appropriate to needs?
- How adequate is the current communication system?

### Management and Staff

- What is the level of experience and competence of managers and employees?
- What is the general incentive/reward system available to employees?
- What is the general level of staff morale?
- What is the overall corporate culture, i.e. the way things get done within the firm?
- Are all employees properly utilised?

### Financial Position and Performance including trends

- What is the total cost per unit?
- What is the liquidity and gearing (leverage) position and trend?
- What is the return on investment, e.g. Return on Equity?
- What are the operating, investing and financing cash flows and trends?
- Does the firm have access to both short-term and long-term funds?

### Security and Risk Aspects

- What is the security of supplies including whether they are being purchased in foreign currency which exposes the firm to foreign exchange risks?
- Are there adequate asset protection systems?
- Is there a risk management system in place?
- What is the effectiveness of all storage facilities?

### Marketing Function

- Is there a strong brand?
- How are customer needs, including customer service, satisfied and monitored?
- Do selling price changes impact on sales demand?
- Is the product portfolio too wide or too narrow?
- How effective is the overall marketing spend?

### Production Function

- What plans are there for improvement in facilities and processes?
- Is there spare capacity?
- How is employee productivity measured?

### Research, Development and Innovation Function

- What is the amount spent on R&D and its trend as % of sales?
- What projects/initiatives are currently in progress?
- How many new products has the firm introduced last year?
- Is the firm ahead or behind its competitors in the area of innovation?

### Accounting and Information Systems

- How frequently are management accounts and key reports prepared?
- Are accounting reports circulated to appropriate persons?
- Are recipients satisfied with the reports they receive?
- What is the percentage of accounting errors discovered within the system?

The results of any internal analysis are crucial in determining the firm's future strategy. Not only does it indicate the, broadly defined, resources that the firm has, it also evaluates how well they have been used in the past. This may lead to an estimate of how well the resources may be used in the future by the same management and whether there is need for additional resources and/or new management.

*Competitive Analysis*

Firm analysis also involves looking at the relative market position of the organization. Market size, market share and market growth are important areas to monitor as these are important drivers of future profitability.

It is also appropriate to analyse the product/service portfolio of the firm. A number of alternative approaches to mapping the portfolio of products/services of a firm have been suggested. One approach illustrated here is the Growth/Market Share matrix that was popularised by the Boston Consulting Group (BCG) during the 1970s to help companies balance their product portfolios in terms of growth versus mature products and cash generators versus cash drains.

The **BCG Matrix** (see **Exhibit 7.3**) shows the expected market growth rate (over the next five years for the market as a whole) on the vertical axis and the relative market share of products on the horizontal axis. The central vertical line identifies the division between high and low (relative) market share. Relative Market Share (RMS) should be used rather than absolute share and this is defined as the market share enjoyed by a firm in a business segment relative to its next largest competitor. It is argued that absolute market share (e.g. 20%) means little because it could mean a very small relative market share if the dominant competitor has 60% of

EXHIBIT 7.3: BCG GROWTH/MARKET SHARE MATRIX

| | | Relative market share of product | |
|---|---|---|---|
| | | High ⟵ | Low |
| Market growth rate | High | 'STARS' Maintain market share by reinvesting profits in price reductions, marketing, product improvement, and discourage competition. Stars become cash cows as product matures. | '???' Invest in market segmentation strategies to reduce competition and increase market share OR Reduce marketing spend and let product become a dog. ↓ |
| | Low | 'CASH COWS' Milk the cash out of the product by reducing marketing to only keep market share. The product is now too long in its life cycle for a strong competitive entry. | 'DOGS' Drop the product. |

the market. Alternatively, absolute market share (e.g. 20%) could be significant if the market is very fragmented and the next largest competitor has only 2% of the market.

The BCG Matrix has four cells and all products are assigned to one of these cells as follows:

1. Stars have high (relative) market share in a growing market. Such products represent the best profit and growth opportunities available. When the market growth falls off, the firm should be very profitable and will generate large amounts of cash and become a *cash cow*. The rule for *star* products is to do whatever is necessary to hold, or if possible, gain market share.
2. Cash Cows represent mature products and likely to be yesterday's *stars*, with high (relative) market share in low-growth markets. Given the combination of low growth but high market share they usually have an entrenched position, which tends to generate substantial cash surpluses over and above that required for investment and growth. *Cash cows* represent a valuable resource because they can be 'milked' so as to generate cash which can be used to develop new *star* products.
3. Dogs have poor competitive position. They suffer from low growth and low market share, and are usually not very profitable. Consequently these products are prime candidates for dropping.
4. ??? are products which have high market growth but a low market share. They pose a dilemma. On the one hand, it is good to be in a high growth market but on the other hand, it is not good to be in a weak (relative) market share position. It will cost the firm a lot of money to move into a *star* position. There are two recommended options: for *???* products – either develop the product into a *star* or divest it as a *dog*.

## *Strategic Implications of BCG Analysis and its Limitations*

The implications of BCG analysis are that firms should have a balanced portfolio of products, which are, most likely, at different stages of their product lifecycle. For the future success of the business, it is important that new products be developed and successfully launched. However, to avoid cash flow problems, new products need to be funded by products at their mature stage and which are currently generating large cash flows.

Like many tools and techniques, there are a number of problems with using the BCG Matrix. First, the BCG Matrix takes into consideration a limited number of factors, in particular the firm's (relative) market share and overall market growth rate. It is logical to suggest that other factors should be taken into consideration in assessing the competitive position of a firm's products. Secondly, there is the practical problem of deciding what is a high or low growth rate for the market and what is the high and low (relative) market share? Thirdly, there is the issue of identifying an appropriate market segment in which the firm operates. For example, is the 'market' defined in terms of the locality or a wider region and how are boundaries defined? Finally, there is the difficulty, on occasions, of getting accurate data for the overall market. In brief, it is fair to say that the **BCG Matrix** is *one* interesting way to look at a firm's product portfolio, but it should be used with caution.

## SWOT Analysis

When the phases of both internal and competitive analysis are completed, managers should have identified the main strengths, weaknesses, opportunities and threats (SWOT) to be specifically considered.

Both strengths and weaknesses are internal to the firm. A strength is something that the firm is good at doing or something that gives the firm reputation. A weakness is something an organisation lacks or performs in an inferior way to the competition. In contrast, opportunities and threats are external to the firm.

An opportunity represents a condition in the external environment which may facilitate the successful performance of the firm. Opportunities will include areas such as new or enlarged markets for existing products, the introduction of new products, improving existing products, cost reductions via new or improved technology, and, even the acquisition of another company to diversify risk.

A threat represents a condition that reduces the possibility of the firm reaching its objectives. Threats could include the introduction of superior products by a competitor, dangers to the stability of raw material supplies, potential labour problems or political upheavals in an overseas country where the organisation has a well-established market.

An illustrative (but incomplete) list of some of the key issues emerging from any SWOT analysis is presented in **Exhibit 7.4** below. A common mistake is to list all the strengths, weaknesses, opportunities and threats since this could lead to 'paralysis by analysis'. Thus, it is recommended that only those items that could be of crucial significance be presented and discussed.

EXHIBIT 7.4: SWOT ANALYSIS – WHAT TO LOOK FOR

| Potential strengths | Potential weaknesses | Potential opportunities | Potential threats |
|---|---|---|---|
| Powerful strategy | No clear strategic direction | Growing market size and new markets | Slowing market growth |
| Strong financial condition | Weak financial position | Falling interest rates | Future financial restrictions e.g. no loans |
| Strong brand name/image/ reputation | Obsolete facilities | Future acquisition of rival firms | Loss of sales to substitute products |
| Cost competitive and profitable | Higher costs than competitors and/or lower profits | Customers are not price sensitive | Adverse shifts in FX rates |

| Potential strengths | Potential weaknesses | Potential opportunities | Potential threats |
|---|---|---|---|
| Good customer service | Internal operating problems | Openings to exploit 'differentiation' | Entry of potential new competitors |
| Good product quality | Product line is too narrow | Expand or adapt product line | Bargaining power of customers or suppliers |
| Alliances or joint ventures | Weak management and functional skills | Alliances or joint venture to expand | Demographic changes |

## 7.3 Strategic Choice

Following the strategic analysis process, we need to look at **strategic choice** – where do we want the firm to be and how do we get there? In this regard it is useful to agree on the firm's vision statement as it is against this vision statement that the more detailed objectives can be written. A **vision statement** is a challenging and imaginative picture of the future role and objectives for an organisation, significantly going beyond its current environment and competitive position. Alternatively, it has been described as a dream about what the company could become and is very much an aspiration. The term 'vision' is often used as a synonym for 'mission', particularly in non-English speaking countries where 'mission' is difficult to translate. But the concepts are different. **Mission** is why a firm exists, i.e. its basic function in society. **Vision** is a view of what the firm could become in the future. Some firms now combine both vision and mission elements into the same statement.

The emphasis on formal vision statements is relatively new and a number of factors account for this trend. First, the modern workforce has changed. Generally, employees are better educated than previous generations, with higher expectations in terms of performance and challenge. Many employees would rather work for a firm they can believe in and, therefore, a firm that proclaims an attractive vision statement is more likely to attract the best recruits and keep them. Also, increasingly, employees are being 'empowered' to undertake appropriate activities within their firms and they will need to understand the organisation's ambitions and their contribution to that purpose. Moreover, modern business is complex, with the added ingredients of increased global competition and rapidly changing technology. A vision statement serves to provide greater organisational purpose and direction and goes beyond the traditional assumption of maximising shareholder value – a rather limited focus as other stakeholders are ignored. Finally, an attractive **vision statement** can result in a company being more respected by its customers and society in general.

## Competitive Advantage and Generic Strategies

The vision/mission statement is aligned to 'strategic choice' since strategic choice reflects how the firm intends to compete in the market place. The acknowledged expert in this field (Michael Porter, 1980) identifies **three main strategic choices**. First, it is possible to target the whole market and adopt an **'overall cost leadership' strategy**, with its low cost focus. Secondly, a firm may target the whole market and adopt a **'product differentiation'** strategy, with the emphasis on being different or unique. Thirdly, the firm may concentrate on a 'niche' or segment of the market and adopt either a **cost leadership** or **product differentiation strategy**. These are presented in **Exhibit 7.5** below.

### Cost Leadership

Cost leadership is a strategy whereby firms outperform their competitors by producing products or services at the lowest cost. Cost leadership could be attributed to high volume, since the cost leader normally has a large market share through low prices and avoids niche markets. Also, economies of scale and/or learning curves may be present which lower unit cost and allow the company to set even lower prices, perhaps eliminating competition.

Cost advantages may also arise from productivity in the manufacturing process, in distribution, or in overall administration. For example, technological innovation in the manufacturing process and labour savings from overseas production are common routes to low cost advantage. Cost leadership companies continuously reduce costs and these cost savings may be passed on to customers in the form of lower prices. Furthermore, low prices limit the growth of competitors and their profitability.

It is also possible to be a cost leader by eliminating discretionary spending. However, it is important not to cut expenditure areas which are important to the long-term position of the firm, e.g. research and development, customer care/service, advertising/marketing and staff training and development. Thus, a potential weakness of the cost leadership strategy is the risk of cutting costs in a way that undermines future demand

EXHIBIT 7.5: MATRIX OF STRATEGIC CHOICES

| | | Strategic Advantage | |
|---|---|---|---|
| | | **Low Cost Position** | **Uniqueness perceived by the Customer** |
| Strategic Target | Industry-wide | 1. Cost leadership | 2. Product differentiation |
| | Niche, i.e. specific segment only | 3. Cost leadership | 4. Product differentiation |

for the product or service. The cost leader remains competitive only as long as the consumer sees that the product or service is (at least nearly) equivalent to competing products that cost somewhat more.

Firms known to be successful at cost leadership are typically very large manufacturers, retailers or low-cost airlines.

*Product Differentiation*

The product differentiation strategy is implemented by creating a perception among consumers that the product or service is unique in some important way, usually by being of higher quality. Brand loyalty will accrue and the perceived better features may allow the company to charge a higher price. The differences may be real or perceived in terms of quality and additional product features. Other differences could be attributable to superior customer service, or even friendliness of staff and cleanliness of premises. However, the characteristics giving rise to product differentiation are capable of being imitated by competitors, although this may be difficult to accomplish in the short term. Alternatively, customers may begin to believe that the perceived difference is not significant – in which situation, lower-cost rival products will appear more attractive. There are differentiated firms in most industries but the appeal of differentiation is especially strong for product lines for which the perception of quality and image is important, as in cosmetics, jewellery and automobiles.

Product differentiation can be identified in a business by comparing the firm with its competitors, using four main headings, with emphasis on the firm's strengths and its competitors' weaknesses:

- Price  Is your price more or less expensive than competitors? Are you considered to be at the top, middle or low end of the spectrum in your market? Is your pricing policy something that sets you apart from your competitors?
- Customer Service  Is there anything about your customer service approach that is unique? Do you provide more assistance including better ongoing customer service, friendlier staff, or provide more attractive terms of service including better on-time delivery?
- Product  Does your product (or service) provide superior value, relative to your competitors, to your customers? Can your product or service be imitated by another firm or substituted by another product? In other words, is your product or service different from existing and potential other product offerings?
- Reputation  How strong is the brand reputation? Who is traditionally attracted to your offerings?

*Focus*

The 'focus' strategy concentrates on a specific 'niche' or segment of a market – as defined, for example, by type of customer, segment of the product line, or geographic area. This strategy is used to choose market niches where competition is the weakest, or where the firm has a strong competitive advantage. The argument here is that the firm succeeds by avoiding direct competition! It has either strong differentiation or low cost advantage (or both) for its market segment. For example, some professional accountancy firms succeed by focusing on tax and personal financial service needs of small clients, in contrast to the audit services offered by the larger international accountancy firms for larger clients. The 'focus' strategy is usually associated with a market segment that is not currently catered for.

An important limitation of the focus strategy is that the niche may suddenly disappear because of technological change in the industry, or change in consumer tastes. A company that specialises only in gourmet coffees, for example, would have a difficult time competing if consumer tastes shifted to other beverages.

The distinctive aspects of these three strategic choices or strategies (cost leadership, differentiation or focus) are summarised in **Exhibit 7.6**. These elements reflect the strategic target, the basis of competitive advantage, product line emphasis, marketing emphasis and accounting orientation.

The accounting information required by managers will vary according to the strategy chosen. With a cost leadership strategy, cost control (and cost reduction), facilitated by traditional budgeting (see **Chapter 14**) and standard costing systems (see **Chapter 15**) will be important. Also, analysis of competitors' cost structures and

EXHIBIT 7.6: DISTINCTIVE ASPECTS OF THE THREE COMPETITIVE STRATEGIES

| Aspect | Cost leadership | Differentiation | Focus |
|---|---|---|---|
| *Strategic target* | Broad cross-section of the market | Broad cross-section of the market | Narrow market segment |
| *Basis of competitive advantage* | Lowest cost in the industry | Unique product or service | Unique product or service or lowest cost in a specific market segment |
| *Product line emphasis* | Limited selection | Wide variety with differentiating features | Targeted to selected market segment |
| *Marketing emphasis* | Low price | Premium price and innovative, differentiating features | Firm's unique ability to serve the selected market segment |
| *Accounting orientation* | Cost control and also market share | Critical success factors relating to quality and service | Critical success factors relating to quality, service *or* cost |

market shares will also receive prominence. In contrast, for firms following a product differentiation strategy, critical factors such as quality, on-time delivery and customer service are likely to be more important for the success of the firm.

## 7.4 Benchmarking

In previous sections we have argued that a firm can only develop its strategy in the context of the firm's position relative to its key competitors. For example, a company's absolute cost level has limited information content – without knowledge of competitor's costs, the firm does not know who the weak and strong opponents are. In the absence of adequate competitor analysis, management must take strategic decisions on very limited information.

An increasingly popular method of comparative analysis is 'benchmarking'. **Benchmarking** is the systematic process of discovery and examination of best practices that lead to superior performance. The resulting **benchmarks** become performance metrics for the company as part of its continuous improvement programme. Benchmarking activities include aspects such as product quality, cost metrics, customer satisfaction and after-sales service and other measures of financial and non-financial performance. Competitive benchmarking can help an organisation avoid being 'ambushed' by competitors since it is a form of environmental scanning which uncovers surprises in the environment (or provides assurances that there are none).

One of the first (published) benchmarking projects was undertaken by Xerox in response to competitive threats from the Japanese. At that time Japanese competitors were selling copiers for less than it cost Xerox to make them in the United States. Launched in 1979, Xerox's competitive benchmarking project was used to examine the cost, operating capabilities, features and mechanical characteristics of similar copier products. This project revealed important performance gaps which Xerox used as a basis for targeting continuous improvement in order to regain its competitive position. Thus, benchmarking relates to the Japanese philosophy of continuous improvement which we mentioned in **Chapter 6**. Continuous improvement is a never-ending commitment to do a little bit better, every day, in every activity. Indeed, the only reason for undertaking a benchmarking exercise is to improve upon existing performance since the benchmarking results are compared with best practice in other companies. The resulting 'benchmark' becomes the standard to be achieved and action is planned to bring current performance up to this level, i.e. to close the gap.

A benchmarking exercise can be extremely useful in exposing incorrect perceptions about the company's strengths and weaknesses. Due to benchmarking the magnitude of the performance gap, relative to competitors, is clearly identified for all to see. Therefore, benchmarked measurements are powerful tools in the change process for every company and benchmarking exercises have become the starting point for process engineering efforts in many organisations.

The performance gap can be either positive or negative. If the gap is slightly positive it indicates that the competition is not too far behind. A large gap on the positive side signals that the company has a competitive advantage that can be exploited in the market place. If the gap is slightly negative, management can look to continuous improvement programmes to reach parity. Unfortunately, the performance gaps may be large on the negative side. As a result, management's initial reaction to them may be one of denial or disbelief, perhaps even suggesting that the benchmarking study was poorly done. Indeed, a large performance gap may be discouraging, causing managers to feel that they cannot possibly catch up on, let alone overtake, the performance of their competitors. However, a large negative gap has only one meaning – radical change is required if the company is to survive.

### Internal Benchmarking

For many companies, internal benchmarking will be the important first step in all external benchmarking exercises. **Internal benchmarking** is the comparison of similar operations or functions across a company, or with associated companies, in order to identify best practice within this common setting. It identifies those centres of excellence within the organisation that can be a source of learning and inspiration for others. Internal benchmarking requires the identification of all existing activities and processes within the various departments of the organisation and their 'drivers', i.e. the causes or triggers of work. Benchmarks cannot be established without a comprehensive understanding of current practices and routines. There are a number of **advantages** associated with internal benchmarking:

- It opens up and improves communication within the organisation. To be successful, benchmarking requires the active participation of every employee in identifying current activities, identifying best practice and facilitating the change needed to match best practice. Benchmarking is about learning from one another and this learning can only take place if everyone feels comfortable in sharing information and can see some benefit from it.
- It allows a company to understand and clearly document its existing practices and procedures. Apart from a benchmarking exercise, it is rare for a company to look at how it does its work in such detail. In many organisations, work processes develop over time and escape scrutiny. Unfortunately, very few tasks are ever discontinued but many enhancements are added over time. The result is incremental and random growth in work procedures, some of which no longer serve a genuine purpose.
- Internal benchmarking can provide immediate opportunities for performance improvement since it identifies good and bad performance within the organisation. This is achieved by assessing whether a particular segment of the company is performing significantly better than others, by exploring the source of this relatively superior performance and by deciding how this superior performance can be emulated by other units within the company.
- It provides an important framework to compare existing internal practices to external benchmark data.

A potential danger of internal benchmarking is that it is confined to internal analysis. In reality, it is the relative performance against competitors that ultimately determines a company's success. In addition, if internal benchmarking is poorly done, it can make subsequent efforts more difficult. This is particularly the case where benchmarking studies are perceived by employees as the first phase of a potential re-engineering programme or redundancy package.

### Using Consultants or Employees?

Benchmarking can be carried out by employees or by external consultants. Companies that have been engaged in benchmarking projects for a number of years believe that a significant amount of money and time can be saved by training their own employees to perform benchmarking projects. Also, some experts believe an in-house effort is more likely to be of higher quality, better targeted and better translated into action. On the other hand, external consultants will have a wide variety of experience and contacts and have the benefit of being more objective in their approach.

In summary, benchmarking is being successfully used by companies in order to identify how to become a world-class performer. The technique is extremely useful in overcoming management complacency and in exposing incorrect perceptions about the company's strengths and weaknesses. However, the adverse gaps between a company's performance relative to best practices can be stunning in magnitude and, as a result, management's initial reaction to them may be one of disbelief with some managers unable to believe that any competitor could be so clearly advantaged. Indeed, a large performance gap may be discouraging, causing managers to feel that they cannot possibly catch up on best competitors. Implementing a benchmarking project cannot ensure success for an organisation. However, it should allow the company to know where its strengths and weaknesses lie. While knowledge is never a sure road to victory, ignorance represents a definite path to failure. As someone once remarked: "If you think education costs money, try ignorance!"

## 7.5  Strategic Management Accounting

It is now generally argued that the traditional orientation of management accounting, based mainly on internally orientated, historical financial data, is not adequate to fully inform managerial decision-making in the modern world. Traditional management accounting information has been described, somewhat uncharitably but nevertheless colourfully, as trying to drive a car down a motorway looking only through a rear-view mirror.

In the market place, competitors try to outmanoeuvre each other with more efficient manufacturing and service delivery processes and better quality. Consumers have also become more sophisticated in their requirements for customer service and value for money. In such an environment, the ability of a firm to be successful is unlikely to happen by chance. Rather, if success is to be achieved (and there is no guarantee that it will be achieved), it will need a carefully thought-out and executed strategy that takes into consideration the important dimensions of a firm's internal and external operating environment.

Not surprisingly, the focus and importance of strategy is, increasingly, being integrated within the discipline of managerial accounting and topics, such as Strategic Management Accounting (SMA), are now appearing on professional management accounting exam papers. Although, there is no generally agreed definition of the term, it would be accepted that the term incorporates topics that have earlier been discussed in this chapter. However, in view of its growing importance, it might be useful if this topic was specifically addressed under a single heading.

There are four main aspects to strategic management accounting which include:

(a)  environmental scanning;
(b)  competitor analysis;
(c)  communicating strategy through performance measures; and
(d)  looking at certain internal data from a strategic perspective.

It should be appreciated that the thrust of strategic management accounting is to focus on areas that traditionally have been perceived as being outside the domain of the management accountant. Each of these is now discussed in turn.

## Environmental Scanning

The essence of SMA is that it focuses managerial attention on the external environment of the company. Environmental scanning involves the monitoring of the environment for possible surprises (or reassurances that there are none). These surprises may be due to technological developments, changes in customer preferences or significant economic changes. Strategic information also includes general information relating to the demographic, social, legal and political environment in which the firm operates. The major external environmental factors relevant to a company are highlighted in **Exhibit 7.7**.

EXHIBIT 7.7: EXTERNAL ENVIRONMENTAL FACTORS

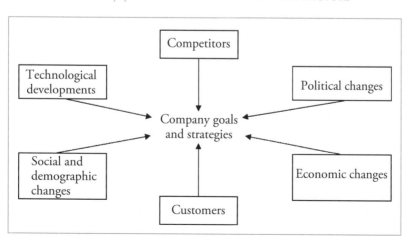

In the context of environmental scanning, the management accountant will also need to collect and analyse various types of market-orientated information. Actual market share is useful as proxy measures for assessing the success of corporate strategy. For example, a market penetration strategy, which involves setting low prices, may yield low profits in initial years and, if judged on purely short-term financial grounds, may appear to have failed. However access to market data may indicate the true position of increased market share. This type of information is best generated in co-operation with the company's marketing department. This interdepartmental co-operation is fundamental if the company's strategic position in the marketplace is to be fully recognised.

## Competitor Analysis

The company can only set meaningful objectives and resulting strategies in the context of its position relative to its key competitors and the variety of external influences in the environment. After all, it is in the market place that customers have to be retained and new customers acquired. All the products available in the market place compete not just on the basis of price but also over a range of important attributes. This perspective views products (goods or services) as a bundle of characteristics. All or some of these attributes appeal to customers and this provides goods with their value. These attributes include a variety of elements including quality, reliability, appearance, performance and after-sales service including maintenance and spare parts.

Competitor analysis can help the firm identify the sources of competitor strengths and those aspects where competitors are most vulnerable. The focus here is on product offering by competitors, their pricing, customer base and financial position. Competitor analysis is akin to setting up a competitor intelligence system and there are many possible sources of information which can be used, including:

- industry trade journals and government statistics
- promotional literature and brochures produced by competitors
- trade exhibitions and physical analysis of competitors' products
- newspaper articles, press releases and reports published on competitors
- mutual customers and suppliers
- own sales force including personnel hired from competitors
- commissioned market research.

## Communicating Strategy through Performance Measures

Strategic management accounting (SMA) recognises that strategy is related to critical success factors (CSFs) and their related performance measures (a topic which will be covered in greater detail in **Chapter 8**). These critical success factors (or key variables) represent the key areas in which superior performance will ensure success. They are the few key areas where 'things must go right' for the business in order for it to be successful. **Exhibit 7.8** presents some examples of critical success factors.

EXHIBIT 7.8: GENERAL EXAMPLE OF CRITICAL SUCCESS FACTORS

| Area of activity | Critical success factor |
| --- | --- |
| Marketing and customer reaction | Sales volume, sales growth and market share |
| | New customers acquired |
| Production and delivery | Quality and on-time delivery |
| | New customers acquired |
| | Plant capacity utilisation |
| Asset management and profitability | Return on Investment (RoI) |
| | Management of working capital |

Thus, the reporting emphasis is shifted from retrospective variance analysis and the range of performance measures will include both financial and non-financial indicators.

## Strategic Perspective on Internal Data

In addition to the increased focus on external information, strategic management accounting (SMA) also looks at the long-term implications of internally generated information. For example, it may be that a reduction in short-term profitability is due to actions undertaken to build market share and secure relative cost advantage, which will help ensure future improvements in profit performance. If the company places too much importance on its short-term profitability, it may be unwilling to invest either in improving its competitive position or in reducing the potential impact of any adverse change in its environment. Conversely, in a strategic context, an increase in short-term profit may be associated with deterioration in its strategic position. This is because the increased profits are due to selling prices being higher than before and above the competitive level, with a consequent reduction in market share.

## Role of the Management Accountant

At this stage, it should be clear that SMA could contribute immensely to the successful performance of an enterprise. However, it can be difficult to set up a formal SMA system. A useful starting point is to identify the type of information that is already available within the firm. To varying degrees, some of the information would be available in different parts of the organisation. However, the information is mostly 'owned' by the different functions that collect them and is not widely disseminated. (Many might be surprised at the range of information that is currently collected by various individuals within the firm.)

As one who is already located at the key junctions of the information infrastructure of the firm and who performs similar tasks for routine control purposes, the management accountant could play a critical and decisive role in setting up the SMA system. It is suggested here that a major role of a strategic management accountant is to coordinate the development of a strategic information infrastructure. This would involve identifying:

(a) the type, collectors and users of strategic information already available in the organisation;
(b) how and when such information is collected and disseminated; and
(c) the necessity for expanding the collection and analysis of appropriate information.

When this is done, the management accountant should accept responsibility for collecting, analysing and disseminating the information to key members in the strategic management team within the firm. This orientation is a long way from the 'retrospective introspection' role of many traditional management accountants. Perhaps this is a role that some management accountants may feel uncomfortable with and badly prepared for? The challenge posed by SMA will move management accountants away from being only financial scorekeepers to being more involved with some of the following tasks:

•   assessment of general economic and technological factors facing the firm and industry
•   analysis of the strengths and weaknesses of both the firm and its competitors
•   designing an internal system to identify value and non-value adding activities
•   conducting customer profitability analyses
•   completing benchmarking exercises
•   identification and measurement of critical success factors (CSFs) and related key performance indicators (see **Chapter 8**).

## Cost and Information Overload

Inevitably, the complaint will be made that the addition of yet another layer of data creates information overload for managers. Also, the cost of acquiring this additional, strategic information must also be considered in the context of its value to decision-makers. However, since management can (and have) made their most costly and fatal mistakes in formulating strategic plans, then strategic information is potentially the most valuable.

SMA is an emerging discipline that is chiefly concerned with the future. This proposal to develop strategic management accounting within firms is not a subtle device to provide a role for unwanted or unemployed management accountants who see their traditional recording role being replaced by computer information systems. Rather this information '**is**' required by managers and, if this leads to better decisions, then the company and all stakeholders will benefit from it. After all, a firm whose employees are insensitive to the future will probably not have one. However, as Mark Twain said: "The art of prophecy is difficult, especially with respect to the future!"

## Conclusion

In conclusion, in this chapter we have discussed the nature of strategic thinking and how it may impact on the discipline of managerial accounting. In the next chapter we turn our attention to the firm's performance measurement system, based on critical success factors which can be used to communicate and drive strategy throughout the company.

## Summary of Learning Objectives

**Learning Objective 1:**  Describe the nature of strategic thinking.

Strategic thinking looks, mainly, to the future and external environment of the firm. By assessing potential strengths and weaknesses, together with opportunities and threats in the environment, the firm is better informed to decide on its long-term goals (or objectives) and agree how these are going to be achieved and are then communicated effectively throughout the organisation.

**Learning Objective 2:** Explain the relevance of PEST factors to strategic analysis.

PEST represents the political, economic, social (or demographic) and technological factors impacting on the firm's environment and the firm itself. Such factors have a most significant impact on the firm and can change the attractiveness of the industry and the competitive positions of competing firms.

**Learning Objective 3:** Outline the process of industry analysis.

When assessing the external environment of a firm it is usual to conduct an industry analysis to determine how attractive the overall industry is and assess its potential in the future. Overall industry profitability is determined by 'Five Forces' namely, the rivalry between existing firms, the threat of new entrants, the threat of substitute products (or services), bargaining power of customers, and the bargaining power of suppliers.

**Learning Objective 4:** Articulate the difference between cost leadership and product differentiation strategies.

Cost leadership is a strategy that concentrates on being the lowest cost producer in the market, so as to undercut actual competitors (or deter future entrants). This low price can be used to build up market share and hence benefit from future economies of scale.

**Learning Objective 5:** Describe the nature of strategic management accounting.

The essence of strategic management accounting is that it focuses attention on the firm's external environment and emphasises the firm's competitors, customers, political, economic, social and technological factors. It is only by a systematic consideration of these factors that an appropriate strategy can be devised. Strategic management accounting also involves the identification of key performance indicators, related to critical success factors. In this way, progress towards strategic intent can be monitored.

**Learning Objective 6:** Discuss the benchmarking process.

Benchmarking could be referred to as a type of inter-firm comparison both in terms of financial metrics and identifying best practice activities. Benchmarking is a useful technique in assessing the competitive position of the firm and identifying areas for improvement. However, a firm's performance in relation to agreed benchmarks may be so inferior to competitors that the results could be treated in a negative rather than in a positive way.

## Questions

### Review Questions

(See Appendix One for Solutions to Review Questions **7.1** and **7.2**)

*Question 7.1 (Strategic Management Accounting)*

**Requirement:** Write a brief note on your understanding of strategic management accounting.

*Question 7.2 (Cost Leadership v. Product Differentiation)*

In the context of strategy, outline the main differences between cost leadership and product differentiation.

### Intermediate Questions

*Question 7.3 (Strategic Management Accounting)*

**Requirement:** What is the relationship between traditional management accounting and strategic management accounting?

*Question 7.4 (Cost Leadership)*

**Requirement:** Briefly explain what factors are important in achieving 'overall cost leadership' and suggest the risks to an organisation of adopting this strategy.

*Question 7.5 (Strategic Management Accounting)*

**Requirement:** Briefly outline the nature of strategic management accounting and suggest the main factors to be considered before implementing it in your firm.

*Question 7.6 (The BCG Growth Share Matrix)*

The Boston Consulting Group (BCG) Growth Share Matrix is based on overall market growth and relative market share.

**Requirement:** Explain the BCG Growth Share Matrix.

*Question 7.7 (Strategy and Porter's Five Forces)*

Michael Porter argues that the overall attractiveness of an industry is determined by the following Five Forces:

- the rivalry amongst current competitors.
- the threat of new entrants to the industry
- the threat of substitute products or services
- the bargaining power of customers
- the bargaining power of suppliers

**Requirement:** Write an explanatory note on each of these.

## Advanced Questions

*Question 7.8 (Strategy and Relevance of Managerial Accounting)*

In their seminal book – *Relevance Lost: The Rise and Fall of Management Accounting* – Johnson and Kaplan argue that: "Today's management accounting information, driven by the procedures and cycle of the organisation's financial reporting system, is too late, too aggregated, and too distorted to be relevant for managers' planning and control decisions" (1987, p. 1).

**Requirement:** Discuss the above statement.

*Question 7.9 (Benchmarking)*

Describe the process of 'benchmarking' and indicate the benefit.

*Question 7.10 (Introduction to Strategic Management)*

The Pony Delivery Company is one of a number of document/letter delivery services by motor cycle courier in Dublin. The company was started some years ago by Tony Redmond and has grown to an organisation which has a total staff of 10 persons. Turnover for the most recent financial year amounted to about €900,000, but the firm was operating at break-even point after deducting Redmond's modest salary.

Tony is the managing director and he has two administrators who deal mainly with the day-to-day administration, i.e. logging calls, arranging pick-ups, checking on delivery of documents and miscellaneous other matters. There are seven couriers engaged as 'contractors'. This means that the couriers are regarded, for tax purposes, as self-employed, and each provides his own motor bike. In return, each courier is paid a gross amount based on the distance involved in each delivery. Such an arrangement is tax efficient for the couriers and easy to administer.

While the following mission statement was framed over Tony's desk, little attention was paid to it. Indeed, Tony only remembered it when an irate customer pointed to it recently. The vision statement read:

> "To cater for the needs of our customers by providing a fast and reliable delivery service in the Dublin area at competitive prices."

Tony did not have any formal management background but, nevertheless, he realised that there may be a need to consider the future for Pony Delivery. He has contacted the major business school near his office to seek advice on how to approach the task of reviewing the future position of Pony Delivery. Their response was to organise a 'seminar' for Tony, where the business school would outline the strategic management process.

**Requirement:** Suggest various issues and recommendations that would be discussed at the seminar and which would have an impact on the management accounting function of this business. You can identify broad or narrow aspects. You can assume that Pony Delivery Company has adequate funds to implement feasible suggestions.

## Question 7.11 (Strategic analysis)

You have just joined the American College, a small, private business school in the centre of Dublin, which offers only a MBA programme.

**Requirements:** Explain:

1. Whether a cost leadership or product differentiation strategy is more appropriate.
2. Whether the relevant industry is growing or declining and explain why or why not this trend should continue in the future.
3. What are the potential and practical threats facing the above organisation?
4. Suggest five performance measures that would reflect critical success factors.

## Question 7.12 Strategic Analysis

You have just joined the Mount Merrion Clinic, which is a residential home that exclusively caters for elderly citizens. The Clinic is partly supported by government funds with an obligation to break-even on an annual basis, taking one year with the next. However, the majority of its funding is generated by private fees and donations from residents and their families.

**Requirements:** Explain:

1. Whether a cost leadership or product differentiation strategy is more appropriate.
2. Whether the relevant industry is growing or declining and explain why or why not this trend should continue in the future.
3. What are the potential and practical threats facing the above organisation?
4. Suggest five performance measures that would reflect critical success factors.

# Performance Management and Measurement

When you have completed studying this chapter you should be able to:

1. Discuss the general limitations of accounting information.
2. Outline the nature and purpose of performance measure systems.
3. Differentiate between the financial, customer, internal and employee perspectives.
4. Describe the 'Balanced Scorecard'.
5. Explain and illustrate the concept of a critical success factor.

## 8.1 The Limitations of Accounting Numbers

In the introductory chapter of this book, and in subsequent sections, we have mentioned that some modern authors have argued that (traditional) management accounting information has lost much of its relevance in the modern business environment. At this point, it is worthwhile to note again some of these **criticisms of traditional management accounting**:

- **Management accounting provides *inaccurate* cost information especially regarding product costs**. This phenomenon is mainly due to the traditional method by which production overheads are absorbed into units of output. Traditionally, such overheads have been absorbed into units of output using, e.g. direct labour hours worked. This is a crude but simple method and probably worked very well in the past; however, it assumes that all production overheads are volume-related. In recent years, overheads have increased dramatically due to automation and an emphasis on customer focus. Many overhead costs do not vary in proportion to volume of output. In addition, direct labour costs, as a percentage of overall cost structure, have become relatively smaller. Therefore, critics argue that traditional cost accounting, using volume-based methods of absorbing production overheads, will result in inaccurate product costs! (This criticism has been addressed in **Chapter 5**, dealing with activity-based costing (ABC).)

- **Management accounting focuses mainly on *internal* data**. While internal data is important to managers in their decision-making tasks, it is also necessary that managers have available to them information relating to the firm's operating environment. For example, it will be of little consolation to the firm if it has a good product, but its competitors have a better one. Such external information will relate not only to competitors but also to the general economic environment and changing customer preferences. (This criticism has been discussed in **Chapter 7**.)

- Management accounting concentrates excessively on **the financial *'results'* for a period under review** rather than providing an adequate explanation of the means by which these financial results were generated, or, more importantly, what activities should be performed differently in the future to generate financial success. The argument here is that 'profit' cannot be directly managed. Rather, profit is generated as a natural consequence of performing well in various areas that include, e.g. customer service, quality, product development and on-time delivery performance. Thus, it can be said that the income statement is a useful but delayed confirmation of a company's competencies.

- **Management accounting concentrates on *short-term* performance**. In fairness, this short-term orientation often extends from the expectations of shareholders and other financiers. Nevertheless, there is a tendency to place a major focus on the achievement of maximum profits in a single accounting period and this creates a mentality of short-termism. If the firm places too great importance on its short-term profitability, it may be unwilling to invest in improving its competitive position, or in reducing the potential impact of any adverse change in its environment. For example, when sluggish sales or rising costs make short-term profit targets hard to achieve, managers often try to boost profits by cutting spending on research and development, marketing, quality improvements and customer care – all of which, of course, are vital to a company's long-term competitive position.

In addition, traditional accounting measurement systems can cause a variety of inappropriate actions, some of which are highlighted below in **Exhibit 8.1**. The first two inappropriate actions, namely the purchase of cheap goods and excess production are self-evident and self-explanatory. With cost centre spending reporting the focus is very much on overall spending limits. The emphasis is on the amount spent (compared with budget) but the quality of service provided is often overlooked. In addition, the annual budgeting process seeks to only justify

EXHIBIT 8.1: INAPPROPRIATE ACTIONS RESULTING FROM ACCOUNTING REPORTS

| Accounting measure | Actions | Overall impact |
|---|---|---|
| Material purchase price variance | Purchase of cheap goods | Excess material usage |
| Overhead absorption based on machine hours | Excess production | Excess stock at end of accounting period |
| Spending variance arising in a cost centre | Focus on spending but ignore overall quality | Incremental approach to budget preparation |

incremental or marginal spending each year rather than questioning the whole budget allocation.

## 8.2 Performance Measurement Systems

The organisation's strategy should be communicated to its employees and monitored. For example, if a firm decides to differentiate itself in the marketplace on the basis of quality, then it should have performance measures in place to monitor and manage quality of production (or service provided). If technological leadership and product innovation are considered to be the key source of the company's competitive advantage, then the firm should measure its performance in these areas, both in absolute terms and also relative to its competitors. In contrast, companies competing primarily on the basis of price (i.e. a cost leadership strategy) would tend to use performance measures relating to cost control, cost reduction and resource utilisation. Thus, the starting point for any well-constructed performance measurement system must be a clear expression of the organisation's vision and objectives and resultant strategy.

An organisation's **vision** is an aspirational statement of what the organisation could become in the future. The term **objective** refers to the specific things the organisation wants to achieve in a definite time period. **Strategy** concerns the matching between what a company can do (given organisational strengths and weaknesses) with what it might do (within the context of environmental opportunities and threats). Thus, an organisation's strategy is the selected route to the destination represented by its objective. In turn, performance measures should drive strategy throughout the organisation so that all people in the organisation understand what the strategy is and how their performance is linked to that overall strategy. While the organisation's vision statement is relatively stable over time, it is likely that objectives may be revised every planning period and strategies will be modified in response to results achieved. The relationship between vision, objectives, strategy, critical success factors and performance measures is depicted in **Exhibit 8.2**:

EXHIBIT 8.2: VISION, OBJECTIVES, STRATEGY, CRITICAL SUCCESS FACTORS
AND PERFORMANCE MEASURES

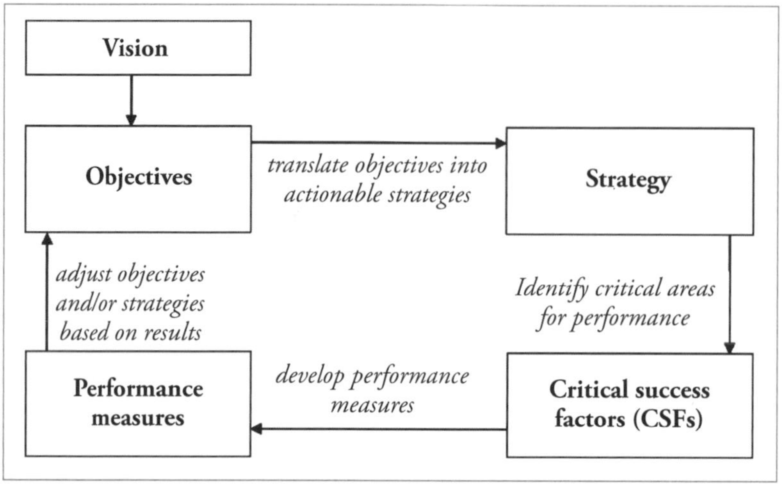

It is only when clear objectives have been set and the strategy to be followed identified that the implementation of a performance measurement system can logically proceed. Ideally, the performance measurement system should focus on the ***critical success factors*** that represent areas in which the firm must excel in order for it to be successful. In other words, they are the areas where 'things must go right' in order for the business to succeed.

## Selecting Performance Measures (or Metrics)

Once the critical success factors have been identified, based on their strategic importance, related performance measures must be established.

A distinction should be made between a performance measure and a performance indicator. **Performance measures** are direct measures, e.g. measuring customer satisfaction by way of survey instruments. In contrast, **performance indicators** involve the use of surrogate or proxy measures.

Thus, in attempting to measure customer satisfaction, for example, managers may assume that reductions in the number of defective returns provide evidence of improved customer satisfaction. Similarly, increases in employee satisfaction may be assumed by reductions in employee turnover or absenteeism. However, it must be recognised that there is a danger of misinterpreting performance indicators. The number of defective returns may subside as customers, for whom quality is a decisive buying criterion, transfer their custom to competitors. Similarly, reductions in employee turnover may be caused by a lack of opportunities for employees outside the company rather than any increased satisfaction they take from their work within the firm.

While each company's set of measures should reflect its own strategies, some principles of design hold true for all companies, for example:

- measures should be linked to corporate strategy
- measures should mirror both internal and external aspects
- measures should be both financial and non-financial.

EXHIBIT 8.3: CRITICAL SUCCESS FACTORS AND PERFORMANCE MEASURES

| Critical success factor | Non-financial measure/indicator |
| --- | --- |
| Customer satisfaction | Number of repeat orders |
| | % of served market achieved |
| | Index of customer satisfaction |
| Quality of production | Percentage of defects |
| | Percentage yield on production |
| | Warranty claims |
| Product innovation | Number of new products |
| | Time to market (for new products) |
| | Number of patents registered |
| Human resources | Percentage of absenteeism |
| | Number of staff promotions |
| | Staff turnover |

Some critical success factors and their related measures are listed in **Exhibit 8.3**. They are based on the assumption that 'what gets measured gets done'. Therefore, the ideal performance measurement system is one that energises people in an organisation to focus on things that really matter.

It should be noted that measures should be both quantitative and qualitative. Quantitative measurement includes both financial and non-financial numbers. Examples of non-financial but quantitative metrics include units sold, number of new customers and new product introductions. Quantitative measures are popular, among other reasons, because of their claim to be objective. Concerns about subjectivity often make managers in general and management accountants in particular, wary of placing undue reliance on qualitative (or non-quantifiable) measurements. Qualitative measures, such as customer or employee satisfaction are inherently subjective. However, they are critically important to business success – companies cannot prosper if their customer base is in continual decline or if their employees are dissatisfied (especially where a firm's success is particularly dependent on employees' know-how and experience).

*Establishing and Communicating Targets*

Measuring performance in isolation has no meaning. Meaning can only be achieved through comparison with targets. At the most basic level, targets can be set relative to past performance. However, this can breed a climate of incrementalism, i.e. making small adjustments each year when more radical improvements may be demanded. The most important question is – how does the firm compare to its competitors? The recognition of the need to establish targets relative to the performance of other firms has resulted in an explosion of interest in benchmarking. **Benchmarking**, as we have previously discussed, is the process of discovery and examination of the best practices, especially among competitors, that lead to superior performance.

There are two main behavioural aspects associated with setting targets for performance measures, i.e. achievability (degree of difficulty) and equity. **Achievability** is concerned with the overall level of difficulty of the targets. Generally, the higher the target, the higher the motivation to achieve. However, the targets must be realistic and perceived as realistic. In other words, the important task is finding a balance between what the superior, as opposed what the subordinate, views as achievable. Frequently, this is a source of conflict.

Finally, **equity** is concerned with perceived fairness within the organisation. In other words, targets should be comparable across similar business units.

## Implementing Evaluation-reward Systems

Since all accounting information is 'behavioural' by definition, mechanisms must be put in place to evaluate performance and to administer rewards. The purpose of implementing such systems is to reinforce positive performance and to modify negative behaviour. It is generally desirable that rewards be based on a range of measurements to ensure that target performance in one area is not achieved at the expense of performance in another (e.g. sales targets achieved by selling at prices that are below acceptable levels).

There are three important **behavioural aspects of the reward process**:

* clarity,
* motivation, and
* responsibility.

**Clarity** First, if one of the main purposes of the performance measurement system is to ensure the successful implementation of company strategy then this should be clearly understood by employees throughout the organisation. Research studies suggest that most employees react well to clear, unambiguous targets together with the knowledge of how these rewards are administered. The issue here is really that of communication, reinforced by previous, observed practice.

**Motivation** The second issue is that of employee motivation and the link to rewards. The rewards available for successful performance must be attractive to the employee and it hardly needs to be stressed that different rewards, e.g. promotion or monetary bonuses, are attractive to different employees.

**Responsibility** Finally, the issue of controllability means that employees should only be held responsible for those elements over which they have control and this is often achieved by some form of participation in the target setting. The implication is that managers would lose interest if their performance was being judged on events outside their control. Rewarding managers (or penalising them) for results achieved over which they have no control runs counter to the motivational goals of rewarding performance. However, one should note, in passing, that managers are often expected to **react** to events that are outside their sphere of influence.

Based on the above, the relevance of non-financial measures of performance is understandable. Moreover, one can also add that non-financial measures are generally unaffected by the level of inflation. In addition, employees do not generally think in terms of financial measures. Rather, for example, in a manufacturing environment employees and managers concentrate on the issues of production and reject rates, on-time deliveries and schedule changes. One important challenge for accountants, therefore, is to design an integrated but comprehensive performance measurement and management system, of which the Balanced Scorecard is one such system.

# 8.3 The Balanced Scorecard (BSC)

A number of integrative frameworks for performance measurement have been proposed in an attempt to remedy the perceived failings of traditional cost systems of which Kaplan and Norton's *Balanced Scorecard* is the best known. The **Balanced Scorecard** was developed as a result of a research project in the early 1990s into advanced performance measurement techniques carried out by Professor Robert Kaplan from the Harvard Business School and David Norton (a management consultant). The research project was conducted in conjunction with 12 US businesses regarded as being at the leading edge of performance measurement. The actual title, the 'Balanced Scorecard', was a variation on the title – Corporate Scorecard – developed by Art Schneiderman, then VP Quality and Productivity at Analog Devices. The resultant template, the Balanced Scorecard (BSC) became an extension of Schneiderman's and was publicised in a pioneering article by Kaplan and Norton in the *Harvard Business Review* (Jan/Feb 1992). Since that time, the concept of the 'Balanced Scorecard' has generated a great deal of interest and practical application.

The essential thrust of the balanced scorecard is based on two fundamental propositions. First, as most people realise, 'what you measure is what you get' and, secondly, managers need a broad range of performance measures in order to manage their business. By way of analogy, they refer to an airline pilot who has a variety of dials and indicators in the cockpit for airspeed, altitude, direction, position, destination, fuel and so on. All of these are needed for a successful flight and relying on a single performance measure can be potentially fatal.

The Balanced Scorecard is, traditionally, divided into different perspectives as outlined in **Exhibit 8.4** below and is intended to provide answers to four basic questions as follows:

- How does the firm look to shareholders? (financial perspective)
- How do customers see the firm? (customer perspective)

EXHIBIT 8.4: THE BALANCED SCORECARD

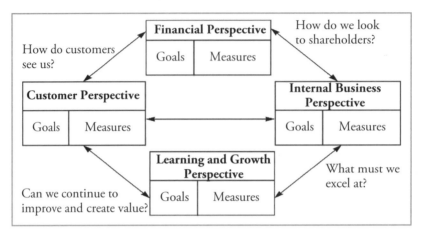

Source: Kaplan and Norton (1992) (adapted)

- What must the firm excel at? (internal perspective)
- Can the firm continue to improve and create value? (learning and growth perspective)

The BSC is 'balanced' in three ways. First, there is a balance between internal and external measures. Secondly, it is balanced by the use of both financial and non-financial measures. Finally, it is balanced in terms of time, i.e. it reflects the past, the present and the future. The financial perspective reflects past decisions and represents the historical, financial performance of the firm. The customer and internal process perspectives represent current performance. The learning and growth perspective represents what must be done in the future that will have a positive, future impact on the firm. Each of these four perspectives will now be discussed in turn.

## Financial Perspective

The financial perspective highlights how the company appears to shareholders (actual and potential) and concentrates on measures relating to financial performance. While profitability as a performance measure has been criticised, it is important to remember that it is an important source of finance. Usually, profit is associated with operating cash flow and offers greater flexibility in the source of finance for corporate investment. Easier access to finance facilitates greater investment which boosts productivity, competitiveness and employment. In a macro context, company profits reflect the health of the economy. Financial measures can be identified along the following themes:

- overall profitability such as return on funds invested
- sales growth

- cost reduction
- cash flow generated, especially from operating activities
- asset utilisation
- financial position, including liquidity and gearing (leverage).

The Balanced Scorecard (BSC) complements these financial measures with three other perspectives that are generally represented by non-financial measures of performance. These are:

(a) the customer perspective,
(b) the internal perspective, and
(c) the learning and growth perspective.

## Customer Perspective

The customer perspective is designed to highlight how customers perceive the business and focus on specific measures that reflect the factors that really matter to customers. One could argue that this perspective is at the heart of the scorecard. Success in any business depends on the ability to establish, maintain and build relationships with customers. However, customer satisfaction does not necessarily mean that your satisfied customers are committed or loyal. On average, a business loses as much as 20% of its customer base each year. To compound the problem, in today's competitive environment, you cannot rely on acquiring new customers to take the place of lost ones. Five generic areas across most kinds of organisations can be cited for the customer perspective:

- Customer satisfaction – since this is considered to be the crucial performance measure for predicting the future success of most companies
- Customer profitability
- Customer retention
- Customer acquisition
- Market share

## Internal Perspective

The internal business perspective is designed to focus on those critical internal activities that must be performed in order to satisfy the expectations of its customers and stem from the entire *value-chain,* which is the sequence of business processes through which value is added to goods and services. Analysis of the value chain leads to the identification of processes that are critical to the organisation's success. There are **three primary activities in the generic value chain** which are stated below:

- **The Innovation Process** Creating entirely new products and services to meet the emerging needs of current and future customers.
- **The Operations Process** Producing and delivering existing products (or services) to existing customers efficiently and reliably.

- **The After-sale Service Process** Satisfying customers after the sale has been high-lighted with prompt attention to their concerns and by providing field service and technical support, as needed.

Thus, the internal perspective represents an analysis of the company's internal processes. We focus on measures for these internal processes that will have the greatest impact on enhancing customer relationships and, therefore, facilitating the achievement of the organisation's financial objectives. It is useful to remember that they represent activities/processes that must be performed within the firm and are usually described as 'verbs'.

## Learning and Growth Perspective

The financial, customer and internal business process objectives of the Balanced Scorecard will typically reveal deficiencies in existing capabilities of employees and internal systems. To close these gaps, businesses will have to invest in re-skilling its employees, enhancing information technology and aligning organisational procedures and routines. These objectives are articulated in the learning and growth perspective. Organisational learning and growth come from three principal sources:

- employee capabilities,
- the information system and procedures, together with
- employee motivation.

At the heart of this perspective are the employees. The learning and growth perspective highlights the fact that, in the face of intense competition, firms must make continual improvement to existing products and processes and have the ability to introduce new products in the future. A generic Balanced Scorecard is shown in **Exhibit 8.5**.

EXHIBIT 8.5: A GENERIC BALANCED SCORECARD

| Critical success factor | Performance measures and indicators |
| --- | --- |
| **Financial perspective** | |
| Overall profitability | Return on shareholders' funds |
| Sales growth | Sales volume trend; sales of new products |
| Cost reduction | Total cost as percentage of total revenue |
| Cash flow | Operating cash flow |
| Asset utilization | Fixed asset turnover; capacity utilisation |
| Financial position | Liquidity and gearing (leverage) ratios |

| Customer perspective | |
|---|---|
| Customer satisfaction | Customer survey index |
| Customer profitability | Average profit per customer segment |
| Customer retention | Number of repeat orders |
| Customer acquisition | Number of new customers acquired & sales € |
| Market share | % of served market achieved |
| **Internal business perspective** | |
| Innovation | Percentage of sales from new products |
| | Expenditure on research and development |
| Operations | Labour and/or machine efficiency ratios |
| | Defect rates including wastage |
| | On-time deliveries |
| After-sales service | Customer complaint response time |
| | Number of visits to customer |
| **Learning and growth perspective** | |
| Employee capability | Days training |
| | No. of graduates in workforce |
| Information systems & procedures | Spending on IT capability |
| | No. of meetings attended by employees |
| Motivation | Employee turnover |
| | Employee satisfaction |

## Advantages and Problems of the Balanced Scorecard

A number of advantages and problems of the Balanced Scorecard will now be discussed briefly. The BSC integrates traditional financial measures with operational, customer and staff issues, which are vital to the long-term success of the firm. Having understood what is important for the business, performance measures are established to monitor performance and targets must be set for improvement. These must then be clearly communicated to all levels of management and staff within the business and appropriate training of all employees should be undertaken. This enables managers and individuals to understand how their own efforts can contribute to the success of the enterprise and the BSC can then become an important instrument in the regular reporting system of the company. However, a scorecard should not be introduced unless it is clear what is to be achieved. No organisation should allow itself to drift into implementing a scorecard unless it has a very good idea of what it expects from it.

Furthermore, it cannot be emphasied enough that top management **must** be committed to the project. They must ensure that the task is given adequate priority. It is also essential to involve as many opinion leaders as possible in the initial process, particularly for the purpose of recruiting a number of highly motivated 'missionaries' for its subsequent implementation.

One should never underestimate the required managerial time in implementing scorecards. The main implementation issue is to accept that it is not a one-, or a two-day project. The process of working down from a vision/mission statement, objectives and strategy to the critical performance measures, standards and rewards takes much time and effort. It may take as long as six months and, even then, the scorecard may subsequently need to be revised.

The cost of acquiring some of this additional information for the various performance measures must also be considered and viewed in the context of its value to decision-makers. Also, it is important to decide 'who' shall have the responsibility to coordinate the additional information. The importance of this information to the firm, coupled with the central role of the management accountant within the organisation, suggests that s/he should become more involved with this information gathering process. The management accountant's office could become the 'information warehouse' of the organisation. Admittedly, there are important organisational and behavioural issues relating to this proposition that should first be addressed.

In developing a range of performance measures, one should be aware of the possible dysfunctional consequences associated with any performance metric. For example, if the measure is the percentage of orders delivered on time, then there is an incentive for managers to sacrifice one late shipment for the sake of other orders that can be delivered on time. Thus, on-time delivery performance looks better when nine deliveries are made on time and one is 10 days late compared with 10 deliveries being made one day late.

In summary, the traditional role of management accountants as the recorders of historical, internal and financial information is changing. Management accountants should realise this and avail of the opportunity to become important facilitators of change. Management accountants who grasp this opportunity will considerably increase their own relevance in modern organisations and increase the capacity of their organisations to prosper. The important issue for management accountants is to reflect on what Albert Einstein once remarked:

> "Not everything that counts can be counted, and not everything that can be counted, counts."

## 8.4 Variations on the Balanced Scorecard

After years of neglect, small and medium-sized enterprises (SMEs) have received additional scrutiny in recent years. This should not be surprising, as they are currently the dominant form of business organisation in all countries, typically accounting for over 90% of all business entities and providing in excess of 60% of total employment. Without their smaller counterparts, few large firms could sustain their sizeable contribution to national and international economies.

However, there is a need to strengthen the managerial capabilities of SMEs. One way to do this is to make small business managers aware of a variation of the BSC tool. Most SMEs do not have sufficient scale to pursue only a strategy of cost leadership. Therefore, they have to differentiate themselves from their competitors. However, while a customer may be prepared to pay a premium for a differentiated product, common sense suggests that there is an overall limit to the premium that can be charged.

Like any useful managerial tool, the one proposed here is based on the premise that businesses are created to satisfy a need, and SMEs are no exception. Successful SMEs need to know their customers and anticipate their future needs; and they must have a solid understanding of their competitors. Logic suggests, and evidence confirms, that SMEs, like most other firms, compete on the basis of:

- price competitiveness,
- quality of product, and
- customer service

(concepts that apply as much to retail and service firms as to those in manufacturing). Arguably, SMEs must satisfy minimum thresholds in all three areas in order to be successful in a competitive and changing market place. There is no fixed position in the triangle in which the SME should ideally place itself in **Exhibit 8.6** in relation to these three variables. Much will depend on the individual SME and its competitive environment – indeed, its position may shift over time, reflecting the changing needs of existing customers or a new customer base. However, it is interesting to ask an SME manager to identify within the triangle (**Exhibit 8.6**) the position he thinks most appropriate for his firm, given its target customers.

There are two immediate advantages to this simple exercise. First, it encourages the manager to think about two external groups: customers and competitors. SMEs can only be successful if they focus on the potential future characteristics of their customers

EXHIBIT 8.6: SOURCES OF COMPETITIVE ADVANTAGE

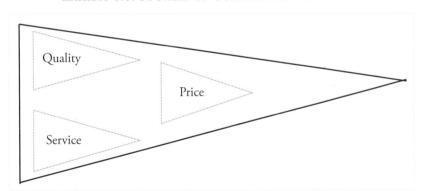

and competitors. Secondly, the exercise forces managers to think in terms of a cause-and-effect relationship and to reflect on two fundamental questions:

- What critical activities should the firm perform in order to deliver quality of product, price competitiveness and customer service?
- How well is the firm currently performing in achieving these objectives?

Based on Kaplan and Norton's Balanced Scorecard, the variation below focuses on four elements integrated in a cause-and-effect relationship (see **Exhibit 8.7**). The cause-and-effect relationship begins with the various internal activities (i.e. 'doing the right things'), moving to the customer perspective ('then our customers will be happy'). However, the internal activities can only be accomplished by employees, supported by appropriate resources. This leads us to a consideration of 'Enablers' ('if we have the right employees and technology'). Finally, on the right hand side of **Exhibit 8.7** we can identify the financial implications ('we will generate financial rewards').

*Internal Activities*

**Internal activities** refer to a relatively small set of actions that have the greatest impact on customer satisfaction and customer loyalty and these usually include aspects of price competitiveness, quality of product and customer service. Such activities are critical to a firm's long-term success and must be monitored through appropriate performance measures in order to ensure that they are carried out effectively and efficiently.

For example, to highlight the importance of quality of finished products, performance measures relating to, say, the number of defects could be used. These defects could be calculated either by internal inspection or on the basis of customer rejects. Likewise, aspects of customer service should be measured, such as the number of on-time deliveries (OTD) or the lead time (i.e. the number of days between receipt of order and final delivery of goods).

EXHIBIT 8.7: CAUSE AND EFFECT RELATIONSHIP

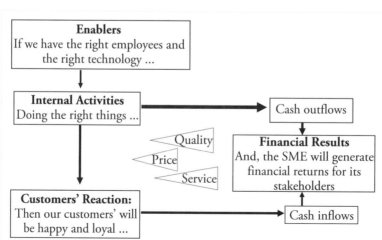

One simple indicator of price competitiveness is **Pc/Po** (i.e. **average price of competitors [Pc] divided by our average price [Po]**). **Internal cost efficiency**, which is the relationship between a product's cost and its price, is similarly important. Internal cost efficiency, which is an important factor in generating profits, can be estimated by calculating total costs (TC) divided by total revenues (TR). In the long run, the price an organisation receives for a product must cover its costs, or it will go out of business. Since customers may purchase goods on the basis of price only, keeping costs low relative to competitors provides an SME with a sustainable competitive advantage.

A small number of easy-to-gather performance measures, with related performance targets for internal activities are presented in **Exhibit 8.8** for illustration purposes only.

*Customers' Reaction*

The reaction of customers and internal activities are mirror images of one another, where the former reflects customers' collective judgement on the performance of a SME in certain critical areas. If the SME fails to satisfy customers in terms of delivering the right product (or service) at a competitive price, it is difficult to see how profits will be generated. At the same time, however, customer satisfaction does not necessarily translate into customer loyalty. It is generally accepted that, on average, a business may lose up to 20% of its existing customer base each year. To compound the problem, an increasingly competitive environment means new customers do not automatically take their place and it costs about five times more to acquire new customers than to retain existing ones. SMEs should focus on three customer-related objectives:

- Customer satisfaction (considered to be the crucial performance measure in predicting future company success)
- Customer loyalty i.e. to what extent do existing customers continue their business association?
- Customer acquisition i.e. how many new customers were acquired during a given period?

EXHIBIT 8.8: PERFORMANCE MEASURES FOR INTERNAL ACTIVITIES

| Objective | Performance measures | Target for period |
|---|---|---|
| Quality of product | % (or number) of customer rejects | (say)< 2% |
|  | % (or number) of internal rejects | (say) < 10% |
| Customer service | On time delivery (OTD) | (say) 90% |
|  | Lead time (days) | (say) 15 days |
| Price competitiveness | Price competitiveness (Pc/Po) | (say) 1.2 |
|  | Internal cost efficiency (TC/TR) $\times$ 100 | (say) 90% |

**Exhibit 8.9** presents objectives, performance measures and related targets for the customer perspective. (These are for illustration purposes only.)

EXHIBIT 8.9: PERFORMANCE MEASURES FOR CUSTOMER PERSPECTIVE

| Objective | Performance measures | Target for period |
|---|---|---|
| Customer satisfaction | No. of complaints | (say) 10 complaints |
| Customer loyalty | Amount (€) of repeat business | (say) 80% of sales from existing customers (or €) |
| Customer acquisition | Sales (€) to new customers | (say) 10 new customers (or €) |

*Enablers*

The third dimension relates to 'enablers' – factors that facilitate internal activities and their improvement. Internal activities are achieved by employees, working with the right technology. Well-trained and motivated employees, through their work attitudes, ethics and behaviour, facilitate customer loyalty through low cost and high quality production, short lead-time for the production of products and delivery of services. Typical objectives, performance measures and related targets for enablers of internal activities are presented in **Exhibit 8.10** (for illustration purposes only):

EXHIBIT 8.10: PERFORMANCE MEASURES FOR ENABLING ACTIVITIES

| Objective | Performance measures | Target for period |
|---|---|---|
| Staff development | Staff training | (say) 1 day per employee |
| Staff morale | No. of suggestions per employee | (say) 1 suggestion per employee |
| Investment (in assets) | € spent on new equipment | (say) €10,000 |

*Financial Results*

The final dimension highlights the financial results that accrue to SME owners (and other stakeholders). It is important to highlight the use of the word 'results', because that is precisely how cash flow and profit arise: they are the result (or residual) of previous activities. Profit is often described as the 'bottom line' and a memorable quotation is:

> "The bottom line is down there where it belongs – at the bottom. Far above it in importance are the infinite number of events that produce the profit or loss."

Three financial objectives, performance measures and related targets for Financial Results are shown in **Exhibit 8.11** below but they are for illustration purposes only:

EXHIBIT 8.11: FINANCIAL RESULTS PERFORMANCE MEASURES

| Objective | Performance measures | Target for period |
|---|---|---|
| Profitability | Return on Investment (RoI) | (say) 20% |
| Liquidity (cash flow) | Cash increase during year (€) | (say) €5,000 |
| Credit control | Average credit days granted to debtors | (say) 40 days |

Two final points should be made about the above presentation. First, an increased emphasis on non-financial measures of performance is an important step towards improving the management capability of SMEs. The above discussion focuses on the 'drivers' of financial success, i.e. the internal activities and those enablers that drive customer satisfaction and loyalty. Secondly, these non-financial performance measures are often much easier and quicker to generate than some of the more traditional financial metrics, which require the preparation of annual financial statements.

## Conclusion

By way of summary and conclusion, we initially discussed in this chapter some of the limitations of accounting numbers. One of these is that, traditionally, accounting information reports the results of historical operations rather than details of how these results were created. The argument, therefore, is that management accountants should expand their traditional system into a more appropriate performance measurement system within their organisation. This performance measurement system must be aligned with corporate strategy and linked to critical success factors. One such system was elegantly explained by Kaplan and Norton in the form of a Balanced Scorecard. However, there are many improvisations of this model, including the 'Cause and Effect Relationship', which may be suitable for SMEs.

## SUMMARY OF LEARNING OBJECTIVES

**Learning Objective 1:** Discuss the general limitations of accounting information.

It can be argued that accounting numbers have the potential to suffer from a number of limitations. Because they mostly reflect the internal operations of the firm, they are not externally orientated. Also, they mainly relate to historical events whereas decision-making requires future estimates. Accounting numbers also represent the 'results' of operations whereas it would be preferable to focus on the 'means' by which these results were generated. Finally, accounting numbers may be inaccurate – as in the case of product costs computed under traditional cost accounting.

**Learning Objective 2:** Outline the nature and purpose of performance measure systems.

Performance measures can be either financial or non-financial and, increasingly, it is argued that non-financial measures of performance are more relevant to responsible managers in their decision-making and evaluation of performance. Performance measures indicate what is important to do within the firm and are related to critical success factors. These critical success factors represent the key areas in which performance must excel if the firm is to be successful. Thus, performance measures are an important method of communicating overall strategy to all employees in the firm. It is usual to report a range of performance measures so that performance in one area is not achieved by poor performance in another area.

**Learning Objective 3:** Differentiate between the financial, customer, internal and employee perspectives.

In order to obtain a balanced set, it is usual to classify performance measures or performance indicators according to four different perspectives. The employee perspective focuses on employees, their skills, training, resources and morale. In turn, employees perform activities and these internal activities are fundamental in achieving customer satisfaction and loyalty. Finally, customer satisfaction and loyalty generates financial rewards that are attractive to shareholders. (It should be noted that other perspectives e.g. community, could be added.)

**Learning Objective 4:** Describe the 'Balanced Scorecard'.

The Balanced scorecard (BSC) is an important management tool, based on four perspectives, which contain a range of performance measures. Typically, each perspective would have about four performance measures (or key performance indicators). The Balanced Scorecard is balanced in a number of ways: it includes both internal and external perspectives; it contains financial and non-financial measures and it reflects historical performance, e.g. financial, with expected performance, employee perspective.

**Learning Objective 5:** Explain and illustrate the concept of a critical success factor.

A critical success factor represents an area in which a firm's performance must be superior in order for it to be successful. While there are a number of generic critical success factors, e.g. customer loyalty, it is important that critical success factors are identified and agreed with reference to the strategic intention of the firm. It is also important that each critical success factor be associated with a relevant performance indicator. Thus, if a firm was pursuing a cost leadership strategy, then cost control (or cost management) would be an important critical success factor and could be measured by reference to cost growth, or actual cost reported against budget.

## Questions

### Review Questions

(See Appendix One for Solutions to Review Questions **8.1** and **8.2**)

#### Question 8.1 (Restoring Relevance to Managerial Accounting)

In recent years it has been suggested that traditional management accounting practice has lost much of its relevance. Specifically, for example, it is argued that management accounting information places undue emphasis on short-term financial results and this should be replaced by reporting only non-financial information.

**Requirement:** Discuss the above statement.

#### Question 8.2 (Non-financial Measures of Performance)

You are approached by a colleague who is aware that you are studying managerial accounting. He is anxious to discuss with you the problems of using profit as a measure of performance and why many companies are using non-financial measures of performance.

**Requirement:** Briefly explain some of the limitations of using profit as a measure of performance and highlight the role of non-financial measures of performance within a management accounting system.

### Intermediate Questions

#### Question 8.3 (Critical Success Factors and Related Key Performance Indicators)

Customer Survey Technologies (CST) Ireland Limited is an Irish subsidiary of an international service provider, enjoying international relationships with many of the world's leading hotel chains. The company's operation in Dublin analyses over 4 million guest comment cards annually, from over 1,000 client hotels and restaurants and other hospitality service outlets, from 80 countries and in 25 languages.

**Requirement:** Identify five critical success factors (CSFs) that will drive the profitability performance of this company in the future and suggest appropriate key performance indicators (KPIs) related to these.

## Question 8.4 (Performance Measures and Non-value-added costs)

You have recently returned from a visit to 'Chindia' – a fictitious country – where the following newspaper article was brought to your attention:

> "Chindia's logistics enterprises must establish an efficient quality control system before they can get in on the fast and lucrative development of the domestic logistics industry, experts have said. Such a system will mean that customers will be reassured that their commodities are safe in transport and that they can check the whereabouts of their products at any time in the process. Without such a system, domestic enterprises will have little chance of competing with foreign logistics companies.
>
> It is accepted that domestic companies are losing customers in competition with foreign companies because of the lack of quality control systems. In addition, lots of value is wasted in inefficient storage, transport and distribution processes. Most domestic logistics enterprises neglect the development of efficient information and quality-control systems. These domestic companies sometimes offer prices as much as 20% lower than those of foreign competitors for cargo delivery, but still fail to get contracts. The major reason they fail to get customers is that they cannot guarantee that they will deliver the customers' products safely and on time. Foreign companies, on the other hand, offer high-quality and transparent delivery systems that reassure their customers."

You are the newly appointed management accountant to OTD Company, a new logistics company based in Chindia. The company delivers small parcels, mail and other items within Chindia, using its own fleet of vehicles and employees.

**Requirements:**

1. Write briefly about the distinction between the terms 'effectiveness' and 'efficiency'.
2. List 10 major 'non-value-added' costs that an inefficient logistics company, such as OTD Company in Chindia, would incur and briefly explain each of them. You should make reference to possible 'opportunity cost' associated with poor delivery service to customers.
3. List 15 key performance indicators which you consider to be drivers of success. In relation to each measure, you should briefly state their importance i.e. justify why you have selected them.

## Question 8.5 (Identifying Performance Measures)

Erin Oil Limited is a newly formed company which retails and distributes central heating oil to domestic and business customers with a vision to be among the most successful in its industry sector. The chief executive of Erin Oil, Mr Barrett, together with his board of directors, has identified major goals and objectives (listed below) which they believe are consistent with the corporate mission.

**Goal 1: Maintain a strong financial performance**
Objective 1. Increase overall financial return
Objective 2. Maintain adequate operating cash flow

**Goal 2: Increase revenue**
Objective 3: Increase the customer base
Objective 4: Increase average volume per customer

**Goal 3: Adopt good management practices**
Objective 5. Ensure on-time delivery
Objective 6. Improve price competitiveness

**Goal 4: Improve human and physical facilities**
Objective 7. Have the best employees
Objective 8. Have the best facilities

The newly-appointed company accountant has suggested that one means of monitoring the progress towards these goals and objectives is to develop a small set of appropriate key performance indicators.

**Requirement:** Outline one measure of performance for each of Erin Oil's objectives stated above.

## Question 8.6 (Performance Measurement and Benchmarking)

The Grafton Hotel is a large high-class hotel situated in the old section of Dublin. Dublin has a resident population in excess of 1 million and attracts a considerable number of European visitors both during the winter and summer time. The Grafton Hotel is part of a worldwide hotel group, with the majority of the shares being held by individual investors – each holding a small number. The remaining shares are owned by institutional investors. The hotel provides full amenities, including an indoor heated swimming pool, as well as the normal facilities of bars, restaurants and good quality accommodation. There are many other hotels in Dublin, some close by, which compete with the Grafton Hotel.

**Requirement:** List appropriate key performance indicators (KPIs) that could be used to assist managers of the Grafton Hotel and suggest ways in which a benchmarking exercise could be carried out to provide comparable information. (**Note:** a description of benchmarking is not required.)

## Question 8.7 (Performance Measurement in the Retail Sector)

The BT Shop specialises in men's clothes and is located in a busy shopping centre in Dublin. The target market is the young professional man who is not very price-sensitive. Rather quality, style and convenience are the dominant considerations for such customers. The shop carries over 200 different brands of various men's clothes. The BT Shop anticipates that sales growth and overall profitability can be achieved provided it is perceived by customers as being a "compelling place to shop". However, this can only be achieved by having well-trained, motivated and dedicated staff, working in a modern, comfortable and prestigious environment.

In order to communicate its strategic imperatives to employees, a balanced score-card was developed with four traditional perspectives, namely, financial, customer, internal activities and learning and growth. The following key performance indicators (KPIs) were selected and the target and actual performance for a recent weekly accounting period were reported:

| Key Performance Indicator (KPI) | Target | Actual |
|---|---|---|
| Sales (€) per employee (p/week) | €4,000 | €4,300 |
| Staff absenteeism (average per shift) | <2% | 1% |
| Total staff suggestions (p/week) | 10 | 7 |
| Hours of training for sales staff (p/week) | 1 hour | 0.5 hours |
| Gross profit margins | 80% | 70% |
| Inventory turnover (days) | 10 days | 12 days |
| Sales growth % (p/week) | 1% | 0.7% |
| Operating cash flow as percentage of sales | 50% | 45% |
| Number of stock-outs (or not available) p/week | <5 times | 2 times |
| Customer satisfaction rating (survey) | 95% | 98% |
| Number of customer complaints p/week | <15 | 12 |
| Price relative to competitors' prices | +7% to 10% | +15% to 20% |

**Requirements:**

1. Classify each of the above performance measures into one of the four BSC perspectives, i.e. financial, customer, internal, and learning and growth.
2. For each KPI indicate whether actual performance is favourable (F) or adverse (A) relative to targets.
3. For each perspective, suggest another KPI that could be used.

## Advanced Questions

*Question 8.8 (Critical Success Factors and Non-Financial Indicators)*

SMC is a private, i.e. fee-paying, secondary school for boys in the Dublin region and its current student enrolment is 600 pupils. The aim of the school is to provide a quality education and learning environment in which each student can develop his full potential, pursue an appropriate career and live his life as a responsible member of society.

**Requirement:** Draft a list of critical success factors and related key performance indicators that are relevant to the above aims of SMC.

*Question 8.9 (Critical Success Factors and Non-Financial Indicators)*

The PGBS is a private, postgraduate business school, offering a variety of masters' programmes such as the MBA together with short executive courses. It also has a suite of specialised masters' programmes. It has about 700 full-time students on various programmes and about 50 full-time academic staff. In addition, there are about 25 administrative staff and about 50 part-time academic staff. There are several other notable institutions in the locality offering similar programmes, although not the same range of programmes are offered in any single institution. The formal mission statement for PGBS is:

> "To be and be seen to be among the leaders in business education in Europe by aiming for the highest international standards in our research and scholarly publications and by the communication of that knowledge to successive generations through excellence in teaching and learning."

**Requirements:**

1. How should PGBS compete against the other institutions? Explain your reasoning.
2. List some critical success factors and related performance measures that are appropriate, in your opinion, in monitoring the achievement of this mission statement.
3. What problems, if any, do you anticipate in the implementation of a performance measurement system?

*Question 8.10 (Performance Measurement Systems)*

The following draft vision statement was agreed at the recent Board of Directors meeting of a manufacturing company producing bulk chemicals:

> We must . . .
>
> **For our Customers:**
> Have a total quality commitment to consistently meet the product, delivery and service expectations of all customers.
> Give customers increased value through processes that continually reduce costs and enhance production efficiency.
>
> **For our Employees:**
> Reward teamwork and performance while treating others with respect.
> Recognise that people are to be cherished and provide them with training and information that enable continuous improvement.
>
> **For our Shareholders:**
> Manage operations to ensure long-term profitability.
> Ensure adequate operating cash flow to cater for short-term obligations.
>
> **For the Community in which we operate:**
> Commit to environmental responsibility.
> Fulfil our responsibility to enhance the quality of community life.

**Requirement:** Develop a set of performance measures the company might use to measure achievement on each of these imperatives.

*Question 8.11 (Performance Measures in a Telecommunications Company)*

The following performance measures were extracted from the annual report of a Telecommunications Company for a recent accounting period:

| | |
|---|---|
| Average training days per employee | 5 days |
| Direct exchange lines per employee | 177 |
| Average line fault per customer (time) | 7.4 years (13.5%) |
| % increase in telephone service revenue | + 7% |
| GSM (% geographical coverage) | 94% |
| Debtor days (average period of credit allowed) | 75 days |
| Return on shareholders' funds (PAT/Equity invested) | 16% |
| Faults and service restored within 1 day | 43% |
| % Annual increase in total operating costs | + 7% |
| Grants (€) paid to children of employees for study | €100,000 |
| Return on sales (PAT/Sales revenue) | 27% |
| Cash inflow from operating activities | €80m |
| Complaint calls answered within 20 seconds | 75% |
| Acquisition (€) of telecommunications plant and equipment | €45m |
| % of paper saved in printing Yellow Pages | 20% |
| Average sick leave per employee | 5 days |
| Provision (%) of fixed telephony service within 1 week of request | 83% |

**Requirements:**

1. For each of the above items, identify what 'critical success factor' (if any) is being measured and indicate why this is important. You should include reference to the likely cause-and-effect relationship between the critical success factor or performance measure and any prior or subsequent performance or happening. Classify each measure into one of the following five perspectives: Financial (F), Customer (C), Internal (I), Enabling (E) (i.e. Learning and Growth) and Public/Social Responsibility (PSR). Please note that it is possible for a performance measure to be included in more than one perspective.
2. Briefly suggest some areas that are overlooked.

*Question 8.12 (Performance Measures and Electricity Supply)*

The Electricity Supply Board (ESB) was established by the Electricity (Supply) Act 1927. Until recently, it was a state monopoly and engaged in the generation and distribution of electricity.

However, legislation now exists that has partially liberalised the electricity market in Ireland. Effectively, the ESB now competes with new players for the 400 (approx.) large industrial users who make up nearly one-third of the electricity market. The immediate challenge is to establish the ESB as the supplier of choice while competing in the generation business. Summarised financial highlights for a recent accounting period indicate an annual turnover in the region of €3.5 billion, generating a surplus after tax of just under €300 million, giving an overall return on capital employed of over 6%. It has about 1.5 million customers and over 16,000 employees (including affiliated enterprises).

The stated strategy of the company is to 'produce and deliver electricity at the lowest possible cost, with the minimum of disruption while preserving the environment'. The following performance measures (adapted for teaching purposes) were extracted from an annual report of the ESB:

| | |
|---|---|
| Average cost of units sold | 6.23c |
| No. of substations installed | 4,145 |
| Reduction in $NO_2$ (nitrogen oxide) emissions | 4% |
| Growth in annual sales turnover | +7% |
| Gearing ratio (LT Loans as % Capital Employed) | 40% |
| Reduction in $SO_2$ (sulphur dioxide) emissions | 5% |
| Return on Capital Employed | 6.6% |
| Capacity installed (kVa) | 483 |
| Number of customers (Total) | 1.5 million |
| Current ratio | 2 times |
| Load factor (average load/peak load) | 60% |
| Average pay/benefits per employee | €35,000 |
| Reduction on $CO_2$ emissions (carbon dioxide from fossil fuels) | 6% |
| Overhead lines installed (km) | 2,652 |
| New dwellings connected | 33,097 |
| Average period of credit allowed | 57 days |
| Sales per employee | €250,000 |
| Surplus (i.e. profit after tax) as % of Sales | 8.5% |
| Number of faults (i.e. reliability) | 99.9% |

## Requirements:

1. For each of the above items, identify what 'critical success factor' (if any) is being measured. Classify each measure into one of the following 5 perspectives: Financial (F), Customer (C), Internal (I), Enabling (E) (i.e. Learning and Growth) and Public/Social Responsibility (PSR). Please note that it is possible for a performance measure to be included in more than one perspective.
2. Briefly suggest some areas that have been overlooked.

# Managerial Decisions and Profit Planning

LEARNING OBJECTIVES

When you have completed studying this chapter you should be able to:

1. Distinguish between strategic and organisational planning and control decisions.
2. Describe the steps in the (rational) managerial decision-making process.
3. Apply profit planning calculations, including break-even point, for single and multiproduct firms.
4. Prepare summarised income statements in contribution format.
5. Estimate the linear relationship between costs and cost drivers using account analysis and the high low methods.
6. Estimate the linear relationship between costs and cost drivers using regression analysis, while also applying measures of reliability.
7. Describe the nature of and perform calculation using the learning curve.

## 9.1 Introduction to Managerial Decision-making

For management accounting purposes, it is useful to classify decisions into three major categories, namely:

- strategic decisions,
- organisational planning, and
- organisational control decisions.

However, in reality, the dividing line between them is blurred. First, there are the **strategic decisions**, which we have outlined in a previous chapter. These should start with a consideration of what is the overall vision for the firm. (Astute readers will note that a firm cannot have a vision in its own right. There is no such thing as a vision **of** the firm. Rather, a vision statement is usually adopted by the key stakeholders of the firm and this represents the vision **for** the firm.) Legitimate vision statements will be developed only after a consideration of the '4Cs' – customers, competitors, competencies and costs. Two of these factors are external to the firm (customers and competitors) and two are internal – competencies and costs. A detailed analysis of these four factors usually results in the identification of the organisation's strengths and weaknesses, together with environmental opportunities and threats. In turn, an appropriate business strategy should be developed.

Many writers on strategy point out that there are two generic strategic choices, referred to as cost leadership and product differentiation. Cost leadership is a strategy in which a firm outperforms competitors by producing products or services at the lowest cost. In contrast, product differentiation is implemented by creating a perception among consumers that the product or service is unique in some important way, usually by being of higher quality or providing an excellent customer service. Brand loyalty, reflecting these better attributes, will allow the company to charge a higher price.

Strategic decisions inevitably lead to organisational planning and control decisions. Organisational planning decisions are short-term decisions, designed to achieve objectives. (Some authors distinguish between goals and objectives by stating that goals represent general aspirations, e.g. to be a profitable company, whereas an objective is a much more specific target, e.g. to earn a return of 10% on shareholders' funds.) It is worth noting that much of the managerial accounting literature dealing with individual behaviour within firms suggests the setting of difficult but attainable objectives. These challenging objectives are intended to motivate individuals whereas unattainable objectives can be demotivating and generally do more harm than good.

Organisational planning, just like strategic planning, is a forward-looking activity with the management accountant assisting in, for example, setting financial targets and providing estimates of future costs and revenues for different alternatives.

Organisational control decisions are concerned with monitoring actual performance and identifying whether the organisation's objectives are likely to be achieved. If objectives are not likely to be achieved, explanations are required and corrective action would usually be taken – if this is possible. This traditional definition views control as a backward-looking activity, with a heavy reliance on providing feedback information about actual performance. The management accountant, typically, facilitates the control process by reporting actual performance against financial objectives and identifying variances, which can either be significant or insignificant.

The definition of a significant variance will be discussed in **Chapter 15**; however, it broadly represents the notion of importance. If the variance is deemed not to be significant, then it is assumed that progress towards objectives is satisfactory. If the variance is significant, managers must identify the cause and make an appropriate response. For example, if a cost overrun has been identified, can different production methods be used to reduce costs, or can the selling price be increased, or can additional units be sold? The difficulty with organisational control decisions is:

1. knowing when a variance is significant, and
2. choosing the most appropriate corrective action.

## Categories of Managerial Decisions

**Exhibit 9.1** summarises these general observations about the categories of managerial activity. It highlights the fact that, because these activities are different, the information requirements of managers are also different.

Managers Involved The strategic planning process typically involves a small number of top management who operate in a very creative way. Middle managers are not usually major participants in the strategic planning process and sometimes may not even be aware that a strategic plan is being prepared. In any event, the time pressures of current activities usually do not allow middle managers to devote the necessary time for strategic reflection. Furthermore, while middle managers are usually very knowledgeable about their own responsibility centre, strategic planning requires a broader knowledge of the entire firm.

Type of Information Required The essence of strategic planning is the future relationship between the company and its environment and much of the information required is externally focused. In contrast, much of the information for organisational planning and control decisions comes from within the organisation itself, from the internal accounting system and is financially orientated.

Time Focus of Information Since strategic thinking is concerned with the future environment and the positioning of the firm within that environment, the time focus of the information presented must be future-orientated and relate to multiple accounting periods. In contrast, organisational planning and control decisions, while also using future-orientated information, will need historical information, often related to the single accounting period under review.

EXHIBIT 9.1: INFORMATION REQUIREMENTS BY DECISION CATEGORY

| | Organisational Planning and Organisational Control | Strategic Planning |
|---|---|---|
| Managers involved | Middle managers | Top managers |
| Type of information required | • Financial<br>• Internal | • Non-financial<br>• External |
| Time focus of information | • Historical<br>• One year period | • Future predictions<br>• Multi-period |
| Required accuracy of information | High accuracy and detail required | Range of estimates |
| Frequency of information | Very frequent and regular | Infrequent and irregular |
| Responsibility centres | These form the basis of organisational planning and control | The focus is the firm itself |

Required Accuracy of Information Because strategic thinking requires much judgement, the information used in the process often consists of approximate estimates. By contrast, the organisational planning and control process usually requires more accurate, reliable and detailed information. Also, because much of the information relating to organisational planning and control has an historical orientation, its level of accuracy and reliability is greater.

Frequency of Information The non-routine nature of the strategic planning process means that the demands for this type of information occur infrequently and at irregular intervals. Important strategic issues do not occur according to a set timetable; rather, they are dealt with when they are perceived to exist. In contrast, information for organisational planning and control is frequently prepared according to a given timeframe.

Responsibility Centres Since organisational planning and control decisions are concerned with implementing strategy, this process relies heavily on 'responsibility centres' and on the individuals who have responsibility for those centres. A responsibility centre can be defined as a part, segment or sub-unit of an organisation whose manager is responsible for a specified set of activities and performance. In contrast, the issue of responsibility centres does not usually arise within the context of strategic thinking since strategic thinking usually involves the firm as an entity, rather than its departments.

## The Three Stages of Decision-Making

It is useful to identify the *three* main stages of decision-making, assuming a rational decision-maker. These stages are as follows:

1. **Define and Agree Objectives** Clearly, the decision-maker(s) must know what result is required, e.g. in terms of profit performance, market share or some other measurable phenomenon. A clear definition of what one is hoping to achieve is essential. In other words, and as somebody once remarked, "if you don't know where you are going, then any road will take you there".

2. **Identify and Evaluate the Alternatives for Action** Having identified the objectives, it is necessary to assess the current position in light of those objectives and to identify what can be done. Any similarities to previous decisions should be highlighted and any possible relevance of their solutions noted. Managers must take care not to rush into accepting what might appear to be the obvious way to tackle the problem. All possible solutions should be evaluated against three criteria:
   (a)  how realistic they are in the light of the available resources and objectives of the organisation,
   (b)  what are their financial implications, and
   (c)  what are the non-quantifiable considerations?

Non-quantifiable (or qualitative) considerations cannot be expressed in numerical terms and they relate to such items as the impact on staff morale if a specific business segment is closed down. Although non-quantifiable, these factors are often highly relevant and important in decision-making. It is important to note that managerial decisions should not be taken solely on the basis of accounting numbers. This is because not all relevant considerations can be translated into accounting numbers and, in any event, the accounting numbers are often estimates of the future.

3. **Select, Implement the Best Solution and Monitor Progress** The best solution will often represent a compromise between all the factors that have been considered and this is especially relevant in a group decision. The preferred solution must now be implemented. Effective implementation of the decision depends on preparing the necessary plans and schedules to ensure that those responsible are clear as to what is required from them, together with the necessary timeline. There should be a clear assignment of authority and responsibility to all concerned and any necessary co-coordinating mechanisms should be established at the outset.

   A system for the regular, periodic reporting of results should also be established so that these can be compared with what was expected and evaluated accordingly. This will enable early detection of any deviations from expectations to allow appropriate corrective actions to be considered and implemented.

We shall now proceed to discuss the use of accounting information in the context of routine managerial decisions and profit planning.

## 9.2  Routine Decisions and the Cost-Volume-Profit Model

In this section we will focus on routine decisions and in the following chapter (**Chapter 10**) we shall focus on non-routine decisions.

**Routine decisions** usually arise in the context of profit planning at the start of the accounting period and their financial implications are included in the annual budget. For example, management might need to decide whether to increase selling prices to boost revenue, or to reduce selling prices in order to generate additional volume.

One of the more important analytical tools used in routine decision-making by management is cost-volume-profit analysis. **Cost-volume-profit ('CVP') analysis** shows how revenues, costs, and, therefore, profits behave in response to changes in the level of business activity. **CVP analysis** can be used by management to answer questions such as the following:

1. What level of sales must be reached to avoid losses, i.e. to break even?
2. How many units must be sold to earn a target level of profit, either on a pre-tax or after-tax basis?
3. Is it worthwhile to spend more on, say, advertising to increase units sold?
4. What products or services should be emphasised in the product line?

To apply **CVP analysis**, costs must be classified in relation to their behaviour with respect to a specified cost driver. It will be recalled that a cost driver is any factor that significantly influences or causes costs. If volume is considered to be the only cost driver in a firm, then the various cost elements can be classified into four categories and graphs of each are presented in **Exhibit 9.2**. Costs (the dependent variable) are presented on the vertical axis and volume (the explanatory variable) is presented on the horizontal axis.

1. **Variable costs** Total variable costs increase or decrease directly and proportionately with changes in volume. If, for example, volume increases by 5%, then total variable costs will also increase by 5%. Petrol is an example of a variable cost for a car, since fuel consumption is directly related to miles driven. As **Exhibit 9.2 (a)** indicates, when volume of output is 'nil', no variable costs are incurred.

2. **Fixed costs** These are costs that remain unchanged in total with respect to changes in volume. Usually, such costs are incurred as a function of time, such as annual insurance or road tax for a car. As **Exhibit 9.2 (b)** indicates, when output is 'nil', a certain level of fixed costs will be incurred but these are not affected by subsequent changes in volume of output.

3. **Mixed costs** In reality, many cost elements are partly fixed and partly variable. These are referred to as mixed or semi-fixed costs. For example, with a car, depreciation is a semi-fixed cost. Some depreciation will occur due to the passage of time, without regard to the miles driven and thus represents a fixed cost. However, the more miles a car is driven each year, the more it depreciates due to wear and tear, which is a variable cost. (There are various techniques for analysing mixed costs into fixed and variable components and these techniques will be discussed later in the chapter.) As **Exhibit 9.2 (c)** indicates, when output is 'nil' a certain level of (fixed) costs are incurred and total costs then increase with additional output.

EXHIBIT 9.2: GRAPH OF COST BEHAVIOUR PATTERNS

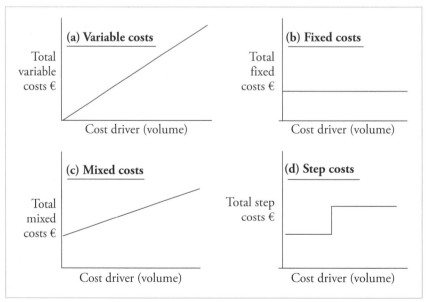

4. **Step costs** Such costs do not change in response to changes in volume within a narrow range of activity. However, once this 'relevant range' of activity is exceeded, additional costs are incurred, representing a stepwise function and these are presented in **Exhibit 9.2 (d).** For example, a university will require extra teaching staff, or be required to hire additional space, when student numbers exceed a certain level.

For convenience, we shall concentrate on just fixed and variable costs. We depict total costs on the vertical axis and the cost driver (e.g. volume) is presented on the horizontal axis. The graph for total costs is shown in **Exhibit 9.3.**

EXHIBIT 9.3: GRAPH OF TOTAL COSTS

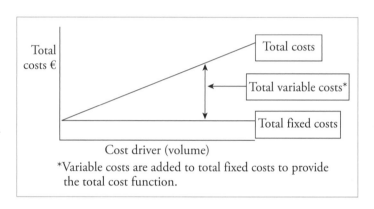

*Variable costs are added to total fixed costs to provide the total cost function.

In relation to the above total cost function, two points are important and can be repeated:

1. The cost function or cost relationship is defined in terms of a single cost driver only and this is assumed to be the volume of output. This assumption is convenient but slightly unrealistic and we have previously seen (when discussing activity-based costing) that there are many plausible non-volume-related cost drivers within an organisation. In addition, it must be acknowledged that costs change for a variety of non-volume reasons, for example, due to inflation. For CVP purposes, we simply focus on the behaviour of costs with respect to changes in volume of output.
2. The cost–volume relationship is valid only within a relevant range of activity. Beyond the relevant range of activity, either fixed costs change due to the new level of output or variable costs change due to, for example, economies of scale.

The importance of the 'fixed or variable' classification lies in the fact that, when the financial impact of changes in output is being studied, attention need only be concentrated on the variable costs, since fixed costs will remain unchanged for different levels of volume within a 'relevant range' of activity. This classification is particularly appropriate in the context of profit planning and decision-making in general.

## Methods of Profit Planning

Once a cost–volume relationship has been established, it can be combined with volume–revenue relationships to provide a simple but useful tool in profit planning. Profit planning provides estimates of profit at various output levels, given information on selling prices, fixed and variable costs. Profit planning can, initially, be done using a graphic approach and is outlined below.

## ILLUSTRATION: GRAPHIC APPROACH TO PROFIT PLANNING

Louth Company sells a single product at €8 each. The operating data is as follows, based on monthly sales which typically range between 6,000 and 10,000 units:

| Louth Company – Monthly Operating Data (per unit €) | |
| --- | --- |
| Average selling price | 8.00 |
| Variable costs: | |
| Purchase cost | 3.80 |
| Sales commission | 0.80 |
| Packaging costs | 0.40 |
| Total variable costs | 5.00 |

Total fixed costs are estimated at €21,000 per month.

A CVP graph of Louth Company is shown below in **Exhibit 9.4** and highlights total revenue, total costs and total profits at different levels of output. The horizontal axis shows the number of units sold per month, based on an upper limit of 10,000 units. The vertical axis is denominated in money terms, presenting both total revenue and total costs. The graph is plotted as follows:

1. The sales revenue line is plotted running from €0 at zero volume of sales to €80,000, representing 10,000 units sold per month at €8 per unit.
2. The monthly fixed costs are plotted as a horizontal line at the level of €21,000 per month.
3. Starting at €21,000 on the vertical axis, the total costs are plotted. Total cost, at any given level of activity, represents a fixed cost element of €21,000 plus a variable cost of €5 per unit for each unit sold. For an output of 10,000 units, total costs are estimated at €71,000.

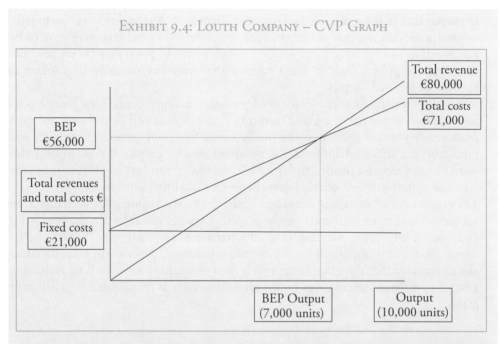

EXHIBIT 9.4: LOUTH COMPANY – CVP GRAPH

The profit expected at any sales level may be read directly from the above graph. One important level of activity is the **break-even point** (BEP). This is the level of activity at which total revenues equal total costs and, therefore, neither a profit nor a loss is generated. The monthly break-even point for the business can be reported either in physical or monetary terms. The physical BEP is 7,000 units and the monetary BEP corresponds to €56,000 in sales revenue. Sales below 7,000 units (€56,000) per month will result in a loss, and sales above this per month will result in a profit.

## Limitations of the Graphic Approach to Profit Planning

The graphic approach to managerial profit planning has a number of major limitations:

1. To be really useful, the graph must be drawn with proper accuracy. Otherwise it will be difficult to determine precisely such information as break-even point and the amount of profit or loss at different levels of output.
2. To show sales revenue as a straight line does not reflect the real position. Sales revenue does not increase in direct proportion to output. In reality, additional sales units can only be achieved if the unit sales price is reduced.
3. Likewise, variable costs do not vary in direct proportion to output and so it is not correct to represent total variable costs as a straight line. For example, the cost of additional materials may increase at a rate which is somewhat less than the increase

in output due to the availability of quantity discounts. Alternatively, raw materials, to meet a sudden increase in demand for the company's products, may have to be purchased at short notice from another supplier whose price may be higher than the regular supplier. Also, it could happen that overtime needs to be worked to produce additional output.

4. Where a firm manufactures a variety of products, a single break-even chart has its limitations because the (weighted) contribution per unit will be different for each product. Any major change in the product mix from one period to the next will invalidate the financial information provided by the graph. A way around this would be to prepare a profit graph for each individual product but this requires the accurate apportionment of fixed costs between individual products.

5. The graph represents a static situation. Thus, if, say, the selling price is changed, an additional line must be drawn on the graph. If several variables are changed – for example, selling price, variable cost and fixed costs – additional lines must be drawn on the existing graph (or a new graph prepared) which will become virtually unreadable. So, the graphic approach does not readily lend itself to evaluating a range of different alternatives unless each alternative is represented by a different graph.

## The Cost–Volume–Profit (CVP) Model

As an alternative to using the graphic approach in profit planning calculations (including break-even point), one can utilise simple formulae based on the contribution per unit. **Contribution per unit** is the difference between sales revenue per unit and variable cost per unit. The CVP model can be derived as follows and is based on four variables:

Profit = sales revenue − total costs
= (sales price × volume) − [fixed costs + (variable unit cost × volume)]
= (sales price − variable unit cost) × volume − fixed costs
where volume represents units sold                                    **Formula 1A**

Since **unit contribution** equals sales price per unit minus variable cost per unit, the above equation can be rearranged as follows:

Profit = (unit contribution × volume) − fixed costs    **Formula 1B**

Contribution per unit is a very valuable piece of information when considering the financial consequences of changing any of the four variables in the CVP model. The contribution per unit tells us how much revenue from each unit sold is available to cover fixed costs. Once enough units have been sold to cover fixed costs (production and non-production) during the accounting period, then the unit contribution from all additional sales represents profit.

The CVP model is widely used in profit planning and decision-making situations. To illustrate, let us consider two decisions in which cost–volume–profit relationships might be used, based on the previous illustration (Louth Company). The first decision concerns reducing unit sales price in order to generate additional sales. The second decision concerns reducing fixed costs that would have a small but adverse impact on volume sales.

## ILLUSTRATION: CHANGING UNIT SELLING PRICE

To increase volume, the manager of **Louth Company** is considering a policy of reducing selling price (and, therefore, contribution) by €1 per unit. (The previous contribution was €8 – €5 = €3 per unit.) Sales are expected to increase from 10,000 to 12,000 units. What is the projected profit at this new level of output? In other words, is the price reduction worthwhile? The calculations are as follows:

| | | |
|---|---|---|
| The current contribution is: 10,000 units × €3 | = | €30,000 |
| The revised contribution is: 12,000 units × €2 | = | €24,000 |
| Profit reduction due to proposal | | (€ 6,000) |

Thus, the revised pricing policy will cause total contribution (and, therefore, profits) to fall by €6,000 since fixed costs will remain unchanged. Therefore, the proposed alternative should be rejected, using only the financial information provided and taking a single period perspective.

## ILLUSTRATION: REDUCING COSTS AND VOLUME

The manager of the Louth Company is considering a proposal to reduce shopping hours by opening two hours later each morning. It is estimated that this policy would reduce sales volume from 10,000 units to 9,000 units but would reduce fixed costs by €1,000 per month. What is the financial impact, assuming the original selling price? The calculations are as follows:

| | |
|---|---|
| Revised contribution: 9,000 units × €3 = | €27,000 |
| Plus: Saving on fixed costs = | €1,000 |
| | €28,000 |
| Less: Current contribution: 10,000 × €3 = | €30,000 |
| Profit reduction due to proposal | (€2,000) |

Assuming the accuracy of the above data and taking a short-term perspective and ignoring all other factors, the proposal is not worthwhile.

## Break-even Point (BEP) and Target Volume

The cost–volume–profit model can also be used to determine break-even point and target volume. The break-even point represents the unique level of activity where total revenues exactly equal total costs. Thus, neither a profit nor a loss is generated at this level of output. The target volume point represents a level of activity which generates a required (pre-tax) profit objective. It is important to note that both of these calculations may be performed either in terms of physical units or monetary values. The basic CVP model was presented in **Formula 1B** as:

$$\text{Profit} = (\text{unit contribution} \times \text{volume}) - \text{fixed cost}$$

At break-even point, profit equals zero. Therefore, the number of units at break-even point can be found by re-arranging the equation as follows:

$$\text{BEP (units)} = \frac{\text{Total fixed costs}}{\text{Unit contribution}}$$

**Formula 2**

### Illustration: Calculation of BEP

Using the Louth Company, the monthly fixed costs amount to €21,000 and the contribution per unit is €3. Therefore BEP (in units) is computed as:

$$\text{BEP (units)} = \frac{€21,000}{€3} = 7,000 \text{ units per month}$$

Sometimes, especially for multi-product firms, it is necessary to calculate BEP in terms of sales revenue. The BEP in sales revenue may be calculated using the Contribution to Sales (C/S) ratio, which is the contribution per unit relative to the unit selling price. (The C/S ratio is sometimes referred to as the Contribution Margin ratio.) Thus:

$$\text{C/S} = \frac{\text{Unit contribution}}{\text{Unit sales price}} \text{ or } \frac{\text{Total contribution}}{\text{Total sales}}$$

The C/S ratio of 0.375 (€3/€8) means that 37.5% of the revenues from each unit sold contributes towards fixed costs, and then entirely to profit after all fixed costs have been covered. This C/S ratio can be used to calculate the BEP in terms of sales revenue. The following formula is derived by multiplying both sides of the BEP (units) equation by the sales price to provide:

$$\text{BEP (in € revenue)} = \frac{\text{Total fixed costs}}{\text{C/S ratio}}$$

**Formula 3**

For the Louth Company, the calculation is as follows:

$$\text{BEP (in € revenue)} = \frac{€21,000}{0.375} = €56,000$$

## Target Volume

Frequently, managers also want to know the level of output that will produce a required profit target. This level of activity is called 'target volume' and, intuitively, it must be above BEP. Formulae 2 and 3 (see above) can be adapted to calculate a target volume, i.e. sales volume (in units) needed to achieve any desired level of profit, as follows:

$$\text{Target volume (units)} = \frac{\text{Total fixed costs} + \text{required profit}}{\text{Unit contribution}}$$

**Formula 4**

## ILLUSTRATION: CALCULATION OF TARGET VOLUME

For example, how many units must be sold by the Louth Company to earn a monthly profit of €6,000? The calculation is as follows:

$$\text{Target volume (units)} = \frac{€21,000 + €6,000}{€3} = 9,000 \text{ units}$$

Alternatively, we can compute the required sales revenue to earn a profit target by substituting the contribution/sales ratio for the contribution per unit in Formula 4. The formula then becomes:

$$\text{Target volume (in sales revenue)} = \frac{\text{Total fixed costs} + \text{required profit}}{\text{C/S ratio}}$$

**Formula 5**

The sales value required for the Louth Company to earn a monthly profit of €6,000 can be computed as follows:

$$\text{Target volume (in sales revenue)} = \frac{€21,000 + €6,000}{0.375} = €72,000$$

## The Impact of Taxes on Target Volume Calculations

In most businesses, tax payable is related to the level of profits generated. We shall assume, for convenience, that accounting and taxable incomes are identical. This allows us to incorporate the impact of taxation into the cost–volume–profit model, e.g. estimating a target volume to achieve a required after-tax profit objective. We shall further assume that tax on corporate income is imposed at a single rate in direct proportion to accounting income. Thus, after-tax profit is equal to the pre-tax profit minus the appropriate tax. However, since CVP analysis is usually performed on a pre-tax basis, then we must use the following simple formula to convert a required after-tax profit figure to a pre-tax profit figure:

$$\textbf{Pre-tax profit} = \frac{\textbf{After-tax profit}}{\textbf{1} - \textbf{tax rate}}$$

## ILLUSTRATION: CALCULATION OF TARGET VOLUME ON AN AFTER-TAX BASIS

The Vartry Company manufactures and sells a standard component in a single size. The following financial information has been provided for the forthcoming accounting year:

| Selling price per unit | €25 |
| Variable costs per unit | €14 |
| Fixed costs (total) | €135,000 |
| Tax Rate on profits | 40% |

**Requirement:** How many units must be sold to generate an after-tax profit of €60,000?

**Solution and analysis:**

| | €   |
|---|---|
| W1. Contribution per unit: | |
| Selling price per unit | 25 |
| Less: variable costs per unit | <u>14</u> |
| = Unit contribution | <u>11</u> |
| Computation of target volume: | € |
| After-tax profit required | <u>60,000</u> |
| Therefore, pre-tax profit is €60,000/(1 − 0.40) | 100,000 |
| Add: Fixed Costs (given) | <u>135,000</u> |
| Required Contribution for target volume | <u>235,000</u> |

Target Volume (units) $\dfrac{\text{Fixed costs and profit}}{\text{Unit contribution}}$ $\dfrac{€235,000}{11}$ = 21,364 units

## Margin of Safety

In addition to planning for profit, managers will be interested in finding out by how much the volume of sales could decline before a loss would occur. This information is particularly relevant where there is great uncertainty regarding future operating conditions. The **margin of safety (MoS)** reflects the relationship between budget sales volume and break-even sales volume. (The calculation is usually done in terms of sales units, but the same result will be achieved if monetary sales values are used.) It is usual to express the margin of safety as a percentage of budgeted or planned sales, as follows:

$$\textbf{Margin of Safety (\%)} = \frac{\textbf{(Budgeted sales (units)} - \textbf{BEP sales (units))} \times \textbf{100}}{\textbf{Budgeted sales (units)}}$$

**Formula 6**

This indicates the percentage by which budgeted sales (units) could decline before the company incurs a loss (holding all other factors constant).

## ILLUSTRATION: MARGIN OF SAFETY

In the Louth Company we identified the BEP (units) as 7,000 units. Therefore, with budgeted sales of, say, 10,000 units, the margin of safety (%) is computed as follows:

$$\text{Margin of safety (\%)} = \frac{(10,000 - 7,000) \times 100}{10,000} = 30\%$$

This means that if forecast sales units fall by less than 30%, then a profit will still be generated, holding all other factors constant. If the sales volume falls by more than 30%, holding all other factors constant, then a loss will be recorded for the period.

If the margin of safety is small, managers may put more emphasis on reducing costs and increasing sales to avoid potential losses. A larger margin of safety gives managers greater confidence in making plans such as incurring additional fixed costs.

## Operating Leverage

The total cost structure of a firm, classified between its fixed and variable elements, allows one to identify the degree of operating leverage. **Operating leverage** represents the risk associated with the firm's current cost structure and, in particular, the risk associated with having fixed costs. (It is especially critical to identify whether direct labour costs represent a fixed or variable element in the overall cost structure.) Fixed costs have the advantage of being relatively easier to plan from year to year, since they do not, by definition, vary with levels of output. However, fixed costs are often difficult to reduce quickly if activity levels fail to meet expectations. This increases the firm's risk of incurring losses.

Operating leverage is usually calculated in terms of contribution, as follows:

$$\text{Operating leverage} = \frac{\text{Total Contibution } €}{\text{Profit for period } €}$$

Operating leverage will indicate how responsive the firm's profits are to changes in sales volume. Firms with a high degree of operating leverage incur more risk of losses when sales decline, due to the excessive incidence of fixed costs. Conversely, when operating leverage is high an increase in sales (once fixed costs are covered) contributes significantly to additional profits. This can be specified as follows:

**% change in profits = % change in sales × Degree of operating leverage**

### Illustration: Operating Leverage

Let us return to the earlier example of the **Louth Company** and we shall present a summarised budget as follows, in contribution format:

| Louth Company – Monthly Operating Data | |
|---|---|
| Sales (10,000 units at €8 each) | €80,000 |
| Total variable costs | €(50,000) |
| Total contribution | €30,000 |
| Fixed costs | €(21,000) |
| Profit | €9,000 |

The operating leverage for the business can be calculated as follows:

$$\text{Operating leverage} = \frac{\text{Total Contribution } €}{\text{Profit for period } €} = \frac{€30,000}{€9,000} = 3.33$$

Thus, if sales increase by, say 20%, the impact on profit can be identified as follows:

% change in profits = % change in sales × Degree of operating leverage
% change in profits = 20% × 3.33
% change in profits = 66.6%

Thus, if sales increase by 20% from their proposed level of 10,000 units, then an additional profit of €6,000 (66.6% × €9,000) will be generated. This calculation can be proved by revising the income summary, based on a 20% increase in sales volume from 10,000 to 12,000 units:

| Louth Company – Revised Monthly Operating Data | |
|---|---:|
| Sales (12,000 units at €8 each) | 96,000 |
| Total variable costs (12,000 units at €5 each) | (60,000) |
| Total contribution | 36,000 |
| Fixed costs | (21,000) |
| Profit (revised) | 15,000 |
| | |
| Profit (original estimate) | 9,000 |
| Additional profit generated | + 6,000 |

The final point to note in relation to operating leverage is that the degree of operating leverage and margin of safety are reciprocals of each other. Thus:

$$\text{Operating leverage} = \frac{1\,(\text{i.e. unity})}{\text{Margin of safety \%}}$$

## ILLUSTRATION: OPERATING LEVERAGE AND MARGIN OF SAFETY

For the Louth Company, the margin of safety based on anticipated sales of 10,000 units was 30%, since the BEP (in units) was calculated at 7,000 units. The degree of operating leverage is thus:

$$\text{Operating leverage} = \frac{1}{0.30} = 3.33$$

The obvious implication is that if the margin of safety is small, the degree of operating leverage is large. Therefore, as fixed costs increase in the overall cost structure, the overall margin of safety, reflecting risk, gets smaller. However, it is important to note that these calculations are specific to different levels of activity. Simply, the figures reflecting both margin of safety and operating leverage will change as activity changes.

## The Importance of Sales Mix in Cost–Profit–Volume Analysis

Most companies sell a variety of different products, which generate different contributions per unit. This applies just as much to a service company (an airline selling different priced tickets) as to a manufacturer producing small, medium and large versions of a product. In such cases, CVP analysis is based on the assumption of a constant sales mix, sometimes referred to as a constant product mix.

### ILLUSTRATION: CONSTANT SALES MIX

Assume a small business sells three types of product – Small, Medium and Large – for which the following financial information is provided:

|  | Small € | Medium € | Large € |
| --- | --- | --- | --- |
| Sales price per unit | 4.00 | 6.00 | 12.00 |
| Less: Variable costs per unit | 2.80 | 3.00 | 6.00 |
| Contribution per unit | 1.20 | 3.00 | 6.00 |
| Contribution/sales ratio (unit) | 0.30 | 0.50 | 0.50 |
| Fixed costs (apportioned) | €6,000 | €7,000 | €9,000 |

**Requirement:** Calculate the break-even point (in monetary terms).

**Solution and Analysis:** There are two ways of calculating BEP (and applying CVP analysis) for a multi-product firm. The first is to calculate the break-even point of each individual product and aggregate the answers. The relevant calculations are as follows:

|  | Small | Medium | Large |
| --- | --- | --- | --- |
|  | € | € | € |
| Fixed costs (above) | €6,000 | €7,000 | €9,000 |
| Contribution/sales ratio | 0.30 | 0.50 | 0.50 |
| BEP (sales revenue) | €20,000 | €14,000 | €18,000 |

In the example above, the BEP (in sales revenue) for the company as a whole is €52,000 (€20,000 + €14,000 + €18,000). This approach assumes that the fixed costs can be accurately apportioned between the various products and that the products can be sold independently of each other. Both of these assumptions may be unrealistic.

Alternatively, the overall BEP can be calculated from an 'average' contribution/sales ratio – on the assumption of a constant sales mix. Such proportions can usually be identified from previous years' sales patterns. Thus, if the three products are sold in the following proportions: 3: 2: 4, the relevant calculations are as follows:

| Product | Mix | Total sales for 9 units | Total contribution for 9 units | |
|---------|-----|-------------------------|-------------------------------|---|
| Small | 3 | €12.00 | €3.60 | |
| Medium | 2 | €12.00 | €6.00 | |
| Large | 4 | €48.00 | €24.00 | C/S ratio = $\dfrac{€33.60}{€72.00}$ |
| Total | 9 | €72.00 | €33.60 | = 0.466 |
| BEP (sales revenue) = | | | $\dfrac{€22,000}{0.466}$ | |
| BEP (sales revenue) = | | | €47,210 | |

The difference in the answers between the two methods stems from the different assumptions. The first method assumes that it is possible to accurately apportion all fixed costs to the individual product lines. In reality, this is difficult to do. The second method assumes that products are sold in a constant product mix. Again, this is not likely to be entirely valid but would appear to be more valid than the first assumption.

## Contribution Format Statements

To facilitate profit planning through the use of CVP analysis, it is recommended to prepare income statements in a contribution format. In **Chapter 2**, **Section 2.2** we introduced this format but it is useful to briefly revise it here:

## ILLUSTRATION: CONTRIBUTION FORMAT INCOME STATEMENTS

Dublin Fashions is a retail company that sells three different product lines: men's, women's and children's clothes. During its most recent financial year the firm made a profit of €30,000 as disclosed in the contribution format income statement:

### DUBLIN FASHIONS
### CONTRIBUTION FORMAT STATEMENT FOR YEAR

|  | Men's € | Women's € | Children's € | Total € |
|---|---|---|---|---|
| Total Sales | 50,000 | 30,000 | 20,000 | 100,000 |
| Variable costs | (20,000) | (10,000) | (15,000) | (45,000) |
| Total contribution | 30,000 | 20,000 | 5,000 | 55,000 |
| Total fixed costs | (11,500) | (8,250) | (5,250) | (25,000) |
| Product profit (loss) | 18,500 | 11,750 | (250) | 30,000 |

Although children's clothes show a small loss of €250 during the period, we would recommend its retention in the product line, in the absence of a specified alternative. The reason for this recommendation is that the product line generates an overall contribution of €5,000 towards fixed costs. The (apportioned) fixed costs (€5,250) would be incurred whether the sale of children's clothes continues or not – at least, we are not informed otherwise. Thus, the notion of contribution, rather than profit, is extremely important in decision-making.

### Assumptions and Limitations of the Cost–Volume–Profit Model

To conclude this section it is worthwhile reviewing the limitations of the CVP model, which stem from the assumptions on which the model is based. These assumptions are:

- Volume/output is the only factor influencing cost. In reality, non-volume cost drivers exist in all firms.
- Sales price per unit remains constant. In contrast, economists like to point out that, in order to sell additional units, the selling price must usually be reduced.
- Variable cost per unit of output remains constant. Thus, we ignore the impact of the learning curve or quantity discounts and assume that there are no economies or diseconomies of scale.

- In a manufacturing business, we assume that units sold equals units produced or, alternatively, stock is valued at variable cost of production. In reality, it is rare that production volume would exactly equal sales. Moreover, many manufacturing firms use absorption rather than variable costing for inventory costing purposes.
- If more than one product is sold, the proportion of the various products sold (sales mix) is assumed to be constant. Assuming a constant sales mix allows CVP calculations to be performed for the firm as a whole. It is important that this sales mix assumption be as accurate as possible and based on previous experience, adjusted for changing circumstances.
- The ability to accurately segregate/classify fixed and variable costs. This assumption is now addressed in the next section.

## 9.3 Establishing Costs and Cost Driver Relationships

One of the important aspects of decision-making is to estimate the financial consequences of each alternative. This section is concerned with estimating valid cost relationships and cost functions.

A **cost function** is an equation used to determine total costs, given an explanatory variable or cost driver. It should be stressed that we are assuming a linear cost function, based on a single cost driver and this is presented as follows:

$$TC = TFC + (VCu \times X)$$

Where TC represents total cost, TFC is total fixed cost for the period under review, VCu is the variable unit cost and X represents the cost driver level, frequently assumed to be the level of output.

When we estimate a cost function, we implicitly assume that total fixed costs remain unchanged with respect to changes in the cost driver and also that the unit variable cost will not change over a relevant range of activity. For example, if the estimated unit variable cost is €5, then no consideration is given to the possibility, unless we specifically state otherwise, that, say, material costs per unit may decrease as larger volumes of direct materials are purchased.

Cost functions can be established by analysing historical data. This does not imply that historical cost data is relevant in decision-making. Historical data relates to the past and, as such, cannot be relevant to the future. However, historical data can be useful in establishing cost functions. It is the predictive ability of historical data that is relevant to decision-making rather than the historical data itself. The following four techniques are often used to estimate cost functions and each will be discussed in turn. It should be expected that each method will provide different estimates of cost relationships:

- the accounts classification method
- the high–low method
- the scatter diagram
- regression analysis.

## Accounts Classification Method

It is useful to begin with the accounts classification method since it requires data relating to a single time period only. This method involves the identification of each element in the overall cost structure and then subjectively partitioning the cost between its fixed or variable components, where relevant. Where costs are considered mixed, they are apportioned on an appropriate percentage basis, using managerial judgement. While this method has the advantage of being reasonably quick and inexpensive, the subjectivity involved can result in significant inaccuracies. Moreover, there are no measures by which one can assess the reliability of the estimated relationship.

## ILLUSTRATION: ACCOUNTS CLASSIFICATION METHOD

The summarised income statement of Kilkenny Limited for the year 20x9 is reported as follows:

| Income Summary for year ... | € | % variability to sales |
|---|---|---|
| Sales (at €1 each) | 400,000 | |
| Less: Cost of sales | (264,600) | 100 |
| General expenses | (29,400) | 25 |
| Cleaning expenses | (2,400) | 10 |
| Delivery expenses | (4,000) | 75 |
| Depreciation expense | (2,000) | nil |
| Salaries and wages expense | (10,000) | nil |
| Rent and heating expense | (13,200) | nil |
| Net profit for period | 74,400 | |

The percentages on the right are considered estimates by appropriate management of the degree of variability of the items concerned in relation to changes in the volume of sales.

**Requirement:** Calculate the break-even point of Kilkenny Limited in terms of sales revenue for 20×9.

**Solution and Analysis:** It is first necessary to analyse each cost element in the overall cost structure in terms of fixed and variable components. The completed schedule is presented below, based on estimates provided by management:

| CLASSIFICATION BETWEEN FIXED AND VARIABLE COSTS | | | |
| --- | --- | --- | --- |
| | Total | Variable | Fixed |
| Cost of sales | 264,600 | 264,600 | Nil |
| General expenses | 29,400 | 7,350 | 22,050 |
| Cleaning expenses | 2,400 | 240 | 2,160 |
| Delivery expenses | 4,000 | 3,000 | 1,000 |
| Depreciation expense | 2,000 | Nil | 2,000 |
| Salaries and wages expense | 10,000 | Nil | 10,000 |
| Rent and heating expense | 13,200 | Nil | 13,200 |
| Totals | 325,600 | 275,190 | 50,410 |

The BEP (€) can be computed using the C/S ratio. The calculations are presented below:

Contribution margin     = (€400,000 – €275,190) =    €124,810

Contribution/sales ratio = €124,810/€400,000    =   0.31

BEP (sales revenue)     = €50,410/0.31         =   €162,613

## The High–Low Method

The high–low method is also called the 'two points' method. This is because two points are selected representing the 'highest' and 'lowest' activity levels, if the data set is large. Associated with these two points of extreme activity levels are the costs whose behaviour with respect to volume is required to be determined.

Assuming identical fixed costs in both periods, the difference between the total costs at these two activity levels must be explained by the behaviour of variable costs, which only respond to changing levels of output. The variable cost per unit is calculated by dividing the difference in total costs by the difference in total activity levels as follows:

$$\text{Variable cost per unit} = \frac{\text{Difference in total costs}}{\text{Difference in activity levels}}$$

Once the variable cost per unit is estimated, fixed costs are calculated by subtracting total variable costs from total costs in either of the two observations. Since we assume fixed costs are identical in both periods, it does not matter whether we estimate fixed costs by using either the high or low activity level.

## Illustration: High–low Method

The total overhead costs for the past four months are reported as follows:

| Month | Overhead costs | Units produced |
|---|---|---|
| January | €70,000 | 20,000 |
| February | €50,000 | 15,000 |
| March | €60,000 | 16,000 |
| April | €40,000 | 10,000 |

The months of highest and lowest activity are January (high) and April (low) respectively. Thus:

| | High January | Low April | Change |
|---|---|---|---|
| Overhead costs | €70,000 | €40,000 | + €30,000 |
| Units of output | 20,000 | 10,000 | + 10,000 |

The additional 10,000 units (between January and April) are associated with additional overhead costs of €30,000. Since only variable costs are assumed to vary with the volume of output, the variable cost per unit can be estimated as follows:

Variable oveahead (per unit) = €30,000/10,000 units = €3 per unit.

Estimated fixed costs per month can now be determined by using either the highest or lowest month. For example, in January, 20,000 units were produced. Therefore, total variable costs can be estimated at €60,000 (20,000 units at €3 per unit). However, since total costs (fixed and variable) are reported to be €70,000 for January, monthly fixed costs can be estimated at €10,000, being the difference between €70,000 and €60,000. In summary, the overhead cost function can be stated as a linear equation as follows:

Y (Total overhead cost per month) = €10,000 + €3 X

where X represents the number of units produced, €10,000 represents the monthly fixed overhead costs, and €3 is our estimate of the variable overhead per unit.

The advantage of the high–low method is its simplicity and ease of use. It can also provide a reasonable check on the estimates obtained by other methods.

The limitations of the high–low method are several. First, only two points are selected and a linear relationship is assumed. Secondly, if the highest and lowest activity points are selected, they may not be representative of the other observations. Thirdly, there may be ambiguity associated with this method since the month with the highest (lowest) activity may not be the month with the highest (lowest) cost. Finally, this method does not provide any measures for assessing the reliability of the relationship between cost and volume.

## The Scatter Diagram

A 'scatter diagram' represents a graph containing historical data over several time periods. Individual observations are represented by appropriate dots on the graph. Once the observations have been plotted, one draws a 'line of best fit'. While plotting the observations is a technical activity, drawing the line of best fit is very much a subjective exercise, based on the visual interpretation of the graph. It is realistic to argue that several individuals faced with the same set of observations will draw a different best-fit line. However, a general rule is to draw a line through the data so that an equal number of observations lie on either side of the line (see **Exhibit 9.5**). The slope of the line of best fit reflects the variable cost element. The intersection of the Y-axis is the estimate of fixed costs.

This method is simple and convenient to use. Also, since it uses a number of observations over time, it provides a good indication of whether a linear relationship exists, whether the relationship is in the form of a step function or whether a curvilinear relationship is more appropriate. In addition, it allows managers to visually examine the data to see whether any 'outliers' exist. An **outlier** can be described as an unusual or non-representative observation and its inclusion can seriously distort cost estimates, especially using regression analysis (which will be discussed below).

The disadvantage of the scatter diagram method is its subjectivity and that, like previous methods, there are no measures with which to assess the reliability of the estimated cost-volume relationship.

EXHIBIT 9.5: LINE OF BEST FIT

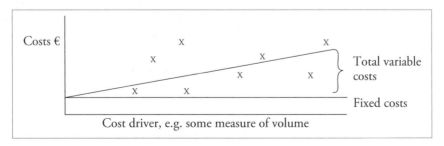

## Regression Analysis

Regression analysis is a statistical technique that allows an objective linear cost function to be identified from a given data set. A linear equation is presented as follows:

$$Y = A + B \times X$$

Where: Y = the dependent variable or value to be predicted, e.g. total cost
  A (alpha) = the constant in the equation, representing fixed costs per period
  B (beta) = the amount of change in Y for each unit change in X
  X = the explanatory variable, e.g. volume of output

Based on a set of past observations for both the explanatory and dependent variables, one can estimate values for both A (alpha) and B (beta) using regression analysis. (The term simple regression is used when there is only one explanatory variable and, if two or more explanatory variables are used, the technique is referred to as multiple regression.)

Regression analysis serves four important purposes:

1. It provides a precise mathematical definition of the cost-volume relationship.
2. It provides measures of reliability for this relationship.
3. It provides the basis for establishing a range for the possible value of Y for a given X value.
4. It provides the basis for establishing a range for the possible value of Beta.

The method for determining the regression equation is the ordinary least squares (OLS) method. This mathematical technique is entirely objective in that two or more persons, using the same data, should arrive at identical regression equations, barring arithmetical errors. The linear equation determined by this technique is unique because it minimises the sum of the squared differences between the estimated regression line and the actual observations, as presented in **Exhibit 9.6**. In other words, it minimises the sum of the vertical squared differences between the estimated and the actual cost for each observation used in the data set.

The immediate implication of the OLS method is that if extreme or outlying values are included in the set of observations on which the regression equation is determined, the resulting regression line may be distorted. Therefore, it is plausible to argue that such outlying values should be eliminated from the data set. Causes of such (cost) outliers could be attributable to, for example, excessive overtime or strikes. If these are not expected to occur as part of normal operating conditions then they should be excluded from subsequent analysis.

The regression equation ($Y = A + B \times X$) can be determined by the following two normal equations and solving for A and B:

$$\Sigma y = NA + B \Sigma x$$
$$\Sigma xy = A \Sigma x + B \Sigma x^2$$

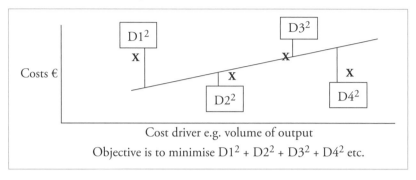

where:   N  = number of observations in the data set
  $\Sigma X$     = the aggregate value of the explanatory variable
  $\Sigma Y$ = the aggregate value of the dependent variable
  A  = Alpha, i.e. a constant (fixed cost) in the equation
  B  = Beta coefficient, i.e. rate of change between $\Sigma X$ and $\Sigma Y$ variables

## ILLUSTRATION: REGRESSION ANALYSIS

The following information is provided for the Clare Company for a random sample of 10-monthly observations (N = 10). The number of units is the explanatory variable (X) and overhead costs are the dependent variable (Y). The accountant presumes a linear relationship. (The figures below were initially expressed in thousands but these have been removed for computational efficiency purposes throughout this example and in the solution/analysis. Thus, our computed estimate of monthly fixed costs of €24.43 represents, in reality, monthly fixed costs in excess of €24,000.)

| No. of units (X) | € Overhead costs (Y) | $X^2$ | XY |
|---|---|---|---|
| 15 | 180 | 225 | 2,700 |
| 12 | 140 | 144 | 1,680 |
| 20 | 230 | 400 | 4,600 |
| 17 | 190 | 289 | 3,230 |
| 12 | 160 | 144 | 1,920 |
| 25 | 300 | 625 | 7,500 |
| 22 | 270 | 484 | 5,940 |
| 9 | 110 | 81 | 990 |
| 18 | 240 | 324 | 4,320 |
| 30 | 320 | 900 | 9,600 |
| 180 | 2,140 | 3,616 | 42,480 |

The two simultaneous equations are:

1. $\sum y = NA + B\sum x$

2. $\sum xy = A\sum x + B\sum x^2$

Substituting the appropriate values into the simultaneous equations, we obtain:

$$2,140 = 10A + 180B$$
$$42,480 = 180A + 3,616B$$

Solving the above simultaneous equations, we get: B = 10.53 and A = 24.43, so that the monthly estimating equation is: Y = 24.43 + 10.53X (but this is subject to rounding errors). This equation can be used to predict monthly overhead costs at different levels of output (units). Because all the 10 observations are used, the results produced by the least-squares method should be superior to other methods previously discussed.

Easy-to-use computer software is available, such as Microsoft Excel®, which performs these calculations very quickly and to a high degree of accuracy. The following represents a summary of the required actions.

Initially, enter the 10 observations relating to the Clare Company (provided above) into Excel and the resulting Excel spreadsheet should look as follows (**Exhibit 9.7**), with cells A5 to A14 containing values for the explanatory variable (units) and cells B5 to B14 containing values for the dependent variable (overhead costs):

EXHIBIT 9.7: EXCEL SPREADSHEET FOR REGRESSION ANALYSIS

| | A | B | |
|---|---|---|---|
| | Book1 | | |
| 1 | Clare company | | |
| 2 | | | |
| 3 | Units | Overhead costs | |
| 4 | | | |
| 5 | 15 | 180 | |
| 6 | 12 | 140 | |
| 7 | 20 | 230 | |
| 8 | 17 | 190 | |
| 9 | 12 | 160 | |
| 10 | 25 | 300 | |
| 11 | 22 | 270 | |
| 12 | 9 | 110 | |
| 13 | 18 | 240 | |
| 14 | 30 | 320 | |
| 15 | | | |
| 16 | | | |

To perform regression analysis on the above data, using Excel, adopt the following sequence:

- Click on **Tools**
- Click on **Data Analysis** (at bottom of drop down menu)
- Select **Regression** and click on OK

*Now you need to 'tell' the program where the appropriate data is located. Proceed as follows:*

- At **Input Y** range prompt – identify cells B5 to B14. This tells the program that the range for Y (the dependent variable – overheads costs) is contained in cells B5 to B14.
- At **Input X** range prompt – key in A5 to A14. This tells the program that the range for X (the explanatory variable – number of units) is contained in cells A5 to A14.
- Click **Output** range and key in (say) A17, which indicates the cell (and surrounding cells) in which the results will be posted. At this stage your screen should appear as follows: (**Exhibit 9.8**)

EXHIBIT 9.8: EXCEL SCREEN FOR REGRESSION ANALYSIS

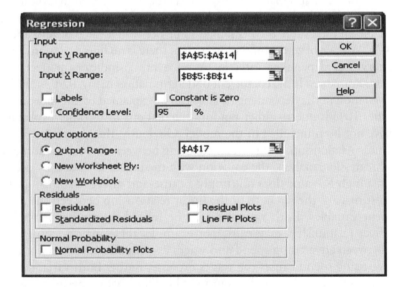

Now, click on **OK**. The solution will print out in cell A17 and surrounding cells and be similar to what appears below.

| Regression Statistics | | | |
|---|---|---|---|
| Multiple R | 0.98 | *Correlation coefficient (R)* | |
| R Square | 0.96 | *Coefficient of determination (R²)* | |
| Standard Error (SEE) | 15.55 | | |
| Observations | 10 | *Number of observations* | |
| | Coefficients | Standard error | T-statistic |
| Intercept | 24.43 | 15.25 | 1.60 |
| X Variable | 10.53 | 0.81 | 13.00 |

## Measures of Reliability

The advantage of using standard computer packages for regression analysis is that measures are automatically provided to assess the reliability of the linear cost–volume relationship. There are two commonly used measures of reliability:

### 1. The Coefficient of Determination

The **coefficient of determination ($R^2$)** is the measure used to assess the reliability of the regression equation. In mathematical terms, the coefficient of determination indicates the percentage variation in the dependent variable that is explained by variations in the independent variable and the value is constrained to lie between a value of zero and an absolute value of '1'. A value of zero would indicate that there is no linear relationship between the explanatory and dependent variable. A value of '1' indicates perfect correlation between the two variables. If the coefficient of determination is, say, 0.90, it indicates that 90% of the variation in the dependent variable can be explained by the independent variable. The other 10% is due to either random fluctuations or to other explanatory variables that have not been included in the model. Obviously, the higher the $R^2$ value, the higher the linear relationship. Thus, when choosing between two cost–volume relations, estimated by regression analysis, the equation with the higher $R^2$ is usually preferred.

However, a high $R^2$ value does not imply a cause-and-effect relationship. Rather, it provides an estimate of the strength of the linear relationship between the explanatory and dependent variables. Both variables may be related to another variable and no cause-and-effect relationship may exist. For example, there may be a high degree of correlation between advertising spend and wages expense; however we would not suggest that advertising spend causes the wages expense. Rather both variables are linked to another (missing) variable – perhaps units sold. Thus, before performing regression analysis, it is important to establish whether the relationship between the two selected variables is, in fact, economically plausible in the first instance. In other words, the relationship should make sense and be intuitive.

In order to avoid potential confusion, it should be noted that the $R^2$ statistic (coefficient of determination) is derived from the coefficient of correlation (R) which measures the 'goodness of fit' between the two variables. The R value is mathematically constrained to lie between a value of −1 to +1. The R value can be either positive – indicating that increasing values of X are associated with increasing values of Y. Alternatively, a negative correlation indicates that increasing values of X are associated with decreasing values of Y.

## 2. T-value of the Beta Coefficient

The second test of reliability of the regression equation is to determine the statistical significance of the **Beta coefficient**. The Beta value for any regression equation estimating cost–volume relationships is usually non-zero, suggesting some positive relationship between the X and Y values. What we need to do is to test statistically whether our computed (non-zero) Beta value in the regression equation could have occurred by chance. If the non-zero Beta coefficient could have occurred by chance, then there is a possibility that the real Beta is, in fact, zero and this would indicate no relationship between X and Y.

The procedure is first to establish a 'T-value' for the Beta co-efficient which is computed as follows:

$$\text{T-value} = \frac{\text{Beta coefficient}}{\text{Standard Error of Beta}} = \frac{10.53}{0.81} = 13$$

To assess the significance of this computed T-value, consult the statistical tables of 'T' to identify the T-statistic for the appropriate degrees of freedom and required confidence level (usually 95%). The appropriate degrees of freedom will be N – p, where N equals the number of observations and p equals the number of parameters in the estimating equation. In simple regression, there are always two parameters: the constant (A) or Alpha and coefficient of the independent variable (B) or Beta.

Using the table (**Exhibit 9.9**) for 8 (10 – 2) degrees of freedom, appropriate to 10 observations, we see that 'T' has a value of 2.306 at the 95% confidence level. This means that there is a 5% probability that the absolute value of T is greater or equal to 2.306. Thus, if the real value of Beta is zero (which would indicate that there is no linear relationship), there is only a 5% probability that the T-value will be **greater** than 2.306. It will be recalled that our computed T-value is 13. Since our computed T-value (13) greatly exceeds the value of 2.306, we can conclude that the above relationship is statistically significant. In other words, it is most unlikely that our computed Beta value of 10.53 could have arisen by chance, if the real Beta value was zero. Therefore, we reject the possibility that B = 0, at the 5% level of significance. If the T-value of Beta was **not** statistically significant, we should not use the estimates generated by the regression model.

It will be noted from **Exhibit 9.9** that, as the overall sample size increases, the statistical T-value reduces. Eventually, it will reach 1.96 indicating that, in a normal probability distribution, 95% of the observations will lie + or –1.96 standard deviations from the mean. Accordingly, many accountants use '2' as a general rule for establishing confidence intervals and also for assessing the statistical significance of the Beta co-efficient.

The two tests of linearity may be summed up as follows. First, the $R^2$ statistic (coefficient of determination) explains the percentage variation in Y explained by X in this illustration, 96%. This indicates that there is a strong linear relationship between the X and Y variables. A second test of linearity is to test the statistical significance of Beta. The computed T-value (10.53/0.81) equals 13, which is statistically significant

EXHIBIT 9.9: STATISTICAL T-VALUES

| Degrees of freedom | For 95% confidence level | Degrees of Freedom | For 95% confidence level |
|---|---|---|---|
| 1 | 12.706 | 13 | 2.160 |
| 2 | 4.303 | 14 | 2.145 |
| 3 | 3.182 | 15 | 2.131 |
| 4 | 2.776 | 16 | 2.120 |
| 5 | 2.571 | 17 | 2.110 |
| 6 | 2.447 | 18 | 2.101 |
| 7 | 2.365 | 19 | 2.093 |
| 8 | 2.306 | 20 | 2.086 |
| 9 | 2.262 | 21 | 2.080 |
| 10 | 2.228 | 22 | 2.074 |
| 11 | 2.201 | 23 | 2.069 |
| 12 | 2.179 | 24 | 2.064 |

since it greatly exceeds the statistical T-value (2.306), corresponding to a 95% confidence level at (N − 2) degrees of freedom.

*Confidence Interval for Y*

A **confidence interval** is a range used to estimate a variable with a specific confidence level – usually 95%. It will be recalled that our regression equation provides an estimated value of Y, given values for A, B and X. Thus, Y will represent, for example, our prediction of total cost for the period under review. However, it is only a point estimate, at a specific level of X. The **Standard Error of the Estimate** (SEE) allows managers to establish a confidence interval for the actual value of Y. A 95% confidence interval for Y is calculated as:

$$Y +/- t95(SEE)$$

It is not necessary to explain the calculation for standard errors since they are computed automatically using an appropriate computer programme. The overall monthly regression equation is:

$$Y = 24.43 + 10.53X$$

where Y = predicted total labour cost; 24.43 = fixed cost per month; 10.53 = the rate of change between X and Y; and X = number of units. Therefore, the total predicted labour cost for a month in which 100 units are produced is €1,077 (24.43 + (€10.53 x 100)).

However, the actual value of Y, at a 95% confidence level, will fall somewhere between: €1,077 +/– 2.306 (15.55) i.e. the values of €1,113 and €1,041.

*Confidence Interval for B*

Finally, a 95% confidence interval for Beta can also be established according to the following formula:

$$B + / - T95(SEb)$$

where SEb represents the standard error of the Beta coefficient (and not SEE). The actual value of Beta is likely to fall between:

10.53 +/– 2.306 (0.81), i.e. between the values of 12.39 and 8.67.

## Multiple Linear Regression

Our previous discussion in relation to cost behaviour has been limited in that it focused exclusively on only one explanatory variable, using a simple, linear model. In some situations a dependent variable is associated with more than one independent variable. For example, often running a simple linear regression and finding that $R^2$ is low, managers might identify another explanatory variable whose inclusion could improve the overall goodness of fit. Indeed, the availability and ease of computer software for regression analysis encourages managers to include additional explanatory variables. Multiple regression uses two or more independent variables, e.g. the volume of output and the skill level of employees. Both simple and multiple regression are everyday tools managers can use in estimating cost–volume relations and cost behaviour in general.

## 9.4 The Impact of the Learning Curve

It will be recalled that one of the fundamental assumptions underlying cost–volume–profit (CVP) analysis is that of a constant unit variable cost for a relevant range of activity. This implies, for example, that as output expands, manufacturing employees will take the same time to produce each successive unit. In other words, the implicit assumption behind CVP analysis was that there was no learning curve. If the labour content per unit is expected to decline, as workers become more familiar with a process, then learning curve principles can be applied. Documented experience in some industries has found that the rate of improvement was so regular that it could be presented as a formula so that the number of direct labour hours required for any given level of output could be predicted with a high degree of accuracy. Learning curve theory is most applicable when a high degree of manual labour is required and there is a high degree of repetition involved in the production process. The fundamental principle of the learning curve can be described as follows:

As the cumulative quantity of output doubles,
the **average** time per unit will fall
*to* a fixed percentage of the previous **average** time.

## ILLUSTRATION: LEARNING CURVE

Thus, assume that an 80% learning curve applies to a specific assembly project. If the first unit requires 100 minutes to produce, then we can estimate the time required to produce, say, four units by way of the following presentation, which initially concentrates on the average time per unit. As output doubles, the average time per unit falls *to* 80% of the previous average (or *by* 20% of the previous average). The cumulative time is found by multiplying the number of units by the average time. The table below indicates that the average time for four units is 64 minutes. Accordingly, an estimate of the total time for 4 units is 256 minutes (4 units at 64 minutes each).

| No. of units | Avg. minutes per unit | Cumulative (total) time |
|---|---|---|
| 1 | 100 (given) | 100 for 1 unit |
| 2 | 80 (80% × 100) | 160 for 2 units |
| 4 | 64 (80% × 80) | 256 for 4 units |

The second method of calculating the average time makes use of log tables. (The following discussion uses logs to the base 10.) This method uses a formula for the learning curve, based on an exponential expression:

$$Y = aX^b$$

Where Y = average time per unit (or average cost per unit)
a = number of hours (or cost) that the first unit requires
X = cumulative number of units
b = the index of learning (which will always be a negative coefficient),
     defined as:

$$b = \frac{\text{Log of learning curve}}{\text{Log 2}}$$

## ILLUSTRATION: LEARNING CURVE

It is possible to convert the above exponential expression to a linear form using logs. Thus, a linear model is:

$$\text{Log Y} = \text{Log a} + b \times \text{Log X}$$

$$\text{and, b} = \frac{\text{Log 0.8 (representing the 80\% curve)}}{\text{Log 2 (representing the doubling effect)}} = 0.322$$

The average time to produce four units is as follows (using log table to the base 10):

$$\text{Log Y} = \text{Log } 100 + \frac{\text{Log } 0.8}{\text{Log } 2} \times (\text{Log } 4)$$

$$\text{Log Y} = 1.806$$

Converting Log Y (using logs to the base 10) of 1.806 to Y we get:

$$Y = 63.97 \text{ minutes}$$

Therefore, the time required to produce four units = 4 × 63.97 = 255.88 minutes.

### ILLUSTRATION: LEARNING CURVE

Tralee Limited manufactures products where the effect of learning on labour cost is very pronounced. A customer has asked for a price quotation on an order for 750 components which would be produced one at a time. It is estimated that the production labour costs of the first unit would amount to €4,000 and that a 80% cumulative learning curve would apply to these production labour costs.

**Requirements:**

1. What is the predicted labour cost if the learning curve is ignored?
2. Using the learning curve, estimate the labour cost of the order of 750 units.

**Solution and analysis:**

1. If the learning curve is ignored, the estimated total labour cost is easily calculated by multiplying the total number of units by the (constant) average cost, as follows:

   750 units @ €4,000 each = €3,000,000

2. To incorporate the learning curve impact, we need to calculate the average labour costs of producing 750 units. It will be noted that 750 units lies, approximately mid-point, between cumulative outputs of 512 and 1,024 units. Therefore, we can calculate:

| Cumulative units | Average cost per unit | Total cost |
|---|---|---|
| 1 | €4,000 (given) | |
| 2 | €3,200 (80% × €4,000) | |
| 4 | €2,560 (80% × €3,200) | |

| Cumulative units | Average cost per unit | Total cost |
|---|---|---|
| 8 | €2,048 (80% × €2,560) | |
| etc. | etc. | |
| 512 | €537 (80% × €671) | |
| 1,024 | 429 (80% × €537) | |
| 750 | €490 (say approx) | Estimate = €367,500 (say) |

Alternatively, we can derive more precise estimates with reference to the learning curve itself:

| $Y =$ | $a X^B$ | |
|---|---|---|
| $\text{Log } Y =$ | $\text{Log } a + b \text{ Log } X$ | |
| $\text{Log } Y =$ | $\text{Log } (4,000) = \dfrac{\text{Log } 0.8}{\text{Log } 2} \times \text{Log } 750$ | |
| $\text{Log } Y =$ | $3.60 + \dfrac{-0.0969}{0.3010} \times 2.875$ | |
| $\text{Log } Y$ | 2.68 (rounded) | |
| $Y =$ | €478 (rounded) | i.e. average cost for 750 units |
| **Total labour cost** | (750 units × €478) = | €358,500 |

Thus, reflecting on our answers to requirements 1 and 2 above, we can note that there are significant differences in the total labour cost estimate depending on whether one assumes, or not, the presence of a learning curve.

## Learning Curve Applications and Implications

The learning curve best applies to those situations that require repetitive effort. Learning curves are not theoretical abstractions but are based on observations of past events. The learning curve could be applied to the following situations:

## Pricing Decisions

The main impact of the learning curve is likely to be in providing better cost estimates to enable better price quotations to be prepared for potential orders. An ability to forecast cost reductions as a result of the learning curve, and consequent selling price reductions, could make the difference between obtaining and losing profitable orders. Indeed, a company could reduce its selling price (through the learning curve effect), which could further increase its volume and market share and eventually force some competitors out of the industry.

## Work Scheduling

Learning curves enable firms to predict their required inputs more effectively and this enables them to schedule more accurate delivery schedules. This in turn can lead to improved customer relationships and possibly result in increased future sales. More accurate production scheduling should also reduce idle time.

## Standard Setting and Variance Reporting

If budgets and standards are set without considering the learning effect, meaningless cost variances are likely to occur. This is because budgets are established assuming constant efficiency whereas actual performance will capture efficiencies due to the learning curve. Significant favourable cost variances are likely to be reported due to the original budgets being incorrect.

## Arguments Against the Use of the Learning Curve

There are a number of arguments against the use of the learning curve and these should be noted. The main arguments are:

- The learning curve generally applies to those situations where the labour input for an activity is large but is not as relevant for automated industries. Given that labour is becoming a less dominant cost in manufacturing and that most manufacturing companies are automated – the relevance of the learning curve is questionable.
- When technological changes take place in the production process or a high level of labour turnover exists – the relevance of the learning curve is doubtful and it is difficult to measure the appropriate rate of learning.
- The variables in the learning curve may not be easy to determine. For example, the first time an operation is performed, both the workers and the operating procedures are untested. The learning process starts from the point when the first unit comes off the production line. However, accurately predicting this rate over a considerable period of time and range of production is a difficult task.
- Application of an incorrect learning curve could prove costly in terms of setting prices and cost estimation. A major problem with the learning curve is the assumption that unit labour costs fall constantly as output is doubled. From a cost budget perspective, there is a danger of underestimating costs if the learning curve is not present as

estimated. This, in turn, can have a negative effect on product pricing and product profitability.
- It is very difficult to apply the learning curve to new situations or new products with no similarity to previous processes or products. While companies may learn lessons from other products in predicting the learning curve impact, the assumed similarities between old and new products may not be as close as anticipated, resulting in inaccurate cost and time estimates.

## Conclusion

In summary, this chapter introduced the topic of managerial decision-making and we paid particular attention to the cost–volume–profit (CVP) model, which allows us to perform, quickly, important profit calculations in routine decision-making situations. However, these calculations are based on a number of assumptions including the ability to accurately segregate fixed and variable costs. We discussed how cost relationships can be estimated using a range of different techniques and introduced the Learning Curve. In the next chapter, we discuss a variety of non-routine decisions including pricing decisions.

## SUMMARY OF LEARNING OBJECTIVES

**Learning Objective 1:** Distinguish between strategic and organisational planning and control decisions.

Strategic decision-making is the preserve of top managers and is concerned with scanning the environment to identify, for example, opportunities and threats, customer preferences and competitor attributes, in order to agree the mission of the company and how this mission is to be achieved. Much of the information required is of a non-financial and external nature. Organisational planning and control decision are made by middle management, designed to achieve objectives arising out of the strategic planning process. Much of the information required is of an internal and financial nature.

**Learning Objective 2:** Describe the steps in the (rational) managerial decision-making process.

The rational decision-making process begins with an agreed objective, i.e. what is to be achieved in the future. Then the decision-maker (or group) identifies the various alternatives and evaluates each of them. Finally, the best alternative, given the financial and non-quantifiable considerations, is selected, implemented and its progress toward achieving the agreed objective is monitored on a regular and frequent basis.

**Learning Objective 3:** Apply profit planning calculations, including break-even point, for single and multi-product firms.

Routine profit planning is driven by four items, namely, the average selling price per unit, the average variable cost per unit, the quantity sold, and the level of fixed costs within the accounting period. These four factors allow us to compute the break-even point both in terms of quantity sold and in terms of sales revenue. With multi-product firms we need to make the assumption of a constant product mix.

**Learning Objective 4:** Prepare summarised income statements in contribution format.

For managerial decision-making it is useful to present income summaries in contribution-based format. Such summaries present total revenue less total variable costs to highlight total contribution. From this figure the total fixed costs are deducted to provide profit (before tax) for the period. Income statements (and product information) in contribution format were presented in the exhibits and illustrations in this chapter.

**Learning Objective 5:** Estimate the linear relationship between costs and cost drivers using account analysis and the high–low methods.

The linear relationship between total costs and cost driver – usually assumed to be some measure of output – can be expressed in equation form as $Y = A + B.X$ – where X is the cost driver). This relationship can be identified by the account analysis method which uses the judgement of a responsible manager to identify how much of a cost element is fixed and how much is variable. Alternatively, the high–low method can be used. The high–low method identifies the change between two representative points in a data set. Both of these methods suffer from the limitation that they do not provide any measures of reliability.

**Learning Objective 6:** Estimate the linear relationship between costs and cost drivers using regression analysis, while also applying measures of reliability.

Regression analysis is a mathematical technique which estimates the value of the intercept (Alpha) and the rate of change (Beta) given a range of dependent (Y) and explanatory (Y) variables. Thus, regression analysis uses all the data provided but, in some cases, data representing 'outliers' may be disregarded. The advantage with regression analysis is that the underlying calculations can be done quickly using, for example, Excel. In addition, the further advantage of regression analysis is that measures of reliability ($R^2$ and the 'T' value of Beta) are automatically produced.

**Learning Objective 7:** Describe the nature of and perform calculation using the learning curve.

The learning curve is an observed phenomenon associated with repetitive tasks, so that when output is increased, workers take, on average, less time to perform the required activity. The reduction in time is formally described as the learning curve. A learning curve of say, 80%, indicates that, when output doubles, the average time per unit will fall to 80% of the previous average time. (A learning curve of

80%, implies a learning rate of 20%.) The implications of the learning curve, e.g. the reduced time to produce additional units, are so significant that this phenomenon should not be overlooked. However, some critics say that the phenomenon will not apply in highly automated plants and, if it is incorrectly applied or assumed, can be harmful. Calculations showing the impact of the learning curve were presented in the exhibits and illustrations in this chapter.

## Questions

### Review Questions

(See Appendix One for Solutions to Review Questions **9.1** and **9.2**)

*Question 9.1 (Profit Planning for a Single Product Manufacturer)*

The Astra Company is the largest producer of tinned dog food in Ireland. The dog food is manufactured under the company's own label and is produced in a single tin size. The product is sold to both supermarket chains and small retail outlets throughout the country. The company's strategy follows the 'cost leadership' model since, in the view of the managing director "you can't sell tinned meat to a dog – you sell the tins to the owner of the dog"! Overall profitability has been satisfactory in previous years due to expanding market share and strict cost control.

However, the managing director is aware of the potential threat of 'globalisation' to a market that has few barriers to entry. He also realises that the Euro currency, together with the Internet, has made selling prices much more transparent within Europe. As a result, he would like to introduce some basic managerial accounting techniques into his business and has asked for your assistance. Based on the firm's income statement, you have extracted the following information for the current year 20x6:

| | | |
|---|---|---|
| Sales units (total) | | <u>11,250 units</u> |
| Sales revenue (11,250 units) | | <u>€450,000</u> |
| | | € |
| Sales price per unit | | 40.00 |
| Less: Variable costs per unit: | € | |
| Direct materials | 4.00 | |
| Direct labour (variable) | 9.00 | |
| Variable production overhead | 3.00 | |
| Selling expenses | <u>3.00</u> | 19.00 |

| Total fixed costs for 20x6 | € |
|---|---|
| Production overheads | 20,000 |
| Administrative overheads | 75,000 |
| Selling overheads | 100,000 |
| | 195,000 |
| Current tax rate on profits | 40% |

**Requirements:**

1. Using the equation method, what is the projected net profit (after tax) for 20x6 assuming an annual sales value of €450,000, i.e. 11,250 units?
2. Calculate the break-even point, in units, for 20x6.
3. Calculate the break-even point, in monetary value, for 20x6.
4. Calculate the target volume, in units, for 20x6 in order to generate a profit (before tax) of €10,000.
5. Calculate the target volume, in monetary values, for 20x6 in order to generate a profit (before tax) of €10,000.
6. Calculate the Margin of Safety percentage (MOS), assuming planned sales for 20x6 are 11,250 units.
7. How many units must be sold in 20x6 to earn a profit (**after** tax) of €15,000?
8. For the financial year **20x7** the following changes are anticipated:
   (a)  Selling price shall increase by 10%; and
   (b)  Variable costs shall increase by 20%; and
   (c)  Fixed costs shall increase by €15,000.

   Based on these anticipated changes, calculate the break-even point (in units) for 20x7.

*Question 9.2 (Accounts Classification and Decision-making in a Retail Company)*

The summarised income statement of Sentra Company, a company that produces a single electronic component, in a standard size, for the **financial year** 20x1 has been provisionally budgeted as follows:

| | € | %* |
|---|---|---|
| Sales (200,000 units) | 500,000 | |
| Direct materials costs | 270,000 | 100 |
| Direct labour costs | 80,000 | 25 |
| Delivery costs | 8,000 | 75 |
| Depreciation | 36,000 | nil |
| Administration costs | 75,000 | nil |
| Net profit for year | 31,000 | |

\* The % figures to the right of each cost item reflect the **percentage variability** with respect to the number of units produced (and sold) and this represents the best attempt by management to use the accounts classification method for cost prediction purposes.

**Requirements:**

1. Classify the above costs into their variable/fixed components using the accounts classification method and present the above income summary in contribution format, based on your analysis. Clearly present your overall cost prediction model for the year, using the number of units produced as the overall cost driver.
2. Calculate the break-even point, in terms of units to be sold.
3. Market research (for 20x1) indicates two possibilities that should be considered:
   (a) A reduction of 5% in the sales price will result in a 30% increase in sales volume; or
   (b) A reduction of 10% in the sales price will result in an increase in sales volume of 50%, provided that an additional €20,000 is spent on advertising.
   You are required to prepare statements in contribution format showing the separate financial results of the above alternatives (a) and (b). What do you recommend?
4. Briefly list five assumptions/limitations of the CVP model.

## Intermediate Questions

### Question 9.3 (Profit Planning with Multiple Products)

Master Limited is a retailer of three main product lines of wooden furniture. It is considering possible amendments to its pricing and product range since some product lines have reported operating losses in the most recent accounting period, as detailed below. Master Limited prepares income statements by product line and all overhead costs are apportioned to product lines. Most of these overhead costs are fixed in relation to volume changes, over a relevant range of activity. They include such items as wages, light and heat, and rates, which are generally apportioned to product lines on the basis of square feet occupied. For the year to 31 December the budgeted figures are as follows (in €000s):

| | Tables and chairs € | Beds € | General furniture € |
|---|---|---|---|
| Sales | 50,400 | 88,000 | 72,000 |
| Cost of sales | 54,000 | 48,000 | 14,400 |
| Gross profit (loss) | (3,600) | 40,000 | 57,600 |
| Selling/distribution costs | 13,000 | 42,800 | 25,700 |

| | | | |
|---|---|---|---|
| Operating profit (loss) | (16,600) | (2,800) | 31,900 |
| 'Unit' basis: | | | |
| Selling price (average) | 14.00 | 22.00 | 30.00 |
| Selling costs (average) | 2.00 | 2.40 | 2.50 |

You have been retained as a consultant to advise Master Limited's board on its policies relating to pricing and product offering.

**Requirements:**

1. Revise the above summarised Income Statement in contribution-based format, and clearly show the number of units of each product line sold.
2. Determine the impact on Master Limited's overall profits of each of the following four proposals, which are independent of each other (i.e. assuming that everything not specified in the particular proposal remains constant):

   (a) The product line of Tables and Chairs is discontinued, but all staff will be retained. The sales of other product lines will not be affected;
   (b) The product line of Tables and Chairs is discontinued with a consequential decrease of 400 Beds being sold, i.e. a 10% fall in the number of beds sold;
   (c) The selling price of the Tables and Chairs product line is increased to €16.00 per unit, with a consequential decrease of one-sixth in the number of Tables and Chairs sold;
   (d) The product line of Tables and Chairs is discontinued, and the space is used to retail a new style of Garden furniture. (Sales of the existing range will not be changed.) It is estimated that 800 of these new sets will be sold at an average selling price of €19 per set. The average purchase cost is €12.00 per set, and the variable selling/distribution costs would be €4.10 per set.

*Question 9.4 (Profit Planning in a Retail Company)*

Abbey's is a small family-owned fish and chip shop, located on the corner of a busy street. Because of its excellent location, the shop attracts a good number of customers and has always been profitable as highlighted by the summarised income for the most recent accounting year:

| | € | € |
|---|---|---|
| **Sales:** | | |
| Fried fish | 40,000 | |
| Chips | 50,000 | |
| Confectionery | 10,000 | 100,000 |

| **Less: Expenses:** | | |
|---|---|---|
| Cost of Fish | 28,000 | |
| Cost of Potatoes | 9,000 | |
| Cost of Confectionery | 8,000 | |
| Cost of frying oil | 8,100 | |
| Depreciation | 5,000 | |
| Wages | 6,600 | |
| Light and heat | 9,000 | 73,700 |
| **Net profit** | | 26,300 |

The following costs are considered fixed in relation to changes in sales volume, over a relevant range of activity:

- depreciation, which is based on a straight-line method
- wages
- a standing charge of €6,000 in respect of light and heat.

**Requirements:**

1. Prepare a report on the three product lines, in contribution format, clearly distinguishing between fixed and variable costs. Overhead costs, where applicable, should be apportioned to the product lines on the basis of sales revenue. Based on your calculations explain whether sales of confectionery should be discontinued. Why or why not?
2. Evaluate the following proposal: Close down the confectionery line and, in which case, half of its sales revenue would be transferred to the sale of chips.
3. What is the additional profit if sales volume of fish increases by 10%, holding all other factors constant?
4. What is the break-even point (in €) for the shop?

*Question 9.5 (Profit Planning with Multi-products)*

Fizzer Company Limited is a pharmaceutical company that currently sells and produces two products – Reactin and Alrite. A new product, Amsick, has just received approval by the government's medical board and it is expected that sales of Amsick will commence in January 20x1. One of the existing products, Reactin, has just come off patent and is expected that it will experience severe competition from generic products next year. This will impact on both sales volumes and sales margins of the product.

You are supplied with the following budget data for the financial year ending 20x0 (based on only two products of Reactin and Alrite):

| Budget for the year ended 31 December 20x0 | |
| --- | --- |
| Sales | €38,000,000 |
| Variable Costs | 6,200,000 |
| Contribution | 31,800,000 |
| Fixed Costs | 7,800,000 |
| Net Profit | 24,000,000 |

**Note 1**: 60% of the above sales revenues and 50% of the variable costs relate to sales of Reactin.

**Note 2**: The selling price of Reactin during the year is €100 per unit and the selling price of Alrite is €400 per unit.

The marketing department have informed you that sales for the new product (Amsick) are expected to be 40,000 units during 20x1. The selling price will be €150 per unit and variable costs will be €20 per unit.

In addition, in view of increased competition, it is expected that sales volumes and sales prices for Reactin will both fall by 20% next year but that the sales volume and selling prices for Alrite will remain unchanged. The total impact on fixed costs resulting from the above changes will be to increase annual fixed costs by a total of €1,800,000 from their 20x0 budgeted level.

**Requirements:** Calculate the break-even point in both unit volume and sales revenue terms for next year (i.e. 20x1).

## Question 9.6 (Choice of Cost Driver and Regression Analysis)

Ian Murphy, the Director of Cost Operations of Indell (Ireland) Limited, is confronted with the problem of identifying appropriate cost drivers for their circuit board assembly plant. Indell (Ireland) carries out the detailed assembly operation whereby absolute accuracy is required and this is achieved by special machines, operating at a precision level equivalent to one two-thousandth of a human hair! Therefore, production overheads are a significant cost in the overall cost structure and Murphy has directed his cost accountant to provide data on overhead costs and two potential cost drivers, i.e. direct labour hours and the number of boards completed. He wants to use regression analysis to demonstrate which cost driver best explains overhead costs and the following information has been obtained:

| Week | Overhead Costs € | Direct labour hours | Units completed |
| --- | --- | --- | --- |
| 1 | 66,900 | 7,619 | 2,983 |
| 2 | 62,200 | 7,678 | 2,830 |
| 3 | 64,300 | 7,816 | 2,413 |

| Week | Overhead Costs € | Direct labour hours | Units completed |
|------|------------------|---------------------|-----------------|
| 4 | 59,900 | 7,659 | 2,221 |
| 5 | 64,400 | 7,646 | 2,701 |
| 6 | 64,000 | 7,765 | 2,656 |
| 7 | 63,000 | 7,685 | 2,495 |
| 8 | 63,300 | 7,962 | 2,128 |
| 9 | 59,200 | 7,793 | 2,127 |
| 10 | 60,100 | 7,732 | 2,127 |
| 11 | 61,400 | 7,771 | 2,338 |
| 12 | 64,000 | 7,842 | 2,685 |
| 13 | 63,400 | 7,940 | 2,602 |
| 14 | 58,300 | 7,750 | 2,029 |
| 15 | 59,300 | 7,954 | 2,136 |
| 16 | 58,400 | 7,768 | 2,046 |
| 17 | 65,000 | 7,764 | 2,786 |
| 18 | 65,400 | 7,635 | 2,822 |
| 19 | 59,600 | 7,849 | 2,178 |
| 20 | 60,000 | 7,869 | 2,244 |
| 21 | 59,800 | 7,576 | 2,195 |
| 22 | 61,400 | 7,557 | 2,370 |
| 23 | 58,200 | 7,569 | 2,016 |
| 24 | 62,700 | 7,672 | 2,515 |
| 25 | 66,500 | 7,653 | 2,942 |

**Requirements:** Use regression analysis in Excel (or other appropriate software) to identify equations using each of the two cost drivers, i.e. direct labour hours and number of boards completed. Which regression equation would you recommend? Explain.

*Question 9.7 (The Application of the Learning Curve)*

The Learning Company has manufactured a special component for the Brady organisation. This component has not been manufactured previously and its production is labour intensive. The first component consumed the following resources (incremental costs):

| Cost item | € |
|---|---|
| Direct materials (1,000 kgs × €2 per kg) | 2,000 |
| Direct labour (1,000 hours × €10 per hour) | 10,000 |
| Variable production overhead (150% × direct labour cost) | 15,000 |
| Fixed production overhead | N/A |
| Special moulds | 10,000 |
| | 37,000 |

The managers of the Brady organisation are impressed with the quality of work, including on-time delivery, of the Learning Company. They would like the Learning Company to produce an additional three components and have asked them to prepare a bid for the three additional units. In analysing the situation, the Learning Company would like to prepare a bid that would ensure a €30,000 contribution on the new order. The production manager of the Learning Company believes that the special moulds used for the first component will be usable for the additional 3 batches. Based on previous experience, the Learning Company estimates that the employees should experience a 80% learning curve for this job.

**Requirement:** Prepare an estimate of the bid, based on incremental cash flows, that the Learning Company should submit to the Brady organisation for the additional three batches (to include the planned contribution).

## Advanced Questions

### Question 9.8 (Cost Prediction and Profit Planning for a Gym)

Olga Carr has just graduated with an MBA degree and prior to this study she had graduated as a qualified fitness instructor. Within two weeks of receiving her (accredited) MBA degree she received a most interesting job offer – to become the manager of her own gym. The previous owner of the gym wanted to retire and he had enquired whether Olga was interested in taking it over. To make matters more attractive, the previous owner was prepared to invest €30,000 by way of share capital in the business – this would be the only share capital invested – and, in return, he would receive a royalty of 10% of members' subscriptions. Effectively, Olga would manage the gym on behalf of the previous owner but she would keep all the profits generated.

Olga quickly made some tentative enquiries. The location was excellent since it was close to the city centre and business district and had ample car-parking facilities. A recent survey by one of her MBA colleagues indicated the following reasons for choosing a gym (**Exhibit 1**):

|  | % responses |
| --- | --- |
| Location of the gym | 47% |
| Variety of the facilities | 56% |
| Professional trainers | 85% |
| Quality of equipment | 48% |
| Opening hours | 72% |

Her target market was expanding as people, in general, were becoming more health conscious. Indeed, a recent report on health and lifestyle in a local paper highlighted the need for adults to take more regular exercise and such publicity would certainly boost membership enquiries. The number of members cannot be known in advance but, given similar gyms in the locality, she will charge a membership fee of €250 per annum (assume members are admitted on the first day of opening). In accordance with fire and safety regulations, general comfort levels and facilities offered by other gyms in the area, it would not be possible to enrol more than 500 members in the first year. A lower enrolment would be preferable.

In addition to the investment from the owner, Olga agreed to borrow €15,000 from the local bank by way of a three-year loan at a fixed rate of 10% per annum. This loan was to be repaid in equal instalments at the end of each year.

This bank loan was conditional on providing some basic management accounting information. The initial task for Olga for next year is to engage in some form of profit planning. She has prepared provisional income and/or cash flow projections for her first year of trading (**Exhibit 2**) based on 300 paid-up members. Due to time restrictions you have not been able to assess the credibility of all these figures. In addition, you notice that the figures do not include any amount for Olga's salary as manager. The exhibit indicates the percentage variability with respect to volume – where volume is defined in terms of number of members.

Exhibit 2: Estimated Income, Expenses and Cash Flows for First Year of Operations

|  | € |
| --- | --- |
| Membership income (300 × €250) | 75,000 |
| Cost of gym and assessment equipment (Useful life 3 years) | 30,000 |
| Cost of office equipment and software (Useful life 5 years) | 10,000 |
| Cost of audio equipment, loudspeakers and CDs (Useful life 4 years) | 2,000 |

| | |
|---|---|
| Annual repayment of loan (including interest, see Note 1) | 6,000 |
| Rent (to owner) on premises per annum (100% fixed) | 2,000 |
| Insurance on property per annum (100% fixed) | 1,000 |
| Electricity per annum (100% fixed) | 2,000 |
| Water and soap per annum (25% fixed, 75% variable) | 2,000 |
| Cleaning including towels per annum (40% fixed, 60% variable) | 1,500 |
| Advertising per annum (100% fixed) | 1,600 |
| Labour costs of instructors per annum (75% fixed, 25% variable) | 2,000 |
| Administration costs per annum (60% fixed, 40% variable) | 3,000 |
| Royalty payable (based on 10% of member's fees) (100% variable) | 7,500 |
| Miscellaneous costs per annum (90% fixed, 10% variable) | 1,000 |

Olga is both excited and frightened by the imminent decision before her. She invites you to coffee and, after initial pleasantries are exchanged, she asks for your advice.

**Note 1:** The loan is for a period of three years and carries a 10% rate of interest.

**Requirements:** (Please ignore the impact of VAT on your calculations):

1. Determine the overall cost structure (template attached) and apply the 'accounts classification' method to the overall cost structure in order to estimate the variable cost per **member** and the annual amount of fixed costs.
2. Calculate the BEP (in annual membership numbers) based on total expenses including depreciation and interest on loans.
3. Calculate the cash BEP (in annual membership numbers). Why might a BEP in terms of cash flow be more appropriate than your calculation in (2) above?
4. Calculate the profit per annum if annual membership figures amount to 300.
5. What 'issues' should you discuss with Olga or what questions would you ask?

| Present value of €1 received in N years hence at a discount rate of X% p.a. – rounded | | | | | | |
|---|---|---|---|---|---|---|
| **Year** | 4% | 6% | 8% | 10% | 12% | 14% |
| 1 | .962 | .943 | .926 | .909 | .893 | .877 |
| 2 | .925 | .890 | .857 | .826 | .797 | .769 |
| 3 | .889 | .840 | .794 | .752 | .712 | .675 |

| Present value of an annuity received each year for N years at X% p.a. - rounded | | | | | | |
|---|---|---|---|---|---|---|
| **Year** | 4% | 6% | 8% | 10% | 12% | 14% |
| **1** | .962 | .943 | .926 | .909 | .893 | .877 |
| **2** | 1.886 | 1.833 | 1.783 | 1.736 | 1.690 | 1.647 |
| **3** | 2.775 | 2.673 | 2.577 | 2.487 | 2.402 | 2.322 |

*Question 9.9 (Cost prediction, Regression Analysis and Outliers)*

The management of CEIBS Company requires more accurate prediction of overhead costs in order to plan its financial needs better. Data on the number of units and the respective monthly overhead costs incurred were collected for the past 12 months. The raw data are as follows:

20X4

| Month | No. of units | Overhead costs € |
|---|---|---|
| January | 21,000 | 86,000 |
| February | 24,000 | 93,000 |
| March | 23,000 | 93,000 |
| April | 22,000 | 87,000 |
| May | 20,000 | 80,000 |
| June | 18,000 | 76,000 |
| July | 12,000 | 67,000 |
| August | 13,000 | 71,000 |
| September | 15,000 | 73,000 |
| October | 17,000 | 72,000 |
| November* | 5,000 | 99,000 |
| December | 18,000 | 75,000 |

* During the month of November, an industrial dispute severely curtailed the output. This was a most unusual occurrence and is not expected to occur in the foreseeable future. As a result, you perform two regressions, one using the full 12 months' data and the other using only 11 months, with the month of November being treated as an 'outlier'. Using linear regression, the following data was obtained:

| 1. | No. of observations in sample | 12 | 11 |
|---|---|---|---|
| 2. | Co-efficient of determination (R2) | .03 | .91 |
| | Co-efficient of regression equation: | | |
| 3. | Constant | 75,554 | 39,347 |
| 4. | Explanatory variable | 0.31 | 2.17 |
| 5. | Standard error of the Estimate | 10,695 | 2,910 |
| 6. | Standard error of the Beta co-efficient | .59 | .23 |
| 7. | T-statistic for a 95% confidence interval | 2.228 | 2.262 |

**Requirements:**

1. Interpret the above results with reference to tests of reliability and recommend which one to use for cost prediction purposes.
2. Using the results of the regression analysis, estimate the monthly overhead costs assuming that 22,500 units were produced.
3. Establish a 95% confidence interval for your Y estimate in (2) above.
4. Establish a 95% confidence interval for your Beta estimate.

## Question 9.10 (The Application of the Learning Curve)

The LC Company manufactures prototypes that incorporate advanced technological features. Each prototype involves labour intensive operations and, as a result, the impact of the learning curve on labour time (and cost) is very pronounced.

A customer has asked for a price quotation on an order for 512 components to be produced by the LC Company. The production manager estimates that an 80% cumulative learning curve would apply to labour operations. It is estimated that direct production labour would amount to €2,000 for the first component.

**Requirements:**

1. What is the predicted labour cost if the learning curve is overlooked?
2. Using the learning curve, estimate the labour cost of the order of 512 units.
3. The customer feels that the bid based on your estimate in (1) is too high. You are unwilling to reduce your bid for this quantity, but the customer has suggested that you resubmit on the basis of a total production run of 700 units. Prepare a new cost estimate.

## Question 9.11 (Profit Planning)

Pizza World operates a chain of three restaurants in a large city in three different locations, providing different types of customer service and each with different operating capacity i.e. the number of pizzas that can be made and sold per **month**. Relevant information is provided to you as follows:

Location A – sit down restaurant only – 7,000 units, per month
Location B – sit down restaurant and takeaway – 8,000 units, per month
Location C – takeaway only, no seating – 9,000 units, per month

Each restaurant sells one standard meal (pizza and drink) for a different price, depending on whether it is a sit down (€20 per meal) or takeaway (€15 per meal) and these prices have not changed for some time. Based on historic records, it is estimated that Location B sells equal numbers of meals as sit in and as takeaway.

Each meal costs the same in terms of ingredients (materials) and preparation (excluding labour) and this cost, at €7 per meal, is fully variable. The employees in each location are all paid €11 per hour and labour costs are considered fixed in response to volume changes over a relevant range of activity. Each location incurs total labour hours in a month as follows:

Location A – a total of 5,000 hours.
Location B – a total of 3,500 hours.
Location C – a total of 3,500 hours.

Employees will be paid for these hours regardless of the level of sales. In addition, trade union rules prohibit any hours beyond these levels in each location.

All administration and advertising is handled by a central office and the monthly cost of this is €75,000 which, to determine overall profitability, is apportioned equally to each location. As part of an incentive scheme, employees in Location A only are paid a percentage commission on all meals sold. During the period under review, based on 7,000 meals sold, sales commission paid to employees amounted to €3,500 and this rate will continue in future.

**Requirements:**

1.  Calculate the total monthly break-even revenue of Pizza World for each location.
2.  Management are considering the possibility of paying staff in Locations B and C a percentage commission on all meals sold of 4.5% of sales price. In return for this, staff will accept a pay cut from €11 per hour to €9 per hour. Looking only at Locations B and C, and based on the above sales forecasts, do you recommend that management make this change?

Source: Chartered Accountants Ireland, Management Accounting and Business Finance, Paper 3, Autumn 2005

*Question 9.12 (The Application of the Learning Curve)*

'The importance of the learning curve is heavily overstated in the modern business environment. It is of relevance to very few organisations and it is too cumbersome and costly to use as a budgeting tool.'

**Requirement:** Critically discuss the above statement, outlining both sides of the argument, before coming to an appropriate conclusion.

Source: Chartered Accountants Ireland, Management Accounting and Business Finance, P3, various papers (adapted)

# Relevant Costs for Decision-making Including Pricing Decisions

When you have completed studying this chapter you should be able to:

1. Distinguish between a sunk and incremental, out of pocket, cash cost and describe their relevance in managerial decision-making.
2. Calculate selling prices using full cost and marginal cost techniques.
3. Discuss the various factors relevant to selling price decisions.
4. Discuss the importance of qualitative (non-quantifiable) factors in managerial decision-making.
5. Apply incremental analysis and opportunity costs in decision-making situations.
6. Describe the economist's approach to deriving profit-maximising prices.
7. Explain the target costing process for new product introduction.

## 10.1 Relevant Costs in Decision-making

This section focuses on a variety of decision-making situations that managers may face. Some of these decision situations may arise due to unforeseen opportunities or threats. Others may arise as a result of reviewing current operations. Therefore, a variety of decision situations outlined in this section do not arise according to a regular timetable. Also, very often, they are unique in that the exact situation is not likely to reoccur.

Typical decision situations explored in this section include:

1. The choice between alternatives that make similar use of facilities.
2. To close down a facility or continue with current operations. (This is often referred to as the 'continued existing use' decision.)
3. To continue to manufacture a product or to subcontract its production to another company, either locally (outsourcing) or in another country (off-shoring). (This is often referred to as the 'make or buy' decision.)

Thereafter, in **Sections 10.2 to 10.4** we shall look at some special aspects associated with pricing decisions.

The uniqueness of each of the above situations poses potential problems in trying to identify relevant information for the decision-maker to use. Relevance is determined by the specific decision situation and, therefore, information may be relevant to one decision situation but not to another. Furthermore, since decisions can only affect the future, relevant information for managerial decisions must be defined in terms of future cash inflows and future cash outflows. In contrast, irrelevant information relates to the past, or will not vary with the alternatives being considered. If irrelevant information is used by managers then it is likely that incorrect decisions will be made.

Most of our discussion on decision-making concerns the identification of 'relevant' costs and it is useful to note that (in exam questions) two categories of cost will always be presented to the reader, namely:

- historical or sunk costs
- incremental, out of pocket cash costs.

## Historical or Sunk Costs

Historical or sunk costs represent costs that have already been incurred or committed and cannot be changed no matter what future action is taken. (Sometimes they can be referred to as committed or fixed costs.) The essential characteristic of this type of cost is that, since they have already been incurred or committed, they are irrelevant and should be ignored in decision-making. (In many cases, historical or sunk costs will also be fixed costs.) Typical examples of historical or sunk costs are the cost of raw materials already purchased, a commitment to pay employees even though they may be idle, or the historical cost of fixed assets. Likewise, costs that have already been incurred on design works are 'sunk' in deciding whether or not to go ahead with the manufacture of a new product. These costs cannot be changed by any decision that will be made in the future. Therefore, it is only future or incremental cash costs, and not historical or sunk costs, that are relevant for decision-making.

Nevertheless, historical cost data *can* play a role in decision-making. When past conditions are not expected to change significantly, historical costs are useful for predicting future costs. For example, if a product's specification will not change, then the quantity used in the past is useful in estimating material usage in the future. However, although historical data may often be used as a guide to prediction, it is never relevant *per se* to the decision itself. In some cases, historical or sunk costs even fail to provide reliable guides for future performance, especially when it is not likely that conditions prevailing in one period will repeat themselves in a subsequent period. Changes in raw material prices and other costs incurred in obtaining outside services may make historical costs relating to these resources irrelevant.

It is important to note that sometimes managers are reluctant to ignore the issue of historical costs in decision-making. Take the dramatic example of a machine purchased for €25,000, which, due to no fault of the firm, has become unusable the day after acquisition! Its estimated value for scrap is now €5,000. In making the decision now to sell the machine, the original purchase price (historical cost of €25,000) is irrelevant as is the 'accounting loss' of €20,000 (i.e. €25,000 − €5,000). Nevertheless, the (financial) accounting treatment of historical costs and resulting losses may make it psychologically difficult or embarrassing for managers to consider them as irrelevant to decision-making.

## Incremental, Out-of-pocket Cash Costs

In order to highlight the significance of 'incremental' costs and to give them greater focus, we shall describe them as 'incremental, out-of-pocket cash costs'. A useful definition of an incremental, out-of-pocket cash cost is the cash outlay that results from choosing a particular alternative. These out-of-pocket costs are always relevant in decision-making because they will only be incurred if an alternative is selected. It is important to note that incremental cash costs and sunk costs are opposites. An incremental cash cost is a cash outlay that results immediately or in the near future from a particular decision. Conversely, a sunk cost is a prior investment of cash resources of the company resulting from a previous decision and cannot be changed. In managerial decision-making, the general rule is that a choice *between* alternatives should be made on the basis of comparing the ***incremental cash inflows*** less ***incremental cash outflows*** of each alternative, subject to any non-quantifiable factors. We are now going to apply these two cost concepts to a variety of decision situations, typically faced by managers.

## *1. To Choose Between Alternatives that Make Similar Use of Facilities*

In the illustration below, the decision-maker must chose between alternatives that make similar use of facilities. A typical situation could involve a manufacturer who must choose between manufacturing, say, Product A or Product B. Alternatively, a retail company could be faced with the decision to sell, for example, Product X or Product Y in a particular space. The illustration below relates to a taxi driver who provides a service to customers.

## Illustration: To Choose Between Alternatives that Make Similar Use of Facilities

A Dublin taxi driver is on his way to the airport to accept a passenger who will pay a fare of €25, which will involve a petrol cost of €5. He receives two urgent calls on his mobile. One potential customer wants to be driven to Galway and the other potential customer wants to go to Limerick – cities that are an equal distance from Dublin and will consume €15 in petrol costs. However, the Galway customer offers a fare of €120, whereas the Limerick customer offers only a fare of €90. No other customers are likely for the remainder of the day and only one fare can be accepted due to the urgency of the situation. Thus, the alternatives are mutually exclusive.

**Requirement:** Ignoring the ethics of the situation and using the accounting information only, which alternative should be accepted?

**Solution and analysis:** Clearly this represents a choice between options, of which there are three. The first option is to continue 'as is', i.e. to continue to the airport and accept the initial customer. The second is to accept the Galway fare and the third alternative is to accept the Limerick fare.

The decision should be based on incremental cash flows (ignoring, for convenience, non-quantifiable factors) of each alternative. The concept of incremental cash flows is an easy one, yet, in some decision situations, their accurate calculation can be a little difficult. To reduce the possibility of errors, a three-column presentation is recommended and is presented below. **Column 1**, on the left hand side of the table, reports the total cash consequences associated with 'continue as is'. **Column 3**, on the right hand side, reports the total cash consequences associated with the alternative. The advantage of this presentation is that it confirms to the decision-maker that one option is always to continue 'as is'. However, there are two other choices to be considered, i.e. drive a new customer to Galway or drive the alternative customer to Limerick. They are mutually exclusive.

The first part of the table below reflects the cash flows associated with the Galway alternative and the second table reflects the cash consequences of the Limerick alternative. Using accounting information only, the taxi driver can approach the decision in either of two ways, each of which will provide the same answer. The first is to focus on the total cash surplus (or financial consequences) of each alternative, i.e. €20 for 'continue as is', €105 for the Galway fare, and €75 for the Limerick fare. Clearly, accepting the Galway fare has the greatest (net) cash inflows of the three alternatives.

A different approach is to focus on the incremental cash consequences of the two situations, given that he is already on his way to collect the airport passenger. The

INCREMENTAL CASH FLOWS ASSOCIATED WITH THE GALWAY ALTERNATIVE

|  | 1. Cash consequences of 'continue as is' | 2. Incremental cash flows | 3. Cash consequences of Galway fare |
|---|---|---|---|
| Cash inflows | 25 | +95 | 120 |
| Cash outflows | (5) | (10) | (15) |
| Cash surplus | 20 | 85 | 105 |

2. INCREMENTAL CASH FLOWS ASSOCIATED WITH THE LIMERICK ALTERNATIVE

|  | 1. Cash consequences of 'continue as is' | 2. Incremental cash flows | 3. Cash consequences of Limerick fare |
|---|---|---|---|
| Cash inflows | 25 | +65 | 90 |
| Cash outflows | (5) | (10) | (15) |
| Cash surplus | 20 | 55 | 75 |

Galway fare provides an incremental cash flow of €85 compared to the incremental cash flow of €55 from Limerick. Again, the Galway alternative is preferable.

The important point is to note that the incremental cash flows can be identified either by comparing the totals presented in **Columns 1 and 3**, or simply by identifying the incremental cash flows which are automatically contained in **Column 2**. The above presentation can prevent silly computational errors being made since **Column 3** must always equal **Columns 1+2**, but always bear in mind that cash flows can either be positive or negative.

## 2. To Close Down a Facility or Continue with Operations

This decision could face a retail company which must decide, for example, whether to delete a product line from its store. Alternatively, a similar type of decision could face a manufacturer who must choose between, say, retaining a production facility, or to close down operations. Likewise, a hotel may decide between closing down operations during the winter season or staying open. The illustration below concerns an oil exploration company that has already spent a great deal of money on drilling costs. Oil has now been discovered, but it will be costly to produce. Should the oil company close down its facility or continue with operations, i.e. engage in the production of oil?

## ILLUSTRATION: TO CLOSE DOWN A FACILITY OR CONTINUE WITH OPERATIONS

The Tipperary Company has previously paid a foreign government €15 million for the rights to explore for oil in that country. According to the formal agreement, if oil is found, the Company is required to pay a royalty to the government of €60 for every barrel produced.

To date, in addition to exploration rights, the company has spent €8 million on drilling operations. It has just discovered an oil field. Management estimates that it will be able to recover 4 million barrels of oil from the field which can be sold, at current prices, for €75 per barrel. However, the production costs are estimated at €9 per barrel. Unfortunately, the government has recently imposed an additional fee of €5 per barrel, by way of a pollution levy, to pay for damages caused by oil spills that might take place in the future.

**Requirements:** Should the company begin producing oil or close down the oil field? Prepare an incremental cash flow analysis to support your recommendation.

**Solution and analysis:** This is a straightforward situation and involves the comparison of two (given) alternatives, namely to continue with operations or to close down. The decision should be made with reference to the incremental cash flows (ignoring non-quantifiable factors).

It is recommended that a constant format is adopted so that incremental cash flows (inflows and outflows) can be quickly and accurately identified. **Column 1** on the left hand side identifies the total cash flows associated with existing conditions, i.e. immediately ceasing operations. **Column 3** on the right hand side presents the total cash flows associated with the production decision being considered. Therefore, **Column 2**, the middle column, indicates the incremental cash flows that are relevant to the decision.

| | 1. Existing cash flows € | 2. Incremental cash flows € | 3. Total cash flows of production € |
|---|---|---|---|
| Payment for drilling rights | (15m) | N/A | (15m) |
| Drilling costs incurred to date | (8m) | N/A | (8m) |
| Sale of oil (4m at €75 each) | N/A | +300m | +300m |

|  | 1. Existing cash flows € | 2. Incremental cash flows € | 3. Total cash flows of production € |
|---|---|---|---|
| Production roy-alty (4m at €60 each) | N/A | (240m) | (240m) |
| Production costs (4m at €9 each) | N/A | (36m) | (36m) |
| Pollution levy (4m at €5 each) | N/A | (20m) | (20m) |
| Total net cash flow | €(23m) | +€4m | €(19m) |

If the company does nothing (and closes down the oil field, and we assume that this is feasible, without incurring any additional costs or revenues), this will result in zero revenues (no oil will be sold) and no additional costs will be incurred. The €23 million already spent on exploration rights (€15 million) together with drilling costs (€8 million) is irrelevant to the production decision. They represent sunk costs as they have already been incurred. The alternative is to produce the oil (4 million barrels). Based on the financial information detailed below, the decision to produce the oil should be taken since it generates an overall cash surplus of €4 million. The presentation highlights the irrelevant nature of costs already spent, i.e. payment for drilling rights (€15 million) together with drilling costs incurred to date (€8 million).

This illustration shows the distinction between a good decision and a good outcome. The former consists of accumulating all the available information and using it in the proper decision context. However, a good decision can never be protected from the element of bad luck or uncertainty. Thus, if the government had *not* recently imposed a pollution levy on the oil industry, which now is estimated at €20 million, the initial decision to explore for oil would have produced a slightly favourable cash outcome of €1 million.

### 3. To Manufacture a Product or Subcontract, i.e. the 'Make or Buy' Decision

The third type of decision situation is the 'make or buy' decision. Like the previous situations, this represents a choice between alternatives, i.e. to continue manufacturing or to subcontract production to an external supplier, and the decision should be based on incremental cash flows.

## ILLUSTRATION: TO MANUFACTURE A PRODUCT OR SUBCONTRACT – THE 'MAKE OR BUY' DECISION

Dodder Limited is a wholly-owned subsidiary of a multinational company which manufactures a range of components for the computer industry. Top management has recently become concerned about the efficiency of the Irish subsidiary and, in particular, about component **CE 100**. The Irish plant produces 100,000 units per annum of this component at the following costs:

| Summary annual cost statement of the Irish plant for CE 100 | |
|---|---:|
| | € |
| Materials (100,000 @ €5 each) | 500,000 |
| Direct labour (12 employees @ €21,000 pa) | 252,000 |
| Manager's salary | 65,000 |
| Depreciation of machinery | 20,000 |
| Cash production overhead (fixed) | 500,000 |
| Administration and advertising costs | 200,000 |
| Total costs | 1,537,000 |
| Cost per unit | €15.37 |

Top management has now received an offer from Lee Limited to supply the annual requirement of 100,000 components at a price of €10 per unit. Since this is considerably cheaper than the average cost of €15.37 for the Irish plant, top management is considering subcontracting their requirements to Lee.

Before a final decision is made the management accountant is provided with the following information for the Irish plant and has been asked to advise top management on the financial and other implications of their proposed decision, e.g. to continue producing the component in Ireland or to subcontract their annual requirement of 100,000 units to Lee Limited, which would result in closing down a small part of the overall Irish operations. The following additional information is provided for the period of the contract:

1. Since the company operates a JIT purchasing system, no closing inventory is carried. Material costs are expected to increase immediately by 10% and will remain at this level during the period of the contract.
2. If this section is closed down, nine of the direct labour operatives would be employed elsewhere in the company at an annual salary of €22,000. This redeployment would eliminate the recruitment of nine new operatives, who

would also be paid €22,000 each per annum. The other three direct labour operatives would be retired on pensions, payable by the company, equal to two-thirds their present salaries. Furthermore, if this section of the plant is closed, the current section manager would be employed in a more senior position elsewhere in the subsidiary at an annual salary of €75,000, since such a vacancy currently exists.

3. Cash production overhead represents the apportionment of general production (and administrative) overheads including items such as rent and this amount will continue to be incurred.

4. Advertising costs consist of €100,000 associated with advertising components CE 100. If the production of these components is outsourced, management will not in future incur such advertising costs. The administration costs consist of salaries of employees who would be made redundant if the manufacture of component CE 100 is subcontracted to Lee, but at no cost to the company for so doing, since they have no employment contracts.

**Requirement:** Prepare a cost statement to advise top management on whether the Irish plant should continue to manufacture component CE 100, or whether the offer from Lee Limited should be accepted.

**Solution and Analysis:** There are two alternatives to be analysed, i.e. to continue to produce the 100,000 components in the Irish plant, or to subcontract and close down this section. Such a decision will be based on incremental cash flows and the alternatives can be evaluated as follows:

| | Cash consequences of 'continue as is' | Incremental cash flows | Cash consequences of accepting Lee's offer and close down |
|---|---|---|---|
| Materials used (100,000 at €5.50) | (550,000) | +550,000 | Nil |
| Direct labour (9 employees at €21,000) | (189,000) | (9,000) | (198,000) |
| Direct labour (3 employees at €21,000) | (63,000) | +21,000 | (42,000) |
| New direct labour (9 employees at €22,000) | (198,000) | +198,000 | Nil |
| Manager's salary | (65,000) | (10,000) | (75,000) |

| | Cash consequences of 'continue as is' | Incremental cash flows | Cash consequences of accepting Lee's offer and close down |
|---|---|---|---|
| New manager | (75,000) | +75,000 | Nil |
| Depreciation | N/A | N/A | N/A |
| Production overhead | (500,000) | Nil | (500,000) |
| Advertising | (100,000) | +100,000 | Nil |
| Administration staff | (100,000) | +100,000 | Nil |
| Purchase of components | N/A | (1,000,000) | (1,000,000) |
| Total cash flows | (1,840,000) | +25,000 | (1,815,000) |

Some explanation of these figures is required, but mainly in relation to the labour costs. If operations continue 'as is' 12 operatives will continue in employment at an annual salary of €21,000 each, giving a total outlay of €252,000 (€189,000 +€63,000). In addition, nine additional staff will be recruited elsewhere in the plant at an annual salary of €22,000 each (total, €198,000). The existing manager will stay on and a new manager, in another section, will be recruited at an annual salary of €75,000.

What happens to these costs if a section of the Irish plant closes? There is a considerable cost saving. First, nine of the existing staff will be reassigned at an extra cost of only €1,000 each per annum. Therefore, the nine existing vacancies do not have to be filled, giving a total incremental cash saving of €198,000. Secondly, three of the operatives staff will be made redundant and this will generate an overall cost saving of €21,000 (3 × ¹/₃ × €21,000). Thirdly, the advertised managerial position does not need to be filled, as the existing manager will assume this position, but at an additional salary cost of €10,000 per annum. The net saving on the manager's salary is €65,000 if this section of the Irish plant closes.

There are no cash flows associated with depreciation since this is simply a book-keeping entry. The allocated amount of cash production overhead will not change between alternatives since this is a general overhead and will continue to be incurred. However, there is a saving of advertising costs and a saving in administrative salaries.

It should be noted that there are a number of different ways in computing the figures presented above. The important aspect is that we make decisions between alternatives on the basis of incremental cash flows. Clearly, costs that are fixed or already committed cannot be incremental. Likewise, costs that do not vary between alternatives cannot be incremental. On purely financial grounds, the acceptance of the Lee offer is (marginally) attractive since it generates a cash surplus of €25,000. However, we would point out that the following factors should be taken into consideration:

- impact of staff morale due to outsourcing
- the quality and reliability of supply from a new supplier
- will the price of €10 per component from Lee be stable over future years?
- can another use be made of the closed down facilities?

It is likely that the significance of these non-quantifiable factors would outweigh the marginal cash benefit of €25,000 per annum for the subcontracting option.

## 10.2 Full Cost and Special Pricing Decisions

In this section, we discuss pricing decisions, even though some reference to this topic has already been made in **Section 3.2**. We shall look at different aspects of pricing decisions, namely, how are full cost prices determined and whether 'special' prices might be computed or accepted in a given situation? First, we shall put the importance of pricing decisions in context and briefly review the important factors influencing the pricing decision.

### The Importance of Selling Price Decisions

Pricing decisions have wide-ranging implications both for the business itself and the environment in which it operates. Unfortunately, owners and managers of businesses too often fail to recognise the fundamental importance of pricing decisions and their implications in the following areas:

- Pricing is a major determinant of both the profitability and cash flow of a business. If prices are too low, costs will not be covered by sales revenue and the firm will incur a loss. Alternatively, if prices are high in order to cover 'costs', demand may be restricted and again total sales revenue may be insufficient to cover costs.
- Prices are an essential element in generating market share. However, pricing is only one of the ways in which the business can influence the demand for its products. It can advertise, expand its sales force, improve product presentation and product features, in addition to lowering the selling price.
- Prices help to generate a particular 'image' for the product, which will influence future growth. Thus, a product may be considered 'exclusive' or a luxury item because of its high sales price.
- Prices may have an impact on the whole national and international economy. This is particularly true for key raw materials such as oil, gas and steel. Furthermore, in most countries, there is an increasing scrutiny of pricing policies of both State and semi-State institutions which are part of an extensive Government involvement in the economy, e.g. electricity, health and postage charges. All these factors have generated a renewed interest in pricing policy decisions.

## Factors Influencing Pricing Decisions

In the real world, selling prices are rarely 'given', rather they must be determined by managers. Pricing decisions represent one of the truly interdisciplinary tasks in any business. Clearly, the marketing people in the business will have a major contribution to make to the product pricing decision based on their judgement and intuition. The marketing manager will rely on his earlier study of behavioural science and basic economics before recommending a pricing decision. The marketing manager will be conscious that, generally, lower prices will be associated with greater demand. He will also be aware of the importance and impact of advertising and promotion and that prices help to generate a particular 'image' for the product which will influence future growth and market share. Thus, a product may be considered by consumers 'exclusive' or a luxury item because of its high selling price.

The production manager will also be consulted to ensure that there is adequate production capacity which can be utilised so that anticipated demand can be satisfied on time and with the required quality.

A similar consideration applies to the manager responsible for logistics and distribution.

The management accountant also plays a part in providing information and evaluating the financial consequences of different pricing policies. There are four main factors that should be considered in making selling price decisions:

- company objectives
- demand
- competition, and
- costs.

These are discussed below.

### 1. Company Objectives

Pricing decisions are not an end in themselves; rather, they act as a means of attaining the objectives of the company. The objectives of a company are the specific goals to be achieved within a definite time period. Many of these specific goals will be based on financial targets since financial objectives are relatively well understood by managers and their specific nature facilitates measurement. It should be appreciated that pricing decisions represent a means to an end; the financial objectives are the 'end result'. Typical financial objectives for a company, as stated in business textbooks, include:

**Maximising Shareholders' Wealth** This objective assumes that all managerial decisions are made to achieve profit maximization. While it may be a useful assumption in relation to the theory of the firm, empirical evidence indicates that, in practice, this does not appear to be a commonly sought after objective. There are three possible reasons for its lack of practical application. First, there may be a moral objection or social stigma associated with the concept. As a result, firms do not want to be perceived as pursuing the goal of profit maximisation. Secondly, as we shall see in **Section 10.3** (when we discuss profit maximisation) there are computational difficulties associated with this approach which requires an accurate estimation of the firm's demand curve. Thirdly, organisation theory suggests that managers are often happy to accept an outcome that is satisfactory rather than continually seeking an alternative that maximises profits.

**Achieving Target Profits**  This requires a company to earn a specific rate of return and prices are set accordingly. This target profit is usually an 'adequate' profit which in turn may be determined by last year's profit. Thus, companies will start their budgeting process with, say, a required profit margin on sales or required return on shareholders' funds and develop sales prices accordingly.

**Achieving Market Share/Volume**  This is also an important factor or objective influencing pricing decisions, and is particularly relevant for companies introducing new products to the market. Pricing in this context is a means for gaining entry to the market or increasing the penetration and positioning of the product in the market. Essentially, there are two different strategies:

> **Price Skimming (Market Skimming)**  This involves setting a high selling price to cream off the top of the market. The selling price includes a premium which will be paid by a group of buyers who are willing to pay more for that product than other groups of buyers. This reason could be that of perceived prestige of the product and is usually associated with luxury or status goods. It only applies, however, when unit costs remain fairly constant since otherwise unit costs of a low volume of production may be high thus offsetting the sales price premium. Price skimming is basically a short-term policy since, once the 'premium' segment is saturated, price is gradually reduced to appeal to the more price sensitive segments of the market. The main advantage of this policy is that it is easy to subsequently lower selling prices. In fact, the selling price is often the most flexible product characteristic. For example, the selling price could be changed overnight whereas changing other product characteristics, e.g. special features, can be a more lengthy process. The principal disadvantage with this approach is that if the sales price premium is very large it may entice competition.

> **Penetration Pricing**  This involves initially setting a low price to generate large demand for the company's product and it is based on the assumption that the market is very price sensitive. Therefore, low prices are seen as effective in generating a high market share. In addition, this policy may be very appropriate where there are economies of scale present, e.g. a learning curve. The essence of the learning curve is that average unit costs decline as output increases mainly due to learning by employees who perform a repetitive task. Hence, a low price coupled with large volume of production enables a company to produce at low cost. The principal problem associated with this approach is that prices may be set too low and thereby generate excess demand – the firm foregoes profits which could have been earned at a higher selling price. In addition, it is assumed that the low initial price discourages actual and potential competition and this may not necessarily be the case.

## 2. Demand

Demand represents the relationship between price and consumer behaviour and, consequently, demand is an important factor in any pricing decision. The general principle is that extra units can only be sold at reduced prices. Conversely, higher prices are generally associated with lower demand. The responsiveness of the level of demand to price changes is reflected by price elasticity. If a small change in price brings about a large change in volume, the product is said to be very elastic. In contrast, for price inelastic products, e.g. birthday cards, changes in price are not associated with changes in demand. Obviously the availability of product substitutes has an important bearing on price elasticity as has the reaction of competitors to a firm's price changes.

### 3. Competition

The existence of competition in the marketplace tends to set an upper limit on the price which can be charged by a company. Much depends on whether products are perceived as either homogeneous (similar) or heterogeneous (dissimilar). If products are perceived in the market place as being homogeneous, then a price cut of one product would greatly increase sales at the expense of the other (homogeneous) products. Consequently, retaliatory price cuts can be expected from the competition so that company's overall market share would remain more or less the same. The companies are therefore disadvantaged by lower profits and the only beneficiaries are the consumers who have benefited from lower prices.

If the products are viewed as heterogeneous based on, for example, quality or value, some degree of brand loyalty can be expected and so price changes would not necessarily be associated with price retaliation by competitors. In this case, companies do not compete on the basis of selling price but compete by 'differentiating' their product from others using characteristics other than price. In the chapter dealing with strategy (especially **Section 7.3**) we discussed the issue of product differentiation.

### 4. Costs

At a fundamental level, sales prices must ultimately cover costs in order to ensure the profitability and financial viability of the firm. Consistently selling below full costs could lead to bankruptcy and, if the firm is to survive, it must sell at prices that will not only cover costs but yield a sufficient profit. This consideration has led to the development of cost-plus pricing policies. Costs can either be 'full' costs or 'marginal' costs, and both approaches will give different cost figures. Both of these approaches are illustrated below.

Full costs include all variable costs in addition to an appropriate amount of fixed costs. The paradox of this approach is that in order to cover fixed costs you need to first estimate the demand in units. Thus, with full-cost pricing, demand (in units) determines unit costs and sales price, whereas economic theory suggests that sales price should determine sales volume and demand. As a result, as we shall see below, there is no guarantee that full-cost pricing will generate a profit. The marginal cost approach is particularly suited to short-run pricing decisions, especially pricing in the context of spare capacity situations.

## Determining Full Cost Selling Prices

Firms cannot be profitable unless the sales price exceeds total costs and this has led to the popularity of full-cost pricing. (Many businesses adapt their full cost calculations to include a profit margin which is added to total cost to determine selling price.) Thus, the computed selling price for a manufacturing firm will be based on four different figures: 1. direct costs, 2. production overhead, 3. non-production overhead, and 4. a required profit margin. (We shall assume a job costing accumulation system.)

Thus, in addition to computed product costs (1 and 2), firms will need to add both a portion of non-production costs (3) and a profit margin (4) to estimate their selling price. Therefore, two issues need to be clarified:

- how does one include an appropriate portion of non-production costs into total cost calculations, and
- what profit margin is appropriate?

To avoid possible confusion, we shall refer to the 'recovery' of non-production overheads in contrast to the 'absorption' of production overheads for product costing and stock valuation purposes. Non-production overheads are usually recovered using some cost base, e.g. total production cost. A logical calculation being as follows, with the amount of non-production overhead to be recovered expressed as a percentage of total production cost:

$$\text{Recovery of non-production overhead} = \frac{\text{Total non-production overhead} \times 100}{\text{Total production cost}} = X\%$$

This indicates the estimated amount of non-production overhead to be included in our estimate of total cost for selling price decisions. It is usually a predetermined percentage of the computed production cost of each job.

In turn, a profit margin will be added and this is usually calculated with reference to total cost, i.e. production and non-production cost with a typical calculation being as follows:

$$\text{Profit margin (or mark-up on cost)} = \frac{\text{Required profit} \times 100}{\text{Total cost}} = Y\%$$

Cost plus pricing can be considered as consisting of three separate, but related, stages. First, there is a separate calculation of production cost and this figure would also be used in valuing the manufactured goods if there were unsold products at the end of the accounting period. In turn, for pricing purposes, we add a portion of non-production overhead to give a total cost figure. Finally, we add a mark-up on total cost to provide a profit margin. In reality, pricing decisions will be made taking into account other (non-cost) considerations but it is useful that managers have access to total cost figures in making selling price decisions, even though they may not be fully utilised.

## ILLUSTRATION: FULL COST PRICING

Galway Toys Ltd manufactures a range of wooden toys according to specifications of their large department store customers and therefore operates a job costing system. The toys are produced in two different departments: **Department A** is labour-intensive and **Department B** is machine-intensive. Appropriate cost information, together with operating data for the forthcoming year, is budgeted as follows, with direct labour being considered a variable cost:

|  | Department A | Department B | Total |
|---|---|---|---|
| Direct materials | €100,000 | €90,000 | €190,000 |
| Direct labour hours | 15,000 | 23,000 |  |
| Direct labour cost (variable) | €150,000 | €230,000 | €380,000 |
| Machine running hours | 7,500 | 4,500 |  |
| Production overhead (fixed) | €150,000 | €180,000 | €330,000 |
| Total production cost |  |  | €900,000 |
| Non-production overhead (fixed) |  |  | €180,000 |

During January 20x1, the firm completed only *two* orders for specific clients. Actual costs and other data pertinent to these orders are given below and you may assume that direct labour is paid at the rate of €10 per hour.

The company operates a normal job costing system whereby production cost is calculated with reference to actual direct materials used, actual direct labour incurred, and production overhead is assigned using a predetermined, departmental overhead absorption rate. In addition, in order to estimate total cost, non-production overhead is recovered on the basis of total production costs.

|  | Job J1 | Job J2 |
|---|---|---|
| **Direct materials cost:** |  |  |
| Department A | €6,000 | €5,000 |
| Department B | €4,000 | €3,000 |
| **Direct labour hours worked:** |  |  |
| Department A @ €10 | 600 hours | 650 hours |
| Department B @ €10 | 800 hours | 1,200 hours |

|  | Job J1 | Job J2 |
|---|---|---|
| **Machine running hours:** | | |
| Department A | 300 hours | 325 hours |
| Department B | 150 hours | 250 hours |

**Requirements:**

1. Compute predetermined production overhead absorption rates for the two departments, using direct labour hours for Department A and machine hours for Department B as the appropriate cost drivers.
2. Calculate a normal selling price for both jobs, assuming that a 10% profit margin is added to the total cost of each job.
3. Provide an estimate for the marginal cost of both jobs and comment on the importance of your figures.

**Solution and Analysis:**

1. Since the company operates a normal job costing system, the first calculation required is that of the predetermined production OHAR, which is computed as follows:

|  | Department A | Department B |
|---|---|---|
| Overheads € | €150,000 | €180,000 |
| Cost driver | 15,000 | 4,500 |
| OHAR = | €10 per labour hour | €40 per machine hour |

2. Initially, we calculate the (normal) production cost for each job, as follows:

|  | Job J1 € | Job J2 € | |
|---|---|---|---|
| **Direct material cost:** | | | |
| Department A | 6,000 | 5,000 | |
| Department B | 4,000 | 3,000 | |
| **Direct labour cost:** | | | |
| Department A | 6,000 | 6,500 | |
| Department B | 8,000 | 12,000 | |
| **Production overhead:** | | | |
| Department A (€10 × 600) | 6,000 | 6,500 | (€10 × 650) |
| Department B (€40 × 150) | 6,000 | 10,000 | (€40 × 250) |
| **Production cost** | 36,000 | 43,000 | |

The normal production cost figures indicated above would be used for inventory valuation purposes. However, for determining selling prices, they need to be adjusted to include both a portion of non-production overhead (related to total production cost) and also a required profit margin (related to total cost). These final calculations are as follows:

|  | Job J1 € | Job J2 € |
|---|---|---|
| Production cost (above) | 36,000 | 43,000 |
| Non-production overheads (W1) @ 20% | 7,200 | 8,600 |
| Total cost | 43,200 | 51,600 |
| Profit margin (10% on cost) | 4,320 | 5,160 |
| Selling price (full cost pricing) | 47,520 | 56,760 |

**W1**: Recovery of non-production overheads, based on total production cost, is calculated with reference to the budgeted figures provided and is calculated as follows:

$$\text{Recovery of non-production overhead} = \frac{€180,000 \times 100}{€900,000} = 20\%$$

It should be remembered that the 'full cost' selling price in this illustration was determined using normal costing principles, i.e. actual direct costs incurred together with a predetermined amount of overhead costs. In many situations, selling prices must be estimated in advance of production (for a manufacturer) and therefore budgeted data only will be used but these will be informed by previous out-turns. Finally, it should be noted that the above calculations provide a guide to the final selling price. The limitation of cost-plus pricing is that there is no guarantee that a customer will purchase the goods at the price thus quoted.

3. Marginal Cost: The marginal cost represents the change in total cost as a result of producing one additional unit (or extra units in this case) and is often equated with the variable cost per unit. In this illustration the only variable costs provided are direct materials and direct labour. Therefore, the marginal cost of both of these jobs is presented as follows:

|  | Job J1 € | Job J2 € |
|---|---|---|
| **Direct material cost:** | | |
| Department A | 6,000 | 5,000 |
| Department B | 4,000 | 3,000 |

|  | Job J1<br>€ | Job J2<br>€ |
|---|---|---|
| **Direct labour cost:** | | |
| Department A | 6,000 | 6,500 |
| Department B | 8,000 | 12,000 |
| **= Marginal cost** | 24,000 | 26,500 |

The identification of marginal costs in decision-making is important. Marginal costs represent the lowest price a company can quote for its products if it wants to avoid incurring a loss on this transaction. As long as the company sets its selling price in excess of marginal cost then it will earn a contribution towards its fixed costs. Therefore, marginal costs are often used to identify possible selling prices for 'one-off' orders, especially if the company has, currently, idle capacity. However, the problem with using marginal costs for determining a selling price for one customer is that other customers may demand similar pricing concessions. In addition, if all selling prices are determined with reference to marginal costing principles, then, it is possible that a company may not generate any profits. This is due to the fact that fixed costs, in aggregate, are in excess of the contribution generated from each product.

Surveys of pricing policies suggest that cost-plus pricing is very common and the following reasons can be cited:

- By relating price to unit costs, the firm simplifies its pricing task considerably and it does not have to make frequent adjustments as demand or market conditions change. Generally, plausible prices can be found with ease and speed. Although managerial efforts are made to move away from cost-based policies, there is generally less uncertainty about costs than about demand. Thus, cost plus calculations provide a starting point from which the process of fixing selling prices can begin. Managerial judgement can then focus on determining the amount of the adjustment to cost to cater for market conditions.
- Where all firms in the industry use cost plus pricing, their prices are likely to be similar if their cost structures and mark-ups are similar. Price competition is therefore reduced, which would not be the case if firms paid attention to demand variations when pricing their products and services.
- There is the belief that cost plus pricing is socially fairer to both the buyer and seller. The firm selling the product or service does not take advantage of the buyer when his need is pronounced, while the selling firm earns a fair return on its investment.
- Other approaches to pricing, such as the economist's method of pricing (**Section 10.3**), are treated with a degree of scepticism due to the requirement of a known

and accurate demand curve. If a firm is seeking to maximise profits then a price/demand schedule should be established and this should be compared with costs at different volume levels, and different prices, to locate the maximum profit point. The practical problem with this approach is the complexity of estimating this demand/price relationship for the many products or services which a typical firm offers. Alternatively, target costing (**Section 10.4**) is relatively new and has not received due consideration on the curriculum of many undergraduate or post-graduate programmes.

In summary, when making pricing decisions, an exclusive focus on cost information is not appropriate. It is important to determine what the customer will pay, but price-demand prediction is difficult. Market information is as important as (internal) cost information and the collection of market data diverts the information search from being too inward looking. Factors such as advertising and promotion, packaging and distribution methods all affect the sales demand level, in addition to the sales price. Therefore, it is necessary to establish a routine system that will regularly monitor the following factors – sales forecasts compared with actual, competitors' prices, customer enquiries and complaints, market share and market growth. An important contribution the management accountant can make to discussions with other executives on pricing is a comparison of variable cost, fixed cost, sales revenue, total contribution and overall profit at various volume levels and flexing the assumed values of the above variables.

## Special Pricing Decisions

On occasions, managers may be asked to quote a special price for a 'one-off' job or to accept/reject a price offered by a potential customer for such an order. We refer to these situations as 'special pricing decisions' (a topic that often appears on managerial accounting exams). **Special pricing decisions** can be described as evaluating **an** (i.e. one) alternative, rather than choosing **between** alternatives. The general rule for such decisions is that the firm should be as well off after accepting the special order as it was before the order. When an alternative, i.e. one alternative, is to be evaluated, it implies that the benefits of the other alternatives are no longer available – effectively that they have already been rejected. Therefore, in evaluating an alternative we must consider a new cost concept – an opportunity cost.

However, before we progress, let us look at two decision situations in which we might find ourselves as managerial decision-makers. In the first situation, we could be asked to choose between Option A and Option B. This decision will be based on incremental cash flows and let us assume that Option A is preferable to Option B (based on incremental cash flows).

## ILLUSTRATION: OPPORTUNITY COST

To highlight this situation, assume a company had to choose between only two alternatives: (a) to continue with existing work or (b) to undertake a special contract. The alternatives are mutually exclusive and the cash flows are as follows:

|  | (a) Existing work € | (b) Special contract € |
|---|---|---|
| Incremental cash inflows | 15,000 | 30,000 |
| Less: Incremental cash outflows | (6,000) | (26,000) |
| Less: Fixed costs | (2,000) | (2,000) |
|  | 7,000 | 2,000 |

The above fixed costs are irrelevant because they will not change as a result of the decision being contemplated and should be ignored. If the above decision is made only on the basis of incremental cash flows (ignoring non-quantifiable factors), it will result in the decision to continue with existing work, which generates an incremental cash flow of €9,000 (€15,000 − €6,000), compared with an incremental cash flow of €4,000 (€30,000 − €26,000) from undertaking the special contract. Thus, the offer of the special contract is rejected on financial grounds, using the information currently available.

However, there is another way we can look at the above situation. We could ask or be asked the question: "What is the minimum price for the special contract that would make it as attractive to us as the existing work"? Thus, this 'new' price would cause us to change our minds. In such situations, the notion of relevant costs must be expanded to include any opportunity cost associated with the decision (incremental cash costs will continue to be relevant as before).

A useful definition of an **opportunity cost** is the net cash benefit that would be obtained if the resources to be committed to the decision were used in the next best alternative. Opportunity cost is always relevant in evaluating the financial consequences of *an* alternative since it implies rejection of other alternatives. However, in some cases there may be no opportunity cost associated with using resources, e.g. the use of idle facilities. In addition, an opportunity cost does not involve an immediate cash outlay and, therefore, it is more subtle to identify and quantify in financial terms. In brief, it is important to stress that **opportunity cost is not used in deciding *between* alternatives. Its relevance is in evaluating the financial consequences of *an* alternative**.

To return to the above illustration, we recall that the special contract was not as attractive as continuing with existing work. Indeed, the special contract will have to be priced at €35,000 to cover its incremental cash costs (€26,000) plus the opportunity cost involved. The opportunity cost (€9,000) is the cash contribution that would have been generated by opting for the next best alternative.

## ILLUSTRATION: SPECIAL PRICING DECISIONS

The directors of Slaney Company are considering whether to undertake a contract for a customer located in the United States with whom they have not conducted any business previously. The proposed contract requires 50,000 special components to be produced during a period when Slaney has slack capacity. (Slaney Company is currently producing about 400,000 components, equivalent to 80% capacity.) Slaney needs to quote a price and the following information relates to client specifications for these special components:

**Raw materials:** Each special component requires two different types of raw materials, designated X and Y respectively, and you are provided with the following information from the company's records:

| Raw material | Units required per component | Units now in stock | Historical cost | Current replacement cost | Current realisable value |
|---|---|---|---|---|---|
| X | 1 | 100,000 | €2.00 | €2.50 | N/A |
| Y | 2 | 200,000 | €3.00 | N/A | €1.10 |

The company uses Material X continuously and stocks are always replenished. The current stock of Y is in excess of the company's requirements and, unless used to manufacture these special components, Material Y would be sold.

**Labour:** The production of each of these special components requires a $1/2$ hour of labour, which is paid at the rate of €5 per hour. However, because of the cancellation of another contract, Slaney expects to have over 35,000 surplus labour hours available during the coming year. Because of the impact on staff morale, the directors have decided not to dismiss any workers in the foreseeable future.

**Overheads:** Fixed overheads for Slaney Company are absorbed to products on the basis of direct labour hours and the production absorption rate for the coming year is €4 per labour hour. In addition, variable overhead costs for this component are estimated at €2.40 per labour *hour worked.*

**Packaging materials:** The firm has already committed to a contract to purchase 270,000 special packaging units at a cost of €5 per unit, giving a total purchase cost of €1.35 million. However, this order will have to be increased by 50,000 units to accommodate the production of these special components. The supplier offers a discount of €0.50 per unit (on all units) whenever the total purchase size exceeds 300,000 units per annum.

**Packaging equipment:** A specialised packaging machine needs to be purchased for the production of these special components. It is unlikely to be used in any other contract. The current cost of this special equipment is €24,000 and its estimated residual (disposal) value is €10,000 at the end of the contract.

**Requirements:**

1. What is the minimum price (in order to incur neither a profit nor loss on the contract) that Slaney could bid for this special order? Prepare a schedule of relevant costs to support your recommendation and your schedule should distinguish between incremental, out of pocket cash costs and opportunity costs.
2. What non-financial considerations are relevant to this decision and how are they relevant?

**Solution and analysis:**

1. The solution below is presented in terms of a schedule of incremental cash flows, together with the inclusion of any opportunity costs, where applicable. Both of these add up to the total relevant cost figure contained in the right-hand column.

| Cost item | Incremental cash flows € | Opportunity cost € | Total relevant costs € |
|---|---|---|---|
| Material X: (50,000 @ €2.50) | 125,000 | | 125,000 |
| Material Y: (50,000 × 2 × €1.10) | | 110,000 | 110,000 |
| Labour (Idle) | Sunk cost | Sunk cost | Sunk cost |
| Fixed Overhead | Sunk cost | Sunk cost | Sunk cost |
| Variable Overhead (50,000 × ¹/₂ × €2.40) | 60,000 | N/A | 60,000 |
| Packaging Materials: (€1.44m − €1.35m) | 90,000 | N/A | 90,000 |
| Packaging equipment (€24,000 − €10,000) | 14,000 | | 14,000 |
| Total cash flows | 289,000 | 110,000 | 399,000 |

Some explanations to the above schedule are appropriate. First, Material X is used regularly by the company and, if used on this special order, must be replaced.

Thus, the incremental cash flow corresponds to the replacement cost. In contrast, Material Y is surplus to requirements and would otherwise be sold. Thus, the use of Material Y in this special order generates an opportunity cost – the cash contribution that would otherwise be generated from its best alternative use – equivalent to its net realisable (disposal) value.

Labour is currently idle and management have agreed that employees will be paid. Therefore, there is no incremental cost associated with these employees being engaged in the special order. Likewise, fixed overheads are irrelevant since they do not, by definition, respond to changes in the volume of output. However, variable overhead is an incremental cash flow and is therefore relevant.

Packaging materials can avail of a quantity discount. The cost of the existing order is €1.35 million (270,000 units × €5) and this will increase to €1.44 million (320,000 units × €4.50) for the increased order size. Therefore, the incremental cash flow associated with additional packaging materials is €90,000. Finally, packaging equipment needs to be purchased for the special order for €24,000. However, since it has an estimated residual value of €10,000 at the end of the contract period, the incremental cash outflows are €14,000.

Thus, the overall relevant cost for this special order is €399,000, or €7.98 per component, and this represents the minimum price that Slaney should charge for this special order, in the present circumstances.

2.  A decision should never be made, exclusively, on financial grounds. There are always non-quantifiable factors that should be taken into consideration. In this situation, the following factors should be noted:

• There may be pressure from other customers to reduce overall prices.
• Can quality of additional production be guaranteed? For example, the order for 50,000 special units will bring plant usage to 90% capacity.
• The above relevant costs are contingent on the circumstances currently prevailing, e.g. surplus labour. Thus, for a repeat order in the future these costs may be significantly different.
• Foreign exchange implications may be relevant since the overseas customer may request being invoiced in US Dollars.
• Is there a guarantee of payment since there is no previous trading history with the new customer?
• This new customer (new market and new product) may have great potential.

In summary, the relevant cash flows in decision-making situations are highlighted in **Exhibit 10.1** below, based on two situations presented in this section, i.e. choose between alternatives and evaluate an alternative:

EXHIBIT 10.1: RELEVANT CASH FLOWS IN DECISION-MAKING

|  | Decision situation: Choose between alternatives | Decision situation: Evaluate an alternative |
|---|---|---|
| Relevant cash flows | Incremental cash inflows Less Incremental cash outflows | Incremental cash inflows Less Incremental cash outflows and Opportunity cost, if any |

## 10.3 The Economist's Approach to Pricing and Profit Maximisation

In a previous chapter (especially **Section 9.2**) we examined the issue of profit planning, which was based on a linearity assumption, i.e. the selling price and unit variable cost are constant over a relevant range of activity. In determining selling prices, economists make different assumptions from accountants in relation to price/demand relationships and total cost behaviour in respect to volume changes. Specifically, economists assume that, as a general rule, price increases are associated with reduced sales volume and price reductions are associated with increased sales volume. In simple terms, the lower the price, the greater the quantity demanded; the higher the price, the smaller the quantity demanded. Reflecting the inverse relationship between price and quantity demanded, the demand curve is downward sloping from left to right and indicates the quantity customers will purchase at any given prices and is presented in **Exhibit 10.2.**

The overall slope of the firm's demand curve is important and this is linked to the concept of price elasticity of demand, which reflects the responsiveness of quantity demanded of a good (or service) to changes in that good's own price. **Price elasticity of demand** is always a negative number, but is usually expressed as an absolute term and can be formally calculated as:

$$|E| = \frac{\Delta Q}{\Delta P} \times \frac{P}{Q}$$

where $\Delta Q$ is the change in quantity demanded, $\Delta P$ is the change in price, $Q$ is the quantity demanded at current price and $P$ represents the current selling price. At high prices, demand is normally elastic; at low prices, it is likely to be inelastic. It should also be obvious that price elasticity can either be greater or less than 1. If $|E|$ is less than 1, we say that demand is **inelastic** and indicates a relationship where a change in price has only a small effect on the quantity demanded. If $|E|$ is greater than 1, the demand is **elastic** and this indicates a relationship where a small change in selling price has a large effect on the quantity demanded.

EXHIBIT 10.2: THE DEMAND CURVE

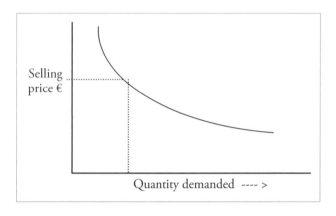

ILLUSTRATION: PRICE ELASTICITY OF DEMAND

To illustrate this formula, suppose a selling price is currently €5 and the corresponding quantity demanded is 1,000 units. If the price increases to €5.75 per unit, the quantity demanded will fall to 800 units. The price elasticity of demand is calculated as:

$$|E| = \frac{200}{0.75} \times \frac{5}{1,000}$$
$$= 1.33$$

Thus, over the range of prices between €5.00 and €5.75, quantity falls at a rate of 1.33% for every 1% change in selling price. It follows that price elasticity will be different at different points along the demand curve.

If a product is perceived by customers as unique and no substitute products are available in the market place, then this product will probably be inelastic, especially if the customer incurs significant costs by switching to an alternative product. In contrast, a product is likely to be elastic if it does not have any unique features to differentiate it from competitors. Essentially, the firm is producing a commodity for which demand is often price-sensitive.

**Profit Maximising Selling Prices**

The profit maximising selling price can be explained in either of two ways. **Exhibit 10.3 (a)** below indicates total revenue and total costs at different levels of output. (The astute reader will notice that neither total revenue nor total costs are linear. Rather, to sell additional quantities the selling price needs to be reduced. Also, additional fixed costs may need to be incurred at higher levels of output.) The profit maximising price

EXHIBIT 10.3: PROFIT MAXIMISING PRICES

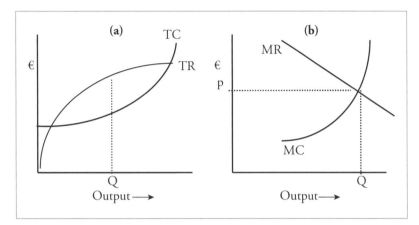

is identified as the point of greatest (positive) difference between total revenue (TR) and total cost (TC) and this is highlighted by 'Q' in the Exhibit. Thus, it is usual to prepare a schedule indicating total revenues and total costs at various levels of output and selecting the output (and therefore selling price) that provides the greatest amount of profit. This approach is recommended in preference to the alternative approach (below) that utilises marginal revenue and marginal cost and is based on **Exhibit 10.3 (b)**.

Economic theory indicates that maximum profits are achieved when marginal revenue (MR) equals marginal cost (MC) and this is depicted in **Exhibit 10.3(b)**. Marginal revenue represents the increase in total revenue due to the sale of an additional unit. Marginal cost is the increase in total cost due to the production of an additional unit. However, it should be remembered that MR and MC are estimates and will rarely be exactly correct. If the firm would like to increase its profit then:

- If MR > MC, the firm can increase its overall profit by selling more, and to do this it should lower its selling price.
- If MR < MC, the firm can increase its overall profit by selling less, and to do so it should increase its selling price.
- If MR = MC, the firm cannot increase its profit either by increasing or decreasing output. It follows that both output and price must be at their optimal levels.

### Requirements for Economic Pricing

Before we examine how to apply the principles of marginal revenue and marginal cost it is worthwhile to stress some fundamental points:

1. We assume that the goal of the firm is to maximise profits and that managers are rational in this regard. However this assumption, as a model of predicting managerial behaviour, is open to question. Some critics argue that managers prefer to earn a satisfactory profit rather than trying to achieve maximum profits. Indeed, 'maximising' implies that there is a way of finding the maximum amount that a company can earn. The reality is that this is not the case. For example, managers cannot know

or consider all the alternatives available and the impact on profitability of each since they would spend all their waking hours thinking about different alternatives.

In addition, it is unrealistic to assume that managers are responsible only to share-holders. Many people would and do argue that modern (commercial) firms consist of multiple stakeholders: customers, employees, its suppliers and the community in which the firm operates. Thus, the sole focus on maximising profits is limited in an environment in which managers are expected to exercise greater social responsibility, which includes acting ethically. Nevertheless, the reality is that, if managers did not attempt to earn the largest amount of profit consistent with industry performance and its own resources, then the firm would either disappear or its management would be replaced by others that would better serve shareholders' interest.

2. The application of economic theory to maximize profits requires knowledge of the firm's demand curve, which is usually presented as follows:

$$P = A - B \times Q$$

Where P = selling price, A is the constant in the equation and represents, in theory, the lowest price at which demand will be zero. The B coefficient represents the relationship between price changes and quantity demanded (but this is **not** the same as price elasticity of demand) and Q is the quantity demanded. The negative B coefficient highlights the inverse relationship between price changes and quantity demanded. In reality, the price/demand relationship is difficult to accurately identify. This is because price is only one of the determinants of demand. Other factors, such as how competitors react to price changes, are important elements in determining demand levels. If, for example, all firms reduce prices, then very little extra volume may be achieved. In addition, the incomes and tastes of customers, product promotion and advertising need to be considered. Of course, attempts are made to estimate price/demand relationships using, for example, the informed judgement of managers, based on past experience, or by price experimentation, whereby different prices are charged to evaluate the sensitivity of quantity demanded to price changes.

3. We need an estimate of marginal cost, i.e. the cost of producing one extra unit of output. In some cases, marginal cost may well equate with unit variable cost but this is not necessarily so. However, we shall assume that marginal cost equals variable cost unless there is evidence to the contrary.

## ILLUSTRATION: PROFIT MAXIMISING PRICES

Rathnew Company produces a single laptop computer and its current price and current annual sales volume are:

| Sales price | Sales volume |
|---|---|
| €1,090 | 14,000 units |

The Board of Directors is considering a change in pricing policy since they are unsure whether additional profits could be generated by different prices. The directors argue that a €50 price increase on the laptop would reduce sales by 2,000 units per annum and a price decrease would give a similar increase. The finance department has produced the estimate of total annual costs, appropriate to various level of output as follows, with a minimum capacity of 10,000 units and maximum capacity being 18,000 units per annum.

| No. of units (per annum) | Total annual costs €000 |
|---|---|
| 10,000 | 8,137 |
| 12,000 | 9,415 |
| 14,000 | 10,753 |
| 16,000 | 12,196 |
| 18,000 | 13,734 |

**Requirements:** Based on the above information, compute the price to be charged in order to maximise profits. Indicate the profit earned at this level of output.

**Solution and analysis:**

There are two methods by which a respectable answer can be provided, based on the many assumptions we shall make, including the accuracy of the responsiveness of quantity demanded to price changes and also the accuracy of the total cost data.

The first method is based on **Exhibit 10.3 (a)** and involves the preparation of a schedule of total revenue and total costs for various levels of output. Currently, at a price of €1,090, the related demand is 14,000 units. If price is increased by €50, then demand changes by 2,000 units. The following schedule can be completed:

### Schedule of Outputs, Revenues, Costs and Profits

| Output (annual) Q | Sales Price P | Total sales (P × Q) | Total costs | Profit (TR − TC) |
|---|---|---|---|---|
| | | €000s | €000s | €000s |
| 10,000 | €1,190 | €11,900 | €8,137 | €3,763 |
| 12,000 | €1,140 | €13,680 | €9,415 | €4,265 |
| 14,000 | €1,090 | €15,260 | €10,753 | €4,507 |
| 16,000 | €1,040 | €16,640 | €12,196 | €4,444 |
| 18,000 | €990 | €17,820 | €13,734 | €4,086 |

Based on the above schedule, which is based on the expectation of demand at different price levels, the price which generates the largest amount of profit is €1,090, which is, coincidently, the current price charged. Therefore no change in price is recommended.

The alternative method, and more precise approach to determining the profit maximising selling price, is based on marginal revenue and marginal cost. Marginal cost represents the additional cost of producing one additional unit and the best estimate of marginal cost is the variable cost. Due to the limited amount of information provided, we shall estimate variable cost per unit by applying the high–low method (see **Section 9.3**).

The high–low method is based on the two most *appropriate* points in the above data set, which may or may not be the highest and lowest. The above schedule confirms that profit maximising price must lie between 12,000 units (profit €4,265,000) and 16,000 units (profit €4,444,000). Therefore, the two most appropriate points to base our high–low calculations on are the total costs corresponding to 12,000 and 16,000 units respectively. Applying the high–low (two points) method we can compute the (estimated) variable cost per unit as follows:

|  | Volume (units) | Costs (000s) |
|---|---|---|
| High | 16,000 | €12,196 |
| Low | 12,000 | €9,415 |
| Change | +4,000 | +€2,781 |
| Variable costs (per unit) rounded | €695 | (€2,781,000/4,000 units) |

In addition, fixed costs can be computed as the difference between total costs (given) and total variable costs calculated for, say, 16,000 units of output. The fixed costs are computed as follows:

Fixed costs (€12,196,000 − (€695 × 16,000)) = €1,076,000 per annum

Both fixed and variable unit cost estimates can now be combined to give the annual total cost equation, namely: €1,076,000 + 695 Q (where Q is the output for the period).

Next, we need to derive an estimate of the firm's demand curve which is written as: $P = A - B \times Q$. Since we know both the current price (P) and the current quantity demanded (Q), we can present the demand curve at two levels of output, say, 12,000 and 16,000 units, as follows:

(i) €1,040 = A − B × 16,000 units

And

(ii) €1,140 = A − B × 12,000 units

By solving the above simultaneous equations, we obtain estimates of A and B with A = 1,440 and B = 0.025. (It should be noted that the Beta coefficient will always have a negative sign reflecting the inverse relationship between selling price and quantity demanded.) Therefore, we can write the firm's demand curve as:

Demand curve                                        P = 1,440 − 0.025Q

If we multiply both sides of this equation by 'Q' we get:

Total revenue (Price × Quantity)                    = 1,440Q − 0.025Q$^2$

And marginal revenue is obtained by using differential calculus:

Marginal revenue (MR) = dy/dx                        = 1,440 − 0.05Q

Our previous estimate of marginal (i.e. variable) cost is:   €695

In order to maximize profit we let
MR = MC, as follows:                                 1,440 − 0.05Q = 695

Therefore we can estimate the value of Q, which is:   Q = 14,900  units

The value of P (Demand curve: P = 1,440 − 0.025 × 14,900) is:                                       P = €1,067$^{50}$

The profit maximising price is similar (but not exactly the same) as the price earlier computed (€1,090). The previous calculation reflects the approximations of our assumptions rather than the accuracy of the calculations based on marginal revenue and marginal cost.

## Conclusion

The economist's approach is a useful framework for considering pricing decisions since it explicitly considers price/demand relationships. However, despite its conceptual merit, the economic approach to pricing is seldom applied in the rigid way outlined here. First, the economic model requires precise information regarding marginal revenue and marginal cost for all the products that a firm sells and this information may not be available in reasonable time and at a reasonable cost.

Secondly, it is plausible to argue that many managers are more likely to be motivated towards achieving a number of goals (such as job security for themselves and other employees, or being a 'good' corporate citizen) rather than strive for a single profit maximisation objective.

Thirdly, there is ample evidence that managers often are content to earn a satisfactory return rather than trying to maximise profits – a managerial approach which carries, in modern times, a certain social stigma.

Finally, some managers may have forgotten their differential calculus, which is a requirement of the economist's approach!

## 10.4 Target Costing and Life Cycle Costing

In recent years, it has been frequently remarked that Japanese companies use accounting information to motivate employees to act in accordance with long-term manufacturing strategies rather than to provide senior managers with precise and essentially short-term data on cost and cost variances. It is claimed that Japanese management accounting plays more of an 'influencing' rather than 'information' role in the managerial process. The emphasis of cost management in Japanese enterprises has shifted from controlling costs at the production stage to controlling costs at the design stage. This approach is a simple recognition that design decisions automatically determine a significant proportion of product costs.

Japanese enterprises have adapted their costing systems to focus on what are termed target costs and they represent product costs that must be achieved in order for the enterprise to enjoy competitive advantage. When contemplating a new product, the Japanese like to establish target costs linked to estimates of a competitive market price. In reality this amounts to moving back from a desired market share to a selling price and, further down, to a required target cost of production. Japanese managers then establish various procedures to ensure progress towards meeting this target cost objective.

Target costing is an approach that is suited to new product development. Under this process a target selling price is estimated, based on required market share, together with a required profit. A target cost can then be computed and the product designed in such a way that it is possible to produce it at its target cost. It is a system that requires top management commitment and proper time and resources to implement. It can slow down the product development process but it will prevent costly long-term mistakes being made – particularly where products are designed with complexity. It is interesting to note that Japanese companies' target costs are usually determined by engineering rather than accounting personnel. The following three phases can be identified:

### 1. The Strategic Process (Determine Market Price, Desired Profit and Target Cost)

Initially, an idea for a product, together with its functionality and features needs to be developed to a stage where it can be suggested to potential customers. The (internal) individuals involved at this stage can come from a variety of sections of the organisations – the marketing department may be involved as they will know the needs of customers, the R&D department will be involved as they have the technical expertise, the production department may be involved as they will understand the capabilities of the existing production processes. In turn, a required market share for the new product, the selling price needed to meet that market share and target profits are agreed with reference to the firm's strategic plan. The required selling price will normally involve market research. At this stage the company should also generate some information on customer demand levels and product specifications. Target profits are usually set with reference to Return on Sales. At this first stage, and in the context of achieving these objectives, the initial target cost of a product is estimated by subtracting the target profit from the required selling price as follows:

**Target cost = Competitive selling price for desired market share**
**Less: Desired profit, based on return on sales**

In turn, the target cost will be analysed into relevant cost elements.

## 2. Value Engineering

This target cost calculation is then compared with current cost calculations, i.e. the cost estimate of producing the product based on current production facilities and product features. In many cases, the current cost will exceed the target cost and so the second phase of the process begins – referred to as value engineering. In essence, the company now needs to determine whether it can produce the product at the required target cost. The production engineers and the R&D department would be closely involved at this stage as they need to design a product that can be manufactured within the target cost using the existing production capacity of the business. In addition, features of the product may be deleted to cut costs while appreciating the potential impact on customers. Essentially, value engineering involves an evaluation of all aspects of a product (its design, specifications, materials and production and sales processes) with a view to reducing current costs towards the desired target cost.

It is interesting to note that value engineering originated in the United States during the Second World War, as production managers and product designers were forced to design products with fewer parts, due to shortages arising from the war effort. Crucial to this phase is consumer analysis, which identifies critical consumer preferences that determine the desired functionality of the new product. For some products, functionality can be added or deleted relatively easily and this is especially relevant where consumer preferences change frequently. In some cases, an 'allowable cost' is agreed which represents a cost figure – in excess of target cost – but which will subsequently be reduced by *Kaizen* costing principles.

## 3. Kaizen Costing

*Kaizen* costing occurs at the manufacturing phase and represents a commitment to 'continuous improvement', i.e. to reduce the allowable costs for a product, with a specific design and functionality, towards the agreed target cost. This continuous process of cost reduction involves:

- the use of advanced manufacturing technology
- the application of cost management techniques including ABC
- rewarding employees for higher productivity
- increased emphasis on quality management.

## ILLUSTRATION: TARGET COSTING

The Rosslare Footwear Company Limited (RFCL) is a manufacturer of casual shoes and has sustained strong growth in the export market – mainly the UK. To expand the business, the directors are considering exporting one of its men's shoes to the US market, where comparable shoes sell for an average of €90. RFCL requires a 20% return on its sales. The current cost of manufacturing RFCL's shoes is €72. This cost includes a range of special features unique to the US market. These features are costed below, together with their importance to US customers:

| Features desired in the US | Costs of feature (in €) | Importance Rating (4 is most important) |
|---|---|---|
| Colourfast material | €6 | 4 |
| Lighter weight | €5 | 1 |
| Extra-soft insole | €3 | 3 |
| Longer-wearing sole | €4 | 2 |

In addition, RFCL recognizes that the US market requires additional distribution and advertising costs which would increase the cost of each pair of shoes by €10. These additional selling and distribution costs cannot be waived or reduced in the short term.

**Requirements:**

1. Using the above information, highlight both the: (a) 'current cost' and, (b) 'target cost'.
2. Which features, if any, should RFCL include in its men's shoes? Support your argument with reference to your target cost calculation.
3. Based on your calculations in (2) above and with reference to an 'allowable cost', suggest how this might be subsequently lowered and comment on RFCL's decision to begin selling shoes in the US.

**Solution and Analysis:**

| | |
|---|---|
| **1. (a)** The current cost is the the cost estimate of producing the product based on current production facilities and product features. This current cost, with all special features, is given and amounts to | €72 |
| **1. (b)** Target cost (in €) | |
| US sales price (given) | €90 |

| | |
|---|---|
| Less: Profit margin (20% given) | (18) |
| = Total cost | 72 |
| Less: Additional transport cost to US | (10) |
| Target production cost | 62 |

**2.** Features to be deleted *

| | |
|---|---|
| Current cost (given) | €72 |
| Eliminate: lighter weight | (5) |
| Eliminate: longer-wearing shoe | (4) |
| = Allowable cost (to be subsequently reduced by Kaizen costing) | €63 |

Special features to be included:

Colourfast only

Extra soft insole

* Other suggestions are acceptable.

**3.** Comments: The allowable cost can be described as an 'acceptable' cost and is close to the desired target cost. However, much effort will be directed towards lowering this cost, subsequently by, for example, improving the production process to generate additional cost savings including the elimination of non-value-added costs. Also, savings in distribution costs will be sought. Thus, the allowable cost is only, temporarily, acceptable and every effort will be made to subsequently lower it towards the target cost level.

Strategically, the decision to sell shoes in the US makes very good sense. To compete effectively in a competitive global market, a firm has to have an effective presence in all the key markets, which would include the US. The experience of competing in the US should bring additional profits if only due to economies of scale. In addition, there are benefits associated with the knowledge obtained from dealing with the different customers and establishing a global brand and market presence. This experience can be used to improve the firm's competitiveness in other markets. However, since the products may be sold in US Dollars (the above calculations are in €) this exposes RFCL to considerable FX fluctuations and risks which can have an enormous impact on profitability unless these FX exchange risks are 'hedged' in some way.

## Life Cycle Costing

Traditional costing systems have tended to focus on the production phase of a product's life. Life-cycle costing, in contrast, is concerned with the three key stages in a product's life cycle, which are identified below. The amount of costs incurred at these three stages can vary from industry to industry:

1. **Development**: This is the design and planning stage in which market research activities takes place and the idea for a new product is brought to its operational stage.
2. **Production/Sales**: The product is manufactured and sold. This is the operational stage.
3. **Post-production:** When production ceases or is abandoned, additional costs may be incurred. Industries in the chemical and mining sectors need to consider the significant costs, e.g. environmental costs to be incurred when the production facility is closed down.

Taking this approach to costing allows a greater appreciation of the full cost of a product through its entire life cycle. This should allow more accurate cost forecasting which should in turn lead to better business decisions being made. In the modern era, post-production costs can be a significant issue as societies around the world become more environmentally conscious.

## Conclusion

To summarise this chapter, we initially examined the meaning and application of relevant costs in decision-making and identified three types of costs that are usually present in decision-making situations:

- incremental, out-of-pocket cash costs,
- sunk costs, and
- opportunity costs.

We then discussed three approaches to selling price decisions:

- cost plus pricing,
- the economist's approach and
- a more modern approach referred to as target costing.

In the next chapter we shall continue our discussion of managerial decision-making and introduce the complexity of scarce resources, also referred to as limiting factors.

## Summary of Learning Objectives

**Learning Objective 1:** Distinguish between a sunk and incremental, out of pocket cash cost and describe their relevance in managerial decision-making.

A sunk (historical or committed) cost is a cost that has been incurred and thus, will not change as a result of the decision being contemplated. (We can include fixed costs in this category.) In contrast, incremental, out-of-pocket costs are costs that will change as a result of the decision being evaluated. While such costs depend on the context of the decision, all variable costs will be included in this category. The importance of this distinction is that sunk costs are never directly relevant to the decision and should be ignored in the analysis. However, incremental, out of pocket costs are always relevant to the decision and should also be included in the evaluation process.

**Learning Objective 2:** Calculate selling prices using full cost and marginal cost techniques.

Selling prices can be calculated using either full costs or marginal costs. Using full costs, both variable and an appropriate amount of fixed costs are included in the computation. However, in order to assign fixed costs for product costing one first needs to estimate in advance the required sales units. Using this method of computation, sales units determine sales price! Marginal costs are the incremental costs associated with the production and sale of the product. Selling prices determined with reference to marginal costs only should always be competitive but they do not provide for any contribution to fixed costs being generated. In addition, such competitive prices may be requested by other customers. Moreover, it may be difficult to subsequently raise selling prices for subsequent contracts initially won on the basis of marginal costs tendering.

**Learning Objective 3:** Discuss the various factors relevant to selling price decisions.

The selling price decision is influenced by a number of factors. First, overall company objectives must be considered. A company interested in surviving an economic crisis may be willing to set selling price decisions on the basis of marginal costs. In contrast, a more profit-oriented firm will probably use some form of cost-plus pricing. Demand is also an important factor since there is no point in setting a selling price above that which customers are prepared to pay. Customer attitudes may be influence by the presence of competition. Therefore, the existence of competition usually places a maximum selling price which a company can charge. Finally, overall cost must be taken into consideration since, if a price does not cover its costs, then overall profitability will not be achieved.

**Learning Objective 4:** Discuss the importance of qualitative (non-quantifiable) factors in managerial decision-making.

Decision-making involves an identification and evaluation of all relevant factors. Some factors can easily be quantified such as cost levels. However, there are always a range of factors which are relevant to the decision but whose impact cannot be readily quantified and these are referred to as qualitative or non-quantifiable factors. While qualitative factors vary with the specific decision situation, some generic factors can be mentioned. For example the closing down of a segment of a manufacturing plant would have an impact on the morale of the remaining employees, or winning a contract may bring a long-term association with a new customer and market opportunities.

**Learning Objective 5:** Apply incremental analysis and opportunity costs in decision-making situations.

Incremental costs are the additional, out of pocket cash costs associated with a decision alternative. Because they change in response to a decision they are always relevant. In some decision situations opportunity costs may also be relevant. Opportunity costs are represented by the cash contribution foregone as a result of choosing one alternative and therefore overlooking another alternative. Opportunity costs are always relevant but they can be more difficult to identify and calculate.

**Learning Objective 6:** Describe the economist's approach to deriving profit maximising prices.

Economists assume that the objective of any profit-orientated firm is to maximise its profits. Economists further assume that selling prices must be reduced in order to increase sales. Specifically, economists argue that, in order to maximise profits, a firm's marginal cost per unit must equal the marginal revenue. In most cases, marginal costs will be equivalent to variable costs.

**Learning Objective 7:** Explain the target costing process for new product introduction.

Cost plus and the economist's approach are the two traditional methods of setting selling prices. The more modern approach is referred to as *target costing* and will involve accounting, marketing, production and engineering personnel. Target costing starts with the selling price required to achieve a required market share. From this price a required profit margin is deducted to provide a target cost. The firm will try to produce this product at or below this target cost. If that is not feasible, some product features may be deleted or the production and distribution process will be reviewed to provide the necessary cost savings.

## Questions

### Review Questions

(See Appendix One for Solutions to Review Questions **10.1** and **10.2**)

*Question 10.1 (Relevant Costs and Decision-making)*

The Marday Hotel is a large family-owned three-star hotel in an Irish seaside town. The hotel opens for business on 1 March of each year and closes again on 30 September (for the purpose of your calculations, you should assume that each month is four weeks long and that the hotel opens for seven days per week, when operating). It has been trading successfully for many years but the owners now recognise that significant renovations are essential to compete in the future. These renovations will allow the hotel to upgrade to a four-star establishment. It is hotel policy to treat all renovation costs at revenue expenditure – no element is capitalised.

Currently, as a three-star hotel, the Marday Hotel has 80 rooms available for occupation. However, while the renovations and upgrading are being undertaken, the hotel will only have 70 rooms available. Historically the Marday Hotel's daily occupancy rates have been as presented below. 'Occupancy rate' is calculated as the number of rooms occupied divided by total rooms in the hotel and management expect to achieve the same percentage occupancy rates in 2007 operating as either a three- or four-star hotel.

| Month | Occupancy rate | Month | Occupancy rate |
|-------|----------------|-------|----------------|
| March | 40% | July | 90% |
| April | 50% | August | 80% |
| May | 70% | September | 40% |
| June | 90% | | |

The room rate, as a three-star hotel, is fixed at €90 per room per night but, as a four-star hotel, the rate will be fixed at €110 per room per night. These rates apply all year round and are never discounted.

Staffing the hotel during the March to September seasons costs €5,000 per week in wages, regardless of occupancy levels, plus €5,000 per month in salary for the manager. (Only the manager is permanent and he works at the hotel for the entire year even during renovations; all other staff can be hired and laid off as required and are only hired in weeks when rooms are occupied.) The other non-labour costs are on a room basis – where a room is occupied, this costs the hotel €25 per room as a four-star hotel and €20 per room as a three-star hotel.

**Three options** are currently being considered:

**Option 1**: Renovations will begin on 1 January 2007

These renovations will take three months and will result in the hotel only being open from 1 April 2007 onwards. The total cost of these renovations will be €100,000 plus a further €8,000 per month for the renovations period payable to the project manager. However, as a four-star hotel, the Marday Hotel will, for the first time, be able to open at Christmas for a three-week period during which it will have 45 rooms occupied. Staff will have to be re-hired for these three weeks and paid at normal rates plus 25%.

**Option 2**: Renovations will begin on 1 March 2007

If renovations begin on 1 March they will be completed on 30 June 2007. During this four-month period the hotel will remain a three-star establishment and 50% of the rooms will be unavailable to guests. In which case, there will only be 40 rooms available in each of these months and all will be fully occupied in the months of April to June (inclusive) since demand patterns exceed rooms available. The cost of renovations will be lower at €60,000 plus a further €2,000 per month payable to the project manager for the duration of the renovations. From 1 July 2007 onwards, the hotel will be four-star and will open for three weeks at Christmas as in **Option 1**.

**Option 3**: Renovations will begin 1 October 2007

These renovations will be completed on 31 December 2007, but will result in the hotel being unavailable for Christmas bookings. During the year, the hotel will operate normally as a three-star hotel. The renovation cost will be €70,000 but there will be no need for a project manager as the full-time, permanent hotel manager will supervise the work.

**Requirements:**

1. For each of the three options above, calculate the expected profit for the Marday Hotel for the year ended 31 December 2007 and recommend to management, based on the calculation, what option to take.
2. Outline **two** additional pieces of qualitative information you would need from management before finalising your advice.

Source: Chartered Accountants Ireland, Management Accounting and Business Finance, P3
Summer 2006

*Question 10.2 (Pricing Policy and Economic Theory)*

The Newman Computer Company manufactures a single computer (PC 286) and the current demand and price levels are as follows:

|        | Sales price | Sales volume |
|--------|-------------|--------------|
| PC 286 | €1,728      | 7,000 units  |

The Board of Directors is considering a change in pricing policy. The directors argue that a price change of €300 would give a 1,000 unit change in unit sales in both directions. In addition, the finance department has produced the estimate of total costs, associated with different levels of output, in any given period:

| No. of units | Total costs €000 |
|:---:|:---:|
| 4,000 | 3,700 |
| 5,000 | 4,500 |
| 6,000 | 5,300 |
| 7,000 | 6,200 |
| 8,000 | 7,100 |
| 9,000 | 8,200 |
| 10,000 | 9,200 |

## Requirements:

1. Calculate the current profit (loss) level for the given sales price and sales volume.
2. Using the high–low method to estimate variable cost and based on the limited data above, advise on the price to be charged in order to maximise profits. What is the maximum profit level?
3. What selling prices would maximise revenues? Calculate profits at these prices.
4. What assumptions have you made in the above calculations?

Intermediate Questions

*Question 10.3 (Relevant Costs and Pricing Decisions)*

The Wang Corporation is a manufacturer of specialised household furniture in Hangzhou. In recent times, the company has operated with some spare capacity and the management of the company is anxious to consider any way of increasing the overall utilisation of the company's plant.

They have recently been approached by Palmart – a large international retailer – who is willing to buy 10,000 wooden garden swings as part of its garden furniture range for its China outlets. Palmart has offered Wang €100 per swing. This is a market for which Wang Corporation has never competed but it acknowledges its growth potential in the future, especially with the increased leisure time and overall spending power of Chinese people. Because garden swings are used in the open-air, Wang will have to use tropical hardwoods in their manufacture, which will have to be properly varnished with chemicals to prevent deterioration during the harsh winter months and blistering hot summers. In addition, each swing will have a special 'gravity rope lock' which is a special safety feature and prevents the garden swing from overturning by accident.

You have been asked to investigate this proposal and have been provided with the following information:

**Entertainment and hospitality:** Senior managers of Wang Corporation have already incurred expenditure in the amount of €10,000 in entertaining Palmart buyers and in obtaining product specifications for this order.

**Raw materials:** Each garden swing would require four different types of raw material i.e. (i) hardwood, (ii) fabric and cushions, (iii) a gravity rope lock and (iv) a chemical spray to improve the weather-resistant qualities of the hardwood. Quantities required, current stock levels and cost of each material are as follows:

| Item | Requirement per swing | Current Stock level (total units) | Historical cost per unit € | Current market price per unit € | Net realisable value per unit € |
|------|----------------------|-----------------------------------|----------------------------|---------------------------------|---------------------------------|
| Hardwood | 10 sq. feet | 140,000 sq feet | 2.00 | 3.00 | 2.50 |
| Fabric/ cushions | 2 sq. feet | 10,000 sq feet | 1.00 | 2.00 | 0.80 |
| Gravity rope lock | 1 lock | Nil | N/A | 5.00 | N/A |
| Chemical spray | 1 gallon | 2,000 gallons | €8 | €12 | See below |

The company uses the hardwood continuously in other product types e.g. office furniture, and stocks are always replenished. The current stock of fabric/cushions is in excess of the company's requirements and, unless used to manufacture these wooden swings, would be sold. The company does not have any gravity rope locks in stock. The chemical spray in stock is surplus to the company's requirements. If it is not used in the manufacture of garden swings the chemical would have to be disposed of by Wang at a *cost* of €3 per gallon. (This is in accordance with local anti-pollution regulations.)

**Labour:** Production of each garden swing requires both skilled and unskilled labour. Four hours of skilled labour are required per garden swing in order to apply the special water/sun resistant chemical spray. Current wage rates are €5 per hour. However, the necessary skilled labour can only be obtained by temporarily ceasing production of another product, details of which are set out below.

| Alternative product | Revenue/costs per product |
|---------------------|---------------------------|
| Selling price per unit | €44 |
| Direct material cost | 10 |

| Alternative product | Revenue/costs per product |
|---|---|
| Skilled direct labour (2 hours) | 10 |
| Fixed overhead | 20 |

Also, temporarily ceasing production by these skilled labourers will involve a penalty cost of €20,000 for non-delivery. It is considered that any lost sales of this alternative product will not be recovered.

Unskilled labour is also required for assembly purposes. It is estimated that the assembly of each garden swing will require 1 hour of unskilled labour and the current wage rate is €2 per hour. However, because of the cancellation of another contract, Wang Corporation expects to have over 25,000 surplus unskilled labour hours available during the coming period which could be used to manufacture these swings. Because of the impact on staff morale and the difficulty of recruiting unskilled labour, the directors have decided not to dismiss any workers in the foreseeable future and will continue to pay their normal wages.

**Overheads:** Fixed production overheads for Wang Corporation are assigned to all products on the basis of skilled labour hours and the production overhead absorption rate for the coming year is €1 per skilled labour hour. Such fixed production overheads include items such as depreciation of machinery on a straight-line method, rent, property taxes and insurance of buildings. In addition, variable overhead costs for each garden swing are estimated at €1 per unit.

**Containers:** Each garden swing will have to be packaged in a special cardboard container. Wang has already committed to a contract to purchase 200,000 of similar cardboard containers (for another product) at €3 per unit. However, this order size will have to be increased to accommodate the distribution of the garden swings. The supplier has agreed a price of €2.90 for all units for an order size of 210,000 units, provided that the revised order is quickly confirmed.

**Packaging equipment:** Specialised packaging machines, purchased by Wang Corporation some years ago, would be used for this proposed contract. While the machinery has an estimated useful life of two years, it will not be used in any other contract and is available for immediate sale. Its current book value is €30,000 and its estimated net realisable value is currently €10,000. It is estimated that these values would be €15,000 and €1,000 respectively at the end of the contract.

**Transport:** Palmart will pay all distribution costs which are estimated at €5 per unit.

### Requirements:

1. Using the information provided, clearly indicate whether the production of 10,000 wooden garden swings is worthwhile on financial grounds only. Prepare a schedule of relevant costs to support your conclusion. Your schedule should distinguish between incremental (out of pocket cash) costs and opportunity costs.

2. Assuming that some form of negotiation on the proposed special order is forth-coming, clearly recommend the minimum acceptable price to Wang Corporation for this special order, applying relevant costing principles, and briefly indicate the reasoning behind your recommended price.
3. List four other considerations, which have not been taken into account in your financial evaluation, that should be considered relevant to this decision and briefly indicate why they are relevant.

## Question 10.4 (Relevant Costs in Decision-making)

Sirocco Limited is an e-consultancy company which specialises in designing and maintaining web sites for small companies and charities. The company employs three people, Anna and Jack who jointly set up the business three years ago, and David who has commenced working for the company having completed a degree in computer studies. The company has recently been approached by a national sporting organisation (NSO) to complete a major web consultancy project. The project would entail:

(a) researching and preparing an e-commerce strategy for the organisation
(b) designing a state-of-the-art web site to promote its activities and to facilitate inter-action with local clubs and individual members; and
(c) training staff regarding e-commerce issues.

Anna and Jack are anxious to accept this new business since they are not very busy at the moment and would appear to have adequate spare time to work on this NSO project over the next six months. However, both Anna and Jack consider that a thorough examination of the financial implications of taking on this new project must first be conducted and so they have asked for your help. They have gathered the following information to assist your evaluation:

1. It is estimated that it would take Sirocco Limited 6 months to complete the NSO project and Anna and David would have to work full time on the project for its duration. Anna currently earns a salary of €80,000 per annum and David earns €50,000 per annum. Two new employees would be specially recruited by Sirocco Limited on 6-month contracts to complete the ongoing work of the company while the NSO project was in progress. Each of the two new employees would earn €20,000 for the contract period.
2. Sirocco Limited currently conducts its business from a small suburban office. Anna and Jack consider that alternative office space would be required if they take on the NSO project. Sirocco Limited currently pays €1,000 per month for the rent of its existing office space and, while the landlord could immediately relocate the company to a larger office in the same complex for the duration of the NSO project, he would charge a €3,500 arrangement fee. The rental payments on the new office space would amount to €2,000 per month.
3. Sirocco Limited has recently contracted with a computer supplier to purchase three new PCs and printers at a total price of €5,400 to conduct the company's regular business. If Sirocco accepts the NSO project, Jack and Anna consider that it would be appropriate to improve the specification of the new PCs which would result in the

total price charged by the supplier increasing to €7,800. In addition, two basic PCs for the new contract employees would be required at a price of €1,500 each.
4. To complete specific aspects of the NSO project, Sirocco Limited would need to purchase new software at a cost of €1,800. This software would not have any additional use thereafter.
5. Anna and Jack estimate that other running costs of Sirocco Limited would increase from €700 to €1,100 per month if the NSO project is undertaken.
6. Costs incurred by Sirocco Limited to date in evaluating whether or not to accept the NSO project include €500 of research costs and €650 entertainment costs.

**Requirements:**

1. Prepare a statement outlining the incremental costs which Sirocco Limited will incur if it accepts the NSO project. Show clearly all your calculations and state any assumptions that you make.
2. If Sirocco Limited requires an incremental profit margin of 25% on sales price on each new project, what is the minimum price which the company must charge for the NSO project?
3. Outline **three** qualitative issues which you believe Sirocco Limited should consider in deciding whether or not to accept the NSO project.

Source: Chartered Accountants Ireland, Management Accounting and Business Finance, P3,<br>Summer 2003

*Question 10.5 (Decision-making involving Subcontract or Manufacture)*

Tolka Limited is a wholly-owned subsidiary, situated in Dublin, of a multinational company which manufactures a range of components for the computer industry. Top management have recently become concerned about the efficiency of the Irish subsidiary and, in particular, about component SAT 100. The Irish plant produces 100,000 units per annum of this component at the following costs:

SUMMARY ANNUAL COST STATEMENT OF THE IRISH PLANT – SAT 100

| | | € |
|---|---|---|
| Materials | (100,000 @ €4) | 400,000 |
| Direct labour | (12 employees @ €20,000) | 240,000 |
| Manager's salary | | 60,000 |
| Depreciation of machinery | | 20,000 |
| Production overhead (fixed) | | 400,000 |
| Administration and advertising costs | | 200,000 |
| Total costs | | 1,320,000 |
| Cost per unit | | €13.20 |

Top management have now received an offer from Major Ltd to supply the annual requirement of 100,000 components at a price of €11 per unit. Since this is considerably cheaper than the average cost of €13.20 for the Irish plant, top management are seriously considering subcontracting their requirements of these components to Major Ltd.

Before a final decision is made, the management accountant is provided with the following information for the Irish plant and has been asked to advise top management on the financial and other implications of their proposed decision e.g. to continue producing the component in Ireland or to subcontract their annual requirement of 100,000 units to Major Ltd, which would result in closing down a small part of the overall Irish operations.

The following additional information is provided:

1. Since the company operates a Just in Time (JIT) purchasing system, no closing inventory is carried. Material costs are expected to increase by 20% in the forthcoming year.
2. If this section is closed down, three-quarters of the direct labour operatives would be employed elsewhere in the company instead of hiring nine new operatives at annual salaries of €20,000 per annum each. The other quarter of the direct labour operatives would be retired on pensions, payable by the company, equal to two-thirds their present wages. The manager could be employed in a more senior position elsewhere in the company at an annual salary of €70,000, since such a vacancy currently exists.
3. Production overhead represents the apportionment of general production overheads including items such as rent, which are considered fixed in relation to changes in the volume of output.
4. Advertising costs consist of €50,000 associated with advertising components SAT 100. If the production of these components is outsourced, management will not in future incur such advertising. The administration costs consist of salaries of employees, amounting to €150,000, who would be laid off if the manufacture of components SAT 100 is subcontracted to Major, but at no cost to the company for so doing.

**Requirement:** Prepare a cost statement to advise top management on whether the Irish plant should continued to manufacture component SAT 100, or whether the offer from Major Limited should be accepted.

*Question 10.6 (Target Costing, Pricing and Value Engineering)*

Benchmark Furniture Limited produces wooden garden swing **seats** (for two persons) as part of its garden furniture range. The company's web site proclaims that 'our major achievement today is our customer's confidence, built through quality and reasonable prices'. Since the eighteenth century, teak was the traditional material for garden furniture. However, in recent years its use has provoked criticism from the environmental lobby and forced manufacturers, in general, to switch from tropical hardwoods. The company uses Sheesham in all its furniture, which is an Indian wood that is similar to teak, but more coarsely grained.

A new managing director has just been appointed who has some experience of Target Costing and Value Engineering principles. He has been informed by his marketing manager that sales targets for the garden swing are difficult to achieve because of aggressive pricing by competitors all over the world. The budgeted selling price of the swing seat for the year just ended was €900 (wholesale) and this selling price was achieved only by aggressive persuasion techniques directed at long-standing customers. Competitors now sell a comparable swing seat for, on average, €850 (wholesale). The marketing manager considers that reducing the price of the company's swing seat to €850 is necessary to retain the firm's annual market share of 10,000 units. In addition, the company would like to achieve a profit per unit, based on budgeted data, as presented below.

The following actual and budgeted cost data has been provided to you for the last accounting period, and actual costs incurred exceeded budget in all cases due to poor cost control. It is anticipated that some of these inefficiencies could be eliminated in future with proper managerial input:

|  | Budgeted data | Actual data |
|---|---|---|
| Units of output | 10,000 units | 10,000 units |
| Selling price per unit | €900 | €900 |
| Total revenue | €9,000,000 | €9,000,000 |
| Total costs: | | |
| Direct materials (basic wood) | €2,600,000 | €2,700,000 |
| Special water/sun resistant varnish | €2,900,000 | €3,000,000 |
| Sanding of finished product | €450,000 | €500,000 |
| Fabric (weather resistant) | €900,000 | €1,000,000 |
| Direct labour (assembly) | €450,000 | €500,000 |
| Direct labour (engraving) | €150,000 | €170,000 |
| Direct labour (gravity rope lock) | €400,000 | €500,000 |
| Machine set-ups (external help) | €800,000 | €800,000 |
| Total costs | €8,650,000 | €9,170,000 |
| Profit/(Loss) for period | €350,000 | (€170,000) |

Because of storage problems the garden swings are produced in batch sizes of 500 units although it may be possible to produce them in batch sizes of 1,000 if additional storage facilities were made available to this division. The cost of these additional storage facilities amounts to about €50,000 per annum.

Based on the analysis of competitors' products and customer feedback, the coating of special water/sun resistant paint, sanding, and provision of fabric are considered essential, as is the fitting of the gravity rope lock system. The furniture features a 'gravity rope lock' system that enables the user to adjust the height and depth of the swing and is considered an essential feature for ultimate comfort. However, the engraving at the back of each swing seat is not appreciated much by most customers.

**Requirements:**

1. Prepare a schedule comparing the budgeted and actual profit per unit, based on the above data, to reveal cost overruns.
2. Calculate the target cost per unit for a sales price of €850 if the original budgeted profit per unit is to be maintained. Also, indicate by how much actual current costs need to be reduced in order to reach this target cost.
3. How much of the current cost per unit is attributable to non-value-added activities?
4. Apply the principles of Value Engineering to attain the target cost calculated in requirement 3 above, and pay particular reference to current production inefficiencies, the possible elimination of non-essential features and also new production methods. Explain your reasoning and assumptions and prove your calculations.

*Question 10.7 (Target Costing)*

Client Y is one of the largest manufacturing clients of your practice and they have asked you to prepare a memorandum for their next board meeting. One of the items on the agenda is a proposal to introduce a target costing system in the company. The directors are not very familiar with this topic. They require clarification on the topic and also whether it will require a lot of extra work for them. They have sought your advice.

**Requirement:** Prepare a memorandum for the Board of Management specifically addressing the role, key stages of, and personnel involved in target costing.

Source: Chartered Accountants Ireland, Management Accounting and Business Finance, Paper 3, Summer 2007

## Advanced Questions

*Question 10.8 (Decision-making and Credit Control)*

Tiga Sales Limited (Tiga) sells to the general public by way of catalogue, telephone and internet sales. The credit controller of Tiga has been reviewing the debtors ledger balances as well as the procedures in the credit control section.

The result of the credit controller's review are summarised in the table below. Tiga divides its sales into three separate geographic regions (Area 1, Area 2 and Overseas Area) and the sales for each region are given in the table below. The average outstanding debtor balances over the year for customers in the various Areas are also shown in the table below. Thus, in Area 1 the average balance per debtor is €500 and there are 1,000 customers in that area. The cost of collecting, or attempting to collect, outstanding amounts varies from Area to Area, with overseas customers costing the greatest amount. In spite of the efforts of the Credit Control Department (as can be seen from the table below), 22% of the total sales to the Overseas Area turn out as bad debts during the course of the year.

All products sold by Tiga produce a contribution of 40% of selling price from which collection costs and bad debts have to be deducted. These vary by area also, e.g. from the table below it can be seen that the overseas area has the highest percentage in terms of both collection costs and bad debts.

| Area | Sales €m | Average balance per customer (€) | Number of customers | Collection costs % of average balance | Bad debts % of area sales |
|---|---|---|---|---|---|
| Area 1 | 8 | 500 | 10,000 | 0 | 0 |
| Area 2 | 7 | 300 | 30,000 | 8 | 18 |
| Overseas | 6 | 600 | 17,000 | 10 | 22 |

The credit controller has had discussions with Domba Limited (Domba), a factoring company, who believes it can improve the overall profitability of Tiga by introducing better credit control and incorporating new and strict guidelines for sales personnel to follow that will speed up debt collection and reduce the bad debt problem. It will charge an annual sum of €2 million for its administration, thereby cutting out all existing collection costs.

Domba has offered to take over the administration of the sales ledger, debt collection and general management of the debtors. However, it will not take over any losses arising from bad debts. It will lend funds to Tiga at 8% p.a. for the amount and period of the outstanding debtor balances, e.g. for every Area 1 customer it will lend €500 at 8% per annum. It predicts that its operating profit efficiency and credit guidelines for sales personnel will cut the bad debts' percentages in respect of Area 2 and Overseas Area customers to 8% and 10% respectively. It will also mean that total Overseas sales will decline by €2 million, with a proportionate effect on balances outstanding. The existing interest rate on Tiga's overdraft is 7% per annum.

**Requirements:**

1. Prepare a table of results which show the various revenues and costs for each Area under both the existing approach and the suggested Domba plan for Tiga.
2. Write a brief report, including your recommendations, on your findings in (1) above for the credit controller of Tiga.
3. Outline the advantages and disadvantages of using short-term debt, as opposed to long-term debt, in the financing of working capital.

Source: Chartered Accountants Ireland, Management Accounting and Business Finance, P3, Summer 2006

*Question 10.9 (Decision-making, Relevant Costs and Cost Prediction)*

Dave Barry, an electrical engineer, is the manager of the Beta Company which manufactures special electrical components to order. He took up his present position some years ago after obtaining an MBA degree. The company has been relatively profitable in recent years although sales, in volume terms, have shown little increase. A potential new customer to purchase a special component has recently approached him. Barry is unsure if the proposal would enable him to make any money on the project. One of his problems is that his firm's weekly production overhead has fluctuated widely in recent weeks. These fluctuations have made it difficult to estimate the level of production overhead that will be incurred for any single week.

The proposal, which Barry is considering, is for the production of 5,000 electrical components. These components require labour-intensive operations since they are, essentially, an assembly-type activity. However, some machine processing is also required. Each electrical component would require an input of one direct labour hour and 10 minutes of machine time. Since the company was already operating at near capacity, Barry realised that the necessary work would have to be performed on an overtime basis. Workers in such circumstances were paid at time and a half.

Barry estimates that, on an overtime basis, the entire job would take 12 weeks to complete and would be finished by mid-December. The current price offer of €50 per unit represented an initial contract of €250,000. The production manager and shop steward were enthusiastic about the proposal since it would boost employees' earnings prior to the Christmas holidays. Currently production workers were paid a basic hourly rate of €6.

Each unit produced requires three different types of raw materials designated A, B and C. Quantities required and additional information are as follows:

| Material type | Kgs required per unit | Current stock level (kilos) | Historical cost per unit | Replacement cost per unit | Net realisable value per unit |
|---|---|---|---|---|---|
| A | 1 | 5,000 | €2 | €4 | €1 |
| B | $1/_2$ | 9,000 | €3 | €5 | €2 |
| C | 2 | NIL | NIL | €6 | NIL |

Material A is used regularly by the company in the production of other electrical components. However, Material B is in excess of the company's requirements and unless used in the production of these units would be sold. The required amount of Material C, since none are in stock, would be specially purchased.

However, the estimating department were unable to provide reliable estimates of the amount of production overhead to be incurred. The sales manager of the firm, Jack Russell, argued that they were irrelevant for pricing purposes because, by definition, they couldn't be attributed to an individual product. He argued that if only direct labour and materials were included in the costing it would enable a very competitive contract price to be quoted. A keen price would virtually guarantee the contract this time – profits could then be generated on subsequent business. If production over-heads were included in the quotation the company could set its price at too high a level relative to the competition.

Dave Barry was not convinced by the argument of the 'irrelevancy' of produc-tion overheads in such circumstances. Rather he believed that an accurate classifica-tion of overheads was essential in both planning and controlling the operations of the firm. Barry remembered from his management accounting course during the MBA that the first thing he had to do was to relate production overheads to some type of activity within the firm. However, he is unsure whether to use direct labour hours or machine running hours as the best measure of activity. Ultimately a choice would have to be made between these two bases in order to determine a cost behav-iour pattern and the first place to start, Dave reasoned, would be an analysis of historical data.

The following data (**Exhibit 1**) on total production overheads, direct labour hours and machine running hours for the most recent 12-week period are collected and Barry noted that they showed sufficient variability in activity levels to provide a useful start for prediction purposes:

EXHIBIT 1: PRODUCTION OVERHEADS INCURRED AND
OPERATING LEVELS OF ACTIVITY

| Week | Direct labour hours | Machine running hours | Total production overheads € |
|------|---------------------|-----------------------|------------------------------|
| 1 | 1,250 | 111 | 29,900 |
| 2 | 1,497 | 132 | 34,600 |
| 3 | 1,184 | 121 | 28,900 |
| 4 | 1,499 | 147 | 34,300 |
| 5 | 1,356 | 154 | 32,400 |
| 6 | 1,300 | 125 | 31,200 |
| 7 | 1,222 | 122 | 28,700 |
| 8 | 1,259 | 131 | 29,400 |
| 9 | 1,109 | 120 | 27,000 |
| 10 | 1,435 | 144 | 33,400 |
| 11 | 1,121 | 112 | 27,700 |
| 12 | 1,433 | 145 | 34,100 |

Barry was confident that the above observations were representative of the current production process and that the relationships would be valid for the forthcoming year. There had not been any significant technological change in the production process in recent times and none was anticipated. His own informal work-study calculations suggested that there was no experience or learning curve phenomenon in the production process. Having quickly revised a basic management accounting text dealing with cost prediction, Barry understood the various methods proposed for determining a cost behaviour pattern.

**Requirements:**

1. Determine the historical cost behaviour pattern of the production overhead costs using the high–low method. Justify your choice of independent i.e. explanatory variable.
2. Determine the historical cost behaviour pattern of the production overhead costs using the regression analysis. Justify your choice of independent i.e. explanatory variable.
3. Assume the following results were obtained from two simple linear regressions.

|  | Regression No. 1 | Regression No. 2 |
|---|---|---|
| Dependent variable (Y) | Production over-head costs | Production over-head costs |
| Independent variable (X) | Direct labour hours | Machine running hours |
| y intercept | €5,519 | €11,682 |
| Coefficient of independent variable | 19.49 | 147.96 |
| Coefficient of correlation (R) | 0.99 | 0.77 |
| Coefficient of determination (R²) | 0.97 | 0.59 |
| Standard error of estimate | 448 | 1800 |
| Standard error of regression coefficient for the independent variable | 0.98 | 38.00 |
| No. of observations | 12 | 12 |
| T-statistic for a 95% confidence interval: 10 degrees of freedom | 2.228 | 2.228 |

(a) Apply two tests to assess the linearity of both regressions. Which regression would you recommend to use? Why?

(b) Calculate a 95% confidence interval for the variable production overhead per unit based on your preferred regression equation. To what extent could this confidence interval influence your recommendation of accepting or rejecting the order? Explain.

4. Would you recommend that Barry accept the proposal? How did you arrive at your conclusion? Would your recommendation change if the company were operating at considerably below maximum capacity?

### Question 10.10 (Relevant Costs in Decision-making)

Kraven Limited is a multinational company in the shipping business. One month ago, management were informed that one of its 10 ships – the *Mirissa* – had sunk. Thankfully, all of the crew were rescued without injury. However, the ship's cargo – agricultural machinery – went down with the vessel. All of the machinery was stored in watertight compartments, guaranteed not to be breached by water for four months. The machinery has a valuation of €5 million and is fully insured. In the event that Kraven Limited cannot retrieve the machinery, the customer will have to place a new order and wait three months for the order to be filled. It is unlikely that this customer will use Kraven Limited for shipping if this machinery needs to be re-ordered.

Management have requested that costings be prepared to assist them in making a decision on whether to attempt to salvage the *Mirissa* (saving the ship and cargo) or not. The following information is available:

1. Kraven Limited has received an urgently commissioned report from an expert on salvage operations which concludes that an attempt to re-float the *Mirissa* would take three months and be successful. This report cost €15,000, the cheque for which is due to be written next week.
2. The *Mirissa* cost €70 million to build six years ago. The insurance company has confirmed that, if the ship is not re-floated, it will pay out 80% of this amount. In addition, it will pay 100% of the €5 million replacement cost of the cargo and this cheque will be endorsed by Kraven to the machine's owners. In such a scenario, Kraven Limited will need to buy a replacement ship (second-hand, of similar age and condition) at a cost of €60 million. The insurance company has also advised that such a claim will result in total premiums payable by Kraven Limited increasing by €200,000 per annum for this year and next year (after which point total premiums are expected by Kraven Limited's management to revert to normal levels).
3. If the salvage operation goes ahead, salvage equipment will need to be purchased at a cost of €3 million. It is estimated that, after the operation, this equipment will have a re-sale value of €500,000.
4. Four specific members of the senior management team will be re-assigned for three months to supervise the salvage operation if it goes ahead. Two of these individuals are currently involved in routine duties that can be handled by their deputies with no increase in workload. The other two members are working on a project (Project M) that must be completed within the next three months or it will not come to fruition. No other employees within Kraven Limited possess the required skills to complete Project M. Upon completion, it has been estimated that Project M would earn Kraven Limited a €2 million contribution, before the senior managers' salaries. All members of the senior management team earn monthly salaries of €15,000.

5. Additional staff will need to be hired to man the salvage operation at a cost of €1 million for the three-month period. The insurance company will reimburse 40% of this cost, with no impact on future premiums.
6. Head office has indicated that it will be charging €175,000 of Administrative fixed costs to the salvage operation if it goes ahead. Included in this amount is €75,000 of actual incremental costs arising specifically from the salvage operation.
7. If no attempt is made by the company to salvage the ship, a fine of €700,000 will be imposed on Kraven Limited by the government's environmental agency.
8. Based on Kraven Limited's normal accounting policies, equipment already owned by the company and used in the salvage operation will be depreciated by €400,000 over a three-month period.

### Requirements:

1. Prepare a statement showing the relevant costs, cost savings and revenues for Kraven Limited should it decide to salvage the ship, as opposed to abandoning it.
2. Detail **four** other factors (which may be quantitative or qualitative) that Kraven Limited should take into account before arriving at a final decision.

Source: Chartered Accountants Ireland, Management Accounting and Business Finance, P3,<br>Summer, 2004

*Question 10.11 (Relevant Costs in Decision-making)*

Sesmatic Limited (Sesmatic) is engaged in the manufacture of specialised hospital equipment. It has just received a notice from one of its customers, a private hospital called The Westchester, cancelling an order for the construction of a specialised piece of radiography equipment. The contract price had been agreed at €1.5 million. The hospital paid a non-refundable deposit of 15% when the contract was signed and Sesmatic had also agreed to a further payment of 20% of the contract price if the contract was cancelled by them.

The construction of this type of equipment is usually done in two phases. Phase 1 has just been completed and costs of €493,000 have been incurred as follows:

|  | € |
|---|---|
| Direct materials | 93,000 |
| Skilled labour (at €10 per hour) | 150,000 |
| Unskilled labour (at €5 per hour) | 25,000 |
| Overheads (150% × *skilled* labour) * | 225,000 |
|  | 493,000 |
| *OHAR: fixed overheads at 120% of skilled labour | |
| *OHAR: variable overheads at 30% of skilled labour | |

The Board of Directors are unsure how to proceed and three alternatives have been identified:

- The **first option** is to sell the equipment, in its current state the equipment could be sold without adaptation for €105,000.
- The **second option** is to dismantle the equipment and sell the individual components for €130,000. Dismantling would require 750 hours of skilled labour at €10 per hour and such employees will be hired specially for the task. In addition, there would be direct expenses of dismantling of €3,500 and transport costs of €5,000. Moreover, an independent consultant for the environmental protection agency would have to sign off on the dismantled equipment/components to ensure that no harmful radioactive material is released in the process. This certification process usually costs €3,000 for a job of this size.
- The **third option** is to adapt the equipment and sell it to another customer for €500,000. This customer has already been identified but no agreement has been reached. The following data has been provided in relation to adaptation by way of Phase 2:
  1. The contract is complete with regard to Phase 1. Phase 2 requires the same input of skilled labour which will continue to be paid at the rate of €10 per hour.
  2. Phase 2 will also require 1,000 additional hours of unskilled labour. However, unskilled labour are currently idle and they have already been given a commitment by management not to be laid off in the foreseeable future. A total of 5,000 unskilled labour hours would be available if necessary.
  3. The contract is 40% complete with respect to material cost. However all remaining material has already been purchased, and is in stock, in order to avail of quantity discounts. The historical cost of the materials in stock amounts to €100,000 and will be replaced since this type of material is used regularly by the company. The replacement cost of these materials is currently €145,000 and their net realisable value is €126,000. However, these materials could be used as a perfect substitute on an alternative project which would earn gross revenue of €350,000 from which incremental costs of €175,000 would have to be paid.
  4. As Sesmatic is in the business of manufacturing hospital equipment it may have potential future liabilities in relation to product faults. Sesmatic pays an annual insurance fee of €40,000 and this policy includes product liability cover. Sesmatic also provides a substantial warranty on new products. To meet this cost the company maintains a warranty provision of 1% on the sales value of each contract and this is considered to be a realistic amount.

**Requirements:** Prepare a report for the Board of Directors of Sesmatic, recommending a specific course of action, based on the following:

1. The quantitative factors which should be considered in relation to each of the three options.
2. The qualitative factors which should be considered by Sesmatic in making its decision.

Source: Chartered Accountants Ireland, Management Accounting and Business Finance, Paper 3
Autumn 2007 (adapted)

*Question 10.12 (Relevant Costs in Decision-making)*

Tom Byrne had been in his new office in Relcost Limited for about 15 minutes before the phone rang. Tom had just taken up the newly created position as Business Analyst with the company and the voice at the other end of the phone quickly indicated the nature of the phone call – management of Relcost had to make a quick decision to accept or reject a proposal which would involve the company producing a new chemical product.

Relcost Limited manufactured a wide range of cleaning products for the household and laundry market. While the process was relatively simple i.e. it involves mixing chemicals, it was also highly dangerous. Simply put, if the wrong type of chemicals were mixed together or mixed in the incorrect amounts, then explosions could occur. There were also other personal health and safety considerations. Thus, safety issues are paramount. Financial considerations were also important and the proposal from Blow Up Limited was rejected by the Cost Accountant as being a total loss-making exercise! Tom was asked to investigate further and discovered the following:

The proposal from Blow Up Limited requires Relcost to manufacture and deliver 50,000 one-gallon drums of special industrial cleaner, designated as PJC 100, within the next month. To date, the company has not produced any industrial cleaner such as PJC 100, since it prefers to supply the household and commercial laundry market. However, the directors believe that the industrial market segment is one in which Relcost should have a presence. A guide price of €30 per one-gallon drum has been initially suggested by Blow Up but the final price is to be determined by negotiation between the two parties.

The proposal was given to the cost accountant a week ago together with product specifications and he quickly rejected the proposal (see below). No explanation was provided but the directors of Relcost were most unhappy at his projected unit cost of €52.60 as they believed that this was unrealistic in the prevailing market conditions. Thus, Tom Byrne was asked to investigate and advise the Board of Directors.

On investigation Tom Byrne discovered the following information and he quickly realised that this would have a significant impact on the relevant costs of this special order. In many instances, he disagreed with the previous cost analysis.

## FINANCIAL EVALUATION OF PJC 100 (50,000 ONE-GALLON DRUMS)

| | | |
|---|---|---|
| Ingredient X | 50,000 litres at historical cost | 150,000 |
| Ingredient Y | 100,000 litres at historical cost | 330,000 |
| Ingredient Z | 150,000 litres at historical cost | 150,000 |
| Skilled labour | 150,000 hours at €7 | 1,050,000 |
| Unskilled labour | 25,000 hours at €5 | 125,000 |
| Production overhead: fixed | 175,000 hours at €3 | 525,000 |

| Production overhead: variable | 50,000 units at €1.20 each | 60,000 |
| Safety packing containers | 50,000 at market price | 200,000 |
| Depr. of packing equipment | €40,000/2 years | 20,000 |
| Travel and hospitality costs | Already incurred | 20,000 |
| Total costs | | 2,630,000 |
| Cost per unit | €2,797,500/50,000 | €52.60 |

**Raw materials**: Each drum would require three different types of chemical raw materials, designated X, Y, and Z. Quantities required, current stock levels and cost of each raw material are as follows:

| Chemical | Litres per one-gallon drum | Current stock (litres) | Historical cost € | Current market price | Net realisable value € |
|---|---|---|---|---|---|
| X | 1 | 100,000 | 3.00 | 5.50 | 1.80 |
| Y | 2 | 60,000 | 3.30 | 2.80 | 1.10 |
| Z | 3 | 100,000 | 1.00 | 0.80 | Nil |

The company uses chemical X continuously and stocks are always replenished.

The current stock of chemical Y is in excess of the company's requirements and, unless used to manufacture PJC 100, chemical Y would be sold.

The company has a stock of chemical Z in hand which is surplus to requirements. However, because chemical Z is toxic then, if it is not used in this order, the material will have to be disposed at a **cost** to the company of €2 per litre. (This is in accordance with local anti-pollution guidelines.)

**Labour:** Production of each one-gallon drum would require skilled and unskilled labour. Three hours of skilled labour are required per one gallon and current wage rates are €7 per hour. However, additional skilled labour can only be obtained by ceasing production of another product, details of which are set out below and also incurring a penalty cost of €10,000 for non-delivery.

| Another product | Revenue/costs per gallon |
|---|---|
| Selling price per gallon | €21 |
| Direct material cost | 3 |
| Skilled direct labour | 14 |
| Fixed overhead | 3 |

The production of PJC 100 requires ½ hour of unskilled labour per one-gallon drum which is paid at the rate of €5 per hour. However, because of the cancellation of another contract requiring unskilled labour, Relcost Ltd expects to have over 100,000 surplus unskilled labour hours available during the coming year. Because of the impact on staff morale, the directors have decided not to dismiss any workers in the foreseeable future.

**Overheads**: Fixed production overheads for Relcost Ltd are assigned to products on the basis of direct labour hours and the production overhead absorption rate for the coming year is €3 per labour hour. Such fixed production overheads include items such as depreciation of machinery on a straight-line method, rent, property taxes and insurance of buildings. In addition, variable overhead costs for PJC 100 are estimated at €1.20 per unit produced. This represented mainly additional liquids which were added to the special chemicals to make up the total liquid contents of each one-gallon drum.

**Safety packing containers:** The company has already committed to a contract to purchase 270,000 of special safety containers for other orders at a unit (i.e. cost per gallon) cost of €5 per unit. However, this order will have to be increased by an additional 50,000 units to accommodate the production of PJC 100. The supplier has agreed a price of €4.50 for all containers for an order size of 320,000 units, provided that the revised order is quickly confirmed.

**Packaging equipment**: Specialised safety packaging machines, purchased by the company some years ago, would have to be used for the PJC 100 contract. While the machinery has an estimated useful life of two years, it will not be used in any other contract. Its current book value is €40,000 and its estimated realisable value is currently €24,000. It is estimated that these values would be €30,000 and €10,000 respectively at the end of the contract.

**Hospitality costs:** Relcost had already spent €10,000 on a trip to Blow-Up's plants which included expenditure on hospitality for Blow-Up's executives.

### Requirements:

1. Critically comment on the approach and figures used by the company's Cost Accountant in evaluating (and rejecting) Blow Up's offer.
2. Using the information obtained by Tom Byrne, clearly indicate whether the production of 50,000 one-gallon drums of PJC 100 is worthwhile on financial grounds only. Prepare a schedule of relevant costs to support your conclusion. Your schedule should distinguish between incremental, out of pocket cash costs and opportunity costs.
3. Assuming that some form of negotiation on the price of the proposed special order is forthcoming, clearly specify the minimum acceptable price to Relcost Limited for the production of 50,000 one-gallon drums of chemical, given the above circumstances. You may assume that short-term financial considerations only are relevant.
4. What non-quantifiable (i.e. qualitative) considerations are relevant to this decision and how are they relevant?

# 11

# Decision-making with Scarce Resources

LEARNING OBJECTIVES

When you have completed studying this chapter you should be able to:

1. Differentiate between a limiting factor and a constraint.
2. Calculate contribution per limiting factor.
3. Apply the graphic approach to profit maximisation.
4. Apply the linear programming technique and interpret optimal solution.
5. Describe the importance of sensitivity analysis.

## 11.1 Introduction to Scarce Resources

In analysing routine and non-routine decisions to date, we have overlooked one very important factor, namely the limited availability of physical resources necessary for production (or provision of services). In the context of management accounting, these scarce resources are referred to as limiting factors. **Limiting factors** represent resource or input constraints that restrict the ability of a business to produce goods or provide services. Limiting factors cannot be eliminated in the short term and include:

- Shortage of raw materials, both in terms of quantity and quality
- Shortage of labour (skilled or unskilled)
- Shortage of machine running hours, i.e. a capacity constraint
- Shortage of shelf space in a retail outlet, i.e. a capacity constraint.

The long-term solution to such situations is to acquire additional materials, labour or capacity. However, this may not be feasible, especially in the short term, for a variety of reasons, including the non-availability of finance. Another possible solution, based on economic pricing theory, is to increase selling prices to reduce demand. Again, however, this might not be realistic if customer goodwill and loyalty is to be maintained. Thus, faced with limiting factors, managers often must curtail production of some products since they do not have adequate resources to produce all they would like.

There are three different techniques that can be used in the context of limiting factors and all assume the short-term objective of 'profit maximisation'. Each technique will identify an optimal solution, i.e. a product mix that will generate an amount of profit that cannot be surpassed by any other (feasible) combination of products. Thus, the focus will be on deriving an optimal plan, also referred to as an optimal production mix or an optimal product mix. **Exhibit 11.1** presents these three techniques. The use of a particular technique is determined by two considerations:

- the number of products that the company is producing; and
- the number of limiting factors.

The techniques discussed in this chapter are:

1. contribution per limiting factor,
2. the graphic approach, and
3. linear programming.

EXHIBIT 11.1: DECISION-MAKING WITH SCARCE RESOURCES

| No. of limiting factors | Number of products in product portfolio | |
|---|---|---|
| | **Two only** | **More than two** |
| **Single** | Contribution per limiting factor (CpLF) | Contribution per limiting factor (CpLF) |
| **Two or more** | Graphic Approach | Linear Programming |

It should be noted that managers are also faced with what are termed constraints. A constraint is conceptually different from a limiting factor as constraints are self-imposed restrictions by management. Typical constraints are represented by maximum demand levels. In this case, management could produce in excess of estimated demand levels. However, such excess production would not generate profits since profits are only generated from sales. Thus, in order to maximise profits for a given accounting period, management will voluntarily restrict products to the estimated number of units that they can sell. The generic term 'scare resources' is often used to describe both limiting factors and constraints.

## 11.2 Contribution per Limiting Factor

Regardless of the number of products in the product portfolio, if there is a si
factor, then managers should always apply the general rule of ranking products a
to their **contribution per limiting factor (CpLF)**. This means that a firm should a
its limited resources in a manner that will maximise the contribution per unit of t
scarce resource. If this is done, the selected mix of products chosen will maximise profits
and there is no alternative product mix that can generate a greater amount of profit. The
application of contribution per limiting factor is done in four steps as follows:

1. Identify the contribution per unit. The contribution per unit is the sales price per
   unit less the unit variable cost. In calculating contribution per unit, always exclude
   any fixed costs that may be provided by way of information.
2. Calculate the amount of scarce resource a unit of each product or service requires.
   The amount of scarce resource can be stated either in physical terms (machine hours)
   or in monetary terms (cost of raw materials required per product). It is important to
   be consistent with the treatment across products, i.e. the input of scarce resources per
   unit should be stated in physical terms (e.g. hours) for all products. Alternatively, the
   input should be stated in monetary terms, e.g. cost per kg for all products.
3. Calculate the contribution per limiting factor for each unit or service by dividing
   contribution per unit (1) by the amount of scarce resource required (2).
4. Rank the products (or services) in descending order relative to contribution per
   limiting factor. This ranking forms the basis of selecting products to be produced.
   The most attractive product is the one that generates the greatest CpLF and will
   be the first product to be produced. Then we produce the second most attractive
   product, and continue this process until the total amount of the limiting factor has
   been utilised. Thus, the production of the least attractive product in terms of CpLF
   will be curtailed.

ILLUSTRATION: CONTRIBUTION PER LIMITING FACTOR

The directors of Donegal Company are preparing a production schedule for the
forthcoming quarter, based on the following data for its four products:

| Unit data | A € | B € | C € | D € |
|---|---|---|---|---|
| Selling price | 20 | 40 | 30 | 25 |
| Direct material | (8) | (20) | (15) | (10) |
| Direct labour (variable) | (3) | (6) | (3) | (4) |
| Fixed overhead | (2) | (2) | (2) | (2) |
| Profit | 7 | 12 | 10 | 9 |

material. However, suppliers of raw materials
ble to deliver more than €80,000 worth of
nent accepts that this shortage of vital raw
production and sales. However, they do not
from the product range. Accordingly, with a
ducts available to customers in general, they
00 units of each product during the forthcom-
ls should be used in the most profitable man-
s of each product per quarter, as follows:

|           | Maximum sales units |
|-----------|---------------------|
|           | 3,000               |
| Product B | 1,400               |
| Product C | 1,600               |
| Product D | 2,000               |

**Requirement:** Calculate the quantities of each product that the company should produce in the forthcoming quarter, and show the forecast contribution for the period.

**Solution and analysis:** The first step in the process is to compute the contribution per unit. This is fairly evident from the above data per unit, provided care is taken to exclude the fixed overhead cost per unit. It is indicated in this case that direct labour is a variable cost. The unit contributions are as follows:

|                  | A € | B € | C € | D € |
|------------------|-----|-----|-----|-----|
| Sales price      | 20  | 40  | 30  | 25  |
| Variable costs   | (11)| (26)| (18)| (14)|
| Unit contribution| 9   | 14  | 12  | 11  |

The second and third steps involve the identification of the input of scarce resource for each product and the computation of the contribution per limiting factor for each product. Since raw materials are in scarce supply, management will want to generate the maximum contribution per input of raw material. This is done by ranking products according to their CpLF, which is, effectively, a measure of efficiency. The calculation below indicates that a unit of product A requires an input of €8 of raw materials and generates a contribution of €9, providing a ratio (1.12) to reflect the efficient use of scarce materials. The other relevant figures indicate that a unit of Product B requires €20 input of raw materials and yields €14 in contribution; a unit of Product C requires €15 input of raw materials and yields €12 in contribution margin; finally, Product D requires a raw material input of €10 and provides a unit contribution of €11.

| | A | B | C | D |
|---|---|---|---|---|
| Unit contribution (calculated above) | €9 | €14 | €12 | €11 |
| Input of raw materials (limiting factor) | €8 | €20 | €15 | €10 |
| Contribution per limiting factor (ratio) | 1.12 | 0.70 | 0.80 | 1.10 |
| Ranking | 1st | 4th | 3rd | 2nd |

Thus, even though a unit of Product B yields the highest contribution per unit (€20), it is the least profitable product in terms of contribution per input of raw material (0.70). If sales of the other products do not depend on the sales of product B, and there are no operational problems involved in varying the production mix of the four products, the production of Product B should be kept to a minimum. This is particularly appropriate since Donegal cannot meet the demand for all products because of limited supply of raw materials.

The contribution per limiting factor is used to assign production capacity to the four products. Product A makes the greatest use of the scarce raw materials, then Product D, followed by Product C, and finally Product B. However, in assigning capacity to production, a minimum of 1,000 units of each product is to be produced. This minimum production quota will require €53,000 of raw materials as is shown below.

| | Minimum units produced | Material cost per unit | Total material cost for minimum production |
|---|---|---|---|
| A | 1,000 | €8 | €8,000 |
| B | 1,000 | €20 | 20,000 |
| C | 1,000 | €15 | 15,000 |
| D | 1,000 | €10 | 10,000 |
| | | | 53,000 |

The balance (at cost) of raw materials to be assigned amounts to €27,000 (€80,000 – €53,000) and this should be used in the most profitable manner. This is done by using the remaining raw materials to produce Product A. However, since only a maximum of 3,000 units of A can be sold (and 1,000 units are included in the minimum production quota), an additional 2,000 units of Product A will then be produced, which requires an input of €16,000 of raw materials, as follows:

| | € |
|---|---|
| Raw materials available | 27,000 |
| A (2,000 units @ €8 each) | (16,000) |
| Balance available | 11,000 |

The next most profitable product is D. However, a maximum of only 2,000 units can be sold. Since 1,000 units are already included in the minimum production quota, only 1,000 extra units of Product D will then be produced, requiring €10,000 of raw materials, as follows:

|  | € |
|---|---|
| Balance available (above) | 11,000 |
| D (1,000 units @ €10 each) | (10,000) |
| Balance available | 1,000 |

The remaining €1,000 of raw materials will be assigned to Product C, the next most profitable product. Since each unit of C requires €15 of raw materials, only 66 (rounded) additional units of C (€1,000/€15) can be produced, which uses up the balance of the remaining raw materials, as follows:

|  | € |
|---|---|
| Balance available (above) | 1,000 |
| C (66 units @ €15 each) | (1,000) |
| Balance available | Nil |

Based on the analysis above, the optimal production plan and related contribution is produced below. The schedule indicates a total contribution of €75,792. This schedule is optimal in the sense that no other combination of products will generate a greater contribution.

### OPTIMAL PRODUCTION AND PROFIT STATEMENT

| Product | Units | Unit Contribution | Total Contribution |
|---|---|---|---|
| A | 3,000 | €9 | €27,000 |
| B | 1,000 | €14 | €14,000 |
| C | 1,066 | €12 | €12,792 |
| D | 2,000 | €11 | €22,000 |
|  |  |  | €75,792 |

The above optimal production plan utilises all the available raw materials. The presence of fixed costs has been ignored in our calculations since they represent sunk costs and are, therefore, irrelevant for decision-making.

However, there are always non-quantifiable factors to be considered in decision making. For example, Product B may be important to the firm in terms of generating company image or customer satisfaction. In such circumstances, some additional units of Product B might be produced. This, in turn, will further curtail the production of a more attractive product and results in an opportunity cost, i.e. the cash contribution lost as a result of producing an additional unit of a less attractive product rather than the more attractive product.

## 11.3 The Graphic Approach

Having discussed how a single limiting factor can be incorporated into managerial decision-making we now turn to a situation where there are several limiting factors but where only two products are manufactured. In such situations, the graphic approach is used, as explained below. However, the graphic approach can only be used where there are two products since there are only two axes on a graph: the horizontal and vertical axes. Nevertheless, the graphic approach provides a useful introduction to more complex problems, which are generally solved using linear programming.

ILLUSTRATION: GRAPHIC APPROACH

Carlow Company aims to maximise its short-term profits. In one factory, it manufactures two liquid products called Alpha and Beta. Each is a mix of readily available ingredients that passes through three successive processes of heating, blending and cooling. Carlow's management accountant has prepared the following up-to-date cost statement for the two products:

|                                          | Alpha € | Beta € |
|------------------------------------------|---------|--------|
| Selling Price per unit                   | 25      | 30     |
| Direct materials cost per unit           | 15      | 17     |
| Variable processing overheads per unit:  |         |        |
| Heating process                          | 4       | 1      |
| Blending process                         | 1       | 5      |
| Cooling process                          | 2       | 3      |
| Contribution per unit                    | 3       | 4      |

Each product is assigned variable processing overheads at the rate of €1 per hour of process time in each department. Thus, product Alpha requires four processing hours in the heating department (€4), one hour in blending (€1) and two hours in heating (€2). However, based on existing information, the amount of processing time is limited to 3,000 hours in each of the three departments. These limits cannot be removed in the short term and unused processing hours in one department cannot be used by another department.

**Requirement:** Identify the Carlow Company's optimal production plan and related contribution, assuming that it wants to maximise its profits.

**Solution and analysis:** The first step involving graphic analysis is to derive the objective function, which indicates the contribution from each product. The objective will be to maximise this objective function, where the number of Alphas and Betas to be produced is unknown, but their respective coefficients are represented by their unit contributions. The objective function can be written as follows:

Maximise: 3 Alpha + 4 Beta

The second step is to develop an equation for the use of each limiting factor where the coefficients represent the amount of limiting factor required for each product and the total amount of the (limited) resources being, in this example, 3,000 processing hours in each of the heating, blending and cooling departments. Therefore, the value of the objective function (stated above) is to be maximised subject to the following restrictions:

Subject to:   4 Alpha + 1 Beta ≤ 3,000 heating hours
1 Alpha + 5 Beta ≤ 3,000 blending hours
2 Alpha + 3 Beta ≤ 3,000 cooling hours

We need to find values for both Alpha and Beta and these can be ascertained using the graphic approach. The graphic approach involves assigning one product (Alpha) to the vertical axis of the graph and the other product (Beta) to the horizontal axis.

There are three limiting factors, namely, processing hours in each of the heating, blending and cooling departments. Starting with the heating department, the Carlow Company could produce either 750 units of Alpha (3,000/4) or 3,000 units of Beta (3,000/1). Alternatively, the Carlow Company could produce any mix of Alpha and Beta in the heating department along a straight line starting with 750 units of Alpha and joining with 3,000 units of Beta. Secondly, the blending department is also limited to 3,000 processing hours. The company could use all these blending hours to produce 3,000 units of Alpha (3,000/1) or 600 units of Beta (3,000/5). Alternatively, Carlow could produce any mix of Alpha and Beta in the blending department along a straight line starting with 3,000 units of Alpha and joining with 600 units of Beta. The same procedure applies to the cooling department which has only 3,000 processing hours available. The company could produce 1,500 units of Alpha (3,000/2) or 1,000 units of Beta (3,000/3) in the cooling department. Alternatively, it could produce any mix of products along a straight line joining 1,500 units of Alpha with 1,000 units of Beta in the cooling department. The resulting graph appears below in **Exhibit 11.2**.

EXHIBIT II.2: GRAPHIC SOLUTION

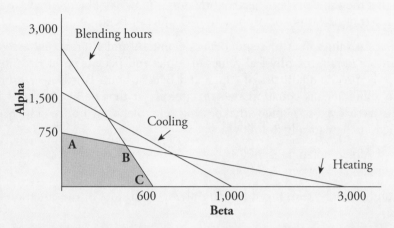

When all the limiting factors (and any constraints) are plotted on the graph, the next stage is to identify the feasible region. This is the (shaded) area within which the optimal solution must lie because the feasible region satisfies simultaneously all the restrictions imposed on the company. The firm can produce any combination of products within the feasible region. However, in order to maximise its profits, the optimal solution will always be a corner point of the feasible region. This statement can be proved mathematically but it is not necessary here. In a minority of situations, it is possible that two corner points could provide the identical contribution and, therefore, both would represent the optimal solution.

The final step in the graphic approach is to identify which of the corner points represents the optimal solution. This is done by calculating the number of units to be produced at each corner point, together with the associated total contribution. The point corresponding to the highest total contribution represents the optimal solution. For example, with Carlow Company there are three corner points referred to as A, B and C respectively. The units of product Alpha and Beta and total contribution are as follows:

CALCULATION OF OPTIMAL SOLUTION

|  | Point A | | Point B | | Point C | |
|---|---|---|---|---|---|---|
| Alpha @ €3 | 750 = | 2,250 | 632 = | 1,896 | Nil = | Nil |
| Beta @ €4 | Nil = | Nil | 473 = | 1,892 | 600 = | 2,400 |
|  |  | €2,250 |  | €3,788 |  | €2,400 |

It can be seen from the above that point B represents the optimal solution, since this generates a contribution of €3,788, which is higher than the contribution generated by either point A or point C. In the context of management accounting we say that the value of the objective function is €3,788. The optimal production mix consists of 632 units of Alpha and 473 units of Beta.

The physical values of Alpha and Beta at points A and B are easily ascertained. How did we obtain the physical values of Alpha and Beta at point B? In order to identify the precise quantities of Alpha and Beta at point B it is necessary to use the two simultaneous equations which intersect at that point. At point B, two limiting factors exist, namely the heating and blending hours. These can be explained mathematically as follows:

(i)   4 Alpha + 1 Beta ≤ 3,000
(ii)  1 Alpha + 5 Beta ≤ 3,000

Equation (ii) can be rearranged by multiplying both sides of the equation by 4 as follows:

(ii)  4 Alpha + 20 Beta ≤ 12,000

Therefore, equations (i) and (ii) can be presented as follows:

(i)   4 Alpha + 1 Beta ≤ 3,000
(ii)  4 Alpha + 20 Beta ≤ 12,000

By subtracting equation (i) from equation (ii) we obtain:

19 Beta = 9,000
1 Beta = 473 units (rounded)

The value of Alpha can be determined by substituting 473 for Beta into either equation (i) or equation (ii). If equation (i) is used, then:

4 Alpha + 1 (473) = 3,000
4 Alpha = 632 units (rounded)

Alternatively, the optimal solution can be identified by selecting an arbitrary total contribution of, say, €1,200 (or any other figure that can be divided by the respective unit contributions). To achieve this total contribution the company can produce either 400 units of A (€1,200/€3), or 300 units of B (€1,200/€4.) We can, therefore, draw a line from the point (A = 400 and B = 0) to the point (A = 0 and B = 300). This line is represented by the dotted line in **Exhibit 11.3** and is sometimes referred to as the iso-profit line, i.e. a line of equal profits. (Actually, the term should really refer to contribution and not profit.) Each point along this dotted line represents all the possible combinations of Alpha and Beta that will yield a total contribution of €1,200. The iso-profit line suggests that rational managers should be indifferent, in an economic sense, to whether they produce 400 units of

A, 300 units of B or any combination of A and B along this dotted line. To maximise the value of the objective function, additional iso-profit lines can be drawn parallel but to the right hand side of the line just highlighted. The final corner point touched represents the optimal solution – point B in this case.

EXHIBIT 11.3: GRAPHIC SOLUTION

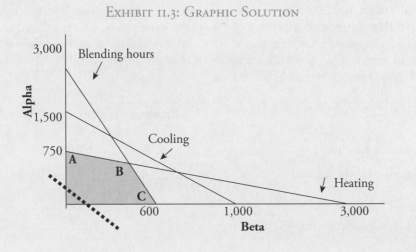

## 11.4 The Application of Linear Programming and 'Solver'

The technique of Linear Programming (LP) can be used to solve the more complex situation associated with managerial decision-making. Based on **Exhibit 11.1** (presented earlier) it is recommended that linear programming be used in a multi-product firm, faced with several limiting factors. The mathematical technique of linear programming allows the identification of the optimal production plan, which is the unique combination of products, given the various restrictions under which the firm operates, that will provide a profit level that cannot be surpassed by any other (feasible) combination of products. The necessary calculations, which can be complex and cumbersome, no longer need to be performed manually. Rather, the optimal solution can now be found quickly, using computer software. One such application is Solver (within Excel) which will be used in the illustration below. In the illustration the firm can produce three different products but machine processing hours are limited in the firm's two operating departments (Departments 1 and 2). In addition, there are both maximum and minimum sales quotas for each product.

## ILLUSTRATION: LINEAR PROGRAMMING

Roscommon Ltd manufactures and sells three consumer products, namely A, B and C. Each product is machine processed through Departments 1 and 2. However machine capacity for each department is limited in the forthcoming period to 300,000 and 400,000 machine hours respectively. In addition, the directors have agreed that minimum quantities of 20,000 of each product be produced in order not to disappoint certain customers. The maximum units of each product that can be sold are 70,000 units and selling price changes are not feasible. The following unit data is presented:

|  | Product A | Product B | Product C |
|---|---|---|---|
| Unit contribution | €9 | €10 | €5 |
| Machine hours per unit: |  |  |  |
| **Dept 1** (maximum 300,000 hours) | 2 | 2 | 1 |
| **Dept 2** (maximum 400,000 hours) | 2 | 3 | 2 |

**Requirements:**

1. Discuss and present the above problem as a mathematical model and, using Solver (in Excel), identify the optimal solution both in terms of physical quantities and monetary contribution.
2. Discuss the role of sensitivity analysis and identify the impact, if any, on the optimal production plan and on profit of the following independent events:

   (a)  Selling price of A reduced by €2 per unit
   (b)  Selling price of B increased by €2 per unit
   (c)  Minimum production quota for A is eliminated
   (d)  Maximum sales quota for B is increased by 5,000 units

**Solution and Analysis:**

**1.** The objective is to maximise overall contribution, and therefore overall profit, by producing a unique combination of products, within the given restrictions. The coefficients in the objective function below represent the unit contributions and the objective function can be written as follows:

$$\text{Maximise: } (9A + 10B + 5C)$$

Secondly, all limiting factors (together with any demand constraints) must be considered. According to the data provided, there is a limited amount of machine hours available in both processing departments for the forthcoming period. The limiting factors represented by machine processing hours can be mathematically expressed as:

$$2A + 2B + 1C \leq 300{,}000 \text{ (Dept 1 hours)}$$
$$2A + 3B + 2C \leq 400{,}000 \text{ (Dept 2 hours)}$$

The above coefficients represent the specified number of machine hours required per unit of product A, B and C respectively. These inequalities indicate that the total number of machine hours used to produce quantities of A, B, and C must be equal or less than 300,000 hours in Department 1 and 400,000 hours in Department 2. Thus, the total machine hours utilised according to our optimal production plan must not exceed the amounts specified.

In addition, maximum and minimum quantities of unit sales of each product have been specified and agreed. They can be expressed as:

A ≥ 20,000 (Minimum sales of A) and
B ≥ 20,000 (Minimum sales of B) and
C ≥ 20,000 (Minimum sales of C) and
A ≤ 70,000 (Maximum sales of A) and
B ≤ 70,000 (Maximum sales of B) and
C ≤ 70,000 (Maximum sales of C)

In summary, we have attempted to represent a real decision situation by a mathematical model with an objective function – expressed in terms of maximising total contribution – together with various limiting factors and constraints. In earlier times, this problem would have been solved using 'simplex' calculations. However, it is more appropriate to show how modern computer software is used to solve this type of problem. The use of Solver (in Excel) will now be illustrated, and related to the above information.

The first step is to enter the above information (in terms of labels, data and formulae) into an Excel spreadsheet, which can be subsequently used by Solver. (The same format applies to all optimisation models.) To input and solve the model you must specify the following, using an ordinary Excel spreadsheet:

• The 'Target Cell' that you want to maximise (or minimise). This corresponds to the monetary value of the objective function.
• Specify the 'Changing Cells', which will, subsequently, contain the physical values for all products according to the optimal solution.
• Specify constraints that must comply with certain limits.

The spreadsheet model is presented below. It should be noted that text information provides signposts for the user and all text information is presented in *italics* below (but alternative presentations are acceptable):

| Cell reference | Text, data or formula |
|---|---|
| Cell A1 | *Roscommon Limited (i.e. name of problem)* |
| Cell B4 | *Product A (product identification)* |
| Cell C4 | *Product B (product identification)* |
| Cell D4 | *Product C (product identification)* |
| Cell A5 | *Changing cells* |
| Cell B5 | 0 (i.e. zero but, when Solver is run, this will be replaced with the optimal number of units of A) |
| Cell C5 | 0 (i.e. zero but, when Solver is run, this will be replaced with the optimal number of units of B) |
| Cell D5 | 0 (i.e. zero but, when Solver is run, this will be replaced with the optimal number of units of C) |
| Cell A7 | *Unit contribution* |
| Cell B7 | 9 (representing unit contribution of A) |
| Cell C7 | 10 (representing unit contribution of B) |
| Cell D7 | 5 (representing unit contribution of C) |
| Cell A9 | *Using Dept 1 hours* |
| Cell B9 | 2 (i.e. hours required by each unit of A in Dept 1) |
| Cell C9 | 2 (i.e. hours required by each unit of B in Dept 1) |
| Cell D9 | 1 (i.e. hours required by each unit of C in Dept 1) |
| Cell A10 | *Using Dept 2 hours* |
| Cell B10 | 2 (i.e. hours required by each unit of A in Dept 2) |
| Cell C10 | 3 (i.e. hours required by each unit of B in Dept 2) |
| Cell D10 | 2 (i.e. hours required by each unit of C in Dept 2) |
| Cell A11 | *Minimum sales units* |
| Cell B11 | 20,000 (i.e. minimum units of A to be produced/sold) |
| Cell C11 | 20,000 (i.e. minimum units of B to be produced/sold) |
| Cell D11 | 20,000 (i.e. minimum units of C to be produced/sold) |
| Cell A12 | *Maximum sales units* |
| Cell B12 | 70,000 (i.e. maximum units of A to be produced/sold) |
| Cell C12 | 70,000 (i.e. maximum units of B to be produced/sold) |
| Cell D12 | 70,000 (i.e. maximum units of C to be produced/sold) |
| Cell A14 | *Target cell* |
| Cell B14 | Insert the formula for the objective function = (B5*B7 + C5*C7 + D5*D7). (When run, Solver will give this monetary value.) |
| Cell A16 | *Constraints* |
| Cell B16 | *Item* |

| Cell reference | Text, data or formula |
|---|---|
| Cell C16 | *Used* |
| Cell D16 | *Limit* |
| Cell B17 | *Dept 1 hours* |
| Cell B18 | *Dept 2 hours* |
| Cell B19 | *Minimum sales A* |
| Cell B20 | *Minimum sales B* |
| Cell B21 | *Minimum sales C* |
| Cell B22 | *Maximum sales A* |
| Cell B23 | *Maximum sales B* |
| Cell B24 | *Maximum sales C* |
| Cell C17 | = (B5*B9 + C5*C9 + D5*D9) formula for Dept 1 hours used |
| Cell C18 | = (B5*B10 + C5*C10 + D5*D10) formula for Dept 2 hours used |
| Cell C19 | = (1*B5) formula for units of A produced/sold |
| Cell C20 | = (1*C5) formula for units of B produced/sold |
| Cell C21 | = (1*D5) formula for units of C produced/sold |
| Cell C22 | = (1*B5) formula for units of A produced/sold |
| Cell C23 | = (1*C5) formula for units of B produced/sold |
| Cell C24 | = (1*D5) formula for units of C produced/sold |
| Cell D17 | 300000 (i.e. maximum hours available in Dept 1) |
| Cell D18 | 400000 (i.e. maximum hours available in Dept 2) |
| Cell D19 | 20000 (i.e. minimum units of A to be produced/sold) |
| Cell D20 | 20000 (i.e. minimum units of B to be produced/sold) |
| Cell D21 | 20000 (i.e. minimum units of C to be produced/sold) |
| Cell D22 | 70000 (i.e. maximum units of A to be produced/sold) |
| Cell D23 | 70000 (i.e. maximum units of B to be produced/sold) |
| Cell D24 | 70000 (i.e. maximum units of C to be produced/sold) |

The completed spreadsheet should appear in **Exhibit 11.4** but it should be noted that different presentations and layouts are acceptable.

EXHIBIT 11.4: EXCEL SPREADSHEET FOR ROSCOMMON LTD

|  | A | B | C | D |
|---|---|---|---|---|
| 1 | Roscommon Ltd | | | |
| 2 | | | | |
| 3 | | | | |
| 4 | | Product A | Product B | Product C |
| 5 | Changing cells | 0 | 0 | 0 |
| 6 | | | | |
| 7 | Unit contribution | 9 | 10 | 5 |
| 8 | | | | |
| 9 | Using Dept 1 hrs | 2 | 2 | 1 |
| 10 | Using Dept 2 hrs | 2 | 3 | 2 |
| 11 | Minimum sales | 20000 | 20000 | 20000 |
| 12 | Maximum sales | 70000 | 70000 | 70000 |
| 13 | | | | |
| 14 | Target cell | 0 | | |
| 15 | | | | |
| 16 | Constraints | Item | Used | Limit |
| 17 | | Dept 1 hours | = (B5*B9+C5*C9 +D5*D9) | 300000 |
| 18 | | Dept 2 hours | = (B5*B10+C5*C10 +D5*D10) | 400000 |
| 19 | | Min. sales A | = (1*B5) | 20000 |
| 20 | | Min. sales B | = (1*C5) | 20000 |
| 21 | | Min. sales C | = (1*D5) | 20000 |
| 22 | | Max. sales A | = (1*B5) | 70000 |
| 23 | | Max. sales B | = (1*C5) | 70000 |
| 24 | | Max. sales C | = (1*D5) | 70000 |

The Excel input describes the decision situation in terms of three essential aspects of decision-making under scarce resources, i.e.:

(a) the decision variables, i.e. products A, B and C, which are labeled in Cells B4, C4 and D4, together with their physical values to be obtained from the optimal solution, which will be presented in cells B5, C5 and D5, when Solver is run;

(b) the objective function value (referred to as the target cell), i.e. the monetary value of the optimal solution, which will be presented in cell B14 (and the label is indicated in cell A14);

(c) the explicit constraints, which are labeled in cells B17 to B24, together with amounts to be used (cells C17 to C24), and the limit/maximum values of these scarce resources (cells D17 to D24).

*Running Solver*

The second stage is to use Solver to compute the optimal solution. We need to click on **Tools** and **Solver** to activate and proceed as follows:

1. We **Set (the) Target Cell** at the top of the Dialog box. This Target Cell is represented by Cell B 14 and corresponds to the monetary value of the objective function, based on the optimal mix of products. (When entering the data, we have already entered in this cell a formula relating to the number of units in the optimal solutions multiplied by the respective unit contributions.)
2. Next move to the 'Equal to' row and click on '**Max**' (to maximise) in order to indicate that we want to maximise the value of the objective function, rather than, say, minimise the costs involved.
3. We need to define the decision variables (three products in this case) that Solver will change or adjust to provide an optimal solution. Thus, in the '**By Changing Cells**' box we enter the reference to the cells which refer to the number of units of each product – in this case we enter simply – Cells B5:D5. Please note that these cell values must be related to the target cell.
4. Next we need to add the constraints. This is done by clicking on the '**Add**' button which will cause the Add Constraint dialog box to appear. The constraints should be added, one at a time. The 'Cell reference' area represents the formula for the left hand side (LHS) of the constraint, i.e. the amount to be used, based on the optimal solution. These values should be less than or equal to the right hand side (RHS) of the boundary values. Thus, for example, C17 ≤ D17 and press OK when entered, and this is followed by C18 ≤ D18 (OK) and C19 ≤ D19 (OK). Make sure that all eight constraints are entered (referring to cells C17 to C24 inclusive). However, please note that, due to space restrictions, only six constraints are listed in the screen shot below. After adding values for the last constraint, click 'OK', which will return you to the Solver Parameters dialog box and your screen should appear as follows:

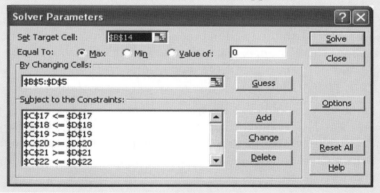

5. Next click '**Options**' in the Solver parameters dialog box and here select both 'Assume Linear Model' and 'Assume Non-Negative' and click 'OK'. This will return you to the Solver parameters box.
6. Now click on '**Solve**' at the top RHS and a Solver results box will appear. Here click all two RHS reports, i.e. 'Answer' and 'Sensitivity'. Thus, in addition to the solution, you will be provided with two separate reports which are useful in interpreting the overall solution. Then click 'OK'. The initial spreadsheet will now change to reflect the optimal solution and is reproduced below:

## Identification of Optimal Solution (Physical and Monetary)

Roscommon

| | A | B | C | D | E |
|---|---|---|---|---|---|
| 1 | Roscommon Limited | | | | |
| 2 | | | | | |
| 3 | | | | | |
| 4 | | Product A | Product B | Product C | |
| 5 | Changing cells | 65000 | 70000 | 30000 | |
| 6 | | | | | |
| 7 | Unit contribution | 9 | 10 | 5 | |
| 8 | | | | | |
| 9 | Using Dept 1 hrs | 2 | 2 | 1 | |
| 10 | Using Dept 2 hrs | 2 | 3 | 2 | |
| 11 | Minimum sales | 20000 | 20000 | 20000 | |
| 12 | Maximum sales | 70000 | 70000 | 70000 | |
| 13 | | | | | |
| 14 | Target cell | 1435000 | | | |
| 15 | | | | | |
| 16 | Constraints | Item | Used | Limit | |
| 17 | | Dept 1 hrs | 300000 | 300000 | |
| 18 | | Dept 2 hrs | 400000 | 400000 | |
| 19 | | Min. sales A | 65000 | 20000 | |
| 20 | | Min. sales B | 70000 | 20000 | |
| 21 | | Min. sales C | 30000 | 20000 | |
| 22 | | Max. sales A | 65000 | 70000 | |
| 23 | | Max. sales B | 70000 | 70000 | |
| 24 | | Max. sales C | 30000 | 70000 | |
| 25 | | | | | |
| 26 | | | | | |

The 'answer report' (**Exhibit 11.5**) indicates the value of the objective function is €1.435 million. This is the maximum contribution which can be generated by the optimal production plan, which is the production of 65,000 units of A, 70,000 units of B and 30,000 units of C.

The 'answer report' also indicates the 'slack' or surplus values associated with the various constraints. For resources that are fully used, indicated as *binding* according to the optimal solution, the slack will be zero. In this case, the machine hours in both Departments 1 and 2 are fully used. Also the maximum sales limit of B (70,000 units) has been reached.

## Exhibit 11.5: Excel Answer Report

| Target Cell (Max) | | | | |
|---|---|---|---|---|
| **Cell** | **Name** | | **Find Value** | *Monetary value of optimal solution* |
| $B$14 | Target Cell Product A | | 1435000 | |

| Adjustable Cells | | | | |
|---|---|---|---|---|
| **Cell** | **Name** | | **Find Value** | *Optimal mix of products* |
| $B$5 | Changing cells Product A | | 65000 | |
| $D$5 | Changing cells Product B | | 70000 | |
| $D$5 | Changing cells Product C | | 30000 | |

| Constraints | | | | *Indicates if constraint is binding or slack* |
|---|---|---|---|---|
| **Cell** | **Name** | **Cell Value** | **Formula** | **Status & slack** |
| $C$17 | Dept 1 hours used | 300000 | $C$17<=$D$17 | Binding = 0 |
| $C$18 | Dept 2 hours used | 400000 | $C$18<=$D$18 | Binding = 0 |
| $C$19 | Min. sales A used | 65000 | $C$19>=$D$19 | Not binding = 45000 |
| $C$20 | Min. sales B used | 70000 | $C$20>=$D$20 | Not binding = 50,000 |
| $C$21 | Min. sales C used | 30000 | $C$21>=$D$21 | Not binding = 10000 |
| $C$22 | Max. sales A used | 65000 | $C$22<=$D$22 | Not binding = 5000 |
| $C$23 | Max. sales B used | 70000 | $C$23<=$D$23 | Binding = 0 |
| $C$24 | Max. sales C used | 70000 | $C$24<=$D$24 | Non-binding = 40000 |

None of the other constraints are binding – a fact reflected in positive slack values in all the remaining rows and highlighted as '***non binding***'. For example, in relation to the maximum sales quota of 70,000 units of Product C, we produce only 30,000 units which provide a slack or surplus amount of 40,000 units.

### Sensitivity Analysis

Another report generated is referred to as the 'sensitivity report'. The information contained in this section is highly relevant to the decision process because of the certainty implied by our mathematical model. Yet certainty is a luxury rarely experienced by the modern manager. Rather, uncertainty is the norm and usually prompts the question 'what if'? These 'what if' questions serve as a useful introduction to the role of sensitivity analysis. Sensitivity analysis is concerned with how possible changes or errors in the input variables affect the optimal solution. In other words, how responsive is the optimal solution to changes in the input data? As such, sensitivity analysis can serve as an important aid in improving the basis for managerial decisions. It also provides guidance for allocating resources to additional data collection such as improving the accuracy of some of the specific numbers utilised in the model.

Information for sensitivity analysis initially starts with the consideration of the coefficients in the objective function, which represent the contribution per unit from each product. These contributions (€9, €10 and €5 for A, B and C, respectively) represent current best estimate values for unit selling prices less variable unit costs. Changes in the value of either of these elements may or may not affect the (physical) optimal solution and the value of the objective function.

The 'adjustable cells' section of the Sensitivity Analysis Report (**Exhibit 11.6**) indicates the ranges of the objective function coefficients within which the optimal solution remains valid. The columns 'Allowable increase' and 'Allowable decrease' indicate by how much the current contribution of each product may be increased or decreased without changing the physical mix of the optimal production plan, while all other variables in the model remain unchanged. For example, the optimal solution, based on a €5 unit contribution from Product C, is highly sensitive to a change in unit contribution in excess of €0.50 (upwards or downwards). In other words, if the change in unit contribution is more than 50c (in either direction) the optimal mix will change. In this context, it may be beneficial to spend additional resources in obtaining better estimates of the contribution margin of Product C. On the other hand the unit contribution of Product B can increase to infinity without affecting the optimal production plan. However, the unit contribution of Product B can decrease by up to 50c per unit without changing the optimal mix of products. Obviously as the unit contribution of any product varies within this 'allowable increase/allowable decrease' so will the total contribution associated with the optimal solution change. However, the physical quantities in the optimal solution remain the same within these unit contribution ranges.

In addition, the sensitivity report provides us with information on shadow prices. The shadow price indicates the increase in total contribution (i.e. the objective function value), if a marginal unit of scarce resource becomes available, while all other factors are held constant. (Conversely, these shadow prices represent the decrease in profit association with only one less unit of this resource available.) Thus, if an additional machine hour was available or could be acquired in Department 1, total contribution would increase by €4 – the shadow or dual price. One additional machine hour in Department 2 would increase overall profit by €0.50. Thus, shadow prices represent an internal opportunity cost to the company represented by the contribution foregone for want of an extra unit of a specified scarce resource. Accordingly, the company would be prepared to pay a maximum premium (over and above the existing variable cost per unit for that

EXHIBIT 11.6: EXCEL SENSITIVITY REPORT

**Adjustable Cells**

| Cell | Name | Final Value | Reduced Cost | Objective Coefficient | Allowable Increase | Allowable Decrease |
|---|---|---|---|---|---|---|
| $B$5 | Changing cells Product A | 65000 | 0 | 9 | 1 | 4 |
| $C$5 | Changing cells Product B | 70000 | 0 | 10 | Infinity | 0.5 |
| $D$5 | Changing cells Product C | 30000 | 0 | 5 | 0.5 | 0.5 |

*Ranges within which the physical mix of optimal solution will not change*

**Constraints**

| Cell | Name | Final Value | Shadow Price | Constraint R.H. Side | Allowable Increase | Allowable Decrease |
|---|---|---|---|---|---|---|
| $C$17 | Dept 1 hours used | 300000 | 4 | 300000 | 5000 | 40000 |
| $C$18 | Dept 2 hours used | 400000 | 0.5 | 400000 | 40000 | 10000 |
| $C$19 | Min. sales A used | 65000 | 0 | 20000 | 45000 | Infinity |
| $C$20 | Min. sales B used | 70000 | 0 | 20000 | 50000 | Infinity |
| $C$21 | Min. sales C used | 30000 | 0 | 20000 | 10000 | Infinity |
| $C$22 | Max. sales A used | 65000 | 0 | 70000 | Infinity | 5000 |
| $C$23 | Max. sales B used | 70000 | 0.5 | 70000 | 10000 | 10000 |
| $C$24 | Max. sales C used | 70000 | 0 | 30000 | Infinity | 40000 |

*Shadow price indicates financial impact of a marginal unit*

resource), equivalent to the shadow price, to acquire an additional unit of scarce resource. It should be stressed that the premium is over and above the existing variable cost in the case of inputs. A zero shadow price indicates that the relevant constraint is not binding and is reflected by slack variables. Thus, there is no benefit to the firm to be gained from acquiring an additional unit of resource that is currently in surplus. The impact on total contribution is nil.

It is important to note that shadow prices are valid provided the relevant constraints are varied individually and this represents one of the limitations of linear programming. In addition, the interpretation and use of dual prices must be restricted to a specific range in values, since they are valid only within this range. The appropriate range appears on the Sensitivity Analysis Report (**Exhibit 11.6**) in the 'allowable increase' and 'allowable decrease' columns. Thus, the shadow price of €4 per unit of machine hour in Department 1 is valid for an allowable increase of 5,000 hours and an allowable decrease of 40,000 hours. Therefore, if an additional 3,000 machine hours in Department 1 could be made available, then total contribution would be increased by €12,000 (3,000 hours × €4). If an additional 6,000 machine hours became available, then the dual price is no longer valid due to the relevant range assumption being violated.

For the maximum sales quota of Product C of 70,000 units, the relevant constraint is inactive, indicated by the zero shadow price. Hence, if the maximum sales quota of Product C could be increased by any amount, the constraint will still remain inactive and the dual price will stay at zero. There is no benefit to management if this sales constraint is removed, and any managerial activity in trying to do so is worthless.

2.  The second requirement of this (Roscommon) illustration involves specific questions relating to sensitivity analysis and the specific impact of the following independent events:

(a) Selling price of A reduced from €20 to €18, i.e. by €2
    The reduction in contribution per unit is within the allowable range and the physical mix of products remains unchanged. However, profits would be reduced by €130,000, i.e. 65,000 units × €2.

(b) Selling price of B increased from €25 to €27
    The increased contribution per unit of €2 is within allowable range and the physical mix of products remains unchanged. However, profits would increase by €140,000, i.e. 70,000 × €2.

(c) Minimum sales quota for A is eliminated
    The elimination of the minimum production quota for Product A will have no financial or physical impact as the company is already producing in excess of minimum quota.

(d) Maximum sales quota for B is increased by 5,000 units
    Profit will increase by €2,500, i.e. 5,000 units × €0.50 each. Because of extra capacity, the physical mix of products will change. However, we can only comment on the additional contribution, based on the information provided. We do not know the physical impact.

In summary, sensitivity analysis can answer the following three important questions in relation to linear programming:

- What is the impact (physical and financial) of a change in unit contribution?
- What is the value of one extra unit of the relevant right-hand side constraint?
- Within what range is the shadow price valid?

Based on sensitivity analysis, the decision-maker has three options:

1. to implement the optimal solution with its specific production plan;
2. to adopt a different production plan based on sensitivity analysis; or
3. to acquire additional information to provide better estimates of the input data.

This final alternative is particularly appropriate where the objective coefficient ranges are extremely tight and/or where the allowable increases or decreases in the constraints are also small.

It is important to note the limitations of linear programming. The first limitation is whether our mathematical model adequately represents the real world? In other words, can complex business problems be reduced to a single maximisation objective function? Secondly, linear programming incorporates various constraints on managerial behaviour whereas it can be argued that managers should be proactive in trying to remove limiting factors rather than accepting them as implied in the mathematical model. Thirdly, non-quantifiable factors are overlooked, especially the important behavioural dimension. For example, the optimal solution may not be acceptable to sales managers who earn, for example, commission based on the number of products sold. They may not be happy with an optimal solution which requires that the production of certain products be curtailed. Therefore, the optimal solution generated by the technique of linear programming should be interpreted with caution.

To sum up, modern computer software makes linear programming an efficient method of determining the optimal solution when the decision-maker is faced with a number of limiting factors. The objective function is usually specified in terms of maximising profits (or minimising costs) but it is difficult to reduce complex business problems to a single objective function. Linear programming models also include constraints facing a company. However, it is important to understand the financial implications of having additional or fewer units of this scarce resource available. Likewise, it is important to understand the consequences of changes in the unit contribution of each of the products. In the next chapter, we turn our attention to the topic of risk and uncertainty in decision-making. In other words, how should managers cope with the possibility that their predictions may not materialise with 100% accuracy?

## Summary of Learning Objectives

**Learning Objective 1:** Differentiate between a limiting factor and a constraint.

A limiting factor represents a physical constraint imposed on a decision situation. These limiting factors could be shortage of machine running hours or availability of labour hours. In a manufacturing firm, limiting factors will restrict the firm in producing all the products that it would like and for which demand exists. A **constraint** can be described as a voluntary restriction accepted by managers. For example, if maximum sales are agreed, then managers will not, voluntarily, produce in excess of this limit since profits would not be maximised. A firm generates profits (and therefore operating cash flow) by selling products rather than overproducing and placing such excess production in inventory.

**Learning Objective 2:** Calculate contribution per limiting factor.

The contribution per limiting factor is a crucial calculation when decision-makers face restrictions. It is calculated by computing the unit contribution and then dividing this by the input of scarce resource required to generate that unit contribution. Effectively, contribution per limiting factor is a ratio of efficiency and is used to rank products in determining the optimal production plan.

**Learning Objective 3:** Apply the graphic approach to profit maximisation.

Where a firm has only two products then the optimal solution can be computed using the graphic approach. The graphic approach will identify the feasible region, and the optimal solution (where the firm seeks to maximise profits) will always be one of the corner points of the feasible region. The optimal solution will be determined by the slope of the iso-profit line which is the line of the respective unit contributions of the two products.

**Learning Objective 4:** Apply the linear programming technique and interpret optimal solution.

Linear programming can now be applied using, for example, 'Solver' in Excel. Linear programming begins by specifying the objective function which is based on the unit contribution of all the available products. Also, linear programming requires the related limiting factors and constraints to be identified so that an optimal solution can be identified. One advantage of linear programming, using Solver, is that subsidiary statistics are automatically generated with which to perform sensitivity analysis.

**Learning Objective 5:** Describe the importance of sensitivity analysis.

The optimal solution is based on assumptions regarding, for example, unit contributions and the availability of scarce resources. Sensitivity analysis can be described as 'what if' analysis and presents the financial consequences of changing either unit contribution or the availability of scarce resources. Binding constraints are associated with positive dual prices. The limitation of sensitivity analysis is that only one variable can be flexed at a time.

## Questions

### Review Questions

(See Appendix One for Solutions to Review Questions **11.1** and **11.2**)

*Question 11.1: (Contribution per Limiting Factor)*

The management of **Bayview Ltd** is frequently faced with the problem of what products to manufacture, given that some input resources may be in scarce supply during the forthcoming period. You are provided with the following information of its three products:

| Item | Product A | Product B | Product C |
|------|-----------|-----------|-----------|
| Machine hours required per unit | 12 | 10 | 16 |
| Labour hours required per unit | 2 | 12 | 8 |
| Material cost per unit | €24 | €45 | €42 |
| Labour hour rate | €2 | €3 | €4 |
| Variable overhead rate per hour | €1 | €3 | €2 |
| Fixed overhead per unit | €10 | €15 | €9 |
| Sales price per unit | €35 | €150 | €110 |

**Requirements:**

1.  In what order of priority should the products be produced when:

    (a)  Adequate amounts of machine capacity is available but labour is scarce
    (b)  Adequate amounts of labour is available but machine capacity is scarce.

**Note**: in both of the above cases, the limiting factor imposed makes it impossible to manufacture all products to meet the demand available.

2.  Briefly outline the limitations associated with the above calculations.

*Question 11.2 (Contribution per Limiting Factor (CpLF))*

The potential impact of genetically modified organisms (GMOs) in the future is enormous but the issue is also very controversial. For example, scientists are developing a GM grass that will not grow beyond a particular height, thus making the mowing of lawns no longer necessary. The adverse effect of this is that many middle-aged men will no longer get their weekly exercise performing this necessary gardening chore! Scientists are also developing GM drought-resistant crops, which are meant to help farmers cope in an increasingly water-scarce world.

While the EU has dithered, other parts of the world have forged ahead with GM crops and the technology is now accepted in more than 20 countries. On one estimate,

GMOs made up more than half of the world's soya crop by area, a quarter of its corn and over one-tenth of its cotton. According to the UN health agency, GM foods are unlikely to pose greater health risks than their conventional counterparts. However, it is accepted that some consumers have remained sceptical, and the use of genetically modified organisms (GMOs) may involve potential risks for human health since some of the genes used in GMOs have not been in the food chain before. Typically in GMO foods scientists have changed DNA sequences in the genetic makeup of a plant to add a specific trait, such as insect resistance, from another organism.

Since genetically modified foods were first introduced in the mid-1990s, the list of those marketed internationally has grown to include strains of maize, soybeans, potatoes, rice and tomatoes. It is now estimated that GM crops cover almost 4% of total global arable land. The United States planted about 60% of the world's total transgenic crop area with Argentina in second place with 20% followed by Canada and Brazil with 6% each.

Ben Johnson Limited is a company located in Puxi and manufactures four different types of consumer product, made from GM soya beans. Information on the estimated selling price and cost per unit is as follows:

|  | A € | B € | C € | D € |
|---|---|---|---|---|
| Unit selling price | 20 | 40 | 30 | 35 |
| Direct materials (variable) | (7) | (20) | (15) | (15) |
| Direct labour (variable) | (3) | (6) | (3) | (4) |
| Variable overheads | (2) | (4) | (3) | (2) |
| Contribution per unit | 8 | 10 | 9 | 14 |

The regular supplier of the GM Soya bean ingredient (raw material) is based in the US and the imported GM materials must pass very stringent government regulations but importation is allowed. This is a very time-consuming process. As a result, the management of Ben Johnson Limited realise that they will be unable to purchase more than €77,000 worth of materials per month for the foreseeable future.

Management realise this will result in curtailment of production and sales. However, they have already signed legally-binding contracts with various customers to supply 1,000 units of each product for the next month. After providing for these minimum quantities, management want to use any remaining raw materials in the most profitable manner possible. Total fixed costs per month amount to €30,000.

**Requirement:** You are required to compute the quantities of each product which the company should produce next month, bearing in mind the restricted supply of raw materials. In addition, you should prepare a summarised profit budget based on your optimal production plan.

## Intermediate Questions

*Question 11.3: (Contribution per Limiting Factor)*

The LF Company Limited is engaged in the manufacture of three products: A, B and C, for the household consumer market which are sold to customers at selling prices of €26, €37 and €22 (excluding VAT) for A, B and C respectively.

The following information has been provided to you in relation to the three products and which are considered representative of the next accounting period:

| | Product A | Product B | Product C |
|---|---|---|---|
| Cost data per unit | € | € | € |
| Direct materials | 6 | 8 | 3 |
| Direct labour (variable) | 4 | 7 | 5 |
| Variable production overhead costs | 4 | 7 | 5 |
| Variable selling costs (commission) | 2 | 1 | 3 |
| Fixed production overhead (total) €80,000 | | | |
| Fixed selling and Admin. Costs (total) €20,000 | | | |

The direct material cost is based on a single raw material and is used in all three products. Direct labour is considered a variable cost. In addition, each product is the responsibility of a separate sales agent, who is partly remunerated on the basis of sales commission and this commission is paid at the rate of €2, €1, and €3 per unit for products A, B, and C respectively.

While planning production schedules for each product for next year it is noted that imported raw material now faces a problem of quota restrictions imposed by the sole supplier and a long lead-time for delivery. Orders for raw materials are placed about one year in advance and the supply of raw materials cannot be increased for the current year (20x1). The raw material quota for next year is 42,500kgs, equivalent to €85,000.

The sales manager considers that, based on last year's performance, it would not be possible to sell more than 6,000 units of each product during the forthcoming year. The general manager remembers attending some lectures on optimal production plans some years ago at college but he could not now remember the specific details. He has asked your assistance.

**Requirements:**

1. Assuming profit maximisation, prepare the optimal production plan and related total contribution and profit.
2. Briefly discuss the role of 'sensitivity analysis' in the context of the above decision. Highlight your answer with reference to **increasing** the unit contribution of Product B.

3. What is the maximum price the company could pay to acquire an extra 30 kgs of raw material? Explain your reasoning in terms of out of pocket cash costs and opportunity costs.
4. Suggest reasons why the various sales agents in this situation may be happy or unhappy to comply with your optimal production plan in (2) above.
5. The computation of the optimal production plan does not appear to take into consideration the complementary demand between the products. To what extent does this make the optimal production plan unreliable, and how could the complementary demand be included in your computation? You do not need to rework your figures.

## Question 11.4: (Decision-making with Scarce Resources)

The Shannon Assembly Company produces and sells three products, which it assembles from components, supplied by its sister company in China. The cost data related to these products for the six months ended 30 September are projected as follows:

|  | Unit Cost Data | | |
|---|---|---|---|
|  | A | B | C |
|  | € | € | € |
| Selling price | 50 | 76 | 66 |
| Cost of components | (12) | (20) | (14) |
| Labour | (16) | (32) | (24) |
| Variable overhead | (10) | (8) | (16) |

The components cost the Shannon Company €2 each. Therefore, product A requires six components, B requires 10 components and C requires seven components. In addition, each direct labour hour costs €8 and labour is considered a variable cost with respect to volume changes.

Fixed overheads are estimated at €39,000 for the six-month period ended 30 September. After the initial sales budget has been drawn up, the Chinese Company announce that the maximum supply of components available during the six-month period will be 48,000 units.

## Requirements:

1. Calculate CpLF and identify the most profitable way to utilise the resources available to the company during the six-month period. You can assume that there is unlimited demand for all three products.
2. Calculate the Break-even Point (in sales units) of the option identified by you.
3. If the maximum demand for each of Products A, B and C for the six months ended 30 September is estimated at 4,000 units each, calculate the optimal production plan if the company wishes to maximise its profits and state what the profit would be.
4. Distinguish between quantitative and qualitative factors in decision-making, using examples to illustrate your answer.

## Question 11.5: (Graphic Approach to Limiting Factors)

The Lindo Graphic Company aims to maximise its profits. In one factory, it manufactures two liquid products called Alpha and Beta. Each is a mix of readily-available ingredients, which passes through three successive processes of heating, blending and cooling. Based on existing information the amount of processing time is limited to 3,000 hours in **each** of the three departments. These hours are not interchangeable between processes due to the separate nature of the three processes. The limited availability of processing hours in each process cannot be removed for the forthcoming accounting period.

Lindo's management accountant has prepared the following up-to-date (unit) information for the two products:

|  | Alpha € | Beta € |
| --- | --- | --- |
| Selling price per unit | 25 | 30 |
| Direct materials per unit | (15) | (17) |
| Variable processing overheads: |  |  |
| Heating process | (4) | (1) |
| Blending process | (1) | (5) |
| Cooling process | (2) | (3) |
| Contribution per unit | 3 | 4 |

Variable processing overheads are absorbed at the rate of €1 per machine processing hour. Thus, product Alpha requires four hours in the heating department, one hour in blending, etc.

**Requirement:** Identify Lindo's optimal production plan and related contribution.

## Question 11.6: (Application and Interpretation of Linear Programming)

The RB Company Limited produces two products, referred to as Red and Blue. These products have a unit contribution of €8 and €6 respectively. Both products require the input of three components, namely, X, Y and Z. Each Red requires three components of X and three components of Y. Each Blue requires two components of X and four components of Y. However, the supply of both component X and Y is restricted to 480 and 600 components respectively. In addition, the production of Red and Blue is also limited by the availability of material Z. Each Red requires 0.5 units of Z and each Blue requires one unit of Z. It is estimated that 140 units of Z will be available in the forthcoming accounting period.

The market demand for both Red and Blue exceeds the production limit imposed by the limited availability of these raw materials.

You are aware that the management accountant has formulated and solved this problem using Linear programming (Solver in Excel). However, only the computer printout is to hand (attached overleaf) and the accountant is not available to answer questions from the management at the forthcoming meeting.

**Requirements:** Answer the following questions, based on the output of the LP model for this problem.

1. What is the maximum number of components of X, Y and Z available during the period?
2. What is the current contribution margin for Red and Blue respectively?
3. What is the optimal solution in terms of units of Red and Blue produced and the related contribution?
4. What would be the impact on profits if one extra X were available? One extra unit of Y?
5. How many units of Z are available? Are all these units being used?
6. What is the range within which the contribution of Red can fluctuate without changing the optimal mix of products?
7. For what range of Y will its shadow prices remain valid?
8. Briefly explain which is the most binding factor on the company, at present.

SOLVER PRINTOUT FOR RB COMPANY

|  | Product Red | Product Blue |  |
|---|---|---|---|
| **Changing cells** | 120 | 60 | |
| **Unit contribution** | 8 | 6 | |
| **Using units of X** | 3 | 2 | |
| **Using units of Y** | 3 | 4 | |
| **Using units of Z** | 0.5 | 1 | |
| **Target cell** | 1320 | | |
| **Constraints** | Item | Units used | Max units available |
| | Units of X | 480 | 480 |
| | Units of Y | 600 | 600 |
| | Units of Z | 120 | 140 |

ANSWER REPORT

| Cell | Name | Value | | | |
|---|---|---|---|---|---|
| $B$13 | Target cell | 1320 | | | |
| Adjustable Cells | | | | | |
| Cell | Name | Value | | | |
| $B$5 | Changing Red | 120 | | | |

| $C$5 | Changing Blue | 60 | | | |

## Constraints

| Cell | Name | Cell Value | Formula | Status | Slack |
|---|---|---|---|---|---|
| $C$17 | Units of X used | 480 | $C$17<=$D$17 | Binding | 0 |
| $C$18 | Units of Y used | 600 | $C$18<=$D$18 | Binding | 0 |
| $C$19 | Units of Z used | 120 | $C$19<=$D$19 | Not Binding | 20 |

### SENSITIVITY ANALYSIS REPORT

| Cell | Name | Final Value | Reduced Cost | Objective Coefficient | Allowable Increase | Allowable Decrease |
|---|---|---|---|---|---|---|
| $B$5 | Changing Red | 120 | 0 | 8 | 1 | 3.5 |
| $C$5 | Changing Blue | 60 | 0 | 6 | 4.67 | 0.67 |

| Cell | Name | Final Value | Shadow Price | Constraint R.H. Side | Allowable Increase | Allowable Decrease |
|---|---|---|---|---|---|---|
| $C$17 | Units of X used | 480 | 2.33 | 480 | 120 | 120 |
| $C$18 | Units of Y used | 600 | 0.33 | 600 | 60 | 120 |
| $C$19 | Units of Z used | 120 | 0 | 140 | infinity | 20 |

## Question 11.7: (The Application of Linear Programming)

The Managing Director of AE Company Limited is trying to plan his production activities for the forthcoming accounting period. The Company assembles computers from bought-in component parts, using a computer-controlled robotic assembly line. Highly qualified computer engineers then test the assembled computers before they are packaged for dispatch to overseas locations. The company currently produces five different computers, which are considered to be independent of each other in terms of overall demand. For simplicity purposes, these products are referred to as products A to E.

It is anticipated that AE Company will operate under a number of restrictions during the forthcoming year. For example, it is considered that the maximum demand for any computer will be 1,000 units. In addition, there are physical limitations. First, assembly hours are limited to 4,500 hours; inspection time is limited to 9,000 hours and packing hours is limited to 11,000 hours for the forthcoming period.

You are provided with the following basic information regarding each computer product:

| Product | Maximum sales units | Contribution per unit € | Assembly hours per unit | Inspection hours per unit | Packing hours per unit |
|---------|---------------------|-------------------------|-------------------------|---------------------------|------------------------|
| A | 1,000 | 24 | 2 | 2 | 4 |
| B | 1,000 | 15 | 3 | 1 | 2 |
| C | 1,000 | 24 | 12 | 6 | 8 |
| D | 1,000 | 15 | 1 | 3 | 1 |
| E | 1,000 | 39 | 8 | 8 | 6 |

The total amount of fixed costs is expected to amount to €30,000 during the forthcoming period but they are not included in the above table.

You have also been provided with a computer printout (using Solver) showing the result of the LP model, based on the above data. (This printout is shown below.)

**Requirements:** Answer the following based on the output of the LP model provided:

1. How many units of A, B, C, D and E will be produced based on the optimal solution?
2. What is the monetary value of objective function?
3. Which is the most binding limiting factor/constraint? Explain your answer.
4. What would be the impact on profits if
   (a) One extra Assembly hour was available?
   (b) One extra Inspection hour was available?
   (c) One extra Packing hour was available?
5. How many inspection hours are actually used?
6. What is the physical and monetary impact if the selling price of 'A' increases by €10?
7. What is the monetary impact if 100 additional Assembly hours are available?
8. What is the BEP in total units, based on the constant product mix of the optimal solution?
9. Briefly list four limitations of using LP in managerial decision-making.

## SOLVER PRINTOUT FOR AE COMPANY

|  | Cell | Name |  | Value |  |  |
|---|---|---|---|---|---|---|
| **Target Cell (Max)** | $B$13 | Target cell |  | 46500 |  |  |
| **Adjustable Cells** | **Cell** | **Name** |  | **Value** |  |  |
|  | $B$5 | Changing A |  | 1000 |  |  |
|  | $C$5 | Changing B |  | 500 |  |  |
|  | $D$5 | Changing C |  | 0 |  |  |
|  | $E$5 | Changing D |  | 1000 |  |  |
|  | $F$5 | Changing E |  | 0 |  |  |
| **Constraints** | **Cell** | **Name** | **Cell Value** |  | **Status** | **Slack** |
|  | $C$17 | Ass hrs | 4500 |  | Binding | 0 |
|  | $C$18 | Insp hrs | 5500 |  | Not Binding | 3500 |
|  | $C$19 | Packing hrs | 6000 |  | Not Binding | 5000 |
|  | $C$20 | Max sales A | 1000 |  | Binding | 0 |
|  | $C$21 | Max sales B | 500 |  | Not Binding | 500 |
|  | $C$22 | Max sales C | 500 |  | Not Binding | 500 |
|  | $C$23 | Max sales D | 0 |  | Not Binding | 1000 |
|  | $C$24 | Max sales E | 1000 |  | Binding | 0 |

## SENSITIVITY REPORT

| Adjustable Cells | Cell | Name | Final Value |  | Objective Coefficient | Allowable Increase | Allowable Decrease |
|---|---|---|---|---|---|---|---|
|  | $B$5 | Changing A | 1000 |  | 24 | 1E+30 | 14 |
|  | $C$5 | Changing B | 500 |  | 15 | 21 | 0.38 |
|  | $D$5 | Changing C | 0 |  | 24 | 36 | 1E+30 |
|  | $E$5 | Changing D | 1000 |  | 15 | 1E+30 | 10 |
|  | $F$5 | Changing E | 0 |  | 39 | 1 | 1E+30 |
| **Constraints** | **Cell** | **Name** | **Final Value** | **Shadow Price** | **Constraint R.H. Side** | **Allowable Increase** | **Allowable Decrease** |
|  | $C$17 | Ass hours | 4500 | 5 | 4500 | 1500 | 1500 |
|  | $C$18 | Insp hours | 5500 | 0 | 9000 | 1E+30 | 3500 |
|  | $C$19 | Pack hours | 6000 | 0 | 11000 | 1E+30 | 5000 |
|  | $C$20 | Max sales A | 1000 | 14 | 1000 | 750 | 750 |
|  | $C$21 | Max sales B | 500 | 0 | 1000 | 1E+30 | 500 |
|  | $C$22 | Max sales C | 500 | 0 | 1000 | 1E+30 | 500 |
|  | $C$23 | Max sales D | 0 | 0 | 1000 | 1E+30 | 1000 |
|  | $C$24 | Max sales E | 1000 | 10 | 1000 | 1312.5 | 1000 |

## Advanced Questions

*Question 11.8: (Decision-making with Scarce Resources)*

Merrion Products Limited is a company owned by the Carroll family. The company manufactures hand-made chocolate biscuits from imported South American cocoa which it sells to a small number of large retail outlets. Initially, a plain chocolate biscuit (Type A) was manufactured and resulting profits were adequate to satisfy the family shareholders. A few years ago, it was decided to introduce new products based on the same cocoa but refined in different ways to suit different Irish tastes. These products, in various sizes, can be referred to as Type B, C and D respectively. The company is now the brand leader in the segment for home-made, quality biscuits made from real cocoa and the company has always been able to meet demand.

According to the audited financial statements, Merrion Products Limited was a profitable company with excellent cash flow. The various family members concentrated mainly on the administrative and selling side of the business and each family member was paid a basic salary. In addition, they shared a sales commission of 10% of total sales revenue for the year.

The Carroll family believed that the company's profitability was mainly attributable to two factors. First was the high quality of its products with guaranteed delivery dates. Michael Carroll, the managing director of the firm, often boasted that the number of customer complaints in any one year could be counted on the fingers of one hand. The second reason was due to subtle marketing and presentation so that each product was perceived by the public as different and was sold to different types of retail outlet. In other words the products were similar (in terms of ingredients and production, they were not considered complementary and had their own unique brand loyalty). Thus the sales of one product could fluctuate without affecting the sales of the other products, or the refusal of orders for one product would not lead to cancellation of orders for the others.

Each chocolate biscuit was produced from South American cocoa. Until recently this raw material was available in unlimited quantities and was purchased by Merrion quarterly in advance as required. However recent political instability in the exporting country resulted in a severe restriction on the availability of this raw material. A recent fact-finding visit to the exporting country only served to confirm the restricted availability of the imported raw material for the forthcoming year. On his return home Michael Carroll called a directors' meeting to discuss the problem and its impact on the budget for the forthcoming quarter.

Una Carroll, the only daughter in the family, filled the role of company accountant. After obtaining a business studies degree at college she immediately joined the family firm. Her role was to maintain the basic financial accounting records and keep control over accounts receivable and payable. She also monitored progress towards agreed budget targets. However, the budget setting process for each quarter was unsophisticated in that output levels were determined by amiable consensus among family members. Preference was usually given to the highest priced item since this procedure maximised sales commission for the family members. Una tried to persuade the other members of the family that there was a more scientific method available to determine best production plans. However, whenever she mentioned the phrase 'profit maximisation' in discussion her family always retorted, "But that's only theory Una and has nothing got to do with practice." Being the youngest in the family Una felt she lacked a great deal of authority and credibility.

The Carroll family felt that the business did not need a management accountant since they considered the overall operations to be fairly simple. Neither did they require the services of a production manager or a marketing manager since they could virtually sell everything they produced. Una knew from experience that as long as budgeted profit was higher than last year then everyone was happy. Generally, the actual financial performance met the budget targets pretty well.

At the start of the meeting Michael Carroll relayed to participants details of his foreign trip. He explained, "Unfortunately our worst suspicions have been confirmed. I saw things at first hand and also had discussions with our Embassy officials. I made direct contract with our usual supplier and he indicated that he will be unable to deliver more than €72,000 of raw materials per quarter until conditions improve and that's not going to be for some time. The basic problem, he tells me is that cocoa butter is not available in his country due to the current political situation and a bad harvest. Since my return home I have made extensive enquiries regarding possible alternative suppliers of the same raw material in other countries. There just isn't any which we could tap at this short notice. Like many simple problems, it's insoluble in the short-term. We've just got to accept it for now!"

Una interrupted: "I expect that our budgets for the next quarter shall have to be carefully prepared". She circulated basic cost and operating data for the forthcoming quarter, based on previous estimates, to participants (**Exhibit 1**).

EXHIBIT 1: SCHEDULE OF COST AND OPERATING DATA FOR QUARTER

| | A | B | C | D | Total |
|---|---|---|---|---|---|
| Budget sales (units) | 1,500 | 2,000 | 2,000 | 1,500 | 7,000 |
| **Product** | | | | | |
| Sales price | 20 | 40 | 30 | 20 | n/a |
| Direct material (imported) | 7 | 16 | 13 | 10 | n/a |
| Packaging costs | 3 | 4 | 6 | 4 | n/a |
| Production overhead (var) | 2 | 1 | 3 | 3 | n/a |
| Production overhead (fixed) | 2 | 4 | 3 | 2 | n/a |
| Total production cost | 14 | 25 | 25 | 19 | n/a |
| **Non-production costs:** | | | | | |
| Selling costs including commission | | | | | 25,700 |
| Administration Costs | | | | | 19,900 |
| Interest expense | | | | | 800 |
| | | | | | 46,400 |

Una continued "In my opinion there is no scope for any reduction in costs. We can't change, at least in the short term, our direct material costs. Neither can we change our packaging costs. Likewise variable production overheads will be incurred if we want to produce and our fixed overheads (both production and non-production) are already down to an absolute minimum. Sales commission is the only thing that we could effectively cut."

Michael Carroll interjected: "No, I recommend that the sales commission be left alone. We're all in this venture together and I reckon we're going to have to sell our way out of our problems. We need to retain the incentive to sell and keep our selling prices intact."

Everyone agreed. Patrick Carroll, the eldest member of the family, who was chiefly responsible for sales, raised the possibility of maximum sales levels of each product. He said, "We must take into consideration that there is a definite limit on the amount of goods which we can sell at existing prices next quarter."

Michael Carroll accepted that the point was valid. After much discussion all family members agreed that maximum sales value of each product at current prices for the forthcoming quarter would be as follows:

| Type | € |
|------|-----|
| A | 60,000 |
| B | 88,000 |
| C | 63,000 |
| D | 40,000 |

Subsequently everyone at the meeting realised that due to the definite shortage of raw materials it was not possible to produce simultaneously all these quantities. Michael Carroll added, "I think we shall have to be more selective in what we produce in future. However, I recommend that we produce a minimum of 1,000 units of each product during the forthcoming quarter. This would, at least, keep the company's products in the minds of the public and satisfy our major customers. It's important to do this. Any remaining materials should be used in the most profitable manner. Una, now is the ideal time to put some of that theory of yours into practice. If you feel that there is a single, best way to utilise our production facilities in these circumstances now is the ideal time to let us know."

**Requirements:**

1. Prepare a statement showing the most profitable production plan for Merrion Products Ltd for the forthcoming quarter. Prepare an income statement to accompany your recommendation. Explain your workings.
2. Calculate the firm's break-even point for the forthcoming quarter. What fundamental assumptions have you made?
3. What is the 'opportunity cost', if any, associated with the minimum production of 1,000 units of each product?

4. Assuming it was possible to increase all selling prices by €7 per unit without influencing demand, would this price increase impact on your analysis? Explain. (It is not necessary to rework your optimal production plan.)

*Question 11.9: (Decision-making with Scarce Resources)*

The Done Group owns a large numbers of retail stores around the country. Managers of each store are given discretion over the range of items offered for sale in their store provided they are drawn from a range of products that are purchased centrally. The manager of one store, located in the busy city centre, has asked your advice on what product lines should be sold as he is in the process of planning his counter arrangements for the coming month. There are only seven counters available in his store, each counter will hold one product group only for the month and each counter is of similar size. Monthly rent for the store amounts to €20,000. The manager is anxious to maximise profits each month and he has provided you with the following estimates of product turnover (in terms of sales per counter) and the respective contribution/sales (C/S) ratios. These figures are based on the annual figures for each product, divided by 12.

| Product | Sales (€) from each ordinary counter | Contribution/sales ratio per counter |
|---|---|---|
| Confectionery | 18,000 | 20% |
| Stationery | 4,000 | 40% |
| Clothes | 7,200 | 40% |
| DVDs | 6,000 | 50% |
| Food | 5,000 | 40% |
| Toys | 8,000 | 55% |
| Hardware | 3,000 | 40% |
| Gardening | 5,000 | 35% |

Two of the seven counters can be situated at the entrance to the store – off the main street. Products placed on entrance counters have a greater opportunity of attracting impulse buyers and it is estimated that products placed on these counters in any one month will experience double their expected turnover in that month.

The manager is not compelled to offer all product groups. He may offer the product on two different counters but not more than two. (If the same product is offered on two counters, sales from the second counter, regardless of its location, are only half the amount of those shown in the above Table.)

**Requirements:**

1. Determine the product range which the manager should offer in order to maximise his profit for the coming month and the amount of such profit. Explain briefly the process you followed to achieve this.
2. What other factors should be considered before deciding on a counter layout based strictly on such a programmed approach to decision-making?

3.  Identify a range of performance measures (financial and non-financial) that can be used to evaluate the performance of each store manager and describe how this can be distorted and/or generate inappropriate behaviour.

*Question 11.10 (Decision-making with Scarce Resources)*

Hazydays Limited is a large furniture manufacturer based in the west of Ireland. It is a family-owned business which commenced trading in the mid-1960s. Over the last 40 years the business has thrived, and now employs six skilled carpenters and trainees, and one secretarial assistant.

While most years have seen profits grow, the business has experienced some financial difficulties in the last number of years. According to the manager, these problems were caused by an attempt to manufacture too many different types of furniture and, as a result, too many labour hours, different skill-sets and material types were required. The problem reached its climax in late 2005 when over 40% of orders went unfilled and had to be cancelled. Not only did this cause a dramatic reduction in revenue for the year but many of these customers explicitly stated they would not deal with Hazydays again.

In response to the problems, the manager of Hazydays felt that drastic action had to be taken. As a result, the company has stopped producing customised furniture and the wide range of products it had previously offered. Instead, it now focuses solely on two mass-produced items, namely kitchen tables and bookshelves. There are only two main costs associated with the production, which are skilled labour and timber. Resource requirements and contribution information regarding each product are shown below:

|  | Labour (Hours/Unit) | Timber (Kgs/Unit) | Contribution (€/Unit) |
|---|---|---|---|
| Bookshelves | 1 | 40 | 40 |
| Table | 2 | 30 | 50 |

Hazydays has 40 hours of labour and 1,200kgs of timber available per day. The manager wants to know how many bookshelves and tables to produce each day in order to maximise contribution and he has asked you to resolve this problem by adopting a linear programming approach.

**Requirements:**

1.  Set out the objective function and the model constraints in a mathematical format.
2.  Draw a diagram which includes the objective function and constraints as set out in (1) and thus determine the mix of bookshelves and tables which maximises contribution.
3.  The company is finding it difficult to recruit the labour required to meet demand. In addition, the timber required is also in short supply and the company is considering the following options:

    • Using an employment agency to hire 10 extra hours of labour per day. What is the maximum that Hazydays should be willing to pay the employment agency per hour of extra labour?

**or**
- Finding a new timber supplier to supply 200kgs extra of timber per day. What is the maximum price per kg for the extra timber that Hazydays should be willing to pay?
4. Based on your calculations in (3) and assuming the options are mutually exclusive, recommend which option, i.e. extra labour or extra timber, the company should choose. Outline two other factors that should be considered before acquiring either the extra hours or the extra timber.

Source: Chartered Accountants Ireland, Management Accounting and Business Finance, P3, Summer 2007

## Question 11.11: (Decision-making with Scarce Resources)

ACF Instruments Ltd holds patents for three electronic measuring instruments, A, C and F, for all of which demand exceeds the company's ability to supply due to shortage of machine running hours in each of the company's operations departments (machining, winding and assembly). The standard costs and selling prices of the three instruments are as follows, and labour is considered a variable cost:

| Per unit data | A € | C € | F € |
|---|---|---|---|
| Selling price | 80.0 | 70.0 | 90.0 |
| Direct material | 29.4 | 17.4 | 37.0 |
| Machining labour (variable) | 9.6 | 7.2 | 8.0 |
| Winding labour (variable) | 4.8 | 6.0 | 4.2 |
| Assembly labour (variable) | 3.2 | 2.4 | 4.8 |
| Variable overhead | 3.0 | 2.0 | 3.0 |
| Fixed overhead | 12.5 | 15.6 | 14.8 |

The above data, together with various limiting factors relating to machining capacity was formulated as a linear programming model and the computer output is provided below.

### COMPUTER PRINTOUT FOR ACF COMPANY

| | |
|---|---|
| 1. Max 30A + 35C + 33F | (Objective function) |
| ST | Subject to (the following restrictions) |
| 2. 12A + 9C + 10F < 3,600 | Maximum machining hours |
| 3. 8A + 10C + 7F < 2,400 | Maximum winding hours |
| 4. 4A + 3C + 6F < 2,400 | Maximum assembly hours |
| Objective function value | €11,286 |
| A | Nil |
| C | Nil |
| F | 342 (units) |

| Row | Slack or surplus | Dual (shadow) price |
|---|---|---|
| 2. (machining) | 171 | Nil |
| 3. (winding) | Nil | 4.71 |
| 4. (assembly) | 342 | Nil |

## Sensitivity Analysis

| Variable | Current coefficient € | Allowable increase € | Allowable decrease € |
|---|---|---|---|
| A | 30.00 | 7.00 | infinity |
| C | 35.00 | 12.00 | infinity |
| F | 33.00 | infinity | 6.00 |

## Right hand side ranges

| Row | Current RHS | Allowable increase | Allowable decrease |
|---|---|---|---|
| 2. (machining) | 3,600 | infinity | 171 |
| 3. (winding) | 2,400 | 120 | 2,400 |
| 4. (assembly) | 2,400 | infinity | 342 |

**Requirements:** Answer the following based on the output of the LP model provided:

1. How many units of A, C, and F will be produced based on the optimal solution?
2. What is the value of the objective function?
3. Which of the three constraints, i.e. machining, winding and assembly hours is the most binding and why is this?
4. What is the maximum number of hours available in each of the three departments?
5. What is the current contribution margin for A, C and F?
6. What would be the impact on profits if:
   (a) One extra machining hour were available?
   (b) One extra winding hour were available?
   (c) One extra assembly hour were available?

7. How many Machining hours are being USED in production?
8. What is the absolute range (i.e. maximum and minimum contributions) within which the contribution of A can fluctuate without changing the optimal mix of products?
9. For what range of machining hours will its shadow prices remain valid?
10. What is the physical and monetary change if the unit selling price of F increases by €5?
11. What is the monetary impact if an additional 100 Winding hours are available?

*Question 11.12 (Decision-making with Scarce Resources)*

The Puxi Company is a family-run firm, with about 20 employees, which manufactures and retails a variety of consumer health foods, based on Soya beans, and the company has been in business for five years. The goods are produced in a small premises in Dublin city centre and are sold in a shop which adjoins this manufacturing unit. Mr Puxi is the Managing Director of the firm; his son Patrick oversees the manufacturing side and the other son, Peter, manages the retail activities. However, for accounting purposes both the manufacturing and retail activities are reported as a single responsibility centre and you observe that the current management accounting and information system (MAIS) is rather basic. For example, manufactured products are transferred to the retail section without any transfer price being noted or recorded. For convenience purposes the three consumer health products can be referred to as Alpha (A), Beta (B) and Cappa (C).

Soya is an excellent source of high quality protein, is low in saturated fats and is cholesterol-free. Recent research has indicated soya has several beneficial effects on health in addition to its nutritional benefits. Soya beans contain high concentrations of several compounds which have demonstrated anti-carcinogenic activity and the relatively low incidence of breast and colon cancer in China and Japan has been partially attributed to the high consumption of soya products. Soya foods include, for example, tofu, miso and soya dairy alternatives. Not surprisingly, foods containing soybeans are on sale in many Irish outlets and the increase in customer awareness of soya foods and their health benefits has had a positive impact on the market and helped boost consumption. Nevertheless, the market remains relatively immature and many Irish consumers have yet to be 'converted' to soya products. Many of those that enter the shop often require extensive information, advice and encouragement before making a purchase.

Over half of the world's soybean production occurs in the US. However, recently soybean crops have been displaced in the US to make way for more lucrative corn – the so called 'war of acreage'. It is estimated that last year American farmers planted 20% more land with corn while soybean acreage fell by about 15%. In addition, in Asia, people are consuming more meat, which means more cows require feedstuff.

The bulk of the world's soybean crop is used for animal feed – without the protein offered by soy, the world would not be able to maintain its current level of livestock productivity. This explains why demand for soybeans as feedstuff has been surging in China, already the world's largest importer. The increased demand for soybean for animal foods together with additional acreage being devoted to growing subsidised biofuels has resulted in the limited availability of soybeans.

A further complication is that over half of the world's soybean crop was genetically modified, a higher percentage than for any other crop. Genetic modifications impart resistance to insect attack, providing cost and yield improvement for the farmer and this gives a tremendous competitive advantage to those using it. Thus, in the United States – the world's largest producer – nearly 90% of its production is genetically modified (GM). Indeed, a survey of soya-based foods, including baby foods, undertaken by the Food Safety Authority of Ireland (FSAI) revealed that a majority of products tested contained genetically modified ingredients. The presence of GM in our food supply has stimulated great discussion and concern about our health, potential damage to the environment and moral debates about how this modern gene technology should be used. Some of this debate is misinformed but the practical implication is that the majority of consumers are opposed to purchasing foods that are labelled as genetically modified. In keeping with its mission of being one of Dublin leading health food shops, Puxi does NOT purchase or use GM soybeans. Indeed, soybeans are becoming more difficult to obtain and this restriction needs to be incorporated in next year's budget. In light of prevailing market conditions it was agreed that only 500,000 kgs of soybeans would be available to Puxi next year and production of some of the firm's three products would have to be curtailed accordingly.

The production process within Puxi is relatively simple. Initially, soybeans are 'pressed' to produce a liquid oil and this is done in the 'Pressing Department'. This is a machine intensive rather than a labour intensive process. In the Filling Department, the derived oil is refined for food use, bottled and packaged for sale. Again, this is a machine intensive process. Direct labour is a relatively small amount in the overall cost structure and, as a result, direct labour cost is combined with production overhead costs into a 'conversion cost' category. The final product is then transferred (without any transfer price) to the adjacent retail store. The operating costs of the retail store are entirely 'fixed' in relation to volume changes and are classified as 'selling and administration' costs. However, both production departments are operating near maximum processing capacity. After discussion it was agreed that the machine hour availability in the Pressing Department would be restricted to 3,000 hours (180,000 minutes) due to obsolete machinery and the machine hour availability in the Filling Department would be restricted to 2,000 hours (120,000 minutes) due to shortage of machine parts.

The following information is provided regarding the three products:

| Product information | Alpha (A) | Beta (B) | Cappa (C) |
|---|---|---|---|
| Selling price per unit | €20 | €26 | €38 |
| Soya bean ingredient cost @ €1 per kg | €3 | €4 | €6 |
| **Variable conversion costs *** | €6 | €8 | €12 |
| **Machine minutes required per unit:** | | | |
| Pressing dept (maximum 3,000 hours) ** | 1 minute | 1 minute | 2 minutes |
| Filling dept (maximum 2,000 hours) ** | ¾ minute | 1 minute | 1¼ minutes |

* Variable conversion costs represent variable direct labour and variable production overheads but excludes direct material cost. Fixed costs (production and non-production) are not relevant to the above production information but amount, in total, to €1 million per annum.
** Note: For availability of machine time and processing time, it is desirable that you work consistently in 'minutes'.

It was noted that contracts had already been signed to produce a minimum of 10,000 units of each product next year to a large supermarket chain, using the chain's own label. In addition, given sales growth in previous years, it was realistic to assume that a maximum of 60,000 units only of each product could be sold next year at existing prices. It was agreed that selling prices would not be changed.

After discussion and review, the various 'constraints' were presented to you and your advice, as a management consultant, was requested:

1. Supply of Soybeans is limited to 500,000kgs for next year, equivalent to a total cost of €500,000

2. Machine hours availability in the Pressing Department is restricted to 3,000 hours (180,000 minutes) next year due to obsolete machinery

3. Machine hour availability in the Filling Department is restricted to 2,000 hours (120,000 minutes) next year due to shortage of machine parts

4. Contracts have already been signed with various customers to supply a minimum of 10,000 units of each of the three products for next year. The minimum units that must be produced next year are as follows:
   Alpha (A)  >= 10,000 units
   Beta (B)    >= 10,000 units
   Cappa (C) >= 10,000 units.

5. Because no increase or decrease in selling price would be made, the maximum demand for the three products for next year was as follows:
   Alpha (A)  <= 60,000 units
   Beta (B)    <= 60,000 units
   Cappa (C) <= 60,000 units.

After looking at the information, you quickly present the above data as a Linear Programming model and run Solver. Your computer printout is attached (see **Exhibits 1 and 2**).

EXHIBIT 1

| Row | | Alpha (A) | Beta (B) | Cappa (C) |
|---|---|---|---|---|
| 1 | | | | |
| 2 | | | | |
| 3 | | Alpha (A) | Beta (B) | Cappa (C) |
| 4 | Changing cells | 60,000 units | 50,000 units | 20,000 units |
| 5 | | | | |
| 6 | Unit contribution | €11 | €14 | €20 |
| 7 | | | | |
| 8 | Using Soya (kgs) | 3 kgs | 4 kgs | 6 kgs |
| 9 | Pressing minutes | 1 minute | 1 minute | 2 minutes |
| 10 | Filling minutes | 0.75 minutes | 1 minute | 1.25 minutes |
| 11 | | | | |
| 12 | Target cell | €1,760,000 | | |
| 13 | | | | |
| 14 | | | | |
| 15 | Constraints | Item | Used | Constraint |
| 16 | | Soya (kgs) | 500,000 | 500,000 |
| 17 | | Pressing minutes | 150,000 | 180,000 |
| 18 | | Filling minutes | 120,000 | 120,000 |
| 19 | | Min. sales of A | 60,000 | 10,000 |
| 20 | | Min. sales of B | 50,000 | 10,000 |
| 21 | | Min. sales of C | 20,000 | 10,000 |
| 22 | | Max. sales of A | 60,000 | 60,000 |
| 23 | | Max. sales of B | 50,000 | 60,000 |
| 24 | | Max. sales of C | 20,000 | 60,000 |

EXHIBIT 2A: ANSWER REPORT

| Cell | Name | Final Value | | |
|------|------|-------------|---|---|
| B12 | Target cell value | €1,760,000 | | |
| Cell | Name | Final Value | | |
| B4 | Changing cells (Alpha) | 60,000 units | | |
| C4 | Changing cells (Beta) | 50,000 units | | |
| D4 | Changing cells (Cappa) | 20,000 units | | |

**Constraints**

| Cell | Name | Cell Value | Formula | Status | Slack/Surplus |
|------|------|-----------|---------|--------|---------------|
| C16 | Soya used (kgs) | 500,000 | C16<=D16 | Binding | 0 |
| C17 | Pressing minutes used | 150,000 | C17<=D17 | Not Binding | 30,000 |
| C18 | Filling minutes used | 120,000 | C18<=D18 | Binding | 0 |
| C19 | Min sales A (units) | 60,000 | C19>=D19 | Not Binding | 50,000 |
| C20 | Min sales B (units) | 50,000 | C20>=D20 | Not Binding | 40,000 |
| C21 | Min sales C (units) | 20,000 | C21>=D21 | Not Binding | 10,000 |
| C22 | Max sales A (units) | 60,000 | C22<=D22 | Binding | 0 |
| C23 | Max sales B (units) | 50,000 | C23<=D23 | Not Binding | 10,000 |
| C24 | Max sales C (units) | 20,000 | C24<=D24 | Not Binding | 40,000 |

EXHIBIT 2B: SENSITIVITY REPORT

| Cell | Name | Final Value | Objective Coefficient | Allowable Increase | Allowable Decrease |
|------|------|-------------|-----------------------|--------------------|--------------------|
| B4 | Changing cells (Alpha) | 60,000 units | 11 | Infinity | 0.50 |
| C4 | Changing cells (Beta) | 50,000 units | 14 | 0.67 | 0.67 |
| D4 | Changing cells (Cappa) | 20,000 units | 20 | 1.00 | 2.50 |

**Constraints**

| Cell | Name | Final Value | Shadow Price | Constraint R.H. Side | Allowable Increase | Allowable Decrease |
|---|---|---|---|---|---|---|
| C16 | Soya Used | 50,000 | 2.50 | 500,000 | 3,000 | 8,000 |
| C17 | Pressing hours used | 150,000 | 0.00 | 180,000 | Infinity | 30,000 |
| C18 | Filling hours used | 120,000 | 4.00 | 120,000 | 1,667 | 6,667 |
| C19 | Min sales A units | 60,000 | 0.00 | 10,000 | 50,000 | Infinity |
| C20 | Min sales B units | 50,000 | 0.00 | 10,000 | 40,000 | Infinity |
| C21 | Min sales C units | 20,000 | 0.00 | 10,000 | 10,000 | Infinity |
| C22 | Max sales A units | 60,000 | 0.50 | 60,000 | 53,333 | 13,333 |
| C23 | Max sales B units | 50,000 | 0.00 | 60,000 | Infinity | 10,000 |
| C21 | Max sales C units | 20,000 | 0.00 | 60,000 | Infinity | 40,000 |

**Requirements:**

1. Using the computer printout and your own calculations, prepare a summarised income statement in contribution format, based on the optimal solution provided.
2. Show your calculation of the annual BEP (in €), using the C/S ratio and assuming the constant product mix of the optimal production plan. What assumptions have you made?
3. Write a properly formatted memorandum to the Managing Director explaining whether a cost leadership or a product differentiation strategy would be appropriate for Puxi to follow. You should also include in your memo FOUR critical success factors (CSF) that should be used to communicate strategy throughout the company and present for each CSF an appropriate performance measure.
4. Clearly identify the impact, if any, on the optimal production plan and on profit of the following independent events and you should present your answer by way of a matrix presented below. You may simply answer whether the physical mix will 'change' or 'no change' (as appropriate) and also clearly indicate the financial impact, as appropriate:

| | Impact on physical plan (Indicate: Change or no change) | Total financial impact (Please specify €) |
|---|---|---|
| (a) Selling price of product A increased by €1 | | |
| (b) An additional supply of 1,000 kgs of Soya beans is available | | |
| (c) An additional 1,000 minutes of Pressing time becomes available | | |
| (d) An additional 1,000 minutes in Filling time becomes available | | |

5. What is the maximum price that one would pay for one extra kg of Soybean ingredient, bearing in mind that the current price is €1 per kg? Briefly explain your answer.

6. The retail manager has noticed that a price reduction of Cappa (C) by €2 per unit would increase sales by 1,000 units. Current sales of Puxi amount to 20,000 units at a price of €38. Present your calculation for a profit maximising price for Cappa for the forthcoming budget period.

Source: University College Dublin, Advanced Management Accounting, Summer 2009

# Decision-making under Risk and Uncertainty

LEARNING OBJECTIVES

When you have completed studying this chapter you should be able to:

1. Distinguish between decision-making under risk and uncertainty.
2. Construct a pay-off matrix reflecting alternatives and states of nature.
3. Calculate and discuss the concept of expected value.
4. Apply maximin, maximax, EMV and least regret criteria.
5. Prepare decision trees to reflect sequential decision situations.
6. Calculate the expected value of perfect information.

## 12.1 Introduction to Risk and Uncertainty

In this chapter we will discuss decision-making under conditions of risk and uncertainty. Coping with '**risk and uncertainty**' is a fact of life and it represents a situation whereby there is doubt regarding future events. In a perfect world there would be no uncertainties and decisions would be easier. Managers would be able to accurately predict the future and to use management accounting information to make the 'perfect' decision. However, in the real world of uncertainty, the decision-maker may forecast a demand of, say, 150,000 units but actual demand may be 100,000 or 200,000 units, or any volume in between.

Some textbooks differentiate between risk and uncertainty. Risk represents a situation in which probabilities can be reasonably assigned to potential outcomes. Thus, in relation to the outcome of a football match, we may assign a 70% probability to winning, a 20% probability to losing, and a 10% probability for a draw. Uncertainty, on the other hand, is characterised by a situation where probabilities cannot be reasonably assigned to potential outcomes. This could reflect the fact that a similar decision situation has not occurred previously. Thus, decision-making under risk and uncertainty is characterised, in general, by the situation where the decision-maker does not know which future event or future outcome will occur.

## 12.2 Decision-making under Uncertainty

It is useful to highlight several elements in a decision situation characterised by uncertainty:

- As in all decision situations, there will always be a number of alternatives available to the decision-maker. If there were no alternatives, there would be no decision to make. The decision-maker must select one of these alternatives.
- There is a set of relevant events that will affect the ultimate outcome. In management accounting, these events are referred to as '**states of nature**' and are usually outside the direct control of the decision-maker. Examples of states of nature include the level of sales demand and reaction by competitors. The states of nature are assumed to be mutually exclusive. This means that no two events can happen simultaneously. To return to our football match analogy above, the result of a football match can be a win, loss or draw but not a combination of these. In addition, it is assumed that the list of states of nature is exhaustive – only the states of nature (or events) listed can occur.
- Bearing in mind the distinction between decision alternatives and states of nature, the decision-maker can construct a pay-off matrix to facilitate the decision. A payoff matrix represents the monetary value of each unique combination of managerial decision/ alternative and particular states of nature that may occur. The alternative chosen and the states of nature determine the amount of the payoff. The completed pay-off matrix represents the total range of decision alternatives and related outcomes that can occur.

A simple pay-off matrix associated with the decision to bet on either 'heads' or 'tails' on tossing a coin is depicted in **Exhibit 12.1** below. Each decision alternative (A1 and A2) has two possible outcomes (heads or tails). Thus, there are four (2 x 2) unique combinations of decision alternative and outcomes, and each of these will have a monetary pay-off, which can be positive or negative, and these are labelled 1 to 4.

EXHIBIT 12.1: PAY-OFF MATRIX: TOSSING A COIN

| | | States of nature (outcomes) | |
| --- | --- | --- | --- |
| | | Heads | Tails |
| A1 | Bet on heads | 1 (win money) | 2 (lose money) |
| A2 | Bet on tails | 3 (lose money) | 4 (win money) |

The alternative selected by the decision-maker will depend on his attitude to uncertainty. It is usual to distinguish between three fundamentally different attitudes to uncertainty which are as follows:

1. **Maximin** This is the most conservative approach to decision-making. In this case, the objective of the decision-maker is to eliminate losses, where possible. This is done in two stages:
   (a) identify the worst or minimum pay-off associated with each alternative, and
   (b) select the best of these alternatives.

   This approach avoids the worst pay-offs. It is important to note that the maximin criterion does not make use of probabilities.

2. **Maximax** This is the most optimistic approach to decision-making. The decision-maker selects the alternative that offers the greatest pay-off. Again, like the maximin criterion, the probabilities of the various states of nature are not used.

3. **Least regret** This decision criterion is associated with the concept of opportunity cost. The decision-maker realises that there is likely to be a difference between what he predicts and the actual outturn. Thus, the decision-maker minimises this difference by using the least regret criterion. This criterion is used when it is important to justify your choice afterwards in the context of accountability. To apply this criterion another pay-off matrix must be prepared in terms of opportunity cost.

   The application of the above three criteria will now be illustrated using the illustration of the Cavan Company.

## ILLUSTRATION: DECISION-MAKING UNDER UNCERTAINTY

Cavan Company produces hamburgers and the managing director is currently considering the number of hamburgers to produce for the forthcoming rugby international. Unfortunately, due to the location of the ground, the hamburgers must be produced prior to match day, and hamburgers unsold at the end of the match day must be disposed of, free of charge, to a local charity. Each hamburger will sell for €1, and the variable cost of production is estimated at €0.45 per unit. The managing director is uncertain how many units can be sold at the forthcoming match but, based on previous experience, he assumes that demand will be 10,000, 20,000, 30,000 or 40,000 units. Therefore, he must decide on whether to produce 10,000, 20,000, 30,000 or 40,000 units.

**Requirement:**

1. Prepare a monetary pay-off matrix to represent the four possible decision alternatives, i.e. the production of either 10,000, 20,000, 30,000 or 40,000 units, and the four separate states of nature.
2. What decision should be selected using the (a) Maximin, (b) Maximax, and (c) Least Regret criteria?

**Solution and Analysis:** A pay-off matrix represents the monetary pay-off associated with each alternative and each possible state of nature. There are four alternatives, each with four states of nature, thus providing 16 unique combinations which are presented in the following pay-off matrix:

PAY-OFF MATRIX

| Decision alternative ↓ | <———States of Nature (Demand)———> | | | |
|---|---|---|---|---|
| | 10,000 units | 20,000 units | 30,000 units | 40,000 units |
| A1: 10,000 units | €5,500 | €5,500 | €5,500 | €5,500 |
| A2: 20,000 units | €1,000 | €11,000 | €11,000 | €11,000 |
| A3: 30,000 units | (€3,500) | €6,500 | €16,500 | €16,500 |
| A4: 40,000 units | (€8,000) | €2,000 | €12,000 | €22,000 |

Some words of explanation and clarification are necessary. In particular, note that any excess production is penalised by having to dispose of the unsold hamburgers, free of charge and which cost €0.45 each to produce on the previous day. If, for example, 20,000 units are produced but the demand is only 10,000 units, then the payoff will be €1,000 representing sales revenue of €10,000 (10,000 units × €1) less production costs of €9,000 (20,000 units × €0.45). In addition, sales cannot exceed the number of units produced. Thus, if only 10,000 units are produced (A1), the maximum units that can be sold is also 10,000 units, irrespective of the demand and the payoff is €5,500 (10,000 units × (€1.00 – €0.45)). Having prepared the above pay-off matrix, the different decision criteria can be applied as follows:

1. **Maximin** This is the conservative or pessimistic approach to decision-making. The worst that can happen under each alternative is €5,500 for 10,000 units produced, €1,000 for the production of 20,000 units; a loss of €3,500 for a production of 30,000 units; a €8,000 loss for the production of 40,000 units. The alternative chosen will be the production of 10,000 units because it guarantees a contribution of, at least €5,500, with no possibility of an overall loss. In other words, the decision-maker selects the best of the worst outcomes associated with each decision alternative. The decision-maker who adopts the maximin criterion is described as risk averse – he will always avoid an alternative which is associated with potential, unfavourable outcomes.

2. **Maximax** This is the optimistic approach to decision-making. The best that can happen under each alternative is a contribution of €5,500 for the production of 10,000 units increasing to a contribution of €22,000 for the production (and sale) of 40,000 units. Using the maximax criterion, the alternative selected is to produce 40,000 units. The decision-maker who adopts the maximax criterion

is described as a risk lover – he will select the alternative with the possibility of the highest return.

3. **The Least Regret** criterion requires the preparation of a second payoff matrix, based on the difference between the expected payoff and what decision would have been made if we knew in advance what was going to happen. Thus, if the production alternative of 10,000 units were adopted but, subsequently, 40,000 units were demanded, then there is a significant opportunity cost associated with our decision. With hindsight, we should have produced 40,000 units. Therefore, the 'regret' associated with the initial decision (to produce 10,000 units) amounts to €16,500, i.e. the difference between €5,500 and the maximum contribution (€22,000) that could have been earned. Thus, the value for each cell in the least-regret matrix is calculated from the initial pay-off matrix and represents the difference, in the original matrix, between the maximum payoff in each column and the payoff computed for each cell. For each decision alternative (i.e. production level of 10,000, 20,000, 30,000 or 40,000 units) the 'regret' or opportunity cost is presented below and the largest of these opportunity costs is underscored for reference. The alternative which provides the 'least' or smallest of those opportunity costs is then selected. In this situation, decision Alternative 3 is selected (i.e. the production of 30,000 units) which represents the least regret of €9,000. The maximum 'regrets' of the other alternatives are €16,500 (10,000 units), €11,000 (20,000 units) and €13,500 (40,000 units).

PAY-OFF (LEAST REGRET)

| | <————States of Nature (Demand)————> | | | |
|---|---|---|---|---|
| | 10,000 units | 20,000 units | 30,000 units | 40,000 units |
| Decision alternative ↓ | | | | |
| A1: 10,000 units | Nil | €5,500 | €11,000 | €16,500 |
| A2: 20,000 units | €4,500 | Nil | €5,500 | €11,000 |
| A3: 30,000 units | €9,000* | €4,500 | Nil | €5,500 |
| A4: 40,000 units | €13,500 | €9,000 | €4,500 | Nil |

* i.e. based on the actual loss of €3,500 per previous matrix. However, if we knew in advance that demand would be 10,000 units, we would have produced 10,000 units providing a contribution of €5,500. Therefore, the 'regret' amounts to €9,000 being the monetary difference between the anticipated loss (−€3,500) and the contribution (€5,500) that would have been generated if we had prior knowledge of which state of nature would occur.

In summary, there are three criteria that can be applied in decision-making under uncertainty, of which maximin and maximax are the most popular and commonly advocated. The important issue is that these criteria do not utilise probabilities either because they cannot be reasonably determined or, alternatively, the decision-maker is either a complete pessimist or optimist!

## 12.3 Decision-making Under Risk

We have already noted earlier in this chapter that 'risk' represents a situation in which probabilities can be reasonably assigned to potential outcomes or states of nature. It is generally recommended that the expected monetary value (EMV) criterion be used in such situations. The EMV represents the weighted average pay-off for each alternative where the weights are the probabilities of each state of nature and these are applied to the respective monetary pay-offs. In relation to the probabilities (i.e. decision-making under risk), two points are worth stressing:

1. Each state of nature will be assigned a probability of between 0 and 1. A value close to 1 indicates that there is a good chance that an event will occur, with a value near to zero indicating only a small likelihood of a particular state of nature occurring.
2. The sum of the probabilities of all the states of nature or possible outcomes must equal 1, implying certainty that one of the identified states of nature will occur.

Therefore, we often say that the states of nature are both exclusive and exhaustive. By exclusive we mean that only one of the states of nature can occur. By exhaustive we mean that there is no possibility that a state of nature, other than those specified, can occur. We shall now return to the illustration of the Cavan Company and the payoff matrix previously prepared.

## ILLUSTRATION: EXPECTED MONETARY VALUE (EMV)

The manager of the Cavan Company (as in the previous illustration) is uncertain how many units can be sold at the forthcoming match, but is willing to place probabilities on his estimates as follows:

| Estimated unit sales | Probability |
|---|---|
| 10,000 | 0.1 |
| 20,000 | 0.4 |
| 30,000 | 0.3 |
| 40,000 | 0.2 |

**Requirement:** Which of these four decision alternatives should be selected using the EMV criterion?

**Solution and Analysis:** The pay-off matrix represents the monetary pay-off associated with each possible alternative and each possible state of nature. There are four alternatives and four states of nature providing a total of 16 different possible outcomes. These are presented below and the pay-off matrix has two additional features. First, we have included the probabilities of the various states of nature. Secondly, we have included an additional (right hand side column) indicating the expected monetary value (EMV) of each of the four alternatives:

PAY-OFF MATRIX

| Alternative ↓ | <———States of Nature (Demand)———> | | | | |
| --- | --- | --- | --- | --- | --- |
| | 10,000 Units (0.1) | 20,000 Units (0.4) | 30,000 Units (0.3) | 40,000 Units (0.2) | EMV |
| 10,000 units | €5,500 | €5,500 | €5,500 | €5,500 | €5,500 |
| 20,000 units | €1,000 | €11,000 | €11,000 | €11,000 | €10,000 |
| 30,000 units | (€3,500) | €6,500 | €16,500 | €16,500 | €10,500 |
| 40,000 units | (€8,000) | €2,000 | €12,000 | €22,000 | €8,000 |

The EMV represents the weighted average pay-off of each alternative. There are four alternatives and each has its own EMV. For the production of 10,000 units a pay-off of €5,500 is guaranteed no matter which state of nature occurs. The production of 20,000 units is estimated to produce an EMV of €10,000 (i.e. €1,000 × 0.1 + €11,000 × 0.4 + €11,000 × 0.3 + €11,000 × 0.2), etc. Using the EMV criterion, 30,000 units would be produced (and sold) because this alternative has the greatest expected average pay-off. The decision-maker that adopts the EMV criterion is described as risk neutral – he neither likes nor avoids risk.

The EMV criterion can be supplemented to include the variability of expected return, i.e. the spread of potential outcomes. This spread or variability is usually measured by the standard deviation which is defined as the measure of variation of values around the mean. It is routinely calculated by any statistical package including Excel, and is produced below for only decision Alternative 2 (produce 20,000 units) and decision Alternative 3 (produce 30,000 units), based on the four states of nature (actual level of demand) and their respective probabilities. (The reader should note that, in relation to the decision alternative to produce 20,000 units, the payoff of €1,000 will occur in one out of 10 times, whereas a payoff of €11,000 will occur nine times out of 10 and all 10 values are included in our calculation of standard deviation.) As indicated by the lower standard deviation (3,162), the spread of outcomes associated with Alternative 2 is narrower and this indicates that this alternative is less risky than Alternative 3. The standard deviation of Alternative 3 is 6,992. However, it should be recalled that the EMV – actually the mean value – of Alternative 3 (€10,500) is slightly higher than the EMV – the mean value – of Alternative 2 (€10,000).

| Alternative 2: Produce 20,000 units | | | Alternative 3: Produce 30,000 units | | |
|---|---|---|---|---|---|
| 1,000 | Mean | 10,000 | −3500 | Mean | 10,500 |
| 11,000 | Std Dev | 3,162 | 6500 | Std Dev | 6,992 |
| 11,000 | No. of values | 10 | 6500 | No. of values | 10 |
| 11,000 | | | 6500 | | |
| 11,000 | | | 6500 | | |
| 11,000 | | | 16500 | | |
| 11,000 | | | 16500 | | |
| 11,000 | | | 16500 | | |
| 11,000 | | | 16500 | | |
| 11,000 | | | 16500 | | |

## Limitations of EMV

The use of the EMV criterion is often recommended in managerial accounting texts. However, it is important to be aware of its many limitations. First of all, using EMV, the decision alternative selected may differ depending on the probabilities of the states of nature. This places extreme importance on how estimates of probabilities should be made. Two types of probabilities can be distinguished, namely, objective and subjective. Objective probabilities are probabilities that can be determined without judgement – for example, tossing a coin or rolling a dice. They can be tested and proved either by logical reasoning or physical observations. Historical data may, or may not, be a valid method of calculating such probabilities. In contrast, subjective probabilities are those probabilities determined by the judgement of experienced people. They cannot be tested in the same way as objective probabilities but are usually formed on the basis of past experience. Subjective probabilities can be very fallible. For example, it has been observed that higher probabilities are often assigned to those states of nature which make sense and are understood by managers relative to more ambiguous situations. Also, subjective probabilities can be distorted by memory. If the probabilities are biased, the resulting decision will be biased.

Secondly, EMV represents the long-run pay-off of an alternative and assumes that the same decision can be taken many times. Thus, in the above Cavan Company illustration, if there were 10 rugby internationals to be played in a season, the company would expect to earn, on average, €10,500 per match, assuming it consistently used the EMV criterion, which selected the production of 30,000 units. However, in many decision situations, there may not be the availability or benefit of repetition especially since one bad experience could force the company out of business.

Thirdly, EMV is appropriate if the decision-maker is risk-neutral. This means that the decision-maker neither likes risk (risk averse) nor is afraid of it (risk lover). Yet many decision-makers are risk-averse, especially when an alternative requires the commitment of a high percentage of the decision-maker's resources. For example, it is often indicated that the EMV associated with insuring a house against fire is negative – suggesting that we should not insure our houses. Yet, we all insure our houses because of the remote possibility of a significant financial loss due to fire. Fourthly, we have assumed that the states of nature are discretely distributed. This means that demand, for example, will be 10,000, 20,000, 30,000 or 40,000 units. In reality, most probability distributions are continuous rather than discrete.

In concluding this section, it is useful to note that we can make a distinction between a good decision and a good outcome. The former represents a situation where relevant information is gathered, critically assessed and judiciously used by the decision-maker. However, there is no guarantee of success. The anticipated or expected 'state of nature' may not materialise and a good decision can be translated into a bad outcome. Of course, the opposite may also occur in that a bad decision may convert into a good outcome, with the benefit of luck.

## 12.4 Decision Trees

Thus far, we have concentrated on a situation in which a single decision alternative has to be selected. However, there is another more complex situation in which a series of decisions have to be made, at different time periods with each decision influenced by the information available and states of nature. Thus, a company may be required to select between building a small plant now with an option of expanding it in future years, or constructing a larger plant immediately. A convenient analytical tool for such a problem is the decision tree.

In its simplest form a **decision tree** is a diagram that shows the various decisions which the decision-maker can make and the various outcomes or states of nature that can occur. Conceptually there is no difference between decision trees and other methods of analysing decision problems: we focus on the decision alternatives and the financial consequences.

A decision tree, for a simple decision situation involving sequential decisions, is illustrated in **Exhibit 12.2**. It should be noted that, when preparing a decision tree, a square box depicts a decision alternative and is formally described as a decision node. 'Circles' represent the various states of nature that can occur, e.g. levels of demand.

EXHIBIT 12.2: DECISION TREE

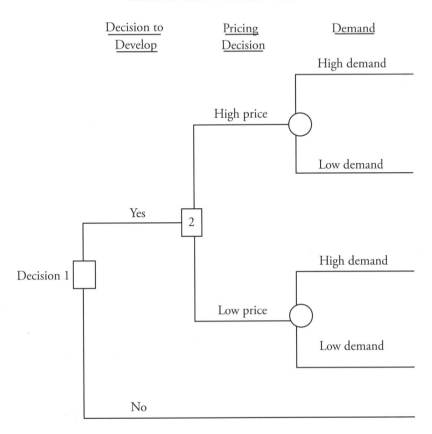

In **Exhibit 12.2** (which represents an artificial situation) there are two (sequential) decisions that need to be made. The first decision (Decision 1) concerns whether to produce a new product or not. This is subsequently followed by the second decision (conditional on the development decision) to set either a high or low price. In turn, there are two possible outcomes (or states of nature) associated with this high–low pricing decision, i.e. either a high or low demand may occur.

It will be recalled that, in decision situations, the decision-maker has control over which alternative to select. However, the decision-maker has no control over which state of nature will occur. Such states of nature could reflect the level of demand, or the reaction of competitors. However, managers will try to influence such states of nature but they cannot be controlled.

In a more elaborate form of decision tree, the estimated probabilities together with monetary pay-offs of each event's outcomes are indicated, which are in turn combined to give an expected monetary value for each 'branch'. Thus, a decision tree, like a pay-off matrix, shows the financial consequences of each unique combination of decision alternative and states of nature. The following illustration indicates how a decision tree works.

## ILLUSTRATION: DECISION TREE

The Corrib Company has some spare manufacturing capacity and is faced with sequential decisions regarding possible use (for a single time period). First, it must decide whether to develop a new product or expand its existing product range. It is estimated that the development of the new product will cost €100,000, which may or may not be technically feasible, i.e. successful. This corresponds to Decision 1 and the decision is simply: 'yes or no'. There is a 70% probability that the development effort will be successful (technically feasible) and, therefore, there is a 30% probability that the development effort will be considered unsuccessful, i.e. technically not feasible. If the new product is successfully developed, it must be manufactured and marketed. The production process requires additional, specific fixed costs of €50,000 with variable costs of €2 per unit. However, another decision must be made regarding the sales price to be charged to customers. After discussion among managers, and bearing in mind competitors' prices, only two possible prices have been suggested, i.e. a high price at €6 per unit and a low price at €4 per unit. In turn, future demand levels have been reduced to two levels (large and small demands) and their respective probabilities are anticipated to be:

| Demand | Probability | Units sold |
|---|---|---|
| Large demand | 0.6 | 100,000 |
| Small demand | 0.4 | 50,000 |

Alternatively, the company could use the above capacity to expand the existing product range. This is the easy option and, with virtual certainty, will generate a surplus of €40,000 during this time period.

**Requirement:** You are asked to present a decision tree to assist in the decision whether or not to develop the product.

**Solution and Analysis:** It should be noted that there are two decisions to be made by managers. The first decision is to develop the new product or expand the existing product range. The second decision concerns the selling price of the new product – assuming its development is successful – and whether to set a high or low price for the product. There are four separate states of nature, i.e. the new product development will be successful or not, and, if successful, and after setting the selling price, the demand for this new product will either be high or low. The completed decision tree is presented in **Exhibit 12.3**.

Each state of nature represents a set of possible events that are both 'mutually exclusive' and 'exhaustive'. By **mutually exclusive**, we mean that no two outcomes can occur at the same time. By **exhaustive**, we mean that the set of states of nature (possible outcomes) represent the entire range of possible events. In other words, there is no possibility that another non-represented outcome might occur.

We assign monetary values or pay-offs to each 'branch'. There are six branches – numbered 1–6 in the Exhibit – and the monetary consequences of each branch is presented under the 'pay-off' heading on the extreme right hand side of the Exhibit.

Thus, if a high price is set and high demand occurs (Branch (1)), the pay-off is €250,000, being the additional contribution of €400,000 ((€6 – €2) × 100,000 less €50,000 for specific fixed costs less €100,000 being the cost of development). Other payoffs (2 – 6) are similarly calculated, using selling prices and demand levels, less any costs incurred. If a decision to proceed with the development is taken but it is not successful (Branch 5), then the net cash outflow is negative €100,000. If the decision is taken to expand the existing product range, the (given) payoff is €40,000 for Branch 6 and this payoff is considered certain

EXHIBIT 12.3: COMPLETED DECISION TREE

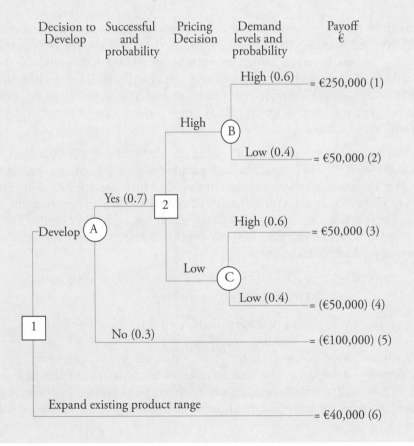

– in order to simplify the illustration. In addition to assigning monetary values to each branch, we also assign probabilities to each state of nature, i.e. the estimated likelihood that each of the uncertain outcomes will occur. (It should be remembered that each state of nature is indicated by a 'circle' on the decision tree.) We know, for example, that the probability of the successful development of the new product is 0.7 and, therefore, that the probability of an unsuccessful outcome is 0.3. In addition, the probability of a high demand is 0.6 and the probability of a low demand must be 0.4.

The sequence of decisions and outcomes in the decision tree reads from left to right. When constructed, it highlights those decisions or events that must logically precede certain other events and decisions. In other words, a logical dependence is portrayed. However, in choosing an alternative, the decision tree must be 'collapsed' or 'folded back' from right to left using these two rules:

1. replace each 'circle' with the expected value of that event's states of nature; and
2. at each decision point (square), choose the alternative with the highest expected value.

The states of nature, equivalent to Circle 'B' has an expected monetary value of €170,000 ((€250,000 × 0.6) + (€50,000 × 0.4)) and the states of nature of Circle 'C' has an expected monetary value of €10,000 ((€50,000 × 0.6) − (€50,000 × 0.4)). In such circumstances, at Decision Point 2, the decision-maker will select the 'high price' option (equivalent to an EMV = €170,000). Thus, we can now ignore the lower price option. We now move back to the earlier decision (Decision 1) to be made.

Circle 'A' has an expected monetary value of €89,000 ((€170,000 × 0.7) − (€100,000 × 0.3)). This must be compared with the pay-off associated with expanding the existing product range (Branch 6) which has a (given and certain) payoff of €40,000. Faced with a choice between these two alternatives, the decision-maker will select the 'develop' option, which has an EMV of €89,000. It is interesting to note that the €89,000 pay-off (for the development option) can be alternatively calculated as follows:

$$EMV = (0.7 \times 0.6 \times €250,000) + (0.7 \times 0.4 \times €50,000)$$
$$- (0.3 \times €100,000) = €89,000$$

However, one must always be aware of the potential inaccuracy of accounting information in decision-making situations. For example, it is likely that some important factors or considerations have not been incorporated within the above decision model, e.g. the strategic significance, if any, of the new product. Moreover, all decision-making suffers from the biased view of managers and this includes the assignment of dubious probabilities to various states of nature.

COMPUTATION OF MONETARY PAYOFFS – IN ABOVE EXHIBIT

| | Cost of development | Additional fixed costs | Revenue generated (demand × unit contribution) | Payoff |
|---|---|---|---|---|
| 1 | (€100,000) | (€50,000) | 100,000 × €4 = €400,000 | €250,000 |
| 2 | (€100,000) | (€50,000) | 50,000 × €4 = €200,000 | €50,000 |
| 3 | (€100,000) | (€50,000) | 100,000 × €2 = €200,000 | €50,000 |
| 4 | (€100,000) | (€50,000) | 50,000 × €2 = €100,000 | (€50,000) |
| 5 | (€100,000) | N/A | | (€100,000) |
| 6 | — | — | — | €40,000 |

## 12.5  Decision-making and Rationality

It is frequently implied in management accounting textbooks that managers are rational in their decision-making. By this we mean that in decision-making managers adopt the sequence presented in **Chapter 9, Section 9.1**, i.e.:

- agree objectives,
- identify and evaluate alternatives, and
- select and implement the best solution.

**However, the rational model may be inadequate in explaining the actual decision-making processes of managers for several reasons:**

1. Some decisions tend to be made with undue haste which reflect the context of the decision.
2. Managers, like any individuals, allow biases to colour their decisions. Biases are preconceived notions that are adopted by managers without adequate reason. For example, a manager who dislikes change may reject a proposal that might improve operating efficiency. Similarly, a manager who likes the prestige of leading a large, publicly quoted company might promote a merger or takeover that reduces shareholder value. Managerial biases cause decision-makers to ignore important limitations in their preferred course of action and prevent them from adequately evaluating or investigating alternatives.
3. Managers sometimes search for a satisfactory rather than an optimal solution to a particular problem. Once a satisfactory solution is determined, the search for 'better' alternatives ceases.
4. The rational approach does not take into account the wide range of political and personality factors involved in decision-making. For example, many managerial decisions are dominated by internal politics that may override the rational process.

## Decision-making by Groups

It is interesting to note that many important managerial decisions are made in a group context, rather than by an individual manager, and group decisions may be heavily influenced by the manager with the strongest personality rather than the manager with the strongest argument. All decisions require two fundamental elements, namely knowledge of the objectives to be achieved, and also the cause-and-effect relationship between action (decisions) and outcomes. In group decisions, the interaction of these two elements becomes complicated and this can be highlighted by constructing a simple two-by-two **matrix** showing, on the horizontal axis, the relative agreement by decision participants on the objectives to be achieved. The vertical axis shows the relative degree of certainty/uncertainty of the cause-and-effect relationship between the decision and outcome. In reality, each axis should be viewed as a continuum rather than two extreme points.

Thus, the matrix presented in **Exhibit 12.4** below represents the approach to group decision-making. The top left-hand box of the matrix is labelled 'decision-making by computation'. This depicts a situation where the objectives are agreed by all decision participants and the probable cause and effect relationships are well understood and accepted by all participants. Hence, managerial decisions are 'computed' by using the available accounting information. The bottom left-hand box represents a situation where the objectives are again agreed but the cause-and-effect relationship between decision alternative and probable outcome is poor. Therefore, managers do not know, in advance, which decision is most likely to provide the best result. In this situation, decisions must be based on the judgment of participants and this is referred to as 'decision-making by judgement' – reflecting the uncertainty surrounding the decision. The top right-hand box of the matrix indicates a situation where the objectives are not agreed (and different individuals sometimes have different objectives), but there is a reasonable cause and effect relationship that can be established between a decision alternative and probable outcome. In this situation, decisions emerge by a process of negotiation between participants and this is referred to as 'decision-making by compromise'. Such situations will require accounting information in order to justify or support particular arguments but it is unlikely that an optimal decision will be made in this context.

EXHIBIT 12.4: OBJECTIVES AND UNCERTAINTY IN GROUP DECISION-MAKING

|  | Agreement on Objectives | |
|---|---|---|
|  | Relative agreement | Relative disagreement |
| ***Certainty of cause and effect relationship*** | Decision-making by computation | Decision-making by compromise |
| ***Uncertainty of cause and effect relationship*** | Decision-making by judgment | Decision-making by inspiration |

Finally, the bottom right-hand box of the matrix indicates a situation where objectives are not agreed, and the probable cause-and-effect relationship between decision alternative and outcome is poor. In such situations, it is inevitable that managerial decisions are made on the basis of inspiration with, perhaps, accounting information playing a very minor role.

In a textbook on managerial accounting it is difficult to incorporate, in a meaningful way, the context and implications of group managerial decision-making. As a result, many texts are written as if managerial decisions correspond, in the main, to the top left-hand box of **Exhibit 12.4**, i.e. decision-making by computation. There is nothing wrong with this approach provided one appreciates that the described decision situation may be a little artificial. Specifically, described situations often ignore the fact that, in group decision-making, objectives are often conflicting and ambiguous, and predictive models regarding alternatives and outcome are imperfect. In addition, one should accept that accounting information always suffers from limitations and also that non-financial considerations are important in managerial decision-making. All this suggests that, in reality, managerial decision-making is rather complicated for a number of reasons.

## 12.6  An Introduction to Information Economics

Managerial accounting is concerned with the provision of information for decision-making and, traditionally, most texts on the discipline have focused attention on the type of information that should be provided in a specific decision context. However, rather less attention has been devoted to the cost of acquiring this information. This is a regrettable oversight, since the acquisition of information in a decision situation may not necessarily be cost-effective. As a general rule in decision-making, only that information that has an expected value greater than its acquisition cost should be acquired. In other words, information can be viewed as an economic commodity, the acquisition of which should be subject to cost-benefit analysis.

The purpose of this short section is to illustrate the concept of expected value of information. We shall focus on a situation where perfect information is available, i.e. we assume that we can acquire advance knowledge of what specific event or state of nature shall happen in the future. Such information has, potentially, great value for decision-makers.

ILLUSTRATION: VALUE OF PERFECT INFORMATION

The directors of Bandon must choose between the production of two different types of products, namely, product X and product Y. For the sake of simplicity, we assume that there are only two outcomes or states of nature, namely, buoyant market conditions, which has an estimated 70% probability, and depressed market conditions with an estimated 30% probability. We adopt a single period model using only monetary values and a hypothetical monetary pay-off matrix is shown below:

PAY-OFF MATRIX

| | Buoyant conditions (0.7) | Depressed conditions (0.3) | EMV |
|---|---|---|---|
| Action 1: Product X | €6,000 | €2,000 | €4,800 |
| Action 2: Product Y | €4,000 | €5,000 | €4,300 |

If we assume that the decision-makers are risk neutral, then the choice between the two alternatives should be made on the basis of maximising expected monetary value. In this situation the directors shall choose A1, which involves producing Product X. However, prior to making a decision, decision-makers often have the option of expanding their existing information set. Such options inevitably cost money, which automatically begs the question of whether it is cost effective to engage in such an acquisition.

It should be stressed that only information which has an expected monetary value greater than its acquisition cost should be acquired. However, the expected value of this additional information must be determined in advance and we now look at how to calculate the expected value of **perfect information**. Perfect information means that we know with certainty which state of nature shall occur in the future. The **expected value of perfect information (EVPI)** represents the difference between the expected monetary value, given advance knowledge of an outcome, and the expected monetary value, given current information. If buoyant conditions were known to occur with certainty then A1 would be chosen. However, this information has no value since our decision would be the same, given the existing information set. However, if depressed conditions were known in advance with certainty, then A2 would be chosen and this represents a changed decision and this information, therefore, has value. The EVPI is, accordingly, calculated as follows:

Expected Monetary Value, given perfect information =    €5,700
(6,000 × 0.7 + 5,000 × 0.3)
Expected Monetary Value, given existing information = <u>€4,800</u>
Therefore, EVPI <u>€900</u>

Thus, the difference between the expected payoff given advance perfect information and the expected payoff given current information is €900. This represents the maximum amount which the directors of Bandon should now pay to acquire perfect information. The value of €900 can easily be proved. If a 'buoyant conditions' message was received the manager of Bandon will still proceed with action A1. In this situation the additional information has no value since it does not change the decision. However, if a 'depressed conditions' message is received (which has a probability of 0.3), then the manager will change his decision and select alternative A2 with a consequent monetary gain of €3,000. The current probability of this happening is 0.3, providing an overall expected value of €900 (€3,000 × 0.3), which is the monetary saving multiplied by the estimated probability.

Therefore, the acquisition of information should be viewed like any other economic resource and subject to cost–benefit analysis. The option of acquiring additional information represents but one of the alternatives facing decision-makers. Only that information that has an expected value greater than its cost should be acquired. In determining this, an added complication is the fact that perfect information is rarely, if ever, available to decision-makers. Information that uses approximations, estimates or is in some other way less than 100% reliable, is said to be 'imperfect information'. Clearly, the value of imperfect information must be less than the value of perfect information. It is possible to calculate the expected value of imperfect information using methodology similar to EVPI. However, such calculations are beyond the scope of this book and some may consider such calculations as impractical. However, their relevance is that they highlight the fact that acquiring additional information has the potential to reduce future uncertainty but that this additional information is costly to acquire and is rarely 100% accurate. In other words, acquiring and using additional information, itself, represents a decision under conditions of risk and uncertainty.

## Summary of Learning Objectives

**Learning Objective 1:** Distinguish between decision-making under risk and under uncertainty.

In decision-making, it is rare that the outcomes – also referred to as the states of nature – associated with the various alternatives can be predicted with 100% accuracy. Rather, there is always the possibility that the predicted outcome may not materialise. If the possible outcomes, for example, tossing a coin will yield 'heads' or 'tails', can be assigned probabilities, this situation can be described as decision-making under risk. Alternatively, if the possible outcomes cannot be assigned reasonable probabilities, for example, estimating the demand for a new product, this situation can be described as decision-making under uncertainty. Thus, the presence of respective probabilities differentiates between decision-making under risk and uncertainty.

**Learning Objective 2:** Construct a pay-off matrix reflecting alternatives and states of nature.

A pay-off matrix represents each unique combination of decision alternative together with the financial consequences of each possible outcome or state of nature. For example, betting on a two horse race reveals four possible combinations. These are (1) betting on horse A, which can: (a) win or (b) lose; alternatively, (2) one can bet on horse B, which can: (c) win or (d) lose. The construction of a pay-off matrix was presented in the exhibits and illustrations in this chapter.

**Learning Objective 3:** Calculate and discuss the concept of expected value.

The expected value is a calculation related to each decision alternative whereby the possible outcomes are multiplied by the respective probabilities. Thus, expected value requires the underlying probabilities to be available and used. If the consequences are stated in financial terms, then the term expected monetary value (EMV) is used and this can be positive or negative. However, it is important to stress that EMV represents the long-run pay-off of a decision alternative. In other words, if the same decision was made on a number of occasions, the overall benefit would be represented by the EMV. Unfortunately, some decisions are one-off events.

**Learning Objective 4:** Apply maximin, maximax, EMV and least regret criteria.

In the absence of probabilities, or where the decision-maker prefers not to utilise underlying probabilities, other criteria must be used. The maximin criterion is the pessimistic criterion. In which case, the decision-maker selects the best of all the worst possible outcomes. Alternatively, the maximax criterion is the optimistic approach to decision-making and assumes that the best possible outcome will occur. The least regret represents an opportunity cost approach to decision-making. In this case, the decision-maker is conscious of making an incorrect decision, so he or she minimises the regret associated with making an incorrect decision.

**Learning Objective 5:** Prepare decision trees to reflect sequential decision situations.

Some decision situations can involve a series of sequential choices. In other words, a first decision, e.g. to develop or not develop a new product, can be followed by a decision to, say, set a high or low selling price. It is useful to map such situations by way of decision trees. A decision tree represents a diagram that shows the various alternatives which the decision-maker can select and the various outcomes or states of nature that can occur. To highlight the diagram, decision alternatives are represented by a square box and outcomes (states of nature) are represented by way of circles. If probabilities are available, the expected monetary value can be calculated for each branch of the decision tree.

**Learning Objective 6:** Calculate the expected value of perfect information.

Most decisions are based on imperfect information. Simply, one does not know for certainty what state of nature will occur. Thus, one alternative in decision-making is to obtain additional information before a final decision is made. However, this additional information may be costly to acquire so that one can compute the expected value of perfect information (EVPI). EVPI represents the monetary difference between the current expected value, given the available information set, and the revised expected value given perfect information, i.e. given a 100% accurate prediction on what will happen in the future. EVPI sets a monetary limit on the cost one should pay to acquire perfect information in any decision situation. However, perfect information is rarely available.

## Questions

### Review Questions

(See Appendix One for Solutions to Review Questions **12.1** and **12.2**)

#### Question 12.1 (Risk and Uncertainty)

Write a short note on the 'Maximax' and 'Maximin' criteria in decision-making and provide a practical example to illustrate your answer.

Source: Chartered Accountants Ireland, Management Accounting and Business Finance, Paper 3, Autumn 2005 (adapted)

#### Question 12.2: (Decision-making with Risk and Uncertainty)

Andy Company is developing a new product which will have a life cycle of only one year. The selling price is €13 per unit. The company is unsure as to how many units can be sold and the sales director has suggested that there are three possible outcomes, namely, medium, low and high. Thus, the medium outcome is associated with the sale of 30,000 units of this product; a pessimistic (low) view suggests 24,000 units may be sold whilst the optimistic (high) view represents 36,000 units, which is considered the maximum that could be sold. (Unsold units can be recycled without any additional cost.) Cost estimates have revealed the following:

|  | Per Unit € | Per Annum € |
|---|---|---|
| Material cost | 2.50 |  |
| Fixed costs |  | 85,000 |

In addition, there are conversion costs that are estimated as follows:

| No. of units | Per annum € |
|---|---|
| 24,000 | 50,000 |
| 30,000 | 57,500 |
| 36,000 | 65,000 |

Resources diverted to this product could continue to be employed earning an annual net profit of €60,000. This profit is fairly certain as it is from selling an existing product to established customers.

**Requirements:**

1. Calculate the profit attributable to the new product for the three volume levels indicated.
2. Upon further investigation it is agreed that probabilities may be subjectively applied to the three volume levels (low, medium and high) as follows:

| Unit Sales | Probability |
|---|---|
| 24,000 | 0.3 |
| 30,000 | 0.5 |
| 36,000 | 0.2 |

In addition, it is noted that material costs could change during the year. It is considered that there is a 30% probability that an increased material price of €3 per unit will occur. Thus, there is a 70% probability that the material cost (€2.50 per unit) will be unchanged. Using the probabilities provided extend, as you think appropriate, the profit projections in (1) above and draw some conclusions about the new product development.

3. What are your views on the use of probabilities in this type of decision?

Intermediate Questions

*Question 12.3: (Forecasting Demand using Expected Monetary Value)*

In preparing its 20x1 budget, the EMV Company conducted a market research study in order to estimate future sales levels for one of its products. Since the demand for this product is not very sensitive to price changes, the sales price for the forthcoming year (20x1) has already been agreed and decided. The company's management accountant received a Memorandum from the head of market research with the following summary:

"It is impossible to predict 20x1 sales with certainty, especially in the present economic climate. If the economy continues as it is, i.e. remains stable, unit sales will be 400,000. However, if the current recession deepens, we expect 300,000 units to be sold this year. Nevertheless, there are signs of 'green shoots' and if this translates into future economic growth, we could expect annual sales of 500,000 units. Our resident economist predicts a 40% probability of a stable economy, a 40% chance of a faltering economy, and a 20% chance of a robust recovery."

**Requirements:**

1. What demand estimate would an optimist (maximax) and a pessimist (maximin) make?
2. Using the EMV criterion, what unit sales would you forecast for 20x1?
3. What are the benefits and limitations of using the EMV calculation?

*Question 12.4: (Decision-making under Conditions of Risk)*

The Top Company Ltd is currently examining the feasibility of producing a new generic pharmaceutical product in its existing manufacturing facility. The proposed selling price in the first year is €35 per unit and this will be increased to €45 in years 2 and 3. Past experience indicates that the life cycle of new products is three years and the following sales projections were made for the new product and the company intends to operate a Just in Time (JIT) system for this new product:

ESTIMATED UNIT SALES AND PROBABILITY

|  | Probability | Year 1 | Year 2 | Year 3 |
|---|---|---|---|---|
| Demand: – above average | 30% | 40,000 | 85,000 | 20,000 |
| – average | 60% | 23,000 | 55,000 | 15,000 |
| – below average | 10% | 7,000 | 30,000 | 5,000 |

The estimated material and labour costs are as follows:

| Direct materials | 3 kgs @ €2/kg |
|---|---|
| Direct labour | 2 hours @ €6/hour |

Management, however, are having difficulty estimating the amount of overhead applicable to this product. The accounting staff suggested that simple linear regression be used to determine the behaviour pattern of total overhead cost. Two separate regression equations were performed, based on historical data, one using direct labour hours and the other using total units sold as the relevant explanatory variables. The information derived from these two regressions, based on historical monthly observations, is as follows:

|  | Explanatory Variables | |
|---|---|---|
|  | Direct labour hours | Total units sold |
| Coefficients of the regression equation: | | |
| Constant | 42,000 | 54,000 |
| Independent variable | 5.0 | 4.5 |
| Coefficient of determination ($R^2$) | 0.90 | 0.64 |
| Coefficient of correlation | 0.95 | 0.80 |
| Standard error of estimate | 2,840 | 3,940 |
| Standard error of coefficient | 0.42 | 2.5 |
| T-statistics required for a 95% confidence interval: | | |
| 12 degrees of freedom | 2.18 | 2.18 |
| 10 degrees of freedom | 2.23 | 2.23 |

### Requirements:

1. Which regression equation should be used in cost prediction?
2. Prepare projected income statements for the three years (including fixed costs) arising from this decision using the EMV criterion but ignoring the time value of money.
3. What do you advise the company to do? Make your recommendation with reference to incremental cash flows and you may ignore the incidence of fixed costs, due to sharing of existing facilities.

*Question 12.5: (Decision-making under Risk and Uncertainty)*

Bective Limited is a small family-run company. It produces hamburgers which are sold to wholesalers and street vendors. As such, it does not conduct any retail business. Recently, the directors of the company have become interested in the street-retailing side of hamburgers, especially where large crowds gather for a short period of time. Specifically, they are considering whether to produce and sell hamburgers for the forthcoming rugby international. Unfortunately, due to the location of the ground, the hamburgers must be produced prior to match day, and hamburgers unsold at the end of match day must be disposed of to charity. Each hamburger will sell for €1.00 and the variable cost is estimated at €0.45 per unit. The directors consider that there are no other costs associated with this venture as the cabin location for sales will be provided free.

The sales manager considers that, given the current production facilities and logistical considerations, the company should consider producing one of four levels of output, i.e. 10,000 units, 20,000 units, 30,000 units or 40,000 units. He estimates that the level of demand is likely to be somewhere between 10,000 and 40,000 units, with much depending on the crowd and weather conditions. To facilitate the decision-making process he assumes that the level of demand (states of nature) will correspond to one of his four capacity levels. He is willing to place probabilities on his demand estimates as follows, which are discretely distributed:

| Estimated unit sales | Probability |
|---|---|
| 10,000 | .1 |
| 20,000 | .4 |
| 30,000 | .3 |
| 40,000 | .2 |

**Requirements:**

1. Prepare a payoff matrix to represent the four possible production alternatives (i.e. producing 10,000, 20,000, 30,000 or 40,000 units) using variable costs and revenues.
2. What alternative should be selected using the following criteria:
   (a) Maximin criterion
   (b) Maximax criterion and
   (c) Expected monetary value (EMV) criterion? In addition, calculate an overall measure of variability in relation to the expected return associated with Alternative 2.
3. What alternative would be selected using the **least regret** (opportunity cost) criterion?
4. Briefly distinguish between a discrete and continuous probability distribution in relation to sales demand.

*Question 12.6 (Decision-making under Uncertainty)*

Trobe Limited operates a chain of hotels in different locations. The company's business has, in recent years, seen something of a downturn and profits have come under pressure. This has prompted management to seek new sources of income. The following have been identified.

New American Travel Group ('NATG') has approached Trobe Limited and asked the company to quote a price per room/night for a total of 5,000 nights per annum for American tours. Trobe is confident that, at a rate of €50 per room/night, it will be successful and this represents the most likely scenario. However, it also believes that there is a possibility that €60 per room/night would be accepted but this is rather optimistic.

German Tours International ('GTI') has also asked Trobe to quote for 3,000 room/nights per annum for its tours. At a rate of €45 per room/night, Trobe believes that it will most likely win this business. Any higher price is unlikely to be accepted.

In the case of both offers, Trobe must only accept them in full – any less than the number of nights being sought will not be acceptable and the groups will approach other hotels. The groups will provide a list of the required dates on their acceptance of the quotes.

In total, Trobe has 32,000 room/nights available per annum, with an average annual occupancy rate of 70%. A fixed rate of €55 per room/night applies all year round and this rate has not changed for three years. If the quotes are not accepted, it is believed that these rates will continue for the coming year. Management are of the opinion, however, that should the quotes be successful, the tours will be in addition to historic occupancy rates.

In terms of costs, management believe that the wages and salaries charge will need to rise by a minimum of 5% on the previous year although, because of union pressure, this will probably be 8%. However, it is possible that union negotiators may press for higher claims but they have been advised by hotel management that any increase greater than 10% will not be sanctioned. Management have stated that whether the quotes are accepted or not will have no bearing on employee numbers.

Other variable overheads are expected to increase by 4% on the previous year. However, if either (or both) quotes are accepted, this will instead give rise to a 6% increase in this regard.

The summarised income statement for the previous year is as follows (and you may disregard any fixed overheads):

|  | € |
|---|---|
| Sales | 1,232,000 |
| Wages & Salaries | (600,000) |
| Other variable overhead | (600,000) |
| Profit for year | 32,000 |

## Requirements:

1. From the information above, prepare three budgeted income statements for the next year using the following headings:
   Most likely
   Optimistic
   Pessimistic

2. Based on the budgeted income statements produced, write a short report to management outlining your observations. In the report you should comment on whether the quotes should be pursued or not.

Source: Chartered Accountants Ireland, Management Accounting and Business Finance, P3,
Autumn 2004

*Question 12.7: (Decision-making under Uncertainty)*

Parka Limited is a manufacturer of electrical components. The company operates in an uncertain market, with new competitors and products appearing annually. As a result, arriving at accurate estimates of the next three months' sales is proving to be problematic. The company is trying to overcome this by incorporating probability factors into its calculations and deliberations. You have been provided with the following information:

**Market size**: Traditionally, Parka has a 50% share of the national market for this particular type of component and this market share is expected to continue. However, there is uncertainty over the size of the total national market. Three market research experts have been consulted and each has given a different estimate as to the national market share in the forthcoming three months. The estimates are as follows:

| Market Researcher | Total National Market (3 months) |
|---|---|
| Expert A | 64,000 units |
| Expert B | 88,000 units |
| Expert C | 124,000 units |

Management believe that each of the above total market size is equally probable to be correct and none stands out as being more likely or unlikely than the others.

**Sales:** Parka sells its components at a price of €200 per unit. On average, 70% of all units are sold to DIY stores, with the balance being sold through a major distributor. Parka operates a rebate system with this distributor **only** such that, at the end of each three-month period, if sales exceed specified levels, Parka pays the distributor a rebate. This is calculated as follows:

| Where Unit Sales Exceed | Rebate on all Sales € |
|---|---|
| 10,000 units | 2% |
| 20,000 units | 3% |

**Material purchase cost:** The current unit cost of materials is €100. However, a price increase is expected to take effect just before the start of the three-month period. Based on historical records, there is a 15% chance that the increase will be 7%, a 60% chance that the price increase will be 10% and a 25% chance that the price increase will be 15%.

**Labour cost:** Each completed unit takes four labour hours to finish. The basic rate of pay is currently €12 per hour. Currently, there are 190,000 hours of direct labour available, and which will be paid for, during the next three months. Any additional labour hours required for production would have to be paid at overtime rates (time and a half).

**Requirement:** Based on the above information, calculated the expected profit for the three-month period. (You may assume that overtime will be worked, when required.)

Source: Chartered Accountants Ireland, Management Accounting and Business Finance, P3
Autumn 2006 (adapted)

## Advanced Questions

### Question 12.8: (Decision-making under Risk and Uncertainty)

Windsupply Limited manufactures large components for use in wind farms and it has just developed a new product – a rotator device. This type of product has recently experienced significant growth due to increased demand for alternative sources of electricity and strong sales are anticipated for the new product.

The company's marketing department has just conducted extensive market research with potential customers to try and establish a selling price for the product and the anticipated sales demand at that price. The market research report contains the following information:

| € 1,500 Selling Price | | € 1,400 selling price | |
|---|---|---|---|
| Annual demand | Probability | Actual demand | Probability |
| 2,500 | 0.25 | 2,200 | 0.20 |
| 3,000 | 0.45 | 3,200 | 0.35 |
| 3,500 | 0.30 | 3,600 | 0.45 |

The following information is also available:

| | € |
|---|---|
| Direct materials | 425 per unit |
| Direct labour | 250 per unit |
| Variable selling and distribution costs | 150 per unit |
| Packaging cost | 75  per unit |
| Fixed costs (per annum) | €650,000 (between 2,000 to 3,000 units) |

Demand for the company's products has increased dramatically and production is close to capacity. The current advice from the manufacturing manager is that, should demand exceed 3,000 units, then a new factory will need to be rented (in addition to the existing factory).

Due to union agreements already made, the company will be unable to transfer existing production to the new factory – only new/additional production can be produced in the new factory. The new factory has a 1-year lease term at a cost of €250,000. In addition, selling, administration and distribution overheads of €150,000 along with €100,000 of additional factory overheads, will be incurred.

However, the new factory layout should permit a more efficient production process and the variable labour cost per unit will decrease to €200 per unit only for the extra units.

Windsupply Limited is currently engaged in formulating its budget requirements for next year's production and sales, and it has decided to use a probability approach to budgeting to determine anticipated profit.

## Requirements:

1. Calculate the expected value of profit and show the range of profits that may occur at a unit selling price of €1,500 and €1,400.
2. Based on your calculations in (1), advise management as to how they should proceed. What other relevant information should be considered?
3. Windsupply Limited has entered into discussions with two new potential customers in an attempt to provide additional production for the new factory should a decision be taken to lease this factory on a permanent basis. The following information has been obtained:

   - It is likely that a Dutch company called Alpha will enter into a contract to purchase 1,200 units at a reduced price of €1,300 per unit. The company is a new entrant to the Irish market and it is therefore anxious to build relations with national suppliers.
   - A company called Beta that did not display any interest at the original selling prices of €1,400 and €1,500 expressed an interest in purchasing 800 units of the product at a reduced price of €1,300. However, Beta has been doing business with its existing supplier for a number of years and it is unlikely to switch to a new supplier like Windsupply.
   - There is also a strong possibility that wage costs and materials may increase by 10% in the coming year due to renegotiation of wage agreements and a potential rise in material costs.
   - If the company is successful in winning both customers, there will be a further capacity issue as a new machine will need to be purchased. If only one customer is obtained, there is enough capacity in the existing machines. A new machine can be leased on an annual basis at a cost of €300,000 per annum.

   Calculate the budgeted contribution to be earned from the two potential customers, based on your assessment of the most likely and the most optimistic scenarios described above.

4. Advise management of any factors that should be considered before making a decision to lease the new factory on a permanent basis and entering into a formal business arrangement with the two new customers.

Source: Chartered Accountants Ireland, Management Accounting and Business Finance, P3, Summer 2007 (adapted)

## Question 12.9: (Decision Trees and EMV)

Phoenix Limited produces and sells mobile phones in various countries in Europe. The company now has its sights set on the lucrative Irish market and their strategy is to aim at the younger age group, i.e. 15–25 year olds, and they are constantly adjusting their product to meet the demands of the particular group with innovative and fashionable updates.

The most recent high specification creation is called the 'Sonic 5' and they are planning to launch this phone in Ireland as they believe it will be an excellent breakthrough product. However, a competitor, French Phones Limited, has also set its sights on the Irish mobile phone market and they have had similar success to Phoenix in the European market.

The demand for 'Sonic 5' will be influenced by the action of French Phones as they are about to launch a rival product which is very similar to the 'Sonic 5'. Phoenix Limited estimates that there is a 40% probability that French Phones will also enter the Irish market at the same time and this will adversely impact on the Irish sales of the 'Sonic 5'. Phoenix Limited has calculated the sales units of 'Sonic 5' in its first year on the Irish market based on two possible pricing points (€150 and €120) and taking the direct competitor into consideration. Details of the potential pricing points and the anticipated sales have been estimated as follows:

|  | Price of Sonic 5 €120 | Price of Sonic 5 €150 |
| --- | --- | --- |
| Competing product by French Phones | 70,000 units | 40,000 units |
| No competing product | 90,000 units | 60,000 units |

In addition, in order to sell the Sonic 5 on the Irish market, Phoenix must pay a special licence fee to the mobile phone regulator. The regulator has not been able to give a final price to Phoenix as they are awaiting clarification on some matters, but they have given an estimate of the price range and their related probabilities. There is a 20% chance the licence fee will be €3 million. However, there is an 80% probability that it will cost €5 million.

The variable costs associated with each unit of Sonic 5 consist of production costs amounting to €30 together with selling and distribution costs amounting to €26.

**Requirements:**

1. Draw a decision tree which should identify all the potential outcomes associated with the pricing of the Sonic 5. Based on this decision tree, calculate the expected monetary value of the pricing decision (i.e. a price of €150 or €120) and make a recommendation, from a financial perspective only, as to which price Phoenix should charge for the Sonic 5.
2. Outline four qualitative factors specific to these circumstances that should be taken into account before a decision is made.

Source: Chartered Accountants Ireland, Management Accounting and Business Finance,<br>P3, Summer 2008

*Question 12.10 (Decision-making under Risk, Uncertainty and Rationality)*

ICS Limited (ICS) is an Irish computer-software company, producing games for the local market only. The company expects that it will earn total profits of €180,000 in the year just ending – 30 June 20x5. It will launch three new games on to the market on 1 July 20x5: 'Space Runner' (SR), 'Football Frenzy' (FF) and 'Cricket Coach' (CC). These are the only three products which the company will be producing and selling in the financial year ending 30 June 20x6. Management are attempting to get an estimate of the likely profits for that year (ending 30 June 20x6). However, because of the inherent riskiness of the computer games market, agreement has not been reached on a number of key estimates, details of which are set out below.

**Sales units (volume)**: Historically, ICS has sold 12,000 units in any year and management consider that there is a 40% probability that this figure will be repeated for the next year (ending 30 June 20x6). In addition, there is a 40% probability that 10,000 units will sell, and a 20% probability that only 1,200 units will sell.

However, predicting which of the three games will be the top seller is even more difficult. Based solely on opinion, management consider that, if 12,000 units are sold, there will be an even split between all three games, but at sales of 10,000 units and below, they expect that SR and FF will each sell twice as many units as CC. As ICS management are risk takers, they have decided that, from a production perspective, they will make 12,000 units regardless (i.e. 4,000 units of each product). Any unsold units (which will be returned to ICS by the wholesalers) will be given away for free at the end of the year.

**Sales price (to wholesalers)**: SR and FF are each expected to sell for €50 per unit, while CC is likely to sell for €40 per unit.

**Variable costs**: The variable costs of production consist of the cost of a CD (€1 each) and the cost of packaging and delivery (to the wholesaler) (€6 each). These costs are the same for all three products and have not changed for two years. However, there is a 40% chance that these costs may increase by 25% in the coming year (with a 60% chance that there will be no change).

**Semi-fixed costs**: ICS outsources the programming and design of its software to freelance software writers. For any game that makes it to the market, ICS pays the programmer an annual payment of €50,000 plus 5% of its gross sales (excluding any units returned by wholesalers).

**Fixed costs**: ICS employs two staff to look after all production, distribution and administration duties, and pays them €25,000 each per annum.

**Requirements:**

1. Using probability theory, show the range, and associated probabilities, of the profits/losses of ICS and calculate the likely profit of ICS for the year ending 30 June 20x6. (Clearly show all workings.)
2. State the probability that, in the year ending 30 June 20x6, ICS will:
   (a) make a loss, using only six mutually exclusive options based on three different sales levels and two different levels of variable costs;
   (b) make a profit in excess of €180,000;
   (c) make a profit in excess of €250,000.
3. What are the implications of your answer to parts (1) and (2) for ICS management?

4. Outline briefly **two** other ways in which the management of ICS could improve profitability.

Source: Chartered Accountants Ireland, Management Accounting and Business Finance,
P3, Summer 2005

*Question 12.11: (Decision-making using EMV Criterion)*

Sportsco Publishers Limited (Sportsco) is a newly formed Irish company that publishes sports books for the Irish market. The company will produce all publications in-house and sell only to retailers who, in turn, sell the books to consumers.

Management are preparing for a forthcoming meeting at which the likely profits for the financial year 2007 will be discussed, based on the launch of four new titles. The titles are *Irish Rugby Greats* (IRG), *A History of Irish Cricket* (HIC), *Olé, Olé, Olé: Irish Soccer* (OIS), and *Great GAA Matches* (GAA). IRG and OIS will be sold to distributors at a price of €30 per book, while HIC and GAA will be sold at €25 per unit. The recommended retail price will be €40 for IRG and OIS, and €35 for HIC and GAA.

Sportsco expects the market to be buoyant in 2007 because of the number of high profile sporting events scheduled for the year. However, they are unable to agree the level of demand and costs that should be assumed for the year. They have provided you with the following details:

**Demand**: Management believe that there is a 40% probability that total book sales of all four volumes will be 100,000 volumes during 2007 as they believe that the titles and authors will have a stronger market appeal than the authors and topics of other companies. However, due to uncertainty regarding the actions that may be taken by rival publishing companies, management believe that there is also a 40% chance that only 75,000 publications will be sold and a 20% probability that only 50,000 publications will be sold.

Management are aware that the appeal of the authors to the market is uncertain and hard to predict. In their opinion it is reasonable to estimate that if 100,000 units are sold the mix will be evenly spread across all titles, while if less than 100,000 books are sold they predict IRG and OIS will sell twice as many copies as HIC and GAA.

In view of the uncertainty, and the requirement to have books published in advance of sales, management have decided to produce 100,000 books.

**Variable costs**: Management has identified four different variable costs, i.e. paper, printing, binding and royalties. Paper currently costs €1 per book, print costs (€2.50 per book), and binding (€0.5 per book). These variable costs will be the same for each title. However, due to potential cost increases management believe that there is a 75% chance that both paper and binding costs will increase by 10% for the financial year 2007. The authors of the books will be paid a royalty of €2 per title printed.

**Labour costs**: Labour consists of skilled and unskilled workers. Skilled workers operate the printing presses. Based on current projections, the skilled employees can complete 78,750 books within normal hours per annum for a total cost of €78,750. The additional books will require a skilled labour cost of €9 per book.

Unskilled labour is required for the 'Finishing' process only. The books are finished in batches of 10,000 units and the unskilled labour cost for each batch is €30,000. There are no economies of scale or learning curve.

**Fixed overheads**: Fixed overheads are estimated at €320,000 per annum. In addition, the company will need to employ three staff to manage all production/administration at a cost of €20,000 each per annum. Furthermore, each book author will receive a one off payment of €10,000. Finally, marketing and distribution costs are €100,000 and book launches will each cost €2,500, i.e. a total outlay of €10,000.

**Requirements:**

1. Based on the information above and using EMV, prepare an income statement showing the range and associated probabilities of Sportsco and calculate likely profit for the financial year 2007.
2. Provide management with an overview of the numbers calculated, in part (1) of the question, for the Board meeting.

Source: Chartered Accountants Ireland, teaching material

## Question 12.12: (Decision-making and the Value of Perfect Information)

The directors of Taurus Limited must choose between high and low production runs for the forthcoming accounting period.

There are only two outcomes, viz. buoyant market conditions (SI) which has an estimated 70% probability and depressed market conditions (S2) with an estimated 30% probability. The monetary payoff matrix is produced below in summarised form:

PAYOFF MATRIX

| | States of Nature | |
|---|---|---|
| Actions | Buoyant demand (p = 0.7) | Depressed demand (p = 0.3) |
| A1: Produce High | €7,000 | €1,000 |
| A2: Produce Low | €3,000 | €2,000 |

A consultant can be engaged who will report that there shall either be buoyant or depressed market conditions. Unfortunately this consultant is by no means infallible.

**Requirements:**

1. "Perfect information has a value, but it comes at a price." Briefly discuss this statement.
2. What decision should be taken in the absence of the consultant's report?
3. What is the maximum amount which should be paid for perfect information, if available?

# 13

# Evaluation of Capital Expenditure Proposals

LEARNING OBJECTIVES

When you have completed studying this chapter you should be able to:

1. Define capital expenditure decisions.
2. Evaluate capital expenditure proposals using the payback period.
3. Describe the time value of money.
4. Distinguish between and apply the techniques of net present value and internal rate of return.
5. Calculate the weighted average cost of capital for use in capital expenditure proposals.
6. Discuss the separate impact of taxation and inflation on capital expenditure decisions.

## 13.1 The Nature of Capital Expenditure

Some of the most significant decisions made by management involve considerable and immediate cash outlay which is anticipated to provide long-term benefits, for example, to expand production capacity, to develop new products or to enter new markets. Such projects are often referred to as **capital expenditure (CapEx) proposals** and the process of planning and evaluating such proposals is generally referred to as **capital budgeting**.

Capital expenditure proposals share three common characteristics. First, they involve an immediate and significant outlay of cash and these amounts are usually included as part of the financial highlights included in the Annual Report of most companies. Once the expenditure has been incurred, the funds may be extremely difficult to recover. For example, much of the costs incurred in, say, research and development or drilling for oil, have little resale value, if any.

Secondly, capital expenditure proposals are long-term in nature, i.e. the benefits are expected to accrue to the firm over a number of years. This requires estimates of future operating cash flows over the project's estimated useful life and they should have the ability to exceed the capital expenditure outlay. Without this (excess) return, the company will not be able to generate additional internal funds for future investment projects.

Thirdly, the significant outlay and the long-term nature of such proposals increases the overall risk of such proposals, not only because the future is always uncertain but also because erroneous data may have been included in the analysis. Managers, by definition, are essentially optimistic. For example, those sponsoring a capital expenditure proposal have a tendency to estimate both the cash inflows and outflows from an optimistic perspective. This means that they will likely overstate the estimated cash inflows and understate the estimated cash outflows. At the very minimum, their natural optimism reduces the validity of any of the evaluation techniques outlined below, because all of them use managerial estimates of cash inflows and cash outflows as the basis of evaluation.

Because of the magnitude of the financial resources involved, together with the, often, strategic nature of such decisions, capital expenditure decisions are crucial in determining the future financial health of the enterprise. If managers do not treat capital expenditure decisions with the seriousness they deserve, they run the risk of making poor decisions. In brief, firms benefit from good capital expenditure decisions. In contrast, if these proposals do not perform as well as the company hoped, then this could lead to financial disaster. Certainly, the magnitude of capital expenditure decisions requires serious analysis before such projects are undertaken.

There are many techniques for evaluating the financial considerations in such situations, but they all use decision concepts outlined in **Chapter 10**, which emphasised the future-orientated nature of decisions, together with the concept of relevant costs, i.e. incremental, out-of-pocket cash costs together with any opportunity cost which may be appropriate. The main difference between capital expenditure decisions and previously discussed decisions is that they involve identifying future cash flows over several years and this will introduce the concept of the 'time value of money' (to be explored subsequently). The most common methods used in evaluating capital expenditure decisions, which will be discussed in turn, are:

1. Simple Payback Period
2. Net Present Value (NPV)
3. Internal Rate of Return (IRR)

### Simple Payback Period

The **payback period** is the length of time necessary to recover the initial capital expenditure from future net cash flows. In selecting between alternative capital expenditure opportunities, a short payback period is desirable since it reduces the risk associated with changes in future economic conditions. In addition, the sooner the amount of the investment is recovered, the sooner the funds may be put to another use. The principal advantage of the payback period is the caution it introduces to the capital expenditure decision and, generally, it produces satisfactory results. Also, it is simple to apply and understand. The application of the payback method will be illustrated using the example of the Monaghan Company.

## Illustration: Payback Period

The Monaghan Company is considering the immediate purchase of equipment for €21,000 that has a four-year life, with an estimated salvage value of €1,000 at the end of these four years. The additional profit from this capital expenditure will be €2,000 per annum, summarised as follows:

|  | € |
|---|---|
| Additional sales revenue (all cash sales) | 17,000 |
| Additional depreciation (€21,000−€1,000)/4 years | (5,000) |
| Additional cash costs | (10,000) |
| Additional profit | 2,000 |

**Requirement:** Calculate the payback period.

**Solution and Analysis:** Since all sales revenues are received in cash and all costs other than depreciation are paid for in cash, the expected annual net operating cash flow from this project is €7,000 (€17,000 – €10,000). Alternatively, the annual net operating cash flow exceeds estimated profit by the amount of the depreciation expense, since depreciation is purely a book-keeping exercise and does not represent a cash flow. The calculation of the payback period is as follows:

$$\frac{\text{Amount invested}}{\text{Estimated annual net cash flow}} = \frac{€21,000}{€7,000} = 3 \text{ years}$$

There are two **limitations associated with the payback period**. First, it ignores the total life of the project and, therefore, the total profitability of the investment. Secondly, it disregards the time value of money. The concept of 'time value of money' is discussed below and will be used in applying both the NPV and IRR methods.

## 13.2 The Time Value of Money

The **time value of money** arises because the projected cash flows from the capital expenditure proposal will extend over a number of future years. Thus, we need to take into consideration the **timing** of those future cash flows. Money received today is preferable to receiving money at some later date due to the fact that, if cash is available now, it can be invested to earn a return. This increase in value over time due to accrued investment income is referred to as the **time value of money**. The relationship between present values and future values is demonstrated in the following example.

### ILLUSTRATION: THE TIME VALUE OF MONEY

If an investment of €100 is made at a 7% rate of interest, compute the future value after two years. The relevant figure is derived from (rounded) compound interest calculations, as follows:

| | |
|---|---|
| Amount to be invested | 100 |
| Interest: Year 1 (€100 × 7%) | _7 |
| Amount to be received in one year (future value) | 107 |
| Interest: Year 2 (€107 × 7%) | _8 |
| Amount to be received in two years (future value) | 115 |

Thus, if €115 would be received two years in the future, the investment would be worth €100 in today's currency. In other words, the future value (FV) of €115 at the end of two years has a current or present value (PV) of €100.

The relationship between present and future values can be expressed by the following equation:

$$PV = \frac{FV}{(1+R)^n}$$

where PV = Present value; FV = Future value; 1 = Unity (or 1)
R = Rate of interest (return); and, N = Number of years

## Present Value Tables

When calculating the present value of future cash flows, one can use discount tables which are included in any standard textbook on finance and an extract is reproduced in **Exhibit 13.1** with an additional extract being provided in the **Appendix** to this chapter. These tables contain a listing of appropriate discount factors to use, depending on the rate of interest and the number of years involved. To convert future value (FV) amounts to present value (PV) amounts, simply multiply the future value amount by the appropriate discount factor. For example, using **Exhibit 13.1**, the present value of €107 to be received in one year, discounted at 7% per annum, is €100 (€107 × 0.935). The present value of €115 to be received in two years, at 7%, is also €100 (€115 × 0.873).

## Classification of Cash Flows

In evaluating capital expenditure projects, it is convenient to divide cash flows into three distinct phases or groups as follows:

- **Initial investment** The initial cash outlay is assumed to take place immediately, sometimes designated '$t_0$' representing time period zero. This amount should also include any additional investment in working capital – for example, stock and debtors – to support the additional volume of sales. Such investment will involve a cash outlay and should be treated accordingly.
- **Operating cash flows** These correspond to cash flows arising from the sale of goods together with payments for day-to-day operating expenses, including any payments for taxation. For convenience purposes, operating cash flows are typically divided into one-year periods and these cash flows are deemed to occur at the end of each respective accounting period. If proposals involve an opportunity cost then, since an opportunity cost is equivalent to a cash outflow, it should be included in the calculations. It is important to remember that we concentrate only on

EXHIBIT 13.1: PRESENT VALUES OF €1 DUE IN N PERIODS

| No. of years | <————————Discount rate————————> | | | | |
|---|---|---|---|---|---|
| | 7% | 10% | 12% | 15% | 20% |
| 1 | .935 | .909 | .893 | .870 | .833 |
| 2 | .873 | .826 | .797 | .756 | .694 |
| 3 | .816 | .751 | .712 | .658 | .579 |
| 4 | .763 | .683 | .636 | .572 | .482 |
| 5 | .713 | .621 | .567 | .497 | .402 |

future cash flows rather than accounting profits or income, because cash is the only resource that is available for reinvestment or for discharging liabilities. Thus, depreciation of non-current (fixed) assets must be ignored since it is a non-cash item of expenditure. In making short-term decisions in earlier chapters, the fact that there is a difference between accounting profits and cash flows was sometimes ignored. This difference must now be acknowledged due to the long-term nature of capital expenditure decisions and the time value of money, i.e. cash.

- **Exit cash flows** These cash flows are generated at the end of the project's life and represent the disposal or salvage value of any non-current (fixed) assets together with any disinvestment of working capital, e.g. reduction in stock levels.

These three groups are summarised in **Exhibit 13.2**. It is convention to describe the start of the project as **time period zero**, i.e. $(t_o)$ and the end of the project $(t_n)$ as **time period n**. The intervening years are usually described as $t_1$, $t_2$ etc.

EXHIBIT 13.2: CLASSIFICATION OF CASH FLOWS FOR LONG-TERM DECISIONS

| Time period $(t_o)$ | Time periods $(t_1, t_2, t_3)$… | Time period $(t_n)$ |
|---|---|---|
| Initial investment<br><br>• Cost of acquiring fixed assets<br>• Increase in working capital requirements | Incremental cash flows<br><br>• Incremental cash inflows<br>• Incremental costs including tax payments | Exit cash flows<br><br>• Sale of assets at end of project<br>• Disinvestment of working capital |

Once all relevant cash flows have been identified, their present value (PV) can be calculated. The present value of a future cash receipt is the amount that a knowledgeable investor would pay today for the right to receive that future receipt. The advantage of using present values in evaluating capital expenditure decisions is that all future cash flows, regardless of when they occur, can be translated to a common base (present value), which facilitates the comparison of alternatives. The present value will always be less than the future amount because cash received today can be invested to earn interest and thereby becomes equivalent to a larger amount in the future. The exact amount of the present value depends upon:

1. The amount of the future receipt.
2. The future time period in which the cash will be received.
3. The rate of return required (called the discount rate) or cost of capital.

The technique that takes into account the timing of future cash flows is called **discounting cash flows (DCF)**. In other words, **discounting** is the process of determining the present value of future cash flows.

## Illustration: NPV

We now return to the Westmeath Company, which is considering the purchase of equipment for €21,000 that has a four-year life, with an estimated salvage value of €1,000. The additional income from this investment will be €2,000 per annum, as follows:

|  | € |
|---|---|
| Additional sales (all cash sales) | 17,000 |
| Additional depreciation: (€21,000 − €1,000)/4 years | (5,000) |
| Additional cash costs | (10,000) |
| Additional profit | 2,000 |

**Requirement:** Calculate the NPV for this proposal, assuming a discount rate of 10%.

**Solution and analysis:** The objective of the NPV technique is to find out whether a given capital expenditure proposal generates a return at least equal to the minimum acceptable rate, i.e. 10% in this case. The discount rate is set equal to the cost of capital (to be explained later). If the NPV of a proposal is positive, the benefits from the expenditure will exceed its costs. In other words, the NPV of a proposal is the difference between the total present value of future cash flows and the cost of the investment. The calculation of NPV is as follows:

| Time period | Cash Flows € | Discount Factor | Present Value € |
|---|---|---|---|
| End of year 1 | 7,000 | .909 | 6,363 |
| End of year 2 | 7,000 | .826 | 5,782 |
| End of year 3 | 7,000 | .751 | 5,257 |
| End of year 4 | 7,000 | .683 | 4,781 |
| End of year 4 (disposal) | 1,000 | .683 | 683 |
|  |  |  | 22,866 |
| Less: Capital Expenditure (payable in advance) |  |  | (21,000) |
| Net Present Value (positive) |  |  | 1,866 |

## Profitability Index

The **profitability index** is an index of the values of alternative capital expenditure projects. The index is calculated by dividing the present value of the project's cash inflows by the initial investment.

### ILLUSTRATION: PROFITABILITY INDEX

To illustrate, we return to the above example (let us refer to it as Project A), which has a present value of cash inflows of €22,866, compared with the initial investment of €21,000. The profitability index is 1.09 times (€22,866 divided by €21,000).

Let us assume that there is another project (Project B), whose present value of cash inflows amounts to €16,000 generated from an investment of €12,000. Both projects have positive NPVs and are acceptable. However, due to scarcity of funds, we may want to rank the projects in order of preference. The profitability index for Project B is 1.33 (€16,000 ÷ €12,000). We would rank Project B higher than Project A because Project B's profitability index value is 1.33 compared to Project A's lower index value of 1.09. Thus, the profitability index is a tool that allows a ranking of competing projects.

## Computer Applications and NPV Calculations

It is useful to briefly look at how computers facilitate the calculation of NPV since their software usually contains functions which calculate NPV quickly and accurately and this is done in **Exhibit 13.3** for the Westmeath Company. The explanatory text is included in **Column A** (and in **Cell B1**). The operating cash flow data is entered in

EXHIBIT 13.3: USING SPREADSHEETS TO CALCULATE NPV

|   | A | B | Explanation |
|---|---|---|---|
| 1 | **Year** | **Cash flow** | |
| 2 | 1 | 7,000 | |
| 3 | 2 | 7,000 | |
| 4 | 3 | 7,000 | |
| 5 | 4 | 8,000 | |
| 6 | PV | 22,872 | *i.e. = NPV(0.10,B2:B5)* |
| 7 | Outlay | 21,000 | |
| 8 | NPV | 1,872 | **i.e. = B6−B7** |

**Column B (Cells B2 to B5)** and the final year's cash flow includes the salvage value of the fixed assets. The initial investment is presented in **Cell B7** (but not as a negative number).

**Cell B6** is entered as a formula as follows = NPV (0.10,B2:B5) and some explanation of this is necessary. The '=' sign indicates a formula, and the NPV notation signifies a NPV calculation. This is followed by a bracket containing the discount factor which is followed by a comma. The 'B2:B5' insert indicates the range of values representing operating cash flows and which require to be discounted. When this formula is inserted in **Cell B6**, the amount of PV €22,872 appears automatically. Finally, the amount of the initial investment must be deducted from the PV and this is done by entering the final formula in **Cell B8** as follows = B6 − B7. This command automatically deducts the initial outlay from the total PV of operating cash flows and this is why the initial investment is originally entered without a negative sign. (Alternatively, if a negative sign is used, then the formula in Cell B8 would use a positive sign and read: = B6 + B7.)

The **advantage** of the NPV technique is that it is concerned with the total lifespan of the proposal and the timing of all cash flows. NPV suffers from the **disadvantage** that it is very sensitive to the choice of discount rate used. The greater the discount rate, the smaller the present value of a given stream of future cash flows. In addition, for computational purposes, restrictive assumptions must be made such as that all cash flows, apart from the initial investment, are deemed to take place on the last day of the accounting period.

## The Internal Rate of Return

Although the NPV method indicates whether a project's return is lower or higher than the required rate of return, it does not show the project's overall percentage return.

The overall percentage return generated by a capital expenditure proposal is referred to as the Internal Rate of Return (IRR). Alternatively, it can be described as the discount rate at which the net present value of a proposal is zero. If the proposal's IRR is greater than its cost of capital, then the project is acceptable. If the IRR is less than the discount rate, the project is unattractive. The calculation of IRR is a trial-and-error process involving the selection of discount rates at random and applying them to future cash flows until one gets two discount rates, one of which gives a negative NPV and the other a positive NPV.

ILLUSTRATION: INTERNAL RATE OF RETURN

Using the earlier example of the Westmeath Company, applying a discount rate of 10%, we calculated that the NPV was (positive) €1,866. Using a discount rate of 14%, the NPV is (negative) €17 (readers are encouraged to prove this for themselves). The actual IRR must, therefore, lie between 10% and 14% and very close to 14%. The IRR is the discount rate at which NPV equals zero and this can be approximated by interpolating between our two points and we can present the range of our values as:

$$4\%\begin{bmatrix}10\% & PV = €1,866 \\ 14\% & PV = -€17\end{bmatrix} €1,883$$

The 4% represents the range between the two percentage points (10% and 14%). The PVs associated with both these discount rates are presented and the total range between these two values is €1,883, bearing in mind that we have a range from (positive) €1,866 and (negative) €17. The IRR is calculated as follows:

$$\text{Approximate IRR} = 10\% + \frac{€1,866}{€1,883} \times (4\%) = 13.96\%$$

## Speeding up Calculations

Discounting future cash flows can be a time-consuming exercise. Fortunately, the calculations can be considerably speeded up using annuity tables. An **annuity** represents the receipt of a constant amount of cash for a specified amount of time, e.g. €1,000 to be received at the end of each of the next four years. The PV of this inflow can be calculated as follows (assuming 10% interest):

|  | Future cash flows | | Present value |
|---|---|---|---|
|  | € | Discount factor | € |
| Year 1 | 1,000 | .909 | 909 |
| Year 2 | 1,000 | .826 | 826 |
| Year 3 | 1,000 | .751 | 751 |
| Year 4 | 1,000 | .683 | 683 |
|  |  |  | 3,169 |

The PV of €1,000 to be received at the end of each of the next four years is €3,169, based on a 10% return. This calculation can be performed more quickly using annuity tables, but such tables can only be used for *constant* cash flows. A partial annuity table is provided below in **Exhibit 13.4** and a further extract of annuity tables appears in the **Appendix** to this chapter.

EXHIBIT 13.4: PV OF AN ANNUITY OF €1 PER PERIOD FOR N PERIODS

| Years | 10% | 14% | 15% | 20% |
|-------|-----|-----|-----|-----|
| 1 | .909 | .877 | .870 | .833 |
| 2 | 1.736 | 1.646 | 1.626 | 1.528 |
| 3 | 2.487 | 2.320 | 2.283 | 2.106 |
| 4 | 3.169 | 2.912 | 2.854 | 2.589 |

Annuity tables are compiled by simply aggregating the individual discount factors in the PV table (**Exhibit 13.1**) for the appropriate number of years. For example, the individual discount factors for 10% on the Present Value table (for four years) are .909, .826, .751 and .683 respectively. When aggregated, these discount factors amount to 3.169. This corresponds to the factor equivalent to four years and 10% in the annuity table (**Exhibit 13.4**). Thus the PV of an **annuity** of €7,000 for each of four years can be quickly ascertained as:

$$\text{Present Value} = €7,000 \times 3.169 = €22,183$$

Annuity tables can be used in the approximation of Internal Rate of Return (IRR) by applying the following steps, and we use the figures from our earlier Westmeath Company illustration:

1. Calculate the payback period of the project (assume three years, i.e. €21,000/ €7,000).
2. Ascertain the project's life (four years) and consult the annuity tables corresponding to four years (the life of the project). The annuity table (**Exhibit 13.4**) indicates that the factor nearest to 3 (the pay-back period), based on four years, is found in the 14% column. (The nearest factor is 2.912.) Thus, the IRR on this project is 14% approximately, but this is a crude and quick estimate.

## 13.3 The Cost of Capital

Discounted cash flow calculations (NPV and IRR) require a discount rate and this is linked to the firm's cost of capital. Clearly, different sources of funds will have different costs and taxation considerations are also important. The cost of debt (Kd) is the annual rate of interest (net of tax) charged by the lender, based on the current market value of the debt. For example, if a company raises €800,000 debt for 10 years at 12% per annum, the gross rate of interest is 12%. However, interest paid on debt finance is tax-deductible and so the after-tax cost of debt finance must be calculated and used. Assuming a tax rate of 40%, then the after-tax cost of debt is 7.2% (12% × 60%). The amount of interest a company pays on debt is easy to determine because it is reported on the firm's income statement or in the notes to the financial statements.

The calculation of the cost of equity capital (Ke) is more complicated and can be approached by using the following argument. The owner of equity shares can either sell the shares or retain them. It is logical to suggest that the shareholder will sell his shares unless they provide him with an 'adequate' return based on the risk-free interest rate plus a premium for risk associated with this investment. The amount of this premium will depend on the investor's perception of the riskiness of the project under review. However, firms do not know the preferences of individual shareholders. What firms must do is try to determine what percentage return equity shareholders generally expect on their investments and use that percentage as the cost of equity capital. How do we measure the return expected by shareholders in general? Basically there are three approaches to estimating the cost of equity capital, each will be discussed in turn:

1. Gordon's Dividend Growth Model
2. The Capital Asset Pricing Model (CAPM)
3. The Bond-yield Adjustment

## Gordon's Dividend Growth Model

In the Gordon dividend growth model, an estimate of the required rate of return on equity is obtained by solving for a discount rate that equates the market price of the stock with the expected one-step ahead dividend per share and the long-term growth rate. Therefore, if we assume that dividends in the future will grow at a constant rate of G%, the rate of return expected by the market will be calculated by the following formula:

$$Ke = \left\{ \frac{D_1}{P_0} \right\} + G$$

Where:  Ke = Required rate of return, equivalent to the cost of equity from a company's perspective
$D_1$ = Expected dividend (but the current dividend is sometimes used)
$P_0$ = Current market price
G  = Constant growth in dividends

If the share receives a return of Ke % in the following period, the value of the share should remain unchanged.

## ILLUSTRATION: GORDON'S DIVIDEND GROWTH MODEL

For example, assume a company has a current dividend of 14c per share with a current price of 1,000c. If dividends are expected to grow at a constant rate of 7% per annum, then the expected future dividend ($D_1$), in the next accounting period, is 15c (i.e. 14c × 1.07). Using the Gordon's dividend growth model, the relevant calculation for cost of equity capital is:

$$Ke = \left\{ \frac{15}{1,000} \right\} + 0.07 = 0.085 = 8.5\%$$

The Gordon's dividend growth model is a simple, yet meaningful, approach to estimating the cost of equity capital. However, for convenience purposes, sometimes the current dividend per share is used. For example, the current dividend yield is 1.4% ((14c/1,000c)×100), which, when added to the constant growth rate (7%), provides an estimated required rate of return on equity of 8.4%.

### Estimating Future Dividends

One of the difficulties in applying Gordon's dividend growth model is the prediction of future dividends. It is usual to predict future growth rates in dividend payments from an analysis of the historical growth rates in dividends over the past few years.

## ILLUSTRATION: ESTIMATING DIVIDEND GROWTH RATES

For example, assume that in Year 1 a company paid total equity dividends of €150,000 and in Year 5 they amounted to €262,350. Thus the dividend growth over **four** years can be modelled as:

$$(1+G)^4 = \frac{262,350}{150,000} = 1.749$$

$$(1+G) = \sqrt[4]{1.749}$$

$$(1+G) = 1.15$$

$$G = 0.15 = 15\%$$

One of the major problems associated with Gordon's dividend growth model is that some companies do not pay dividends to shareholders. This may be because the company is unprofitable or because the company has a policy of not paying dividends. Therefore, alternative methods of calculating the cost of equity capital are needed.

## The Capital Asset Pricing Model

The Capital Asset Pricing Model (CAPM) is a commonly presented method in corporate finance textbooks for estimating the cost of equity capital. The CAPM evolved out of modern portfolio theory which argues that there exists a linear relationship between the expected return on a security and its level of 'systematic risk'. This argument requires some explanation.

The total risk of an investment can be divided between systematic and non-systematic risk. Systematic risk cannot be eliminated by diversification because it relates to the market as a whole. For example, interest or exchange rate movements or changes in the level of taxation rates impact on all companies. Since these factors cause returns to move in the same direction they cannot be eliminated, *per se*, and systematic risk will always be present in investment decisions. However, some securities will be more sensitive to market forces than others and will, therefore, have a higher level of systematic risk.

In contrast, unsystematic risk can be described as specific or diversifiable risk and can reflect, for example, the nature of the business and particular problems which may occur within a company. It may be possible to cancel out these firm-specific factors as an investment portfolio increases in size and becomes more diversified. For example, investing separately in alcohol and non-alcohol manufacturing companies is a form of diversification. The CAPM is based on the assumption that one can diversify away a considerable amount of risk by holding a large volume of investments. So, the only risk that an investor needs to accept – and the only risk that will be rewarded – is the risk that one cannot avoid, namely the systematic risk.

The CAPM can be used to estimate the required rate of return on equity (RoE). CAPM argues that the cost of equity capital is determined by the formula:

$$Ke = Rf + (Rm - Rf)Be$$

Where:

Ke  = required rate of return on equity
Rf  = the risk-free rate of interest, indicated by the return on government stock
Rm = the return on the market portfolio
Rm – Rf = the expected market premium
Be  = Beta or systematic (or non-diversifiable) risk of a particular security

Beta is a measure of a security's volatility, i.e. how the price of a security will move in relation to the overall market. Therefore, it reflects non-diversifiable or systematic risk. Beta should not be viewed as indicating how attractive or otherwise a particular investment may be. Rather it is a measure of risk. By definition, the market itself has an underlying Beta of 1.0 and individual securities are ranked according to how much they deviate from the overall market. A Beta of 1.0 indicates a stock that rises and falls in complete harmony with the overall market. A security that swings more than the market over time (i.e. is more volatile), has a Beta above 1.0. If a stock moves less than the market, that stock's Beta is less than 1.0. More specifically, a stock that has a Beta of 2 will follow the market in an overall decline or growth, but does so by a factor of 2.0; meaning when the market has an overall decline of, say, 3%, a stock with a Beta of 2.0 will fall by 6%. Betas can also be negative, meaning a stock moves in the opposite direction of the market: a stock with a Beta of $-3.0$ would decline by 9% when the market goes up by 3% and conversely would climb by 9% if the market fell by 3%. Generally, Betas tend to be positive.

## ILLUSTRATION: USING CAPM FOR KE

Thus, if the risk-free interest rate is 5% and the market premium is 6%, with a company's Beta of 0.8, the CAPM provides a required rate of return on equity for this company of 9.8% as follows:

$$Ke = 5\% + 0.8 \times (11\% - 5\%) = 9.8\%$$

While CAPM is widely used in computing the cost of equity capital, several empirical studies show that Beta alone does not **fully** account for the observed average return on equity over time. Critics point out that the 'market-risk premium' may not be static, but appears to change in a dynamic way with the business cycle. In addition, it is debatable whether Beta remains stationary over a long period of time in the real world. Finally, Beta calculations are based on historical data and it is argued that historical returns are poor proxies for future, expected returns.

### The Bond Yield Adjustment

The bond yield adjustment approach is a much simpler approach to estimating the cost of equity capital than either of the two approaches presented above. With this approach, the long-term yield of bonds is used as a base rate upon which an equity premium, based on managerial judgement, is added. However, because interest expense payable on bonds is tax-deductible, we use the after-tax cost.

## ILLUSTRATION: BOND YIELD ADJUSTMENT

Thus, if risk-free bond investments had a gross cost of 10%, with a tax rate of 40% and the estimated risk-premium was 5%, then using this method, the required rate of return on equity capital would be estimated at about 11% as follows:

$$(10\% \times 60\%) + 5\% = 11\%$$

## The Weighted Average Cost of Capital (WACC)

Since most commercial firms have a mixture of both debt and equity in their capital structure, it is advisable to use the weighted average cost of capital (WACC) in evaluating capital expenditure decisions. There are a number of advantages associated with the WACC:

1. A weighted cost gives recognition to the fact that a company's capital structure has both debt and equity elements. Different capital structures are to be found in different industrial sectors and in different countries. It is suggested that all capital expenditure proposals should be evaluated at this composite rate, thus enjoying some benefit from cheaper debt finance. However, this method ignores variations in risk among projects. If a project involves little risk, then a lower discount may be more appropriate. Conversely, a higher discount rate would be appropriate for a project which is associated with higher risk.
2. The WACC reflects the long-term future capital structure which, over time, the company finances capital expenditure proposals in the proportions specified. It can be argued that the capital structure changes slowly over time. Therefore the marginal cost of new capital should be roughly equal to the WACC.

It is important for companies to assess carefully the cost of capital relevant to a capital expenditure proposal, since this is the figure at which it should discount the project's cash flows to determine its NPV or IRR. Projects that have positive net present values at the appropriate cost of capital are likely to increase a company's share price. Those with negative net present values will decrease a company's share price and should not be undertaken.

### ILLUSTRATION: WACC USING THE DIVIDEND GROWTH MODEL

The capital structure of Offaly Company is summarised as follows:

| | |
|---|---|
| Equity | €6 million |
| Debt (7%) | €4 million |

The current level of dividend is 10c per share and this has been growing at 6% per annum in recent years. The market price of the company's equity shares is 200c. The market value of debt is equal to its par value. The tax rate on corporate profits is 50%.

**Requirement:** Compute the weighted average cost of capital to be used as a discount rate in project appraisal, using Gordon's dividend growth model.

**Solution and analysis:** Using Gordon's growth model, the cost of equity capital (Ke) is given by:

$$Ke = \left\{ \frac{D_1}{P_0} \right\} + G$$

Where:

$D_1$ = expected dividend per share;
$P_0$ = market price per share and
$G$ = dividend growth per annum.

Since the current dividend is 10c per share, which is expected to grow by 6% per annum, then the next expected dividend is 10.6c. Thus:

$$Ke = \left\{ \frac{10.6}{200} \right\} + 0.06 = 0.113$$

$$= 11.3\%$$

The weighted average cost of capital (WACC) is based on the firm's capital structure and can be computed as follows:

|  | €000 | Cost | €000 |
|---|---|---|---|
| Equity | 6,000 | 11% (rounded) | 660 |
| Debt | 4,000 | 3.5% net after tax | 140 |
|  | 10,000 |  | 800 |

Weighted Average Cost of Capital = 8% ((800/1000)×100)

Because of the difficulties encountered in determining the cost of capital, many firms will adopt a discount rate which they consider appropriate without complicated mathematical analysis, i.e. adopt the bond yield adjustment method. This selected discount rate would be based on the risk-free rate in the market with an adjustment for the risk inherent in the capital expenditure proposal. Thus, a project considered as being virtually risk free might be evaluated using a discount rate of, say, between 7% and 9%, whereas a high-risk proposal may be evaluated using a discount rate of, say, 15% to 20%. While there are probable errors in making calculations based on the above figures, these inaccuracies can be overcome by utilising sensitivity analysis.

## 13.4 The Impact of Taxation on Capital Expenditure Decisions

In most Western economies, the tax rate on corporate profits typically ranges between 25% and 40%. These high tax rates mean that the payment of tax liabilities, generated by profits arising from the capital expenditure proposal, is a most important component of cash flow and must be taken into consideration in evaluating capital investment proposals.

There are **two separate tax issues to be considered**. First is the different treatment of the amount of capital expenditure for taxation and for accounting purposes. For accounting purposes, capital expenditure is recorded under the heading of non-current (fixed) assets on the balance sheet and this expenditure is written off to the income statement by way of depreciation over the estimated useful life of the asset. However, the taxation authorities often do not allow a deduction of accounting depreciation in computing profits for taxation purposes. Instead, 'capital allowances' are granted on the cost of qualifying fixed assets at specified rates. In special circumstances, some companies may write off the entire cost of the qualifying plant and equipment immediately on purchase against taxable profits. These are referred to as **accelerated capital allowances**. The general result of this treatment is that a company would not have to make tax payments in the early years of capital expenditure programmes. Rather, the payment of tax liabilities would be effectively postponed to later years when the present value of those cash payments would be much lower. Effectively, companies would use the investment in fixed assets to postpone (but not eliminate) the payment of tax liabilities to future time periods.

Secondly, one needs to determine the actual amount of tax to be paid on profits and when this payment should be made. Obviously, the actual tax rate in force should be used. It should be noted that in some circumstances the actual tax rate could be as low as 10%. Corporate tax liabilities are usually paid in the year subsequent to the year of assessment. However, depending on how the exam question is phrased, one may assume that corporate tax liabilities are paid in the year to which they relate. Thus, the date of corporate tax payments should be clarified before you engage in computations.

When estimating the NPV of capital expenditure proposals involving taxation it is useful to prepare two separate calculations. First, it is necessary to calculate the amount of taxable profits for each year using normal accounting conventions such as the accruals concept. However, depreciation expense should not be included since it is not an allowable expense for taxation purposes; instead, the appropriate capital allowances should be deducted. The purpose of this calculation is to determine the amount of the tax liability, if any, for each accounting period.

The second set of calculations is to determine the NPV of all the cash flows associated with the proposal which will include the payment of any tax liability. Likewise, any 'exit' cash flows should be included, e.g. disinvestment of working capital and any cash received on the eventual disposal of the fixed asset. However, such disposal may attract an additional tax liability, which can be referred to as a balancing charge, representing the excess of the cash proceeds over the tax written down value. (The opposite phenomenon is a balancing allowance – an additional tax loss – which represents the excess of the tax written down value of the fixed assets over the cash proceeds on disposal.)

## ILLUSTRATION: TAX IMPLICATIONS

The Laois Company is evaluating a capital expenditure proposal that will increase annual profits by €40,000 (before depreciation) over the next three years. The proposal requires an immediate investment in new plant and machinery costing €90,000. This machinery has an estimated life of three years with an estimated scrap value of €20,000. Accelerated capital allowances are available. The current rate of taxation is 40% and tax is payable in the year to which it relates.

**Requirement:** Is the proposed expansion worthwhile, assuming the firm's cost of capital is 10% (after tax)? You can assume that the gain on sale of fixed assets is taxed at the normal rate.

**Solution and analysis:** We first compute the amount of tax to be paid (see **W1** below). In Year 1, annual profits of €40,000 (before depreciation) are generated from which (100%) capital allowances are claimed. Therefore a tax loss of €50,000 is created and this is carried forward to Year 2. Since profits amount to €40,000 in Year 2, the tax loss for this year (€10,000) is carried forward to Year 3. Therefore, corporate tax liabilities will accrue in Year 3, based on an annual profit of €40,000 less the tax loss carried forward of €10,000. However, since the relevant fixed assets were sold in Year 3 for €20,000, this creates a (taxable) balancing charge of the same amount since the tax written down value at date of disposal was zero. Therefore, total taxable profits in Year 3 amount to €50,000 which are assessed at 40%.

### W1: COMPUTATION OF TAX PAYABLE

|  | Year 1 | Year 2 | Year 3 |
|---|---|---|---|
| Additional profit | 40,000 | 40,000 | 40,000 |
| Less: Capital allowances | (90,000) |  | * 20,000 |
| Tax loss | (50,000) ⟶ | (50,000) |  |
| Tax loss |  | (10,000) ⟶ | (10,000) |
| Taxable profits |  |  | 50,000 |
| Tax @ 40% | Nil | Nil | 20,000 |

* In effect, the company has claimed capital allowances in total of €90,000, whereas the actual depreciation suffered was only €70,000 (€90,000 – €20,000). This excess claim is now being clawed back by the taxation authorities as a taxable item, referred to as a balancing charge.

The second step is to compute the NPV of all future cash flows. The cash flows are partitioned into appropriate years and discounted by the firm's cost of capital (10%) as presented below:

| COMPUTATION OF NPV OF FUTURE CASH FLOWS | | | | | |
|---|---|---|---|---|---|
| | Investment €| Cash flows € | Tax paid € | Net flows € | PV factor | PV € |
| Now | (90,000) | | | (90,000) | 1.0 | (90,000) |
| Year 1 | | 40,000 | | 40,000 | .909 | 36,360 |
| Year 2 | | 40,000 | | 40,000 | .826 | 33,040 |
| Year 3 | 20,000 | 40,000 | (20,000) | 40,000 | .751 | 30,040 |
| NPV | | | | | | 9,440 |

Based on the after-tax cost of capital (10%), this proposal should be accepted due to its positive NPV, amounting to €9,440.

## Sensitivity Analysis

In evaluating capital expenditure proposals, one initially assumes the accuracy of all estimates. In reality, however, estimates are rarely perfect and managers must never lose sight of the uncertainty inherent in the decision process. Simply speaking, managers cannot forecast the future with complete accuracy. One way to assess uncertainty is to use sensitivity analysis. In brief, **sensitivity analysis** is the examination of the financial impact of changes or errors in any of the variables in a decision model.

If, by changing any variable in the decision model, the new outcome is significantly different from the original forecast, management is forewarned that the original solution is extremely sensitive to certain changes in the parameters of the model. Decision-makers are well advised to use sensitivity analysis to test their original computation before committing their economic resources. The important point is that sensitivity analysis enables decision-makers to better appreciate the uncertainty existing in any decision process.

## Capital Expenditure and Inflation

Since capital expenditure involves long-term financial considerations, it is appropriate to briefly discuss the impact and correct treatment of inflation. **Inflation** represents the decline in the general purchasing power of money so that, over time, more and more money is needed to purchase the same quantity of goods and services. Unless the impact of inflation is correctly incorporated in the analysis of long-term decisions, incorrect decisions could occur. Thus, we must be careful to use the correct cost of capital to discount the correct future cash flows.

The cost of capital to be used in discounting may either be the money (nominal) rate of interest or, alternatively, the real rate of interest. The **money rate of interest** is the rate of interest that is quoted in the 'market' and is probably the rate of interest with which most people are familiar. It will automatically include an element attributable to anticipated inflation. In contrast, the **real rate of interest** is significantly lower than the money rate of interest and, in an inflationary environment, may be negative. The money rate of interest is linked to the real rate of interest by the expected rate of inflation. Thus, it is often assumed by managers that, if the money rate of interest is 10%, with inflation running at 6%, then the real rate of interest is 4%. (Actually, this calculation is not entirely accurate but this should have little impact on the calculation of NPV due to rounding of discount factors.) Likewise, future cash flows may either be stated in money terms, i.e. anticipating future price increases, or in real terms.

These alternatives present us with two choices for calculating NPV. First, we could estimate future cash flows (incorporating anticipated inflation) and discount them at the money rate of interest. In many situations this is the simplest approach as it is usually easier to make monetary cash flow projections. Alternatively, NPV can be computed by estimating **real** future cash flows and discounting at the **real** cost of capital. However, working in real terms does, in effect, involve a double set of calculations, i.e. converting future cash flows to real terms and then discounting these by the real cost of capital. This increases the time to be spent on calculations and also the risk of computational error.

Nevertheless, both methods should provide identical NPVs, though the first alternative is strongly recommended. The important thing is **not** to confuse the two methods. Thus, it is **incorrect** to use the real rate of interest to discount money cash flows. Likewise, it is **incorrect** to use the money rate of interest to discount real cash flows. Indeed, if one of these incorrect methods is used, the capital expenditure process will be biased and most probably lead to wrong decisions.

In summary, decision-makers, in capital expenditure decisions, have a choice of two methods for incorporating inflation into NPV calculations. They may discount money cash flows by the money cost of capital or, alternatively, discount real cash flows by the real cost of capital. Both methods produce identical net present values, subject to small but inevitable rounding errors.

## ILLUSTRATION: CAPITAL EXPENDITURE PROPOSALS AND INFLATION

Newbridge Limited is considering a capital expenditure proposal, costing €4.5 million which has an expected life of four years. The preliminary financial analysis reveals the following information:

|  | Time period | | | | |
|---|---|---|---|---|---|
|  | $t_0$ €000 | $t_1$ €000 | $t_2$ €000 | $t_3$ €000 | $t_4$ €000 |
| Investment in new plant | 4,500 | | | | |
| Investment in additional stock | 300 | | | | |

|  | Time period | | | | |
|---|---|---|---|---|---|
|  | $t_0$ €000 | $t_1$ €000 | $t_2$ €000 | $t_3$ €000 | $t_4$ €000 |
| Sales |  | 3,500 | 4,900 | 5,320 | 5,740 |
| Operating cash costs |  | 1,655 | 2,350 | 2,800 | 3,250 |
| Research costs already incurred |  | 875 | 875 | 875 | 875 |

You have ascertained the following information:

1. The projected sales and operating costs have been computed using current prices (i.e. at $t_0$). However, due to inflation, sales prices are expected to increase at a rate of 2% per annum. Operating costs are expected to increase by 3% per annum.
2. Capital allowances are allowed at a rate of 25% per annum on the reducing balance method on the new plant and equipment.
3. Corporation tax is 18% and is payable one year in arrears.
4. The estimated scrap value of the relevant plant and equipment at the end of Year 4 is zero.
5. The company has already incurred costs of €3.5 million in researching the product. It is the policy of the company to write off research costs to the income statement over a four-year period.
6. The company's (nominal) required rate of return on all projects is 10% (after tax) and this should be used as the discount rate.

**Requirement:** Calculate the Net Present Value for the proposed investment and provide a recommendation.

**Solution and analysis:** The first step is to calculate the capital allowances to be claimed on the qualifying fixed asset, using 25% per annum on a reducing balance method **(W1)**. In addition, at the end of the project, the fixed asset has a zero disposal value, generating an additional deduction, corresponding to the balancing allowance.

**W1. COMPUTATION OF CAPITAL ALLOWANCES (INCLUDING BALANCING ALLOWANCE)**

|  | $t_1$ €000 | $t_2$ €000 | $t_3$ €000 | $t_4$ €000 |
|---|---|---|---|---|
| Cost/tax written down value | 4,500 | 3,375 | 2,531 | 1,898 |
| Annual (25% Reducing balance) | 1,125 | 844 | 633 | 475 |
| Tax written down value | 3,375 | 2,531 | 1,898 | 1,423 |

**Balancing allowance/charge on disposal**

| | |
|---|---|
| Tax written down value (at sale) | 1,423 |
| Sales proceeds | Nil |
| Additional Allowance (Year 4) | 1,423 |

The next stage is to compute the corporate tax payable and this is done by preparing a taxation computation for each year (**W2**). Since tax is payable on monetary cash flows, cash flows must be adjusted for the appropriate rate of inflation and this is a **compound** calculation. Capital allowances are also included.

W2. COMPUTATION OF TAX PAYABLE (IN INFLATED MONETARY TERMS)

| | $t_1$ €000 | $t_2$ €000 | $t_3$ €000 | $t_4$ €000 |
|---|---|---|---|---|
| Sales (+ 2%) | 3,570 | 5,098 | 5,646 | 6,213 |
| Operating costs (+ 3%) | (1,705) | (2,493) | (3,059) | (3,658) |
| Inflated net cash flows | 1,865 | 2,605 | 2,587 | 2,555 |
| Capital allowances (W1) | (1,125) | (844) | (633) | (475) |
| Balancing allowance (loss) | | | | (1,423) |
| Taxable profits | 740 | 1,761 | 1,954 | 657 |
| Tax at 18% | (133) | (317) | (352) | (118) |

Finally, we progress towards the computation of NPV. The approach taken below is to discount money cash flows by the money rate of interest. It avoids a double set of calculations and, in any event, the money cash flows have already been computed. It should be noted that we have not included any reference to the research costs already incurred. These are irrelevant since they are in the nature of a sunk cost and they cannot be changed. We have included the additional investment in working capital and reversed this cash flow when the project is finished. Finally, it should be noted that corporate taxation is paid one year in arrears.

COMPUTATION OF NET PRESENT VALUE (NPV)

| | $t_0$ €000 | $t_1$ €000 | $t_2$ €000 | $t_3$ €000 | $t_4$ €000 | $t_5$ €000 |
|---|---|---|---|---|---|---|
| Capital expenditure | (4,500) | | | | | |
| Working capital investment | (300) | | | | 300 | |

| | $t_0$ €000 | $t_1$ €000 | $t_2$ €000 | $t_3$ €000 | $t_4$ €000 | $t_5$ €000 |
|---|---|---|---|---|---|---|
| Annual operating cash flows | | 1,865 | 2,605 | 2,587 | 2,555 | |
| Taxation paid | | | (133) | (317) | (352) | (118) |
| Net Cash flows | (4,800) | 1,865 | 2,472 | 2,270 | 2,503 | (118) |
| Discount factor at 20% | 1 | 0.909 | 0.826 | 0.751 | 0.683 | 0.621 |
| PV cash flows | (4,800) | 1,695 | 2,041 | 1,705 | 1,709 | (73) |
| **NPV =** | | | + €2.277k | | | |

The NPV of the project is positive at €2.277k. The NPV decision criterion suggests that all projects generating a positive NPV should be viewed as feasible as they cover the company's required rate of return. Therefore, in this case, management of Newbridge Limited should therefore proceed with this project, based on the information provided.

## A Strategic Focus

It is important to remember that discounted cash flow (DCF) analysis can give only a general impression as to the possible economic outcome of an investment project. It should be appreciated that there are often too many non-quantifiable factors that have not been considered. This being so, there is really no justification for indulging in mathematical fine-tuning when evaluating such proposals. Indeed, it could well be inappropriate since usually it can only result in spurious accuracy and so mislead management as to the reliability of any ultimate figures. It is far better to examine the project in terms of its overall commercial strategy and long-term financial plans. It should be clear that measuring the financial benefit of capital expenditure projects – as DCF or payback methods attempt to do – is only one step in the decision-making process.

Consequently, management should spend some of its time improving the quality of the assumptions and ascertaining that the strategic questions have been asked, rather than being concerned with more refined mathematical calculations. Explicit attention to the major assumptions, together with use of sensitivity analysis, is strongly recommended. There is little value in refining an analysis that does not utilise sound assumptions and ask strategic questions. In some capital expenditure analyses reviewed by managers, the major assumptions are either not provided or are buried in the supporting detail.

Someone once remarked that capital expenditure proposals do not begin life in a filing cabinet awaiting only the collection of accounting information necessary for their evaluation. Such proposals must be created, and so the capital expenditure process within the firm should be regarded as a socio-political, as well as a financial process.

## SUMMARY OF LEARNING OBJECTIVES

**Learning Objective 1:** Define capital expenditure decisions.

Capital expenditure decisions are characterised by a number of features. These include an immediate and significant cash outflow. It is expected that this cash outflow will generate a future stream of cash inflows over a long period of time, some of which will generate additional tax payments on corporate profits. In evaluating such spending proposals, decision-makers may use the time value of money. However, other decision-makers may adopt more conservative approaches to evaluation, such as computing and selecting between proposals on the basis of the payback period.

**Learning Objective 2:** Evaluate capital expenditure proposals using the payback period.

The payback period is the length of time it takes to cover the initial capital expenditure outflow. In applying this technique, it is usual to concentrate on absolute cash flows, without reference to the time value of money, i.e. discounting techniques are not applied. (However, a 'discounted' payback period could be computed.) Many argue that the payback period is an appropriate method to use when evaluating capital expenditure proposals because of the conservatism it introduces to the decision-making process, especially when the future environment is very uncertain.

**Learning Objective 3:** Describe the time value of money.

Money in hand is more valuable than the promise of the same amount to be received in the future. This is due to the fact that money in hand can be invested to earn a rate of return in the form of interest. Therefore, in absolute terms, the future value will always be higher than the present value of the same amount and this can be referred to as the time value of money. When using the time value of money to evaluate capital expenditure proposals, we 'discount' future cash flows to their present value so that all cash flows are then stated in common currency and can be added together or subtracted, as appropriate.

**Learning Objective 4:** Distinguish between and apply the techniques of net present value and internal rate of return.

The time value of money involves 'discounting' all future cash flows (inflows and outflows) to their present value. In mathematical terms, this is equivalent to applying compound interest calculations backwards. Net present value is an absolute monetary amount and can be either positive or negative. If positive, this indicates that a proposed capital expenditure proposal earns in excess of the required rate of return. In contrast, internal rate of return (IRR) is a percentage and represents the exact discount rate that will give a net present value of zero. IRR is usually computed using interpolation, based on two observations, namely, a positive and negative net present value.

**Learning Objective 5:** Calculate the weighted average cost of capital for use in capital expenditure proposals.

The appropriate discount rate to use in evaluating capital expenditure decisions is based on the firm's weighted average cost of capital (WACC). WACC is calculated using the respective proportions of debt and equity in the capital structure of a firm. The cost of debt capital is the after-tax cost, because interest paid on loans is tax deductible. The cost of equity is mainly calculated with reference to either Gordon's dividend growth model or the Capital Asset Pricing Model (CAPM).

**Learning Objective 6:** Discuss the separate impact of taxation and inflation on capital expenditure decisions.

Since capital expenditure decisions are expected to generate additional cash benefits it is important to factor into the analysis the taxation consequences of such decisions. Initially, capital expenditure may qualify for capital allowances (equivalent to tax depreciation). Also, the additional cash flows may generate additional tax liabilities on corporate profits. Finally, when long-term assets are sold, they may generate either a balancing allowance (tax loss) or a balancing charge (tax gain). In addition, due to the long-term nature of capital expenditure decisions, it is important to correctly adjust for the impact of inflation, for which there are two methods. First, future (money) cash flows may be discounted by the (money) cost of capital. Alternatively, the real WACC should be used to discount the real cash flows arising in the future.

## Appendix 13.1

(a) Present value of €1 received in N years hence at a discount rate of X% p.a.

| N | 4% | 6% | 8% | 10% | 12% | 14% |
|---|-----|-----|-----|------|------|------|
| 1 | .962 | .943 | .926 | .909 | .893 | .877 |
| 2 | .925 | .890 | .857 | .826 | .797 | .769 |
| 3 | .889 | .840 | .794 | .751 | .712 | .675 |
| 4 | .855 | .792 | .735 | .683 | .636 | .592 |
| 5 | .822 | .747 | .681 | .621 | .567 | .519 |
| 6 | .790 | .705 | .630 | .564 | .507 | .456 |
| 7 | .760 | .665 | .583 | .513 | .452 | .400 |
| 8 | .731 | .627 | .540 | .467 | .404 | .351 |
| 9 | .703 | .592 | .500 | .424 | .361 | .308 |
| 10 | .676 | .558 | .463 | .386 | .322 | .270 |

(b) Present value of annuity of €1 received each year for N years

| N | 4% | 6% | 8% | 10% | 12% | 14% |
|---|-----|-----|-----|------|------|------|
| 1 | .962 | .943 | .926 | .909 | .893 | .877 |
| 2 | 1.886 | 1.833 | 1.783 | 1.736 | 1.690 | 1.647 |
| 3 | 2.775 | 2.673 | 2.577 | 2.487 | 2.402 | 2.322 |
| 4 | 3.630 | 3.465 | 3.312 | 3.169 | 3.037 | 2.914 |
| 5 | 4.452 | 4.212 | 3.993 | 3.791 | 3.605 | 3.433 |
| 6 | 5.242 | 4.917 | 4.623 | 4.355 | 4.111 | 3.889 |
| 7 | 6.002 | 5.582 | 5.206 | 4.868 | 4.564 | 4.288 |
| 8 | 6.733 | 6.210 | 5.747 | 5.335 | 4.968 | 4.639 |
| 9 | 7.435 | 6.802 | 6.247 | 5.759 | 5.328 | 4.946 |
| 10 | 8.111 | 7.360 | 6.710 | 6.145 | 5.650 | 5.216 |

## Questions

### Review Questions

(See Appendix One for Solutions to Review Questions **13.1** and **13.2**)

### Question 13.1 (Introduction to Capital Expenditure Decisions)

Briefly outline the nature of capital expenditure decisions and describe the procedures which should be adopted for approving and reviewing such projects.

### Question 13.2 (Methods of Evaluating Capital Expenditure Decisions)

The American Plant in Dublin had been a trouble spot in the group for a few years, thought George Frost, the Managing Director of LA Group, a large international company based in France. Some years ago, as part of its corporate strategy, it had begun to diversify into packaging, pharmaceutical and consumer products. One of its packaging plants was situated in Dublin but, based on the monthly returns, it was an inefficient operation. The monthly operating report contained sales figures, production figures and overall profit and return on investment.

Frost would visit the packaging plant once a month, usually unannounced. However, many of the plant's senior managers were not available to brief him fully on developments and, not surprisingly, Frost grew very critical of the Dublin operation. In addition to being inefficient, Frost felt that many managers were not committed to the job and many had lost their technical curiosity. Resulting from his most recent visit, Frost set out rigid guidelines on future capital expenditure requests from the Dublin plant. Frost thought that he might not be able to improve the efficiency of the Dublin plant but he could veto future capital expenditure requests that did not make economic sense.

According to Frost's directive, most proposals for capital expenditure would have to be personally sanctioned by him or one of his assistants. The procedures to be followed were contained in considerable detail in a capital expenditure manual that was distributed to the key financial personnel at the Dublin plant. The capital expenditure manual contained an explicit set of requirements including, among other things, a minimum payback period of less than three years and that all proposals would earn at least 10%.

The capital expenditure manual also contained an explicit categorisation of capital expenditure requests such as cost reduction schemes. There was also a distinction drawn between new capital expenditures and regular capital expenditures.

One of the assistant managers in the Dublin plant, Frank Ross, had recently submitted a capital expenditure proposal. Frost looked at the summary sheet (below) requiring a choice between two alternatives to implement a cost reduction scheme by investing in new equipment. However, Frost quickly realised that the capital expenditure analysis was incomplete. The proposal had simply included a detail of cash flows with no further analysis except a recommendation to accept 'Project L' rather than 'Project S'.

Since Frost was busy that evening, he has provided you with the summarised data.

OPERATING DATA FOR CAPITAL EXPENDITURE PROPOSALS

| | Project S €000 | Project L €000 |
|---|---|---|
| Initial cash outlay | (1,000) | (1,000) |
| Future cash savings | | |
| At end of year 1 | 500 | 100 |
| At end of year 2 | 400 | 300 |
| At end of year 3 | 300 | 400 |
| At end of year 4 | 100 | 600 |

**Requirement:** Analyse the data, and advise George Frost on which alternative to accept. Use the Payback Period together with NPV and IRR calculations.

## Intermediate Questions

*Question 13.3 (Computing NPV with Taxation)*

The Moore Company manufactures and sells a wide range of durable products. Currently it is evaluating the possible introduction of a new product, the Alpha. It is anticipated that sales and costs of Alpha over the next four years will be as follows:

| Year | UNIT SALES | UNIT SELLING PRICE € | UNIT VARIABLE COST € |
|---|---|---|---|
| 1 | 20,000 | 44 | 40 |
| 2 | 26,000 | 45 | 39 |
| 3 | 21,000 | 50 | 39 |
| 4 | 20,000 | 50 | 40 |

Production of Alpha requires an immediate investment in new plant and machinery costing €200,000. This machinery has an estimated life of four years with an estimated scrap value of €10,000. Accelerated capital allowances can be claimed on this item for tax purposes.

In addition, a special advertising campaign would cost €250,000 and be launched immediately. Additional investment in working capital would also be required in the amount of €80,000, which would be disinvested at the end of year four.

The current rate of taxation is 40% and is payable one year in arrears.

**Requirement:** Is the proposed expansion worthwhile, assuming the company's cost of capital is 10% (after tax)?

## Question 13.4 (NPV and Generally Accepted Accounting Principles (GAAP)

The Arkle Company has an opportunity to manufacture 100,000 custom-designed units on contract for Taffe Corporation. The Taffe Corporation would pay €8 for each of the first 50,000 units delivered plus €10 for each of the next 50,000 units. Deliveries would be 15,000 units this year, 45,000 units next year, and 40,000 units in the third year and Taffe's payments for these units would be made at the time of delivery. However, to facilitate the liquidity position of Arkle, Taffe Corporation would advance €100,000 by way of interest-free loans to Arkle and this would be recovered when the final delivery of goods was made.

Arkle would need to buy special equipment for €110,000 immediately and management estimates that the new equipment would have a €20,000 market value at the end of the third year. It seems very unlikely to have any usefulness to Arkle after that time. In addition, manufacturing costs are estimated as follows:

| Raw materials | €2 a unit |
| Direct labour | €3 a unit |
| Production overhead | €70,000 a year |

Arkle would invest €50,000 in cash to purchase the initial materials inventory which would be maintained for the duration of the three-year contract by way of safety stock. The remaining raw materials would be purchased as required. However, towards the end of the contract stock levels would be reduced and the purchase of raw materials would be curtailed accordingly. All raw materials would be completely used up by the time work on the contract was completed. There would be no work in process at the end of any year.

Total production overhead would be only €60,000 for the **first** year because the new facilities would not be in operation for the whole year. The annual overhead costs (above) includes €30,000 in depreciation on the new equipment. No allocations of divisional or corporate overhead costs are included in these figures.

Additional selling and administrative costs of €45,000 would be incurred in each of the next three years.

Arkle's management evaluates all capital expenditure proposals using the net present value method. The tax rate is 40%. Use accelerated capital allowances on new equipment for tax purposes. Tax would be paid at the end of the year in which it is accrued.

The Arkle Company's capital structure consists of equity (60%) and debt (40%). Debt carries a gross interest of 9% whereas the cost of equity is unknown. However, the current level of dividend is 10c per share and this has been growing at 6% per annum in recent years. The current market price is estimated at 150c.

**Requirements:**

1. Calculate Arkle's WACC using Gordon's dividend growth model.
2. Using NPV, calculate the net present value of this proposal. Should the contract be signed?

*Question 13.5 (Computing NPV with Taxation)*

The Holly Company is evaluating a capital expenditure proposal that will allow the introduction of a new product that will increase profits by €40,000 (before accounting depreciation) over the next three years.

The proposal requires an immediate investment in new plant and machinery costing €90,000. This machinery has an estimated life of three years with an estimated scrap value of €20,000.

Accelerated capital allowances, at the rate of 100% of the capital expenditure, are available for tax purposes. The current rate of taxation is 40% and is payable in the year to which it relates.

**Requirement:** Is the proposed expansion worthwhile? Assume the firm's cost of capital after tax is 10%.

*Question 13.6 (Estimating the Cost of Capital)*

**Requirements:**

1. Based on the information below, calculate the cost of equity capital for LUBOK plc – a quoted company – as at the beginning of 2006, using the following:
   (a) The dividend growth model;
   (b) The capital asset pricing model.
2. The market price per share on the Stock Exchange at 1 January 2006 was €1.20, ex dividend, and the annual dividend per share for recent years was as follows:

| Year | Cent per share |
|------|----------------|
| 2001 | 7.63 |
| 2002 | 8.31 |
| 2003 | 8.88 |
| 2004 | 9.35 |
| 2005 | 10.00 |

| | |
|---|---|
| Beta coefficient for LUBOK plc shares | 0.7 |
| Expected rate of return on risk-free securities | 8% |
| Expected return on the market portfolio | 12% |

State, for each model separately, the main simplifying assumptions made, and express your opinions as to whether the models yield results that can be safely used in practice.

Formula for the dividend growth model: $\dfrac{D_o\,(1 + g)}{MV} + g$

Formula for CAPM $\qquad\qquad\qquad r_f + \beta(r_m - r_f)$

Where

| | | |
|---|---|---|
| $D_o$ | = | Current dividend per share |
| g | = | Average annual dividend growth rate |
| MV | = | Market value of share |
| $r_f$ | = | Risk-free rate of interest |
| $r_m$ | = | Current dividend per share |
| $\beta$ | = | Beta or systematic (or non-diversifiable) risk of a particular security |

Source: Chartered Accountants Ireland, Management Accounting and Business Finance,
P3, Autumn 2006

## Question 13.7 (Aspects of Capital Expenditure Decisions)

Describe how the following factors can impact on the capital expenditure decision:

1. Cost of capital
2. Tax
3. Working capital

Source: Chartered Accountants Ireland, Management Accounting and Business Finance,
P3, Summer 2005

## Advanced Questions

## Question 13.8: (Estimating the Cost of Capital)

Bindaroo PLC presented the following balance sheet items at 31 December 20x1:

| | € |
|---|---|
| Authorised ordinary share capital of €1 each (€1,000,000) | |
| Issued share capital of €1 each | 500,000 |
| 8% irredeemable preference shares | 100,000 |
| Revaluation reserves | 200,000 |
| Retained earnings | 400,000 |
| 4% Debentures (redeemable in 2016) | 300,000 |
| | 1,500,000 |

The following information is also available:

1.  The market value of the ordinary shares is €3.60 per share (ex div).
2.  The 8% irredeemable preference shares are quoted at €1.09.
3.  In the year to 31 December 20x1, a dividend of €0.06 was paid on the ordinary shares. Recent trends indicate that Bindaroo increases its dividend payments on average by 3% per annum.
4.  The risk-free rate of interest is 2.5%. The market rate of return is 6%.
5.  The Beta factor applicable to the equity of Bindaroo is 1.04.
6.  Profit before interest and tax (PBIT) for the year ended 31 December 20x1 amounted to €650,000.
7.  Assume that taxable profit is identical to accounting profits and assume an effective corporation tax rate of 20%.

**Requirements:**

1.  Calculate, in respect of Bindaroo, the following:
    (a)  The profit retained for the year ended 31 December 20x1
    (b)  The capital (balance sheet) gearing and income gearing (times interest cover)
    (c)  The cost of equity capital using both the Gordon growth model and CAPM
    (d)  WACC, using current market values and your CAPM calculation, at 31 December 20x1.
2.  Explain why the two methods of calculating the cost of equity noted above provide different results. State which method is superior, in your opinion, and why.

Source: Chartered Accountants Ireland, Management Accounting and Business Finance,<br>P3, Summer 2004

*Question 13.9: (Evaluation of Capital Expenditure Proposals)*

LAZER plc is a large engineering company, entirely financed by equity, whose financial year ends on 31 December. The company's objective is to maximise shareholder wealth, and it generates sufficient taxable profits to relieve all capital allowances at the earliest opportunity. Currently, one of the company's divisional managers has to fulfil a particular contract, and he can do this in one of two ways. Under the first (**Proposal 1**), he can purchase plant and machinery; while under the second (**Proposal 2**), he can use a machine already owned by the company.

The end-year operating net cash inflows in nominal (i.e. money) terms, and before Corporation Tax, are as follows:

|            | 2008   | 2009   | 2010   |
|------------|--------|--------|--------|
| **Proposal 1** | 40,000 | 55,000 | 70,000 |
| **Proposal 2** | 70,000 | 70,000 | NIL    |

**Proposal 1:** Under this proposal the company will incur an outlay of €62,500 on 31 December 20x7 for the purchase of new plant and machinery. The plant and machinery is expected to be scrapped on 31 December 2010, with the nominal cash proceeds at that date being projected at €5,000. This has not been included in the nominal net cash inflows given above. Under this proposal, existing machinery, which has no further use, would be scrapped on 31 December 2008, realising €60,000.

The labour force required under this proposal will have to be recruited locally, and budgeted wages have been taken into account in preparing the estimates of the future nominal net cash inflow given above.

**Proposal 2:** This second proposal covers a two-year period from 31 December 20x7. It will require the company to use a machine which was purchased for €150,000 a number of years ago when 100% first year capital allowances were available and which is therefore fully written down for tax purposes. The company has no current use for the machine and it would otherwise be sold on 31 December 2008 for an estimated €60,000. However, if used under this proposal, the expected residual value of the machine would be zero at the end of the two-year period.

The labour force required under this proposal would be recruited from elsewhere within the company and, in end-year nominal cash flow terms, would be paid in total €20,000 and €21,600 respectively for 2008 and 2009. However, the staff that would have to be taken on in other divisions to replace those switched over to the new project would, in corresponding end-year nominal cash flow terms, cost, in total, €22,000 for 2008 and €23,760 for 2009.

The end-year nominal net cash inflows of €70,000 for both 2008 and 2009 which are associated with this proposal are, after deducting the remuneration of the work force, actually employed on the project.

**Working Capital Requirements:** For **both** proposals, working capital requirements, in nominal money terms, at the beginning of each year are estimated at 10% of the end-year operating net cash inflows referred to in the table above. The working capital funds will be released when a proposal is completed. There are no tax effects associated with changes in working capital.

The corporation tax rate is expected to be 30% over the planning period, tax being payable 12 months after the accounting year-end to which it relates.

The annual tax allowance for plant and machinery is given at the rate of 20% on a straight line basis. The allowance is given in the year which the asset is first put into use, and a balancing allowance may occur in the year of disposal. Any balancing charges or allowances are calculated for individual assets (i.e. they are not part of the general pool for tax purposes).

The company's nominal cost of capital is 6% (after tax).

**Requirements:**

1. Calculate the net present value at 31 December 20x7 of each of the two mutually exclusive proposals.

2.  Indicate briefly any reservations you might have about basing an investment decision on these figures.

Source: Chartered Accountants Ireland, Management Accounting and Business Finance, P3,
Summer 2007 (adapted)

## Question 13.10: (Capital Expenditure Decisions and Inflation)

Describe how inflation should be incorporated within the capital expenditure decision.

Source: Chartered Accountants Ireland, Management Accounting and Business Finance,
Paper 3, Summer 2005

## Question 13.11 (Capital Expenditure Decisions and Inflation)

You have recently been appointed finance director of Brisk Plc. The company is considering investing in new plant and equipment which will facilitate the production of an electronic security device with an expected market life of four years. The previous finance director had undertaken an analysis of the proposed project. The main features of his analysis are shown below.

|  | Time period | | | | |
|---|---|---|---|---|---|
|  | $t_0$ €000 | $t_1$ €000 | $t_2$ €000 | $t_3$ €000 | $t_4$ €000 |
| Investment in depreciable assets | 4,500 |  |  |  |  |
| Investment in working capital | 300 |  |  |  |  |
| Sales |  | 3,500 | 4,900 | 5,320 | 5,740 |
| Direct materials |  | 535 | 750 | 900 | 1,050 |
| Labour costs |  | 1,070 | 1,500 | 1,800 | 2,100 |
| Overhead expenses |  | 50 | 100 | 100 | 100 |
| Research costs |  | 875 | 875 | 875 | 875 |
| Depreciation of relevant assets |  | 900 | 900 | 900 | 900 |

You have ascertained the following information:

1.  All of the above projected figures have been computed using current prices (i.e. at $t_0$). However, due to inflation, sales prices are expected to increase at a rate of 2% per annum. Costs of materials, labour and overheads are expected to increase by 3% per annum.

2. Capital allowances are allowed at a rate of 25% per annum on the reducing balance basis on the new plant and equipment.
3. Corporation tax is 18% and is payable 1 year in arrears.
4. The estimated scrap value of the relevant plant and equipment at the end of Year 4 is zero.
5. The company has already incurred costs of €3.5 million in researching the product. The payment for this research is due in Year 1. It is the policy of the company to write off research costs to the profit and loss account over a 4-year period.
6. The company's (nominal) required rate of return on all projects is 20% (after tax) and this should be used as the discount rate.

## Requirements:

1. Calculate the relevant inflated cash flows that would arise from the proposal for each of the four years and determine both the Net Present Value and the Payback period (after tax) for the investment and recommend, with reasons, whether the company should proceed with this investment.
2. Outline briefly some of the limitations of the appraisal you have prepared above.

Source: Chartered Accountants Ireland, Management Accounting and Business Finance, P3, Autumn 2004 (adapted)

*Question 13.12: (Capital Budgeting Decisions and Inflation)*

You have recently been appointed finance director of NewBrisk Plc ('NewBrisk'). The company is considering investing in the production of an electronic security device with an expected market life of four years. The previous finance director had undertaken an analysis of the proposed project. The main features of his analysis are shown below.

|  | Time period | | | | |
|---|---|---|---|---|---|
|  | $t_0$ €000 | $t_1$ €000 | $t_2$ €000 | $t_3$ €000 | $t_4$ €000 |
| Purchases of plant and equipment | 4,500 | | | | |
| Investment in working capital | 300 | | | | |
| Sales | | 4,000 | 5,000 | 5,550 | 6,000 |
| Materials | | 535 | 750 | 900 | 1,050 |
| Labour | | 1,070 | 1,500 | 1,800 | 2,100 |

| | Time period | | | | |
|---|---|---|---|---|---|
| | $t_0$ €000 | $t_1$ €000 | $t_2$ €000 | $t_3$ €000 | $t_4$ €000 |
| Overheads | | 50 | 100 | 100 | 100 |
| Interest paid on new loans | | 550 | 550 | 550 | 550 |
| Research costs already incurred | | 300 | 300 | 300 | 300 |
| Depreciation on new plant | | 1,125 | 1,125 | 1,125 | 1,125 |

You have ascertained the following information:

1. All of the above projected items have been computed in terms of current prices (i.e. prices at $t_0$). However, due to inflation, selling prices, together with materials, labour and overheads are expected to increase by 3% per annum. For convenience of computation it is assumed that inflation will occur at the last day on the accounting year.
2. The new plant and equipment will be exclusively financed by a new loan with fixed interest payments. Thus, interest costs will remain unchanged over the life of the project.
3. Capital allowances are allowed at a rate of 25% per annum on the reducing balance basis on the new plant and equipment. The estimated scrap value of this plant is zero at the end of Year 4. Corporation tax is 20% and is payable 1 year in arrears.
4. The company has already incurred costs of €1.2 million in researching the product. It is the policy of the company to write off research costs to the income statement over a four-year period.
5. The company's (nominal) cost of capital is 20% (after tax).

**Requirements:**

1. Calculate the relevant inflated cash flows for this proposal for each of the four years.
2. Calculate the Net Present Value and the Payback period for the investment and recommend, with reasons, whether the company should proceed with this investment.

Source: Chartered Accountants Ireland, Management Accounting and Business Finance, P3, Autumn 2004 (adapted)

# 14

# Budgets and Budgetary Control

LEARNING OBJECTIVES

When you have completed studying this chapter you should be able to:

1. Discuss the advantages of budget preparation in the context of planning and control.
2. Prepare operating budgets.
3. Prepare master budgets.
4. Describe the use of spreadsheets in budgeting.
5. Outline the weaknesses of traditional budgeting practices and suggest improvements.
6. Distinguish between a static and flexed budget.
7. Explain why flexed budgets are needed in performance evaluation.
8. Calculate the financial impact of both sales volume and sales price variances.
9. Calculate both market share and market size variances.

## 14.1 Introduction to Business Plans and Financial Control

In our everyday lives we routinely make estimates of future income and expenditure. Sometimes these may be done for a weekly time period or, more formally, for a longer period of time. This is the essence of financial planning or, simply, budgeting. There are a variety of reasons why we engage in some form of financial planning. The end result, however, is that, usually, we want to achieve a future financial target. Individuals, for example, may estimate their future income and, accordingly, may curtail their expenditure. Thus, an inevitable implication of budgets (or any control system) is to influence or restrict behaviour in some way or other.

When we talk about financial plans in management accounting we usually use the expression 'budget'. A **budget** can be described as an approved financial plan, reflecting expectations for a defined, future period of time. This forward-looking perspective is an important aspect of any budgeting process. This future period is usually one year, with appropriate subdivisions, though it can be either shorter or longer. (A **rolling budget** is a plan that is always available for a specified future period by adding, say, a month in the future as each current month elapses.) Not only does a budget reflect expectations, it also reflects a commitment by subordinates to attain agreed budget objectives.

Research indicates that virtually all organisations engage in some form of budgeting, though its extent varies from one business to another. Large, well-managed companies generally have carefully prepared budgets for every aspect of their operations. Smaller businesses may prepare, for example, only a sales budget.

As we shall see below, budgets facilitate budgetary control. This means that, during the accounting period, actual results are compared to budget to reveal favourable or unfavourable variances from plan. If actual revenue is greater than the budgeted amount or costs are lower than budgeted, then the variance is classified as a **favourable variance**. In contrast, if the actual revenue is lower than the budgeted amount or actual expenditure is in excess of the budgeted amount, then the resulting variance is identified as an **adverse variance**. Thus, with budgets we link both the planning and control functions of the management accountant.

## 14.2 The Advantages and Use of Budgets

We have already defined a budget as a formal financial plan for a defined, future period of time. To appreciate fully the role of budgeting in the modern organisation, one must consider its advantages. Four advantages are usually cited in favour of the budgeting process:

### 1. Budgeting ... Provides an Enhanced Managerial Perspective

In preparing a meaningful budget, managers are forced to make estimates of, and anticipate future economic conditions, including, for example, demand for the company's product, level of competition and even proposed changes in legislation. Thus, budgeting increases management's awareness of the company's external economic environment. In the absence of the necessity to prepare a budget, managers could spend most of the time on routine matters rather than thinking about the future. The budgeting process requires that managers should consider how conditions might change next year and what implications such changes might have for the business.

### 2. Budgeting ... Improves Coordination and Provides Advance Warning of Internal Problems

Successful organisations need to coordinate the various internal aspects of their business and this includes sales, production and distribution functions. For example, in preparing sales budgets, managers will usually forecast a number of activities including, e.g. the volume of goods to be sold. Using these estimates, production plans are developed to determine the resources required, including production targets, raw materials required, number of employees etc. Alternatively, if the sales manager introduces a new advertising campaign in order to boost sales of the company's manufactured products, then it is important that the production manager be aware of this so as to ensure adequate production levels. The various activities within a company are better coordinated and communicated by the preparation of budgets and they provide an advance warning of potential internal logistical problems.

Also, since a budget shows expected financial results, management is forewarned of impending financial problems. If, for example, the cash budget shows the company will exceed its overdraft limit in future months, management has advance warning of the need to reduce expenditure or to obtain additional finance. Budgeting, therefore, improves internal communication and coordination and reduces the need for crisis management.

## 3. Budgeting ... and the Motivation of Individuals

It has been said that budgeting is both a technical and behavioural process. Budgets provide financial (and non-financial) targets that responsible individuals are expected to meet. Typically, a separate budget is prepared for each responsibility centre within the organisation. The responsible manager is informed (after negotiation) about what is expected of him and is held accountable for meeting budget targets. Successful performance usually leads to rewards and so managers are motivated to achieve results. However, in general terms, **in order to motivate employees, three elements must be present in the budgeting process**:

(a) **The budget target should be difficult to achieve but attainable**. This is sometimes interpreted as having a 50/50 chance of success. Thus, open-ended goals, e.g. more is better, are not usually desirable as research has shown that motivation is reduced when goals are not specific. A substantial amount of research indicates that the desire to achieve within individuals is strongest when goals are perceived to be challenging; motivation is reduced if goals are perceived as too difficult, too easy or ambiguous. If budget targets are perceived as too hard, people will give up; if targets are too easy then significant employee effort will not be required. Ambiguous targets can result in confusion about priorities. Perceptions regarding budget difficulty and fairness can be impacted by subordinates participating and having some influence over the budgetary process.

In addition to improved motivation, there are two other benefits of employee participation in the budgetary process. First, the subordinate has the benefit of local knowledge and often knows more about certain aspects than his superior. Secondly, it can improve communication between superior and subordinate. However, it should be noted that, sometimes, superiors agree relatively easy budget targets to avoid the potential embarrassment of confronting a subordinate with inadequate performance. For all these reasons, budget targets are usually the end result of consultation and negotiation.

(b) **There must be a reward promised (and delivered), contingent on successful performance.** The purpose of providing such rewards is to reinforce positive behaviour and to modify negative behaviour. Practical implementation is, however, particularly dependent on organisational culture and the management philosophy of the firm. However, where companies have decided to make a significant portion of a manager's remuneration flexible – determined by successful performance – a balance of measures helps to ensure that target performance in one area is not achieved at the expense of performance in another area, e.g. production targets met by compromising on quality targets. In addition, measures on which any particular manager's remuneration depends should only be based on that manager's sphere of influence. Rewarding managers (or penalising them) for results achieved over which they have no control runs counter to the motivational goals of rewarding performance.

(c) **The rewards must be attractive to the individual.** These rewards are not necessarily monetary and can include promotion or other non-monetary benefits. While individuals vary significantly in the values they place on formal organisational rewards, nevertheless such reward systems are likely to have a substantial impact on employee motivation. Yet money, for instance, has different meanings for different persons and so a carefully designed reward system will hardly motivate a person for whom money has little value. The implication is that a pay/reward structure will have the most impact on the performance of employees with the greatest need for money per se and less impact on those individuals concerned with satisfying social or aspirational needs.

However, budgets can create negative or dysfunctional behaviour. This occurs when the budgetary control system influences behaviour in a manner which is not consistent with organisational goals or strategies. The problem tends to be associated with the evaluation/reward system, i.e. companies tend to get what they measure. Thus, for example, employees are very conscious of the 'ratchet effect' whereby budget targets are continually adjusted upwards by their superiors, based on prior successful performance. If the 'ratchet' phenomenon is present on a regular and frequent basis, then some employees will have the incentive to perform just *under* budget in order to ensure that subsequent targets are not increased. (We shall return to this topic in **Section 14.7.**)

## 4. Budgeting ... Provides a Framework for Control

The final advantage of preparing budgets is that they provide a yardstick or framework against which to compare actual performance. The resulting variances may indicate the need for corrective action, if appropriate. (It is usual that variance reports operate on the principle of management by exception, in that only significant variances are reported. If the variance is not considered significant, then performance is considered satisfactory.) Thus, if a company's expenditure to date is in excess of target (and therefore profit targets have not been met), then future expenditure plans could be reduced.

Alternatively, management could revise plans to generate additional revenues. This is the essence of control, which involves a continual monitoring of performance to date and comparing it with what the organisation intended it to be. Thus, we use the phrase 'budgetary control' to capture the initial financial planning process and, subsequently, the control function facilitated through the evaluation of current performance against budget.

The discipline of management accounting emphasises budgetary control, which we can also describe as **control by comparison** or **results control**. The traditional orientation to this type of control was to regard it as an *ex post* exercise – monitoring actual performance, comparing it with targets and, if there were adverse variances, taking corrective action. However, it should be obvious that setting easy-to-achieve targets would ensure that an in-control situation was always achieved. Thus, we need to integrate both planning and traditional control phases. Planning and control are two sides of the same coin. Without planning, there cannot be control. Similarly, planning is virtually useless unless there is a control mechanism in place. **Three important elements of a 'control by comparison' system** can now be specified.

1. **The Financial Target or Objective** The first element is the financial target or objective to be achieved. Objectives are stated in specific terms, preferably in such a way that one can determine whether the objective is being achieved or not.

2. **Evaluation of Actual Performance against Plan** The second element in the control system is the monitoring and evaluation of actual performance against original plans, typically, the financial targets set in the planning stage. Clearly, this requires an internal reporting system and reports generated must be timely in the sense that they must be produced within the accounting period to allow corrective action to be taken. If the reports are received after the end of the accounting period, then they are too late! Reports should also be accurate although there is an inevitable trade-off between timely and accurate information. Most important is that the reports should be relevant, but it is the user of the reports rather than the preparer of the report who determines relevance. To be relevant, reports should focus on those aspects that are the responsibility of the individual recipient. Individuals should feel that they will not be unfairly penalised or blamed for variances outside their control. Different levels of management have different responsibilities and different needs for performance information. If information is not relevant, not timely, or not understandable, then it ceases to be useful for control purposes.

   This monitoring and evaluation of actual performance against budget usually reveals a variance that can be positive or negative, favourable or adverse. In many respects, this is the most important part of the control system since the manager must decide what variances are significant. In other words, the manager must exercise his judgment on whether the system is, or is not, in control. This is referred to as the **control decision point**. There is no easy way to determine what represents a 'significant' variance. Many managers determine significance in terms of the percentage variation. Other criteria that can be used relate to the absolute amount of variance under consideration, or the trend in the variance over time or the nature of the process. Moreover, it may be company practice to be concerned with, say, only adverse variances. In other cases, managers may be concerned if the variance occurs very infrequently. The key issue in determining the significance of variances is that of managerial judgment.

3. **The 'Control Action'** The third and final element in the control system is the 'control action', i.e. deciding on and implementing the most appropriate action in relation to the significant variance. A number of points should be mentioned in this regard. First, the cause of the variance must be determined. In some cases, the variance may be entirely random and would not be expected to occur again. In other cases, the cause of the variance may be permanent, e.g. a price increase in raw materials. In other cases, the variance may be due to incorrect standards in the first place – the calculation of the required input of direct labour hours may have been incorrect. However, if the variance is due to operational causes (malfunctioning of machines or labour inefficiency, for example), corrective action should be taken, subject to cost/benefit considerations. The appropriate response is still a matter of judgment. This is the **control action point**. However, the corrective action to be taken may not be obvious, e.g. costs may be too high, but there may be no obvious or easy method of reducing them. Indeed, there may be several possible alternatives and management must exercise judgment as to what corrective action is most appropriate.

Before looking at the preparation of budgets and performance reports, there are two points worth stressing regarding budgetary control:

1. **Financial variances only represent signals that the system is in or out of control.** Thus, a sales report may indicate that sales are not achieving target levels. However, it is crucial to understand that this unsatisfactory performance could be due to optimistic sales forecasts, the uncompetitive sales price or a problem with product quality or customer service. The control system requires a managerial response, based on an understanding of the underlying problem. The managerial response is the essence of control.

2. **Control is time-specific**. This means that one can only control an event that is in the process of happening. This requires regular and periodic reporting of actual performance against budget. One cannot control an event that has already occurred though one can learn from the experience. Thus, a variance can be included in subsequent discussion including the agreeing of targets for the following accounting period.

Implicit in the above process is the acceptance that, once approved, the budget can be changed or revised only under specified conditions. Clearly if a budget could be revised at will by the subordinate, there would be very little point approving the budget in the first instance. On the other hand, if the budget assumptions turn out to be so unrealistic that the comparison of budget with actual performance is meaningless, budget revisions may be desirable.

There are two general types of procedure regarding budget revisions, namely, (a) systematic revision and (b) special circumstances. **Systematic revision** means that the budget is updated on a regular and agreed basis during the relevant accounting period. However, this is a time-consuming process. Thus, some companies budget for a year but only the figures for the first six months are approved. The subsequent six months are revised before being approved. Revising budgets, based on special circumstances, is self-evident, but the problem with this approach is defining what constitutes 'special circumstances'. The important aspect is that permission to make revisions due to special circumstances should be made difficult to obtain and should be properly approved and communicated.

## Control and Stop/Go Controls

The managerial accounting discipline makes a distinction between '**control**' and '**controls**'. The former is associated with the (financial) condition to be achieved in the future, e.g. the sales or profit target. With reference to progress towards this condition, the performance of the organisation can be described as being either in control or out of control. On the other hand, 'controls' represents the various means by which 'control' can be achieved. Thus 'controls' represent the entire set of procedures and systems that organisations use to guide, influence and motivate all employees. Within the discipline of management accounting, controls are generally of two types, which we can refer to here as 'control by comparison' (or results control) and 'stop/go' (or action) controls.

'**Control by comparison**' can be described, essentially, as an error-based system and one disadvantage of this system is that variances or errors are allowed to occur. This is particularly disadvantageous in systems where time lags occur between the occurrence of an error, its reporting and the implementation of corrective action.

In contrast, '**Stop/go**' controls are intended to regulate activities *before* they happen and, thus, they can be described as preventative controls as their purpose is to prevent an undesirable situation happening. These controls are part of the wider system of internal control that exists within the organisation. Within the discipline of managerial accounting, spending authorisation limits are an example of such controls, since spending above these limits is not allowed or, at least, the excess spending should have prior sanction before these limits can be breached. Organisations usually have a variety of 'stop/go' controls, based upon specified practices and procedures. Employees are expected to comply with these routine procedures and policies but there is rarely any reward or recognition for complying with them. In contrast, if they are not complied with, employees usually face sanctions.

However, 'stop/go' controls suffer from a number of limitations:

1. Because they represent specified behaviour, 'stop/go' controls can restrict behaviour in certain circumstances in a manner that can be considered inappropriate. For

example, if overall spending limits are enforced, the ability of the firm to respond to market opportunities may be significantly reduced, or at least it may be cumbersome to react to such opportunities.

2. Related to this is the impact on employee morale and motivation. Effectively, stop/go controls generally curtail discretionary human behaviour and this is capable of reducing the challenge facing employees and their overall job satisfaction. In a previous chapter, we have mentioned that, in modern organisations, employees are better educated and trained than employees of previous decades. Thus, they are often more comfortable in jobs that provide challenge and flexibility than in situations whereby a specific response or action is predetermined.

3. Due to the complexity of modern business, it would be impossible to regulate all possible activities by way of specific procedures. In other words, 'stop/go' controls cannot be designed for every conceivable possibility.

4. Finally, it is difficult to control human behaviour. Different individuals behave in different ways – look at how different drivers react to amber traffic lights! Even our own behaviour to such situations differs from time to time. Since the most pervasive control system within organisations is that of 'control by comparison', assisted by the existence of budgets, we shall now discuss how operating budgets are prepared.

## 14.3 Preparation of Operating Budgets

Organisations usually follow a formal series of steps to prepare budgets but the most important is to review its current strategy. As we have discussed in Chapter 7, such a strategic review usually begins with an assessment of external factors that affect operations, which typically include political, economic, social and technological considerations. Such an analysis can reveal both opportunities and threats.

In turn, an internal analysis should be undertaken and this would consider, for example, the financial position and performance of the company, managerial expertise, product development, and staff competencies. This internal analysis facilitates the identification of the company's strengths and weaknesses.

Matching the firm's strengths with identified opportunities, while minimising the adverse impact of threats and weaknesses, allows the firm's strategy to be properly evaluated. Only when this issue has been addressed adequately should consideration turn towards preparing detailed financial projections for a forthcoming period of time.

### Budget Preparation in Large Manufacturing Firms

We shall now turn to the preparation and integration of detailed budgets. For convenience, we shall focus on a financial year, with quarterly subdivisions. (However, the income statement and balance sheet presented here are based on annual data.)

The preparation of quarterly budgets is recommended where there is a significant seasonality factor associated with the firm's operations. Indeed, seasonality can create unique problems for budgeting since accounting data for one quarter may be unrepresentative of a subsequent period. The issue of seasonality usually impacts on budgets in some of the following ways (which are not listed in order of importance):

1. Quarterly (or monthly) demand levels (e.g. ice cream sales) are likely to fluctuate. Excess demand over production capacity in one quarter must be compensated for by excess production in a prior period.
2. The seasonality of sales demand may have important implications for the recruitment/retention of staff.
3. Overall occupancy costs are likely to vary with seasons/months, e.g. heating costs.
4. In months of 'low' trade, losses may be incurred which may put the firm under cash flow pressures. However, the advantage of quarterly budgets is that they provide an early warning system so that action may be taken to prevent this occurrence or, alternatively, adequate bank loans are negotiated in good time.
5. Operating costs, e.g. agricultural products, may vary from season to season and quarterly budgets are likely to provide more realistic figures compared to annual figures which require an average cost per annum.

Here, we shall illustrate budgeting procedures for a manufacturing firm, which is the most complex type of organisation. The emphasis will be on the preparation of a series of operating budgets. Operating budgets usually refer to operational activities and consist of the following sequence for a manufacturing firm:

1. Sales budget
2. Production budget
3. Raw materials purchase budget
4. Various expense budgets.

In the next section (**Section 14.4**) we shall discuss how these operating budgets, together with any capital expenditure budget, will be integrated with a master budget (or budgeted financial statements) as represented by the:

5. Cash budget
6. Budgeted income statement
7. Budgeted balance sheet.

Each of these budgets will now be discussed in turn.

## 1. Sales Budget

The sales budget will be prepared based upon estimates of general business and economic conditions, expected levels of competition and consumer demand. In this context, it is worthwhile highlighting the difference between a budget and a forecast.

A forecast is merely a prediction of what will most likely happen in the future and the forecaster does not accept any responsibility for meeting the forecasted results. Moreover, forecasts are not normally approved by a higher authority and they are usually updated as soon as new information suggests that there is a change in relevant conditions. In contrast, budgets represent specific targets to be achieved in the future and they can be used as both a planning and control tool by management.

The sales budget is the simplest of all budgets to **prepare** since it consists of two variables only – sales volume (in units) and average selling price. However, it is a difficult budget to **agree** since it is a prediction of expected unit sales by product and average selling price for a defined future period.

The sales budget is the first budget to be prepared since it will impact on virtually all other budgets in the organisation. For example, the sales budget will have an immediate and direct impact on the production budget and various expenses budgets. The format of the sales budget for a single accounting period is as follows:

**Sales Budget for…**

Sales in units × Sales price per unit = Total budget sales revenue

In turn, the total budget sales revenue will be partitioned between anticipated cash receipts during the period (transferred to the cash budget) and accounts receivable at the end of the period (transferred to the closing balance sheet), and described on the balance sheet as **Accounts Receivable** or **Trade Debtors**.

## ILLUSTRATION: SALES BUDGET

For illustration purposes, let us work through the budgeting process of Waterford Limited – a recently incorporated company – which manufactures 'widgets', which will be sold for €30 each. The quarterly sales forecast, in units, for 20x9 is as follows:

| Quarter | Sales units |
|---------|-------------|
| 1 | Nil |
| 2 | 2,000 |
| 3 | 3,000 |
| 4 | 4,000 |
| | 9,000 |

It is expected that 20% of total sales will be for cash and the remainder will receive three months' credit. Therefore, ignoring bad debts, the sales (revenue) budget, together with cash collections, is:

## W1. Sales Budget and Cash Collections for Year...

| | Q1 | Q2 | Q3 | Q4 |
|---|---|---|---|---|
| Units | Nil | 2,000 | 3,000 | 4,000 |
| Revenue @ €30 each | Nil | €60,000 | €90,000 | €120,000 |
| Cash collections: | | | | |
| Cash sales | Nil | €12,000 | €18,000 | €24,000 |
| From debtors | Nil | Nil | €48,000 | €72,000 |
| Total cash collections | Nil | €12,000 | €66,000 | €96,000 |

The amount to be collected in cash each quarter is also presented above. It is antici-pated that 20% of total sales will be for cash and the remainder will receive three months' credit. Thus, cash collections in Q2 will amount to €12,000 (20% × €60,000). Accounts receivable or trade debtors at the end of Q4 amounts to €96,000 (80% × €120,000 – the sales revenue in the final quarter). Please note that it is purely coincidental that the accounts receivable at the end of Q4 is a similar figure to the amount of cash collected during Q4.

In some instances, product demand is fairly stable and easily predictable but this is unusual. More normally, product demand varies widely depending on many factors external to the organisation and hence beyond its direct control. The need for a sound sales forecasting system is now accepted by almost all businesses. There are different approaches to sales forecasting, which are summarised as follows:

- **Surveys of buyers' intentions** In this method, the organisation bases its sales fore-cast on a survey of buyers' intentions – it asks its major customers for a schedule of their expected future purchases by product and price. Obviously, this method could not be applied where there are a large number of small customers: it tends to be most useful where there are a relatively small number of larger, industrial customers who must be co-operative and are able to forecast their own demand with reasonable accuracy.
- **Sales force estimates** With this method, the various sales personnel are asked to forecast the future product sales for their own particular areas. This method is based on the belief that the person nearest to the customer is best placed to judge market conditions. However, this method suffers from the possible optimism of sales personnel, with the resulting potential overstatement of demand.
- **Statistical method** This involves projecting the sales patterns of previous accounting periods according to various statistical relationships. It has the advantage that cyclical trends and seasonal variations can be more easily identified and allowed for. (The technique of regression analysis is frequently used – see **Section 9.3 above**.) Usually, these statistical methods are used in combination with the other two methods.

The importance of the sales budget will encourage businesses to seek better methods of estimating future sales demand. However, increasing competition, both nationally and internationally, will inevitably complicate the background against which such budgets are made. Organisations should recognise that sales budgets are, at best, reasoned estimates of future demand and operational plans must be as flexible as possible to allow for errors.

## 2. Production Budget (Units)

The purpose of the production budget is to determine the physical number of finished goods that must be produced during the forthcoming accounting period. This budget is prepared only for a manufacturing enterprise, and is directly related to the sales forecast. It is prepared in terms of finished units only (and not in financial terms). If the company does not embrace Just in Time (JIT) philosophy, then one must be careful to adjust for opening and closing stocks of finished goods on hand to identify the number of completed units that must be produced. The format for the production budget is as follows, for a hypothetical company:

### Production Budget for...

| | |
|---|---|
| Number of units to be sold as per sales budget (say) A | 1,000 units |
| Add: Closing stock of finished goods required (units) B | 200 units |
| Less: Opening stock of finished goods (units) (C) | (300) units |
| = Units to be produced (production requirements) <br> D = A+B−C | 900 units |

If the number of units to be produced exceeds current operating capacity, the management may have to decide whether to subcontract, plan for overtime, acquire additional capacity or reduce production of some items. If the number of units to be produced is less than capacity, then additional opportunities should be considered by management, e.g. to tender for special order decisions which would utilise this spare capacity.

### ILLUSTRATION: PRODUCTION BUDGET

To continue with our illustration, let us assume that Waterford Limited will commence production on 1 January 20x9 and it is intended to hold 1,000 finished units in stock at the end of each quarter. There is no opening inventory (stock) of finished goods at the start of the year since this is a newly established company.

However, the closing stock at the end of quarter 1 will represent the opening stock of Quarter 2 and so forth. The (quarterly) production budget, in completed units, appears for the first year as follows:

**W2. Production Budget of Finished Units for Year… Quarter**

|                      | 1     | 2       | 3       | 4       |
|----------------------|-------|---------|---------|---------|
| Units sold           | Nil   | 2,000   | 3,000   | 4,000   |
| Add: Closing stock   | 1,000 | 1,000   | 1,000   | 1,000   |
| Less: Opening stock  | Nil   | (1,000) | (1,000) | (1,000) |
| Units to be produced | 1,000 | 2,000   | 3,000   | 4,000   |

### 3. Raw Materials Purchase Budget

The raw (or direct) materials purchase budget indicates the physical amount of raw materials to be purchased in order to satisfy the above production requirements, together with the purchase costs involved. This budget starts by identifying the physical raw materials to be used in production (from the production budget). If the company does not embrace JIT philosophy, then one must adjust for any required opening or closing stock of raw materials. Such stock holdings are influenced by storage space and costs, trends of materials' prices and such factors. It can be presented as follows:

**Raw Materials Purchase Budget for…**

| | |
|---|---|
| Units to be produced (as per production budget) | A |
| Kgs required per unit | B |
| Kgs required for total production | $C = A \times B$ |
| Add: Closing stock of raw materials required (say) | D |
| Less: Opening stock of raw materials (say) | (E) |
| Kgs to be purchased this period | $F = C + D - E$ |
| Cost per kg € | G |
| Total cost of raw materials purchased € | $H = F \times G$ |

In turn, the total cost of raw materials purchased will be partitioned between cash paid to suppliers during the period (reported in the cash budget) and accounts payable (or trade creditors) at the end of the period (transferred to the closing balance sheet).

## ILLUSTRATION: RAW MATERIALS PURCHASE BUDGET

To continue with our illustration, let us assume that, for Waterford Limited, the production of each 'widget' requires 2kg of raw material at a cost of €4 per kg. The initial purchase of raw material will take place during Quarter 1, and there is no opening stock of raw materials since this is a newly established company. The company requires 5,000 kgs of closing stock at the end of each quarter. The raw material purchase budget, together with related cash payments for the year, is as follows:

### W3. Raw Materials, Purchase Budget and Cash Payments for Year

| | Quarter | | | |
| --- | --- | --- | --- | --- |
| | 1 | 2 | 3 | 4 |
| Units produced each quarter | 1,000 | 2,000 | 3,000 | 4,000 |
| Materials required (× 2 kgs per unit) | 2,000 | 4,000 | 6,000 | 8,000 |
| Add: Closing stock required (kgs) | 5,000 | 5,000 | 5,000 | 5,000 |
| Less: Opening stock (kgs) | Nil | (5,000) | (5,000) | (5,000) |
| Purchases (kgs) | 7,000 | 4,000 | 6,000 | 8,000 |
| Cost per kg | €4 | €4 | €4 | €4 |
| Total cost of purchases | €28,000 | €16,000 | €24,000 | €32,000 |
| Cash payments to suppliers | Nil | €28,000 | €16,000 | €24,000 |

The above presentation includes the cash impact on the overall cash budget for the year. We have assumed that Waterford Limited receives three months' credit from its suppliers. Thus, the first payment (€28,000) takes place in Quarter 2. At the end of Quarter 4, €32,000 will be owing to suppliers and this will be listed as **Accounts Payable** or **Trade Creditors** on the balance sheet at that date.

## 4. Expense Budgets

A variety of expense budgets can be prepared and these can include, for example, labour, production overhead and support expense budgets, such as selling, distribution and administration. The expense budgets are driven by the figures contained in either the production or sales budget. For example, the labour budget depends on the number of units to be produced since this will determine the number of labour hours required. The total number of hours multiplied by the anticipated wage rate provides a budget for labour cost. The preparation of other budgets, for example, for fixed costs is straightforward but care should be taken with the treatment of depreciation, where appropriate, since this is a non-cash item of expenditure. Depreciation will appear in the firm's budgeted income statement but will be excluded from the cash budget.

## ILLUSTRATION: EXPENSE BUDGETS

In Waterford Limited, the remaining variable cost structure per unit of output is anticipated:

|  | € |
|---|---|
| Direct labour per unit | 2 |
| Variable production overhead per unit | 3 |

Direct labour and variable overheads will be paid in the quarter in which they are incurred. For convenience, the direct labour and variable production overhead figures are combined in the calculation presented below since they both relate to the number of units produced. Since the total cost amount will be paid as incurred, the same amount will be reflected in the cash budget for each quarter:

### W4. Direct Labour and Variable Overhead Budget for Year ...

|  | Q1 | Q2 | Q3 | Q4 |
|---|---|---|---|---|
| Units produced | 1,000 | 2,000 | 3,000 | 4,000 |
| Cost per unit | €5 | €5 | €5 | €5 |
| Total cost | €5,000 | €10,000 | €15,000 | €20,000 |

In addition, Waterford Limited will incur fixed production overheads amounting to €10,000 in Quarter 1 and €12,000 in each of the remaining three quarters. These amounts will be paid when incurred and they can be budgeted as follows:

### W5. Fixed Production Overhead Budget for Year ...

|  | Q1 | Q2 | Q3 | Q4 |
|---|---|---|---|---|
| Total cost | €10,000 | €12,000 | €12,000 | €12,000 |

Waterford Limited anticipates it will incur Selling and Administration overheads amounting to €10,000 per quarter and these will be paid as incurred. This budget is presented below and the amounts will be recorded in both the projected income statement and budgeted cash flow statement for the financial year.

### W6. Selling and Administration Budget For Year ...

|  | Q1 | Q2 | Q3 | Q4 |
|---|---|---|---|---|
| Total spending | €10,000 | €10,000 | €10,000 | €10,000 |

Depreciation of fixed assets has not been included in the above fixed overhead figures. Waterford Limited calculates depreciation on its planned capital expenditure as follows:

1. plant and equipment (costing €100,000) at 20% on cost per annum;
2. motor vehicles (costing €20,000) at 25% on cost per annum, and
3. factory premises (costing €100,000) at 2% on cost per annum.

The depreciation budget is based on the historical cost of the assets and the relevant depreciation policy as follows, assuming all items are purchased at the start of the year, since this is a new business.

### W7. Depreciation Budget for Year ...

| | | € | |
|---|---|---|---|
| Factory premises | 2% × €100,000 | 2,000 | |
| Plant | 20% × €100,000 | 20,000 | |
| | | 22,000 | (production overhead) |
| Motor vehicles | 25% × €20,000 | 5,000 | (distribution overhead) |

It is worth repeating (since many students make mistakes in this regard) that depreciation of fixed assets should never be included in the cash budget! Depreciation does not represent a cash flow. Depreciation is simply a book-keeping entry made at the end of the year in accordance with generally accepted accounting principles. However, it is a legitimate expense of the business and will be recorded as such in the budgeted income statement for the period under review.

## 14.4 Preparation of the Master Budget

When all the operating budgets have been prepared, it is usual to integrate them into a master budget. A **master budget** typically consists of a cash budget, an income statement and projected balance sheet. If there are capital expenditure plans, these can also be integrated into this phase since they will impact heavily on all three accounting statements.

## ILLUSTRATION: CAPITAL EXPENDITURE BUDGET

For Waterford Limited, the following capital expenditure will be required during January 20x9:

|  | € |
|---|---|
| Factory premises | 100,000 |
| Plant and equipment | 100,000 |
| Motor vehicles | 20,000 |
|  | 220,000 |

In addition, the newly-formed company will have an issued share capital of €100,000 which will be subscribed for in full during Quarter 1. Furthermore, the parent company will advance €50,000 per quarter by way of an interest-free loan.

### 5. Cash Budget

The cash budget summarises (monthly or quarterly, as required) cash receipts and cash payments. Cash receipts will arise from operating, financing or investing activities. Operating cash receipts depend upon the sales forecast and the company's experience in collecting amounts receivable from customers. In addition, there may be cash inflows due to financing activities, e.g. issue of capital or loans. Investing cash inflows arise from the sale of fixed assets or long-term investments.

Likewise, cash payments can be divided into operating, financing or investing activities. Operating cash payments depend upon the budgeted levels of materials' purchases as well as credit terms offered by suppliers. In addition, there are operating expenses such as production, selling, distribution and administration expenses. Furthermore, there may be cash payments associated with investing activities, e.g. purchase of fixed assets, or financing activities, e.g. repayment of capital or loans. A typical (summarised) format for the cash budget is as follows:

### CASH BUDGET FOR …

| Cash inflows | All itemised |
|---|---|
| Cash outflows | All itemised |
| Net cash flows | Difference between cash inflows and cash outflows |
| Opening cash balance (say) | Usually given |
| = Closing cash balance | Reported on closing balance sheet |

## ILLUSTRATION: CASH BUDGET

The Cash Budget for Waterford Limited for the year ended 31 December 20x9 is
as follows:

### Cash Budget for Year Ended 31 December 20x9

|  | Q1 | Q2 | Q3 | Q4 |
|---|---|---|---|---|
| **Cash Inflows:** | € | € | € | € |
| Cash collected from sales W1: | | | | |
| Cash sales (20%) | Nil | 12,000 | 18,000 | 24,000 |
| Credit sales (80%) | Nil | Nil | 48,000 | 72,000 |
| Capital invested | 100,000 | Nil | Nil | Nil |
| Loan received | 50,000 | 50,000 | 50,000 | 50,000 |
| Total cash inflows (€474,000) | 150,000 | 62,000 | 116,000 | 146,000 |
| **Cash Outflows:** | | | | |
| Purchase of fixed assets | 220,000 | Nil | Nil | Nil |
| Payments to suppliers W3 | Nil | 28,000 | 16,000 | 24,000 |
| Labour and var. overhead W4 | 5,000 | 10,000 | 15,000 | 20,000 |
| Fixed production costs W5 | 10,000 | 12,000 | 12,000 | 12,000 |
| Selling and admin. costs W6 | 10,000 | 10,000 | 10,000 | 10,000 |
| Total cash outflows (€424,000) | 245,000 | 60,000 | 53,000 | 66,000 |
| Net cash flows per quarter | (95,000) | 2,000 | 63,000 | 80,000 |
| Opening cash balance | Nil | (95,000) | (93,000) | (30,000) |
| Closing cash balance | (95,000) | (93,000) | (30,000) | 50,000 |

The total cash inflows for the year amount to €474,000 compared with total cash
outflows of €424,000. Thus, the projected bank balance at the end of the financial year amounts to €50,000 (in funds). This will be shown on the balance sheet
under the heading of current assets.

## 6. Budgeted Income Statement

This budget is based upon the sales revenue forecast and estimates of the cost of goods sold and various operating expenses. It is prepared on the normal accrual basis of accounting and does not require estimates of the timing of cash receipts and cash payments. A typical income statement for a manufacturing firm would be as follows and this is presented for the year. (Quarterly figures could also be presented, if required.)

### INCOME STATEMENT FOR YEAR ...

|  | € |
|---|---|
| Sales | |
| Less: Cost of sales | |
| = Gross profit | |
| Less: Selling, distribution & administration costs (all itemised) | |
| = Operating profit (or loss) for year | |
| Less: Interest payable | |
| = Profit before tax | |

The projected income statement for the year summarises sales revenue, cost of sales and all the operating and other expenses. The residual will either be a net profit or a net loss.

### ILLUSTRATION: BUDGETED INCOME STATEMENT

For Waterford Limited, it is useful to calculate the cost of sales (9,000 units) from the budgeted unit cost, assuming (for convenience, in this instance) that finished goods are valued at variable cost of production.

#### W8. Computation of Unit Cost (Variable Costing)

|  | € |
|---|---|
| Direct materials (per unit) | 8 |
| Direct labour (per unit) | 2 |
| Variable overhead (per unit) | 3 |
| Total unit (variable) cost | 13 |
| Total cost of sales (€13 × 9,000 units) | = €117,000 |

Since the number of units sold during the period was 9,000, the cost of goods sold amounts to €117,000 (9,000 × €13). However, according to the production budget, 10,000 units will be produced during the year, leaving an estimated 1,000 units in stock at the end of the accounting period. These will be valued at €13,000 (€13 × 1,000) and shown on the closing balance sheet under the heading of **Current assets**. The projected income statement for Waterford Limited for the year is as follows:

**Income Statement for year ...**

| | | € |
|---|---:|---:|
| Sales (9,000 units @ €30) W1 | | 270,000 |
| Less: Cost of sales | | |
| Variable costs (9,000 units @ €13) W8 | (117,000) | |
| Fixed production overheads W5 (total) | (46,000) | |
| Depreciation of premises and plant W7 (total) | (22,000) | (185,000) |
| Gross profit | | 85,000 |
| Selling and Administration costs W6 (total) | | (40,000) |
| Depreciation of distribution vehicles W7 | | (5,000) |
| Net profit for year (ignoring taxation) | | 40,000 |

## 7. Budgeted Balance Sheet

The final budget to be prepared is the forecast balance sheet at the end of the budget period. All assets will be disclosed together with all liabilities and shareholders' funds. The closing bank balance will be the closing balance as per the forecast cash budget. The retained earnings for the period (to be included in shareholders' funds) will be related to the forecast income statement for the period. A typical projected balance sheet would appear as follows:

BALANCE SHEET AS AT. . .

| | € |
|---|---|
| Non-current assets (net book amount) | |
| Current assets | |
| = Total assets | |
| Financed by: | |
| Shareholders' funds | |
| Liabilities | |
| = Total liabilities and shareholders' funds | |

## ILLUSTRATION: BUDGETED BALANCE SHEET

The projected balance sheet for Waterford Limited is now presented. The advantage of preparing this financial statement is twofold. First, it highlights the overall financial position at the end of the budget period and this is of interest to most business managers. Secondly, a properly balanced balance sheet is an indication of the arithmetical accuracy of the budgeting process (but compensating errors may still be present in our calculations).

### Balance Sheet as at 31 December 20x9

| | € Cost | € Agg. Depr. W7 | € Net |
|---|---|---|---|
| Non-current (fixed) assets | | | |
| Premises | 100,000 | 2,000 | 98,000 |
| Plant | 100,000 | 20,000 | 80,000 |
| Vehicles | 20,000 | 5,000 | 15,000 |
| | 220,000 | 27,000 | 193,000 |
| Current assets | | | |
| Inventory (Stocks): | | | |
| Raw materials (5,000 kgs × €4) | | 20,000 | |
| Finished goods (1,000 units × €13) | | 13,000 | |
| Debtors (80% × €120,000) W1 | | 96,000 | |
| Bank balance (see cash budget) | | 50,000 | 179,000 |
| | | | 372,000 |

| Financed by | |
|---|---:|
| Share capital | 100,000 |
| Add: Retained earnings (see income statement) | 40,000 |
| | 140,000 |
| Interest-free loan | 200,000 |
| Current liabilities: | |
| Trade creditors (100% × €32,000) W3 | 32,000 |
| | 372,000 |

The process of developing a master budget, together with the underlying operating budgets, becomes increasingly complex as organisations become larger. For one thing, communication and agreement become more difficult the more people that are involved. In addition, one needs to consider, for example, possible foreign exchange implications for those firms involved in international trade, the state of the national economies and uncertainties associated with inflation.

In the above presentation we have concentrated on a manufacturing concern. However, different types of organisation will prepare different types of operating budgets although most commercial organisations would prepare a sales budget, since revenue generation (and subsequent cash collections) is a key activity. In contrast, a retail shop would not prepare a production budget, since it does not manufacture goods for resale. A service company would not prepare a production or raw materials budget, for the same reason. The preparation of other budgets, such as a research and development budget, may depend on the overall size of the organisation and the significance of the amounts involved. As a useful guide to budgetary activities, **Exhibit 14.1** represents budgets that might be prepared for different manufacturing, retail and service firms.

EXHIBIT 14.1: BUDGETS FOR DIFFERENT ORGANISATIONS

| Type of budget | Manufacturer | Retailer | Service |
|---|:---:|:---:|:---:|
| Sales Budget (Sales units and price) | Yes | Yes | Yes |
| Production Budget (i.e. units to be produced) | Yes | No | No |
| Raw materials purchase budget (Quantity and cost of raw materials to be purchased) | Yes | Purchase of finished goods only | No |

| Labour cost budget (Labour hours required and rate per hour) | Yes | Yes | Yes |
|---|---|---|---|
| Overhead cost budget (A range of budgets representing production and non-production activities, as appropriate) | Yes | Yes | Yes |
| Cash budget (Projected cash inflows and cash outflows) | Yes | Yes | Yes |
| Forecast income statement (Budgeted sales revenues less all budgeted costs) | Yes | Yes | Yes |
| Projected balance sheet (Projected assets, liabilities and shareholders' funds) | Yes | Yes | Yes |

## 14.5 Accounting for Value Added Tax (VAT)

In Ireland, approximately one-third of all tax revenue is represented by VAT. Value Added Tax is a tax on spending or transactions and as such it is a discretionary tax – if you don't want to pay the tax, don't buy the goods! However, this is easier said than done since VAT applies to most items of expenditure. Effectively, registered firms are obliged to charge VAT on its sales to customers at the appropriate rate. At the end of the VAT period, usually two months, the firm must pay over the VAT charged to its customers – even though they have not been paid for the goods – less VAT that it paid on its purchases during the period. Thus, most firms will have a VAT liability at the end of the VAT period.

However, it is also possible, but not very common among firms in general, that a firm may be in a VAT refund situation at the end of the VAT period. The **essentials of any VAT system** can be summarised as follows:

- A registered firm should charge VAT on the supply of goods (or services) at the appropriate rate. Thus, the payment of VAT by consumers is automatic since it is built into the final price which is paid for the goods or services. This can be referred to as a tax on Outputs. For accounting purposes, the VAT exclusive sales figure is transferred to the income statement.
- VAT is paid by the registered firm on its purchases and other expenses, at the appropriate rate. This can be referred to as a tax on Inputs. For accounting purposes, the VAT exclusive figure is transferred to the income statement.

- The difference between VAT on outputs and VAT on inputs is essentially a tax on 'value added' and must be remitted to the tax authorities at the appropriate time. (Alternatively, a VAT refund can be expected.) However, the administrative burden falls on the various business entities, which are registered for VAT. In this context, businesses act as unpaid tax collectors, but nevertheless incur certain costs in doing so. In addition, the rates of VAT change over time, adding complexity to the system.

There are three main rates of VAT, i.e. zero, 13.5% and 21%. (There is also an exempt status which applies to, for example, education and hospital services. This status means that VAT is not applied to transactions involving such services. The only advantage is that the exempt trader is not obliged to make VAT returns or maintain VAT records.) Examples of goods and services taxable at the various rates are as follows:

1. **Zero:** Exports, children's clothing and footwear, food, oral medicines, fertilizer and farm animal feedstuffs. The implication of this status is that the trader, technically, is able to charge VAT at a 0% on his sales (outputs). Thus, when he is charged VAT on his inputs (goods and services), he is in a VAT refund situation.
2. **21% (standard rate):** Adult clothing and footwear, household goods and furniture, motor vehicles, office equipment and stationery, accountancy and legal services, telephone bills, alcohol and soft drinks.
3. **13.5%:** Building materials including concrete blocks and repairs, immovable goods (e.g. houses), agricultural contractors, cinemas, restaurant and hotel meals and accommodation, domestic heating oil, theatres, and certain bakery products.

## ILLUSTRATION: ACCOUNTING FOR VAT

It has already been noted that the basis of VAT liability is the invoices issued to customers during a two-month taxable period together with the invoices received from suppliers. VAT should be charged to each customer whereas VAT is paid on most purchases (and other qualifying expenses). We shall assume the following transactions for two separate illustrations:

1. A firm produces the following summary of Sales (Outputs) and Purchases and other expenses (Inputs) for a recent taxable period:

| Transactions | VAT inclusive amount | VAT amount | VAT exclusive amount |
|---|---|---|---|
| Sales €5,000 (plus VAT @ 21%) | €6,050 | €1,050 | €5,000 |
| Purchases €2,000 (plus VAT @ 21%) | €2,420 | €420 | €2,000 |
| Other inputs €1,000 (plus VAT @ 21%) | €1,210 | €210 | €1,000 |

| Computation of VAT liability: | | |
|---|---|---|
| VAT charged on sales (above) | | €1,050 |
| Less: VAT borne on purchases (above) | (€420) | |
| Less: VAT borne on other inputs (above) | (€210) | (€630) |
| = VAT due at end of period | | €420 |

2. A trader who sells goods both at the zero and 21% rates of VAT presents you with the following budgeted information for the months of January and February. For convenience, we shall assume that the trader accounts for VAT on an invoice basis.

| Sales of product A | €42,000 | Zero rate |
|---|---|---|
| Sales of product B | €84,700 | Inclusive of VAT at 21% |
| Purchases and expenses | VAT inclusive | |
| Purchase of product A | 25,000 | Zero rate |
| Purchase of product B | 48,400 | Inclusive of VAT at 21% |
| Other inputs (VAT non-deductible) | 1,210 | Inclusive of VAT at 21% |
| Electricity | 2,270 | Inclusive of VAT at 13.5% |
| New equipment | 6,050 | Inclusive of VAT at 21% |

**Requirements:**

1. Prepare the budgeted trading summary for the period. (Ignore opening and closing stock levels, which are insignificant.)
2. Show the balance sheet extracts in relation to property, plant and equipment and VAT payable or refundable.

**Solution and discussion:**

### W1. Computation of VAT payable for period

| Sales (outputs) | € VAT exclusive | € VAT | € Total value |
|---|---|---|---|
| Sales of product A | 42,000 | Nil | 42,000 |
| Sales of product B | 70,000 | 14,700 | 84,700 |
| | 112,000 | 14,700 | 126,700 |

| Purchases (inputs) | | | |
|---|---|---|---|
| Purchases of product A | 25,000 | Nil | 25,000 |
| Purchases of product B | 40,000 | 8,400 | 48,400 |
| Expenses (inputs) | | | |
| Other expenses * | 1,210 * | n/a * | 1,210 |
| Electricity | 2,000 | 270 | 2,270 |
| Equipment | 5,000 | 1,050 | 6,050 |
| Total VAT recoverable | | 9,720 | |
| VAT payable | | 4,980 | |

* VAT deduction is not allowed.

### Income Summary (Extract) and Balance Sheet (Extract) Based on above Information

| | € |
|---|---|
| Sales (total) – always shown exclusive of VAT | 112,000 |
| Purchases (total) – always shown exclusive of VAT | 65,000 |
| Expenses (total) – always shown exclusive of recoverable VAT | 3,210 |
| Property, plant and equipment (cost) – non-current asset | 5,000 |
| Vat Payable – current liability | 4,980 |

## Cash Basis of Accounting

The previous discussion indicated that the sales invoice is a most important document in accounting for VAT. Many traders normally account for VAT on an invoice basis, following the method outlined above. However, two problems emerge with applying the invoice basis:

1. Accounting for VAT on an invoice basis can create cash flow problems for traders where extended credit is given to customers. As each invoice is issued, the trader becomes liable to remit the VAT charged (less VAT on inputs) to the tax authorities and must do so for each two-month period. However, it may be that, with extended credit given, customers may not have paid their account and this creates cash flow problems for the trader.

2. Many traders do not issue invoices to customers and it would clearly be absurd to require them to do so, e.g. publicans, newsagents. Consequently, certain registered persons may be allowed to use the cash receipts basis of accounting instead of the usual sales invoice basis. (However, VAT on inputs will still be based according to invoices received.)

### Bad Debts, etc.

Since VAT liability is determined by the selling price, it is only fair that this liability should be reduced if bad debts are incurred or discounts are made or goods returned. A taxable person may adjust his liability for tax in respect of returned goods, discounts or price adjustments to the goods. However, in the case of bad debts, prior approval should be obtained from the tax authorities.

### Annual Accounting for VAT

In order to facilitate the efficient running of the VAT system, the tax authorities are authorised to permit registered traders to make an annual, i.e. a single return, and pay their VAT on an annual basis instead of the bi-monthly return. This represents a significant concession to traders, especially small traders who do not have ready access to book-keeping services. However, this arrangement is granted only at the discretion of the tax authorities and is not an automatic concession.

## 14.6 The Use of Spreadsheets in Budget Preparation

A spreadsheet program is the electronic equivalent of a pencil, an eraser and a large, blank piece of paper ruled with horizontal lines to give rows, and vertical lines to provide columns. This paper analogy, in fact, highlights the origin of spreadsheets for instructional purposes. In the classrooms of years gone by, for example, budgets were constructed on vertically ruled paper, with various inputs listed on the left hand margin, e.g. sales price, demand levels, etc., and their financial impact in successive periods was shown sequentially in columns of the sheet. While this provided a convenient format to trace the consequences of variations in the inputs, considerable calculation was required.

According to Dan Bricklin, who conceived the idea of the electronic spreadsheet, he did so while watching his MBA professor at Harvard create a financial budget on a blackboard. When the professor found an error or wanted to change a parameter, he had to tediously erase and rewrite a number of sequential entries in the table. This caused Brickin to realise that he could replicate the process on a computer using an 'electronic spreadsheet', based on underlying formulae. Eventually the idea was translated into reality with the development and distribution of **VisiCalc** in 1979, which was the first spreadsheet program available for personal computers and is generally credited for fuelling the rapid growth of business computing. The software was designed for Apple computers and its considerable success motivated IBM to enter the PC market which they had been ignoring until then.

Though the electronic spreadsheet was a revolutionary idea, Bricklin was advised that it would be unlikely that he would be granted a patent, so he failed to profit significantly from his invention. At that time, patents were not available for software in the US, so it was thought that the product could only be copyrighted, and as copyright deals with form rather than ideas, competitors could quickly copy the concept and present the result in a different layout without infringing the copyright! This was done through the development of successive types of electronic spreadsheets.

The electronic spreadsheet was designed to facilitate recalculation which was necessary whenever a budget was revised in any way. However, electronic spreadsheets can be used for any application in which relationships between numerical values are established. Each figure is entered in a specific cell which is identified by its row **number** and a column **letter**, giving it a unique address. Although only about 20 rows and 10 columns can appear on the computer screen at any time, several thousand cells are available for modelling purposes. The various cells are linked by way of hidden formulae.

## ILLUSTRATION: ROWS AND CELLS

For example, if cell A1 contains a sales value for year 1 and cell B1 contains a sales value for year 2, then cell C1 could contain a command to calculate the average sales value for the two years. Cell C1 will contain the hidden command, which is written in the format: $= (A1+B1)/2$), but this cell will also reveal the output desired. Thus:

|   | A | B | C |
|---|---|---|---|
| 1 | 10,000 | 11,000 | 10,500 $= (A1 + B1)/2$ |
| 2 | etc. | etc. | etc. |

Those familiar with the concept of spreadsheets should realise their potential in the area of financial computation and analysis. A **complex matrix of relationships** can be established using formulae to express the dependency of the value in one cell to the value in another. Ultimately, a change in one input cell can have a ripple effect (which takes place almost instantaneously) to cause changes in hundreds of other cells, and on the final output in which one is interested. Automatic recalculation is one of the most useful features of electronic spreadsheets.

The advantage of **speed of calculation** should also be noted. In fairness, developing spreadsheet solutions to a problem might, initially, take longer than simply using a pencil, paper and calculator. However, if recalculation is required, the electronic spreadsheet is much quicker than the manual effort. Also, the model or template can be stored and used repeatedly in the future, with consequent time saving.

In addition, many spreadsheets allow automatic calculation of certain variables. These variables include, for example, commonly used statistical values such as the 'average' or 'standard deviation' for a given set of variables or more advanced statistics such as $R^2$ – the coefficient of determination. Spreadsheets can also be used to cross-analyse variables, e.g. sales vs marketing spend. This builds up an understanding of what drives the business and aids planning and decision-making.

Furthermore, spreadsheet software is now integrated in the sense that the user can easily switch from, for example, modelling to business graphics and back. This avoids the frustration of having to transfer data from one application to another. However, one danger of spreadsheets is that, through unnecessary complexity and poor layout, the setup of the spreadsheet becomes corrupted. In other words, the apparent ease of model building leads to poorly constructed models which, sometimes, may be incorrect. If this limitation can be avoided, spreadsheets offer users an extremely powerful means of building a useful predictive tool.

An added advantage of electronic spreadsheets is in the area of **sensitivity analysis** or **what if analysis**. When creating business models, one must make certain assumptions about the future and it is advisable to explore what would happen if some of these assumptions were to change. The ease with which sensitivity analysis can be carried out has made the electronic spreadsheet a valuable tool for management accountants and decision-makers. Thus, the user may change any variable (i.e. cell value) and see the resulting implication immediately. Thus, if cell B1 is changed in the above illustration to a value of €14,000, then the value of cell C1 is updated immediately to €12,000. In simple terms, **sensitivity analysis** allows the user of computer spreadsheets to see the financial implications of any change to assumptions and this assists in the review and negotiation of budgets.

In the area of financial analysis, other important benefits need to be stressed such as the advantage of **consistency**. For example, if accounting information relating to several units is properly input, then a consistent set of accounting/financial indicators are produced. This consistency of calculation facilitates both the comparison of a unit's performance over time and a comparison of a unit's performance with other units.

## 14.7 Weaknesses of Traditional Budgeting and 'Beyond Budgeting'

"Any technique of management reaches maturity when, after its earlier mistakes have antagonised human beings sufficiently, it emerges with a new outlook and practice that is in harmony with the basic motivations of people. Budgeting now seems to be undergoing this metamorphosis."

The above quotation would not be out of place in many current publications which refer to the 'Beyond Budgeting' debate – a phrase that has gained currency in recent times. To paraphrase the current debate into a few words is a dangerous task; however, the argument is that budgeting, as most companies practise it, should be abolished or, at least significantly amended! Yet, it is remarkable to note that the above quotation is not a modern one, but rather appeared in 1954 in the *Harvard Business Review*. It would appear that little progress on refining and adapting budgeting practices has been made over the past five decades.

## The Evolution of Budgets in Commercial Organisations

The practice of budgeting was initially popularised by governments who, by the Nineteenth Century, presented to their parliaments an annual statement of revenues and expenditure and projected surplus or deficit. Clearly, this highlighted the need for financial planning, e.g. the amount of revenue to be raised. It also facilitated overall control of expenditure since, in theory, no funds could be spent without prior approval of parliament.

The technique of budgeting in commercial organisations grew in popularity in the early Twentieth Century. This increased emphasis on business planning and budgeting was facilitated by the emergence of comprehensive texts on budgeting and managerial accounting. Notable among these was a text by McKinsey (1924), whose career, prior to the establishment of the consulting firm bearing his name, included a distinguished period as Professor of Accounting at the University of Chicago. Subsequently, the topic was perceived to be so important that the first International Conference on Budgeting took place in Geneva in 1930. The purpose of the Conference was to provide an opportunity for a discussion between practical and theoretical specialists on the principles and methods of budget control. Remarkable for that time, it drew an attendance of some 200 delegates from 27 countries.

The technique of budgeting spread, especially after the Second World War, from America to Europe and from large firms to small firms. However, mainly due to the difficulty associated with forecasting sales, the technique was used as a system to control costs. Nevertheless, the popularity of budgetary control grew due to its perceived usefulness.

One of the limitations of current budgeting practices is that they represent fixed performance contracts in many firms. In other words, managers commit themselves to annual budget targets and are provided with strong incentives to meet them. The potential for dysfunctional behaviour is obvious and, in a pioneering and highly influential study in 1952, Chris Argyris brought to our attention the significant behavioural effects of budgeting in organisations. In particular, this study highlighted that the use of budgets could cause dysfunctional behaviour in subordinates. Indeed, the previously mentioned *Harvard Business Review* article (1954) suggested that:

> "men have become so frustrated under maladministered budgets that they have resorted to all sorts of tricks to conceal the actual results and have padded their budgets to give themselves breathing room. It is here that staff have usurped authority,

merited pay increases have been denied because of budget limitations, and tales have been carried around (and) up to the top under the guise of budget reporting."

## The Problems of Current Budgeting Practices

Traditional budgeting is now ingrained in all areas of organisational activity. We have seen earlier in this chapter that budgets serve an important integrative function within the organisation and also provide a most important framework for performance evaluation with reference to the original target. Nevertheless, current budgeting practices have been widely criticised. While not exhaustive, some of the main criticisms of the annual budgeting process are presented below, but not in order of importance:

- Budgets are typically prepared without regard to company strategy. Thus, the agreed budget does not communicate strategy throughout the organisation. In such circumstances, the implementation of strategy is confined to top management rather than every employee in the organisation.

- The focus of the budgetary process is on financial numbers only. They typically exclude all other metrics such as performance measures relating to critical success factors.

- Since the business environment is changing so rapidly, it is argued that realistic budgets for the future cannot be prepared.

- The annual budgeting process becomes an incremental activity within organisations. This represents justifying annual increases/decreases based on the outturn of the previous year. Most targets include some reference to historical data and this is understandable. Because most budget centres will start the accounting period with some facilities, e.g. employees, it is common to base the budget on existing levels, modified for certain changes due to, either external forces, or changes in internal factors. However, such an approach rarely encourages innovative thinking within organisations.

With incremental budgeting, the annual budget reflects a continuation of normal operations from year to year, adjusted for inflation. Inevitably, inefficiencies are usually carried forward from year to year. Also, it may be difficult to obtain funding for new activities since existing activities usually take precedence and, as a result, the firm may not benefit from potential opportunities or be aware of potential threats in the environment.

In contrast, **zero-based budgeting (ZBB)** is a method of budgeting in which managers are required to justify all costs as if the proposals involved were being considered for the first time. The aim is to get away from tendencies for budgets to grow incrementally over time. Under ZBB every activity to be carried out by the organisation must be fully justified by the sponsoring manager and prioritised in order to be included in the budget, as if it were being included for the first time. The prioritising of activities is important since this allows senior managers to review these activities and cut back on those that appear to be less critical or whose costs do not appear to be justified. Thus existing activities have to be justified in exactly the same way as new proposals, with all unnecessary costs stripped out. Effectively, the baseline is zero rather than last year's budget. However, ZBB has a number of practical shortcomings which have limited its successful application. ZBB is most suited to discretionary costs where management are free to decide how much or how little to spend on an activity. In addition, the complexity involved in identifying, costing and ranking various activities can lead management to the conclusion that the effort and cost does not justify the benefit. Many organisations would accept that, while ZBB has the potential to improve existing budgeting practices, incremental budgeting is preferable due to its simplicity of preparation and the regular budgetary cycle and process is commonly understood and accepted.

• The cost of budget preparation is enormous in terms of managerial time, effort and monetary resources consumed. The exercise is protracted and is characterised by the need for regular reworking associated with changed assumptions. It has been suggested that large companies would typically take between two to three months to complete the annual budget process and it can consume about 20% of manager's time.

• People 'play games' with budgets such as setting revenue targets that are easily achieved. Alternatively, managers may incorporate some 'budgetary slack' in their cost budget. In other words, in submitting budgets, managers may understate revenue and overstate costs. These have the effect of making the budget profit targets easier to achieve and reduce the risk of the manager not achieving them. Furthermore, agreed budgets become a 'fixed performance contract' between superiors and subordinates, and subordinates are usually incentivised to reach the agreed targets by whatever means at their disposal. In other cases, managers may deliberately overspend budget allocations in case the budget is reduced for next year. Moreover, expenditure on discretionary items, e.g. advertising, staff training or research and development, may be curtailed to achieve short-term financial profit targets. This behaviour is sometimes referred to as 'short-termism' whereby short-term profit performance is rewarded more than long-term achievement. Such actions could place the long-term position of the firm at a disadvantage. Also, budget evaluation and the provision of rewards create tension and anxiety among employees, which, in an extreme case, could lead to the manipulation of reported data.

• Budgeting can create conflict between superiors and subordinates, for example, in the process of agreeing targets for next year, especially where a better-than-budget performance in one year becomes the target performance in the following year. This is referred to as the 'ratchet effect'. If this phenomenon is perceived by subordinates to be present, then it may be difficult to motivate employees to achieve budget targets.

• Budgets can create a climate of 'by the book' within organisations whereby achieving budget target is all that matters and is all that will be rewarded. This approach can considerably restrain individual behaviour, especially innovative behaviour. It is inevitable that some innovative behavior will have an impact on a company's expenditure levels. However, it is possible that, if a proposed innovative behaviour has not been included in the annual budget, its approval will be rejected or at least deferred by sceptical seniors, who prefer to adhere to budget targets of expenditure.

- It is sometimes difficult to assign proper responsibility to individuals for their performance in relation to budgets. This is particularly the case if non-controllable factors are included in the performance evaluation. Allied to this point is the fact that some items of overhead expenditure, especially in large organizations, are not assigned to responsible individuals when the original budget is being agreed. Due to this absence of assigning responsibility, such overhead costs receive annual increments in keeping with the practice of increment budgeting. Thus, it is not surprising that these overhead costs are often difficult to reduce except through the simple but inappropriate expedient of mandating, say, a 10% reduction in all areas of expenditure.

## Beyond Budgeting?

Recently some authors have argued, based on many of the points outlined above, that the annual budget is a barrier to effective management in today's competitive environment. It is also argued that companies can gain substantial benefits from managing without budgets. Strong support for this controversial argument comes from a number of sources and this includes case studies of some big European and American companies that have successfully abandoned their traditional budgeting practice. It is convenient, but by no means complete, to categorise the **critics of traditional budgeting practice** and their suggestions into two groups:

- One group advocates **maintaining and improving the budgeting process** (to which this author subscribes).
- The other group is more radical and proposes that **budgeting should be abandoned**. Both of these viewpoints are now briefly presented. Retaining budgets as they are currently practised is not an option!

### Maintain and Improve?

This viewpoint can be conveniently described as the **activity-based budgeting (ABB)** school. The ABB approach focuses on generating a budget from an activity-based model of the organisation. The ABB model begins with estimated demand for products and services and, using activity-based concepts, converts these into activity requirements. It is only when the operational model is balanced, i.e. resources required to fill demand are matched by resources available (capacity) that the operational model is translated into a financial plan, and checked to see whether it meets a pre-determined financial target. If the initial financial plan is not acceptable then, for example, activities and resource consumption will be adjusted and reworked.

In contrast, traditional budgeting procedures do not collect information on activities. Since the ABB approach focuses on activities and resources, it is capable of highlighting potential inefficiencies and bottlenecks. In addition, ABB budgets can be used to clarify who is accountable for specific activities that cut across different departments. Furthermore, critical success factors will become apparent under ABB. Since these are often physical measures, they are more easily understood and accepted by managers, and more easily communicated.

### Abandon Budgeting?

The abandon budgeting approach is much more radical. It is based on the argument that budgetary practices which combine financial planning and subsequent performance evaluation lead to poor budget estimates and dysfunctional or perverse behaviour on the part of employees. Therefore, in order to avoid this annual 'performance trap', change is needed in the way we evaluate performance or, alternatively, by the complete abandonment of the budget. This performance trap is associated with evaluating managers by reference to financial targets that are dubiously set but remain fixed for the budget period. To avoid such perverse behaviour, it is argued that performance evaluation should be based on hindsight (together with a greater range of non-financial measures). Essentially, this means that evaluation of performance should be done by looking back at the actual operating conditions that prevailed during that period, rather than the original budget targets. Also, it is recommended that performance rewards be based on much more subjective evaluations as, it is argued, this will encourage employee initiative. The new objective is to foster an attitude of doing what is best for the organisation in light of prevailing circumstances and employees should be empowered to make decisions that are consistent with the vision and strategy of the organisation.

### Some General Implications

Some general implications associated with the debate can be identified as follows:

- Cost control is still important in most businesses and underpins the 'cost leadership' strategy. Unfortunately, 'cost leadership' is capable of being eroded, especially with the rapid diffusion of best practices within an industry. Perhaps less capable of being imitated is the 'differentiation' strategy whereby companies create a perception among consumers that the company's product or service is unique in some important way. Approaches to product differentiation include an emphasis on product quality, with emphasis on superior customer service and brand loyalty. Yet, these considerations are rarely made explicit in traditional budgeting practices. In simple terms, we have previously argued that the essence of strategy is about being different. **Beyond budgeting** companies continuously review their strategic position and are continuously looking for opportunities and threats in the future rather than continuously looking backwards at historical performance.
- Related to strategy and the success of organisations is their performance in relation to critical success factors. Critical success factors are those few, key areas that are most important in determining long-run profitability for the company. Such factors include, for example, quality, service, lead time and on-time delivery, customer satisfaction and loyalty, production flexibility and product innovation. In

**beyond budgeting** companies, measurement and reporting are confined to a few performance indicators, and it is the quality and relevance of the information that is more important than the quantity of the information.

- The **beyond budgeting** approach assumes that effective organisational performance is likely to be associated with giving employees the training and authority to make decisions, and rewarding them accordingly. Yet we have discussed the possibility that traditional budgets may suppress employee creativity and innovation. Therefore, it is argued that, in order to be successful, modern organisations need to replace their traditional budgeting systems with a system that empowers and facilitates actions based on value propositions of the firm.

- **Beyond budgeting** companies have changed both the target and reward systems. Rewards are now based on group rather than individual performance. Also, rewards are structured around beating the competition – a term that is widely defined and includes comparable sections within the company. Thus, the focus is on relative, competitive performance and not on comparative performance in relation to previously agreed budget targets. Thus, no matter how well one is doing, in terms of rewards, in **beyond budgeting** companies it is always advantageous to do better.

However, budgets, as we currently understand the term, will still be important in terms of forecasting and planning. For example, no one would suggest that cash flow forecasts should be abandoned and, indeed, rolling forecasts will be increasingly used. Also, cost forecasts will be required, for example, in setting predetermined overhead absorption rates in manufacturing firms which use either normal or standard costing systems. However, their use in performance evaluation will be diminished. It may be difficult for managers and management accountants to accept the various propositions associated with the **beyond budgeting** debate. Personally, this author is sympathetic to the argument that, in order to survive, companies will have to plan and control their operations in a different way in the future. At a minimum, the current criticisms of traditional budgeting practices should prompt us to question the efficiency and effectiveness of current financial control systems within organisations. Better budgeting practices should allow us to move forward with constantly improving methods of management accounting. The result should be a better alignment of accurate forecasting with corporate strategy, which, in turn, should be integrated with attempts to motivate managers and employees in a positive manner.

## 14.8 Flexible Budgeting and Reporting Revenue and Basic Cost Variances

In the previous sections we have noted that budgets are prepared based on certain assumptions about the level of future sales and other operating data. Such budgets are used for planning and motivational purposes and can be referred to as static budgets – since they will typically refer to a specified volume of production or output. However, it is unlikely that, for example, sales volume expectations will be exactly met simply because the future is never certain. Therefore, it is important, in the evaluation and control process, to compare like with like.

For example, it would not be realistic to compare the budgeted cost for 10,000 units of output with actual costs of an output of 12,000 units, especially where many costs are considered variable with respect to volume. Thus, in order to properly evaluate actual performance, we need to determine actual and budgeted revenue and costs for the same level of activity. This is the essence of flexible budgeting and flexed budget reporting.

**Flexible budgets** are budgets that are prepared at the end of the period, based on actual output. Therefore, they reflect what costs should have been incurred for an attained level of activity and they are used as a framework for calculating and analysing variances. In brief, they could be described as the budget that would have been prepared if one knew the actual level of output in advance! It is important to stress that flexed budgets are prepared for evaluation and control purposes rather than for planning purposes. Generally, they are relatively straightforward to prepare, provided one distinguishes between fixed and variable costs and the appropriate cost driver(s) involved. For the sake of illustration, we shall assume in this section that the most significant cost driver relates to volume of output.

Differences between flexed budget figures and actual results are referred to as **budget variances** and we typically relate them to their impact on profit performance. Thus, if actual revenues are higher than budget, or if actual costs are lower than budget, the variance is classified as a **favourable (F) variance**. In contrast, if actual revenues are lower than budget, or if actual costs are higher than budget, the variance is classified as an **adverse (A) variance**.

It is important to note that a favourable cost variance, for example, could reflect an unsatisfactory situation! For example, under-spending on research and development activities could reflect inactivity or lack of progress in this important area. Likewise, under-spending on direct material cost, for example, in a fast food restaurant may reflect poor quality meat or a reduction in the quantity of input per unit – both of which could adversely impact on customer satisfaction in the longer term. Thus, in evaluating performance it is necessary first to compute the appropriate variance and then to identify reasons why the 'significant' variances occurred. This information will then be used to suggest corrective action.

In the illustration below we shall prepare a basic financial performance report, using flexed budget principles. To vary the illustrative material, we shall use the example of a retail company – an oil distribution company – which is a single product firm.

## Illustration: Flexed Budget Reporting

The Limerick Company retails central heating oil and it encounters wide fluctuations in volume (activity) levels from month to month. The following (summarised) data refers to expected sales and costs for a normal level of activity of 20,000 gallons per month and the actual costs incurred in the month of June.

| | Budget | Actual |
|---|---|---|
| Sales units (actual) | 20,000 units | 18,000 units |
| | € | € |
| Sales revenues | 100,000 | 108,000 |
| Fuel costs (variable) | (60,000) | (81,000) |
| Fixed costs | (30,000) | (26,000) |
| Profit for month | 10,000 | 1,000 |

**Requirement:** Prepare a performance report for the above month, comparing actual performance with the flexed budget.

**Solution and Analysis:** In order to compare 'like with like' we need to flex the static budget (prepared for anticipated sales of 20,000 gallons) to the actual level of output (18,000 gallons). The presentation below introduces an additional column of information into the reporting process, i.e. the flexed budget column. Essentially, this indicates that if we knew in advance that 18,000 gallons would be produced and sold, then a profit of €6,000 for the month would have been projected. In addition, we have included an additional column for variances between flexed and actual. It should be noted that the actual selling price was €6 per gallon compared with a budgeted selling price of €5 per gallon.

### Flexed Budget Reporting

| | Static budget | Flexed budget | Actual | Variance |
|---|---|---|---|---|
| Sales gallons (actual) | 20,000 gallons | 18,000 gallons | 18,000 gallons | |
| | € | € | € | € |
| Sales revenues | 100,000 | 90,000 | 108,000 | +18,000 |
| Fuel costs | (60,000) | (54,000) | (81,000) | (27,000) |
| Contribution | 40,000 | 36,000 | 27,000 | (9,000) |
| Fixed costs | (30,000) | (30,000) | (26,000) | + 4,000 |
| Profit for month | 10,000 | 6,000 | 1,000 | (5,000) |
| Profit variance | **(€4,000) A** | | | |
| Profit variance | | **(€5,000) A** | | |

The above table indicates two main categories of variances. First is the adverse profit variance between the static and flexed budgets (€10,000 − €6,000 = Adverse €4,000). This is attributable to one factor only – the level of sales was less than anticipated. Consequently, this is referred to in management accounting as the sales volume variance.

The second category of variances represents the difference between the flexed budget profit (€6,000) and the actual outturn (€1,000) – an adverse profit variance of €5,000. This overall profit variance is due to operational factors of which three can be usually identified. First is the variance arising from the actual selling price per gallon (€6) being higher than budget (€5) and this is identified above as €18,000 favourable. This variance is referred to as the sales price variance. The second element of operational variances is attributable to variable costs. In the above case, total adverse variable cost variances amounted to (€27,000). Finally, fixed costs variances amount to €4,000 F, indicating that expenditure on fixed costs was less than anticipated. Using the above variances, the difference between the static budget profit (€10,000) and the actual profit (€1,000) can be reconciled and presented in a simple report as follows:

**Profit Reconciliation: Static Budget and Actual Profit ....**

|  | € |  |
|---|---|---|
| Profit as per static budget | 10,000 |  |
| Less: Sales volume variance | (4,000) A | (10%) A |
| = Profit as per flexed budget | 6,000 |  |
| Add: sales price variance | 18,000 F | 20% F |
| Less: Variable cost variances (fuel) | (27,000) A | (50%) A |
| Add: Fixed cost variances | 4,000 F | 13% F |
| = Actual profit for period | 1,000 |  |

Thus, for the month under review, the decline in sales volume reduced overall profits by €4,000 (2,000 gallons × €2 contribution per gallon). This is equivalent to 10% of the original contribution. Alternatively, the reduction in volume (2,000 gallons) is equivalent to 10% of the budgeted volume (20,000 gallons). In contrast, the increase in average sales price by €1 per unit generated additional profits of €18,000 (€1 × 18,000 gallons). Alternatively stated, the increase of €1 in average selling price is equivalent to an increase of 20% on the budgeted selling price. However, the most significant item was the change in fuel costs which were €27,000 more than anticipated. This represents a cost over-run of

50% – calculated with reference to the flexed budget. Finally, this additional cost of fuel was partially offset by less than anticipated fixed costs – a favourable €4,000 variance, equivalent to a cost saving of about 13% on the original budget figure. We shall see in the next chapter how a standard costing system allows us to further analyse these cost variances.

In summary, flexed budgets enable a more meaningful evaluation of current performance to be made and should be used as the basis for all variance analysis. It is based on the simple concept that, to evaluate current performance against budget, one should compare like with like and this assumes an ability to identify fixed and variable costs and other input/output relationships.

### Alternative Calculation of Sales Variances

We shall now explain how the two sales revenue variances (sales volume and sales price variances) can, alternatively, be calculated by way of formula. (**Chapter 15** explains how flexible budgeting is the basis for evaluating current performance when a company operates a standard costing system and it is useful to be able to compute sales revenue variances quickly and without reference to flexed budget calculations.)

### ILLUSTRATION: ALTERNATIVE CALCULATION OF SALES VARIANCES

We shall start with the previous flexed budget report. The static budget (20,000 units) has been flexed by using actual output (18,000 units) and is reproduced below:

#### Flexed Budget Report for Month of......

|  | Static budget | Flexed budget | Actual | Variance |
|---|---|---|---|---|
| Unit sales | 20,000 | 18,000 | 18,000 |  |
|  | € | € | € | € |
| Sales revenue | 100,000 | 90,000 | 108,000 | 18,000 F |
| Fuel costs | (60,000) | (54,000) | (81,000) |  |
| Fixed costs | (30,000) | (30,000) | (26,000) |  |
| Net profit | 10,000 | 6,000 | 1,000 |  |
| Sales volume variance | (€4,000) A |  |  |  |

The two variances that are relevant to this discussion are the sales volume and sales price variances. The sales volume variance is €4,000 adverse – reflecting a lower sales volume than anticipated. The sales price variance is €18,000 favourable, highlighting a higher average sales price than anticipated. Both of these variances can be calculated using the following formula:

### Calculating sales variance using formulae

| | |
|---|---|
| Sales volume variance: (Actual sales quantity – budget sales quantity) × budget unit contribution | $(18,000 - 20,000) \times €2 = €4,000$ A |
| Sales price variance: (Actual average selling price – budget selling price) × Actual quantity sold | $(€6 - €5) \times 18,000 = €18,000$ F |

Our calculations confirm the adverse variance of €4,000 relating to *sales volume*. Common sense dictates that (under variable or direct costing) this variance represents the difference in sales volume, multiplied by the budgeted unit contribution. Since 2,000 fewer gallons were sold, the anticipated profit impact was adverse in the amount of €4,000. Likewise, the sales price variance indicates the profit impact resulting from the increase in average selling price from €5 to €6 per unit, multiplied by the number of units sold – a favourable variance of €18,000.

## ILLUSTRATION: SALES VARIANCES

Antrim Limited is a retail company, selling products J and E, and the following represents the budget for the year 20x1:

| | Budget units | Budget sales price € | Budget variable cost € |
|---|---|---|---|
| Product J | 5,000 | 32 | 24 |
| Product E | 10,000 | 24 | 20 |

During 20x1, the following represented the actual sales performance:

| | Actual sales units | Actual sales price € | Actual variable cost € |
|---|---|---|---|
| Product J | 6,000 | 31 | 24 |
| Product E | 9,000 | 25 | 20 |

**Requirement:** Calculate appropriate sales revenue variances. (It should be noted that in this example, in order to reduce complexity, there are no cost variances.)

**Solution and Analysis:** In order to concentrate only on the sales revenue variances, the above actual cost figures are exactly in line with budget. Also, fixed costs are ignored as they are assumed to be insignificant. The first working is to prepare static and flexed budgets and report overall actual performance, for each product individually, as follows:

|  | Static budget | Flexed budget | Actual | Variance |
|---|---|---|---|---|
| **Product J** |  |  |  |  |
| Sales units | **5,000** | **6,000** | **6,000** |  |
|  | € | € | € | € |
| Total sales revenue | 160,000 | 192,000 | 186,000 | (6,000) A |
| Total variable costs | (120,000) | (144,000) | (144,000) | Nil |
| Total profit | 40,000 | 48,000 | 42,000 | (6,000) |
| **Product E** |  |  |  |  |
| Sales units | **10,000** | **9,000** | **9,000** |  |
|  | € | € | € |  |
| Total sales revenue | 240,000 | 216,000 | 225,000 | 9,000 F |
| Total variable costs | (200,000) | (180,000) | (180,000) | Nil |
| Total profit | 40,000 | 36,000 | 45,000 | 9,000 F |
| Overall volume variance | **€4,000 F** |  |  |  |
| Overall price variance |  | **€3,000 F** |  |  |

The sales volume variance can be calculated for each product and summarised as follows and the respective product contributions should be noted:

### Sales volume variance

|  |  | € |
|---|---|---|
| Product J | (6,000 − 5000) × €8 | 8,000 F |
| Product E | (9,000 − 10,000) × €4 | (4,000) A |
|  |  | 4,000 F |

The above analysis indicates that, although the total number of units sold (15,000) was the same as budgeted, the company sold more of the more profitable product (J had a budgeted unit contribution of €8) and less of the less profitable product (E had a budgeted unit contribution of €4). Therefore, there is an overall, favourable profit variance due to the changed mix of products sold.

In addition, there is an overall sales price variance caused by selling at a price higher (lower) than budget, with respect to the number of units sold. The sales price variance for each product can be calculated and summarised as follows:

### Sales price variances

|  |  | € |
|---|---|---|
| Product J | (€31 − €32) × 6,000 units | (6,000) A |
| Product E | (€25 − €24) × 9,000 units | 9,000 F |
|  |  | 3,000 F |

The analysis of the sales price variance above indicates that there was a €1 per unit price reduction in product J, reducing overall profits by €6,000. In contrast, there was a €1 increase in product E, proving an overall increase of €9,000 to overall profits. Thus, the overall price variance (for both products) amounted to €3,000 favourable. A summarised financial report can be presented as follows:

### Profit Reconciliation for Year 20×1

|  | € |
|---|---|
| Static budget profit (€40,000 + €40,000) | 80,000 |
| Add: Sales volume variances | 4,000 F |
| = Flexed budget profit | 84,000 |
| Add: Sales price variances | 3,000 F |
| = Actual profit | 87,000 |

Based on these variances, management may want to find why there were price changes and also why sales targets were exceeded for Product J but were not achieved for Product E. It is plausible that the price reduction for Product J was associated with an increase in demand for that product. In contrast, the price increase in Product E may be associated with the reduction in sales volume. The purpose of the analysis is to identify causes that need to be corrected or adjusted in planning for future periods.

## 14.9  Market Share and Market Size Variances

The variance information relating to sales we described in the previous section do not necessarily indicate how a firm is performing relative to its competitors. For example, changes in sales volume may simply reflect changes in the market size due to changes in general economic conditions. Thus, the market size variance does not tell us much about the marketing manager's performance because it is largely determined by factors outside the manager's control. In contrast, market share represents the firm's proportion of the total business in a particular market and an increase, for example, does reflect on the firm's overall marketing effectiveness. A firm's market share can be calculated as follows:

$$\text{Market Share} = \text{Firm's Sales/Total Market Sales}$$

It should be noted that the figures for 'sales' may be determined on a value basis (sales price multiplied by volume) or on a unit basis (number of units shipped or number of customers served). While the firm's own sales figures are readily available, total market sales are more difficult to determine. Usually, this information is available from trade associations and market research firms.

Many companies place much greater emphasis on market share rather than market size variances. This is because they believe that the market share variance reflects the competitive performance of the company and is a good indicator of future sales growth. Accordingly, companies will usually include market share aspirations in their budget targets. Before we look at some of the detailed calculations, it is worthwhile to note **some of the advantages associated with increased market share:**

- **Increased overall profitability** – higher volume can be instrumental in developing a cost advantage due to economies of scale, especially since a large player has strong bargaining power in negotiations with suppliers and distribution channels.
- **Future sales growth** – increased market share is usually a good indicator of future sales growth.
- **Reputation** – market leaders have 'clout' or bargaining power that they can use to their advantage.
- Market share is the responsibility of the marketing manager, whereas market size can depend on economic factors outside his direct control.

However, an **increase in market share is not always desirable.** For example:

- If the firm is near its production capacity, an increase in market share might necessitate investment in additional capacity. If this capacity is underutilised, higher unit costs will result.
- Overall profits may decline if market share is gained by decreasing prices and a price war might be provoked if competitors attempt to regain their share by lowering prices.

- A small niche player may be tolerated if it captures only a small share of the market. If that share increases, a larger, more dominant competitor may decide to take remedial action.
- Monopoly or anti-competition issues may arise if a firm dominates its market.

In the previous section we calculated both the sales price and sales volume variance. In this section we illustrate how to subdivide the sales **volume** variance into a market size and a market share variance. The market size indicates the profit impact on a company (using budgeted contribution figures) of a changed market size. The market share variance indicates the profit impact on a company (using budgeted contribution figures) of a changed market share obtained by the company. The calculations are as follows:

### Market Size and Market Share Variances

Market size variance:
  (Actual market size – budget market size) × *budget* market share × budget unit contribution

Market share variance:
  (Actual market share – budget market share) × *actual* market size × budget unit contribution

## ILLUSTRATION: MARKET SIZE AND MARKET SHARE VARIANCES

You are provided with the summarised information relating to Athy Company for a recent accounting period:

|  | Budget | Actual |
|---|---|---|
| Sales (units) | 100,000 | 90,000 |
| Selling price (per unit) | €20 | €24 |
| Variable cost (per unit) | €10 | €10 |
| Fixed cost (total) | €300,000 | €300,000 |

The Athy Company operates exclusively in the Republic of Ireland market and the national market was estimated at 1 million units at the time of setting the budget and Athy estimated that it would obtain a 10% share of this market. However, at the end of the year reliable industry figures indicated that the Irish market for the above period expanded to 1,200,000 units. (To focus our attention on the sales revenue variances, we have eliminated any cost variances.)

**Requirement:** You are required to calculate the normal sales volume and sales price variances, from the above data, and separate the sales volume variance into its market size and market share variances, using the above information. Briefly discuss the meaning and implications of these variances.

**Solution and Analysis:** In order to calculate the normal sales revenue variances (volume and price) it is useful, but not necessary to prepare a flexed budget report as follows, so as to put the figures into context:

### Flexed Budget Report for Year

|  | Static budget | Flexed budget | Actual | Variance |
|---|---|---|---|---|
| Sales (units) | 100,000 | 90,000 | 90,000 | |
| Sales revenue | €2,000,000 | €1,800,000 | €2,160,000 | 360,000 F |
| Var. costs | (1,000,000) | (900,000) | (900,000) | Nil |
| Contribution | 1,000,000 | 900,000 | 1,260,000 | |
| Fixed costs | (300,000) | (300,000) | (300,000) | Nil |
| Profit | 700,000 | 600,000 | 960,000 | 360,000 F |
| Sales volume var. | | **(€100,000) A** | | |

Alternatively, the usual sales variances can be calculated as follows:

| | |
|---|---|
| Sales volume variance: (Actual sales quantity – budget sales quantity) × Budget unit contribution | (90,000 − 100,000) × €10 = (€100,000) A |
| Sales price variance: (Actual average selling price – budget selling price) × Actual quantity sold | (€24 − €20) × 90,000 = €360,000 F |

The profit reconciliation statement can be presented as follows:

### Profit Reconciliation Statement for Year

| | € |
|---|---|
| Static profit (above) | 700,000 |
| Sales volume variance: | |
| (90,000 − 100,000) × €10 contribution per unit | (100,000) A |
| = Profit per flexed budget | 600,000 |
| Sales price variance: | |
| (€24 − €20) × 90,000 | 360,000 F |
| Actual profit for year | 960,000 |

The overall sales volume variance (€100,000 A) can, in turn, be subdivided into a market size and a market share variance. The market size indicates the profit impact (using budgeted contribution figures) of a changed market size. The market share variance indicates the profit impact (using budgeted contribution figures) of a changed market share obtained by the company. The calculations are as follows:

| | |
|---|---|
| Budgeted unit contribution (€1,000,000/100,000) | €10 per unit |
| Budgeted market share % (100,000/1,000,000) | 10% (given) |
| Actual market share % (90,000/1,200,000) | 7.5% |
| Market size variance: | |
| (1,200,000 − 1,000,000) × 10% × €10 | €200,000 F |
| Market share variance: | |
| (7.5% − 10%) × 1,200,000 × €10 | (€300,000) A |
| | (€100,000) A |

The market size variance is favourable because the overall market increased in size, from 1 million units to 1.2 million units. Of greater significance is the adverse market share variance (€300,000) caused by the firm's market share decreasing from a budget figure of 10% to an actual market share of 7.5%. Such an adverse performance has implications for future sales growth and future unit cost calculations.

## Conclusion

In summary, this chapter was devoted mainly to **control by comparison.** Within the discipline of managerial accounting, this process involves setting financial targets (or financial objectives) that reflect a desired state or condition. These financial targets then become the reference point for the evaluation of actual performance. However, it is important to compare 'like with like' and this introduced us to the practice of flexible budgeting.

Many people consider budgeting to be a purely technical issue. However, there is an important behavioural dimension that should not be overlooked. Added to this is the relatively recent debate that traditional budgeting practices within companies need to be critically examined to see whether they can be improved upon. In the next chapter we shall discuss another aspect of control by comparison – standard costing.

## Summary of Learning Objectives

**Learning Objective 1:** Discuss the advantages of budget preparation in the context of planning and control.

A budget represents a projected statement, prepared in financial or non-financial terms for a specified period of time and which represents targets which managers and employees are expected to attain. The advantages of preparing budgets include providing an enhanced managerial perspective regarding the future, improving internal coordination and communication, helping to motivate responsible individuals and providing a framework to evaluate actual performance.

**Learning Objective 2:** Prepare operating budgets.

Operating budgets are prepared for various operating activities. For a manufacturing firm, operating budgets would include budgets for sales, production, materials purchasing, labour and other costs. Operating budgets relate to activities under the control of a responsible manager. The preparation of various operating budgets was presented in the exhibits and illustrations in this chapter. The figures contained in these operating budgets will be used in preparing the master budget of the business entity.

**Learning Objective 3:** Prepare master budgets.

Master budgets typically contain a projected income statement, a cash flow forecast together with a balance sheet for the end of the accounting period. A master budget is a summary document and highlights the important financial targets for the business entity. The preparation of master budgets was illustrated in the exhibits and illustrations in this chapter. The preparation of master budgets (and operating budgets on which they are based) is facilitated by the use of computer spreadsheets.

**Learning Objective 4:** Describe the use of spreadsheets in budgeting.

This chapter described a computer spreadsheet as the electronic equivalent to a pencil, an eraser and a large blank piece of paper ruled with horizontal lines to give rows and vertical lines to provide columns. This electronic spreadsheet facilitates automatic and immediate recalculation which is necessary whenever any of the budget variables are revised in any way. This includes a situation where the decision-maker may want to highlight the sensitivity of a proposed solution to changes in any of the underlying assumptions.

**Learning Objective 5:** Outline the weaknesses of traditional budgeting practices and suggest improvements.

For well over half a century, traditional practices have been criticised by many authors. A few criticisms can be highlighted. Many commentators point out that traditional budgeting practices are associated with incrementalism whereby small annual changes are made to last year's figures. In this way the annual budget reflects a continuation of normal operations from year to year and this approach rarely encourages innovative thinking. In addition, the annual budget can be prepared without regard to company strategy and important non-financial metrics are often overlooked. Others argue that, since the business environment is changing so rapidly, realistic budgets cannot be prepared for the future. Finally, budgets can promote various types of dysfunctional behaviour in budget participants.

**Learning Objective 6:** Distinguish between a static and flexed budget.

A static budget is the budget prepared at the start of the year, given a set of assumptions regarding, for example, sales volume. The static budget is prepared for planning, coordination and motivation purposes. Alternatively, the flexed budget is finalised, typically, at the end of the period and is based on the actual volume of activity, e.g. units sold. In this way, one should compare the flexed budget with actual performance and this comparison should reveal important operating variances. The comparison between static and flexed budget will reveal the profit variance arising from selling either more or less units than anticipated and which is described as the sales volume variance.

**Learning Objective 7:** Explain why flexed budgets are needed in performance evaluation.

Flexed budgets are required in order to compare like with like, i.e. compare actual performance with flexed budget which coincides with actual output for the period. In this way important operating variances can be identified. Otherwise, one would confuse variances due to changed volume with variances due to operational circumstances. Three important variances can be identified when comparing flexed budget with actual performance namely, sales price variance, total variable cost variances and total fixed cost variances.

**Learning Objective 8:** Calculate the financial impact of both sales volume and sales price variances.

The sales volume variance is calculated with reference to higher/lower sales volume multiplied by the budgeted unit contribution. This highlights the change in profits associated with achieving higher/lower sales volume relative to the static budget. The sales price variance is calculated with reference to the change in average actual selling price compared to budget, multiplied by the actual quantity sold. This calculation isolates the change in profits associated with a higher/lower (average) sales price. In some firms, there is an accepted trade-off between a favourable sales volume variance and an adverse sales price variance. The sales price and sales volume variances can be calculated for manufacturing, retail and service firms.

**Learning Objective 9:** Calculate both market share and market size variances.

The sales volume variance can be described as a physical variance in that it identifies the profit impact of a higher/lower sales volume than anticipated in the static budget. In turn, the sales volume variance can be divided into the market size and market share variance. The market size variance isolates the financial impact on a firm's overall profitability associated with the overall size of the market increasing or decreasing. The market share variance isolates the financial impact on a firm's overall profitability associated with the firm's market share increasing or decreasing during the accounting period. It is important to monitor both the market size and market share variances because a positive sales volume variance could be achieved as a result of an expanding market size but in which the firm's market share is declining.

## Questions

### Review Questions

(See Appendix One for Solutions to Review Questions **14.1** and **14.2**)

*Question 14.1 (Basic Cash Budgeting)*

Clock Limited is preparing its budgets for the next quarter. The company's management accountant has collated the following information to assist with the preparation of these budgets. The company sells 10% of its goods for cash. The remainder of customers receive one month's credit. The projected sales revenue for the four months ending 31 December 20x1 are estimated as follows:

| September | €12,500 |
| October   | €13,600 |
| November  | €17,000 |
| December  | €16,800 |

Payments to creditors are made in the month following purchase. Direct material purchases for the four months ending 31 December 20x1 are estimated as follows:

| September | €3,450 |
| October   | €3,780 |
| November  | €2,890 |
| December  | €3,150 |

Wages are paid as they are incurred, and are budgeted at €1,300 per month. Production overheads are estimated to be €3,200 per month, while selling, distribution and administration overheads amount to €1,890 per month. Included in the amounts for overhead given above are depreciation charges of €300 and €190 respectively. Clock Limited takes one month's credit on all overheads.

In addition, Clock Limited intends to purchase a delivery vehicle in November 20x1 for a cash payment of €9,870. The forecast cash balance at the end of September 20x1 is €1,235.

## Requirements:

1. Prepare a cash budget for each of the months October to December 20x1.
2. Explain, using your answer to (1) above, how a spreadsheet may be used to assist in the preparation of cash forecasts.
3. Explain how a cash forecast is an example of both feed-forward and feedback control mechanisms.

### Question 14.2 (Preparation of a Master Budget in a Service Firm)

Olga Carr has just graduated with an MBA degree from CIIM. Prior to this study she had graduated from Moscow University as a qualified fitness instructor. Within two weeks of receiving her (accredited) MBA degree she received a most interesting job offer – to become the manager of her own gym in Nicosia, Cyprus! The owner of the gym, a friend of one of her fellow MBA students, had enquired whether she was interested in taking it over.

Olga quickly made some tentative enquiries. The location was excellent since it was close to the city centre and business district of Nicosia and had ample car parking facilities. Also, her target market appeared to be expanding as Cypriots were becoming more health conscious. Indeed, a recent report on the health and lifestyle of Cypriots highlighted the need for them to take more regular exercise and such publicity would certainly boost membership enquiries. Her father agreed to provide €30,000 capital to the business. In addition, Olga agreed to borrow €15,000 from her local bank.

The following financial information was provided to Olga on a confidential basis and, due to time restrictions, she had not been able to assess its credibility. You may assume that all transactions are undertaken by cash/bank unless otherwise stated or where this assumption would be inappropriate. However, you note that there is no provision made for Olga's salary as manager.

| | € |
|---|---|
| 1. Share capital invested in business | 30,000 |
| 2. Long-term loan received (three years) – see Note 1 | 15,000 |
| 3. Cost of gym and assessment equipment (Useful life three years) | 30,000 |
| 4. Cost of office equipment and software (Useful life five years) | 10,000 |

| | |
|---|---|
| 5. Annual repayment of loan (including interest, see Note 1) rounded | 6,000 |
| 6. Rent (to owner) on premises (per annum) | 10,000 |
| 7. Electricity and water (per annum) | 4,000 |
| 8. General cleaning including towels etc. (per annum) | 3,000 |
| 9. Advertising (per annum) | 5,000 |
| 10. Labour costs of instructors and administration (per annum) | 6,000 |
| 11. Membership income (cash): 300 members at €250 per annum | 75,000 |
| 12. Depreciation of gym equipment | ?? |
| 13. Depreciation of office equipment | ?? |

**Note 1**: The loan is for a period of three years and carries a 10% rate of interest. The loan including interest is to be paid at the end of each of the three years, in equal instalments of €6,000 each.

The initial task for Olga for next year is to do some budgeting for the first year of operations. The number of members cannot be known in advance but it is assumed to be 300 members. Moreover, given similar facilities in Nicosia, annual membership will be €250 per annum (assume members are admitted on the first day of opening). In accordance with fire and safety regulations, general comfort levels and facilities offered by other gyms in the area, it would not be possible to enrol more than 500 members in the first year. Olga is both excited and frightened by the imminent decision before her. She invites you to coffee and, after initial pleasantries are exchanged, she asks for your advice.

**Requirements:** Based on the information provided, you are required to prepare the following budgets for the first year of operations:

1. Budgeted income statement
2. Budgeted statement of cash flows for the first year of operations
3. Budgeted balance sheet at the end of the first year of operations.

Present value of a €1 annuity received each year for N years at X% p.a.

| | 4% | 6% | 8% | 10% | 12% | 14% |
|---|---|---|---|---|---|---|
| 1 | .962 | .943 | .926 | .909 | .893 | .877 |
| 2 | 1.886 | 1.833 | 1.783 | 1.736 | 1.690 | 1.647 |
| 3 | 2.775 | 2.673 | 2.577 | 2.487 | 2.402 | 2.322 |
| 4 | 3.630 | 3.465 | 3.312 | 3.170 | 3.037 | 2.914 |
| 5 | 4.452 | 4.212 | 3.993 | 3.791 | 3.605 | 3.433 |
| 6 | 5.242 | 4.917 | 4.623 | 4.355 | 4.111 | 3.889 |
| 7 | 6.002 | 5.582 | 5.206 | 4.868 | 4.564 | 4.288 |

## Intermediate Questions

### Question 14.3 (Preparation of a Master Budget for a Manufacturer)

Manacco Company is a company that is to be formed with an issued share capital of €105,000. This share capital will be issued in January – the first month of the new accounting period. Also, in January, the company will purchase (and pay for) fixed assets costing €100,000. The company expects a period of rapid growth and the estimated sales in units are as follows:

|          | Units  |
|----------|--------|
| January  | 4,000  |
| February | 6,500  |
| March    | 8,500  |
| April    | 11,000 |
| May      | 14,000 |

The sales price per unit is €30. Twenty per cent of sales will be paid for in cash and the remainder will be received in the month following sale. There were no debtors (accounts receivable) on 1 January.

The stock of finished goods and raw materials at 1 January was Nil and the company has now decided to institute a stocking policy of having in hand 80% of next month's sales of finished goods and 100% of next month's raw materials required for production. The production process is very rapid and there is no 'work-in-progress', i.e. units are started and completed in the same day. Production of one unit requires 2 kilos of material at €3.50 per kilo and 2.5 hours of labour at €5 per hour. Material is purchased one month before it is required for production and is paid for immediately (in cash). Direct production labour is paid for in the month in which it is used. In addition, variable production costs amount to €1 per unit and this will be paid as incurred. There are no fixed production overheads but administration costs amount to €10,000 per month.

For the purposes of the requirements below, you can assume that the Company has agreed generous bank overdraft facilities to cover any cash shortfall as might arise.

**Requirements:**

1.  Prepare the following monthly budgets (January – March)
    (a)  Sales and cash collections
    (b)  Production
    (c)  Material purchases and payments
    (d)  Labour
    (e)  Variable production overhead
    (f)  Cash Budget for each of the three months of January, February and March
    (g)  Budgeted Income statement for the quarter (January to March)
    (h)  Balance Sheet at end of March
2.  Comment briefly on the budgeted financial performance and position.

*Question 14.4 (Preparation of a Master Budget for a Retailer (with VAT))*

The SW Company was formed a number of years ago by two college friends to distribute central heating oil to domestic customers in a provincial town in Ireland. The business is relatively easy to administer and organise. In brief, central heating oil is purchased from an importer based in Dublin and is stored in large tanks. In turn, the oil is sold and distributed to domestic customers. The business is administered from a small rented office.

Forward planning has never been a strong characteristic of the SW Company, and the previous 18 months have seen a succession of problems, especially regarding cash management, which might well have been avoided. In particular, the recent liquidity problem has prompted the management of the company to consider introducing a system of budgetary control.

Derek Young has been appointed as consultant to provide expert assistance. His initial brief is specific: 'To provide financial budgets for the next financial year'. He began by examining carefully the latest balance sheet (**Exhibit 1**).

EXHIBIT 1: BALANCE SHEET AT 31 DECEMBER 20X0

|  | € | € |
|---|---|---|
| Fixed Assets (net) |  | 100,000 |
| Current Assets |  |  |
| Stocks (200,000 litres) | 100,000 |  |
| Debtors (Q4 20x0) | 350,000 |  |
| Bank | 1,000 |  |
|  |  | 451,000 |
|  |  | 551,000 |
| **Financed by** |  |  |
| Ordinary Share Capital |  | 200,000 |
| Retained earnings |  | 161,000 |
|  |  | 361,000 |
| Current liabilities |  |  |
| Trade creditors | 100,000 |  |
| Corporation tax payable | 70,000 |  |
| VAT payable | 20,000 | 190,000 |
|  |  | 551,000 |

Then with the help of the management team estimates were compiled, discussed, amended and refined. A summary of the final data is presented below.

1. Sales and stock are budgeted as:

|  | Sales litres | Closing stock (litres) |
|---|---|---|
| Quarter 1 | 250,000 | 200,000 |
| Quarter 2 | 320,000 | 300,000 |
| Quarter 3 | 450,000 | 400,000 |
| Quarter 4 | 530,000 | 300,000 |

2. The average selling price per litre is €1 (excluding VAT) to which is added VAT at 20%. Customers, on average, take one quarter's credit to pay their account.
3. The average purchase cost is €0.50 (excluding VAT) per litre, in addition to VAT at 20%. On average, purchases of oil are paid for in the quarter following purchase.
4. Depreciation is calculated on fixed assets at the rate of 20% based on the book value at the end of the financial year. New fixed assets will be purchased (for cash) at the start of Quarter 1, in the amount of €30,000.
5. The following items of expenditure will be paid for during each quarter.

|  | Q1 | Q2 | Q3 | Q4 |
|---|---|---|---|---|
| General expenses | €15,000 | €17,000 | €21,000 | €23,000 |
| Distribution costs | €15,000 | €18,000 | €19,000 | €22,000 |

6. The arrears of corporation tax payable at the start of the year will be paid during the first quarter. Corporation tax liability for 20x1 is estimated at €200,000. VAT is payable quarterly in arrears. (VAT applies only to purchases and sales of oil.)

**Requirements:**

1. You are required to prepare for each quarter of 20x1:
   (a) a sales budget (showing vat-exclusive and vat-inclusive amounts)
   (b) a purchases budget (showing vat-exclusive and vat-inclusive amounts)
   (c) a cash budget
   (d) a budgeted income statement for the year ended 31 December 20x1
   (e) a budgeted balance sheet as at 31 December 20x1.

*Question 14.5 (Budgeting and Impact of Different Financing Options)*

You have just been employed as Assistant Financial Controller in YUKI plc. The capital structure of the company is set out below.

|  | € millions |
|---|---|
| Equity shares of €100 each | 20 |
| Retained earnings | 10 |
| 9% Preference shares of €100 each | 12 |
| 7% Debentures | _8_ |
| Total capital employed | _50_ |

The company earns a pre-tax return (using PBIT) on capital employed of 12%. Corporation tax is 25%.

The company requires a sum of €2,500,000 to finance an expansion programme which is also expected to generate a pre-tax return on investment of 12%.

The following three funding alternatives are available to the company:

Issue of 20,000 equity shares at a premium of €25 per share
Issue of 10% preference shares at par
Issue of 8% debentures

It is estimated that the following Price Earnings ratios will apply in respect of each of the financing options:

| Equity | 17 times |
|---|---|
| Preference | 16 times |
| Debentures | 15 times |

**Requirements:**

1. Calculate the expected earnings per share and market price per share under each of the three alternatives.
2. Write a memorandum to the Financial Controller explaining the impact of each funding alternative on this company's share price, gearing and level of financial risk.

Source: Chartered Accountants Ireland, Management Accounting and Business Finance, P3, 2007
(adapted)

## Question 14.6 (Budgeting and Working Capital Management)

Dippa Publishing is a children's book publisher and has asked your bank to lend €250,000 for working capital finance. You are provided with the following financial summaries:

**Dippa Publishing Limited**
**Balance Sheet at 31 December 20x7**

|  | € |
|---|---|
| Non-current assets (fixed assets) (net) | _925,000_ |
| Current assets |  |
| Inventory (stock) | 510,000 |

| | |
|---|---:|
| Accounts receivable | 375,000 |
| Cash on hands | 50,000 |
| | 935,000 |
| Total assets | 1,860,000 |
| **Financed by:** | |
| Shareholders' funds | 1,082,000 |
| Long-term debt | 475,000 |
| Current liabilities: | |
| Accounts payable and accrued expenses | 203,000 |
| Short-term loans | 75,000 |
| Current portion of long-term lease | 25,000 |
| | 303,000 |
| Total liabilities and shareholders' funds | 1,860,000 |

### Income statement for year ended 31 December 20x7

| | € |
|---|---:|
| Sales | 4,622,800 |
| Cost of sales | (3,504,100) |
| Gross profit | 1,118,700 |
| Total operating expenses | (893,000) |
| Profit before interest and tax | 225,700 |

**Requirements:**

1. Discuss the implications of adopting a conservative approach, as opposed to an aggressive approach, to working capital management. (Working capital may be defined here as consisting of inventory, trade debtors and trade creditors.)
2. Assuming a 365-day year, calculate the company's cash operating cycle (or cash conversion cycle).
3. What general concerns might you have regarding this loan request?

Source: Chartered Accountants Ireland, Management Accounting and Business Finance, PE3, 2007
(adapted)

## Question 14.7 (Preparation of a Master Budget for a Retailer (with VAT))

James Wang realised two things about himself – he was good at selling things to other people, but he was bad at accounting and financial matters. James had recently fulfilled his life's ambition of opening his own retail shop. Initially, he would focus on the sale of Chinese wines for the domestic market in Shanghai.

In a global context, China is not well know for its wine or wine consumption. Figures suggest that the amount of wine per capita consumed by Chinese people in the country stood at 0.3 litres in 2004, only 6% of the global average. However, the consumption is much higher in the more affluent coastal cities and the figures indicate the great potential of the wine market in China. (Comparative figures for Italy and France, for example, are about 50 litres per head – significantly down from about 90 litres per head in the 1980s.) In countries such as Ireland and the UK, sales of wine have soared and a number of different factors explain this. First of all, more people are affluent and have more time and money to spend on luxuries such as wine. Secondly, there is a trend for people to drink more at home before going out, while many other simply prefer to have friends over and this has increased the 'drinking at home culture'. Women are also driving the increased consumption of wine and it is interesting to note that, in the UK, women make 70% of wine purchases in supermarkets.

It is estimated that the Chinese wine market will grow by about 15%–20% per annum for the next few years. The main reasons for this rapid growth of wine consumption is due to the increased number of people with high incomes, the introduction of some Western lifestyle choices, greater knowledge about wine as a drink and the recent reduction of some import tariffs on imported wines. (The reduction in import tariffs from about 40% to about 15% may encourage foreign players to enter the market but they will only be successful if they have efficient distribution networks.) Currently, the Chinese alcohol market is dominated by four products – beer (85%), spirits (9%), yellow wine (5%) and wine (1%). Market analysts believe that beer has already developed to a mature stage, traditional spirit consumption has declined of late, and yellow wine is popular only in certain regions.

The Chinese (domestic) wine market is dominated by four brands – Changyu, Great Wall, Dynasty and Tonghua – and they control about 60% of the market. James has agreed to sell various brands for these producers and he is confident that his business model – good quality wines at affordable prices – will be successful.

James began by preparing some financial estimates for his first year of trading and has provided you with the following information and seeks your assistance. His business is subject to VAT at the rate of 10% on purchases and sales of wine. These estimates have been provided by an external consultant and can be considered reliable. You should also assume that temporary bank overdraft facilities are available during the year, if required.

1. He would invest €30,000 by way of share capital in the business.
2. He would borrow €26,000 from a bank for a seven-year period. This loan would be repaid in equal instalments (with interest) at the end of each year. The implicit rate of interest of this loan was 8%, but he does not know how much the annual repayment will be.
3. Various other financial information is provided as follows:

|  | € |
|---|---:|
| Cost of equipment (Useful life three years) – paid immediately | 30,000 |
| Total sales of which 90% will be received in cash and 10% will be receivable at the end of the year. All sales are inclusive of VAT at 10%. | 330,000 |
| Wine purchases of which 80% will be paid during the year and 20% payable at the end of the year. Purchases are inclusive of VAT at 10%. | 165,000 |
| Rent paid for premises (two years paid in total i.e. €30,000 per annum) | 60,000 |
| Advertising costs | 10,000 |
| Wages and salaries | 50,000 |
| Miscellaneous costs | 10,000 |
| Payment of VAT on account during first year | 5,000 |
| Depreciation of equipment (straight line with nil residual value) | ?? |
| Repayment of loan including interest (see 2 above) | ?? |

The initial task for James was to do some budgeting for the first year of operations. He invites you to coffee and quickly asks for your advice.

**Requirements:**

1. You are required to record the above financial information using the attached template, and you may assume that temporary bank overdraft facilities are available. You should adjust your figures for closing stock of wine amounting to €20,000 (excluding VAT).
2. Having recorded the transactions, you are required to prepare the following budgets for the first year of operations:
   (a)  A budgeted income statement and calculate the BEP (in sales revenue)
   (b)  A cash budget for the first year of operations, clearly showing the cash surplus or cash deficit at the end of the year, and
   (c)  A budgeted balance sheet at the end of the first year of operations.

Present value of an annuity received each year for N years
at X% p.a. (with rounding)

|  | 4% | 6% | 8% | 10% | 12% | 14% |
|---|---|---|---|---|---|---|
| 1 | .962 | .943 | .926 | .909 | .893 | .877 |
| 2 | 1.886 | 1.833 | 1.783 | 1.736 | 1.690 | 1.647 |
| 3 | 2.775 | 2.673 | 2.577 | 2.487 | 2.400 | 2.322 |

|   | 4% | 6% | 8% | 10% | 12% | 14% |
|---|-----|-----|-----|------|------|------|
| 4 | 3.630 | 3.465 | 3.312 | 3.170 | 3.037 | 2.914 |
| 5 | 4.452 | 4.212 | 3.993 | 3.791 | 3.605 | 3.433 |
| 6 | 5.242 | 4.917 | 4.623 | 4.355 | 4.111 | 3.889 |
| 7 | 6.002 | 5.582 | 5.200 | 4.868 | 4.564 | 4.288 |

## Advanced Questions

### Question 14.8 (Preparation of a Master Budget for a Manufacturer)

Somerton Ltd is a manufacturer of wooden children's toys and these are sold to retail shops, but, for simplicity purposes, these toys are referred to as product Y and Z.

Its balance sheet at 31 December is attached overleaf. On the basis of sales forecasts, it is anticipated that 40,000 units of Y and 12,500 units of Z will be sold (all on credit) in the forthcoming year at selling prices of €10 and €16 respectively.

Management are anxious to introduce a basic management control system into the organisation and the first step in this process is the preparation of budgets for the forthcoming year. The following information is presented to you:

At the end of the year, management require 1,200 units of Y and 800 units of Z to be held in stock. In addition, 7,000 kg of raw material are also to be held.

The production inputs and costs of each product are as follows:

|   | Y | Z |
|---|---|---|
| Raw Materials | 2 kg | 3 kg |
| Cost of Raw Material | €1/kg | €1/kg |
| Direct labour | 3 hours | 2 hours |
| Direct labour rate per hour | €1.50 | €1.50 |
| Other production overheads (variable) | 50c/unit | €1/unit |

The following costs are anticipated during the year:

| Selling expenses | €65,000 |
|---|---|
| Light and Heat | €3,600 |
| Administration | €22,000 |
| Rent and Rates | €25,000 |

During the year €35,000 of new fixed assets will be purchased. In addition, 60,000 new shares will be issued at €1 each. Depreciation is calculated at the rate of 10% on the book-value of fixed assets in existence at end of year.

Strict credit limits will be imposed on customers. It is agreed that the average period of credit allowed to customers will be 45 days (based on a 360-day year) and this figure is to be used in budget calculations. Creditors are anticipated to increase by 20% on the opening balance.

### Somerton Limited – Balance Sheet as at 31 December 20x8

|  | € |
|---|---|
| **Non-current assets** | |
| Cost less aggregate depreciation | 260,000 |
| **Current Assets** | |
| Stocks of finished goods | |
| 500 units of product Y at €7 | 3,500 |
| 500 units of product Z at €7 | 3,500 |
| Raw materials at cost: 5,000kg at €1.00 | 5,000 |
| Debtors (accounts receivable) | 24,000 |
| Cash/Bank | 29,500 |
|  | 65,500 |
| Total assets | 325,500 |
| **FINANCED BY** | |
| Issued share capital of 50c each | 240,000 |
| Retained earnings | 73,500 |
|  | 313,500 |
| Current Liabilities (Creditors) | 12,000 |
| Total liabilities and shareholders' funds | 325,500 |

### Requirements:

1. Prepare a cash budget for the year to 31 December 20x9 (monthly figures are not required).
2. Prepare an income statement for the year ended 31 December 20x9 together with a balance sheet assuming closing stock of finished goods is valued at variable cost of production.

*Question 14.9 (Cash Budgeting)*

Garner Limited (Garner) is a house construction company in the Leinster region. It has a central depot located in Dublin city centre into which inventories are received and from which they are distributed to sites throughout the region. However, local site managers are also empowered to order materials directly from local suppliers to be delivered straight to the individual sites. These are referred to as 'purchases to contract' and they are generally consumed almost immediately after receipt of goods but the relevant invoices are paid by head office.

Due to the downturn in the construction sector, the profit projection for the forthcoming quarter reveals three months of consecutive losses. Thus, the directors of Garner wish to introduce a monthly cash budgeting system and have asked your assistance. You are provided with the following monthly income statements, which serve as the management accounts:

**Income summary for quarter ended 31 December 20x1**

|  | Sept €000s | Oct €000s | Nov €000s | Dec €000s | Jan etc. (1) €000s |
|---|---|---|---|---|---|
| Contracts invoiced (2) | 2,000 | 320 | 600 | 720 | €800 |
| Opening stock and WIP | 2,352 | 1,771 | 2,187 | 2,252 | |
| Materials purchased (HO) | 209 | 201 | 150 | 220 | |
| Purchases to contract | 511 | 400 | 330 | 400 | |
| Wages | 60 | 75 | 60 | 72 | |
| Closing stock and WIP | (1,771) | (2,187) | (2,252) | (2,364) | |
| = Cost of sales | 1,361 | 260 | 475 | 580 | |
| S & Admin for month | 172 | 177 | 142 | 152 | |
| Royalties | 100 | 15 | 30 | 35 | |
| Rent for month | 8 | 8 | 8 | 8 | |
| Depreciation for month | 5 | 5 | 5 | 5 | |
| Total expenses | 1,646 | 465 | 660 | 780 | |
| Profit (loss) before tax | 354 | (145) | (60) | (60) | |

**Notes**

1. The contracts invoiced are for €800,000 for each of January, February and March.

2. Customers are generally required to pay part of the final price in stages, and some of this must be paid in advance. Research into the pattern shows that, of the total sales invoiced, the amounts are paid for in equal instalments as follows:

> 25% on signing of sales agreement, which is three months before final invoicing
> 25% on house inspection, which is one month before final invoicing
> 25% on the day of final invoicing
> 25% on the month after final invoicing.

The contracts invoiced above in the income summary represent the 'final' invoice amounts for each month.

3. To improve the cash collection rate, a commission to Garner employees is being introduced at the rate of 2% (rounded upwards to the nearest €000) on cash receipts from contracts. The scheme will start with October sales and the commission will be paid one month in arrears.

4. Of the total purchases, one-third of the amounts will be paid for in the month of purchase and a 2.5% discount will be received on this payment. The balance will be paid, on average, in the month following delivery but no discounts will accrue when the balance is discharged.

5. Wages, selling and administrative expenses are paid for in the month in which they are incurred.

6. Royalties and rent are both paid quarterly in arrears on 31 March, 30 June, 30 September and 31 December based on the quarter to which they relate.

7. Outlays on capital expenditure are expected as follows: October…€80,000, November…€40,000 and December…€100,000.

8. The opening cash balance on 30 September is €120,000 (in funds).

**Requirements:**

1. Prepare a cash budget for the months of October, November and December, and
2. Comment briefly, by way of a memorandum to the Board of Directors, on the cash position at the end of each of the three months.

> Source: Chartered Accountants Ireland, Management Accounting and Business Finance, Paper 3, Autumn 2007 (adapted)

## Question 14.10 (Sales Revenue Variances and Market Share Variances)

Fenwick Limited is a retailer of plastic garden furniture. It deals in two basic products, i.e. tables and chairs, which are purchased from manufacturers and resold to customers. The budgeted selling price of these independent products is shown below, and they can be sold in any mix required by the customer. Sometimes a customer will buy only a table, i.e. to replace an existing table; other customers will buy a number of chairs and others will buy different mixes of the two products.

| Tables (Selling price) | €100 per unit |
| Chairs (Selling price) | €25 per unit |

Alternatively, customers can buy a furniture 'set', consisting of a table and two chairs, as a special package. If customers choose this option, they will receive a special discount for this combination which is included in the budgeted selling price of €140.

In order to improve the management control system within the firm, management prepared the following sales targets for the most recent financial year, and no opening or closing inventory (stock) was assumed since the accounting year end coincides with the middle of winter when stock of such items are insignificant:

| Tables (Budget sales) | 1,000 individual units |
| Chairs (Budget sales) | 4,000 individual units |
| Sets (Budget sales) | 9,000 sets |

However, the following actual sales were achieved during the corresponding year:

| Tables | 500 units | €50,000 sales revenue |
| Chairs | 5,500 units | €110,000 sales revenue |
| Sets | 8,800 sets | €1,320,000 sales revenue |

The standard variable cost per unit is as follows and, during the current accounting period, this was the same as the actual cost, due to negotiated purchase agreements:

| | Standard units cost (and actual) |
| Tables | €10 each |
| Chairs | €17 each |
| Sets | €44 each |

## Requirements:

1. Write a short note, using practical examples, to clearly illustrate your understanding of the term market share variance.
2. For each of the three products (tables, chairs and sets) calculate both sales price and sales quantity variances and reconcile your calculations with reference to the static and flexed budgets and actual profit reported during the year. You may ignore fixed costs in your calculations.
3. Fenwick's budgeted sales of sets was prepared on the assumption that the company would secure 25% of the available 'sets' market. It transpires that the sales achieved by Fenwick were, in fact, 22% of the actual sets market. Calculate both the market size and market share variances for this product i.e. sets, only.

Source: Chartered Accountants Ireland, P3, Autumn 2006, various (heavily adapted)

*Question 14.11 (Discussion on Issues in Budgeting)*

Write an essay on one of the following:

1.  "The budgeting process is complicated by the presence of subordinates. To get the job done, it is suggested that we must have everyone's input and work to a consensus. In reality, this may not be practical."

    Discuss the above statement in the context of budget setting and suggest factors that might influence the effectiveness of participation.

    > Source: Chartered Accountants Ireland, Management Accounting and Business Finance,
    > Paper 3, various, including Autumn 2007 (adapted)

2.  Conflicting arguments have been made in relation to Zero Based Budgeting (ZBB) as witnessed by the following statement: 'Zero based budgeting beats incremental budgeting hands down every time but, unfortunately, it's great in theory but not so good in practice!'

    > Source: Chartered Accountants Ireland, Management Accounting and Business Finance,
    > Paper 3, various (adapted)

3.  It has been recently suggested that budgeting, as most firms practise it, should be abolished. This is because it has been argued that traditional budgeting techniques are no longer relevant in the current business and economic climate and proponents of 'beyond budgeting' in particular would advocate such an opinion.

    Discuss the arguments supporting a move towards 'beyond budgeting' from more 'traditional' techniques.

    > Source: Chartered Accountants Ireland, Management Accounting and Business Finance,
    > Paper 3, Autumn 2007 (adapted)

*Question 14.12 (Critical Analysis of Budgeting Practices)*

The pharmaceutical sector is one of the greatest examples of Ireland's economic success. For instance some 16 of the top 20 of the world's largest pharmaceutical firms have established subsidiaries here. Many produce some of the world's best-known drugs, from Pfizer's Lipitor and Viagra to Eli Lilly's antidepressant Prozac to GlaxoSmithKlein's Panadol and Solpadeine, to Janssen's Imodium. The pharmaceutical and chemical sector in Ireland employs about 24,000 persons (one-third of them are third-level graduates). In addition, for every job directly created it is estimated that at least another is created in the local economy in a number of support industries from process design to health safety and environmental specialists. The sector exports about €40 billion each year – about one-third of Ireland's total exports. They are also significant contributors to the Irish Exchequer since they pay over €1.1 billion in corporation tax – about one-fifth of the total corporation tax take. This tax take is in spite of Ireland's low tax rate (12.5%) and such favourable tax treatment is also provided by Puerto Rico and Singapore – which are Ireland's main competitors in the field.

In May 20x7, John Fleming, the managing director of XT Pharm, a manufacturing division of a large (US) multinational company located in Dublin, was disappointed with his company's failure to meet budgeted sales and profits during the first four months of the current year. The company does not experience seasonal fluctuations so that the annual budget figures were reduced pro rata based on the number of months in the reporting period. Currently sales and profit were running significantly below budget, according to preliminary statements (**Exhibit 2**). XT Pharm produces two (patented) products – Terzone, which is a pain-killing drug, and Xamate, which is used in the treatment of osteoporosis. (For simplicity sake, both products are hereafter referred to as product 'T' and product 'X' respectively.)

EXHIBIT 2: ACTUAL AND BUDGETED PROFIT PERFORMANCE
JANUARY–APRIL, 20X7

|  | Budgeted € | Actual € |
|---|---|---|
| Sales | 2,713,000 | 1,900,000 |
| Direct Labour (variable) | 900,000 | 700,000 |
| Direct Materials (variable) | 600,000 | 410,000 |
| Production overhead (fixed) | 500,000 | 300,000 |
| Marketing and selling (fixed) | 200,000 | 80,000 |
| New advertising campaign (fixed) | 100,000 | 100,000 |
| Administration (fixed) | 93,000 | 101,000 |
| Research & development (fixed) | 115,000 | 40,000 |
| Profit | 205,000 | 169,000 |

Fleming, as managing director, is held responsible for his company's profit performance, measured in terms of return on equity (ROE). Of greater significance to Fleming was the possible ramification for him personally. He was widely tipped to be promoted to head office before the end of the year. However, a ROE of anything less than 20% would seriously impair his chances of this much sought after promotion.

The annual budgetary process in XT Pharm typically began a few months before the start of the new financial year. The first step in the process was to prepare a detailed estimate of expected sales for the forthcoming year. These estimates were gathered from two sources: the marketing manager who was responsible for the overall promotion of the firm's products, and two senior sales managers who were responsible for the individual product's sales. However, the sales managers, unlike the marketing manager, had responsibility for an individual product and were remunerated by way of basic salary, commission and performance-related pay linked to their ability to achieve budget targets. Fleming felt that one estimate would serve as a good check on the other, and also believed that participation in setting the sales plan was one way to ensure its effectiveness. The marketing manager prepared his estimates by subdividing the market into two parts: sales resulting from normal industry growth at current levels of market penetration and increased sales resulting from further penetration of the market with existing products. At the same time the senior sales representatives predicted the volume of orders that each customer would place in 20x7.

The sales representative produced an estimate of product X sales of €3 million for 20x7, and the marketing department estimated sales of €3.4 million which was similar to the previous year's sales turnover. Fleming felt that the two estimates were in reasonable agreement and incorporated the higher of the two figures into the profit plan. The marketing manager estimated sales of product T at €4 million, while the best (i.e. most optimistic) forecast of the sales representative was only €3 million. Sales for product T had been €1 million in 20x5 and €2 million in 20x6. Fleming discussed the discrepancy with both individuals. On reflection, he decided that the sales manager had submitted a conservative estimate and agreed that the figure submitted by the marketing manager was the appropriate target.

Once the total sales estimate of €7,400,000 was provisionally decided upon by Fleming, the process of estimating production costs began. Each product is manufactured in separate departments under the responsibility of individual production managers. The two production managers were furnished with the sales (volume) estimates and asked to forecast direct labour costs, supervisory salaries and production overhead expenses. (Material costs were estimated by the purchasing department.)

The production department responsible for product X had been a problem area within the division for some time. Four department managers had resigned or been fired during the last three years. A new production manager, David Ryan, had just been appointed and was informed by Fleming that he was expected to have his department on budget by the end of the year. In response, Ryan indicated that his new department had performed poorly in recent years and that he had been in charge for only two months. Fleming then replied, 'I'm expected to meet my profit targets. The only way that can occur is if my subordinates exercise control over their costs and achieve their budgets.' Since the sales value of Product X was more or less the same as the previous year, Ryan inflated last year's cost figures by 10% to cover 'cost inflation and slippage' and submitted them to Fleming for inclusion in the budgeted figures.

The manager responsible for Product T responded to the budget request in prompt fashion. Since the budgeted output was exactly double that of the previous year, he doubled budgeted costs under his responsibility (but which excluded direct materials) compared with the previous year. He then reduced his individual cost estimates by 5% to allow for increased efficiency.

Fleming, a pharmacist by profession, requested the purchasing department to provide estimates of direct material costs for both products, given the agreed and required volumes. Since the purchasing manager thought that it was impossible to predict what all the raw material prices would be, especially given fluctuating dollar/Euro exchange rates, he increased last year's standard prices by 10%. The marketing, administration and research departments forecast their own expenses. Due to Fleming's inexperience in these areas, these estimates were accepted largely without discussion.

With the various forecasts in hand, the accounts department estimated a profit of €560,000 for the year, based on a (provisional) sales value of €7.4 million. Once this draft profit figure had been drawn up, Fleming reviewed it in relation to the specific sales and profit targets required by head office for his company. In reviewing the plans of each department, it became obvious that the combined plans of the company were not sufficient to meet the overall required target of a Return on Equity (Return on Shareholders' funds) of 20%. Fleming confirmed his suspicion by consulting the firm's financial position at 31 December 20x6 (**Exhibit 3**).

EXHIBIT 3: BALANCE SHEET AT 31 DECEMBER 20X6

|  | € | € |
|---|---|---|
| Tangible fixed assets at cost | 3,900,000 | |
| Less: aggregate depreciation | (2,100,000) | 1,800,000 |
| Current Assets | | |
| Stock | | 1,400,000 |
| Trade debtors | | 500,000 |
| Bank balances | | 400,000 |
| | | 2,300,000 |
| Total assets | | 4,100,000 |
| *FINANCED BY:* | | |
| Shareholders' funds | | 2,800,000 |
| Current liabilities | | |
| Trade creditors | | 1,300,000 |
| | | 4,100,000 |

Based on his initial calculation of forecast RoE, the planned sales figure for XT Pharm was therefore revised by Fleming upward by 10% to €8,140,000 and profit to €615,000. Fleming thought that this was a difficult but achievable plan and one that would satisfy head office.

By mid-May, Fleming was very concerned about the poor profit performance of his division relative to budget and contemplated three alternatives to improve the situation. First, he was considering the elimination of €30,000 from the advertising budget for the remainder of 20x7, but had not discussed it with the marketing department.

Secondly, he thought of postponing the addition of two new scientists to his staff until next year. He had already made plans to hire two research personnel by the middle of the current year. One scientist would investigate certain production processes that were yielding excessive labour processing inefficiency variances. The other would conduct clinical studies into 'BetaB', which was a new compound for the treatment of Alzheimer's disease. (In 1906 Alois Alzheimer, a German neurologist, first found clumps of fibrous protein that are characteristic of the disease that now bears his name. These 'amyloid plaques' have become synonymous, not just with Alzheimer's disease, but with a number of other illnesses that wreak havoc in the brain. Only recently have researchers managed to get a better understanding of how and why amyloid forms in the first place.) In preliminary animal studies, BetaB prevented the build-up and reduced the level of amyloid plaque that is considered to be one of the main causes of Alzheimer's disease. To date, BetaB is the only compound for testing the amyloid deposits on the brains of Alzheimer's patients. No pharmaceutical company, currently, has a treatment for Alzheimer's disease. The proposed clinical trials on about 100 patients would take about one year. Fleming estimated that postponing the hiring of these scientists would save €55,000 in salaries and supporting expenses (for the remainder of the year).

Finally, Fleming was thinking about reducing raw material purchases in order to reduce investment in stocks. The reduction in stock levels was an attractive possibility since material stocks accounted for almost 35% of total assets. He recognised, however, that this course of action involved risks.

Fleming realised that top management in head office would not be satisfied with his explanations of failure to meet plans. He understood that he was expected to take whatever remedial and alternative courses of action were needed in order to meet the one-year goals. He was certain that real pressure was building up for him and his managers to meet targets.

**Notes:**

1. Patent protection for drugs begins at the point of filing the patent application and lasts for 20 years. However, it takes an average of 10 to 12 years to turn a promising new compound into a marketable medicinal product that is safe and effective enough to bring to patients. Thus, the average medicine has between 8 and 10 years of effective patent protection left before facing competition from generic equivalents.
2. Every big pharmaceutical company now invests between €2 and €5 billion annually in the quest for new medicines and it is estimated that each new drug to reach the market costs in the range of €600 million to €900 million to develop.

**Requirements:**

1. Using budgeted data, calculate the BEP (in € sales) and MOS % for the year 20x7.
2. What is the budgeted Return on Equity for the year? What is the actual outturn likely to be (assuming no corrective action and assuming no seasonality of data) for the year 20x7?
3. Critically examine the budget practices described and suggest the possible adverse effects if the present method of budget administration is continued.
4. What are the immediate and long-term effects of the three alternatives that Fleming is considering?
5. Identify four performance measures/indicators that you would use to evaluate the Research and Development department and briefly indicate why you have selected them.
6. Some multinationals operating in Ireland maintain their entire nominal ledger accounting and reporting system in terms of dollars. Specify what you consider to be the reasons for this practice.

Source: UCD, B. Comm Advanced Management Accounting, Winter 2004

# Standard Costing and Variance Analysis

When you have completed studying this chapter you should be able to:

1. Outline the nature and advantages of a standard costing system.
2. Calculate and interpret material cost variances in term of usage and price.
3. Calculate and interpret labour cost variances in terms of usage and price.
3. Calculate product overhead costs variance using both absorption and direct (variable) costing.
4. Reconcile profit figures using both absorption and direct (variable) costing.
5. Describe the causes of variances and indicate when variances should be investigated.
7. Calculate both mix and yield variances.
8. Calculate and discuss foreign exchange (FX) variances.
9. Calculate and report planning and operating variances.

## 15.1 Introduction to Standard Unit Costs

In manufacturing firms, a standard costing system is usually integrated within the budgetary control system, although a company may operate a budgetary control system without having a standard costing system. **Standard costing** is best described as a unit (production) costing system and these unit costs are determined in advance. These predetermined unit costs can be compared with actual costs to reveal variances – favourable or otherwise. In addition, standard costs facilitate flexible budgeting. For example, if a standard unit (production) cost is determined at €2 per unit and, if 5,000 units are produced during the accounting period, then the total production cost for the purposes of a flexed budget can be quickly calculated at €10,000. Moreover, the existence of a standard cost for a unit of output enormously simplifies closing stock valuation. This is because, if cost standards are realistic, then products can be valued at their standard cost for financial reporting purposes.

Most of the discussion on standard costing takes place in the context of manufacturing firms, and indeed its origin can be traced back to such firms that began to refine their cost accounting systems in the early Twentieth Century. However, aspects of a standard costing system can relate to any enterprise in which a precise physical relationship can be determined for inputs and outputs. Thus, for example, if a service firm can reasonably estimate that a task requires a specified amount of labour hours, it can apply standard costing principles to that task. Alternatively, a taxi firm may be able to identify a standard cost per mile driven in order to be better able to monitor fuel consumption in its fleet of taxis.

## 15.2 Material and Labour Cost Standards and Variances

Standard costing involves the setting of predetermined cost estimates for a **unit of output**, based on materials, labour and production overhead specifications. Standard costs do not apply to non-production costs because they are not part of the stock valuation process. In addition, it is virtually impossible to establish a valid input-output relationship for these non-production costs since many are in the nature of discretionary, fixed costs. These unit cost standards can be determined in one of three ways, namely, basic cost standards, ideal cost standards or currently attainable cost standards. It is probable that each of these 'standards' will provide different cost figures and this should be borne in mind when computing cost variances – by comparing cost standards with actual performance – and attributing explanation and responsibility for cost variances, either favourable or adverse.

A basic cost standard is a cost standard that is left unchanged over several operating periods. The advantage of this method is that it avoids the complexity and administrative costs associated with revising standard cost data on a regular and frequent basis. Also, it can be argued that the use of a basic cost standard provides greater validity in the calculation of cost variances and their analysis over time. However, the counter argument is that basic cost standards can become out of date and, therefore, the resulting cost variances are not very meaningful. An ideal cost standard is one based on perfect performance. Basically, it represents the lowest minimum cost possible under the most efficient operating conditions. In many cases these ideal cost standards may be very 'tight' or difficult to attain. Therefore, they can be used to motivate those employees who seek challenges at work but, simultaneously, they may not motivate others who perceive ideal cost standards as unrealistic and cannot be achieved!

A further disadvantage is that ideal cost standards will most likely generate only adverse cost variances which may not be fully reflective of performance during the period under review. Therefore, currently attainable cost standards are most commonly used by manufacturing companies and represent costs that should be incurred under expected, but efficient, operating conditions. Effectively, they represent difficult, but not impossible targets to achieve. The main advantage of currently attainable standards is that they provide the most appropriate basis for comparison against actual cost. Furthermore, their identification and computation is usually agreed through participation in the budgeting process by responsible managers. Participation in budget preparation is a positive aspect in terms of getting agreement between superiors and subordinates in addition to using the intimate knowledge of operating managers. Moreover, because the resulting cost standards are attainable, they can be better used to motivate and reward managers. The disadvantage of currently attainable standards is that they can be costly and time-consuming to update during each accounting period – usually a year, as quarterly or shorter time period revisions would be problematic. Finally, it could be argued that currently attainable standards include an amount of tolerated cost inefficiency and, under WCM philosophy, all inefficiency should be ruthlessly eliminated. The important thing to remember is that there are different ways to compute unit standard costs and the underlying methodology should always be borne in mind when computing end of period cost variances.

A standard unit (production) cost is initially determined with reference to two separate standards:

- A standard physical input, i.e. input of labour hours or kilograms of raw materials, for each unit of output, and
- A standard price for each physical unit of input.

Thus, for example, the standard direct material cost per unit is the combination of both a quantity (or physical) standard (Qs) and a price (or monetary) standard (Ps). Therefore, if a unit of output requires 2kg of raw materials (Qs), and each kg costs €3 per kg (Ps), the standard material cost per unit is €6 (Qs×Ps). This is pictured below in **Exhibit 15.1**.

If the standard (direct material) cost is compared with actual cost, **two** important variances can be isolated. These are referred to as a **price variance** and a **usage variance**. (We could alternatively refer to them as a monetary and physical variance.) The price variance is due to the actual price (Pa) of a physical input being higher (or lower) than the standard or budgeted price (Ps). A usage variance occurs when the actual amount of kilograms consumed (Qa) is more or less than anticipated. These price and usage variances are depicted in **Exhibit 15.2**.

Using **Exhibit 15.2** for reference, the price variance can be quickly computed according to the formula overleaf. This price variance highlights whether the average unit purchase price of the production inputs (materials, labour or production overheads) was more or less than budget and computes the total impact on profitability by multiplying the average unit difference by the actual quantity purchased (Qa), or consumed, as appropriate. Therefore, the price variance can be computed as follows:

Price variance:

**(Actual unit price – budget unit price) × actual quantity purchased,**
or in simple terms:

**(Pa − Ps) × Qa**

EXHIBIT 15.1: STANDARD MATERIAL COST PER UNIT

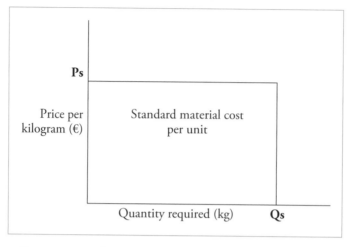

EXHIBIT 15.2: STANDARD MATERIAL COST VARIANCES

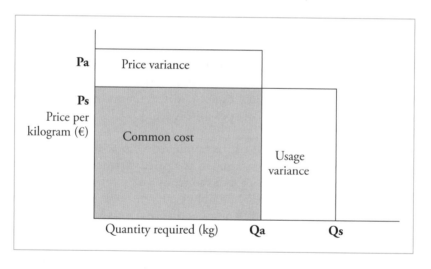

In turn, the usage variance can also be quickly computed by way of formula, based on **Exhibit 15.2**. This variance indicates whether the amount of materials (or other cost inputs) consumed for the actual output produced was more or less than anticipated and the total impact on profitability is computed by multiplying the usage difference by the standard price per unit. Therefore, the usage variance can be computed as follows:

Usage variance:

**(Actual quantity used – budget quantity for actual production) × budget unit cost**, or in simple terms:

$$(Qa - Qs) \times Ps$$

Before we illustrate the calculation of direct materials and direct labour cost variances for a manufacturing concern, it is worthwhile to stress one important point. Standard cost variances (and revenue variances which we discussed in the previous chapter) are described as either Favourable or Adverse with reference to their overall profit impact. The important revenue and cost variances are presented in **Exhibit 15.3** below. But, the calculation of variances below is based on the assumption that the company is operating a standard variable (or direct) costing system. In essence this means that any closing stock of finished goods is valued at variable production cost only. Under a standard variable (or direct) costing system, fixed production costs are written off entirely to the firm's income statement. (The alternative costing system is that based on absorption costing principles and is explained subsequently. Absorption costing is more complicated but, with two exceptions, the variances calculated will be the same.)

The overall profit variance, i.e. the difference between the static budget profit and actual profit for the period, is represented by both sales and cost variances. It will be recalled from **Section 14.7** that the overall sales variance can be divided into two parts which are referred to in **Exhibit 15.3** as a sales volume variance (A) and a sales price variance (B). The total cost variance can be divided between production and non-production costs. Using a standard costing system, it is usual to divide production costs into their constituent elements namely, direct materials, direct labour, variable production overhead and fixed production overhead. **Exhibit 15.3** indicates that, for the variable cost elements, both a price (C) and usage (D) variance can be computed – but their precise titles may change slightly. In simple terms, the price variance highlights the profit impact of the monetary standard not being met. The usage variance highlights the profit impact of the physical standard not being adhered to. Finally, since fixed production overheads are assumed not to vary with output, then the only mean-

EXHIBIT 15.3: PROFIT VARIANCE CHART FOR DIRECT COSTING

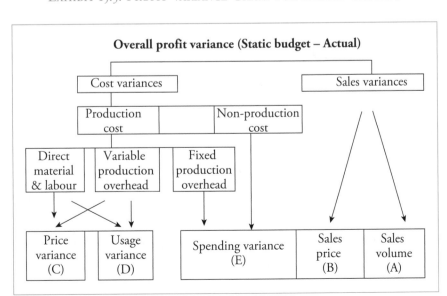

ingful variance is due to spending more or less than anticipated. This difference is simply referred to as a spending variance (E).

The calculation of standard cost variances for both direct materials and direct labour will be illustrated by way of example below. In subsequent illustrations, we shall introduce calculations in relation to both variable and fixed overheads.

## ILLUSTRATION: DIRECT MATERIAL AND DIRECT LABOUR VARIANCES

The Down Company plans to produce 40,000 units of a single product during the coming year. The direct material and direct labour cost figures per unit are budgeted as follows:

| | | |
|---|---|---|
| Direct material | 3kg @ €2 each | 6 |
| Direct labour | 1 hour @ €3 each | 3 |
| Direct cost per unit | | 9 |

However, only 36,000 units were produced and sold during the year. The purchased materials cost €196,000, involving 112,000kg at €1.75 per metre. However, at the end of the period, 2,000kg had not been used. The total labour cost was €142,600 representing 46,000 direct labour hours at €3.10 per hour. For the purpose of variance reporting, the company ignores overhead costs.

**Requirement:** Calculate the direct cost variances under a standard costing system. Please note that it is usual for the total direct materials and direct labour variances to be subdivided into both a price and usage variance and these correspond to variances (C) and (D) in **Exhibit 15.3**. Please note that the labour price variance is better referred to as the labour rate variance and the labour usage variance is more commonly referred to as the labour efficiency variance.

**Solution and Analysis:** It is first useful, but not necessary, to put the relevant figures into a flexed budget reporting format as follows:

| | Static budget | Flexed budget | Actual | Variance |
|---|---|---|---|---|
| Units | 40,000 | 36,000 | 36,000 | |
| | € | € | € | € |
| Direct material | 240,000 | 216,000 | 192,000* | 24,000 F |
| Direct labour | 120,000 | 108,000 | 142,600 | (34,600)A |

*€196,000 less unused stock (2,000kg) valued at standard cost (€2 per kg). It is advisable to always value closing stock of direct materials at standard cost as this ensures the full price variance

is recognised at time of purchase. If closing stock was valued at actual cost, this will result in the price variance being recognised only at time of usage – effectively delaying the recognition of material price variances. It is the purchase rather than the usage of direct materials that causes the price variance to occur.

According to the above presentation, the total material cost variance amounts to €24,000 favourable and the total labour cost variance is €34,600 adverse. The purpose of the standard costing system is to divide both these variances into a price and usage component and they can be calculated according to the following formulae.

Price variance:

(Actual unit price – budget unit price) × actual quantity purchased, or in simple terms: $(Pa - Ps) \times Qa$

Usage variance:

(Actual quality used – budget quantity for actual production) × budget unit cost, or in simple terms: $(Qa - Qs) \times Ps$

In relation to direct materials, the variance calculations are as follows:

|  |  | € |
|---|---|---|
| Material price | (€1.75 − €2.00) × 112,000 | 28,000 F |
| Material usage | (110,000kg* − 108,000kg**) × €2 | (4,000) A |
| Total material cost variances |  | 24,000 F |

* Adjusted for closing stock of 2,000kg
** The number of kilograms which should have been used for actual output of 36,000 units, i.e. 36,000 units × 3kg per unit.

The same type of cost variance calculations are performed for direct labour as follows:

|  |  | € |
|---|---|---|
| Labour rate | (€3.10 − €3.00) × 46,000 | (4,600) A |
| Labour efficiency | (46,000 hrs − 36,000 hrs***) × €3 | (30,000) A |
| Total labour cost variances |  | (34,600) A |

***The amount of direct labour hours which should have been used for actual output of 36,000 units, i.e. 36,000 units × 1 labour hour per unit.

**Alternative presentation:** The calculation of variances can, alternatively, be done using a 'T-account' for each cost element. For direct materials, the left-hand side of the account reflects inputs and actual expenditure and the right-hand side reflects how the amounts used should be accounted for, including any closing stock (which is valued at standard cost). Each side of the account has two columns in which we record both the physical flow of resources and the associated monetary amounts. Using the data above, the direct material ledger account is as follows and represents three consecutive ledger entries:

DIRECT MATERIALS ACCOUNT

| | Kgs | € | | Kgs | € |
|---|---|---|---|---|---|
| Actual input (1) | 112,000 | 196,000 | Standard output (36,000 units) (3) | 108,000 | 216,000 |
| | | | Balance (2) | 2,000 | 4,000 |

The first transaction (1) records that 112,000kg were purchased at a total cost of €196,000. The second entry (2) records the valuation of closing stock which is valued at standard cost (2,000kg × €2). The third transaction (3) is based on the production of 36,000 units which, in standard costing terms, should have consumed 108,000kg in total (3kg × 36,000 units), giving an overall standard cost of €216,000 (108,000kg × €2).

At this stage of the recording process, one must **first** identify the discrepancy in relation to the physical amounts involved. There is an obvious discrepancy between the physical amounts − 112,000kg being traced into the process but only 110,000kg can be accounted for. One can assume that the physical discrepancy is due to the fact that the company used 2,000 more kilograms than anticipated. This is an adverse usage variance (4) and can be recorded as:

DIRECT MATERIALS ACCOUNT

| | Kg | € | | Kg | € |
|---|---|---|---|---|---|
| Actual input (1) | 112,000 | 196,000 | Standard output (3) | 108,000 | 216,000 |
| | | | Usage variance (4) | 2,000 | 4,000 |
| | | | Balance (2) | 2,000 | 4,000 |
| | 112,000 | | | 112,000 | |

The final discrepancy can be found in the monetary columns. Simply, the total of the left hand side (monetary) column must be compared with the total of the right hand side (monetary) column. This final calculation completes the direct materials account and automatically calculates the direct material price variance (5) as follows:

DIRECT MATERIALS ACCOUNT

|  | Kg | € |  | Kg | € |
|---|---|---|---|---|---|
| Actual<br> input (1) | 112,000 | 196,000 | Standard<br> output (3) | 108,000 | 216,000 |
| Price<br> variance (5) | Nil | 28,000 | Usage<br> variance (4) | 2,000 | 4,000 |
|  |  |  | Balance (2) | 2,000 | 4,000 |
|  | 112,000 | 224,000 |  | 112,000 | 224,000 |

The same T-account method can be used to calculate the direct labour cost variances. The direct labour cost account appears as follows:

DIRECT LABOUR ACCOUNT

|  | Hours | € |  | Hours | € |
|---|---|---|---|---|---|
| Actual<br> input (1) | 46,000 | 142,600 | Standard<br> output (2) | 36,000 | 108,000 |
|  |  |  | Efficiency<br> variance (3) | 10,000 | 30,000 |
|  |  |  | Rate<br> variance (4) | Nil | 4,600 |
|  | 46,000 | 142,600 |  | 46,000 | 142,600 |

The first transaction (1) records the expense payment in relation to actual direct labour hours, i.e. 46,000 hours, costing a total of €142,600. The second transaction (2) is based on the production of 36,000 units which, in standard costing terms, should have consumed 36,000 hours in total (1 hour × 36,000 units), giving an overall standard cost of €108,000 (36,000 hours × €3). (Readers should note that there cannot be any closing stock in relation to direct labour hours.)

At this stage of the recording process, one must first identify the discrepancy in relation to the physical amounts involved. There is an obvious discrepancy between actual labour hours provided/consumed (46,000) and the amount of labour hours that **should** have been consumed (36,000). This indicates that 10,000 more hours were used or worked than should have been. This **adverse** labour efficiency variance (3) amounts to €30,000 (10,000 hours × €3). Finally the labour rate variance (4) of €4,600 was also adverse, indicating that the company paid its employees a higher rate per hour than budgeted. Both the labour rate and labour efficiency variances are adverse and will be transferred to the debit (expense) side of the income statement when preparing end of period management accounts. In a subsequent section of this chapter we shall discuss possible causes of these and other variances.

## 15.3 Overhead Cost Variances

Before presenting the calculation of overhead cost variances, we need to again stress the accounting difference between production and non-production overheads. The former are **product** costs and form part of stock valuation calculations (for financial reporting purposes) and are an integral part of any standard costing system. In contrast, non-production overheads, e.g. selling, distribution and administration expenses, are always written off immediately and in their entirety to the firm's income statement as they are considered **period** and not product costs. Variances arising from non-production overheads are simply calculated as the difference between (flexed) budget and actual spending and are generally referred to as 'spending variances'.

In relation to production overheads, one must distinguish between fixed and variable costs: fixed production overheads are assumed to remain unchanged in total with respect to changes in the relevant cost driver level (volume). Conversely, variable production overheads are expected to change in total with respect to changes in the cost driver level. Bearing this distinction in mind when computing production overhead variances, it is recommended that both fixed and variable calculations be performed separately. The distinction between fixed and variable production overheads is also important because of the difference between absorption and variable (direct) costing. In **Section 2.3** we discussed the difference between variable (direct) costing and absorption costing. Variable (or direct) costing values closing inventory at variable cost of production only. In contrast, absorption costing values closing stock at the total cost of production and this includes an element of fixed production overhead.

For variable production overheads, the calculation of both 'monetary' and 'physical' variances is identical under either variable or absorption costing systems. Therefore, just like direct materials and direct labour, the total variable production overhead can be subdivided into price and usage components, corresponding to variances (C) and (D) in **Exhibit 15.3**.

ILLUSTRATION: VARIABLE PRODUCTION OVERHEAD VARIANCE

The Derry Company has budgeted to produce 1,000 units during the coming period. Each unit will require 2 hours of labour processing time and the variable production overhead absorption rate is €20 per direct labour hour. During the relevant period, 900 units were produced, using 2,000 labour hours. The actual variable overhead incurred amounted to €43,000.

**Requirement:** Calculate the variable production overhead variances for the period.

**Solution and analysis:** During the period, variable overheads amounting to €43,000 were incurred in producing 900 units. The variable overheads that should have been incurred amount to €36,000 (900 units × 2 hours × €20).

Clearly, the amount of the variable overhead variance is €7,000 adverse. This can be subdivided into price and usage (efficiency) variances as follows:

**Price (or Rate) variance:**

**(Actual hourly rate − budget hourly rate) × actual hours worked**

The actual absorption rate per hour for variable overheads amounted to €21.50 (€43,000/2,000 hours) compared with a budget rate of €20. Thus, for every hour worked (2,000 hours), there was an hourly rate variance of €1.50. The variable overhead rate variance is computed as follows:

Variable overhead rate variance:
(€21.50 − €20.00) × 2,000 hours = €3,000 A

**Efficiency variance:**
The efficiency variance can be calculated with reference to the following formula:

**(Actual hours worked − budget hours for actual production) × budget hourly rate**

Since variable overheads are absorbed on the basis of labour hours, calculations must be performed using labour hours rather than on the basis of units produced. Under standard costing, the 900 units produced are equivalent to 1,800 hours of work (the standard allowance for actual output). Since 2,000 hours were worked, there is an adverse efficiency variance of 200 hours. The variable overhead efficiency variance is computed as follows:

Variable overhead efficiency variance:
(2,000 − 1,800) × €20 = €4,000 A

**Alternative presentation:**

Rather than using formulae, the variances can be computed using the T-account method. The left-hand side always records the actual amounts expended and the right-hand side records actual output in terms of standard hours and standard cost. The initial entries in this ledger account are as follows:

VARIABLE OVERHEADS ACCOUNT

|  | Hours | € |  | Hours | € |
|---|---|---|---|---|---|
| Actual input (1) | 2,000 | 43,000 | Standard output (900 units) (2) | 1,800 | 36,000 |

The first entry (1) on the debit side of the T-account shows that 2,000 hours were worked at a total cost of €43,000. (The average rate per hour was €21.50 i.e. €21,000/2,000 hours.) The credit entry (2) records the actual output of 900 units in terms of standard hours and standard cost. The ledger entry therefore records 1,800 labour hours and the total standard cost of actual output amounting to €36,000 (1,800 hours × €20).

Next (3) one always identifies the discrepancy in relation to the physical amounts involved. There is an obvious discrepancy since we can trace 2,000 hours going into the account but can identify an output equivalent to only 1,800 hours. Common sense suggests that the company used 200 more hours than anticipated for this volume of output. This is an adverse efficiency or usage (200 hours × €20 per hour = €4,000) variance and can be recorded as:

### VARIABLE OVERHEADS ACCOUNT

|  | Hours | € |  | Hours | € |
|---|---|---|---|---|---|
| Actual input (1) | 2,000 | 43,000 | Standard output (2) | 1,800 | 36,000 |
|  |  |  | Efficiency variance (3) | 200 | 4,000 |
|  | 2,000 |  |  | 2,000 |  |

Finally (4) we identify the discrepancy in the monetary columns. Simply, the total of the left hand side column must be compared with the total of the right hand side column. The final calculation completes the variable overhead account as follows and represents the adverse variable production overhead rate variance in the amount of €3,000:

### VARIABLE OVERHEADS ACCOUNT

|  | Hours | € |  | Hours | € |
|---|---|---|---|---|---|
| Actual input (1) | 2,000 | 43,000 | Standard output (2) | 1,800 | 36,000 |
|  |  |  | Efficiency variance (3) | 200 | 4,000 |
|  |  |  | Rate variance (4) | Nil | 3,000 |
|  | 2,000 | 43,000 |  | 2,000 | 43,000 |

## Fixed Production Overhead and Non-Production Overheads

Under variable (or direct) costing the final set of variances that are calculated concern fixed production overheads ((E) in **Exhibit 15.3**) and non-production overheads.

Since both these cost items are assumed to be fixed in relation to changes in the underlying cost driver level, the only meaningful variance is that of a spending variance. Simply, the spending variance is the difference between the budgeted amount of the expenditure compared with the actual expenditure and can be calculated as:

**Spending variance (fixed overheads) = Budget – Actual**

A comprehensive profit analysis example relating to direct (variable) costing is now presented in the next section.

## 15.4 Profit Reconciliation Using Variable Costing

Profit reconciliation (or analysis) is a technique associated with standard costing systems, and involves presenting all the revenue and cost variances in a single statement. Ideally, to provide reference points for managers, the profit reconciliation statement should clearly show the profit forecast per the static budget, the profit as per the flexed budget and, finally, the actual profit generated for the period under review. This technique is now illustrated with reference to the example below.

### ILLUSTRATION: PROFIT RECONCILIATION

Armagh Company produces a single product and operates a standard costing system, based on variable costing principles. Its budget and actual outturn for 20x8 is summarised as follows:

|  | Budget | Actual |
|---|---|---|
| Sales units | 5,000 | 5,200 |
| Sales revenue | €60,000 | €61,880 |
| Less Cost of production: | | |
| Direct materials | 15,000 | 16,500 |
| Direct labour | 30,000 | 29,250 |
| Variable overhead | 5,000 | 4,800 |
| Fixed overhead | 5,000 | 5,100 |
|  | 55,000 | 55,650 |
| Gross margin | 5,000 | 6,230 |
| Less: Administration costs | 2,500 | 2,560 |
| Profit for year | 2,500 | 3,670 |

In addition, you are provided with the following information relating to the above year:

- The standard selling price and cost per unit (under variable costing) is as follows:

| Selling price per unit | €12 |
|---|---|
| Direct materials (1kg × €3 per kg) | 3 |
| Direct labour (1 hour × €6 per hour) | 6 |
| Variable production overheads (1 hour × €1 per hour) | 1 |
| Budgeted unit contribution | 2 |

- During the year 5,200 widgets were produced. There were no opening stocks of finished goods.
- 6,000kg of raw materials were purchased at a cost of €18,600 during the year of which 700kg remain in stock at the end of the year.
- The total hours worked during the year amounted to 3,900 hours at a total cost of €29,250.
- Variable overheads incurred during the year amounted to €4,800. Fixed production overheads incurred during the year amounted to €5,100. Production overheads are absorbed on the basis of direct labour hours.
- Administration costs, which are considered a fixed cost, amounted to €2,560 during the year.
- Actual unit sales during the year were 5,200 units, which generated sales revenue of €61,880.

**Requirement:** Prepare a profit reconciliation statement, reconciling static profit with actual profit using revenue and cost variances in as much detail as possible.

**Solution and analysis:** The solution below, for variable production costs, is presented by way of T-accounts. The sequence to be followed will always be:

1. Record the actual physical and monetary inputs for direct materials, direct labour and variable production overheads on the left-hand (debit) side of the T-account.
2. Record the physical and monetary standards for the <u>actual</u> output on the right-hand (credit) side of the account.
3. Record any closing (or opening) stock of direct materials at standard cost.
4. Identify the discrepancy in the physical columns. This is commonly referred to as the usage (efficiency) variance, which is multiplied by the standard cost per unit of input.
5. Finally, the remaining discrepancy in the T-account can only be explained by the monetary variance, commonly referred to as the price (rate) variance. This is the final variance since the physical discrepancy has been calculated in (4) above.

Each of the three variable cost elements of Armagh's production is presented below.

### Direct materials at €3 per kilogram

|  | Kg | € |  | Kg | € |
|---|---|---|---|---|---|
| Actual input (1) | 6,000 | 18,600 | Standard output (2) | 5,200 | 15,600 |
|  |  |  | Usage variance (4) | 100 | 300 |
|  |  |  | Price variance (5) | Nil | 600 |
|  |  |  | Balance (3) | 700 | 2,100 |
|  | 6,000 | 18,600 |  | 6,000 | 18,600 |

### Direct labour cost at €6 per hour

|  | Hours | € |  | Hours | € |
|---|---|---|---|---|---|
| Actual input (1) | 3,900 | 29,250 | Standard output (2) | 5,200 | 31,200 |
| Efficiency variance (4) | 1,300 | 7,800 | Price variance (5) | Nil | 5,850 |
|  | 5,200 | 37,050 |  | 5,200 | 37,050 |

**Note**: there is no closing stock, corresponding to (3) above.

### VARIABLE PRODUCTION OVERHEADS (ABSORBED AT €1 PER LABOUR HOUR)

|  | Hours | € |  | Hours | € |
|---|---|---|---|---|---|
| Actual input (1) | 3,900 | 4,800 | Standard output (2) | 5,200 | 5,200 |
| Efficiency variance (4) | 1,300 | 1,300 | Rate variance (5) | Nil | 900 |
|  | 5,200 | 6,100 |  | 5,200 | 6,100 |

**Note**: there is no closing stock corresponding to (3) above.

In the above account variable production overheads are absorbed on the basis of direct labour hours. Therefore, since there is a favourable efficiency variance in labour hours, there must also be a favourable efficiency variance in relation to variable production overheads.

The only other cost variances relate to fixed production overheads and administration costs. Since both cost elements are assumed to be fixed in relation to changes in volume, the only meaningful variance is a spending variance, calculated as the difference between budget and actual expenditure. The spending variances are:

Fixed production spending variance:
(€5,100 − €5,000) = (€100) Adverse

Administration spending variance:
(€2,560 − €2,500) = (€60) Adverse

To complete the illustration, we can compute both sales variances. The sales price variance is computed as the difference between average actual price and standard price multiplied by the number of units sold and is as follows:

Sales price variance:
(€11.90 − €12.00) × 5,200 = (€520) Adverse

The sales volume variance is computed as the difference between actual volume and budgeted volume, multiplied by the budgeted unit contribution. It identifies the overall profit impact due to the change in volume, i.e. an additional 200 units were sold and each unit was anticipated to generate a contribution (sales price less variable costs) of €2. The formal calculation is as follows:

Sales volume variance:
(5,200 units − 5,000 units) × €2 = €400 favourable.

All the sales and cost variances calculated above can be combined to prepare a comprehensive performance report to management. To put the report into context we prepare a flexed budget report (using variable costing principles) but such a report is not really necessary.

FLEXED BUDGET REPORT FOR 20X8

|  | Static budget | Flexed budget | Actual outturn | Variance (FB−A) |
|---|---|---|---|---|
| Sales units | 5,000 | 5,200 | 5,200 | |
|  | € | € | € | € |
| Sales revenue | 60,000 | 62,400 | 61,880 | 520 A |
| Materials | (15,000) | (15,600) | (16,500)* | 900 A |
| Labour | (30,000) | (31,200) | (29,250) | 1,950 F |
| Variable overhead | (5,000) | (5,200) | (4,800) | 400 F |
| Fixed overhead | (5,000) | (5,000) | (5,100) | 100 A |
| Administration | (2,500) | (2,500) | (2,560) | 60 A |

| Net profit | 2,500 | 2,900 | 3,670 | 770 F |

| Sales volume var | + €400 F | | | |

| Price & cost vars | | + €770 F | | |

\* The actual cost of raw materials consumed during the quarter amounted to €16,500. This represents the actual cost of purchases less closing stock, which is valued at standard cost. Since closing stock is valued at standard, this has the effect of recognising the material purchase price variance in the period in which the goods were purchased. This is a logical treatment since the price variance has been incurred. Alternatively, closing stock could be valued at actual rather than standard cost. This would have the impact of recognising the materials price variance only when the materials were used rather than when they were purchased. The former treatment is recommended.

The above variances can be used to reconcile budget with actual profit figures.

RECONCILIATION OF BUDGETED TO ACTUAL PROFIT FOR 20X8 (VARIABLE COSTING)

| | € | |
|---|---|---|
| Net profit as per static budget | 2,500 | |
| Add: Sales volume variance | 400 | 4% F |
| = Net profit as per flexed budget | 2,900 | |
| Sales price variance | (520) | 0.8% A |
| Materials price variance** | (600) | 3.3% A |
| Materials usage variance | (300) | 1.9% A |
| Labour rate variance | (5,850) | 25% A |
| Labour usage variance | 7,800 | 25% F |
| Variable overhead rate variance | (900) | 23% A |
| Variable overhead efficiency variance | 1,300 | 25% F |
| Fixed overhead spending variance | (100) | 2% A |
| Administration costs spending variance | (60) | 2.4% A |
| = Actual profit for year | 3,670 | |

** Using actual and budget rates per unit

The above presentation includes the percentage variation and this is intended to highlight the significant variances – in terms of percentage variation. Clearly, there is a problem with regard to labour standards and this will need to be investigated before corrective action is contemplated.

## 15.5 Profit Reconciliation Using Absorption Costing

We have already mentioned the difference between variable (direct) costing and absorption costing systems (the topic was covered in greater detail in **Section 2.3**). The difference between these two methods is the accounting treatment of fixed production overheads. Under variable (or direct) costing, these fixed production overheads are not included in stock valuation calculations. On the other hand, absorption costing includes a portion of these fixed production overheads in the valuation of closing stock. Thus, the profit impact of these two costing methods is generally different and this has implications for calculating standard cost variances. We now revisit our standard costing calculations and variances using absorption costing. For illustration purposes, we shall repeat the example of Armagh Company which was worked through in **Section 15.4** so that the main differences between the two systems can be better appreciated.

Under absorption costing, there are only two changes to the standard cost variances previously calculated. One represents a change to the method of calculating the sales volume variance and the other change is the calculation of an additional cost variance, referred to as the fixed production overhead volume variance.

The sales volume variance, under absorption costing, is intended to highlight the impact on profit as a result of a change in sales volume. This variance represents the difference between the static budget units and actual units sold. Under absorption costing we multiply the difference in sales volumes by a **profit margin** per unit. This profit margin represents the budgeted selling price per unit less the (full) production costs, which automatically includes a portion of fixed production overhead. (It is important to remember that under variable costing, unit **contribution** was used to calculate the sales volume variance.)

ILLUSTRATION: VARIANCE CALCULATIONS UNDER ABSORPTION COSTING

Returning to the Armagh Company and, under absorption costing, the standard cost and profit margin per unit is calculated as follows:

BUDGETED SELLING PRICE AND STANDARD COST

|  |  | € |
|---|---|---|
| Sales price per unit |  | 12 |
| Direct materials | (1kg × €3 each) | (3) |
| Labour | (1 hour × €6 per hr) | (6) |
| Variable production overhead | (1 hour × €1 per hr) | (1) |
| Fixed production overhead | (€5,000/5,000 units) | (1) |
| Profit per unit |  | 1 |

Thus, under absorption costing, the sales volume variance will be calculated with reference to actual sales volume less budgeted sales volume multiplied by the profit per unit. The profit per unit is the unit selling price less all production costs. The calculation of the sales volume variance (under absorption costing) is as follows:

Sales volume variance: (5,200 units − 5,000 units)×€1 = €200 F

The second difference between variable (direct) costing and absorption costing is the calculation of an additional cost variance – the fixed production overhead volume variance. It should be recalled that the absorption of fixed production overheads is based on estimated volume. Thus, the fixed production overhead absorption rate is calculated, above, as €1 per unit (€5,000/5,000 units). This means that there may be a prediction error in our calculations and this will arise whenever actual output is different to budgeted output. Therefore, there will be a difference between the amount of fixed production overhead **absorbed** during the period and the amount of fixed production overhead budgeted. To cater for this situation, we need to compute an additional cost variance, referred to as the fixed production overhead volume variance.

The fixed production overhead volume variance is calculated as the difference between **standard** hours for the actual output and **budgeted** hours multiplied by the fixed production overhead rate per hour. The calculation is as follows:

Fixed overhead volume variance:
(5,200 hours − 5,000 hours) × €1 = €200 Favourable

This volume variance does not mean that costs were €200 less than anticipated. Rather, it means that additional production, of 200 units, was available to absorb the fixed overheads that were expected to occur and this resulted in an over-absorption of fixed production overheads. (The volume variance can also be adverse. This will occur when actual production volume is less than expected.)

Alternatively, the fixed production overhead variances can be calculated using the 'T-account' method and this is produced below.

FIXED PRODUCTION OVERHEADS (ABSORBED AT €1 PER LABOUR HOUR)

| | Hours | € | | Hours | € |
|---|---|---|---|---|---|
| Actual input (1) | 5,000* | 5,100 | Standard output (2) | 5,200 | 5,200 |
| Volume variance (3) | 200 | 200 | Spending variance (4) | Nil | 100 |
| | 5,200 | 5,300 | | 5,200 | 5,300 |

* The budgeted hours are used as this was the denominator in computing the predetermined fixed production absorption rate.

The sequence by which the transactions are recorded is the same as previously outlined. First (1) we record the actual expenditure but we record '5,000' hours, since this is the number of hours that we have anticipated and used in our calculation of the budgeted fixed production overhead absorption rate. Secondly, (2) we record the actual output (i.e. 5,200 units) at the standard amounts involved, as represented by 5,200 labour hours and an overall standard cost of €5,200 (€1 per hour). Thirdly (3) we note that there is a discrepancy in relation to the physical amounts. Effectively, we 'overproduced' the equivalent of 200 hours, giving a favourable volume variance of €200.

Finally, (4) the monetary variance reflects the overspending, with reference to the original budget, as indicated by a €100 adverse expenditure variance. This fixed production overhead expenditure variance is identical to that calculated under variable (direct) costing.

The inevitable question is, who is responsible for the fixed production overhead volume variance? It is not the production manager since it is usually argued that he does not establish his production schedule in isolation. Rather the volume of production is determined by a group of managers on the basis of anticipated customer orders and other factors. This being so, the fixed production overhead volume variance is not really controllable by the production manager and should not be attributed to him. It is simply a book-keeping variance when a company operates a standard absorption costing system and it is difficult to equitably assign responsibility for this variance.

The profit reconciliation statement under absorption costing appears as follows, and again, highlights the three profit figures, namely, the original profit target, the flexed profit target and the actual profit reported for the period. It should be noted that the fixed overhead volume variance is presented just below the (revised) sales volume variance.

RECONCILIATION OF BUDGETED TO ACTUAL PROFIT FOR 20X8
(ABSORPTION COSTING)

|  | € |
|---|---|
| Net profit per static budget | 2,500 |
| Sales volume variance | 200 F |
| Fixed overhead volume variance | 200 F |
| = Net profit per flexed budget | 2,900 |
| Sales price variance | (520) A |
| Materials price variance | (600) A |

| | |
|---|---|
| Materials usage variance | (300) A |
| Labour rate variance | (5,850) A |
| Labour usage variance | 7,800 F |
| Variable overhead rate variance | (900) A |
| Variable overhead efficiency variance | 1,300 F |
| Fixed overhead expenditure variance | (100) A |
| Administration expense expenditure variance | (60) A |
| = Actual profit for year | 3,670 |

Astute readers will notice that the actual net profit for the year (€3,670) is the same under both variable (direct) and absorption costing! Even more astute readers will recall that both the variable (direct) and absorption costing system provide the same net profit figure whenever there is no increase or decrease in overall stock levels during the accounting period and this is the case with the Armagh Company.

## 15.6 Causes and Investigation of Variances

It should be remembered that variances only represent signals that the firm's operations may or may not be 'in control' and we have previously associated this with the **control decision point**. This point is determined by the perceived significance of a particular variance. **Management by exception** is the process of concentrating only on those areas where differences between budget and actual performance are deemed to be significant or important. These variances represent potential problem areas and should be investigated. If a variance is not significant, then it suggests that actual performance approximates planned performance. The problem with management by exception is that it indicates **when** corrective action should be taken but not **what** specific action should be taken. Common sense suggests that, before any action is taken, it is crucial to understand the causes of the individual variances. However, in many cases it is not obvious what the most appropriate managerial response should be. Nevertheless, it is the managerial response in relation to the receipt of a variance report that represents the control device. We have previously referred to this phase as the **control action** point. Thus, there are three related aspects. First, the manager must decide whether a variance is significant, in other words, whether it is important enough to be investigated. Secondly, the real underlying cause of the variance must be identified. Thirdly, corrective action should be taken where feasible. We shall discuss all these three issues in turn below.

## Significance of Variances

Not all variances from budget or standard can be considered important and worthy of investigation. Thus, managers should confine their analysis to variances that they consider to be important or significant. Managers may use any combination of five techniques to determine the significance of individual variances and these techniques are: (1) the percentage variation, (2) the frequency of the variance, (3) the trend of variance, (4) control charts, and (5) cost-benefit models based on statistical analysis. Each of these is now briefly discussed in turn.

### 1. The Percentage Variation

This involves setting a predetermined limit – say, 10% – and investigating all variances in excess of this limit. The advantage of this approach is its simplicity and ease of implementation. However, some small expense items may vary well in excess of the predetermined limit. For example, most managers would not deem a 20% variation in a budgeted expense item of €1,000 significant. Thus, the percentage rule needs to be supplemented by a rule specifying absolute monetary amounts. What tends to happen is that small percentage variations are used for large monetary amounts and large percentage variations allowed for small monetary amounts. However, the use of any percentage to determine the significance of variances is always arbitrary.

### 2. Frequency of Variance

Some managers investigate a variance based on the infrequency of its occurrence. Thus, a very rare variance may be deemed sufficiently important to warrant investigation in comparison to a variance that occurs on a regular basis.

### 3. Trend of Variance

Some variances may be small in percentage terms, but increasing in size over successive accounting periods. This trend, especially if it is adverse, could signal a variance investigation decision in order to try and prevent a significant variance occurring in a future time period.

### 4. Control Chart

This is a more formal method of investigation and involves setting limits within which variances are considered to be insignificant and therefore operations are deemed to be 'in control'. The approach recognises that many standards represent average performance over a period of time rather than a specific measure during a single accounting period. Thus, one can expect a normal pattern of variability from any particular process under observation. Any measurement outside this acceptable pattern of variability is considered a signal that the process is 'out of control'– the cause of which should be investigated. If the actual performance remains within these limits, then no investigation is deemed necessary.

The acceptable limits are referred to as the upper control limit (UCL) and lower control limit (LCL). Usually samples from the process are taken at regular and frequent intervals and the mean (average) of the sample observations are plotted on a control chart. Upper and lower statistical confidence limits are also placed on the chart. For example, assuming normally distributed means, 95% confidence limits are obtained by setting the control limits equivalent to 1.96 standard deviations from the mean. An observation falling outside such confidence limits would have less than a 5% probability of arising in an in-control process. (One could establish a 99% confidence limit by using 2.58 standard deviations.) A typical control chart is displayed in **Exhibit 15.4** based on a mean (average) value of 10 and a standard deviation of 1. The upper and lower control limits, for 95% confidence, are set at 11.96 and 8.04 respectively (10 ± 1.96 × 1). Successive observations have been plotted on the control chart, with only observation number 4 falling outside the control limits.

Control charts have a number of advantages:

1.  They avoid the unrealistic assumption of a single standard and therefore allow some variability in performance.
2.  They are simple, cheap and quick to operate.
3.  The graphic format of control charts is an excellent way of communicating trends for ready interpretation by the human eye. Returning to **Exhibit 15.4**, we can see a pattern of increasing variances in observations 5, 6 and 7 without hitting the upper control limit. This pattern indicates a shift away from standard operations, but no significance is given by a mechanical rule applied only to the most recent observation – observation 7 is still within the allowable range of acceptable performance.

The main limitation of control charts is that they are based on an arbitrary rule, i.e. investigate a phenomenon if an observation is beyond the specified control limits. In

EXHIBIT 15.4: CONTROL CHART

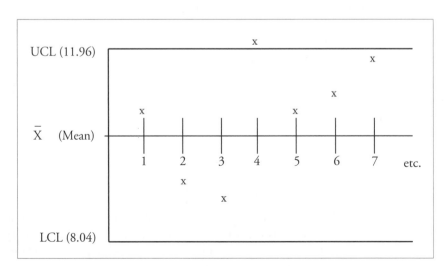

addition, does one use 95% or 99% confidence limits? Associated with these control limits is the possibility of type 1 and type 2 errors. A type 1 error results when an in-control process is investigated and this incurs unnecessary costs because no benefits accrue from the investigation. Type 2 errors result when an out-of control process is *not* investigated. The opportunity cost of type 2 errors is represented by the savings which could have been obtained by investigation and correction. Thus, the wider the control limits, the lower the possibility of a type 1 error but the higher the probability of a type 2 error. The second limitation of control charts is that there is no attempt to associate the cost of investigation with potential savings. This limitation leads us to the final method of investigating variances.

### 5. Cost–Benefit Models

Cost–benefit models acknowledge that the decision to investigate variances represents decision-making under uncertainty. In which case a variance investigation decision should be based on three considerations namely, (1) the cost of investigation, (2) the probability that the process is out of control and (3) the net benefits arising from correcting the problem. Costs of investigation include the cost of shutting down the plant with consequent lost production, salary costs of investigators and the opportunity cost of managerial time. The net benefits to be generated, but only if the cause of the variance is correctable, include savings in the form of eliminated inefficiencies and wastages but they also include the costs of correction. Therefore, investigating variances involves two costs. First, the cost of investigation, which must be spent as part of the investigation process and, secondly, the cost of correction, which represents a contingent cost – this will only be incurred if the system needs to be corrected. The cost-benefit model, like all statistical decision models, is based on the premise that investigation should only take place when the expected value of investigation is positive. If investigation takes place there are two possibilities, i.e.

- Investigation was unnecessary either because the system is in control, i.e. the variance was purely random or the variance is permanent and cannot be corrected.
- The system is out of control and can be corrected. Therefore, there are net benefits to be gained from investigation. Usually, additional costs will be incurred to correct the variance and these costs must be included in the calculation of net benefits.

In order to calculate the expected value of investigation we must estimate the probabilities that the system is in control. If we adopt the following notation, a simple profit matrix can be calculated:

C = Cost of initial investigation
B = Net benefits of correction (gross benefits less correction costs)
P = Probability that the system is in control
1 − P = Probability that the system is out of control

If the system is in control, costs of investigation (C) will be incurred but there are no benefits to accrue. If the system is out of control, there will be net benefits (B) but there will also be the initial costs of investigation (C). It is usual to present the decision by way of a simple payoff matrix as follows:

STATES OF NATURE

|  | In control (P) | Out of control (1 − P) |
|---|---|---|
| Investigate variance? | −C | B − C |

For investigation to be worthwhile, the expected value of investigation must be greater than zero, and this can be depicted as follows:

$$\text{Investigate if: } (-C) \times (P) + (B - C) \times (1 - P) > 0$$

This can be rearranged to provide a simple 'trigger value' or decision rule for investigation as follows:

$$\text{Investigate if trigger value for investigation } \quad \frac{(B - C)}{B} \quad > P$$

The significance of this formula is that we do not need precise estimates of the probability that the system is in control. Approximate probability will usually suffice. Also, the trigger value allows one to estimate a 'break-even' possibility for a variance investigation decision.

## ILLUSTRATION: COST-BENEFIT MODEL OF INVESTIGATION

The Bray Company uses a standard costing system in its factory in which its semi-automated process is rarely out of control. The cost of variance investigation is €500 and, if the process is found to be out of control, its cost of correction is €1,000. However, the gross savings of correction are estimated to be €4,000. Management believes that there is a probability of 80% that the system is in control.

**Requirement:** Should the process be investigated using the cost-benefit model?

**Solution and Analysis:** The 'trigger' value for investigation can be calculated as follows

$$\textbf{Trigger value for investigation} \quad \frac{(€3,000 - €500)}{€3,000} = 0.83$$

The 'trigger value' computed above is 0.83. This is greater than the estimated probability that the system is in control (0.8) and so investigation of the variance should take place, since 0.83 > 0.80.

## Causes of Variances

Before corrective action can be contemplated it is first necessary to determine the cause of identified variances. Management accountants, therefore, act as financial detectives, either discovering appropriate reasons for variances or evaluating the evidence or reasons presented by others. It is useful to suggest that all variances can be classified into one of four groups as follows:

1. **Errors in the accounting system:** These variances arise because the actual data, which is used to compare against standards is wrong! In other words, there is an error in the accounting system. Such errors could be due to, for example, failure to record closing stock of direct materials, or incorrect reporting of other cost data, e.g. labour hours worked, or failure to correctly record the actual level of sales. Such incorrect postings may have been due to genuine errors or, alternatively, due to deliberate data manipulation by employees.

2. **Incorrect standards:** These variances are due to the unrealistic nature of the original standards and are sometimes referred to as prediction or planning errors. If the standards are incorrect then the resulting variances are largely meaningless. It may well be that the monetary standards were unrealistic, e.g. incorrect forecasting of fuel prices, or that the physical standards were inappropriate, e.g. incorrect understanding of the relationship between the amount of direct labour hours required per unit of output.

    Managers may wish to attribute variances to this cause. This is because, if they successfully argue that the original standards were incorrect, there is no need for corrective action (which may be very convenient) and therefore they can avoid confrontation with subordinates. Nevertheless, it should be acknowledged that, in some cases, variances do arise because of incorrect standards. However, one should be sceptical if a significant number of variances are attributed to incorrect standards.

3. **Random errors:** These are errors that are not expected to reoccur or, alternatively, are outside the control of management. However, managers are expected to react to them.

4. **Implementation errors:** These errors are due to operational factors during the reporting period, including incorrect or inappropriate behaviour of employees. These causes should be corrected by appropriate managerial action. A list of possible reasons under this heading is provided (**Exhibit 15.5**), but it is not exhaustive:

EXHIBIT 15.5: POSSIBLE CAUSES OF VARIANCES

Sales volume variances could be attributable to:
    poor sales effort from sales personnel resulting in declining orders
    a general decline in quality of product
    increased selling price (see below)

Sales price variance could be due to:

    unauthorised change in selling price due to prevailing conditions

The direct material cost variance could be attributable to:

    change in price due to, say, quantity discount or new supplier

    change in mix or proportion of materials used

    change in production process including new machines

    equipment malfunction

    theft or other loss of direct materials

The direct labour cost variance could be attributable to:

    change in wages' rates due to overtime

    different mix or proportion of workers, e.g. skilled and unskilled

    change in production process including new machine

    productivity (and experience/training) of employees

    impact of staff morale including improvement in working conditions

    intentional 'go slow' by employees or some industrial dispute

Overhead (production and non-production) cost variances could be attributable to:

    new suppliers or vendors

    change in quantity required

    outsourcing activities

    change in efficiency due to some factors listed above

    changed economic conditions resulting in increased prices

    new equipment and/or different depreciation amounts

    change in number of supervisors and/or change in automation

    agreed change in spending, e.g. advertising spend due to competition

While the benefits of analysing variances should now be obvious, it should be noted that variance analysis may not be a worthwhile exercise in the following situations:

- Where variances are permanent and re-occur period after period, the usefulness of variance analysis is questionable. This would suggest that it is the standard that is at fault – if correctly stated, no variance would have arisen in the first place. For example, where frequent changes in prices of inputs occur, there is a danger that standard costs may be out of date. Standards also become out of date where operations are subject to frequent technological changes or fail to take into account learning curve effects. Investigation of variances falling into this category will only provide feedback on the inaccuracy of the standards and highlight the need to update standards.

- The benefits of variance analysis decrease if the exercise is carried out too long after the event. If performance reports are prepared on a monthly basis, this represents a considerable time lag that is not helpful for the daily control of operations. For operational control purposes, labour and material usage variances should be reported in physical terms in 'real time'.

- Variance analysis is not a worthwhile exercise when no corrective action is taken, even though appropriate. If management do not respond to reported variances, the control function is being damaged.

- Variances should only be investigated where the benefits exceed the cost of the investigation. In cases where the cost exceeds the benefits, the variance analysis exercise would not be worthwhile. However, it is important that all relevant costs and benefits are considered in making such a decision.

- Cost structures have changed in recent years with overhead costs becoming more dominant and direct labour costs diminishing in importance. In other words, more of the firm's costs have become fixed in the short term. Given that standard costing is a mechanism that is most suited to the control of direct and variable costs, but not fixed or overhead costs, the technique of variance analysis has been questioned in relation to overhead cost variances.

- For organisations adopting modern managerial approaches that focus on continuous improvement, minimising stocks, zero defect production and delivery of high quality products and services, standing costing systems and variance analysis may not be appropriate. When standard costs are used, a climate is created whereby the standards represent targets to be achieved rather than creating a climate of continuous improvement, including innovative behaviour.

## Interdependency of Variances

One of the practical difficulties associated with identifying the causes of variances is the phenomenon which can be described as the interdependency of variances. This is a situation when a variance is caused by one manager but is reported in another manager's performance report. A typical example is where inferior but cheap materials are purchased. A favourable price variance may be reported for the purchasing manager but, if this were due to the purchase of inferior materials, it would lead to an adverse efficiency variance as extra materials are consumed in production. Alternatively, workers may require additional production time as a result of the poor quality of materials. Thus, it is useful to remember that standard costing systems *per se* do not reveal the causes of variances. Instead, they reveal areas in which important questions should be asked.

## Corrective Action by Managers

The final sequence associated with variance analysis suggested by this section is the managerial response to variance reports. Since the appropriate corrective action is by no means obvious, this brings us back to the general topic of managerial decision-making which, we have previously argued, should be based on incremental cash flows and opportunity costs, if applicable.

In reality there may be a vast number of alternatives to be considered. Managers must take care not to rush into accepting what might appear to be the obvious way to tackle the problem. All possible solutions should be evaluated against three criteria: (a) how realistic are they in the light of the available resources and objectives of the organisation, (b) what are their financial implications and (c) what are the non-quantifiable considerations? Although non-quantifiable, these factors are often highly relevant and important in decision-making. It is important to note that managerial decisions should not be taken solely on the basis of accounting numbers. This is because not all relevant considerations can be translated into accounting numbers and, in any event, the accounting numbers are often rough estimates of the future.

## 15.7 Overview of Production Mix and Yield Variances

In previous Sections we have illustrated the calculation and importance of both the direct material usage and direct labour efficiency variances. We have referred to them collectively as physical variances, since they represent differences between the amount of resources used and the amount of resources that should have been used to produce a given level of output.

In this Section, we can subdivide efficiency (or usage) variances into two component parts. We shall focus only on direct materials and refer to these two new variances as materials mix and materials yield variances. It is useful to remember that the aggregate of these variances will equate to the materials usage variance.

However, there are three necessary conditions before these variances can be calculated. First, the company must use a mix of materials to produce their products and it should be obvious that many organisations use a multiple of inputs in their production process. If this condition is not present, this variance will not apply. Secondly, the various materials must be interchangeable. For example, a firm producing animal feed can use different combinations of different types of grain and protein to produce its final product. In such circumstances, it can be anticipated that manufacturers will substitute, for example, one type of grain for another depending on price and general availability. Alternatively, the production process may be such that it is difficult to control standard proportions precisely. However, if the materials are not interchangeable, then there cannot be a mix variance. For example, a computer manufacturer cannot substitute a keyboard for a screen. Thirdly, the prices of the various inputs must be different as otherwise a variance would not occur under this heading. If all three conditions apply, management may want to subdivide the direct materials usage variance into mix and yield components.

The **mix** variance shows the profit impact of using something other than the standard mix of inputs. This will occur whenever there is a departure from the standard formula and the financial consequences are favourable, e.g. suggesting the use of cheaper than anticipated materials, or adverse, e.g. a larger proportion of more expensive material has been used.

The **yield** variance reflects the relationship between inputs and outputs. This variance will arise whenever there is a difference between the standard output for a given level of inputs and the actual output attained. Again, this variance can be adverse, e.g. the use of inferior materials, or favourable, e.g. the adoption of better production procedures. We shall briefly illustrate the calculation of all the direct materials cost variances using the following example.

## ILLUSTRATION: MATERIALS MIX AND YIELD VARIANCES

The Boyne Company produces a single grade and size of animal feed using two materials, Barley and Oats. The standard cost of each of these inputs and quantities required per bag is as follows:

|             | Barley | Oats |
|-------------|--------|------|
| Cost per kg | €2     | €3   |
| Kgs per bag | 10     | 5    |

During the accounting period, the company produced 7,000 bags of animal feed and the following prices were paid and quantities used (there was no stock at the start or end of the period).

|                        | Barley    | Oats      |
|------------------------|-----------|-----------|
| Kgs purchased and used | 72,000    | 38,000    |
| Total cost             | €136,800  | €106,400  |
| Cost per kg            | €1.90     | €2.80     |

**Requirement:** Calculate the direct materials price and usage variances, and subdivide the usage variance into its mix and yield components.

**Solution and Analysis:** The calculation of both the direct materials price and usage variances can be performed using, for example, the T-account method. The T-accounts for both Barley and Oats are reproduced below using steps designated (1–5) previously presented:

### DIRECT MATERIALS (BARLEY) AT €2 PER KILOGRAM

|                   | Kg     | €       |                     | Kg     | €       |
|-------------------|--------|---------|---------------------|--------|---------|
| Actual input (1)  | 72,000 | 136,800 | Standard output (2) | 70,000 | 140,000 |
|                   |        |         | Usage variance (4)  | 2,000  | 4,000   |

| | Kg | € | | | Kg | € |
|---|---|---|---|---|---|---|
| Price variance (5) | Nil | 7,200 | | | | |
| | | | Balance (3) | | Nil | Nil |
| | 72,000 | 144,000 | | | 72,000 | 144,000 |

DIRECT MATERIALS (OATS) AT €3 PER KILOGRAM

| | Kg | € | | | Kg | € |
|---|---|---|---|---|---|---|
| Actual input (1) | 38,000 | 106,400 | Standard output (2) | | 35,000 | 105,000 |
| | | | Usage variance (4) | | 3,000 | 9,000 |
| Price variance (5) | Nil | 7,600 | | | | |
| | | | Balance (3) | | Nil | Nil |
| | 38,000 | 114,000 | | | 38,000 | 114,000 |

Both the above adverse usage variances (€4,000 and €9,000) can be divided into two components reflecting the financial consequences of mix and yield variances. Before we illustrate these variances it is important to remember that we are dealing with physical variances together with the relative proportions of the direct materials (or direct labour) involved. Thus, in order to identify the financial consequences of these physical variances we will always use the standard or budgeted cost per ingredient.

The information provided indicates that the standard mix per completed bag of animal feed was 10kg of Barley for every 5kg of Oats, giving a standard proportion of 2/3rds to 1/3rd. It should also be noted that a total of 110,000 (72,000 + 38,000) kilograms of raw materials were actually used during the period.

The mix variance is the difference between the budgeted cost for the actual mix of actual quantity of materials used and the budgeted cost of the standard mix of the actual quantity of materials used. It should be noted that the total amount of materials actually used (110,000kg) must always equal the actual quantity used in the standard proportions (110,000kg). This highlights the nature of the mix variance. It is a physical variance and arises whenever the actual and standard proportions differ. Appropriate calculations are presented below (and rounding differences have been eliminated for presentation purposes):

|  | Barley | Oats | Total |
|---|---|---|---|
| 1. Actual mix used (kgs) | 72,000kg | 38,000kg | 110,000kg |
| 2. Standard mix of actual usage based on standard proportions ($^2/_3{}^{rds}$ and $^1/_3{}^{rd}$) | 73,333kg | 36,667kg | 110,000kg |
| Difference (1−2) | 1,333kg | 1,333kg | Nil |
| Standard cost per kg | €2 | €3 | |
| Mix variance | €2,667 F | (€4,000) A | (€1,333) A |

**Note:** Rounding differences

The yield variance is the difference between the budgeted cost of the standard mix of actual total quantity of direct materials used and the budgeted cost for the standard mix based on actual output. The calculations are performed as follows:

|  | Barley | Oats | Total |
|---|---|---|---|
| 2. Standard mix of actual usage based on standard proportions ($^2/_3{}^{rds}$ and $^1/_3{}^{rd}$) | 73,333kg | 36,667kg | 110,000kg |
| 3. Standard mix based on actual output: | | | |
| 7,000 units × 10kg | 70,000kg | | |
| 7,000 units × 5kg | | 35,000kg | |
| Difference (2 − 3) | 3,333kg | 1,667kg | Nil |
| Standard cost per kg | €2 | €3 | |
| Yield variance | (€6,667) A | (€5,000) A | (€11,667) A |

**Note:** Rounding differences

SUMMARY:

|  | Barley | Oats |
|---|---|---|
| Mix variance | €2,667 F | (€4,000) A |
| Yield variance | (€6,667) A | (€5,000) A |
| Total usage variance | (€4,000) A | (€9,000) A |

It will be noted that, in the above table, the mix and yield variances for both direct materials (Barley and Oats) aggregate to the original direct materials usage variance for both ingredients.

In brief, the mix and yield variances indicate that whenever inputs are interchangeable in the production process a favourable direct material usage variance can arise from two sources: (1) using a cheaper mix of materials to produce a given level of output, or (2) using less input for a given level of output. If the assumption of 'interchangeability' is valid, isolation of the mix and yield variances will give management some useful information. However, if this assumption is not present, our analysis will be an ingenious technical exercise but utterly meaningless!

## 15.8 FX Variances

One of the basic principles associated with variance analysis is that managers should only be held responsible for those events over which they are in a position to influence. Specifically, a **controllable cost** is any cost that is subject to the influence of a responsible manager for a given period of time. Thus, a proper variance reporting system could either exclude all **un**controllable costs from a manager's performance report or it could structure the report in such a way as to separately highlight the controllable and uncontrollable variances.

In reality, controllability of costs may be difficult to determine. First of all there is the situation which we have previously described as 'interdependency of variances'. By this we mean that a variance caused by one person may be reflected in another's performance. To illustrate this we have used the example of a purchase of inferior materials that causes adverse usage variances in the production process. Secondly, variance reports relate to specific time periods and, over time, managers change. Thus, there will inevitably be certain 'legacy' issues whereby a current manager may inherit a predecessor's operating inefficiencies or unfavourable agreements negotiated by him with third parties. While assigning responsibility for variances is important, one should not overlook the fact that the basic purpose of variance reporting is to focus on information gathering rather than control. After all, managers are expected to react to (significant) variances even though they are not in a position to influence them. Thus, variance reporting can be viewed as a device to highlight those persons in the organisation who should be first asked questions rather than who are first to be blamed. The ultimate purpose of variance analysis is to gather information to improve future performance.

The dual purposes of assigning responsibility and obtaining information for future improvement can be highlighted with reference to foreign exchange (FX) transactions. The importance of these transactions will vary from company to company but, with the global economy, increasingly more and more trade is done with our international colleagues. Typically, one-third of Ireland's exports are sold to the UK and another one-third to non-Euro countries including the US. In addition, a significant amount of imports are obtained from non-Euro zone countries. For example, sales by an Irish company to the UK will be invoiced in Sterling and sales to the US will be invoiced in Dollars. Therefore, the potential for foreign exchange (FX) fluctuations is obvious and these fluctuations can be favourable or adverse. For example, towards the end of 2002 the FX rate of the dollar and Euro was about €1 = $1. Towards the end of 2009, the exchange rate was about €1 = $1.50.

Firms try to eliminate or minimise FX risk using a variety of techniques. The simplest technique is to agree with your customers that you will trade only in Euro rather than the local currency and this, effectively, transfers any FX risk to your customers and suppliers. A second technique is to 'hedge' the underlying risk which means undertaking equal and opposite transactions. For example, an Irish company selling to the US (in dollars) would borrow similar amounts in dollars. Therefore, any change in FX rates would generate both a FX gain and FX loss of equal amounts. Finally, companies can purchase FX options which will guarantee receipts or payments at specific and agreed exchange rates.

The implication of FX risk for management accounting and variance reporting is that we should isolate all FX variances. We shall illustrate this with reference to the purchase (importation) of direct materials, in the context of standard costing, but the principles can be equally applied to all costs and revenues. We shall argue that variance analysis will be improved by, first, isolating any FX variance and, then, calculating the standard cost (and sales) variances as normal.

## ILLUSTRATION: FX VARIANCE

The Foy Company produces boxes of chocolate in its highly automated Dublin plant in Ireland. The main ingredients are milk chocolate and glucose syrup. The milk chocolate is imported from Switzerland whereas the glucose syrup is imported from the United States. Both the Swiss currency (Swiss franc) and the US currency (dollar) have flexible exchange rates with the Euro and this exposes the Irish plant to foreign exchange fluctuations. The Foy Company operates a standard costing system, with particular emphasis on raw materials, which amounts to 80% of the final cost of the product. The standard raw material cost per unit is calculated on a normal output of 100,000 boxes per month and includes three separate standards as follows:

1. Budgeted exchange rate for year:
   €1 Euro = $1.50 (US) dollars
   €1 Euro = SF 8 (Swiss) francs
2. Physical standard per box of chocolates:
   $1/_2$ kilogram of glucose syrup purchased from the USA
   1 gallon of milk chocolate purchased from Switzerland
3. Monetary standard:
   Glucose syrup is budgeted to cost $6 per kg (€4 per kg)
   Milk chocolate is budgeted to cost SF8 per gallon (€1 per gall)

During the recent month, the Foy Company produced (and sold) 90,000 boxes of chocolate. The management accountant recorded the following information on actual performance:

- 50,000kg of glucose syrup were purchased (and used) for $350,000 and when converted to local currency amounted to €250,000.

- 125,000 gallons of milk chocolate were purchased for SF 1,125,000 and when converted to local currency amounted to €150,000. Apart from the 25,000 gallons in stock at the end of the accounting period, all milk chocolate was used.

**Requirements:**

1. Calculate the material cost variances using traditional standard costing.
2. Calculate the raw material cost variances, separating the FX variance, and comment on your calculations.

**Solution and analysis:** The first part of the requirement is to calculate the materials price and usage variances, ignoring the impact of FX fluctuations. This is done separately for both ingredients. The recording sequence is as follows:

 (i) Record the actual physical and monetary inputs for direct materials on the left-hand (debit) side of the T-account. This will represent the actual amount paid in local currency.
 (ii) Record the physical and monetary standards for the **actual** output on the right-hand (credit) side of the account.
(iii) Record any closing (or opening) stock of direct materials at standard cost. (There is a closing stock of glucose only.)
(iv) Identify the discrepancy in the physical columns. This is referred to as the usage variance, which is multiplied by the standard cost per unit of input.
 (v) Finally, the remaining discrepancy in the T-account can only be explained by the price variance. This is the final variance since the usage discrepancy has been calculated in (iv) above.

DIRECT MATERIALS (GLUCOSE) AT €4 PER KG (TRADITIONAL ANALYSIS)

|  | Kgs | € |  | Kgs | € |
|---|---|---|---|---|---|
| (i) Input | 50,000 | 250,000 | (iii) Finished | | |
| | | | (90,000 boxes) | 45,000 | 180,000 |
| | | | (iv) Usage var. | 5,000 | 20,000 |
| | | | (v) Price var. | N/A | 50,000 |
| | _____ | _____ | (ii) Balance | Nil | Nil |
| | 50,000 | 250,000 | | 50,000 | 250,000 |

DIRECT MATERIALS (CHOCOLATE) AT €1 PER GALLON (TRADITIONAL ANALYSIS)

|  | Galls | € |  | Galls | € |
|---|---|---|---|---|---|
| (i) Input | 125,000 | 150,000 | (iii) Finished | 90,000 | 90,000 |
| | | | (90,000 boxes) | | |
| | | | (iv) Usage var. | 10,000 | 10,000 |

| | | (v) Price var. | N/A | 25,000 |
|---|---|---|---|---|
| | | (ii) Balance | 25,000 | 25,000 |
| 125,000 | 150,000 | | 125,000 | 150,000 |

The direct material price variance is adverse for both ingredients, amounting to €50,000 and €25,000 for glucose and chocolate respectively. However, these price variances automatically include any variance attributable to movements in foreign exchange rates. Effectively we are assigning responsibility for the entire price variance to the purchasing manager even though the movement in FX rates is beyond his ability to influence. Also, the separate impact of FX movements represents relevant information to managers to enable them to improve future performance. Thus, it is recommended that the direct materials variances be recalculated to, first, isolate the FX variance.

**Isolating the FX variance:** The journal entry to record the direct material purchases is produced below where both purchase transactions are recorded at the budgeted exchange rate and the difference between the budgeted amount and the actual amount is recorded separately and immediately as a FX item.

JOURNAL ENTRIES

| | Dr. | Cr. |
|---|---|---|
| Dr. Materials control a/c ($350,000/1.5) | €233,333 | |
| Cr. Bank a/c (Actual payment) | | €250,000 |
| Dr. FX variance a/c (Adverse) | €16,667 | |
| **(Purchase of glucose)** | | |
| Dr. Materials control a/c (SF 1,125,000/8) | €140,625 | |
| Cr. Bank a/c (Actual payment) | | €150,000 |
| Dr. FX variance a/c (Adverse) | €9,375 | |
| **(Purchase of chocolate)** | | |

The direct materials ledger accounts can now be completed as normal. However, the purchase cost is recorded at the budgeted exchange rate, determined at the start of the year. This will result in a revised price variance, since we have now used different input prices – an average of €4.66 and €1.125 for glucose and milk chocolate respectively. However, the original usage variance remains unchanged for both ingredients. It will be recalled that the usage variance reflects a physical phenomenon and is not impacted by FX movements.

### DIRECT MATERIALS (GLUCOSE) AT €4 PER KG (ISOLATING FX VARIANCE)

| | Kgs | € | | Kgs | € |
|---|---|---|---|---|---|
| Input | 50,000 | 233,333 | Finished | | |
| | | | (90,000) | 45,000 | 180,000 |
| | | | Usage var. | 5,000 | 20,000 |
| | | | Price var. | N/A | 33,333 |
| | | | Balance | Nil | Nil |
| | 50,000 | 233,333 | | 50,000 | 233,333 |

### DIRECT MATERIALS (CHOCOLATE) AT €1 PER GALLON (ISOLATING FX VARIANCE)

| | Galls | € | | Galls | € |
|---|---|---|---|---|---|
| Input | 125,000 | 140,625 | Finished | | |
| | | | (90,000) | 90,000 | 90,000 |
| | | | Usage var. | 10,000 | 10,000 |
| | | | Price var. | N/A | 15,625 |
| | | | Balance | 25,000 | 25,000 |
| | 125,000 | 140,625 | | 125,000 | 140,625 |

It will be noted that the (revised) price and FX variance is equal to the original price variance computed in the traditional way and these are summarised as follows:

| | Glucose | Chocolate |
|---|---|---|
| Revised price variance | (€33,333) A | (€15,625) A |
| FX variance | (€16,667) A | (€9,375) A |
| Original price variance | (€50,000) A | (€25,000) A |

The topic addressed in this section was whether FX variances should be reported separately as part of the variance analysis procedure. It is strongly recommended that FX variances be reported separately since individual managers do not have the ability to influence FX rates but also the separate highlighting of these variances improves the type of information available to managers. This argument applies both to cost and revenue variances. For illustration purposes, we concentrated only on cost variances relating to the purchase of direct materials.

## 15.9  Revision Variances

In standard costing, a variance arises whenever a difference occurs between standard and actual costs. It is likely that most variances within a standard costing system will be due either to operational factors or incorrect standards. The important point is that operational variances are down to performance, whereas variances arising from incorrect standards reflect the accuracy or otherwise of the forecasting process. More important is that, if the standards are considered incorrect and unattainable, then individuals cannot be held fully responsible for meeting these standards. In addition, the resulting variance analysis reports are largely meaningless. Managers, including subordinates, may wish to argue that variances are due to incorrect standards. This is because, if they successfully argue that the original standards were incorrect, there is no need for corrective action (which may be very convenient) and this may avoid confrontation between superiors and subordinates. Nevertheless, it should be acknowledged that, in some cases, variances do arise because of incorrect standards. However, one should be sceptical if a significant number of variances are attributed to incorrect standards.

Some companies will try to separate planning and operational variances but this division can be very subjective and is usually clouded with managerial bias. The practical implication is to revise the original budget or targets to reflect the more realistic standards and prepare a variance analysis report. In essence, we are trying to highlight 'revision' variances, i.e. variances due to significantly incorrect standards. However, to do this, the causes of variances must first be determined. Preparing a budget, based on revision variances, represents revising the original targets to what was, with hindsight, considered realistic. A brief illustration of 'revision' variances is presented below and we shall focus only on cost variances. However, the illustration includes the calculation of a sales volume variance as otherwise the reconciliation of the materials cost figures would be complicated due to changes in sales volume.

### ILLUSTRATION: REVISION VARIANCES

The Ardee Marmalade Company uses oranges as the raw material for its only product. It normally produces 30,000 jars of marmalade each month and the budgeted selling price is €3.00 per jar. Each jar of marmalade was budgeted to contain 0.25kg of oranges with a budgeted cost price of €5 per kg. Actual production (and sales) of marmalade in May 20x5 amounted to 32,000 jars. The actual cost of the 13,600kg used for production was €61,200. There were no closing stocks.

At the end of the period, it was discovered that, because of the exceptionally poor quality of oranges available in May 20x5, a special discount of 10% on the previously agreed invoice price was successfully negotiated with the supplier. In addition, because of the inferior quality, it is now accepted that an input of 0.40 kilos per jar was more realistic given the poor quality fruit. The average, actual selling price achieved during the month amounted to €3 per jar.

**Requirement:** Identify the cost variances for materials for May 20x5:

1. Ignoring the impact of poor quality oranges, i.e. under traditional cost variance analysis, and
2. Incorporating the effect of poor quality oranges into the analysis using revision variances. (You may assume that direct materials cost variances are the only variances that should be revised.)

**Solution and analysis:** To put this topic into context it is useful, but not necessary in order to calculate detailed variances, to show the static and flexed budgets together with actual outturn for the period. We shall initially present these figures using traditional variance analysis and based on the original standards. Therefore our initial calculations will not make use of revision variances and the schedule is presented below. It should be noted that the budgeted contribution per unit is €1.75 (€52,500/30,000) and this is also equivalent to the profit per unit in the absence of fixed costs in this illustration:

| TRADITIONAL VARIANCE ANALYSIS | | | |
|---|---|---|---|
| | **Static budget** | **Flexed budget** | Actual |
| Sales (units) | 30,000 | 32,000 | 32,000 |
| Kg/Jar | 0.25 | 0.25 | |
| Price per kg | €5.00 | €5.00 | |
| Total kgs | 7,500kg | 8,000kg | 13,600kg |
| | | | |
| Sales (revenue) | €90,000 | €96,000 | €96,000 |
| Materials cost | €37,500 | €40,000 | €61,200 |
| Profit | €52,500 | €56,000 | €34,800 |
| Sales volume variance | **€3,500 F** | | |
| Operating variances | | **(€21,200) A** | |

The above schedule indicates that, in addition to the favourable sales volume variance of €3,500 (2,000 units × €1.75), the overall direct materials cost variance is €21,200 (A). In turn, the total direct materials cost variance can be divided into its price and usage components and the relevant ledger account is presented below. This indicates a (favourable) price variance of €6,800 and an adverse usage variance of €28,000. The price variance is due to purchasing oranges at an actual cost of €4.50 per kg compared with a budget cost of €5 per kg. Not surprisingly, the usage variance is large because it fully incorporates the acquisition of poor quality oranges.

### DIRECT MATERIALS A/C (ORANGES) @ €5 PER KG

| | Kgs | € | | Kgs | € |
|---|---|---|---|---|---|
| Input | 13,600 | 61,200 | | | |
| | | | Output | | |
| | | | (32,000 × 0.25) | 8,000 | 40,000 |
| | | | Usage var. | 5,600 | 28,000 |
| Price var. | N/a | 6,800 | | | |
| | | | Balance | Nil | Nil |
| | 13,600 | 68,000 | | 13,600 | 68,000 |

In view of the exceptional circumstances during the accounting period, it is preferable to present cost variances making use of revision variances. Specifically, the purchase price of oranges should be revised from €5 to €4.50 per kg. In addition, the quantity used per jar should be revised from 0.25kgs to 0.40kg per jar. It is useful, but not essential, to present a schedule to reflect the revised budget figures and this is presented below. It should be noted that the budgeted contribution (profit) per unit has changed from €1.75 (static) to €1.20 (revised):

### REVISED BUDGET AND REVISION VARIANCES

| | Static budget | Revised, static budget | Flexed budget | Actual |
|---|---|---|---|---|
| Sales (units) | 30,000 | 30,000 | 32,000 | 32,000 |
| Kgs/Jar | 0.25 | 0.40 | 0.40 | |
| Total kgs | 7,500kg | 12,000kg | 12,800kg | 13,600kg |
| Price per kg | €5.00 | €4.50 | €4.50 | |
| | | | | |
| Sales (revenue) | €90,000 | €90,000 | €96,000 | €96,000 |
| Materials cost | €37,500 | €54,000 | €57,600 | €61,200 |
| Profit | €52,500 | €36,000 | €38,400 | €34,800 |
| Revision variances | **(€16,500) A** | | | |
| Sales volume variance | | **€2,400 F** | | |
| Operating variances | | | **(€3,600) A** | |

In the above presentation we have separately calculated the profit impact of revising variances and this amounts to €16,500 A. In addition, the sales volume variance (€2,400, i.e. 2,000 units × €1.20) is presented as usual (although some authors may report this also as a revision variance). Finally, the above schedule indicates that the total operating (direct materials) cost variance is €3,600 A (€57,600 − €61,200). This, in turn, can be divided into price and usage variances. The ledger account below shows that there is no (operational) price variance. Simply, the revised purchase price was €4.50 per kg and this was the actual price paid. However, there is a usage variance amounting to €3,600 A. This usage variance indicates that 13,600kg were used compared with 12,800kg which should have been used (32,000 × 0.4kg) and the difference between these two physical amounts is multiplied by the (revised) price of €4.50 per kg.

DIRECT MATERIALS A/C (ORANGES) @ €4.50 PER KG

| | Kgs | € | | Kgs | € |
|---|---|---|---|---|---|
| Input | 13,600 | 61,200 | | | |
| | | | Output | | |
| | | | (32,000 × 0.4) | 12,800 | 57,600 |
| | | | Usage var. | 800 | 3,600 |
| Price var | N/A | Nil | Price var. | N/A | Nil |
| | | | Balance | Nil | Nil |
| | 13,600 | 61,200 | | 13,600 | 61,200 |

Finally, a variance analysis report can be prepared and is presented below. It highlights the significant impact of purchasing inferior quality oranges, which was not expected and possibly occurred due to adverse weather conditions:

VARIANCE REPORT (PROFIT RECONCILIATION) FOR MONTH OF....

| | | € |
|---|---|---|
| Profit per static budget | | 52,500 |
| Revision variances: | | |
| Materials price revision | 30,000 × 0.4 = 12,000 × (€4.5 − €5.0) | 6,000 F |
| Materials usage revision | 30,000 × (0.40 − 0.25) × €5 | (22,500) A |
| Profit per revised budget | | 36,000 |

| | | |
|---|---|---|
| Sales volume variance | 2,000 × €1.20 | <u>2,400</u> F |
| Profit per flexed budget | | 38,400 |
| Materials price variance | (see T-account) | Nil |
| Materials usage variance | (see T-account) | <u>(3,600)</u> A |
| Actual profit | | <u>34,800</u> |

The main benefits of preparing variance analysis reports, based on revision variances, are:

1. The above presentation provides additional information to managers since it clearly indicates that the most significant item during the period was the deterioration in the quality of oranges purchased.
2. In addition, the above presentation focuses on those elements that are under the control of managers and, for example, good/bad weather is clearly not under their sphere of influence.
3. Large positive planning variances can indicate that standards are set too low and that staff are achieving these too easily. Thus, the motivational element of standards may not be functioning properly.

However, revision variances also have their limitations:

1. If more than one revision variance exists, it can be difficult to fully establish the extent of each prediction error independently.
2. Revision variances can create a 'climate of revisionism' within organisations. By this is meant that all (significant) variances are attributable to planning errors, suggesting that corrective action may not be necessary.
3. Standard setting is not an easy process, particularly for businesses in volatile industries. Thus, standards can quickly become out of date due to unpredictable factors. Therefore, the need to isolate revision variances is time consuming, it adds complexity to the reporting process and may provide very little additional information to managers.
4. In many cases, the identification of revision variances is arbitrary and, sometimes, controversial. Indeed, who has responsibility for deciding to revise certain standards?

In summary, this chapter has discussed standard costing systems and the computation of variances between standard and actual cost. Since any standard is only an estimate of what is likely to be achieved in reality, variances in virtually all cost elements can be expected to occur. Management by exception helps managers focus their attention on those operations where there are significant deviations between planned and actual results. The problem with management by exception is that it indicates **when** corrective action should be taken but not **what** specific action should be taken. Variances are only signals. Corrective action can only come about after investigation and analysis has been undertaken to find out why the performance was inadequate. We therefore discussed the variance investigation decision. We finished the chapter by looking at some of the advanced aspects of variance analysis, namely, mix and yield variances, FX variances and the impact of revision variances arising out of original standards that are subsequently deemed to be incorrect and inappropriate. In the next and final chapter, we discuss certain issues relating to responsibility centres.

## Summary of Learning Objectives

**Learning Objective 1:** Outline the nature and advantages of a standard costing system.

A standard costing system starts with a unit cost, based on two standards, namely a monetary and a physical standard. The monetary standard indicates the expected price to be paid for inputs such as materials, labour and production overheads. The physical standard indicates the expected usage of material, labour and overhead inputs. By multiplying both unit standards together, one computes the standard cost per unit. Because standard costing is based on two standards, two variances may potentially arise which could be theoretically referred to as a monetary and physical variance, but different titles are used in practice.

**Learning Objective 2:** Calculate and interpret material cost variances in terms of usage and price.

The total material cost variance can be subdivided between the materials price variance and the materials usage variance. The materials price variance reflects the profit impact associated with paying more or less (per unit) for the quantity of materials purchased. The materials usage variance reflects the profit impact associated with using more or less than the amount of materials stated in the flexed budget and this physical variance is multiplied by the standard price to identify the total financial consequences.

**Learning Objective 3:** Calculate and interpret labour cost variances in terms of usage and price.

The total direct labour cost variance can be subdivided into a labour rate variance and a labour efficiency variance. The labour rate variance reflects the profit impact associated with paying more or less (per unit) for actual labour hours worked. The labour efficiency variance reflects the profit impact associated with using more or less labour hours than the amount of labour hours stated in the flexed budget and this physical variance is multiplied by the standard rate per labour hour to identify the total financial consequences.

**Learning Objective 4:** Calculate product overhead costs variance using both absorption and direct (variable) costing.

For end of period inventory valuation purposes, product costs can be computed using either absorption or direct (variable) costing methods. The essential difference between these two systems is the accounting treatment of fixed production overhead. Absorption costing considers fixed production overheads as part of closing inventory valuation. In contrast, direct (variable) costing considers product cost as consisting only of variable production costs so that fixed production overheads are written off in full and immediately as incurred to the income statement. Variable production overhead variances will be identical under both systems. Under variable (direct) costing, the only fixed production overhead cost variance is that arising from either spending too much or too little relative to budget and this is referred to as the expenditure variance. In contrast, under absorption costing, while the expenditure variance remains the same as in variable (direct) costing an additional variance – the fixed production overhead volume variance – is calculated. Calculations involving overhead cost variances were presented in the exhibits and illustrations in this chapter using both absorption and variable (direct) costing.

**Learning Objective 5:** Reconcile profit figures using both absorption and direct (variable) costing.

It is useful to report to management all sales and cost variances arising within an accounting period. (These variances can be either favourable or adverse.) It is usual to highlight the significance of these variances either by reporting the percentage variance and/or using some form of trend analysis. End of period reports will usually start with the profit target as per the static budget and finish with the actual profit reported for the period. Such profit reconciliations or profit analysis can be prepared under both absorption and variable (direct) costing. Profit reconciliations were prepared in various exhibits and illustrations in this chapter using both absorption and variable (direct) costing.

**Learning Objective 6:** Describe the causes of variances and indicate when variances should be investigated.

This chapter identified four general causes of variances namely, an accounting error in reporting actual performance, standards being considered unattainable, random errors which are not expected to reoccur and, finally, operating variances. Operating variances are due to incorrect operating procedures and should be rectified before the next accounting period. There are a wide range of possible causes of operating variances and the underlying cause must first be identified before any corrective action can be taken. Finding out the cause of a variance requires investigation and this investigation can be, at times, costly both in terms of time involved and possible disruption to production. Generally, variances should be investigated when the expected benefits of investigation are greater than the expected costs. However, in some cases managers use simple rules of thumb to indicate when a variance should be investigated.

**Learning Objective 7:** Calculate both mix and yield variances.

The physical or usage variances associated with direct materials (or direct labour) can be subdivided into mix and yield components. These variances can only be calculated when there is a mix of physical inputs and these different inputs are interchangeable. The mix variance indicates the profit impact of using something other than the standard mix of inputs. The yield variance reflects the difference between the standard output for a given level of physical inputs and the actual output achieved.

**Learning Objective 8:** Calculate and discuss foreign exchange (FX) variances.

Sometimes a price variance can be caused by fluctuating foreign exchange rates. Clearly such an occurrence is outside the direct control of, say, the purchasing manager. In order to adhere to the principle of controllability when preparing performance reports it is useful to isolate any price variance arising from fluctuating foreign exchange rates from other price variances. Thus, FX and other price variances are reported separately and it is likely that the corrective actions will be different. For example, FX variances may be minimised by way of hedging transactions while other price variances can be rectified by seeking, say, better prices from suppliers.

**Learning Objective 9:** Calculate and report planning and operating variances.

The final complication arising out of our study of standard costing relates to the segregation of planning from operating variances. Planning (or revision) variances are prepared when it is accepted that the original targets were unrealistic in light of the conditions prevailing during the accounting period under review. For example a bad harvest may cause raw material prices to significantly increase. To attribute all this adverse price variance to the performance of the purchasing manager conflicts with the principle of controllability. Therefore, it is recommended to first isolate any planning variances before calculating the operating variances and assigning appropriate responsibility. The limitation of revision variances is that they can create a 'climate of revisionism' whereby major variances are attributed to unrealistic standards in the first instance, given the conditions prevailing.

## Questions

### Review Questions

(See Appendix One for Solutions to Review Questions **15.1** and **15.2**)

*Question 15.1 (Production Overhead Cost Variances under Absorption Costing)*

The OHAR Company applies overhead on the basis of direct labour hours in department B. Two direct labour hours are required for each product unit. Planned production for the period was set at 9,000 units. Manufacturing overhead was budgeted at €135,000 for the period of which 20% of this cost is considered fixed in relation to volume changes. The company uses an absorption costing system, based on direct labour hours.

During the period, the 17,200 hours actually worked during the period resulted in production of 8,500 units. Variable manufacturing overhead costs incurred were €108,500, and fixed manufacturing overhead costs amounted to €28,000.

## Requirements:

1. Calculate the following production overhead variances:
    the variable overhead spending variance for the period.
    the variable overhead efficiency variance for the period.
    the fixed overhead spending (budget) variance for the period.
    the fixed production overhead volume variance for the period.
2. Who is responsible for the fixed production overhead volume variance?

*Question 15.2 (Profit Reconciliation under Standard Costing (Variable and Absorption))*

You have recently been appointed as management accountant to TOD Limited – a company that manufactures a standard size of aluminium window for the construction industry. The company has just finished its initial three months (i.e. the first quarter) of operations and your first major assignment is to compare actual performance with budget.

Prior to commencing business, the company's financial advisors had prepared the following standard costs and projections, based on the contribution format, for the forthcoming year:

| | | |
|---|---|---|
| Sales price (per unit) | | €25 |
| Direct materials (10 feet @ €0.60 per foot) | €6 | |
| Direct labour (4 hours @ €2 per hour) | €8 | |
| Variable production overhead | €4 | |
| Variable administration costs | €2 | (20) |
| Budgeted contribution (per unit) | | 5 |
| Fixed production overhead per annum | | €120,000 |
| Fixed administration overhead per annum | | 80,000 |

Based on these figures, the company planned to reach break-even point of 10,000 units for the first quarter i.e. 40,000 units per annum.

The actual income statement (in draft format) for the first quarter in which 9,500 units were produced and sold was presented to you as follows:

INCOME STATEMENT – FOR THREE MONTHS ENDING....

|  | € | € |
|---|---|---|
| Sales (9,500 units @ €26 each) |  | 247,000 |
| Direct materials (100,000 feet) | 61,000 |  |
| Direct labour (40,000 hours) | 72,000 |  |
| Variable production overhead | 40,000 |  |
| Fixed production overhead | 18,000 | (191,000) |
| Production margin (surplus) |  | 56,000 |
| Variable administration overhead | 24,000 |  |
| Fixed administration overhead | 22,000 | (46,000) |
| Net profit for quarter |  | 10,000 |

The managing director of TOD Ltd, who has little knowledge of accounting, was pleased to have recorded a profit during the quarter even though the break-even production target was not achieved. He has asked you to prepare a statement showing the variances from budget.

**Requirements:**

1. Prepare both static and flexed budget income statements for the first quarter using variable (direct) cost principles.
2. Prepare a schedule of variances, reconciling budget with actual profit using variable (direct) costing.
3. Prepare a schedule of variances, reconciling budget with actual profit using absorption costing.

## Intermediate Questions

*Question 15.3 (Standard Cost Variances and Decision-making)*

As the assistant management accountant of Horseman Limited, you are responsible for the standard cost variance calculations arising from the use of two machines.

Each machine (number 1 and 2) produces the same end product (X50) from the same raw material (B30). However, Machine 1 is an older version of Machine 2 and as a result it is believed to be less reliable and more likely to break down or produce defective output. There are no other notable differences between the machines.

You have been provided with the following data for the most recent month (May) for each machine:

Machine 1 produced 1,760 units of X50 in May from 9,000kg of B30. Machine 2 produced a total of 2,000 units of X50 by also using 9,000kg of B30. The standard input of B30 required for one unit of X50 (on either machine) is 4kg. The total purchase of B30 for the two machines in the month came to €47,600 (there was no opening or closing stock). The budgeted cost per kg of B30 is €2.19 and each machine was originally budgeted to produce 2,200 units in a month.

Each machine is operated by one dedicated staff member, who must stay beside the machine while it is producing. The standard labour time per unit of X50 is 12 minutes and the contracted (and actually) hourly rate of pay is €10 – there is no overtime premium. The operator of each machine was paid a total of €3,100 for the month. Neither operator performs any other work in the company and they are only paid for the hours they are actually in attendance at the machine (however long that may be). Both operators are equally competent and have no impact on the productivity of the machine.

In six months' time, Horseman intends to cease production of X50 at which point both machines will be decommissioned. Management believe that, for the next six months, the variances of the month of May will be exactly the same for each subsequent month.

**Requirements:**

1. From the information given, calculate the following variances for the month of May:
   > Material Price and Usage
   > Labour Rate and Efficiency

   The Material Usage and Labour Efficiency variances should be split between each machine, based on the information given.
2. (a) Advise management on what is the maximum amount they should be willing to pay a maintenance company to get Machine 1 to operate at the same efficiency and output levels as Machine 2. (In this context efficiency refers to only direct materials and not direct labour.) Management believes that this can be done before the final six-month period commences and that it will be successful, if undertaken. You should confine your analysis to this six-month period.
   (b) Outline **three** other pieces of information that should be sought by management before a final decision is made on using the maintenance company.

Source: Chartered Accountants Ireland, Management Accounting and Business Finance, Autumn, 2006 (adapted)

*Question 15.4 (Planning and Operating Variances)*

The New Chip Marmalade Company uses Spanish oranges as the raw material for its only product. Based on previous experience, it normally produces 32,000 jars of marmalade each month.

Oranges are purchased in standard crates containing 40 kilos of fruit and were expected to cost €200 per crate during 20x5. Because of the exceptionally poor crop of oranges available in May 20x5, however, a special discount of 10% on the previously agreed price was successfully negotiated. The actual cost of 340 crates (i.e. 13,600kg) used for production in May was €61,200.

Actual production of marmalade in May 20x5 amounted to 32,000 jars. Each jar was budgeted to contain 0.25 kilos of oranges but, because of the exceptional circumstances, it is now accepted that 0.40 kilos per jar was more realistic given the heavy incidence of poor quality fruit.

Each jar of marmalade is budgeted to sell at €5.00 per jar. However, during the month of May, the average selling price amounted to €4.00 per jar.

**Requirement:** Prepare a variance analysis report for materials for May 20x5:

1. Ignoring the impact of poor quality oranges, i.e. based on traditional variance analysis, and
2. Incorporating the effect of poor quality oranges into the analysis by the separation of planning and operational variances, i.e. based on revision variances.

Note: Additional calculations have been included in the solution in order to provide an overall context.


## Question 15.5 (FX Variances under Standard Costing)

The EXFX Company produces chocolate bars in its Irish plant. The main ingredient is milk chocolate imported from Switzerland. The company operates a standard costing system, within which a foreign exchange variance in addition to the normal material price and material usage variances is calculated. The standard raw material cost per bar is based on the following:

Budgeted exchange rate for year: 1 Euro = SF 10 (Swiss) francs
Physical standard per bar: 1 gallon of milk chocolate purchased from Switzerland
Price standard: Milk chocolate will cost SF5 per gallon

During the recent month, the EXFX Company produced (and sold) 80,000 bars of chocolate. During that month, 120,000 gallons of milk chocolate were purchased from the Swiss sister company for SF 1,200,000 at a Euros equivalent of €100,000. Apart from the 30,000 gallons in stock at the end of the accounting period, all milk chocolate was used in production.

1. The FX variance for the above period amounts to:
   (a) €120,000 favourable
   (b) €20,000 favourable
   (c) €150,000 adverse
   (d) €9,375 adverse
2. The materials usage variance (after calculating the FX variance) is:
   (a) €120,000 favourable
   (b) €10,000 adverse
   (c) €5,000 adverse
   (d) None of the above

3. The price variance (after calculating the FX variance) is:
   (a)   €120,000 favourable
   (b)   €9,375 adverse
   (c)   €15,625 favourable
   (d)   €60,000 adverse

*Question 15.6 (Reporting Revenue and Cost Variances)*

All characters in this case are fictitious.

One could say, with confidence, that Joe Barrett was born into the domestic central heating oil distribution business. He was born on 11 May 1970, the exact same day that his father, Victor, had signed a contract with a major oil importing company to set up a domestic central heating oil distribution business in North County Dublin. In 1970, domestic central heating was still a relatively rare phenomenon in Ireland. However, Victor Barrett anticipated that the rapid economic development in Ireland around that time would herald a massive house building programme which, in turn, would stimulate a latent demand for domestic central heating systems. It was generally felt that domestic central heating systems were cheaper than electricity, much cleaner than solid fuel systems, e.g. coal or anthracite, and generally much more convenient – heat could be obtained at the touch of a button. In addition, people were generally confident of their oil supplies – that was before the first oil shock!

Few consumers realise that domestic central heating oil comprises either gas oil (oil) or kerosene (kero). Typically, old houses use gas oil in their domestic central heating systems whereas more recently built houses burn kero. (Kero is also used as aviation fuel – a fact that sometimes causes restricted market availability.)

The domestic central heating oil distribution business is a relatively simple one: the local distributor purchases the oil from a major oil importer for an agreed price per litre and then resells it to domestic householders at a higher price. Essentially domestic central heating oil is a commodity – all oil distributors sell the same product. In recent times, the market was becoming increasingly competitive due to the presence of several similar oil distributing companies in the North County Dublin area. Also, with the recent oil price volatility domestic customers were becoming more price sensitive.

After leaving school, Joe Barrett attended a college in Dublin where his social and sporting performance was more notable than his academic achievements. Joe didn't mind, as he couldn't anticipate, then, the problems and decisions which he now had to face. Shortly after Joe's graduation, Joe's father bought an apartment in Spain and left Joe, the only child, to run the business! There was little warning or discussion between parent and son. Victor, literally took his passport and company Visa card, said 'goodbye', and flew Ryanair to Murcia about 12 months ago. He left behind his Spanish mobile number.

During the past 12 months, Joe settled in as Managing Director and was content to answer the phone and take orders from customers and do other things as requirements dictated. The winter months were incredibly busy compared with the more leisurely summer months. He got on well with his staff comprising a secretary, a book-keeper, a receptionist, three sales persons, three drivers and a yardman. There were also a few part-time employees. If there was no work to do during the summer, Joe would head off early to play golf – the links course was beside the business premises. (This location ensured that the development value of his business site was extremely high.)

Joe Barrett has just received his first set of 'management accounts' for the current year end (**Exhibit 1**). He was surprised that they were so brief and that no mention was made of key performance indicators. The management accounts contained only financial information of a bad news variety. He knew that the price of oil had increased during the year and that sales, in volume terms, had fallen as a result. Now after his first year of trading he noted that the business has reported a loss before tax of €760,000, compared to a budgeted profit of €65,000. He quickly realised that he needed some basic financial advice in understanding both what had happened during the year, but also in planning for next year. He has asked for your help.

EXHIBIT 1: BARRETT OIL PRODUCTS:
PROFIT SUMMARY FOR YEAR ENDED 31 DECEMBER 20X1

| Income statement | Budget CY | Actual CY |
|---|---|---|
| Sales (gas oil) | 25,000,000 litres | 24,000,000 litres |
| Sales (kero) | 13,000,000 litres | 12,000,000 litres |
| | 38,000,000 litres | 36,000,000 litres |
| | € | € |
| Sales (gas oil) | 6,000,000 | 6,960,000 |
| Sales (kero) | 3,250,000 | 3,600,000 |
| COGS (gas oil) | (5,000,000) | (6,000,000) |
| COGS (kero) | (2,600,000) | (3,600,000) |
| Gross Margin | 1,650,000 | 960,000 |
| Distribution costs (fixed) | (805,000) | (895,000) |
| Administration Costs (fixed) | (750,000) | (795,000) |
| Operating Profit (Loss) PBIT | 95,000 | (730,000) |
| Interest paid | (30,000) | (30,000) |
| Profit before tax | 65,000 | (760,000) |
| Taxation | (20,000) | (NIL) |
| Profit after tax | 45,000 | (760,000) |

| | | |
|---|---|---|
| Retained earnings at start of year | 388,000 | 900,000 |
| Retained earnings at end of year | 433,000 | 140,000 |

BARRETT OIL PRODUCTS
BALANCE SHEET AT 31 DECEMBER 20X1

| | Actual CY €|
|---|---|
| Non-current assets | |
| Property, plant and equipment (net) | 800,000 |
| Current Assets | |
| Stock | 900,000 |
| Debtors | 900,000 |
| Bank | 100,000 |
| | 2,700,000 |
| Financed By | |
| Shareholders' funds (share capital & retained earnings) | 800,000 |
| Long-term loans payable (6%) | 500,000 |
| Current Liabilities (trade payables) | 1,400,000 |
| | 2,700,000 |
| CY = current year, PY = previous year | |

A number of issues required Joe's immediate attention. He realised that Ireland, in terms of energy requirements, was the most import-dependent country in Europe, importing over 90% of the fuel needed to keep the country running. The country spends, on average, about €100m every week on energy, with 98% of the power being supplied by fossil fuels – mainly oil, gas and coal which create vast amounts of greenhouse gases and are becoming increasingly more expensive for us to use. This creates two major pressures. The first is that the constant haemorrhaging of money out of the country for such consumption is not sustainable. The other is our Kyoto commitment to limit polluting greenhouse gas emissions which will be enforced by the European Union. However, the reality is that Ireland's $CO_2$ emissions will be several million tonnes over limit and some experts believe that this will cost the State about €2 billion – money that will go to purchase the euphemistically called 'carbon polluting credits', allowing us to pump excess $CO_2$ into the atmosphere. This arrangement has been described as paying your neighbour to dump your rubbish on his lawn!

Remarkably, when it comes to renewable energy resources, Ireland is the envy of Europe, with the best wind regime, the best growing conditions for timber and an excellent solar system for certain ground and water heating systems. In addition, solar energy is not a myth. Every year, Ireland receives the equivalent of 600 times its total energy consumption in solar irradiation. And yet these clean energy sources now supply just 2% of Ireland's energy requirements! Joe Barrett, a political activist with the Green Party, wondered about the long-term potential of the product he was exclusively selling.

Related to this was the fact that he had recently been contacted by a National Petrol company offering one of their garages for rent for an annual fee – to be negotiated. The garage has currently an annual turnover (52 weeks) of €2,100,000 (3,000,000 litres) on which a gross profit margin of 10% is generated. In addition, the garage also sells newspapers, sweets and grocery items in the amount of €1,000 per week. The gross profit margin is 28% on these goods and the existing fixed costs of operating and maintaining the site is estimated at €3,000 per week. However, included in this sum is a wages item of €500 per week, which could be filled by a current employee of BOP who was due to retire. The employee concerned was agreeable to moving to the new site for the same salary and waive his pension rights, which would otherwise be paid directly by Barrett Oil Products. In addition, Joe Barrett intended to spend a total of €30,000 for the first year on advertising his new location.

In addition, he was concerned at the high level of distribution costs (€895,000 was actually incurred during the recent year, as disclosed by the management accounts) in his business. The cost elements included under this heading comprised depreciation, maintenance and insurance of distribution trucks, drivers' wages and other miscellaneous distribution costs. He was happy to consider them as a 'fixed cost'. Currently, the same price per litre is quoted to all customers, but, sometimes, discounts are offered to special or valued customers. Barrett realised that the firm's 'cost to serve' was heavily influenced by transportation costs i.e. distance (mileage) between firm and customer, the 'fill rate' i.e. the amount of litres ordered by each customer, together with the number of orders/deliveries made, irrespective of the quantity of oil ordered.

**Requirements:** You are required to draft a report to Joe Barrett in which you should address the following issues (and introduce other issues as you deem appropriate):

(a) Explain to Joe Barrett whether Barrett Oil Products (BOP) should compete on the basis of cost leadership or product differentiation.

(b) Clearly outline the critical success factors for this business and highlight the related performance measures/indicators, which Joe should monitor on a regular basis. (Your answer can be in any Scorecard format.) Briefly justify why you have selected them.

(c) Detail some of the benefits and also some problems associated with introducing your performance measurement system into BOP.

(d) Calculate his BEP (in litres) for the current year using actual data. Specify two crucial assumptions that you have made.

(e) Prepare a financial performance report reconciling the original budgeted profit of €65,000 for the period with the actual reported loss of €760,000 and briefly comment on the most significant items. In addition, comment on the usefulness of your calculations in preparing a budget for the forthcoming year.

(f) What is the maximum rent Joe Barrett should pay for the petrol site assuming a 52-week year and a required 2% return on total sales of the garage?

## Question 15.7 (Discussion Question on Standard Costing)

Write an essay on one of the following topics:

1. Variance analysis is past-focused and therefore, is wasted effort. Critically discuss the above statement, clearly providing arguments supporting and refuting it.

   Source: Chartered Accountants Ireland, Management Accounting and Business Finance, Paper 3, Summer 2006 (adapted)

2. A variance indicates a deviation from a plan, but not all variances should be investigated. Elaborate on this statement in order to explain to your colleague.

   Source: Chartered Accountants Ireland, various exams

3. In recent years, some writers have argued that standard costing and variance analysis is likely to generate behaviour which is inconsistent with the strategic manufacturing objectives that companies need to achieve in order to survive in today's intensively competitive international economic environment. Explain the arguments in favour of the relevance and irrelevance of standard costing and variance analysis in the modern manufacturing environment.

   Source: Chartered Accountants Ireland, various exams

## Advanced Questions

### Question 15.8 (Revenue and Cost Variances and Miscellaneous Issues)

Hex Limited manufactures computer games, and has been involved in the industry for over 20 years. The CEO is proud of the company's achievements so far, especially in what he calls a highly volatile, unpredictable and unstable industry. While Hex has always enjoyed moderate success, it has grown exceptionally since 2002. It has built most of its success on one game called X1, a product which is aimed largely at males aged 18 to 25. This year is the game's fifth year on the market, and the CEO of Hex views this as 'the long-term earner'. Based on this success, Hex recently released two other games on the market called X2 and X3. These are based on the same technology as X1 and are aimed primarily at the same market. The budgeted figures for 20x6 were as follows:

| Product | Volume | Selling price € | Variable cost € |
|---|---|---|---|
| X1 | 12,000 | 8 | 6 |
| X2 | 1,000 | 10 | 6 |
| X3 | 2,000 | 10 | 4 |

The actual figures for 20x6 are detailed below:

| Product | Volume | Selling price € | Variable cost € |
|---|---|---|---|
| X1 | 12,200 | 8 | 7 |
| X2 | 500 | 10 | 6 |
| X3 | 2,000 | 14 | 4 |

While a leading games magazine had predicted at the start of 20x6 that industry sales for these niche games would be approximately 100,000 units, an industry report has stated that these games were more popular than expected, with total sales of 110,000 units registered in 20x6.

**Requirements:**

1. Reconcile the static budget contribution to the actual contribution for Hex for 20x6. Your reconciliation should include a detailed calculation of the following variances:
   (a) Sales price variance
   (b) Sales volume variance
   (c) Variable cost variance.
2. Comment on the possible reasons for your results in (1).
3. Calculate the market size and market share variances for Hex for 20x6.
4. Outline **four** advantages of implementing a standard costing system in a modern manufacturing environment.
5. Outline **four** difficulties arising when establishing a standard costing system.

> Source: Chartered Accountants Ireland, Management Accounting and Business Finance, P3, Summer 2007 (adapted)

*Question 15.9 (Direct Materials and Labour Variances Including Mix and Yield)*

Ellis Limited manufactures a chemical compound called 'Base T' which it sells to the pharmaceutical industry. The standard input of 10 litres should produce 7 litres of

Base T. (Thus there is normal wastage of 3 litres.) The standard inputs of each raw material and standard price are as follows:

| Raw material | Quantity (litres) | Price € | Total € |
|---|---|---|---|
| Chemical X | 5 | 1.40 | 7.00 |
| Chemical Y | 3 | 1.80 | 5.40 |
| Chemical Z | 2 | 1.15 | 2.30 |

The standard cost of labour includes one hour of skilled labour and two hours of unskilled labour at €45 and €15 per hour respectfully. Standard production of output is 10 litres per labour hour (both skilled and unskilled in the standard proportions of 1/3 skilled and 2/3 unskilled). The following were the actual results for June 20x7 in which 72,450 litres were produced:

| Raw material | Quantity (litres) | Actual price € | Total cost € |
|---|---|---|---|
| Chemical X | 48,000 | 1.68 | 80,640 |
| Chemical Y | 32,000 | 1.95 | 62,400 |
| Chemical Z | 20,000 | 1.30 | 26,000 |
|  | 100,000 |  | 169,040 |

The actual number of labour hours worked consisted of 2,900 skilled labour hours which cost €48 per hour and 5,100 hours of unskilled labour hours which cost €16 per hour. You have been asked by the managing director of the company to provide a detailed variance analysis of the material and labour costs incurred for June 20x7.

## Requirements:

1. Prepare a detailed reconciliation of the budgeted costs of both material and labour to the actual costs incurred using the following variances:
   (a) Materials price variance
   (b) Materials usage variance (subdivided into mix and yield components)
   (c) Labour rate variance
   (d) Labour efficiency (usage) variance (subdivided into its mix and yield components)
2. Briefly outline the difficulties when a manufacturing company tries to introduce a standard costing system.

Source: Chartered Accountants Ireland, Management Accounting and Business Finance, P3, Autumn 2007

*Question 15.10 (Revision Variances with Mix and Yield Calculations)*

Sweet Babies Limited produces infant milk formula for sale through retail outlets. Profit margins are tight and, as part of its cost control procedures, the company operates a standard costing system. The products are produced in separate batches and the standard (ingredient) costs for 'Formula 2+' (i.e. for toddlers over two years of age) are as follows:

| Milk proteins | 700kg @10c per kg | €70.00 |
| Fatty acids | 400kg @ 16c per kg | €64.00 |
| Lactose | 99kg @ 33c per kg | €32.67 |
| Minerals etc. | 1kg @ 200c per kg | €2.00 |
| Standard ingredient cost | | €168.67 |

During the previous accounting period, various unforeseen factors caused an increase in costs. For example, bad weather caused the increase in the price of milk proteins by 20% and thus a price of 12c per kg would have been more realistic in the circumstances. In addition, increases in processing cost due to high fuel prices meant that the normal price for fatty acids was 19c per kg, although more aggressive purchasing policy resulted in actual purchase cost being slightly less than this amount. It was decided to incorporate these changes into the standard cost system before the calculation of usual cost variances.

During the above period, only one batch of 'Formula 2+' was produced and the following actual results occurred:

| Milk proteins | 742kg @12c per kg | €89.04 |
| Fatty acids | 428kg @ 18c per kg | €77.04 |
| Lactose | 125kg @ 32c per kg | €40.00 |
| Minerals etc. | 1kg @ 95c per kg | €0.95 |
| Standard ingredient cost | | €207.03 |

**Requirements:**

1. Calculate the total cost variance for the batch produced during the period and divide this total variance into planning (uncontrollable) and operating (controllable) variances.
2. For each of the four ingredients, analyse the total operating variance into price and usage components, using the revised standards applicable during the period.
3. Comment on the advantages and disadvantages of variance analysis using planning and operating variances.
4. Calculate the mix and yield variances, based on the information provided.

Source: Chartered Accountants Ireland, CA Proficiency 2, Strategic Finance and Management Accounting, Sample Paper, 2009

*Question 15.11 (Planning and Operating Variances)*

Brady Limited manufactures a consumer food product. The firm's Production Manager, Ms Mary Smith, has become very concerned about the levels of production efficiency achieved by the firm during the previous year and feels that unless some form of remedial action is taken immediately the company may begin to lose market share to their increasingly cost-efficient competitors.

Eager to investigate this issue further, Mary has accumulated the following actual information for the quarter ended 30 June 2008, in relation to the production of the firm's principal product:

| | |
|---|---|
| Actual production | 20,000 units |
| Actual materials usage | 90,000 kilos |
| Actual cost of materials used | €1,305,000 |

The company has always used a standard costing system and it currently contains the following predetermined standards, having last updated in January 2006:

| | |
|---|---|
| Standard price of materials | €14 per kilo |
| Standard usage of materials per unit | 5 kilos |

In accumulating this information, Mary was informed by the firm's Management Accountant that in the quarter ended 30 June 2008 the market price of materials had increased at the start of the period and had remained static at €15 per kilo. Additionally, the introduction of new production machinery during the quarter resulted in the standard amount of materials used per unit increasing to 5.5 kilos as a result of teething problems with the new machinery. However, Mary is now convinced that these issues have been resolved and consequently she feels that production will be more efficient in the near future.

**Requirements:**

1. Based on the above information, prepare a schedule indicating the total costs of materials based on the original standard, the revised standard and actual cost of materials for the above quarter and indicate the total variances involved.
2. Calculate the materials price variance and the materials usage variance associated with both the revision and operating variances for the period under review.
3. Based on your results from (1) and (2) above, prepare a memorandum for Mary analysing the firm's production efficiency and offering whatever suggestions for improvement you consider appropriate.
4. It has since transpired that, as Mary believes that Brady's standard costing system has become increasingly irrelevant, she is actively considering the possibility of abandoning the entire system altogether. What advice would you offer Mary? Explain your answer fully.

Source: Chartered Accountants Ireland, CA Proficiency 2, Strategic Finance and Management Accounting, teaching material

## Question 15.12 (Planning and Operational Variances)

Ashcroft Limited manufactures a single product, and uses a standard costing system as a routine part of its management control system. However, this standard costing system only applies to direct materials and direct labour due to the insignificance of its overhead costs. The following information per unit is presented to you:

|  | € | € |
|---|---|---|
| Selling price per unit |  | 200 |
| Less: 4kg materials @ €20 per kg | 80 |  |
| 6 hours labour @ €7 per hour | 42 |  |
|  |  | 122 |
| Contribution per unit |  | 78 |

For Period 3, 2,500 units were budgeted to be produced and sold but the actual production and sales were 2,850 units at €200 each. The following information was also available in respect of Period 3:

At the commencement of Period 3 the normal material became unobtainable and it was necessary to use an alternative. Unfortunately, 0.5kg per unit extra was required. The price of the alternative was revised to €16.50 per kg. In the event, actual usage was 12,450kg which cost €18 per kg.

The Trade Union representative pointed out that a previously agreed salary increase had not been paid. In addition, there were unexpected difficulties working with the alternative materials. Management now accept that the hourly rate should be €8 per labour hour and this was the actual rate paid during the period. A total of 18,800 hours were paid for.

After using traditional standard cost variances for some time, Ashcroft Limited is contemplating adapting its traditional variance reporting system to differentiate between planning and operational variances.

### Requirements:

1. Prepare a statement reconciling budgeted contribution for Period 3 with actual contribution, using traditional sales, material and labour cost variances.
2. Prepare an operating statement that reconciles the budgeted contribution for the actual volume of sales to the actual contribution, reporting on the constituent planning and operational variances separately.
3. Explain the meaning of the variances shown in your reconciliation statement in requirement (2).

Source: Chartered Accountants Ireland, CA Proficiency 2, Strategic Finance and Management
Accounting, Summer 2009 (adapted)

# Responsibility Centres and Corporate Structure

LEARNING OBJECTIVES

When you have completed studying this chapter you should be able to:

1. Explain the nature, advantages and limitations of decentralisation.
2. Distinguish between the different types of responsibility centres and the different types of performance measures useful in evaluating such responsibility centres.
3. Calculate, interpret and distinguish between return on investment (RoI) and Residual Income (RI).
4. Calculate and interpret Economic Value Added.
5. Explain the nature of and methods of determining transfer prices.
6. Describe the reasons for both profit boosting and profit depressing transfer prices.
7. Describe contingency theory and its role in managerial accounting.
8. Describe the purpose and elements of a management compensation scheme.

## 16.1  Corporate Structure and Decentralisation

Decision-making and control are meaningful concepts only when an objective exists. An objective is a specific target to be achieved in the future. Individuals have objectives but enterprises do not! Rather there are objectives FOR enterprises. In the context of a business enterprise, each participant is interested in his own economic welfare and it is logical to assume that the interests of different stakeholders are conflicting. Shareholders are interested in earning a return on their investment; employees are interested in secure and well paid employment; customers are interested in a quality product at low cost which provides high customer value. These interests are not necessarily mutually exclusive. There is likely to be some basic level of agreement since it is usually in the interest of all stakeholders if the business continues to exist. We have assumed in this book that consensus on objectives can be reached and that a corporate objective usually takes the form of profit maximisation or, at least, making a satisfactory profit in the circumstances prevailing.

In pursuit of corporate objectives, we have stressed a technical and behavioural element. The technical element represents the flow of information to managers. Some of this information concerns the internal operations of the firm. Other information relates to the environment in which the company operates. This information may be obtained routinely or on an ad-hoc basis and it may be communicated formally or informally to participants. The behavioural element represents the decisions taken by managers in response to this information. It is true to say that information is power.

The final issue that we need to address in this book is that of corporate structure including responsibility centres and how the performance of responsible managers should be evaluated. In small organisations all important decisions are usually made by one dominant individual. However, as an organisation grows and becomes more complex it is difficult and undesirable for one individual to make all the important decisions. Simply, there are too many decisions to be made and no single person can control all functions. It follows that in an organisation of substantial size – measured with reference to, for example, sales revenue, total assets or total employees – there must be an organisation structure in existence. Traditionally this structure is formal and hierarchical, whereby the objectives and strategy of the business are established by top management and these are communicated to members of the organisation. Individual managers must decide on the tasks that are to be performed in order to achieve these objectives and on the resources that are to be used. In turn progress toward the objectives must be monitored through a variety of performance reports (containing financial and non-financial information) and corrective action taken when the need arises. Thus, control consists of the managerial response to performance reports but this managerial activity must take place within an overall structure. If managers are to be held accountable for their performances, they must have clearly defined areas of responsibility based on an organisational structure as otherwise their evaluation would be meaningless. The situation described above is summarised in **Exhibit 16.1.**

EXHIBIT 16.1: PROGRESS TOWARDS CORPORATE OBJECTIVES

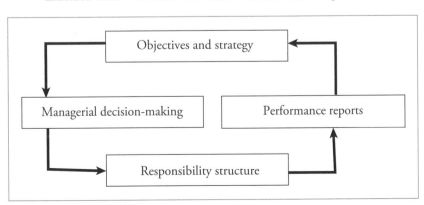

## Decentralisation

As the organisation grows in size and complexity, successful management of it by one dominant individual or a small group of people becomes more difficult. In order to overcome this problem there is general agreement on the need for some form of decentralisation, that is, the breaking down of the organisation into subunits where individual managers have the freedom to make their own decisions. Thus, the essence of 'decentralisation' is the freedom given to managers to make decisions. Such decisions concern, inter alia:

- pricing
- product mix
- purchasing
- operating processes
- customer relations.

In reality, an organisation structure will be partly centralised and partly decentralised. For example, in a university, it makes sense if advertising, administration or even staff recruitment is centralised but, typically, the academic function of the university is facilitated by individual departments which teach specialised subjects, under the direction of a subject professor. The following advantages of decentralisation should be noted:

1. It frees top management from day-to-day operational decision-making thereby enabling it to focus more on strategic matters and providing overall direction for the company. It has been argued by many authors that top managers should spend more of their time on reviewing strategic issues. This means thinking about what the business should become, what trends may emerge that may impact upon it, or what new and exciting development it could initiate itself. This 'helicopter viewing' as it is sometimes called requires a large amount of managerial time and there are often more than enough highly urgent operational issues to distract and absorb a manager's time and attention.

2. It improves the decision-making within the company by ensuring that those personnel thoroughly acquainted with an aspect of the firm make decisions concerning it. In other words, local decision-makers have the benefit of local knowledge. In theory, local managers should be better informed about their customers, suppliers and employees than top management who are remote from the situation. This is particularly appropriate in a multinational corporation whereby important social, legal and language barriers can be minimised by decentralisation. If there is increased efficiency, then this should be good for the organisation as a whole.

3. There is a more rapid response to environmental changes and opportunities by eliminating cumbersome and slow communications which would be required in a centralised firm. This delivers the flexibility to respond quickly to emerging situations.

4. It provides additional motivation for managers due to their increased status within the company as important decision-makers. Decentralised managers have greater freedom in their roles, thus making their activities more challenging while offering

the opportunity to achieve self-fulfilment. In addition, motivation is increased due to the ability of the manager to exercise his individual initiative. At a minimum, managerial attitudes towards the organisation should be improved.

5.  It provides a good training ground for managers. By giving managers of local units the freedom to make decisions, the firm can identify which individuals are or are not good top management material.

The disadvantages of decentralisation must also be noted. Initially there is the cost of investment in formal training. Also, there may be more administration/reporting and possible duplication of functions since each responsibility centre is likely to have, for example, its own information and accounting system. Chiefly there is the possibility of dysfunctional or suboptimal decision-making by individuals. This arises if a manager makes a decision that is beneficial to his own unit or for his own personal benefit, but which is not in the interests of the organisation as a whole. This behaviour may be generated by 'short-termism' i.e. actions aimed at securing higher near-future financial results to the detriment of better long-term results. Because of the rewards on offer, such as pay and/or bonuses which are linked to profit performance, managers are likely to try to maximise profits in the short-term to the detriment of long-term performance. This situation represents a lack of goal congruence or harmony between the goals of the individual manager and the goals of the organisation as a whole. This lack of harmony may be associated with a commitment to a unit rather than to the organisation as a whole. Of course, a certain amount of friendly rivalry may be desirable within organisations but it could lead to friction and uncooperative behaviour. In addition, a decentralised structure creates two further issues which we have not specifically addressed in previous chapters, namely:

1.  What are the appropriate types of responsibility centres and how do you evaluate them? (This is discussed below in **Section 16.2** in relation to both financial and non-financial measures of performance.)

2.  What is the appropriate price to be charged for transfers between decentralised units of the same company? This is the issue of transfer pricing and is discussed in **Section 16.4** below.

## 16.2 Types of Responsibility Centres

### Decentralised units become Responsibility Centres

A **responsibility centre** is any unit within an organisation that is headed by a manager who is accountable for those activities over which he can exert significant control. In a sense, an organisation is a collection of responsibility centres, each of which can be depicted as a box on the organisation chart, and which are arranged in a hierarchical structure. However, from the standpoint of senior managers, the company as a whole can be considered a responsibility centre in its own right, although the term is more commonly used to refer to sections or units within the firm.

All responsibility centres have some form of inputs, which may be physical goods, services or simply cash but all are capable of being converted into monetary amounts. With these resources, certain activities are performed, which can be referred to as outputs. All responsibility centres have outputs, that is, they do something either in providing goods or services for other responsibility centres within the organisation or to customers in the outside world. If the outputs of a responsibility centre are sold to an outside customer, the accounting system measures these outputs in terms of sales revenue. If they are not sold then non-financial measures, such as the number of service units provided, can be used.

Responsibility centres are based on the fundamental principle of 'controllability' whereby an individual (manager) is assigned responsibility for what he can control. To do otherwise will de-motivate the manager and this may affect his performance in the areas which are under his direct control. There are three types of responsibility centre and these reflect the hierarchy of the organisation. The (commercial) organisation itself will typically be an investment centre. In turn, investment centres are composed of profit centres. Lastly, there are cost centres. However, identifying the appropriate type of responsibility centre is often difficult. Nevertheless, the division of the organisation into different types of responsibility centres is important for determining the choice of appropriate performance measures for evaluation purposes. Specifically, the performance measures (financial and non-financial) chosen should be based on the principle of controllability. There are three main issues involved in evaluating these responsibility centres:

- What types of responsibility centres are appropriate for the organisation structure and what financial measures should be used to evaluate such responsibility centres?
- What sort of dysfunctional behaviour is possible in response to these measures?
- What key performance indicators (KPIs) should be used to supplement financial measures?

## Cost (or Expense) Centres

If the accounting system measures the amount of operating costs incurred by a responsibility centre but does **not** measure the value of its output in terms of revenues, the responsibility centre is called a cost or expense centre. A cost centre manager generally has control over a limited amount of assets, but usually has no right to sell those assets or to acquire additional assets. A typical cost centre is the production department whose responsibility is to produce goods. Since a reliable relationship can be determined between inputs and outputs, then this department is referred to as an **engineered** cost centre, or sometimes a 'standard cost centre'. Consequently the comparison between actual input spending and physical output becomes important, e.g. cost per unit, as would standard cost variances.

For other cost centres within organisations, especially those that provide a service, it is more difficult to measure actual outputs or the physical relationship between inputs and outputs may not be evident. Thus, the amount of costs incurred depends on management's judgement about the expenditure that is appropriate under the circumstances. Departments dealing with administration, information technology, maintenance, personnel and research and developments are referred to as **discretionary** cost centres.

Since operating costs, i.e. inputs can be easily determined, for both engineered and discretionary expense centres, they may be evaluated by comparing budget with actual spending. For engineered cost centres, e.g. the production department, a reliable relationship can be determined between inputs and outputs and this facilitates the use of a standard costing system. Therefore, they will be evaluated with reference to their performance in relation to overall budget but also in relation to standard cost variances that are deemed to be controllable by the responsible manager.

However, this budget constrained focus can lead to various forms of dysfunctional behaviour. We have already cited in other Sections the example of postponing essential machine repairs and maintenance in order to achieve spending targets. There is also the situation of deliberate overspending of budget on the assumption that, if the budget is not spent during the current accounting period, then it will be cut in the forthcoming year. Cost centres are not required to generate revenues although cost centre managers can affect the amount of revenue generated by the firm by, for example, the quality and on-time delivery of goods. This suggests that traditional financial measures of evaluating performance should be supplemented by a range of appropriate non-financial measures relating to, for example, on-time delivery, quality of output, customer satisfaction (and customers may be internal rather than external users), and employee satisfaction. The issues of financial evaluation, potential dysfunctional behaviour and key performance indicators for cost centres are summarised in **Exhibit 16.2**.

## Profit Centres

Revenue is the monetary measure of outputs, and expense (or cost) is a monetary measure of resources consumed. Those familiar with basic financial accounting will remember that profit is the difference between revenue and expenses. If performance in a responsibility centre is measured in terms of the difference between the revenue it earns and the expense it incurs, the responsibility centre is a **profit centre**. (Some

EXHIBIT 16.2: EVALUATION OF COST CENTRES

|  | Engineered cost centres | Discretionary cost centres |
|---|---|---|
| Financial measures | Budget v. actual including standard cost variances | Budget costs v. actual |
| Dysfunctional behaviour? | • Standards set too easy<br>• Resistance to standards | • Always overspend<br>• Ignore quality of service |
| Key performance indicators (KPIs) relate to: | • Internal activities<br>• Customer satisfaction<br>• Employees and facilities | • Internal activities<br>• Customer satisfaction<br>• Employees and facilities |

texts describe a situation whereby a manager is responsible only for revenues generated and this is described as a revenue centre. However, such managers are usually accountable for some elements of cost in generating that profit and so it is preferable to evaluate such managers with reference to profit centres.) The profit centre manager will have some responsibility for setting selling prices as otherwise he would not be able to respond quickly, as appropriate, to changes in competitor prices. They have responsibility for the mix of products offered and for marketing the products or services offered. However, the manager of a profit centre does not make decisions in relation to the level of investment in assets. Rather they are provided with a specific amount of fixed (non-current) assets with which to conduct the business. Typical examples of profit centres are video rental stores, local branches of banks, managers of branch retail stores and units within a fast food chain.

A profit centre resembles a business in miniature but without the ability to decide on investments involving long-term assets or capital expenditure decisions. The primary performance measure for a profit centre is the profit generated by the centre. Since one of the objectives of the overall firm is to generate profits, then using profit as a performance measure should generally motivate the profit centre manager to act in the best interests of the entire entity. A profit centre, like a separate company, has its own income statement that shows revenue, expenses, and profit. Most of the decisions made by the profit centre manager impact on profitability and, therefore, this financial statement becomes a key part in the management control process. Typical measures of performance include the absolute amount of profits generated, profits as a percentage of sales and overall cost levels. These financial performance measures would relate both to budget and actual performance.

However, financial measures can generate inappropriate managerial behaviour, much of which is aimed at increasing short-term profits but to the detriment of long-term performance. In addition, profit centres may be linked with other profit centres within the same organisation. For example, customers that have an unsatisfactory experience in one fast food outlet are unlikely to eat in other outlets of the same chain. Therefore, it is appropriate to supplement the evaluation process with a range of relevant non-financial measures relating to, for example, customer satisfaction, quality of output and delivery, and employee satisfaction. The issues of financial evaluation, potential dysfunctional behaviour and key performance indicators for profit centres are summarised in **Exhibit 16.3**.

EXHIBIT 16.3: EVALUATION OF PROFIT CENTRES

| Financial measures | • Budgeted profit v. actual with profit variances |
| | • Profit as % of sales and profit growth |
| Dysfunctional behaviour? | • Manipulate revenue and expense figures |
| | • Too much emphasis on short-term profitability |
| Key performance indicators (KPIs) relate to: | • Customer satisfaction and loyalty |
| | • Internal activities |
| | • Staff and facilities |

## Investment Centres

The third responsibility centre is referred to as an investment centre. The manager of an investment centre has responsibility for the acquisition of long-term assets in addition to generating revenues and incurring costs. Typically, investment centres are independent businesses and, therefore, investment centres consist of several profit and cost centres. An investment centre manager can generally increase profit by increasing the total amount of productive assets. However, increasing the size of the investment centre's assets, without recognising the opportunity costs of the funds invested, can be harmful for the organisation. Therefore, investment centre managers will be evaluated on their ability to generate a sufficiently high return on investment (RoI). Unfortunately, return on investment means different things to different people and is usually defined in one of three ways: (1) Return on capital employed (RoCE), (2) Return on shareholders' funds (RoSF) or (3) Return on total assets (RoTA). It is important that whatever measure is used, it is used consistently and properly communicated. These (RoI) ratios are usually computed by:

1. **RoCE = Profit before interest and tax (PBIT)/capital employed**
2. **RoSF = Profit before tax (PBT)/shareholders' funds** (or this can be calculated on an after-tax basis)
3. **RoTA = Profit before interest and tax (PBIT)/total assets.**

However, all accounting measures of performance are capable of causing dysfunctional behaviour, for example, in manipulating the financial data or undertaking actions that, while they improve short-term performance, are detrimental to the long-term success of the organisation. Thus, financial measures must be supplemented by an appropriate range of key performance indicators. The issues of financial evaluation, potential dysfunctional behaviour and key performance indicators for investment centres are summarised in **Exhibit 16.4**.

EXHIBIT 16.4: EVALUATION OF INVESTMENT CENTRES

| Financial measures | Budgeted RoI v. actual RoI |
| --- | --- |
| Dysfunctional behaviour? | Manipulate revenue and expense figures |
| Key performance indicators (KPIs) relate to: | • Customer satisfaction and loyalty<br>• Internal activities<br>• Employees and facilities |

ILLUSTRATION: RETURN ON INVESTMENT

Return on Investment (RoI) will always be expressed as a percentage (%). Provided one clearly identifies what is meant by 'investment' the calculation is relatively simple. In the illustration below, we shall define investment in terms of total assets, but other definitions could also be used.

The Leinster Group has two major operating investment centres referred to as Division A and Division B respectively. The following summarised results relate to a recent accounting period:

|  | Division A | Division B |
|---|---|---|
| Operating profits (a) | €100,000 | €200,000 |
| Profit before tax | €80,000 | €170,000 |
| Profit after tax (profit for year) | €60,000 | €130,000 |
| Investment in Total Assets (b) | €600,000 | €900,000 |
| Return on Total Assets (a)/(b) | 16.6% | 22.2% |

RoI is commonly used in the context of evaluating the economic performance of investment centres. It has a number of advantages, including:

1. It uses financial accounting information which should be readily available and understood by management.
2. It can be used in a creative way to identify a pyramid of ratios which can be used for identifying financial strengths and weaknesses. One possible pyramid takes shape as follows:

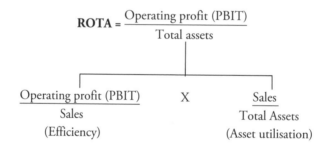

Thus, the overall profitability performance of any enterprise can be determined by reference to two major areas, namely, the profitability of sales and the utilisation of assets. Expanding this notion we observe that overall profitability is determined by the combination of, for example:

- Gross profit to sales ratio, i.e. pricing policy
- Total operating expenses to sales ratio, i.e. cost control
- Turnover of fixed assets, i.e. ability of fixed assets to generate sales
- Stock turnover ratio, i.e. management of stocks
- Debtor days, i.e. credit control

3. It may be used in inter-firm or investment centre comparisons, provided that the units whose results are being compared are in the same sector.

There are a number of disadvantages associated with RoI. Typically:

1. It is difficult to establish a satisfactory definition of and measurement for 'investment'. Several definitions are used which equate investment with (a) total assets, (b) total long-term funds used (i.e. capital employed) or (c) shareholders' funds. However, the denominator in any of these ratios depends on the valuation of total assets and fixed assets in particular. Thus, one could use the current value of fixed assets. While this may allow better economic comparisons between firms, its application is limited since some firms prefer to value their fixed assets at historical cost. If historical costs are used, should one use the net or gross value of fixed assets? If net book-values are used then, ignoring acquisitions, these tend to decline over time and the RoI will tend to increase over time, other things being equal. There are no definitive answers to these issues and the important point, therefore, is consistency of application and communication of the definition used.

2. When comparing ratios of different investment centres, it is necessary that they use similar accounting policies with respect to such items as valuing stocks, fixed assets and the treatment of research and development expenditure. Different accounting treatments of these items will result in different profit figures. (We shall also see in **Section 16.4** that a unit's profitability can be dramatically influenced by transfer pricing practices.)

3. The use of RoI as a performance metric can, in some cases, be associated with incorrect capital expenditure decisions. In other words, in specific circumstances, managers, when evaluated on the basis of RoI, may reject proposals that should be accepted and reject others that should be accepted. This is an important point and will be explained in the illustration below (but the figures are contrived and marginal).

ILLUSTRATION: RETURN ON INVESTMENT (RoI)
AND INCORRECT DECISIONS

The Connacht Group has two major investment centres which are referred to as Divisions A and B respectively. They are currently being reviewed in terms of their target RoI which has been set at 12%. The following information has been extracted from the budgets, provisionally agreed, for the forthcoming year:

INCOME SUMMARIES FOR YEAR ...

|  | Division A € | Division B € |
|---|---|---|
| Operating profit for year | 200,000 | 64,000 |
| Interest payable | (50,000) | (40,000) |
| Profit before tax | 150,000 | 24,000 |
| Taxation | (45,000) | (6,000) |
| Profit after tax | 105,000 | 18,000 |

BALANCE SHEET EXTRACTS AT END OF FINANCIAL YEAR

|  | Division A € | Division B € |
|---|---|---|
| Fixed assets | 800,000 | 650,000 |
| Current assets | 200,000 | 150,000 |
| Total assets | 1,000,000 | 800,000 |
| Shareholders' funds | 400,000 | 300,000 |
| Long-term loans payable | 400,000 | 300,000 |
| Current liabilities | 200,000 | 200,000 |
|  | 1,000,000 | 800,000 |

After the above budget figures have been agreed, two additional proposals have been suggested but neither of them is included in the above figures. Project Alpha is being considered by Division A and Project Beta is being considered for Division B. Relevant information on these two proposals is as follows:

1. Project Alpha will increase annual sales of Division A by €200,000 as a result of undertaking an advertising campaign which will cost €15,000. The sales increase will improve the division's contribution by €30,000 (excluding advertising costs) but will require an additional investment in stocks (and therefore funds invested) amounting to €100,000.
2. Project Beta requires Division B to purchase new equipment costing €200,000 (which is to be financed by additional funds) which will improve annual profits by €22,000, including depreciation, due to increased efficiency.

**Requirements:**

1. Determine the budgeted RoI for each Division, **excluding** consideration of the two proposed projects, and assuming investment is defined in terms of total assets.
2. Calculate the revised RoI for each Division, **including** the two proposed projects. Suggest which of the two projects are likely to be approved (or rejected) by the respective managers. Explain your reasoning.

**Solution and Analysis:** The budgeted and revised RoI for both Divisions are presented below. Investment is defined in terms of total assets and therefore one should divide PBIT, i.e. operating profit, by total assets to obtain the relevant RoI.

| Original RoI (budget) | Division A | Division B |
|---|---|---|
| **Return on total assets** PBIT × 100 Total assets | $\frac{200,000 \times 100}{1,000,000} = 20\%$ | $\frac{64,000 \times 100}{800,000} = 8\%$ |

| Revised RoI | Division A | Division B |
|---|---|---|
| *Return on total assets* | | |
| $\dfrac{\text{PBIT} \times 100}{\text{Total assets}}$ | $\dfrac{215,000 \times 100}{1,100,000} = 19.5\%$ | $\dfrac{86,000 \times 100}{1,000,000} = 8.6\%$ |

Using RoI as the main financial tool for performance evaluation, the manager of Division A would be motivated to reject Project Alpha because it reduces his budgeted RoI from 20% to 19.5%. (We can ignore the fact that this is a marginal decline, but a decline, nonetheless.) This is regrettable from a company-wide view as the extra €15,000 profit generated from the additional investment of €100,000 is above the target rate of 12%.

On the other hand, using RoI, the manager of Division B is motivated to accept Project Beta since his division's RoI will improve – admittedly by a marginal amount. However, the overall return (€22,000) from the investment (€200,000) is 11%, which is marginally below the desired overall rate of 12%. Nevertheless, the manager has the incentive to accept this project since it improves his overall RoI towards the target rate of 12%.

## Residual Income

To overcome this potential dysfunctional consequence associated with using RoI, illustrated above, an alternative measurement to evaluate investment centres has been proposed. This is referred to as **Residual Income (RI)**. It is calculated as the operating profit (PBIT) of an investment centre less the 'imputed' interest on the investment in the centre. The imputed interest is only a notional entry and is not recorded as an accounting transaction and represents the opportunity cost associated with investing funds in a particular organisational unit. The term residual **income** is used rather than residual profit since this measurement was popularised in the United States where the term 'income' is generally used instead of 'profit'. Unlike RoI, it will always be an absolute monetary amount rather than a percentage and can be positive or negative.

### ILLUSTRATION: RESIDUAL INCOME (RI)

The Cobh investment centre has an investment in total assets of €50,000 which generates an operating profit of €15,000. The minimum acceptable rate of return is 14% on this investment. The residual income is computed as:

| | |
|---|---|
| Operating profit (PBIT) | €15,000 |
| Imputed interest (14% × €50,000) | (7,000) |
| Residual income for period | 8,000 |

The main advantage of using RI to evaluate investment centres is that it avoids the possible dysfunctional decision-making associated with RoI. As we have seen, the use of RoI may influence investment centre managers to reject opportunities which could otherwise increase the value of the overall firm. We shall now return to our illustration of the Connacht Group to highlight this important point.

## ILLUSTRATION: RESIDUAL INCOME (RI)

The Connacht Group has two major investment centres which are referred to as Divisions A and B respectively. They are currently being reviewed in terms of their target RoI which has been set at 12%. The following information has been extracted from the budgets, provisionally agreed, for Divisions A and B for the forthcoming year:

### INCOME SUMMARIES

|  | Division A € | Division B € |
|---|---|---|
| Operating profit for year | 200,000 | 64,000 |

### BALANCE SHEET EXTRACTS AT END OF FINANCIAL YEAR

|  | Division A € | Division B € |
|---|---|---|
| Fixed assets | €800,000 | €650,000 |
| Current assets | 200,000 | 150,000 |
| Total assets | 1,000,000 | 800,000 |

After the above budget figures have been agreed, two additional proposals have been suggested but neither of them is included in the above figures. Project Alpha is being considered by Division A and Project Beta is being considered for Division B. Relevant information on these two proposals is as follows:

1. Project Alpha will increase annual sales of Division A by €200,000 as a result of undertaking an advertising campaign which will cost €15,000. The sales increase will improve the division's contribution by €30,000 (excluding advertising costs) but will require an additional investment in stocks (and therefore funds invested) amounting to €100,000.
2. Project Beta requires Division B to purchase new equipment costing €200,000 (which is to be financed by additional funds) which will improve annual profits by €22,000, including depreciation, due to increased efficiency.

**Requirements:**

1. Determine the budgeted RI for each Division, **excluding** consideration of the two proposed projects, and assuming investment is defined in terms of total assets.
2. Calculate the revised RI for each Division, **including** the two proposed projects. Suggest which of the two projects are likely to be approved (or rejected) by the respective managers. Explain your reasoning.

**Solution and analysis:** The budgeted and revised RI for both Divisions is presented below. Investment is defined in terms of total assets and the relevant opportunity cost of funds is assumed to be 12%.

RI BASED ON ORIGINAL BUDGET

|  | Division A € | Division B € |
|---|---|---|
| Profit before interest and tax | 200,000 | 64,000 |
| Less: Notional interest (12% x total assets) | (120,000) | (96,000) |
| = Residual income | 80,000 | (32,000) |

RI BASED ON REVISED BUDGET

|  | Division A € | Division B € |
|---|---|---|
| Profit before interest and tax | 215,000 | 86,000 |
| Less: Notional interest (12% x total assets) | (132,000) | (120,000) |
| = Residual income | 83,000 | (34,000) |

Using RI as the main financial tool for performance evaluation, the manager of Division A would now be motivated to accept Project Alpha because it increases his division's residual income from €80,000 to €83,000. (This project would likely to be rejected using RoI.) On the other hand, using RI, the manager of Division B is motivated to reject Project Beta since his division's RI will decrease from a negative €32,000 to a negative €34,000. (This project would likely to be accepted using RoI.)

The main advantage of RI is, therefore, that it always prevents potential dysfunctional decision-making when considering capital expenditure proposals in a situation where an investment centre is evaluated with reference to RoI. (This has been illustrated above.) Another advantage of using residual income is that investment centre managers are continually made aware of the opportunity cost of funds associated with their responsibility centre.

Nevertheless residual income has some disadvantages. Chiefly, there is the difficulty in identifying the appropriate percentage to use in computing the notional capital charge and also in identifying the appropriate value of assets (or investment) on which the capital charge should be based. Moreover, residual income is not as commonly understood as, for example, return on investment.

Both RoI and RI suffer from the same disadvantage of 'short-termism'. This is a phenomenon whereby managers take actions aimed at securing higher short-term future financial benefits to the detriment of long-term results. Part of this phenomenon may be due to the determination of executive pay, especially where such pay is linked to profit-related performance. Also, for publicly quoted companies, the growth and dominance of financial institutions as shareholders in recent years must be noted. These financial institutions often require good profit performances from companies in order to increase the market value of the company and, therefore, their investment portfolio. For publicly quoted companies, because of the size of such shareholdings, any bulk sale of shares could result in a severe reduction in market value of the company. Related to the issue of short-termism and profit performance is the important issue of ethics, corporate governance and environmental responsibilities. As a result, codes of conduct and/or ethical guidelines are now available in some companies to signal appropriate and inappropriate individual behaviour.

## 16.3 Economic Value Added

Because of the limitations associated with both RoI and RI outlined above another financial metric has been suggested to evaluate the performance of investment centres. This new metric is referred to as Economic Value Added. The term 'Economic Value Added' was coined (and trademarked) by Stern Stewart, a US consulting firm. It can be defined as a business unit's net operating profit after tax (NOPAT) after deducting a notional capital charge. This capital charge is linked to the capital invested in the unit multiplied by the cost of capital. The idea is not new and, in its most fundamental form, EVA is the simple notion of residual income. The objective of EVA is to measure the residual wealth created by a business unit during an accounting period. This residual wealth is obtained by deducting taxes and a capital charge from the (adjusted) net operating profit and this can be presented as follows:

|  | €000 |
|---|---|
| Adjusted, operating profit for period | 100 |
| Less: Tax on operating profits, say | (40) |
| = Net Operating profit after tax (NOPAT) | 60 |
| Less: Capital charge (Adjusted capital x WACC) say | (25) |
| Economic Value Added (EVA) | 35 |

If EVA is positive, the company has created wealth during the period. If EVA is negative, then the company is destroying wealth. Over the long term, only those companies creating wealth can survive.

As previously mentioned, the concept of EVA is similar to that of Residual Income. Indeed, some textbooks do not differentiate between the two terms. In some cases, calculations of both Residual Income and EVA will produce identical figures. However, there are likely to be differences for three reasons:

1. In contrast to Residual Income, EVA uses the firm's cost of capital (WACC) instead of a minimum required rate of return. The cost of capital is obtained by calculating a weighted average of the cost of the firm's two sources of funds – debt and equity. However, for many business units, the minimum desired rate of return and the cost of capital could be approximately the same.
2. The 'income' figure used for EVA is referred to as Net Operating Profit after Tax (NOPAT). The operating profit is usually readily available and reported as profit **before interest** and tax. However, from this we must deduct the tax payable on such operating profits. Since the tax expense is computed **after** deducting interest expense, if any, we must add back to the tax expense the tax benefit of such a deduction. The objective here is to estimate the tax payable on operating profits.
3. Another difference is that EVA does not rely on conventional accounting policies. Under EVA, for example, expenses that contribute to the long-term value of the business unit are capitalised rather than being written off to the income statement when incurred. These expenses include research and development costs and training and employee development. Thus, in calculating EVA, we use the terms 'adjusted earnings' and 'adjusted capital', in order to eliminate the distortion of accrual accounting.

## Adjustments to Eliminate the Distortions of Accrual Accounting

Generally accepted accounting principles require managers to account for transactions on an accrual basis. This accounting treatment is done for two reasons: (1) to better match costs with revenues and (2) to ensure a conservative calculation of profit when there is uncertainty about the timing of future revenues or costs. For some events – such as recording the sale of goods on credit – there is little dispute about the correct accounting period in which to record this transaction. However, there are other entries that accountants record that can potentially distort the economic income of a business. EVA calculations attempt to undo these adjustments to (1) generate a profit number that more closely represents economic cash flows and (2) restate the balance sheet to reflect the true value of resources used to generate income. The main adjustments are described here although many more could be added such as the capitalisation of operating leases:

1. Capitalise expenditures on research and development
2. Do not amortise goodwill
3. Adjust current year's tax expense to eliminate deferred taxation.

## Research and Development Expense

Any asset, by definition, represents a future cash flow or benefit. One of the hotly debated issues in financial reporting over the years is how to account for research and development costs. Are they assets or expenses? Some argue that managers invest in research and development for the sole purpose of developing new products and processes that will generate future cash flows. According to this reasoning, research and development expenditure should be capitalised as an asset and expensed against revenues of future periods. Accountants, however, are suspicious that the amounts spent on research and development may not be fully recoverable in future periods. They argue that some research and development expenditure is inevitably wasted, because experimentation by its nature implies trial and error. Therefore, rather than permitting managers to record research and development expenditures as assets – and amortise them over the lives of new products and processes – financial reporting standards prefer managers to write off to the income statement all research and development expenditure in the period in which the expenditure takes place.

The EVA calculation reverses this thinking. Research and development expenditure is capitalised and shown on the balance sheet as an asset and amortised over some estimated life (typically five – 10 years). This has the effect of increasing profit (earnings) by the amount of the research and development expense (less any amount associated with its amortisation over time) and increasing the value of the asset and the associated capital base recorded on the balance sheet.

### Amortisation of Goodwill

Accountants account for the difference between the purchase price of a company and its identifiable net assets as goodwill. For example, if Company A purchased Company B for €40 million, and the net assets of Company B (assets minus liabilities) were valued at €30 million, the balance of €10 million would be shown on the purchaser's balance sheet as a long-term asset – 'goodwill' – and be subject to annual impairment reviews. This means that goodwill could be amortised over, say, 10 years. Thus, over each of the future 10 years, some portion of the goodwill would be written off against income, thereby reducing reported profits.

For EVA purposes, the goodwill accrual must be adjusted in two ways. First, the reduction in income due to the impairment or amortisation of goodwill in the current period is added back to income. In other words, it is not amortised in order to approximate a cash flow-based operating profit figure. Secondly, the balance sheet is restated to reflect the full purchase price of the acquisition so that managers are held accountable for generating returns on the full value of the assets employed.

### Deferred Tax Expense

Some people think that 'tax expense' in a company's income statement shows the amount of taxes a company is required to pay on its profits to the government. This is only partially true. First we must distinguish between a company's accounting and taxable income. The former is the amount of income reported in the income statement presented to shareholders. This is sometimes referred to as 'book income' and is prepared under generally accepted accounting principles. Taxable income, on the other hand, is the amount of profit that is taxable. Because of the complexities of the corporation taxation code, it is a rarity that these two figures will correspond. In some extreme cases, a company may have considerable accounting or book income but no taxable income.

Generally accepted accounting principles require companies to record a tax expense based on the reported accounting rather than taxable income. The difference between what a company records in its income statement as a tax expense and what it actually pays the tax authorities reflects a **timing difference**. The most common timing difference is due to the treatment of depreciation for accounting and taxation purposes. For example, many companies choose a straight-line method of depreciation for financial accounting purposes to best match revenues with expenses. However, for the calculation of taxable income, companies may adopt some method of accelerated depreciation to minimise taxable income and reduce current tax liabilities. Thus, accounting income and taxable income will differ.

Accountants believe that the taxes 'deferred' this year because of accelerated depreciation for tax purposes will have to be paid in the future. As a result, **tax expense** on an income statement is based on *accounting (or book) income* (e.g. using straight-line depreciation), and not on the income that is calculated on a company's tax return. The difference between the taxes actually paid and the amount that would have been paid using the company's accounting (or book) income is recorded as an additional tax expense in the firm's income statement. In addition, a corresponding liability (referred to as a deferred tax liability) is reported on the balance sheet.

For EVA calculations, the current year's tax expense attributable to the accrual of deferred taxes is added back to income in order to better estimate cash flows labelled as NOPAT. Similarly, deferred taxes payable on the balance sheet are considered part of the adjusted capital of the firm, since the concept of deferred tax liabilities does not exist under EVA.

Many other adjustments could be made in order to compute EVA. However, in reality, research analysts and companies themselves prefer to only make a small number of adjustments (about 5 – 15) to its accounting earnings. The most common adjustments relate to research and development expenditure, goodwill and deferred tax but others, for example, the capitalisation of operating leases, could have been added to our discussion.

## ILLUSTRATION: ECONOMIC VALUE ADDED (EVA)

The following information relates to Tory Ltd for a recent accounting year:

INCOME STATEMENT FOR YEAR...

| | € |
|---|---|
| Gross profit | 2,270 |
| Selling & administration costs | (1,780) |
| Research & development expenses | (180) |

| Goodwill amortised | (20) |
| Profit before interest and tax | 290 |
| Interest paid | (10) |
| Profit before tax | 280 |
| Current tax on profit for year | (99) |
| Deferred tax | (26) |
| Profit for the year | 155 |

BALANCE SHEET AS AT ...

|  | € |
| --- | --- |
| Fixed assets (net) | 110 |
| Research & development costs | Nil |
| Goodwill | 180 |
| Stock (inventory) | 300 |
| Trade debtors | 420 |
| Cash | 280 |
|  | 1,290 |
| **Finance by:** | |
| Shareholders' funds | 625 |
| L. T. Loans (10%) | 100 |
| Deferred taxation | 106 |
| Trade creditors | 360 |
| Tax payable | 99 |
|  | 1,290 |

The following information is provided:

1.  Goodwill acquired at the start of the year is being written off over 10 years. For EVA purposes, this should be capitalised and it is not subject to impairment reviews.
2.  Research and development costs were incurred during the year and were immediately expensed. It would be more realistic to write these costs off over a period of 10 years.
3.  Long-term loans carry a gross interest rate of 10% whereas the cost of equity is estimated at 16% after tax. Assume a tax rate of 45% on profits.

**Requirement:** Calculate the EVA for the above accounting period and comment.

**Solution and analysis:** The first step is to calculate the adjusted earnings and adjusted capital. The adjustments to both earnings and the capital base are detailed below:

INCOME STATEMENT FOR YEAR...

|  | Original € | Adjustments € | Revised € |
|---|---|---|---|
| Gross profit | 2,270 |  | 2,270 |
| Selling & administration | (1,780) |  | (1,780) |
| Research & development | (180) | (i) + 180 − 18 | (18) |
| Goodwill | (20) | (ii) + 20 | 0 |
| Interest paid * | (10) |  | N/A |
| Profit before tax | 280 |  |  |
| Current tax | (99) | (iii) add (10 × 45%) | (103½) |
| Deferred tax | (26) | (iv) + 26 | 0 |
| Net profit | 155 | NOPAT | 368½ |

\* Interest is automatically excluded in calculating operating profit (PBIT).

The first adjustment (i) involves capitalising the full amount of research and development costs incurred and then amortising them over 10 years. The second adjustment (ii) involves writing back the amortisation of goodwill. The full amount of goodwill acquired, therefore, appears on the balance sheet. The third adjustment attempts to calculate the amount of tax payable in relation to operating profits. The quickest way to do this is to adjust the annual tax expense in the income statement. Since the annual gross interest expense (€10) is tax-deductible, the tax benefit of this interest expenditure must be €4$^{1}/_{2}$ (€10 × 45%). Therefore, the tax charge applicable to only operating income, i.e. before interest is deducted, is estimated at €103$^{1}/_{2}$ (€99 + 4$^{1}/_{2}$).

The closing balance sheet is also adjusted and is presented below. The first adjustment (i) involves the capitalisation of research and development costs but amortising this expenditure over 10 years. The second adjustment (ii) involves writing back the amortisation of goodwill. The full amount of goodwill acquired, therefore, appears on the balance sheet. The third adjustment (iii) involves the elimination of deferred tax from the balance sheet since it does not exist under EVA because it is not associated with current cash outflows. Finally, the revised figure for shareholders' funds must be the balancing figure on the revised balance sheet.

BALANCE SHEET AT END OF YEAR...

|  | Original € | Adjustments € | Revised € |
|---|---|---|---|
| Fixed assets (net) | 110 |  | 110 |
| Research & development | Nil | (i) + 180 − 18 | 162 |
| Goodwill | 180 | (ii) + 20 | 200 |

| | | | |
|---|---|---|---|
| Stock | 300 | | 300 |
| Debtors | 420 | | 420 |
| Cash | 280 | | 280 |
| | 1,290 | | 1,472 |
| Financed by: | | | |
| Shareholders' funds | 625 | Balancing figure | 913 |
| LT Loans (10%) | 100 | | 100 |
| Deferred taxation | 106 | − 106 | Nil |
| Tax payable | 99 | | 99 |
| Trade creditors | 360 | | 360 |
| | 1,290 | | 1,472 |

Secondly, WACC must be calculated and this is done along the lines outlined in Chapter 13 (capital expenditure decisions, and specifically **Section 13.3**). The company's WACC is computed as follows:

| | Amount € | Portion % (Rounded) | After-tax cost % | Weighted cost % |
|---|---|---|---|---|
| LT Loans | 100 | 9.8% | 5.5% | 0.5% |
| Equity | 913 | 90.2% | 16% (given) | 14.5% |
| | 1,013 | 100.0% | | 15.0% |

Finally, EVA is computed as:

| | | € |
|---|---|---|
| Adjusted EVA earnings (above) | | 368.5 |
| Adjusted investment (above) | €1,013 | |
| Required return (15% × €1,013) | | 152.0 |
| Economic value added during period | | 216.5 |

The above calculations, based on a NOPAT figure, indicate that this company is generating considerable wealth for shareholders. It is certainly a priority for commercial organisations to generate returns for shareholders and EVA focuses on generating returns in excess of the cost of capital entrusted to managers.

### Benefits of EVA

The first proclaimed advantage of EVA is that its supporters argue that a strong correlation exists between EVA and share price movement. However, some of the results are conflicting. It shall be interesting to see whether this correlation continues as stock markets become more volatile in the future due to rising oil prices, shortages of raw materials, a credit crisis and increasing political uncertainty.

Secondly, EVA can be, and is increasingly, linked to managerial compensation. In this way, managerial compensation is closely linked to wealth creation. While accounting numbers used in external financial statements must comply with GAAP, those in incentive compensation plans need not comply with GAAP. Designers of incentive plans should investigate how to modify the accounting numbers to provide incentives for desired behaviour. For example, suppose top management of a software development company wishes to encourage the company to make substantial investment in research and development. Under GAAP, much, if not all, of that investment will have to be written off as an expense in the period in which the expenditure is incurred. Yet, this company wants to encourage managers to invest in research and development. Consequently, the Board of Directors will probably elect to capitalise these expenditures for the purpose of its incentive compensation plan.

Thirdly, EVA can be used in making decisions regarding various business units because it highlights those units where shareholder wealth is being created or destroyed. Therefore, EVA can be used in deciding which business units should be expanded or reduced.

Fourthly, EVA highlights the cost of capital of a business unit. A number of companies have discovered that EVA helps to encourage the right kind of behaviour from their business units in a way that emphasis on operating income alone cannot. The underlying reason is EVA's reliance on the true cost of capital. Moreover, this focus may encourage senior management to examine the capital structure of the business unit more carefully. In many small and medium-sized businesses, the capital structure is often accepted as a 'given' and rarely receives serious scrutiny. In other words, making the cost of capital explicit may help to concentrate managers' attention on financing the business in a cost-effective manner.

Finally, it is relatively simple for a company to incorporate EVA into the Balanced Scorecard by including it in one of the financial measures in the financial perspective category.

## Limitations of EVA

There are a number of limitations associated with the use of EVA. First of all, it is a single measure of financial performance and should not be used in isolation for evaluation purposes. The recent literature on management accounting is in agreement that performance evaluation should not exclusively focus on a single metric–financial or non-financial. Moreover, any metric is capable of distortion and promoting dysfunctional consequences. In addition, lower level managers and employees may feel helpless to affect earnings or investment and therefore EVA is perceived as being irrelevant to them.

In common with other financial measures of performance, EVA does not explicitly attempt to place a value on all the assets of an organisation. This remains problematic for knowledge-intensive businesses or any business with intangible resources that do not appear on the balance sheet. The result of this is that EVA is not a complete measure of the manager's stewardship of the shareholders' investment and may therefore overstate the wealth generated during an individual accounting period.

In large multi-product organisations the difficulties in calculating EVA will multiply. Common assets and costs will need to be apportioned between divisions and/or products to enable calculation of divisional and/or product EVA. Of course, such problems do not arise solely in the calculation of EVA and already exist in the calculation of RoI or RI.

A major practical issue that arises in the calculation of EVA is how earnings and capital should be defined. In excess of 150 adjustments have been identified, although a small number of key adjustments is preferable. Indeed, it may be difficult for investors or analysts to make all the suggested adjustments because they will only have access to the information disclosed in the published accounts. In addition, adjustments, such as the capitalisation of research and development costs and the determination of the optimal period of amortisation of goodwill, are very subjective. Ultimately it would be more correct to consider EVA as a crude estimate rather than a single unambiguous figure (of course, the same could be said of accounting earnings!).

In conclusion, EVA is conceptually correct since it is based on the fundamental concept of economic profit, which is the profit generated after considering all costs, including the cost of capital, and taxation. The notion that companies earning an economic profit will add wealth to their owners is well grounded in economic theory and in practice. Thus, EVA can be viewed as a serious attempt to make operational the concept of economic profit.

## 16.4 Transfer Prices and their Determination

Transfer prices involve the pricing of goods or services that are transferred (bought and sold) between members of the same corporate family. They can be described as internal prices or intragroup transfer prices. They are to be contrasted with the market price, which measures exchanges between a company and the outside world. Internal exchanges that are measured by transfer prices result in revenue for the responsibility centre supplying the goods (or services) and represent an equivalent cost for the responsibility centre buying the goods and therefore they have the potential to influence the reported profitability of individual business entities.

The relevance of transfer prices developed as a corollary to the decentralisation efforts that took part in many business organisations, especially American companies, during the early part of the Twentieth Century. Under conditions of increased local autonomy, the need arose for a system of internal pricing that would fairly reflect the performance of the responsible managers and their responsibility centres and would motivate managers to operate their divisions efficiently.

In a decentralised organisation the general rule is that, if the objective is to maximise **group** profits, then business units within that group should trade with each other. (Later in this section we shall add the complication of taxation and tariffs.) However, the concept of decentralisation grants freedom to the respective managers to make decisions. In theory, decentralised managers are free to trade with whomever they prefer and are also free to negotiate buying and selling prices for goods and services. However, this freedom creates a potential problem. Transfer prices represent revenue for the selling division and associated costs for the purchasing division. This can create dysfunctional behaviour and is illustrated in the Trim Group example below.

## ILLUSTRATION: PROFIT IMPACT OF TRANSFER PRICING

The Trim Group consists of a number of independent business units which include the Gort and Slane companies. The Gort Company is a manufacturing division of electrical components and it has presented the following summarised budget for the forthcoming financial year:

| | |
|---|---:|
| Sales (50,000 units @ €7.50 ) | € 375,000 |
| Variable costs at €6 per unit | (300,000) |
| Total contribution | 75,000 |
| Less: Fixed costs (excluding interest) | (50,000) |
| Divisional operating profit | 25,000 |

Included in Gort's budget above is the proposed sale of 10,000 components at €7.50 each to Slane Company, another company within the Trim group. (There are no tax or tariff implications on this proposed internal transaction.) However, this is only a proposed transfer and there are no legal agreements involved.

In recent days, a firm external to the group, i.e. an independent manufacturing contractor, has offered to supply Slane Company with the same number of components at €7.20 each. Since this is 30c less than the price being charged by Gort, the manager of Slane wants Gort to reduce the price to this level, otherwise Slane Company will purchase from the external supplier. Under the decentralised group structure, the managers of both Gort and Slane have been given freedom to make decisions regarding selling prices and trading customers.

**Requirements:**

1. Calculate the impact on the total profit of (a) Gort (b) Slane and (c) the Trim Group if Gort meets the €7.20 price and supplies Slane with 10,000 components. In other words, the proposed internal transaction will go ahead but at a reduced price of €7.20 rather than €7.50 for each of the 10,000 components.
2. Calculate the impact on the total profit of (a) Gort (b) Slane and (c) the Trim Group if Gort does not lower its price and Slane purchases the 10,000

components externally. (In other words, the proposed internal transaction will not go ahead.) For various technical reasons, it is not possible for Gort to acquire another customer for these components during the forthcoming accounting period, and therefore, the goods will not be produced.

3. Comment on the implications of your calculations but ignore all taxation considerations.

**Solution and analysis:**

1. If the proposed transfer price is reduced from €7.50 to €7.20 per component the financial consequences can be summarised as follows:
The profits of the Gort division will fall by €3,000 (i.e. €7.50 − €7.20) × 10,000 components. This is the reduction in the proposed unit selling price (€0.30) multiplied by the number of components sold. The profit of the Slane division will increase by €3,000, i.e. ((€7.50 − €7.20) × 10,000). This is the reduction in the proposed unit purchase price (€0.30) multiplied by the number of components purchased.

In other words, there is a simultaneous increase in profit in one company and a corresponding reduction in another. Therefore the profits of the overall group remain unchanged.

2. If Slane purchases from an external company, then intra-group trading will not take place. This decision will usually be to the detriment of the overall group. The financial consequences can be summarised as follows:
The profits of the Gort division will fall by €15,000, i.e. ((€7.50 − €6.00) × 10,000). This represents the lost unit contribution per unit (€1.50) multiplied by the number of units sold. The profits of Slane division will increase by €3,000, i.e. ((€7.50 − €7.20) × 10,000). This is the reduction in the proposed unit purchase price (€0.30) multiplied by the number of components purchased.

The total profits of the Trim Group will fall by €12,000, represented by the reduction suffered by Gort (− €15,000) partly offset by the additional profits generated by Slane (€3,000). Alternatively, this amount can be calculated as follows:
Additional cash outflows from Group due to external purchase:
(72,000)
Cash saving due to non-production                                    + 60,000
Overall decline of group profits
(12,000)

3. The above illustration confirms that it is usually advisable, from the perspective of the group, for business units within the group to trade with each other. Indeed, it is interesting to observe that if the transfer price was €1 per component

then there would be a zero impact on overall group profitability. However, with a transfer price of €1 per component, the profits of the individual companies would be significantly affected. The second important comment is that both managers have an incentive to trade with each other if the transfer price can be set between a range of €7.20 to €6.00. The €7.20 price is determined by the market price currently available. Simply, Slane can buy externally at €7.20 and its manager would not be prepared to pay a higher price than this, if he is evaluated with reference to profits generated. In addition, a price of €6 is the minimum price that Gort would accept and this is determined by its appropriate variable cost per unit.

## Methods of Transfer Pricing

Because of the profit impact of transfer prices on individual companies and the group as a whole, it is preferable that some method of determining transfer prices be established. At this stage it is important to stress that transfer prices do not impact on the PRE-tax profit of the **group**. Transfer prices simply shift pre-tax profits from one business unit to another. However, when taxation and tariffs are involved, then the **post**-tax profits of the group can be significantly changed by transfer prices. Ignoring tax considerations, there are three main methods to determine transfer prices and each will be discussed in turn.

### 1. Market Price

This approach sets the transfer price equivalent to the prevailing market price. This puts the selling and the buying divisions on the same footing as independent contractors and both participants have the incentive to deal with each other. It also preserves managerial autonomy. The buying responsibility centre should ordinarily not be expected to pay more internally than it would have to pay if it purchased from the outside world. Nor should the selling centre ordinarily be entitled to more revenue than it could obtain by selling to the outside world.

The use of market-based transfer prices has two important advantages. First, market prices set an upward limit to the transfer price. This should generate economic efficiency within the transferor division and prevent excessive costs from being passed on. Secondly, market-based transfer prices have the benefit of being relatively objective and they do not depend on the relative negotiating skills of the respective managers. However, market-based transfer prices suffer from a number of disadvantages. In practice, it is sometimes not clear what the market price is because different suppliers may set different prices on essentially identical items. Also, if the goods are highly specialised, a market price may not exist. In addition, market prices can fluctuate considerably and the problem arises as to whether long-run average or current prices should be used. Current prices are normally chosen as it is considered better to evaluate managerial performance in the light of prevailing conditions. Finally, it can be expensive to continually acquire up-to-date market prices in a complex and constantly changing market place.

## 2. Cost-based Transfer Prices

In a great many situations, there is no reliable market price that can be used as a basis for the transfer price. In these situations, a cost-based transfer price is used. If feasible, the cost should be a standard cost rather than actual cost. If it is an actual cost, the selling responsibility centre has little incentive to control efficiency because any cost increases will be automatically passed on to the buying centre by way of the transfer price. However, to allow a business unit to generate profits – otherwise it would be classified as a cost centre – some amount of profit would be included in the transfer price. This may be specified by top management in order to lessen arguments that could otherwise arise. To avoid disputes, any policy statement as to what costs should be used and what the allowable profit margin is must be unambiguously worded. In particular, short-term unit costs may be different from long-term costs. There can also be questions as to whether all of the cost elements normally included in the seller's definition of full cost should be included in the definition of cost used to determine internal transfer prices. Therefore, cost-based transfer prices can refer to either marginal cost or full costs and whether a profit margin is allowed to the supplying company.

If the profit margin allowed on transfer prices is severely restricted by group policy then there is a strong argument that the respective divisions should no longer be evaluated as an investment (or profit) centre. If business units are not considered to be autonomous, then traditional measures of performance, e.g. Return on Investment, no longer apply in evaluating managerial performance.

## 3. Negotiation and Arbitration

Because of the potential areas for disagreement in both market-based and cost-based transfer prices, transfer prices sometimes are negotiated between buyer and seller. In some cases the selling division may be willing to depart from the normal company transfer price policy. For example, the selling responsibility centre may be willing to sell below the normal market price rather than forfeit the business, which could happen if the buying responsibility centre took advantage of a temporarily low outside price. Also, the selling division may have spare capacity. In such circumstances, the two parties negotiate a 'deal'.

Unless both responsibility centre managers have complete freedom to act, these negotiations will not always lead to an equitable result because the parties may have unequal bargaining powers. That is, the prospective buyer may not have the power of threatening to take its business elsewhere, and the prospective seller may not have the power of refusing to do the work. In addition, negotiation can be very time-consuming which can lead to friction between the two divisions rather than co-operation.

In some situations it is unlikely that a single price will meet all the objectives outlined above. For example, if a transfer price is too favourable to the receiving division the supplying division may become demotivated. If it is too favourable to the supplying division the receiving division may not be interested in purchasing. One suggestion for resolving this conflict is to use dual-transfer pricing. Dual-rate transfer pricing allows the supplying division to record the transfer at one price while the receiving division records the transfer at a different price.

## ILLUSTRATION: DUAL RATE TRANSFER PRICES

Division A produces goods at a marginal cost of €10,000 and these are sold to Division B for €12,000. This transfer price allows Division A to record a contribution to profit of €2,000. Meanwhile, Division B records the receipt of the goods at €10,000. Therefore, when Division B tries to sell the goods externally they know what the marginal costs of the goods is to the group as a whole and so are in a position to make better financial decisions.

There are a number of problems with the dual rate transfer prices. The use of two different prices can cause confusion (this is compounded if there are a large number of divisions involved). Also, an inter-company adjustment is required to cancel out double counting of profits made. However, the overriding consideration is whether these transfer prices encourage independent managers to make decisions in the best interest of the group rather than their respective units.

### Profit Switching Transfer Prices

Transfer prices can either be international transfer prices for international trade or domestic prices for trade within one country. Once a company expands into the international business scene, the problem of transfer pricing quickly magnifies. It is estimated that at least 60% of all international trade consists of transfers between related business entities, especially multinational entities (MNEs). A MNE is defined as an enterprise that owns and controls value-adding activities in more than one country. This definition recognises that such firms may produce both goods and services and, indeed, an increasing amount of transfer pricing relates to the provision of services.

The issue of profit switching transfer pricing is often associated with multinational enterprises (MNEs). There are a number of reasons why MNEs developed. Originally, some MNEs needed to gain access to the natural resources of certain countries. These can be referred to as resource seeking MNEs. For example, aluminium processing companies will tend to have bauxite mines in other countries and, for the same reason, tyre companies will tend to own rubber plantations in other countries. The basic motivation was to secure supply of raw materials. In most cases the MNEs' superior access to capital, technology and global markets put them in a stronger position to develop these resources more efficiently than local enterprises. Other MNEs developed in order to seek additional markets. In this case the MNE, rather than exporting to a country, will establish a local manufacturing base in that country due to, for example, transport costs or trade restrictions. An example of this is EU regulations which resulted in some US and Japanese companies setting up in Ireland to supply the EU market. Because the goods were produced in Ireland and exported to the EU no restrictions, i.e. tariffs, applied. Finally, MNEs developed in order to allow a particular overseas division to specialise in a particular product or in a specific stage of a production process. Thus there is product specialisation or process specialisation. The purpose is to make optimal use of the locations suitable for the production of the particular products or to maximise the economies of scale in the manufacture of individual products. This is typically the case with production or assembly in low labour cost countries. In addition, there may be government incentives on offer such as investment incentives and generous tax concessions.

It is frequently alleged in the media that transfer prices are used to manipulate profits of MNEs and we shall refer to these situations as either profit boosting or profit depressing. We shall take a highly simplified example of a parent company and only one foreign subsidiary in a different overseas jurisdiction.

The situation of profit boosting transfer prices is reported in **Exhibit 16.5**. In this case, the parent company (or other companies in the group), sells goods and services to the foreign subsidiary at low prices but buys from it at high prices. The financial impact is to artificially boost the profits in the overseas subsidiary because its input costs have been artificially reduced and its revenues have been artificially inflated. However, under this set of conditions, the national economy of the country in which the subsidiary operates may gain more than the national economy of the country in which the parent company is based. For example, there is more (foreign direct) investment, more taxable income, greater economic growth of the subsidiary, and more export revenues.

EXHIBIT 16.5: PROFIT BOOSTING TRANSFER PRICES

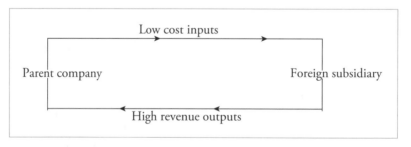

Profit boosting transfer prices can be due to a number of factors. First, transfer prices can be used to effectively reduce tariffs for the overseas subsidiary. Most import duties or tariffs are levied by the Custom authorities on an **ad valorem** (meaning, relating to the value) basis and, in some countries, these duties can be set at very high rates. This means that they are based on the declared value of the transaction, i.e. the declared invoice value, which reflects the transfer price. The financial impact of tariffs can be lessened if the parent company reduces the price for the goods it exports to its foreign subsidiary. Secondly, transfer prices can be used to bypass import restrictions. Some

(Third World) countries try to limit the value of goods that can be imported in order to improve their balance of payments account and protect important foreign currency reserves. Therefore, they impose import restrictions. However, in many cases these import restrictions relate to the value of goods rather than their physical amount. These restrictions can be circumvented by setting low transfer prices invoiced to the foreign subsidiary. Thus, the foreign subsidiary can import twice as many products if they can be purchased at half price, using **creative** transfer pricing practices. Thirdly, transfer prices can be used to benefit an overseas subsidiary which earns a tax credit based on the value of goods it exports. The higher the transfer prices on goods sold and attributable to exported goods, the greater the subsidy received or the value of the tax credit. Fourthly, profit boosting transfer prices will enhance the subsidiary's profitability and this may enable the overseas subsidiary to better qualify for loans or investment in local currency. Fifthly, transfer prices can also be used to provide hidden subsidies to overseas subsidiaries and this may allow it to better compete with local competition. Finally, profit boosting transfer prices can also be used to reduce corporate tax levels by shifting taxable profits to a low tax base country. In this case, overseas profits are taxed at a lower rate than in the parent company's country. Because of the importance of this corporate taxation issue, we shall return to it separately. In summary, profit boosting transfer prices may be due to a number of factors, including:

- High ad valorem import tariffs
- Restrictions on value of goods that can be imported in local economy
- Export subsidy or tax credit based on value of exports
- Local loans based on the financial profit and profitability of subsidiary
- Hidden subsidies in the face of significant competition in the local economy
- Corporate tax rate lower than in parent's country.

Transfer prices can also be used for profit depressing reasons. In **Exhibit 16.6** the parent company sells at high prices to its foreign subsidiary and buys from it at low prices. The financial impact is to artificially reduce the profits in the overseas subsidiary because its input costs have been artificially inflated and its revenues have been artificially reduced.

EXHIBIT 16.6: PROFIT DEPRESSING TRANSFER PRICES

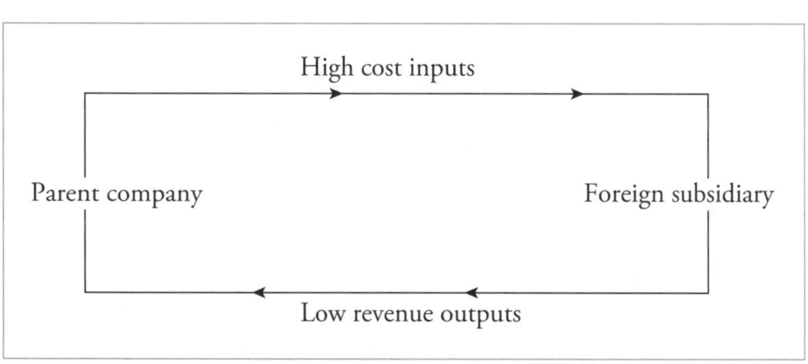

Profit depressing transfer prices can be due to a number of factors. First, transfer prices can be used to circumvent or significantly lessen the impact of financial controls. For example, a government prohibition on dividend remittances to the parent company (or foreign owners) can restrict the ability of a firm to repatriate profits. However, overpricing the goods shipped to the foreign subsidiary in such a country can increase the funds paid out of these countries without appearing to violate dividend restrictions imposed by the government in the host country. (Alternatively, goods may be invoiced to head office from that subsidiary at a cheap price.) In other words, dividend restrictions become irrelevant since the foreign subsidiary does not generate profits in the first instance!

Secondly, transfer prices can also be used to by-pass anti-dumping laws. The parent company can reduce the prices of goods sold to foreign subsidiaries and the foreign subsidiary can then sell them for prices which local competition cannot match. If anti-dumping laws exist on final products, a company can under-price components and semi-finished products to its affiliates. The affiliates can then assemble or finish the product at prices that would have been classified as dumping prices had they been imported directly into the country.

Thirdly, high transfer prices on goods shipped to subsidiaries can also be desirable when a parent wishes to lessen the reported profitability of its subsidiary. This may be because of demands by the subsidiary's workers for higher wages. Alternatively, there may be a joint venture agreement whereby profits are shared with a local partner. Fourthly, profits may be kept deliberately low in a foreign subsidiary due to political instability. Finally, profits may be kept deliberately low so that new competitors will not be lured into the industry by high profits. In summary, the policy of depressing the profits of the subsidiary company may be due to:

- Restrictions on profit or dividend remittances to head office
- Bypassing anti-dumping regulations
- Local partners i.e. joint ventures, or pressure from workers for greater share in profits
- Political instability in local country
- Desire to reduce reported profits to keep competitors out.

However, seldom do the conditions line up as nicely from their standpoint as depicted above. It is far more likely that a country will simultaneously have conditions taken from both exhibits. For example, a country experiencing balance of payments difficulties may restrict dividend payments or the value of goods imported. A company using high transfer prices on sales to its subsidiaries in such a country would gain in terms of taking out more money than it might have been able to otherwise, but would lose by having to decrease the quantity of imported materials its affiliate needs. Alternatively, a country may have high ad valorem tariffs and high corporate tax rates. Under-pricing goods shipped to an affiliate in such a country lessens the tariff duties but also increases subsidiary profits due to lower input costs, resulting in higher taxes for the subsidiary. **Exhibits 16.5** and **16.6** are based on a two-country model. In reality, several countries may be involved and this greatly increases the complexity of using transfer prices to increase global after-tax profits. We shall now turn our attention to the important issue of taxation and tariffs.

## The Impact of Tax on Corporate Profits

Throughout the world, corporate profits are liable to tax. However, countries have different tax rates on corporate profits. There are also different tax regulations. While the issue of international taxation is very complex, it is fair to say that, as a result of double taxation agreements (DTAs), tax is generally paid only in the country in which the profits are generated. Thus, using transfer prices, profits can be shifted from a high-tax jurisdiction to a low-tax jurisdiction. While the pre-tax profit of the group is unchanged (ignoring import/export duties), the post-tax profit of the group will be improved.

It is important to realise that transfer pricing is a very sensitive political issue. Transfer pricing, in general, is the subject of significant debate in international forums, especially in the UN, the EU and the OECD. Initial concerns in these two forums centred on the tax implications of transfer pricing. Developing countries, in particular, felt that MNEs were avoiding taxes and other controls through transfer prices to the detriment of the countries involved. These countries encouraged the UN to establish a code of conduct to require legitimate transfer pricing policies and better disclosure of information to allow the countries to monitor the actions of MNEs.

Because of the tax implications of transfer pricing, some governments, especially the US, insist that all transfer prices between a company and its foreign affiliate be set at arm's length market-based prices. Indeed, in the US, the IRS is allowed to intervene if it feels that significant tax avoidance is taking place. In the UK the Inland Revenue has the power to adjust the taxable income of the UK party. However, the rigour in monitoring the transfer pricing policies of multinational companies varies worldwide. Countries eager to attract foreign investment are regarded by some as not having much interest in transfer pricing issues.

Some companies use deterministic models to determine optimum transfer prices. This means that all the relevant information is included in a model, usually in the form of an algebraic equation, to determine the optimum transfer price. This practice is now illustrated.

## ILLUSTRATION: DETERMINISTIC TRANSFER PRICING MODEL

Clifden Electronics is a diversified international company and the group headquarters is located in Boston. One of its divisions manufactures and sells components in the US where the tax rate on corporate profits is currently 50%. The Chinese market is one of the foreign markets in which Clifden are now interested and it has a 70% owned subsidiary in that country. It is anticipated that the US division will produce and sell the components to the Chinese subsidiary for the Chinese market. However, Chinese import tariffs on such components are 40% of the declared value. These duties are paid by the Chinese subsidiary. The tax rate on corporate profits in China is 20%. There are no other restrictions or taxes affecting the transfer of goods or funds from China to the United States and FX implications can be ignored.

**Requirement:** Develop a deterministic model suitable for predicting cash flows to the shareholders in the group company. Based on your model, should the transfer price be set at high or low levels? Are there any difficulties in getting agreement between the two trading companies regarding this transfer price?

**Solution and analysis:** Apart from the tax and tariff rates, very little additional information is provided. Therefore, we shall have to create a deterministic cash flow model using simple notation. Our cash flow model will indicate the cash flow to each individual entity and the group as a whole, based on the following notation:

C = Cost of production in the US
TP = Transfer price between the two entities
ChSP = Chinese selling price

The cash flow models can be created by following the cash flow sequence associated with product (in the US) and sale in China, together with tariff and taxation implications. Cash inflows are reported as a positive amount and cash outflows are depicted as a negative amount.

|  | USA | China |
|---|---|---|
| (1) Production cost in US (C) | − C | |
| (2) Transfer price (TP) | + TP | − TP |
| (3) Chinese import tariff | | − 0.4 × TP |
| (4) China sale price (BSP) | | + ChSP |
| Therefore, US pre-tax profits | TP − C | |
| Therefore, China pre-tax profits | | ChSP − 1.4 TP |
| USA corporate tax % | 50% | |
| China corporate tax % | | 20% |
| Cash flow after tax | .5 (TP − C) | .80 (ChSP − 1.4TP) |
| % Ownership of subsidiary | | 70% |
| Profit after tax available to group | .5 (TP − C) | .56 (ChSP − 1.4 TP) |

Both of the (individual) cash flow models can be combined to provide a group cash flow model and then simplified as follows:

$$= 0.5 \, (TP − C) + 0.56 \, (ChSP − 1.4 \, TP)$$
$$= 0.5 \, TP − 0.5C + 0.56 \, ChSP − 0.784 \, TP$$
$$= 0.56 \, ChSP − 0.5C − 0.284 \, TP$$

Since the TP coefficient in the above group cash flow model is negative, this indicates that in order to maximise cash flow of the group the lowest transfer price possible should be adopted. It is interesting to note that this low transfer price to China will increase profits in China and this will be acceptable to the minority shareholders in the Chinese subsidiary.

However, transfer prices apply not only to the sale of goods but they can also apply to a range of other transactions and **Exhibit 16.7** indicates the major possibilities. These other transactions can relate to the provision of services such as consulting or accounting services. Transfer prices can also apply to the use of physical assets or, indeed, the sale of these assets between companies. In a similar way, transfer pricing arrangements might relate to the use of funds, involving interest and/or dividend payments as appropriate, but especially with tax considerations in mind. Transfer pricing arrangements can also relate to cost-sharing including joint venture proposals. More recently, there has been a phenomenal growth in transfer pricing practices in relation to the use of intellectual property involving the use of patents, licences and royalty agreements. In many countries, income from patents, royalties and licence agreements receive very favourable taxation treatment. Therefore, it is important to note that the appropriate vehicle to be used for tax driven transfer prices will depend on the tax code in force and, if in existence, the provision of the double-tax treaty between countries.

Finally, the presence of profit switching prices between companies within the same corporate group complicates the performance evaluation of such units, especially overseas subsidiaries. This is because reported profit may be largely determined by a centralised policy on transfer prices rather than the performance of individual managers of the responsibility centres involved.

## 16.5  Contingency Theory

The basic theme of this book is that good managerial decisions require the design of both a relevant information system and an appropriate corporate responsibility structure. As a result, the discipline of management accounting is often taught from the perspective of an optimal system and structure which is applicable to all organisations, in all circumstances. Yet, empirical studies of management accounting practices within organisations over the past few decades indicate significant differences in the type of information generated by the management accounting system, the way that

EXHIBIT 16.7: TRANSACTIONS REQUIRING TRANSFER PRICES

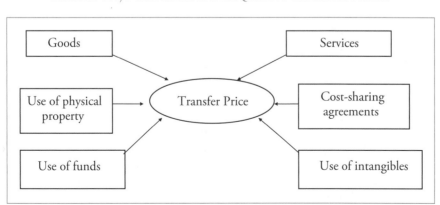

information is used by superiors and subordinates, and the corporate responsibility structure. To some people who are knowledgeable about the discipline, this phenomenon is to be expected and reflects the choices available. For example, in this book we have identified various areas which require choice. These include, for example, the choice between job, process or activity-based costing systems; the choice of methods to be used in evaluating capital expenditure decisions; the use of budgets; the decision to adopt a standard costing system with supporting variances and, finally, the choice of responsibility centres and performance measures to use for evaluation purposes. However, some academics began to theorise regarding these differences and the contingency theory was adopted.

Contingency theory is actually a theory about organisations and argues that there is no universally acceptable model of the organisation that explains the diversity of organisational design. It claims that organisational design depends on the contingent factors relevant to the situation. This theory can and has been applied to the discipline of management accounting and suggests that there is no universally appropriate management accounting system applicable to all organisations in all circumstances. Under contingency theory, the type of accounting system and responsibility structure varies according to the specific circumstances or situations in which the organisation operates. In simple terms, the contingency theory of management accounting argues that there is no one 'best' system; rather specific aspects of an accounting system are associated with certain defined circumstances. Therefore, to offer specific advice to individual enterprises, in relation to their management accounting system, one must be aware of particular aspects within the organisation, the type of people in it and its specific environment.

Starting around the 1980s, several empirical studies have tried to identify factors which influence the design and use of management accounting systems within organisations. The variables that have been identified as important in influencing management accounting systems relate both to external and internal factors.

The external factors include, for example, environmental uncertainty. If the external environment is stable, it has been argued that the use of a budget constrained style of evaluation is appropriate. In other words, performance evaluation is made with reference to meeting financial targets. In contrast, if the firm's environment is dynamic then a more subjective style of evaluation is appropriate. The simple reason for this is that if the environment is rapidly changing then budgets quickly become out of date. In which case, performance evaluation with reference to out of date financial targets is not entirely appropriate.

As well as external factors, contingency theories have identified various internal factors that influence the design of management accounting systems within organisations. These factors include, for example, organisation size, competitive strategy, technology and industry type. It is not surprising that large organisations – which have more resources to spend than smaller firms – tend to be more associated with sophisticated management accounting systems that incorporate a range of new approaches such as activity-based costing, CoQ reports and comprehensive performance measurement systems. Competitive strategy, either in the form of product differentiation or cost leadership, also impacts on the design of management accounting systems. Cost leadership tends to be associated closely with tight control over costs so that budgets and standard costing systems are prevalent. In contrast a product differentiation strategy concentrates on a range of critical success factors that include product quality and high customer satisfaction. With product differentiation, traditional financial control procedures which relate to, for example, budgets and standard costing, are less important. Technology was also found to be an important factor in explaining diversity of management accounting practices. In Chapter 6 we noted a range of different production technologies, including the use of Advanced Manufacturing Technology and JIT systems. Finally, different organisations will have different cost structures and therefore different management accounting techniques will be appropriate. If, for example, a large portion of a firm's cost structure is considered to be variable in response to changes in the level of cost drive (volume) and can be directly attributable to products, then it is easier to establish an input/output relationship and this facilitates both budgeting and especially the applicability of standard costing systems. In contrast, where a large portion of a firm's cost structure is considered 'fixed' in relation to changes in the level of the cost driver (volume), then it is more difficult to establish an input/output relationship. This applies especially to service firms and many costs can be considered as discretionary and based on managerial judgement.

The contingency theory of management accounting is useful in highlighting that no one system of management accounting is appropriate for all organisations, and all circumstances. However, contingency theory is subject to criticisms from a range of sources. First, it can be argued that the above statements regarding the implications of contingency theory are intuitively obvious and one could argue that this hardly provides anything of practical use to management accountants. Logically, one would expect that those researching this topic would have put forward suggestions as to how accounting systems could be improved by demonstrating what systems work well in what circumstances. So far, however, contingency theory seems to have provided little more than a framework for discussing the major influences in the design of management accounting systems within organisations.

Secondly, some critics argue that the definition and measurement of key variables associated with contingency theory need greater clarification. For example, how does one define and measure 'corporate culture'? Indeed in some cases there is little agreement on what the main contingent variables are. In addition, the interconnected nature of these variables suggests that it is difficult to study them in isolation. Thirdly, some of the correlations between variables reported in contingency studies are small and the results of all these studies are not always consistent. Finally, some authors argue that contingency theory overlooks the importance of power. For example, a management accountant who is regarded as having considerable power within the organisation might be able to gain acceptance for 'his' management accounting system which is much more extensive than what would otherwise be required.

However, to its credit, contingency theory has added some academic rigour to the discipline of managerial accounting. It has also broadened the orientation of management accounting and has led to an increase in research into management accounting practices.

## 16.6  Management Compensation

### Agency Theory and Agency Costs

Management or executive compensation is usually discussed in the literature in the context of Agency Theory. An agency relationship exists whenever one party (the principal) hires another party (the agent) to perform some service, and this service requires the principal to delegate some decision-making authority to the agent. The potential problem of this arrangement is that the two may not have the same goals or interests, but the principal, presumably, is hiring the agent to pursue the interests of the former. The costs that arise when agents fail to act in the best interests of principals are referred to as agency costs. In small organisations, agency costs are minimised since the principal can personally oversee agent behaviour. However, in larger organisations, agency behaviour is more difficult to observe and agency costs tend to increase. The following are the more important agency costs related to managerial accounting but some are difficult to quantify:

- Opportunity costs due to poor managerial decisions, arising from, perhaps, lack of effort or commitment on the part of managers. This could also be due to conflicting goals between the principal and agent, and the agent makes decisions which maximise his own self-interest to the detriment of his principal.
- Monitoring costs, i.e. the costs of monitoring agent behaviour which includes the cost of generating appropriate performance reports on a regular basis.
- Incentive costs, i.e. the payments made to senior managers to act in the best interests of the principal.
- Contracting costs, i.e. legal and other professional fees required to negotiate executive contracts.

To encourage top management to take actions that are in the firm's best interests, the owners introduce an executive compensation scheme that enables senior managers to share in the firm's (successful) performance. In theory, executive compensation schemes are intended to fuse together the interests of the principal and the agent.

### Elements of Compensation Schemes

In simple terms, management incentives or compensation schemes consist of policies and procedures intended to reward managers for successful behaviour. The most significant incentive schemes offer financial rewards and consist of three elements namely, salary, benefits (perquisites) and a bonus. However, there are non-financial incentives which may be attractive to managers including the possibility of receiving awards and public recognition, being assigned increased responsibilities with greater autonomy or even relocation to a more attractive location (or office). The attractiveness of financial and intangible rewards will depend on the individual manager and it must be noted that, if the offered rewards are not attractive to managers, they will not have any motivating effect.

Salary represents the fixed, annual payment made to the individual manager. Most organisations also offer perquisites which include special benefits for the manager such as free or heavily subsidised living accommodation, a company car, access to cheap loans, club membership or medical benefits and pension contributions made by the company. The attractiveness or otherwise of such benefits to individual managers depends on whether they are liable to additional tax liabilities as 'benefits in kind' (BIK). Generally, the provision of living accommodation by an employer is a taxable benefit, unless the manager is required under terms of his employment to live in that accommodation. For company cars the BIK is equivalent to 30% of the original market value of the car. Preferential loans also attract a BIK assessment with the benefit depending on whether the loan was used to fund the cost/repair of the manager's principal private residence or was used for other purposes. The BIK for club subscriptions and medical expenses is based on the amount paid by the employer on behalf of the employee. However, the provision of any pension accruing on the retirement or death of a senior manager does not attract a BIK assessment. Both salary and benefits are usually negotiated when a manager is hired or when contracts are renewed. Thus, they are not, per se, influenced by the manager's performance.

Bonuses represent payments made to managers based on the achievement of agreed performance targets during an accounting period. The agreed period could be more or less than one year. There is growing evidence that, prior to the current 'credit crisis' the bonus element of managers' compensation was the fastest growing part and largest amount within the overall package. Some of these bonus payments are difficult to justify. However, it should be acknowledged that payments to, for example, professional football players, movie and rock stars are also relatively high but they attract less criticism – perhaps because they entertain us better!

There are a variety of payment options for bonuses. Cash payments are the most common form of bonus payment, since they can and do apply to all organisations. As the name implies, a cash bonus is paid when the bonus is earned. However, in some cases cash bonuses may be paid by way of deferred compensation. Thus, although the amount of the bonus is calculated annually, payment to recipients is spread over a period of, say, three years. Under this system, managers receive only one-third of their bonus in the year in which it was earned. The remaining two-thirds are paid over the next two years. Therefore, a manager working under this arrangement would receive one-third of his bonus for the current year plus one-third of each of the bonuses for the preceding two years. The objective here could be to retain senior staff as the deferred compensation, depending on the employment contract, may only be payable if the individual manager stays with the company for a specified period of time. The advantage of deferred compensation is that managers can estimate, with better accuracy, their cash income for the forthcoming year. However, all cash bonuses are subject to tax at the manager's marginal rate of tax. Thus, it is usual to arrange bonuses that are more tax-efficient to the individual recipient.

A stock option is a right to purchase shares in the company at or after a given date in the future at a specified price agreed upon at the time the option is granted (usually between 90–95% of the current share price). Such stock options became very popular during the 1980s and 1990s for a number of reasons. First, compensation tied to the value of stock (shares) was viewed as a way to encourage managers to focus on increasing the long-term value of the company and therefore to focus their energies on the longer-term performance of the company for the benefit of all shareholders. The manager gains if, after exercising his option, he sells the stock at a price that exceeds the exercise price. However, many stock options are for 'restricted stock' which means that the managers are not permitted to sell this stock for a specified period – typically three to five years.

Secondly, from an individual manager's perspective, such stock-based compensation is more tax efficient than cash payments. An added advantage of granting stock options is that, until relatively recently, the granting of stock options did not impact on reported net income but rather this event was simply disclosed in footnotes to the financial statements. However, the International Financial Standards Board now requires that the fair value of employee-based compensation be reported as an expense on the company's income statement (see, IFRS 2, Share-based payment). A final advantage of stock options is that they do not require any cash outlay on behalf of the company. However, the attractiveness or otherwise of stock options depends on the future share price of the company and common sense tells us that share prices are sensitive to changes in reported profits. Thus, managers with attractive stock options had the perverse incentive of engaging in 'earnings management' including the adoption of aggressive accounting policies so that a smooth upward earnings trend would be reported, with the result that share prices would also increase in the required manner.

## Performance Criteria for Bonus

Large (quoted) companies now use a combination of three criteria to determine whether a bonus is payable. For a listed company, the share price is normally used, with the bonus depending on the increase in share price over a given period of time, or whether the share price reaches a predetermined target level. This is in keeping with the philosophy of maximising shareholder value. However, the current share price is only an accurate measure of what the company is worth at the point in time when the shares are traded. Unfortunately, the average shareholder does not have access to the same amount of information about the company that top managers have. A second problem with using share price as a performance criterion is the lack of a direct causal relationship between managerial actions and share price performance. Many non-controllable and random events, such as general business conditions, government actions or international developments impact on a firm's share price. (We have also previously mentioned that share price may be manipulated by creative accounting techniques including the adoption of aggressive accounting policies.)

If the company's share price is not considered appropriate (or is not readily available in the case of a non-quoted company) various accounting measures can be used, e.g. the amount of cost savings obtained during the accounting period, the sales growth in terms of monetary or volume terms or the growth in profits for the period under review. These measures may be referenced either to what was achieved in the previous year, budget or in peer companies. (The advantage of using peer companies is that the impact of non-controllable factors is reduced. For example, senior management of a company whose operating profits increased by 10% while the peer group of companies increased by 20% would not be rewarded due to their poor relative performance.) Many people consider that accounting measures are appropriate performance criteria because they represent economic performance and also they are commonly understood. However, it should be noted that accounting measures are short-term metrics and can be manipulated by inappropriate behaviour to increase short-term profits, but this behaviour often has a negative effect on long-term potential. This is especially the case where the bonus element is a large amount of the overall compensation package. In addition, when selecting accounting-based measures, a decision should be made on which adjustments, if any, will be made for uncontrollable factors. Generally, two types of adjustment are made, namely, to eliminate the financial consequences of decisions made by other managers, and to eliminate the financial impact of events not caused by the incompetence of the relevant manager. However, these adjustments are often made with a great deal of subjectivity. It is little consolation to note that organisations often reward or penalise managers for various factors that are beyond their ability to directly influence.

Due to the limitations of using either or both share price and accounting measures as performance criteria in determining bonuses, most firms also determine bonus awards with reference to a range of key performance indicators linked to critical success factors. Such key performance indicators include metrics on market share, customer satisfaction and loyalty, product innovation, on-time delivery, staff training and many others. These key performance indicators, it will be recalled, measure the 'things that matter' to the long-term success of the firm. Increasingly, firms are reviewing and amending their management compensation schemes and it is not uncommon to see compensation schemes that include all three performance criteria.

## Other Considerations

There are some other considerations associated with managerial compensation that need to be briefly mentioned. First of all, the determination of the bonus can be done at a manager-specific or at a general level. Using a specific approach, only the performance in a manager's unit is evaluated. The advantage of a specific pool is that it directly motivates responsible managers since the amount of the bonus for any manager is independent of the performance of the other managers. In contrast, when a general approach is used, the bonus to each manager depends, in some predetermined way, on the performance of the firm as a whole. This represents reality since it should be noted that business units within the same firm are interdependent and one manager's decisions may have an impact on other units within the organisation. Thus, a general bonus pool provides an important incentive for coordination and cooperation among unit managers within the organisation, since all managers share in the greater overall profits. Also, this general system of sharing is appropriate when individual performance is difficult to measure. For example, it is difficult to measure the contribution of the Financial Controller or Chief Management Accountant to the company's overall performance. The sharing arrangements for general level schemes can vary widely. For example, some schemes allow all managers to share equally; other schemes distribute bonuses in proportion to salary. Both of these methods of distribution are easy to understand and implement. However, they assume that either all managers' contribution is equal, or that their contribution is directly proportional to salary earned. In addition, general sharing schemes can be associated with the free-rider problem whereby undeserving managers are automatically entitled to a bonus due to the collective good work of their peers.

The second issue concerns the size of the bonus pool to be shared among managers, and here firms will differ. The simplest approach is to determine the size of the bonus pool with reference to a fixed percentage of reported profit – previously agreed to be either operating profits, profits before or after tax. Some companies allow a minimum bonus to be paid, in spite of low profits or even when the firm is loss-making, in an attempt to retain senior staff who may otherwise be tempted to leave. More recently, firms have been encouraged to adopt the Economic Value Added (EVA) metric which requires the firm to first earn a minimum rate of return on its investment before a bonus can be paid. Thirdly, what is the ideal length of the bonus period? This issue is impossible to adequately resolve. Some bonuses are calculated annually while others may be calculated over a longer period of, say, five years. Short-term schemes may encourage managers to ignore the important long-term considerations. However, long-term schemes may not be very practicable in an organisation where senior managers are regularly changing positions.

In summary, the variety of executive compensation schemes which exist within companies is enormous and this divergence of practice would be explained by contingency theory (**Section 16.5**). However, the objective of any management compensation scheme should be to ensure the achievement of long-term company goals by facilitating the recruitment of managers with relevant ability and expertise, retaining those managers and motivating them by providing rewards based on successful accomplishment and performance. Thus, accounting information is used to measure and evaluate the performance of the organisation but, in accordance with agency theory, it is also used to motivate, measure and evaluate the performance of individual agents. However, one problem with agency theory is that it largely remains an academic concept. There is little evidence that agency theory has resulted in better management compensation arrangements within organisations and this comment is particularly relevant in recent times when excessive managerial compensation, especially in financial institutions, appears to have been the norm rather than the exception. Indeed, many managers are not even aware of the theory. However, agency theory is a useful framework within which to examine the influence of incentives in the motivation and rewarding of managers and is likely to become a more important issue during the next decade. After all, rewarding effective managers is critical to the success of all firms.

## 16.7 Reflection

Congratulations on arriving at the end of this book and I hope you found it relevant to your studies. We have covered a lot of management accounting material, and much of it at an advanced level, but you will discover that there is a great deal more to be learned about the practice of this discipline. It is hoped that this text has provided a very solid practical and theoretical foundation upon which to build subsequent learning as part of a life-long commitment to the subject. At this stage it is worthwhile to reflect on some of the main issues that we have covered.

An initial and very important point is that the discipline of managerial accounting is a human invention. Therefore, it can be described as an art rather than a science. The discipline was invented or created in order to serve a purpose. That purpose, articulated throughout this book, is to influence the decisions of managers. Thus, in many ways the discipline of management accounting is probably as old as accounting itself. However, in terms of academic study, management accounting was popularised only around the 1950s, and this was facilitated by the publication of the first management accounting texts. In contrast, the first books on financial accounting appeared more than 400 years ago!

Because managerial accounting exists to be useful its practice has evolved over the years. It is fair to say that its modern origins lie in a costing tradition, heavily influenced by the industrial revolution which introduced mass production processes. The accountants, and in many cases engineers, of these enterprises were faced with the problem of costing a variety of different products, complicated by the growing amount of overheads. As businesses grew in size, complexity and geographical diversity, managers needed improved systems to provide the information that was necessary for various management decisions, including planning, performance evaluation and control. In addition, there was the necessity to value unsold production at the end of the year for financial reporting purposes. Subsequently, these 'internal' accountants became extremely valuable in trying to control costs, especially when vast amounts of money were expended in the various munitions contracts of the First World War. Thus, it is no coincidence that the two main professional management accounting institutions were founded in the UK and the USA around this time.

Gradually, these cost accountants adapted themselves to become management accountants. By the 1960s, management accounting had become a separate discipline in its own right in both university and professional accountancy exams. Topics such as cost accumulation systems, decision-making, budgetary control and standard costing were regular and frequent examination topics. However, no discipline, especially the practical discipline of managerial accounting, remains static.

In the 1980s the then practice of management accounting was severely criticised by Thomas Johnson and Robert Kaplan in their book *Relevance Lost: The Rise and Fall of Management Accounting* (1987). This book subsequently received an award from the American Accounting Association for the accounting publication with the greatest potential for influencing practice. Johnson and Kaplan examined the evolution of management accounting practice and they suggested that management accounting had lost its relevance in the modern business environment. This is because, for example:

1. Product cost information may be inaccurate due to the traditional method of absorbing production overhead, e.g. based on direct labour hours. This is a crude but simple method of overhead absorption but it assumes that all production overheads are volume-related, i.e. they are linked directly with the level of output.

    In modern firms, overheads are caused as much by complexity of operations as volume of output.

2. Management accounting practice focuses on the financial results for a period under review rather than the means by which these financial results were obtained. It should be obvious to readers that profit, *per se,* cannot be directly managed. Rather profit is generated as a natural consequence of performing well in various areas that include, for example, customer service, quality, product development and delivery performance. We have earlier referred to these as critical success factors and they should be included as part of the set of relevant management accounting information.

3. Traditionally, management accounting information focuses mainly on internal data. While internal data, such as cost per unit, is important to managers in their decision-making tasks, it is also necessary that managers have available to them information relating to the firm's operating environment. For example, we have already stressed that it will be of little consolation to a firm if it has a good product, but its competitors have a better one. Such relevant external information will relate not only to competitors but also to the general economic environment and changing customer preferences.

4. Management accounting reports concentrate on short-term performance. In fairness, this short-term orientation is often the result of the expectations of shareholders and other financiers. Nevertheless, there is a tendency to place a major focus on the achievement of the maximum profits in a single accounting period and this creates a mentality of short-termism. The reaction of management is to take measures that could undermine long-term viability. Typical examples include a reduced emphasis on quality, or cutbacks in advertising expenditure and staff training.

Reflecting recent developments in the broad discipline of management accounting, new titles for courses and textbooks have appeared. These new titles usually include words such as 'Strategic' or 'Strategy', 'Cost Management', or 'Performance measurement'. While these terms have different meanings, it is realistic to suggest that they share common implications for the discipline of managerial accounting. Specifically, they all require the broadening of the type of relevant information that is presented by the management accountant to managers for decision-making, including strategy formulation and monitoring of its implementation. This proposal to expand the scope of managerial accounting is not a subtle device to provide a role for unwanted management accountants, whose traditional recording role may be under threat by increasingly sophisticated computer information systems. Instead, this broad range of information *is* required by managers and, if this leads to better decisions, the company and all its stakeholders will benefit from it. In conclusion, managerial accounting is about looking to the future. After all, if you don't look to the future you probably won't have one.

## SUMMARY OF LEARNING OBJECTIVES

**Learning Objective 1:** Explain the nature, advantages and limitations of decentralisation.

The essence of decentralisation is the freedom given to responsible managers to make decisions. Most modern organisations are decentralised in some way. There are a number of advantages associated with decentralisation. First, there is the benefit of faster response to an emerging crisis using the benefit of local knowledge and an awareness of the local culture and language. Decentralisation also motivates managers who are rewarded on successful performance and decentralised units also provide a useful training ground for managers. However, decentralisation has certain limitations in that it causes some duplication of administrative and accounting activities. Perhaps the biggest limitation is, given freedom to make decisions, managers may make decisions in their own best interest which may not be in the best interest of the group as a whole.

**Learning Objective 2:** Distinguish between the different types of responsibility centres and the different types of performance measures useful in evaluating such responsibility centres.

This chapter highlighted three types of responsibility centre. In an expense centre, the manager is responsible only for costs but has no responsibility for revenue generation. Expenses centres can be either discretionary or engineered. The manager of a profit centre is responsible for costs and generating revenues. The manager of an investment centre is responsible for costs, revenue and capital expenditure decisions. Often, an investment centre is an independent business entity. All responsible centres should be evaluated with reference to appropriate financial and non-financial metrics based on what aspects they have responsibility for.

**Learning Objective 3:** Calculate, interpret and distinguish between Return on Investment (RoI) and Residual Income (RI).

An investment centre is usually evaluated, in financial terms, with reference to either return on investment (RoI) or residual income (RI). RoI is a percentage and represents the average return on the funds invested. The invested funds can be defined in terms of shareholders' funds (equity), capital employed or total assets. RI is an absolute amount and can be either positive or negative. RI is calculated by deducting from operating profits (PBIT) a notional interest charge based on the required rate of return on the investment controlled by the responsible manager. If RI is positive it indicates that the investment centre is earning in excess of its required rate of return. If RI is negative it means that the required rate of return is not being generated from the investment.

**Learning Objective 4:** Calculate and interpret Economic Value Added.

A modern refinement of residual income is referred to as Economic Value Added (EVA). EVA calculates the net operating profit after tax (NOPAT). However, a significant difference between EVA and RI is the type and number of adjustments made to the conventional income statement. For example, no provision is made for deferred taxation, and development and advertising expenditure is typically capitalised and written off over a number of years under EVA. In addition, goodwill is capitalised and is not subject to either annual amortisation or end of year impairment reviews. From NOPAT a notional interest charge is deducted based on the cost of capital and the funds invested. A positive EVA indicates that wealth has been generated during the accounting period whereas a negative EVA indicates that wealth has been destroyed.

**Learning Objective 5:** Explain the nature and methods of determining transfer prices.

Transfer prices are the price at which goods or services are transferred between units of the same corporate family. Ignoring taxes and tariffs, transfer prices do not impact on the overall profitability of the group. However, they do impact significantly on the reported profitability of the individual companies involved in trading by way of transfer price. The three methods of determining transfer prices are based on cost, market value and negotiation. It is generally considered that transfer prices, based on market prices, are conceptually superior but in some instances they may not be available – as in transferring goods which are only partially complete.

**Learning Objective 6:** Describe the reasons for both profit boosting and profit depressing transfer prices.

Transfer prices, especially those taking place across international boarders, can be used to either boost or lower reported profits in an overseas subsidiary. Profit depressing prices may be used because of political instability in the location of the overseas subsidiary or where there are restrictions on profit repatriation from that country. Profit depressing transfer prices can also be used to reduce wage demands in the local economy. In contrast, profit boosting transfer prices can be used to avail of low taxation rates in the location of the foreign subsidiary. They can also be used to circumvent import tariffs or benefit from export credits based on the declared value of the transaction, i.e. the declared transfer price.

**Learning Objective 7:** Describe contingency theory and its role in managerial accounting.

Contingency theory is a theory of organisations which can be applied to the discipline of management accounting. The essence of the contingency theory is that there is no 'best' management accounting system which can exist in all situations and be suitable to all companies. Rather management accounting information systems and their uses should be adapted in order to meet different environmental and organisational circumstances. Contingency theory explains, according to some authors, why some firms have, for example, an activity-based costing system and others do not. However, some critics of contingency theory argue that the definition and measurement of key variables associated with contingency theory need greater clarification. For example, how does one define and measure 'corporate culture' or 'power'? However, to its credit, contingency theory has added some academic rigour to the discipline of managerial accounting.

**Learning Objective 8:** Describe the purpose and elements of a management compensation scheme.

Management compensation schemes consist of policies and procedures intended to facilitate the recruitment of managers with relevant ability and expertise, retaining those managers and providing rewards based on successful accomplishment and performance. Most incentive schemes offer financial rewards and consist of three elements namely, salary, benefits (perquisites) and a bonus. However, there are non-financial incentives which may be attractive to managers, for example, the possibility of receiving awards and public recognition, being assigned increased responsibilities with greater autonomy or even relocation to a more attractive location (or office). The attractiveness of financial and intangible rewards will depend on the individual manager and it must be noted that, if the offered rewards are not attractive to managers, they will not have any significant motivating effect.

## Questions

### Review Questions

(See Appendix One for Solutions to Review Questions **16.1** and **16.2**)

*Question 16.1 (MCQ on Responsibility Centres)*

1. Which of the following is **not** a benefit associated with decentralisation?
   (a) Quicker decision-making
   (b) Increased motivation of sub-unit managers
   (c) Greater responsiveness to local needs
   (d) Decreased costs of gathering information

2. Which of the following is a cost/limitation associated with decentralisation?
   (a) Decreased loyalty toward the organisation as a whole
   (b) Sharper focus of management

    (c)  Better decision-making

    (d)  (a) and (b)

## The following data apply to Questions 3 and 4

Information pertaining to KC's Division for 20x8:

| | |
|---|---:|
| Sales | €610,000 |
| Variable costs | 500,000 |
| Traceable fixed costs | 100,000 |
| Average invested capital | 50,000 |
| Imputed interest rate | 18% |

3.   The ROI, based on invested capital, was
    (a)  40%
    (b)  29%
    (c)  20%
    (d)  18%

4.   The RI was
    (a)  €1,000
    (b)  2%
    (c)  €11,000
    (d)  €20,000

5.   A major advantage of decentralisation is:
    (a)  the elimination of dysfunctional decision-making.
    (b)  the loss of economies of scale.
    (c)  the creation of a more elaborate reporting system.
    (d)  greater awareness of local needs.

6.   The term 'controllability' is often used in the context of performance evaluation. Controllability means:
    (a)  the segregation of different business units.
    (b)  reporting only exceptional or significant variances.
    (c)  the degree of influence that a specific manager has over costs and revenues.
    (d)  controlling the objectives of individual business segments.

7.   Financial performance measures are commonly used as organisational goals. Such a performance measure (e.g. ROI) can result in:
    (a)  manipulation of the performance measure.
    (b)  suboptimisation.
    (c)  management's behaviour being influenced by the performance measure.
    (d)  all of the above.

8.   The term 'incongruent' is often used in the context of performance evaluation. Incongruent means that:
    (a)  one business segment's goals agree with overall organisational goals.
    (b)  one manager's goals conflict with overall organisational goals.

(c)  there are common goals between managers.
(d)  all of the above.

9.  Performance evaluation of a business segment should be measured on the basis of:
(a)  all costs and revenues apportioned to that segment.
(b)  all variable costs and revenues attributable to that segment.
(c)  assets, expenses and revenue of the business segment.
(d)  depends on the type of responsibility centre.

10.  Cost centre managers should be evaluated on the basis of:
(a)  all cost variances.
(b)  flexed budget cost variances.
(c)  controllable cost variances.
(d)  all of the above.

11.  Which one of the following is least likely to impact on the performance of a profit responsibility centre:
(a)  changes in sales volume.
(b)  changes in controllable expenses.
(c)  changes in bank/cash balances.
(d)  changes in depreciation of fixed assets.

12.  If an investment centre generates a positive residual income then:
(a)  actual return on investment < target rate.
(b)  actual return on investment > target rate.
(c)  actual residual income < target rate.
(d)  actual residual income > target rate.

13.  Residual income is used as a performance measure to:
(a)  determine the actual amount by which actual profit exceeds the profit required to meet the minimum ROI.
(b)  determine the amount of profit required to equal the minimum ROI.
(c)  measure the performance of an autonomous profit centre.
(d)  determine the percentage of excess profits.

## Questions 14 to 17 are based on the following information:

|                      | Division 1   | Division 2   |
|----------------------|--------------|--------------|
| Profit attributable  | €400,000     | €200,000     |
| Investment           | €2,000,000   | €1,600,000   |

The company has a 12% cost of capital per annum. There are two projects which are now being considered but neither of them is included in the above figures.

(i)  Project Alpha: Division 1 has the opportunity to increase annual sales by €200,000 by undertaking a special advertising campaign which will cost €20,000. The sales increase will improve the division's contribution by €50,000 (before the additional advertising) but will require an additional investment in assets of €200,000 per annum.

(ii)  Project Beta: Division 2 can purchase some new equipment costing €300,000 which will improve annual profits by €30,000 due to increased efficiency.

14.  The budgeted ROI for Division 1, before and after project Alpha is incorporated, is:

|  | Before | Incorporating Alpha |
|---|---|---|
| (a) | 8% | 19.5% |
| (b) | 20% | 21.5% |
| (c) | 8% | 21.5% |
| (d) | 20% | 19.5% |

15.  The budgeted ROI for Division 2, before and after project Beta is incorporated, is:

|  | Before | Incorporating Beta |
|---|---|---|
| (a) | 5% | 10% |
| (b) | 12.5% | 14.4% |
| (c) | 12.5% | 12.1% |
| (d) | none of the above. | |

16.  The budgeted RI for Division 1, before and after project Alpha is incorporated, is:

|  | Before | Incorporating Alpha |
|---|---|---|
| (a) | €160,000 | €166,000 |
| (b) | 8% | 7.5% |
| (c) | 20% | 19.5% |
| (d) | €160,000 | €8,000 |

17.  The budgeted RI for Division 2, before and after project Beta is incorporated, is:

|  | Before | Incorporating Beta |
|---|---|---|
| (a) | 12.5% | 12.1% |
| (b) | €8,000 | €2,000 |
| (c) | 20% | 12.1% |
| (d) | €8,000 | €8,000 |

18.  The Gamma Division is considering a proposal which will require an additional investment of €500,000. The target return for such projects is 12%. If the residual income is €80,000, the actual profit generated on this investment is:
(a)  12%
(b)  €60,000
(c)  28%
(d)  €140,000

19.  Orion has a target ROI of 20%. Estimated data for the forthcoming year is:

| | |
|---|---|
| Expected unit sales | 10,000 |
| Variable cost per unit | €300 |
| Annual fixed costs | €1m |
| Investment base | €1.6m |

The minimum selling price which could be charged to avoid a negative residual income is:
(a)  €132
(b)  €340

(c) €400

(d) €432

20. The following information relates to the Bull Division of Sharp Limited:

Sales (50,000 units @ €8 each)      €400,000

Variable costs                                      €300,000

Fixed costs                                            €75,000

Investment Base                              €150,000

Target RoI                                                    20%

In addition to the above budgeted data, the manager of Bull Division has the opportunity to sell 10,000 additional units for €7.50 each. However, an additional investment in fixed assets of €20,000 is required. If this proposal is accepted, then residual income will:

(a)  increase by €5,000

(b)  increase by €6,000

(c)  increase by €11,000

(d)  increase by €75,000

## Question 16.2 (Measuring Performance in Responsibility Centres)

'Traditional financial-based measures of performance of responsibility centres may lead to negative effects in the modern business environment. A wider range of measures must now be adopted to provide a fuller picture of the performance of a business branch, sector or division.'

### Requirements:

1. Discuss the limitations of traditional measures of divisional performance, specifying in each case which measures you are referring to.

2. Suggest alternative measures which might be adopted and explain their purpose and significance.

Source: Chartered Accountants Ireland, P3, Management Accounting and Business Finance,
Summer 2000 (adapted)

## Intermediate Questions

### Question 16.3 (Evaluating Financial Performance using RoI and RI)

The ABC Group operates in the fast food industry and is divided into two main retail sections, named Division A and Division B. Each retail division is considered as an investment centre because the managing director of each unit has full authority over all operating, investment and financing decisions. This investment centre structure was introduced in order to motivate managers.

The Head Office management are anxious to introduce a formal evaluation system, based on financial performance, in order to equitably assess the performance of each division. The following information has been extracted from the budgets, provisionally agreed, of Divisions A and B for the forthcoming year:

INCOME SUMMARIES FOR YEAR ENDED...

|  | Division A € | Division B € |
|---|---|---|
| Operating profit for year | €200,000 | €64,000 |
| Interest | (50,000) | (40,000) |
| Profit before tax | 150,000 | 24,000 |
| Taxation | (45,000) | (6,000) |
| Profit after tax | 105,000 | 18,000 |

BALANCE SHEET EXTRACTS AT END OF FINANCIAL YEAR

|  | Division A € | Division B € |
|---|---|---|
| Current assets | 200,000 | 150,000 |
| Fixed assets | 800,000 | 650,000 |
| Total assets | 1,000,000 | 800,000 |
| Shareholders' funds | 400,000 | 300,000 |
| Long-term loans payable | 400,000 | 300,000 |
| Current liabilities | 200,000 | 200,000 |
|  | 1,000,000 | 800,000 |

After the above budget figures have been agreed, two additional proposals have been made but neither of them is included in the above figures. Project Alpha is being considered by Division A and Project Beta is being considered for Division B. Relevant information on these two proposals is as follows:

1. Project Alpha in which Division A has the opportunity to increase annual sales by €200,000 by undertaking a special advertising campaign which will cost €15,000. The sales increase will improve the division's contribution by €30,000 (excluding advertising costs) but will require an additional investment in stocks (and therefore share capital) of €100,000 per annum.
2. Project Beta in which Division B can purchase some new equipment costing €200,000 (which is to be financed by additional share capital) which will improve annual profits by €22,000, including depreciation, due to increased efficiency.

**Note:** The company has a minimum rate of return of 12% per annum on its investment, defined in terms of its **total assets.**

**Requirements:**

1. Determine the budgeted RoI for each Division, **excluding** consideration of the two proposed projects, and assuming investment is defined in terms of (pre-tax) return on shareholders' funds.
2. Determine the budgeted RoI for each Division, **including** the two proposed projects, and assuming that investment is defined in terms of (pre-tax) return on shareholders' funds.
3. Bearing in mind the information generated in parts (1) and (2), which of the two projects are likely to be approved (or rejected) by the respective managers? Explain your reasoning.
4. It has been suggested to management that evaluation of performance would be better done by using Residual Income. Determine the budgeted Residual Income (RI) for each Division both **excluding** and **including** the two proposed projects. Which project, if any, is likely to be sanctioned? Why?
5. What other measures (financial and non-financial) could be used to evaluate the performance of each division?

## Question 16.4 (Evaluation of Responsibility Centres)

The CIIM Group operates in the retail sector of large white, electrical consumer goods. It has a number of retail outlets in various cities. The decision to open a particular shop is taken at the behest of top management. Thereafter, a manager of each location is appointed who is responsible for sales and cost of operations, including delivery to customers. Towards this end, he is given discretion on what items to sell, what suppliers to purchase from and to undertake appropriate delivery requirements to customers.

The manager of general operations for the group will retire shortly next year. A review of the performance, attitudes, and skills of several management employees has been undertaken. The selection committee has narrowed the choice to the managers of Division North and Division South, both of whom have similar educational qualifications and experience within the group. The financial results of their performance in the past three years are reported below (000 omitted).

| | Division North | | | Division South | | |
|---|---|---|---|---|---|---|
| | 20x2 | 20x3 | 20x4 | 20x2 | 20x3 | 20x4 |
| Overall market size | €10,000 | €12,000 | €13,000 | €5,000 | €6,000 | €6,500 |
| Sales | 1,000 | 1,100 | 1,210 | 450 | 600 | 840 |
| Cost of sales | 300 | 352 | 423 | 135 | 168 | 218 |
| Operating costs | 675 | 710 | 621 | 310 | 400 | 480 |

| | Division North | | | Division South | | |
|---|---|---|---|---|---|---|
| | 20x2 | 20x3 | 20x4 | 20x2 | 20x3 | 20x4 |
| = PBIT | 25 | 38 | 166 | 5 | 32 | 142 |
| Interest | 6 | 6 | 7 | 3 | 6 | 7 |
| = Profit | | | | | | |
| before tax | 19 | 32 | 159 | 2 | 26 | 135 |
| Total fixed | | | | | | |
| assets | 200 | 205 | 210 | 100 | 140 | 160 |
| Current assets | | | | | | |
| Inventory | 60 | 70 | 80 | 40 | 50 | 60 |
| Debtors | 60 | 65 | 70 | 30 | 40 | 50 |
| Bank | 10 | Nil | Nil | Nil | 10 | 30 |
| | 130 | 135 | 150 | 70 | 100 | 140 |
| Total assets | 330 | 340 | 360 | 170 | 240 | 300 |
| **Financed by:** | | | | | | |
| Shareholders' | | | | | | |
| funds | 227 | 235 | 245 | 123 | 140 | 170 |
| L Term | | | | | | |
| Liabilities | 63 | 65 | 65 | 27 | 60 | 70 |
| Trade | | | | | | |
| creditors | 40 | 40 | 50 | 20 | 40 | 60 |
| | 330 | 340 | 360 | 170 | 240 | 300 |

**Requirements:**

1. Calculate both RoI (in terms of return on total assets) and RI for both divisions for 20x4, assuming that investment is defined as total assets, and the firm's minimum return on total assets is 15% per annum. Comment on the use of RoI as a performance measure for evaluation purposes.
2. On the basis of the financial information given, which manager would you recommend for the post of manager of general operations? Support your answer.
3. Many believe that a single measure, such as ROI, is inadequate to fully evaluate performance. Give a range of other performance indicators that could be used in evaluation (together with your reasoning for each measure).
4. What factors should be considered in preparing budget figures for 20x5?

*Question 16.5 (Evaluation of Responsibility Centres)*

SV Supermarket Group is a national supermarket chain which is divided into four geographical regions. In the Leinster region there are 40 stores in operation – all owned rather than leased – and it is intended to open additional outlets in the future. The decision to open a new store or not is taken by the regional manager.

Once the decision is taken to open a store, a store manager is appointed and each store manager is responsible for selling price decisions and undertaking in-store promotions. Each store manager, whilst having some freedom within his or her own store, is responsible to the regional manager who, in turn, reports to the head office. However, each store has an administration manager who looks after all administrative, accounting and personnel matters. The responsibility accounting system of the SV Supermarket group makes use of cost centres, profit centres and investment centres.

Each store offers a wide range of goods including food products, clothing and hardware and there is, usually, an in-store cafeteria. SV Supermarkets have an arrangement with large manufacturers to buy most of its products centrally and thereafter the products are sold at agreed prices to each local store.

Store managers have no authority to make capital expenditure decisions above €20,000 per annum. Rather, capital expenditure decisions are taken by the regional manager.

**Requirements:**

1. Distinguish between cost centres, profit centres and investment centres, illustrating your answer by reference to the SV Supermarket group. For each responsibility centre suggest two possible performance measures, one financial and the other non-financial.
2. Discuss the potential problems in using cost, profit and investment centres for managerial decision-making and evaluation.

*Question 16.6 (Economic Value Added)*

The following summarised financial statements relate to Smalltony Limited for a recent accounting year:

INCOME STATEMENT FOR YEAR ENDED ...

|  | € |
|---|---|
| Gross profit | 2,270 |
| Selling & Admin | (1,780) |
| R & D | (180) |
| Goodwill amortised | (20) |
| Profit before interest and tax | 290 |
| Interest paid | (10) |
| Profit before tax | 280 |
| Current tax | (99) |
| Deferred tax | (26) |
| Profit for year | 155 |

BALANCE SHEET AT YEAR END....

| | € |
|---|---|
| Total assets | 1,290 |
| Financed by: | |
| Capital employed | 831 |
| Current liabilities | 459 |
| | 1,290 |

The following information is provided:

1. Goodwill on acquisition of a subsidiary company purchased during the year is being written off over 10 years. For EVA purposes, this should be capitalised.
2. Research and development costs are expensed as incurred. However, it would be more realistic to write these costs off over a period of 10 years. No research and development costs have been incurred previously.
3. Assume a tax rate of 45% on taxable profits.
4. The weighted average cost of capital (WACC) is given as 15%.

**Requirements:**

1. Calculate the EVA for the above accounting period. Show your workings. What do your calculations reveal and imply?
2. Highlight some of the limitations of EVA.

*Question 16.7 (The Profit Impact of Transfer Pricing)*

The Goodman Company Limited is a manufacturing division of electrical components within the Telling Group and it has presented the following summarised budget for the forthcoming financial year:

| Sales | € 375,000 |
|---|---|
| Variable costs @ €6 per unit | (250,000) |
| Contribution | 125,000 |
| Less: Fixed costs (excluding interest) | (50,000) |
| Divisional operating profit | 75,000 |

Included in Goodman's budget above is the proposed sale of 10,000 units at €7.50 each to Sharp Company, another division in the Telling group. (There are no tax or tariff implications on this proposed internal transaction.) However, this is only a proposed transaction and there are no legal agreements involved.

In recent days, a firm external to the group i.e. an independent manufacturing contractor, has promised to supply Sharp Company with the same number of electrical components at €6 each.

Under the decentralised corporate structure, the managers of both Goodman and Sharp have been given freedom to make decisions regarding selling prices and trading customers.

## Requirements:

1. Calculate the impact of the total profit of (a) the Goodman division (b) the Sharp division and (c) the Telling Group, if Goodman meets the €6 price and supplies Sharp with 10,000 units.

2. Calculate the effect on the total profit of (a) the Goodman and (b) Sharp divisions and the (c) Telling Group if Goodman does not lower its price and Sharp purchases the 10,000 units externally. (In other words, the proposed internal transaction will not go ahead.) For various technical reasons, it is not possible for Goodman to acquire another customer for the 10,000 units during the current accounting period, and therefore, the goods will not be produced.

3. Based on your calculations, identify a theoretical minimum transfer price and a theoretical maximum transfer price. What are the implications of these two prices?

## Advanced Questions

### Question 16.8 (Transfer Pricing)

Pizza Place operates a chain of three restaurants in a large city in three different locations, providing different types of customer service and with different operating capacity. Each restaurant sells one standard meal (pizza and drink) for a different price, depending on whether it is a sit down in Location A (€20 per meal), takeaway in Location C (€15 per meal) or mixed i.e. sit down and takeaway (Location B). Based on historic records, it is estimated that Location B sells equal numbers of sit in and takeaway meals.

Each meal costs the same in terms of ingredients (materials) and preparation (excluding labour) and this cost, at €7 per meal, is fully variable. The employees in each location are all paid €11 per hour and labour costs are considered fixed in response to volume changes over a relevant range of activity. Each location incurs total labour hours in a month as follows:

Location A – a total of 5,000 hours.
Location B – a total of 3,500 hours.
Location C – a total of 3,500 hours.

Employees will be paid for these hours regardless of the level of sales. Also, trade union rules prohibit any hours beyond these levels in each location. In addition, as part of an incentive scheme, employees are paid a percentage commission on all meals sold. The unit sales price, unit variable costs and total fixed costs are summarised as follows:

|  | A (sit down) | B (both) | C (takeaway) |
|---|---|---|---|
| Sit down revenue | €20.00 | n/a | n/a |
| Sit down and takeaway | n/a | €17.50 | n/a |
| Takeaway | n/a | n/a | €15.00 |
| Materials | (7.00) | (7.00) | (7.00) |
| Sales commission (10%) | (2.00) | (1.75) | (1.50) |
| Fixed costs per month: |  |  |  |
| Labour | €55,000 | €38,500 | €38,500 |
| Administration | €25,000 | €25,000 | €25,000 |
| Total fixed costs | €80,000 | €63,500 | €63,500 |

Because of the labour hours restriction, management are interested in determining some form of transfer pricing system between the locations. This would involve meals being fully prepared in one location and delivered to another. Specifically, this proposal would apply to transfers only from Location A to Location C and from Location B to Location C. The delivery cost between Locations A and C would be €5 per meal, while between Locations B and C this would be €4 per meal. Staff commissions will be based on the percentages previously agreed i.e. 10% on sales price.

**Requirements:**

1. What are the minimum transfer prices that should be charged under each of the following independent scenarios, on the basis that demand in Location C will be 15,000 meals per month? In each case, you are required to comment on whether the transfer prices would be acceptable to both the providing and receiving locations.
   (a) Location C will only have capacity to prepare 10,000 meals, while Locations A and B will have excess capacity of 2,500 meals each.
   (b) No excess capacity is expected in any of the three locations and overtime is not possible.

2. Outline briefly **three** types of transfer prices, commenting on their individual limitations.

Source: Chartered Accountants Ireland, Management Accounting and Business Finance, P3, Autumn 2005

*Question 16.9 (Transfer Pricing)*

Outdoors is the name of a Group that produces a range of gardening materials. It has two divisions, a manufacturing division known as 'Pulp' and a retail division known as 'Retail'. It also has a head office where group decisions are made. Pulp's main product is wood pulp, which is sold both to external (non-group) customers and internally to the retail division. The Retail division converts the wood pulp into bags of wood chip which is a popular product for gardeners.

The full production capacity of the Pulp division is 5,000 tonnes of wood pulp per month. Currently sales demand is 90% of this capacity and two-thirds of its sales are made to external customers and one-third is sold to the Retail division. The internal transfer price (from Pulp to Retail) was agreed at variable cost plus a 60% mark-up (on variable cost). This price was used for budgeting purposes within the group and the group financial year commences 1 January.

However, due to intense competition in the wood pulp market, the external selling price charged by Pulp was reduced to €135 per tonne and this price became effective on 1 June 20x8 during the current budgetary cycle. The Retail division has voiced its concern in relation to the reduced selling price to external parties and the fact that no change in the internal transfer price has been made. However, Pulp has argued that the original transfer price was agreed, having been proposed by top management for the year, and has argued that internal selling prices must hold for the entire year.

The Retail division produces 100 bags of wood chip from each tonne of pulp it is supplied with every month and it sells each bag for €3.50. The Retail division has carried out some market research and they have estimated that, if it were to reduce its selling price to €3.15 per bag of wood chip, its sales would increase by 50,000 bags per month. (If this price is introduced it would apply to all sales.)

The group costing report for Pulp shows a variable cost of €100 per tonne and fixed costs of €120,000 per month. In the Retail division, the variable cost (excluding the cost of the internal purchase from Pulp) is an additional €0.80 per bag and the fixed costs are €80,000 per month.

**Requirements:**

1. Prepare the estimated income statements for June 20x8 for each division and for the group as a whole on the following scenarios:
   (a) The transfer price currently operating between the two divisions (i.e. variable cost plus 60% mark up) and the selling price in Retail of €3.50 per bag.
   (b) The transfer price currently operating between the two divisions but the selling price in Retail reduced to €3.15 per bag. In this scenario, Pulp would operate at full capacity to fulfil additional demand.

2. The Retail division has successfully argued at group level that it is being unfairly treated under the current transfer pricing agreement. Head Office has agreed that it will allow Retail to source wood pulp outside the group, provided it leads to an increase in overall group profits. Retail has found an alternative supplier who will supply 2,000 tonnes of wood pulp for €125 per tonne and this will allow Retail to sell wood pulp at €3.15 per bag. In turn, Pulp has found a new customer who will pay €135 per tonne for its remaining capacity of 2,000 tonnes but Pulp must pay additional transport costs of €2 per tonne.

Recalculate the estimated income statements for each division and the group as a whole based on the new scenario presented and comment on your results from the perspective of each division and the group.

3. Outline the difficulties of setting a transfer pricing structure that achieves the dual objective of increasing overall group profit whilst enabling equitable evaluation of divisions.

Source: Chartered Accountants Ireland, Management Accounting and Business Finance, P3, Autumn 2007 (adapted)

## Question 16.10 (Determining (international) Transfer Prices)

A US Corporation Company produces 'widgets' which are sold on the domestic market. Profits in the US are liable to a tax rate on corporate income of 40% but this is levied only on American income on foreign profits repatriated.

The American company is keen to expand into the European market and, towards this end, they have established a wholly owned assembly plant in Ireland. This assembly plant qualifies for a corporate tax rate of 10% in Ireland. In reality, the 'widgets' will be manufactured in the United States and these partly completed goods will then be transported and assembled in Ireland. Because of its location within the EU, the goods exported to Europe from Ireland are not liable for any import or export tariff.

The cost of assembly in Ireland, selling and distribution costs in Europe and legal and regulatory expenses are estimated at 20% of final selling price.

The management of the American company is anxious to determine in advance a transfer pricing strategy i.e. a low or high transfer price between the American and Irish plants. However, one can ignore Double Tax Agreements (DTA) between the two countries.

### Requirements:

1. In any decentralised organisation complete autonomy of action is impossible when a substantial level of transfer pricing takes place. In this context briefly explain decentralisation and autonomy of action and outline whether autonomy is good.

2. Develop a deterministic (mathematical) model suitable for predicting cash flows to the American company, the Irish company, and, finally, the overall group, assuming the existence of the American and Irish companies only and clearly specify your recommendation of setting either a 'high' or 'low' transfer price in order to maximise group after-tax profitability.

3. Use your model developed in (2) to predict group cash flows (after-tax) assuming an Irish selling price (ISP) of €100, a transfer price between the US and Ireland of €50; and a production cost in the US equivalent to €20.

4. Rework your figures assuming a transfer price between the US and Ireland of €80, and prove the after-tax cash saving to the group due to using a transfer price of €50 rather than €80.

*Question 16.11 (International Transfer Pricing with Tariffs)*

URI Corporation is a diversified multinational company and the group headquarters is located in Boston. One of its US-based divisions manufactures and sells 'widgets' in the United States where the tax rate (Federal and State) on corporate profits is currently 50%.

The Chinese market is one of the foreign markets in which URI are interested and it now has a 60%-owned distribution subsidiary in that country with the remaining 40% owned by the Chinese government. It is anticipated that the US division will produce and sell the 'widgets' to the Chinese subsidiary for the Chinese market. However, import tariffs are payable by the Chinese subsidiary amounting to 40% of declared invoice value.

The applicable tax rate on corporate profits in China is 35%. There are no other restrictions or taxes affecting the transfer of goods or funds from China to the United States and FX implications in relation to the Dollar and Yuan currencies can be ignored.

**Requirements:**

1. By definition, decentralised units have a great deal of autonomy. Write a brief note outlining the dangers from permitting autonomy of action, and in what ways do interdivisional transfers make complete autonomy impossible?
2. Develop a deterministic model suitable for predicting cash flows to the shareholders in the group holding company. Based on your model, should the transfer price be set at high or low levels? Are there any difficulties in getting agreement between the two trading companies regarding this transfer price?

*Question 16.12 (Evaluation of Responsibility Centres)*

Sesco plc owns and operates 30 supermarket stores selling food and other household supplies in the Irish market and there is considerable competition between the various supermarket chains operating here. In recent years there have been examples of too many supermarkets attempting to operate in the same locality where the size of the customer base was too small to support the number of outlets. Also, there have been examples of national and local price wars breaking out (between Sesco and its competitors) as a result of one or more operators attempting to increase market share.

Performance evaluation and control within Sesco plc is primarily exercised by a review of a range of league tables of key ratios relating to profitability and other indicators. The management of Sesco plc have noticed that there is significant divergence in performance across the stores in the group. Hence, there is a need to review the systems and criteria used for control and performance evaluation. Profitability ratios and indicators per store are compared within the company rather than with industry benchmarks.

Stores that are not affected by price wars or increased competition usually experience sales growth of no more than 3% per annum excluding inflation. Cost controls permit only limited discretion to local management.

Summary financial data and selected data for Stores A, B, and C gathered by internal audit for Sesco plc, are set out in **Appendix 1** in respect of year ended 31 December, 20x9 and in **Appendix 2** in respect of the previous year ended 31 December, 20x8.

**Requirements:**

1. (a) Explain, with reasons, which key ratios you, as management accountant of Sesco plc, would recommend to be used for operational control and performance evaluation of existing stores.
   (b) Comment on the performance of stores A, B and C, using the available information.

2. Set out briefly the risks associated with a 'domestic company', such as Sesco plc, expanding its operations into a foreign country.

3. Discuss the role of management accountants in risk management.

> Source: Chartered Accountants Ireland, CAP 2, Strategic Finance and Management Accounting, Summer 2009 (adapted)

APPENDIX 1: SUMMARY DATA FOR SESCO FOR YEAR ENDED 31 DECEMBER 20X9

|  | Store A | Store B | Store C | Group (30 stores) |
|---|---|---|---|---|
| Floor area (square metres) | 1,200 | 1,000 | 1,100 | 31,500 |
| Number of (FT equivalent) employees | 72 | 70 | 67 | 1,785 |
| Number of competitors in local area | 8 | 4 | 5 | n/a |
| Total no. of customer complaints | 115 | 106 | 98 | 2,800 |
| No. of coding errors per 1,000 transactions | 12 | 9 | 4 | 5 |
|  | €000 | €000 | €000 | €000 |
| Revenue | 7,680 | 7,200 | 7,370 | 192,450 |
| Cost of sales | 5,982 | 5,456 | 5,632 | 149,350 |
| Gross profit | 1,698 | 1,744 | 1,738 | 43,100 |
| Labour costs | 917 | 907 | 886 | 21,700 |
| Other costs | 731 | 647 | 692 | 16,400 |
| Total costs | 1,648 | 1,554 | 1,578 | 38,100 |

| | | | | |
|---|---|---|---|---|
| Operating profit (before interest and tax) | <u>50</u> | <u>190</u> | <u>160</u> | <u>5,000</u> |
| Balance Sheet summaries at 30 April 20x9 | €000 | €000 | €000 | €000 |
| Inventory at end of year | 324 | 329 | 343 | 8,500 |
| Less: Trade payables | (1,241) | (1,164) | (1,191) | (31,100) |
| Other assets | <u>1,117</u> | <u>940</u> | <u>1,122</u> | <u>27,400</u> |
| Capital Employed | <u>200</u> | <u>105</u> | <u>274</u> | <u>4,800</u> |

There are no significant receivables in any store.

APPENDIX 2: SUMMARY DATA FOR YEAR ENDED 31 DECEMBER 20x8

| | Store A | Store B | Store C | Group |
|---|---|---|---|---|
| | €000 | €000 | €000 | €000 |
| Revenue | <u>8,320</u> | <u>6,963</u> | <u>7,038</u> | <u>186,950</u> |
| Gross profit | <u>1,947</u> | <u>1,693</u> | <u>1,655</u> | <u>42,050</u> |
| Operating profit (before interest and tax) | <u>317</u> | <u>232</u> | <u>152</u> | <u>5,700</u> |
| Number of competitors in local area | 6 | 4 | 5 | |
| Total number of customer complaints | 99 | 107 | 101 | |
| No. of coding errors per 1,000 transactions | 8 | 8 | 3 | |

# Appendix One

# Solutions to Review Questions

*Solution 1.1 (Descriptions of Financial or Managerial Accounting)*

| Item | Description | Answer |
|------|-------------|--------|
| a | Accuracy | Financial |
| b | Annually | Financial |
| c | Assets and liabilities | Financial |
| d | Audited | Financial |
| e | Budgets | Managerial |
| f | Cost per unit | Managerial |
| g | Critical success factors (CSFs) | Managerial |
| h | Detailed information | Managerial |
| i | External users | Financial |
| j | External information | Managerial |
| k | Future orientated | Managerial |
| l | Internal users | Managerial |
| m | International Financial Reporting Standards | Financial |
| n | Key performance indicators (KPIs) | Managerial |
| o | Market share | Managerial |
| p | Non-financial performance measures | Managerial |
| q | Objectivity | Financial |
| r | On time delivery of products | Managerial |
| s | Regulated | Financial |
| t | Reports on customer loyalty | Managerial |
| u | Shareholders | Financial |
| v | Strategy | Managerial |
| w | Subjective | Managerial |
| x | Summarised information | Financial |
| y | Threats and opportunities | Managerial |
| z | Vision | Managerial |

## Solution 1.2 (Profit v. Performance Measures)

### (a) Why profit as a measure of performance?

'Profit' summarises the financial consequences of all the trading activities of a business. In other words, all the activities within the firm can be translated into a common currency, i.e. financial terms whose net financial impact is reported as profit (or loss) on the bottom line. Thus, profit is a commonly used measure of performance for all types of commercial enterprises. In addition, firms use financial resources to generate such profits and the overall measure of Return on Capital Employed (RoCE) or Return on Investment (RoI) is commonly used.

Moreover, the calculation and comparison of profit is well understood and relatively easy, despite well-known problems relating to the use of various profit measures.

### (b) Limitations of profit measurement

There are several limitations in using profit as a measure of performance of which the most important are:

- Because its calculation is based on accounting data, it is possible to argue that the profit figure can be distorted. For example, a great deal of subjectivity is required in computing some cost data, e.g. providing for annual depreciation.
- Profit is a result. The profit measure does not disclose the root cause of problems occurring in a business, e.g. where a real problem is excessive set-up times or poor quality or low on-time delivery. Thus, managers require information on the 'means', i.e. what activities cause profits to be generated. One can also add that the profit measure is incomplete. An over-concentration on profit can ignore the important liquidity position of the firm. In addition, profit is an inadequate measure to control all functions of the business as it may be severely affected by uncontrollable factors such as inflation, exchange rates and the effects of the economy in general.
- An undue emphasis on profit as a key measure of performance can give rise to the phenomenon of 'short-termism'. This means that activities are undertaken by managers to generate short-term profit performance to the long-run detriment of the firm. Typical examples are the reduction on marketing spend or cutting down on staff training or research and development costs. Such activities may have a favourable short-term profit impact but can be disadvantageous to the long-run survival prospects of the firm.
- The profit figure reported in the financial statements is an historical measure. It relates to what has happened in the past. For decision-making, managers need estimates of future profitability but historical profits are only a guide to what future profit may be.

## Solution 2.1 (Absorption v Variable (Direct) Costing)

### Memorandum

To:     Managing Director
From:   A Student
Date:   13 September 20x1
Re:     The Introduction of Variable (Direct) Costing

This memorandum has been prepared at the request of the managing director, to provide assistance to company management regarding the possible introduction of variable (direct) costing to value finished goods at the end of the accounting period for financial reporting purposes. Currently, the company uses absorption costing and there is some concern that profits are overstated using this method. This memorandum will explain the difference between absorption costing and variable (direct) costing, list the arguments put forward in support of both methods and explain the impact on profits of using absorption costing as opposed to variable (direct) costing.

**(i)** Absorption costing is also called full costing and refers to a system in which all the fixed production overheads are allocated to products. Product costs then comprise direct materials, direct labour, direct expenses, variable production overhead and an allocation of fixed production overheads.

Variable (direct) costing,  refers to a system in which only variable production costs are assigned to products. Product costs comprise direct materials, direct labour, direct expenses and variable production overheads. Fixed production overheads are considered to be period costs and are not charged to products, but written off immediately to the income statement.

**(ii) Arguments in support of absorption costing:**

- Absorption costing does not understate the importance of fixed costs. The allocation of fixed manufacturing costs to products recognises that sufficient revenue must be generated to cover fixed costs in the long run.
- Absorption costing defers fixed overheads by including them in the closing stock valuation. These fixed overheads will only be recorded as an expense in the period in which the goods are sold. This is in contrast to a variable costing system, which includes fixed manufacturing overheads in the period in which they are incurred and if sales are lower than production may result in fictitious losses.
- Absorption costing is theoretically superior to variable costing. Theory suggests that fixed manufacturing costs are just as much expended in the production of goods as variable manufacturing costs and consequently all costs expended in the manufacture of a product should be charged to the goods produced.
- Absorption costing is based on the revenue production concept. This concept assumes that any cost essential in making a product that may reasonably be expected to be sold represents a cost of obtaining sales revenue. Hence these costs should be deferred and included in the stock valuation so that they can be matched with revenue in calculating profit for the period of sale.

**Arguments in support of variable (direct) costing:**

- Variable (direct) costing provides more useful information for decision-making. Variable (direct) costing separates variable and fixed manufacturing costs and facilitates projection of future costs and revenues for different activity levels and the use of relevant cost decision-making techniques. Relevant costs are required for a variety of short-term decisions, e.g. whether to make a product internally or purchase externally.
- Variable (direct) costing removes the effect of stock changes on profit. Where stock levels are likely to fluctuate significantly, profits may be distorted when they are calculated on an absorption costing basis, since the stock changes will considerably affect the amount of fixed manufacturing overhead charged to an accounting period. This is not the case with variable (direct) costing as fixed manufacturing overheads are not included in the stock valuation.
- Variable (direct) costing avoids fixed overheads being capitalised in unsaleable stocks. If a company has surplus stocks, under an absorption costing system only a portion of the fixed production overheads will be charged as an expense in the period, the remainder will be included in the valuation of surplus stocks. There is a danger that these surplus stocks may be difficult to sell and hence a reduction in selling price may be necessary to sell off the stock. Again this does not arise in variable (direct) costing, as products are not charged with any share of fixed production overheads.

**(iii)** The impact on profit of using absorption costing as opposed to variable (direct) costing may be clearly demonstrated using three situations:

    (a)   Where the production level exceeds the sales level
    (b)   Where the sales level exceeds the production level
    (c)   Where the production level equals the sales level

*(a)    Where the production level exceeds the sales level*

In this case the profit in an absorption costing system will be higher than in a variable (direct) costing system. This is because absorption costing only includes that portion of the fixed manufacturing overheads allocated to the units sold and the remaining fixed manufacturing costs are included in the closing stock valuation. Variable (direct) costing on the other hand includes all fixed manufacturing costs as a period expense.

*(b)    Where the sales level exceeds the production level*

In this case the profit in an absorption costing system will be lower than in a variable (direct) costing system. This arises due to the fact that more fixed manufacturing overheads are being charged against profit than were actually incurred during the period.

*(c)    Where the production level equals the sales level*

In this case profit as calculated under both costing systems will be the same. For the absorption system, the only fixed manufacturing overhead that will be included in cost of sales will be the amount of fixed manufacturing overhead that is incurred for the period.

The company currently has a level of production that exceeds the sales level and the use of an absorption costing system will indeed cause an overstatement of profits. If the present situation is to continue, switching to a variable (direct) costing system will ensure that company profits are more correctly stated. However, the company needs to consider future plans in detail before making significant changes to its costing system.

Moving from the current absorption costing system to a variable (direct) costing system would involve a significant alteration in cost accumulation procedures and may cause difficulties for the company. Therefore, in considering a change of costing system I would advise the company to clearly evaluate its future plans and production levels to ensure that such a change would be appropriate and worthwhile. If you have any further queries or would like additional information about any of the matters mentioned above, please do not hesitate to contact me.

## *Solution 2.2 (Calculation of Unit Cost Data for Pricing Decisions)*

### 1.  Revised Profit Statement of Cortec Ltd after review of costs

|  | ZC100 | ZC150 | ZC200 | Total |
|---|---|---|---|---|
| Quantity | 95,000 | 105,000 | 150,000 | 350,000 |
|  | € | € | € | € |
| Materials (Note 1) | 807,500 | 1,076,250 | 1,650,000 | 3,533,750 |
| Labour (Note 2) | 950,000 | 1,260,000 | 1,500,000 | 3,710,000 |
| Variable Overheads (Note 3) | 199,500 | 294,000 | 435,000 | 928,500 |
| Fixed Overheads (Note 4) – original | 380,000 | 420,000 | 600,000 | 1,400,000 |
| Fixed overheads (Note 4) – revised sum | 166,250 | 183,750 | Nil | 350,000 |
| Total Costs | 2,503,250 | 3,234,000 | 4,185,000 | 9,922,250 |
| Sales (incl 25% mark-up) | 3,129,063 | 4,042,500 | 5,231,250 | 12,402,813 |
| Net Profit | 625,813 | 808,500 | 1,046,250 | 2,480,563 |
| Revised unit selling price (sales/unit) | 32.94 | 38.50 | 34.88 | |

**Note:** The shaded areas indicate figures that have changed.

| Workings: | € |
|---|---:|
| **Note 1 (re information item 1)** | |
| ZC100 materials | |
| 95,000 units × €8.50 | 807,500 |
| ZC150 materials | |
| 105,000 units × €10.25 | 1,076,250 |
| ZC200 materials acquired from new foreign supplier | |
| 150,000 units × €11 | 1,650,000 |
| | |
| **Note 2 (re information item 2)** | |
| Labour to produce 1 unit of ZC100 = 1.25 hours | |
| Cost per unit = 1.25 hours × €8 = €10 × 95,000 units | 950,000 |
| | |
| Labour to produce 1 unit of ZC150 = 1.5 hours | |
| Cost per unit = 1.5 hours × €8 = €12 × 105,000 units | 1,260,000 |
| | |
| Labour to produce 1 unit of ZC200 = 1.25 hours | |
| Cost per unit = 1.25 hours × €8 = €10 × 150,000 units | 1,500,000 |
| | |
| **Note 3 (re information item 3)** | |
| Variable overhead allocated to ZC100 should be €2.10 per unit instead of €2.50 × 95,000 units | 199,500 |
| Variable overhead allocated to ZC150: €2.80 × 105,000 units | 294,000 |
| | |
| Variable overhead allocated to ZC200 should be €2.90 per unit instead of €2.50 × 150,000 | 435,000 |
| | |
| **Note 4 (re information item 4)** | |
| Total fixed overhead in a year 350,000 units × €5 | 1,750,000 |
| Relates to X430 (to be assigned only to ZC 100 and ZC 150) | (350,000) |
| Balance | 1,400,000 |
| €1,400,000 to be assigned to all 3 units (€1,400,000/350,000) = | €4 per unit |
| €350,000 to be assigned to ZC 100 and ZC 150 only (€350,000/200,000) = | €1.75 per unit |

## 2. Critical analysis of revisions proposed

**New foreign supplier:** Based on the new quotation, the company will save on raw material costs. While the price itself is guaranteed, this is only for one year. Thus, one needs to consider the long-term price. The reliability of the new supplier also needs to be assessed – while the local supplier may cost more, if they guarantee on-time delivery, this could be important. Also, the (new) supplier could experience production/delivery problems because of location. In addition, overall quality could also be a concern, but it would be important that further testing was carried out before a decision is made here.

**Time and Motion study:** The study took place on one Monday morning and may not be representative of the true time required for production. Rather, the study should be conducted over an extended period, such as a week, to allow a better average to be determined. This would help to adjust for factors such as participating fatigue, machine breakdowns and other disruptions which could be one-off in nature.

**Correction of variable overhead error:** The company is correct in making this amendment to their costings as working from an incorrect base can lead to inaccurate decisions. It would be important for the company to ensure that all costings exercises are reviewed by persons other than those who derived them as this should help to pick up errors at an early stage.

**Correction of fixed overhead error:** The previous comments are also relevant here. It would be worthwhile for the company to verify that the overhead absorption rate (units of production) is valid for all elements of fixed overheads. There may be costs in this category, such as insurance or rent, that relate to space occupied rather than units produced. The company may want to reclassify such costs and assign them using different OHARs.

**Overall** The net impact of the revisions is to increase the sales price of the ZC100 and ZC150, but reduce the price of the ZC200. This happens because the company sets prices on the basis of a 25% mark up on costs. It is important for the company to be satisfied that increasing the sales price will not adversely affect units sold – the market may react by demanding less of ZC100 and ZC150, particularly if there are substitutes available, while demanding more of ZC200. This may not be in line with the firm's planned production and could result in lower overall profits. The company may need to re-evaluate its approach to pricing by reviewing what is acceptable to the end user and determining its cost base with this in mind:

## Solution 3.1 (Recording Cost Flows under a Job Costing System)

**1.**

### Creditors Control

| | | | |
|---|---|---|---|
| Bank | 50,000 | Balance b/d | 10,000 |
| Balance c/d | 20,000 | Purchases | + 60,000 |
| | 70,000 | | 70,000 |
| | | Balance b/d | 20,000 |

### Direct Materials Control

| | | | |
|---|---|---|---|
| Balance b/d | 20,000 | WIP – Issues | 53,000 |
| Purchases | 60,000 | Balance c/d | + 27,000 |
| | 80,000 | | 80,000 |
| Balance b/d | 27,000 | | |

### Work-in-Progress Control

| | | | |
|---|---|---|---|
| Materials | 53,000 | Finished Goods Control | 70,700 |
| Labour | 22,700 | Balance c/d (see schedule) | 23,400 |
| Factory overhead (applied) | 18,400 | | |
| | 94,100 | | 94,100 |
| Balance b/d | 23,400 | | |

### Finished Goods Control

| | | | |
|---|---|---|---|
| Balance b/d | 40,000 | Transfer to Cost of Sales | 58,250 |
| WIP Control | 70,700 | Balance c/d (see schedule) | 52,450 |
| | 110,700 | | 110,700 |
| Balance b/d | 52,450 | | |

### Production Overhead Control

| | | | |
|---|---|---|---|
| Bank, etc. | 19,000 | WIP control – overhead absorbed | 18,400 |
| WIP Control | | Cost of goods sold | 600 |
| | 19,000 | | 19,000 |

### Cost of Goods Sold

| | | | |
|---|---|---|---|
| Finished Goods Control | 58,250 | Transfer to Income statement (see schedule) | 58,850 |
| Prod'n Overhead Control | 600 | | |
| | 58,850 | | 58,850 |

### Administration Expenses

| | | | |
|---|---|---|---|
| Bank | 20,000 | | |

### Wages Control

| | | | |
|---|---|---|---|
| Bank | 22,700 | WIP – Labour | 22,700 |

+ Balancing (plug) figure

## 2. Schedule:

(a)
Closing work-in-progress – Job 84

| | |
|---|---:|
| Direct Materials | €16,000 |
| Direct Labour | €4,200 |
| Overhead absorbed | €3,200 |
| | €23,400 |

(b)
Closing Stock of Finished Goods

| | Materials | Labour | Overhead | Total |
|---|---|---|---|---|
| Job (opening) – 50% | 9,200 | 6,000 | 4,800 | 20,000 |
| Job 81 – sold | — | — | — | — |
| Job 82 – 50% | 7,500 | 4,250 | 3,600 | 15,350 |
| Job 83 – 75% | 9,000 | 4,500 | 3,600 | 17,100 |
| Job 84 – WIP | — | — | — | — |
| | | | | 52,450 |

(c)
Cost of sales

| | Materials | Labour | Overhead | Total |
|---|---|---|---|---|
| Job (opening) – 50% | 9,200 | 6,000 | 4,800 | 20,000 |
| Job 81 – 100% | 10,000 | 4,000 | 3,200 | 17,200 |
| Job 82 – 50% | 7,500 | 4,250 | 3,600 | 15,350 |
| Job 83 – 25% | 3,000 | 1,500 | 1,200 | 5,700 |
| Job 84 – WIP | — | — | — | — |
| | | | | 58,250 |
| Add: Under-absorbed production overhead (not prorated) | | | | 600 |
| | | | | 58,850 |

## Solution 3.2 (Job Costing and Pricing in a Manufacturing Company)

### 1. (a)
Overhead Analysis (apportionment)
Note: Different bases of apportionment are acceptable.

| Overhead | Basis of apportionment | Total | Manufacturing | Polishing | Packing |
|---|---|---|---|---|---|
| Supervisory Labour | Given | 420,000 | 230,000 | 110,000 | 80,000 |
| Light and heat | Floor space | 48,000 | 21,333 | 16,000 | 10,667 |
| Rent and rates | Floor space | 27,000 | 12,000 | 9,000 | 6,000 |

| Machine maintenance | Machine hrs | 16,000 | 8,000 | 4,000 | 4,000 |
|---|---|---|---|---|---|
| Plant depreciation | Book value | 80,000 | 48,000 | 20,000 | 12,000 |
| Factory canteen | Employees | 35,000 | 15,000 | 15,000 | 5,000 |
| | | 626,000 | 334,333 | 174,000 | 117,667 |

## 1. (b)          Overhead absorption rates (OHARs)

| Overhead absorption per | Machine hours | Direct labour hours | |
|---|---|---|---|
| | **Manufacturing** | **Polishing** | **Packing** |
| Budgeted overheads | 334,333 | 174,000 | 117,667 |
| Budgeted hours | 30,000 | 60,000 | 20,000 |
| OHAR per machine hour | €11.14 | | |
| OHAR per direct labour hour | | €2.90 | €5.88 |

## 2.          Computation of Selling price of Job No 999

| | | € |
|---|---|---|
| Direct materials (given) | (€7,500 + €2,800) | 10,300 |
| Direct labour (given) | (€850 + €3,900 + €1,500) | 6,250 |
| Overheads | | |
|     Manufacturing Department | (50 machine hours × €11.14) | 557 |
|     Polishing Department | (90 labour hours × €2.90) | 261 |
|     Packing Department | (25 labour hours × €5.88) | 147 |
| Total production cost | 80% of selling price | 17,515 |
| Add: Profit margin | 20% of selling price | 4,379 |
| = Recommended Selling price | | 21,894 |

Note: The profit margin given is based on 20% of selling price. This is equivalent to a mark-up on cost of 25%.

*Solution 4.1 (Process Costing with Equivalent Units – Single Process)*

### Process account

| Narrative | Units | € | Narrative | Units | € |
|---|---|---|---|---|---|
| Material control a/c | 1,000 | 2,700 | Finished goods | 600 | 5,400 |
| Labour control a/c | | 2,000 | WIP c/f | 400 | 1,750 |

| Narrative | Units | € | Narrative | Units | € |
|-----------|-------|-----|-----------|-------|-----|
| Overheads a/c | | 2,450 | | | |
| | 1,000 | 7,150 | | 1,000 | 7,150 |

| Working | Materials | Labour | Overheads |
|---------|-----------|--------|-----------|
| Costs to be assigned (a) | €2,700 | €2,000 | €2,450 |
| Equivalent units: | | | |
| Finished goods | 600 | 600 | 600 |
| Closing WIP | 300 | 200 | 100 |
| (b) | 900 | 800 | 700 |
| Cost per equivalent unit (a)/(b) | €3.00 | €2.50 | €3.50 |
| **Total unit cost €9.00** | | | |

*Solution 4.2 (Multi-choice Questions on Process Costing and Spoilage)*

| Question | Answer |
|----------|--------|
| 1 | (b) |
| 2 | (c) |
| 3 | (d) |
| 4 | (a) |
| 5 | (b) |
| 6 | (c) |
| 7 | (b) |
| 8 | (a) |
| 9 | (d) |
| 10 | (c) |

## Solution 5.1 (Limitations of TCA and advantages of ABC)

Companies may introduce ABC systems due to the limitations of their existing TCA systems but also because there are some additional benefits associated with ABC. Therefore, a large number of reasons for introducing ABC may be cited, some of which stem from the limitations of traditional cost accounting. The main reasons can be listed as follows:

- In some manufacturing firms, direct labour is only a small element of a company's overall cost structure, yet direct labour hours are used as the basis for absorbing overheads.
- The traditional system assigns too much overhead to some products, i.e. over costing high volume products. Thus, low volume products are being heavily subsidised by the high volume products.
- ABC is more logical than the traditional overhead absorption system and is easier to explain to non-accounting personnel.

- There is growing cost pressure due to competitive forces. This requires effective activity management including identifying non-value added activities and targeting them for attention, i.e. reduction or elimination.
- There is a lack of strategic information such as customer profitability.

A number of difficulties can be cited regarding implementing an ABC system and include:

- Getting people interested and/or avoiding their resistance. The purpose of an ABC system must be explained in advance, otherwise its introduction may generate staff resistance. However, growing cost consciousness within the organisation facilitates the introduction of ABC.
- Costly to implement (time, software, staff training).
- Identifying appropriate cost pools and cost drivers. This is extremely difficult in real life.
- Reorganising existing cost centres into (new) cost pools, which has implications for the reporting structure within the organisation and individual responsibilities.
- Need to change the computer system and/or maintain a data base in relation to various activities.
- The commonality of some costs means that arbitrary apportionment still exists, e.g. where a purchase order involves different parts used for different products.

## Solution 5.2 (Traditional Cost Accounting v. Activity-based Costing)

### Part 1

**1.**                                    **Summarised cost structure**

|                  | Total     | %    |
|------------------|-----------|------|
| Direct materials | 725,000   | 34%  |
| Direct labour    | 400,000   | 18%  |
| Overheads        | 1,000,000 | 48%  |
|                  | 2,125,000 | 100% |

The most obvious comment is that overheads are the biggest single cost element and therefore we need to be very careful with the method used to trace such overheads to units of output. Also, direct labour cost is the smallest cost element. Thus, one can always question the fundamental assumption of TCA that direct labour (smallest) causes overheads (the biggest).

**2.**                                    **OHAR based on DLH**

$$\text{OHAR} \quad = \quad \frac{\text{€ Overhead}}{\text{DL Hours}} \quad = \quad \frac{\text{€}1,000,000}{400,000} \quad = \quad \text{€}2.50 \text{ per DL Hour}$$

In the above working, there is only one cost pool for the purpose of overhead absorption and all overheads are included in this (plant-wide) cost pool. The cost driver is direct labour hours which is typical for a traditional cost accounting system.

| Unit cost (TCA)                                    | Product X | Product Y |
|----------------------------------------------------|-----------|-----------|
| Direct materials (given)                           | 25.00     | 20.00     |
| Direct labour (given)                              | 15.00     | 5.00      |
| Overhead (€2.50 per DLH, i.e. 15 and 5 hours)      | 37.50     | 12.50     |
| Total cost                                         | 77.50     | 37.50     |
| Sales price                                        | 70.00     | 100.00    |

Based on the limited information and based on full cost rather than marginal costing principles, Product X appears to be a loss-maker and Product Y is (extremely) profitable.

## Part 2

**3.**                                    **Cost driver rates (under ABC)**

The difference in UNIT product costs obtained using TCA v. ABC is highlighted below. (However, the TOTAL costs of the organisation do not change under ABC. Rather, it is the way that overheads are assigned, i.e. absorbed to products and therefore it is the individual product costs that change.) Under ABC, the cost driver can be computed as follows:

(a) Cost driver rate for ordering of materials

$$\text{Ordering of materials} = \frac{\text{Ordering overheads}}{\text{Number of orders}} = \frac{€700,000}{35} = €20,000 \text{ per order}$$

(b) Cost driver rate for machine set ups

$$\text{Set-up overheads} = \frac{\text{Set-up overheads}}{\text{Number of set-ups}} = \frac{€120,000}{240} = €500 \text{ per set-up}$$

(c) Cost driver rate for inspection costs

$$\text{Inspection overheads} = \frac{\text{Inspection overheads}}{\text{Number of inspections}} = \frac{€180,000}{1,200} = €150 \text{ per inspection}$$

With ABC, cost driver rates are used to assign overhead costs to products as shown below. The treatment of direct costs (materials and labour) is identical to the traditional method.

| Unit cost (ABC) | Product X | Product Y |
|---|---|---|
| Direct materials (given) | 25.00 | 20.00 |
| Direct labour (given) | 15.00 | 5.00 |
| Ordering costs (i) | 20.00 | 40.00 |
| Set-up costs (ii) | 0.80 | 20.00 |
| Inspection costs (iii) | 2.40 | 24.00 |
|  | 63.20 | 109.00 |
| Sales price per unit | 70.00 | 100.00 |

(i) X = €20,000 × 25 orders/25,000 = €20 & Y = €20,000 × 10 orders/5,000 = €40
(ii) X = €500 × 40 set-ups/25,000 units = €0.80 & Y = €500 × 200 set-ups/5,000 units = €20
(iii) X = €150 × 400 inspections/25,000 units = €2.40 & Y = €150 × 800 inspections/5,000 units = €24

Summary: The difference in unit costs is explained by the different demands each product places on the resources of the company. TCA, which uses volume-based absorption rates, tends to over-cost high volume products and under-cost low volume products. ABC, on the other hand, is based on the fundamental concept that products consume activities and activities consume resources. These activities often are not proportional to volume of output.

| Unit cost comparison (€) | Product X | Product Y |
|---|---|---|
| Traditional cost accounting | 77.50 | 37.50 |
| Activity-Based Costing | 63.20 | 109.00 |
| Sales price (given) | 70.00 | 100.00 |

## Solution 6.1 (Quality Costs)

1. The following classification system is usually used in relation to costs of quality:

- Prevention costs: these are costs incurred to keep quality defects from occurring and are often associated with costs incurred prior to production.
- Appraisal costs: These are costs incurred in the measurement and analysis of data to ascertain if products and services conform to specifications. They represent costs incurred after production but before sale.
- Internal failure: these are costs incurred as a result of poor quality found through appraisal prior to delivery to the customer.
- External failure: these are costs incurred to rectify quality defects after unacceptable products or services reach the customer and lost profit opportunities caused by the unacceptable products or services delivered.

2. The classification of costs/activities is as follows:

| Lists of costs/activities | P Prevention | A Appraisal | IF Int. failure | EF Ex. failure |
|---|---|---|---|---|
| 1.  Final inspection | | X | | |
| 2.  Warranty repairs | | | | X |
| 3.  Goods returned and scrapped | | | | X |
| 4.  Quality training * | X | | | |
| 5.  Settlement of product liability action | | | | X |
| 6.  Field service personnel | | | | X |
| 7.  Packaging inspection | | X | | |
| 8.  Complaint department | | | | X |
| 9.  Rework units from work-in-progress | | | X | |
| 10. Replacement of defective goods sold | | | | X |
| 11. Lost sales due to quality deficiency | | | | X |
| 12. Scrap (at inspection) | | | X | |
| 13. Product recalls | | | | X |
| 14. Downtime caused by defects | | | X | |

| Lists of costs/activities | P Prevention | A Appraisal | IF Int. failure | EF Ex. failure |
|---|---|---|---|---|
| 15. Inspection of incoming raw materials | | X | | |
| 16. WIP inspection | | X | | |
| 17. Calibration of test gauges | | X | | |
| 18. Salaries of quality personnel | X | | | |
| 19. Quality improvement projects | X | | | |
| 20. Inspection of rework | | | X | |
| 21. Tuition for external suppliers | X | | | |
| 22. Quality awards for employees | X | | | |
| 23. Acquisition of test equipment | | X | | |

* Quality training is usually classified as 'prevention'.

## Solution 6.2 (JIT Systems and Value Adding Activities)

### SCHEDULE OF COSTS

| Cost implications | Current system € | JIT system € |
|---|---|---|
| Materials inspections | 40,000 | Nil |
| Materials storage | 70,000 | Nil |
| Materials movement to Process 1 and 2 | 40,000 | 12,000 |
| Cost of materials | 200,000 | 200,000 |
| Process 1 and 2 costs | 150,000 | 150,000 |
| Inspection – Process 1 work | 50,000 | Nil |
| Inspection – Process 2 work | 10,000 | Nil |
| Packaging of completed goods | 50,000 | 50,000 |
| Final storage (awaiting distribution to customers) | 10,000 | Nil |
| Delivery to customers | 80,000 | 100,000 |
| Staff and vendor training | Nil | 50,000 |
| | 700,000 | 562,000 |

Under the ideal JIT system, there are only six activities associated with the production/distribution process. The use of JIT eliminates or reduces wastage in relation to the inspection of incoming materials together with storage of goods (while waiting to be processed), unnecessary movement of goods and all inspection checks. The result is a leaner production process with non-value added activities eliminated or significantly reduced. While additional costs have been incurred, there is an overall reduction in costs, supporting the argument that 'quality is, indeed, free'.

## Solution 7.1 (Strategic Management Accounting)

Management accounting is sometimes criticised because it emphasises internal and historical information on, for example, costs and revenues. However, this information is of limited relevance in managerial decision-making. Managers require future-orientated information and of an external focus, e.g. looking at customer needs and competitors' capabilities and intentions. Therefore, it is necessary to continually review customer requirements, their satisfaction and loyalty, together with information relating to competition, their products and the markets in which they operate. This may involve benchmarking exercises against competitors. This external and future-orientated focus comprises the emerging discipline of strategic management accounting.

Typical strategic management accounting measures include market share statistics and trends for all major products. Additionally the market prospects of new and existing products must be evaluated along with relevant characteristics of competitors. Using these externally based reference points will improve the relevance of management accounting information.

## Solution 7.2 (Cost Leadership v. Product Differentiation)

The terms 'cost leadership' and 'product differentiation' owe their popularity to Michael Porter, whom many people consider to be the guru of corporate strategy. He argued, convincingly, that these are the two generic strategies for creating and sustaining superior performance.

A cost leadership strategy seeks to achieve the position of lowest-cost producer in the industry. The competitive advantage that results from producing at the lowest cost is that the manufacturer can compete on price with every other producer in the industry and can earn the highest unit profits. A company that relies on cost leadership will place a strong emphasis on cost management and cost control. In addition, low prices usually generate large demand and this will allow the company to benefit from economies of scale, e.g. paying lower prices for higher quantities of purchases, or benefiting from the impact of the learning curve in relation to repetitive labour practices. In turn, the lower prices that prevail in the market place can be an important barrier to entry for potential entrants to the market. Thus, price competition can be avoided.

A differentiation strategy attempts to make the product unique in terms of attributes which are desirable to the customer. This can be achieved either by way of a superior product or a superior service, or both. The assumption is that competitive advantage can be gained through the unique characteristics of a firm's products (or service). With a successful differentiation strategy, loyalty to the firm's products will build up and customers are not so price-sensitive. The firm can then sell its products at a premium price – prices which are considerably higher than the cost of production. The problem with product differentiation strategy is that it is capable of being imitated, or customers can become 'tired' of the product and substitute it. Under a product differentiation strategy, internal cost management practices are not so important. Rather, a detailed knowledge of market opportunities and size, as well as precise and detailed information on competitors, their relative strengths and weaknesses, is required. Thus, there is a shift in the focus for management information from an historical and introspective nature to that focused on the future and external environment.

In conclusion it should be noted that many companies compete on both strategies, although this is not recommended by Porter. Some firms do strive for cost leadership and product differentiation simultaneously.

## Solution 8.1 (Restoring Relevance to Managerial Accounting)

The role of the management accountant is to provide information to managers that is relevant in their planning and control decisions. It is fair to argue that much of this information is financially orientated. This orientation is understandable since there is a single accounting system operating within organisations and much of this information is used to generate external financial statements at the end of the accounting period.

While annual financial statements are required by Company Law, even more regular information, e.g. quarterly results, is required for listed companies, i.e. companies quoted on a Stock

Exchange. Increasingly, managers are under pressure to achieve short-term profit targets in order to meet the expectations of shareholders. If these short-term profit targets are not met, then the company's share price is usually adversely affected. Therefore, it is inevitable that managers focus on maximising profits in the short-term – often to the detriment of long-term performance.

Typical examples of the heavy emphasis on short-term performance include a reduction of expenditure on areas such as marketing, research and development, staff training and quality initiatives. Such decisions will boost short-term profitability but the long-term competitive position of the firm will be adversely affected. This phenomenon is referred to as 'short-termism' and, with this focus, the ability to generate long-term value is ignored or receives scant attention. However, it should be noted that it is competence in a wide range of activities, such as marketing, staff relations, customer service, research and development, product development, quality etc., that generates long-term value.

In many cases, it is not the accounting information that is at fault. After all, accounting numbers reflect the financial consequences of managerial decisions. Rather it is the orientation of managers (and external stakeholders) that needs to be better focused on the longer-term.

## *Solution 8.2 (Non-financial Measures of Performance)*

Profitability remains the principal measure by which the success or failure of a business is judged. While the issue of profit performance can be an emotive one, it is important to remember that profitability allows the company to live up to its responsibilities, e.g. by remunerating fully its employees and paying adequate dividends to its shareholders. However, in spite of its widespread use as a performance measure, profitability does have a number of limitations.

'Profit' is generally historical, i.e. it relates to past performance. For decision-making purposes, it is future orientated information that is relevant. In addition, profit reflects many internal dimensions of performance but it does not directly capture issues such as customer satisfaction or the performance of competitors. In other words, reporting only profit does not indicate WHY profit performance was satisfactory or otherwise. Moreover, profit does not adequately indicate the impact of external factors, such as inflation and general economic conditions.

Secondly, not all organisations have profitability as their main objective, e.g. government bodies and charities.

Thirdly, a commercial firm may have alternative objectives, although these may not be incompatible with the profit objective. Cash flow is an important objective of any firm. A company may be profitable and yet have severe cash flow problems. Thus, profitability is not necessarily an indicator of continued success.

Finally, investors are placing increased emphasis on short-term profit performance. Indeed, managers are aware that their performance bonuses are often based on such short-term profit performance. This short-term profit emphasis may encourage managers to take a short-term view. Managers may cut essential costs like training or research in order to show a profit in the short-term.

While financial performance and position are important, they are limited in that they represent the end rather than the means by which these financial results were created. In other words, accounting information highlights the financial consequences of problems but not the problems themselves. Therefore, to assist managers, management accountants are being asked to generate a suitable range of non-financial measures of performance. These key performance indicators (KPIs) relate to the critical success factors (CSFs) – the areas in which performance must excel if the business is to be successful.

Non-financial measures therefore supplement traditional financial measures but, depending on the decision being made, it is possible to argue that they are more relevant to managers. Effectively, they reflect what responsible managers are expected to do. In addition, they are probably generated on a more timely basis and, often, managers can immediately see the performance in these areas, e.g. on-time delivery. Thus, they are more meaningful and understandable to managers. In addition, non-financial measures are not, generally, distorted by changing price levels, e.g. customer satisfaction. However, they should not replace financial measures, but should supplement them and be integrated with them to improve the relevance of managerial accounting information.

## Solution 9.1 (Profit Planning for a Single Product Manufacturer)

**1.**                                            **Profit projections for 20x6**

Note: Profit Equation: (SP − VCu) × Q − FC

| | | |
|---|---|---|
| Sales price per unit | | €40 |
| Less: variable cost per unit | | (19) |
| = Unit Contribution | | €21 |
| Multiplied by total units sold | | 11,250 |
| | | **€** |
| = Total Contribution | 11,250 × €21 | 236,250 |
| Less: Fixed Costs | | (195,000) |
| Profit Before Tax | | 41,250 |
| Less: Tax (40%) on profits | | (16,500) |
| = Profit After Tax (profit for year) | | 24,750 |

**2. BEP (20x6) in units**        €195,000 ÷ €21 =        9,286 units

**3. BEP (20x6) in €**        € 195,000 ÷ 0.525 =        €371,429
    (€21 ÷ €40 = 0.525)

**4. Target volume (units)**        (€195,000 + 10,000) ÷ 21 =        9,762 units

**5. Target volume (in €)**        (€195,000 + 10,000) ÷ 0.525        = €390,476

**6. Margin of safety %**        ((11,250 − 9,285) ÷ 11,250) × 100        = 17.4%

**7. Target Profit After Tax of €15,000**
        Target Profit **Before** Tax,
        i.e. (€15,000 × 100/60)                        =        €25,000
        Target volume (€195,000
        + €25,000) ÷ €21                        =        10,476 units

**8. BEP for 20x7:**

| | | |
|---|---|---|
| Revised selling price | €44.00 | |
| Revised variable cost | 22.80 | |
| Revised unit contribution | 21.20 | |
| BEP (Units) = (€210,000 ÷ €21.20) | = | 9,906 units |

## Solution 9.2 (Accounts Classification and Decision-making in a Retail Company)

**1.**                    **Fixed and variable cost classification**

| Cost Item | Variable € | Fixed € | Total € |
|---|---|---|---|
| *Direct materials* | 270,000 | Nil | |
| Direct labour | 20,000 | 60,000 | |
| Delivery | 6,000 | 2,000 | |
| Depreciation | Nil | 36,000 | |
| Admin. costs | Nil | 75,000 | |
| | 296,000 | 173,000 | 469,000 |

Variable cost per unit (€296,000/200,000) = €1.48

Cost model: Y = €173,000 + 1.48 X (Where X = Units sold)

### Income summary (in contribution format) for . . .

| | € | € |
|---|---|---|
| Sales (200,000 units) | 500,000 | |
| Less: Variable costs | (296,000) | |
| = Total contribution | 204,000 | €1.02 |
| Less: Fixed costs | (173,000) | |
| = Profit for period | 31,000 | |

**2. BEP (units)**          =          $\dfrac{€173,000}{€1.02}$          =          169,607 units

**3. (a)**                    **Analysis of alternative (i)**

| | Current situation | (i) 5% Price reduction with 30% increase in sales volume | |
|---|---|---|---|
| | € | | € |
| Sales | 500,000 | × 95% × 1.30 | 617,500 |
| Less: Var. costs | (296,000) | × 1.30 | (384,800) |
| = Contribution | 204,000 | | 232,700 |
| Less: Fixed costs | (173,000) | No change | (173,000) |
| = Profit | 31,000 | | 59,700 |

**3. (b)**                                    **Analysis of alternative (ii)**

|  | Current situation | (ii) 10% Price reduction with 50% increase in sales volume with advertising | |
|---|---|---|---|
|  | € |  | € |
| Sales | 500,000 | × .90 × 1.50 | 675,000 |
| Less: Variable costs | (296,000) | × 1.50 | 444,000 |
| = Contribution | 204,000 |  | 231,000 |
| Less: Fixed costs | (173,000) | + 20,000 | (193,000) |
| = Profit | 31,000 |  | 38,000 |

Recommendation: Select (a), assuming the accuracy of the above data, as this provides the greatest overall contribution.

**4.**                    **Assumptions underlying CVP model:**

- Constant selling price, i.e. linear relationship between volume and sales price
- Constant variable cost per unit and no economies of scale
- Ability to accurately segregate fixed and variable costs
- Constant product mix (for a multi-product firm)
- Volume is only (main) cost driver

## Solution 10.1 (Relevant Costs and Decision-making)

**1.**                    **Evaluation of Option 1 (70 rooms available)**

| Room revenue: Month | Rooms let | Days | Room days |
|---|---|---|---|
| March (4 weeks) | n/a | n/a | n/a |
| April (4 weeks) | 50% × 70 = 35 | 28 | 980 |
| May (4 weeks) | 70% × 70 = 49 | 28 | 1,372 |
| June (4 weeks) | 90% × 70 = 63 | 28 | 1,764 |
| July (4 weeks) | 90% × 70 = 63 | 28 | 1,764 |
| August (4 weeks) | 80% × 70 = 56 | 28 | 1,568 |
| September (4 weeks) | 40% × 70 = 28 | 28 | 784 |
| Christmas (given) | 45 | 21 | 945 |
|  |  |  | 9,177 |
| Revenue (9,177 × €110) |  |  | 1,009,470 |

| Costs: | | | |
|---|---|---|---|
| Renovations (given) | | 100,000 | |
| Project Manager (3 months × €8,000) | | 24,000 | |
| Staffing (24 weeks × €5,000) | | 120,000 | |
| Manager (12 month contract) | | 60,000 | |
| Room costs (€25 × 9,177 rooms) | | 229,425 | |
| Christmas staff (€5,000 × 3 × 1.25) | | 18,750 | |
| | | | 552,175 |
| Expected profit | | | 457,295 |

## Evaluation of Option 2 (80 rooms and then 70 rooms available)

| Room revenue: Month | Rooms let | Days | Room days |
|---|---|---|---|
| March (4 weeks) | 40% × 80 = 32 | 28 | 896 |
| April (4 weeks) – fully occupied | 40 | 28 | 1,120 |
| May (4 weeks) – fully occupied * | 40 | 28 | 1,120 |
| June (4 weeks) – fully occupied | 40 | 28 | 1,120 |
| | | | 4,256 |
| July (4 weeks) | 90% × 70 = 63 | 28 | 1,764 |
| August (4 weeks) | 80% × 70 = 56 | 28 | 1,568 |
| September (4 weeks) | 40% × 70 = 28 | 28 | 784 |
| Christmas (given) | 45 | 21 | 945 |
| | | | 5,061 |
| | | | 9,317 |
| Revenue (4,256 rooms × €90) + (5,061 rooms × €110) | | | 939,750 |
| Costs: | | | |
| Renovations (given) | | 60,000 | |
| Project Manager (4 months × €2,000) | | 8,000 | |
| Staffing (28 weeks × €5,000) | | 140,000 | |

| | | |
|---|---|---|
| Manager (12 month contract) | 60,000 | |
| Room costs (€20 × 4,256 rooms) | 85,120 | |
| Room costs (€25 × 5,061 rooms) | 126,525 | |
| Christmas staff (€5,000 × 3 × 1.25) | <u>18,750</u> | |
| | | <u>498,395</u> |
| Expected profit | | <u>441,355</u> |

* The normal room occupancy pattern in May would be 70% suggesting that 56 rooms (80 rooms × 70%) would be let. However, only 40 rooms are available due to renovation.

### Evaluation of Option 3 (80 rooms available; operate as 3 star hotel)

| Room revenue: Month | Rooms let | Days | Room days |
|---|---|---|---|
| March (4 weeks) | 40% × 80 = 32 | 28 | 896 |
| April (4 weeks) | 50% × 80 = 40 | 28 | 1,120 |
| May (4 weeks) | 70% × 80 = 56 | 28 | 1,568 |
| June (4 weeks) | 90% × 80 = 72 | 28 | 2,016 |
| July (4 weeks) | 90% × 80 = 72 | 28 | 2,016 |
| August (4 weeks) | 80% × 80 = 64 | 28 | 1,792 |
| September (4 weeks) | 40% × 80 = 32 | 28 | 896 |
| Christmas | N/A | N/A | <u>N/A</u> |
| | | | <u>10,304</u> |
| Revenue (10,304 rooms × €90) | | | 927,360 |
| Costs: | | | |
| Renovations (given) | | 70,000 | |
| Project manager | | N/A | |
| Staffing (€5,000 × 28 weeks) | | 140,000 | |
| Manager (12 month contract) | | 60,000 | |
| Room costs (10,304 rooms × €20) | | 206,080 | |
| Christmas staff | | <u>N/A</u> | |
| | | | <u>476,080</u> |
| Expected profit | | | <u>451,280</u> |

**2.**                         **Additional information**

Management have provided a large amount of information on which the above calculations have been based. Remarkably, the overall cash consequences are not significantly different but option 1 is slightly more favourable than the other two. Thus, much will depend on the overall accuracy of the figures together with non-financial considerations which include:

- Will the project manager and contractor be available to start on the proposed dates?
- Are estimates for the length of time and cost for each option accurate and reliable?
- Are there provisions in place if the projects overrun in time or cost?
- Is the hotel guaranteed a 4 star rating after the renovations and so quickly?
- Are the occupancy rates realistic?
- Will staff be available for re-hire for a short (3 week) period over Christmas?
- In the case where renovations are carried out while the hotel is open for business, will guests have to endure significant disturbance and, if so, can the hotel still charge full rates during this period?
- In option 2 some existing customers cannot be accommodated during the months of April to June (inclusive) and this may result in a loss of customer loyalty caused by this non-availability.
- Is it realistic to assume that room rates for the Christmas period are the same as at other times?

## Solution 10.2 (Pricing Policy and Economic Theory)

**1.  The current profit figures can be determined as follows:**

| Current profit levels | |
|---|---|
| Volume (given) | 7,000 units |
| Units sales price (given) | €1,728 |
| Sales revenue (P × Q) | €12,096,000 |
| Total costs (given) | € (6,200,000) |
| Current profit | € 5,896,000 |

### W1. Estimate of variable cost (High-low method)

First, identify within what range the profit maximising price will be. Based on the schedule below, the profit maximising price must lie between prices €2,628 (generating demand of 4,000 units) and €2,028 (generating demand of 6,000 units). A price reduction beyond €2,028 will cause further reductions in profit.

| Volume | Sales price (unit) | Total revenue 000s | Total costs 000s | Profit 000s |
|---|---|---|---|---|
| 4,000 | €2,628 | €10,512 | €3,700 | €6,812 |
| 5,000 | €2,328 | €11,640 | €4,500 | €7,140 |
| 6,000 | €2,028 | €12,168 | €5,300 | €6,868 |

High-low method to ascertain variable costs

|  | Output | Costs (000s) |
|---|---|---|
| High | 6,000 | €5,300 |
| Low | 4,000 | €3,700 |
| Change | + 2,000 | + €1,600 |
| Variable costs (per unit) |  | €800 |
| Total costs €500,000 + 800 Q |  |  |

### W2. Estimates of 'A' and 'B'

$$B = 300/1,000$$
$$B = 0.3$$
$$1,728 = A - 0.3\,(7,000)$$
$$A = 3,828$$

**2.** ### Profit maximising price (MR = MC)

| Demand curve | $P = 3,828 - 0.3Q$ |
|---|---|
| Total revenue (Price × Quantity) | $3,828Q - 0.3Q^2$ |
| Marginal revenue (MR) | $3,828 - 0.6Q$ |
| Marginal cost (estimate) see W1 | €800 |
| Let MR = MC (to maximise profits) | $3,828 - 0.6Q = 800$ |
|  | $Q = 5,046$ units (rounded) |
|  | $P = €2,314^{20}$ |
| Total revenue | €11,677,453 |
| Less: variable costs (total) | (4,036,800) |
| Less: fixed costs | (500,000) |
| = Net profit for period | € 7,140,653 |

**3.** ### Sales maximising price

| Demand curve | $P = 3,828 - 0.3Q$ |
|---|---|
| Total revenue (Price × Quantity) | $3,828Q - 0.3Q^2$ |
| Marginal revenue (MR) | $3,828 - 0.6Q$ |
| Let: MR = 0 (to maximise revenues) | $3,828 - 0.6Q = 0$ |
|  | $Q = 6,380$ units |
|  | $P = €1,914$ |

| Total revenue (€1,914 × 6,380 units) | €12,211,320 |
| Less: variable costs (€800 × 6,380 units) | (5,104,000) |
| Less: fixed costs | (500,000) |
| = Net profit for period | € 6,607,320 |

**4. We have made a number of crucial assumptions such as:**
- The demand curve can be correctly identified but, in reality, this is difficult to calculate. Thus, for example, we need to take into consideration how (possible) competitors might react to our price changes. Also, price is assumed to be the only variable impacting on demand.
- The demand curve is linear.
- That estimate of marginal cost is correct and that marginal cost is constant.
- The fixed costs do not respond to changes to volume of output, within a relevant range of activity.

## Solution 11.1 (Contribution per Limiting Factor)

**1.** The initial task is to compute the contribution per unit, as follows:

### W1. Contribution per unit

| | Product A €| Product B €| Product C €|
|---|---|---|---|
| Direct materials | 24 | 45 | 42 |
| Direct labour | 4 | 36 | 32 |
| Variable overhead | 2 | 36 | 16 |
| | 30 | 117 | 90 |
| Sales price | 35 | 150 | 110 |
| = Unit contribution | €5 | €33 | €20 |

(a) **Labour is scarce**

The above calculation allows us to compute the contribution per limiting factor (CpLF), which represents a ratio of efficiency in relation to the use of scarce labour.

| | Product A | Product B | Product C |
|---|---|---|---|
| Contribution (above) | €5 | €33 | €20 |
| Labour hours per unit | 2 | 12 | 8 |
| Contribution per limiting factor | €2.50 | €2.75 | €2.50 |
| Product ranking | 2 joint | 1 | 2 joint |

## (b) Machine capacity is scarce

|  | Product A | Product B | Product C |
|---|---|---|---|
| Contribution | €5 | €33 | €20 |
| Machine hours per unit | 12 | 10 | 16 |
| Contribution per limiting factor | € 0.42 | €3.30 | €1.25 |
| Product ranking | 3 | 1 | 2 |

## 2. Brief outline of the limitations associated with the above calculations:

(i)   The assumption of a constant unit contribution. Thus, we assume a constant sales price and also assume a constant unit variable cost.

(ii)  No consideration is taken of economies of scale including the possible impact of the learning curve.

(iii) Managers accept the above limiting factors and respond to them. It may be more useful for managers to investigate ways of relaxing these limiting factors.

(iv)  We assume that the objective is to maximise profits in the short term.

(v)   We have not included the possibility of complementary demand among products.

(vi)  The 'optimal solution' may not be popular among managers for a variety of reasons.

## Solution 11.2 (Contribution per Limiting Factor (CpLF))

### W1. Contribution per limiting factor

|  | A | B | C | D |
|---|---|---|---|---|
| € Contribution per unit | €8 | €10 | €9 | €14 |
| Limited Factor (€ raw materials input) | €7 | €20 | €15 | €15 |
| Efficiency ratio (Contribution per L F ) | 1.14 | 0.5 | 0.6 | 0.93 |
| Ranking of products | 1 | 4 | 3 | 2 |

### W2. Optimal production plan

| | |
|---|---|
| Raw materials available | €77,000 |
| Less: Minimum production quota: | |
| 1,000 units ((A × €7) + (B × €20) + (C × €15) + (D × €15)) | (57,000) |
| Balance of raw materials available (after minimum production) | €20,000 |
| ∴ Additional units of A to be produced (€20,000 ÷ €7) | 2,857 units |

### Budget for month, based on optimal production plan

| | | |
|---|---|---|
| Product A: 3,857 units × €8 contribution | = | €30,856 |
| Product B: 1,000 units × €10 contribution | = | 10,000 |

| | | | |
|---|---|---|---|
| Product C: 1,000 units × €9 contribution | | = | 9,000 |
| Product D: 1,000 units × €14 contribution | | = | 14,000 |
| | | | 63,856 |
| Less: Fixed costs (given) | | | (30,000) |
| Maximum possible profit | | | 33,856 |

## Solution 12.1  (Risk and Uncertainty)

### The maximax and maximin criteria in decision-making

Decision-making under risk and uncertainty is characterised by a situation whereby a number of different outcomes can occur. These outcomes are referred to as 'states of nature' and, in the context of tossing a coin, the states of nature would represent the occurrence of either 'heads' or 'tails'. In some decision-making scenarios, the various states of nature can be assigned reasonable probabilities and this situation is described as decision-making under risk. The assigned probabilities are constrained to lie between '0' and '+1', with a value close to zero indicating only a slight chance of occurring. A value close to '1' indicates a high likelihood of occurrence.

In some decision situations, it might not be possible to assign meaningful estimates of probabilities to possible outcomes. Strictly speaking, this represents decision-making under uncertainty. When this occurs, either the maximax or maximin criteria may be used. This involves looking at various possible outcomes and making a choice based on one's attitude towards risk, as well as the importance of the result but without reference to the likelihood of occurrence.

Maximax criterion: The maximax criterion is based on the assumption that the best payoff will occur. In other words, the most optimistic outcome is assumed. This is sometimes referred to as the 'best of the best'.

Maximin criterion: The maximin criterion is based on the assumption that the worst possible outcome will always occur. Having identified all the worst possible outcomes for a given decision situation, the decision-maker selects the largest payoff. In other words, he selects the best of the worst scenarios. This is the opposite to maximax and the worst possible outcome is assumed. The term 'best of the worst' is sometimes used here.

Illustration: The CUD Company must choose between purchasing either Machine A or Machine B. Machine A has low fixed costs and high unit variable costs whereas Machine B has high fixed costs and low variable costs. Consequently, Machine A is most suited to low-level demand whereas Machine B is suited to high level demand. Assume there are only two possible demand levels, low and high, but their respective probabilities are unknown or are considered too unreliable to use. The estimated payoff for each demand level is as follows:

| | Low Demand €| High demand €|
|---|---|---|
| Machine A | 100,000 | 160,000 |
| Machine B | 10,000 | 200,000 |

Based on the above, the higher payoffs are €160,000 for Machine A and €200,000 for Machine B. Thus, Machine B would be selected using the maximax criterion.

The worst outcome for Machine A is €100,000 and €10,000 for Machine B. Consequently, A should be purchased using the maximin rule.

## Solution 12.2 (Decision-making under Risk and Uncertainty)

1. **Calculation of the profit attributable to the new product for the three volume levels:**

| Units | 24,000 €  | 30,000 €  | 36,000 €  |
|---|---|---|---|
| Material costs | 60,000 | 75,000 | 90,000 |
| Conversion costs | 50,000 | 57,500 | 65,000 |
| Fixed costs (given) | 85,000 | 85,000 | 85,000 |
| Total cost | 195,000 | 217,500 | 240,000 |
| Sales revenue | 312,000 | 390,000 | 468,000 |
| Profit for year | 117,000❸ | 172,500❷ | 228,000❶ |

2. **If the higher price for materials applies, then costs will rise and profits will fall as follows:**

| Units | 24,000 | 30,000 | 36,000 |
|---|---|---|---|
| Additional costs | 12,000 | 15,000 | 18,000 |
| Revised profits | 105,000❻ | 157,500❺ | 210,000❹ |

Probabilities have been supplied in relation to the sales volume (high, medium and low) and also in relation to material cost (unchanged and higher). Thus, there are six possible combinations of these events.

| Sales volume & prob | Material price & prob | Combined probability |
|---|---|---|
| Low 0.3 | Unchanged 0.7 | 0.21 (a) |
| Low 0.3 | Higher 0.3 | 0.09 (b) |
| Medium 0.5 | Unchanged 0.7 | 0.35 (c) |
| Medium 0.5 | Higher 0.3 | 0.15 (d) |
| High 0.2 | Unchanged 0.7 | 0.14 (e) |
| High 0.2 | Higher 0.3 | 0.06 (f) |
| | | 1.00 |

**The profit levels reported above can be associated with the probabilities thus:**

| Profit € | Probability | | EMV € |
|---|---|---|---|
| 228,000❶ | X 0.14 (.7 × .2) (e) | = | 31,920 |
| 210,000❹ | X 0.06 (.3 × .2) (f) | = | 12,600 |
| 172,500❷ | X 0.35 (.7 × .5) (c) | = | 60,375 |
| 157,500❺ | X 0.15 (.3 × .5) (d) | = | 23,625 |
| 117,000❸ | X 0.21 (.7 × .3) (a) | = | 24,570 |
| 105,000❻ | X 0.09 (.3 × .3) (b) | = | 9,450 |
| | | Expected value | €162,540 |

**Comment:** the EMV of the proposal is positive in the amount of €162,540, and this suggests that the proposal should be accepted. However, the EMV criterion is based on the long-run average payoff but this proposal may be a one-off variety. However, losses are not anticipated or associated with any possible state of nature. It should be noted that the computation of EMV is highly influenced by the assigned probabilities.

3. The use of probabilities in conditions of uncertainty assists the decision-maker by revealing a range of outcomes and their likelihood. Business decisions are rarely made in conditions of certainty and this approach requires a manager to state the degree of confidence in his/her estimates. It must be remembered that the probabilities are not scientifically determined but in most cases are based on managerial judgement. Furthermore the discrete probability distribution assumed regarding possible sales volumes, i.e. low, medium and high, is an over-simplification of the range of possible outcomes in the real world.

## Solution 13.1 (Introduction to Capital Expenditure Decisions)

Capital expenditure decisions are characterised by a large and immediate cash outflow which is expected to generate future financial benefits over a long period of time. In addition, the anticipated value of such cash inflows are expected to exceed the amount of the initial outlay or investment. Because of the amount of immediate cash outlay, together with the future time periods involved, these capital expenditure decisions are more risky than most short-term decisions. As a result, it is normal to apply 'cost of capital' calculations in evaluating such decisions.

The 'cost of capital' can be formally defined as the discount rate which, when used to discount the future cash flows of a business, will leave the value of the business unaltered. The cost of capital can be viewed as the minimum return required by shareholders and should be used when evaluating investment proposals. In order to maximise the wealth of shareholders, the basic decision rule in capital expenditure decisions is that, if total cash flows relating to an investment proposal are negative when discounted using the cost of capital, the proposal should be rejected. However, if the discounted (total) cash flows are positive the proposal should be accepted. Failure to calculate the cost of capital correctly can result in incorrect capital expenditure decisions being made. Where the cost of the capital is understated, investment proposals, which should be rejected, may be accepted. The converse is also true.

It is also important to factor into such decisions the impact of taxation and any anticipated general and specific price changes expected over future periods of time.

It should be noted that, once made, capital expenditure decisions are often irreversible and the effect of the decisions may have a profound impact on future profits of the company. It is therefore important to ensure that adequate procedures exist to approve and review capital expenditure projects.

Proposals for large capital expenditure should be subject to close scrutiny by top management. Initial proposals should take the form of a proposal, which sets out the nature and rationale of the project, the expected costs and benefits and the expected time scale of the project. Investment appraisal techniques should be applied to expected costs and benefits wherever possible to establish the financial viability of the proposal. In assessing the initial proposal, management should be satisfied that the proposal is based on realistic estimates and assumptions and all risks associated with the project have been properly identified. Indeed, a range of possible outcomes should be subject to evaluation. Top management should also be satisfied that the proposal fits in with the overall strategy of the business.

Before receiving final approval and incorporation into the final capital expenditure programme, the proposal should be considered alongside other capital expenditure proposals to ensure the correct 'mix' of investments has been achieved. The funding implications of the proposal must also be considered.

Once the capital expenditure project is under way periodic checks on progress should be made. Comparisons between actual results and earlier estimates should be carried out to see whether there is a significant divergence and, where this occurs, corrective action may be required. Revised estimates concerning future cost and benefits and revised time scales may need to be produced as the project progresses in order to keep top managers informed of significant changes. This may result in a decision to close down a project before the end of its originally forecast life.

At the end of the project a post-completion audit should be carried out to assess past performance and to learn from mistakes made. The post-completion audit should help top management in assessing future capital expenditure proposals and should also help provide a check on the submission of proposals based on over-optimistic assumptions.

## Solution 13.2 (Methods of Evaluating Capital Expenditure Decisions)

### Summary of Analysis

|  | Project 'L' | Project 'S' |
|---|---|---|
| (a) Payback period (W1) | $2^{1}/_{3}$ years | $3^{1}/_{3}$ years |
| (b) Net present value (W2) | + €79 | + €50 |
| (c) Internal rate of return (W3) | 14.5% | 11.8% |

Recommendation: Assuming the accuracy of the above figures and ignoring other considerations, project L should be accepted. It provides the shortest payback period ($2^{1}/_{3}$ years) and also gives a higher NPV. While the difference between NPVs does not seem to be significant in this case, Project L provides an overall IRR of 14.5%, compared with 11.8% for Project S.

### W1. Calculation of payback period

|  | Project 'L' | Project 'S' |
|---|---|---|
| Cash outflow | (€1,000) | (€1,000) |
| Cash inflow − year 1 | 500 | 100 |

|                           | Project 'L'             | Project 'S'             |
|---------------------------|-------------------------|-------------------------|
| = Balance after year 1    | (500)                   | (900)                   |
| Cash inflow − year 2      | 400                     | 300                     |
| = Balance after year 2    | (100)                   | (600)                   |
| Cash inflow – year 3      | 300                     | 400                     |
| Balance after year 3      | + 200                   | (200)                   |
| Cash inflow – year 4      |                         | 600                     |
| Balance after year 4      |                         | + 400                   |
| Payback period (approx.)  | $2^1/_3$ years          | $3^1/_3$ years          |

### W2. Calculation of Net Present Values (NPVs)

#### Project 'L'

| Time          | Cash inflows | Discount factor | Present value |
|---------------|--------------|-----------------|---------------|
| End of Year 1 | €500         | .909            | 455           |
| End of Year 2 | €400         | .826            | 330           |
| End of Year 3 | €300         | .751            | 226           |
| End of Year 4 | €100         | .683            | 68            |
|               |              |                 | €1,079        |
| Less: Amount to be invested (payable in advance) | | | (1,000) |
| Net Present Value (positive) | | | €79 |

#### Project 'S'

| Time          | Cash inflows | Discount factor | Present value |
|---------------|--------------|-----------------|---------------|
| End of Year 1 | €100         | .909            | 91            |
| End of Year 2 | €300         | .826            | 248           |
| End of Year 3 | €400         | .751            | 301           |
| End of Year 4 | €600         | .683            | 410           |
|               |              |                 | €1,050        |
| Less: Amount to be invested (payable in advance) | | | (1,000) |
| Net Present Value (positive) | | | €50 |

### W3. The Internal rate of return (IRR)

The Internal Rate of Return (IRR) is defined as the discount rate at which net present value is zero. The calculation of the IRR is a trial and error process involving the selection of discount rates at random, applying them to future cash flows until one gets two rates, one of which gives a negative NPV and the other a positive NPV.

Using the above example, at a discount rate of 10% the NPV of Project 'L' was +€79 and the NPV of project 'S' was +€50. Clearly the IRR for both these projects must be greater than 10%. Using a 15% discount rate for 'L' and a 12% rate for 'S' the net present values are negative as follows:

Project 'L'

| Time | Cash inflows | Discount factor | Present value |
|---|---|---|---|
| | | (15%) | |
| End of Year 1 | €500 | .870 | 435 |
| End of Year 2 | €400 | .756 | 302 |
| End of Year 3 | €300 | .658 | 197 |
| End of Year 4 | €100 | .572 | 57 |
| | | | €991 |
| Less: Amount to be invested (payable in advance) | | | (1,000) |
| Net Present Value | | | €–9 |

Project 'S'

| Time | Cash inflows | Discount factor | Present value |
|---|---|---|---|
| | | (12%) | |
| End of Year 1 | €100 | .893 | 89 |
| End of Year 2 | €300 | .797 | 239 |
| End of Year 3 | €400 | .712 | 285 |
| End of Year 4 | €600 | .636 | 382 |
| | | | €995 |
| Less: Amount to be invested (payable in advance) | | | (1,000) |
| Net Present Value | | | €–5 |

For project 'L' the IRR must lie between 10% and 15% and very close to 15%. For project 'S' the IRR must lie between 10% and 12% but close to 12%. The IRR is the discount rate at which NPV equals zero and this can be approximated by interpolating between two points as follows:

**Interpolation**

| 10%        PV = €79 positive | 10%        PV = €50 positive |
|---|---|
| 5% { Difference €88 } | 2% { Difference €55 } |
| 15%        PV = − €9 negative | 12%        PV = − €5 negative |
| Approximate IRR for 'L' | Approximate IRR for 'S' |
| $10\% + \dfrac{79}{88} \times 5\% = 14.5\%$ | $10\% + \dfrac{50}{55} \times 2\% = 11.8\%$ |

## *Solution 14.1 (Basic Cash Budgeting)*

### 1. Cash budget for October, November and December 20x1

|  | October € | November € | December € |
|---|---|---|---|
| Sales receipts: |  |  |  |
| 10% in cash | 1,360 | 1,700 | 1,680 |
| 90% in one month | 11,250 | 12,240 | 15,300 |
| = Total receipts | 12,610 | 13,940 | 16,980 |
| Payments: |  |  |  |
| Material purchases (one month credit) | 3,450 | 3,780 | 2,890 |
| Direct wages | 1,300 | 1,300 | 1,300 |
| Production overheads (W1) | 2,900 | 2,900 | 2,900 |
| Selling, distrib. & admin. overhead (W1) | 1,700 | 1,700 | 1,700 |
| Delivery vehicle | = | 9,870 | = |
| Total payments | 9,350 | 19,550 | 8,790 |
| Net cash inflow/(outflow) | 3,260 | (5,610) | 8,190 |
| Opening cash balance | 1,235 | 4,495 | (1,115) |
| Closing cash balance at the end of the month | 4,495 | (1,115) | 7,075 |

**W1:** Depreciation has been excluded from the overhead payment figures because it is not a cash item.

2.  The layout given above could be used as the model upon which a spreadsheet-based monthly cash forecast could be prepared. The basic layout of the model would be based on the separation of input areas from display areas, so that the cash forecast itself simply picks up data which is

input into another cell of the spreadsheet containing the data and the underlying relation-ships to be used. With this kind of layout it becomes easy to see the effect of changes to either the raw data, or to the assumptions underpinning the model of the cash flows produced.

In practice, cash budget information will be sourced from many areas from within a large organisation, to be pulled together within the accounting department, so that the overall impact upon cash flow can be predicted.

The great advantage of the spreadsheet lies in its speed of calculation, and in its flexibility in the context of 'what-if' or sensitivity analysis. The danger is that, through unnecessary complexity and poor layout, the data becomes corrupted or poorly presented through the set up of the spreadsheet itself – the apparent ease of model building leading to poorly constructed models. If this can be avoided, spreadsheets offer to users an extremely powerful means of building a useful predictive tool.

3. Feedforward control represents a situation when predictions are used to modify action so that potential, future threats or adverse variances are avoided or opportunities exploited. A cash forecast may indicate that insufficient cash will be generated to enable objectives to be achieved. By being forewarned, action to improve cash flow can be taken, so that the objectives are in fact achieved through the modification of immediate actions.

Feedback control is exercised by comparison of actual against forecast, any difference identified being explained and used (although it is by definition, historical) to control current operations. Thus, the reasons for a cost overspend, for example, during the period under review would be sought, and the implications for the future determined.

## Solution 14.2 (Preparation of a Master Budget in a Service Firm)

1.
### Olga Carr (Nicosia Gym)
### Budgeted statement of cash inflows and cash outflows ...

|  | € |
|---|---|
| Cash inflows: |  |
| Obtaining share capital | 30,000 |
| Obtaining bank loan | 15,000 |
| Membership fees (see above) | 75,000 |
| Total cash inflows | 120,000 |
| Cash outflows: |  |
| Purchase of gym equipment | 30,000 |
| Cost of office equipment | 10,000 |
| Loan repayment (including interest) | 6,000 |
| Rent paid to owner | 10,000 |
| Electricity and water | 4,000 |
| General cleaning costs | 3,000 |
| Advertising | 5,000 |

| | |
|---|---:|
| Labour costs and administration | 6,000 |
| Total cash outflows | 74,000 |
| Projected closing cash balance (B/S) | + 46,000 |

**2.**

**Olga Carr (Nicosia Gym)**
**Budgeted income statement for first year of operations**

| | € |
|---|---:|
| Membership fees | 75,000 |
| Less: Costs: | |
| Loan interest | 1,500 |
| Rent of premises | 10,000 |
| Electricity and water | 4,000 |
| General cleaning | 3,000 |
| Advertising | 5,000 |
| Labour costs and administration | 6,000 |
| Depr. of gym and assessment equipment | 10,000 |
| Depr. of office equipment | 2,000 |
| Projected profit for first year of operations (T/f to Balance Sheet) | 33,500 |

**3.**

**Olga Carr (Nicosia Gym)**
**Projected Balance Sheet at end of first year of operations**

| | € |
|---|---:|
| Non-current assets | |
| Gym equipment (at net book value) | 20,000 |
| Office equipment (at net book value) | 8,000 |
| Current assets | |
| Stock (inventory) | Nil |
| Accounts receivable (debtors) | Nil |
| Cash/Bank balance | 46,000 |
| Total Assets | 74,000 |
| Financed by: | |
| Share Capital | 30,000 |
| Retained profits | 33,500 |
| Long-term loan payable | 10,500 |
| Current liabilities | |
| Accounts payable (creditors) | Nil |
| Bank overdraft | Nil |
| Total Liabilities and Shareholders' Funds | 74,000 |

## Solution 15.1 (Production Overhead Cost Variances under Absorption Costing)

### 1. Calculation of the production overhead variances:

The standard cost elements for the variable and fixed production overhead are:

| | Budgeted costs ÷ | | Normal output = | Standard cost |
|---|---|---|---|---|
| Var. OH: €135,000 | × 80% = | €108,000 | 9,000 units | €12.00 per unit |
| | | | | (€6.00 per hour) |
| Fixed OH: €135,000 | × 20% = | €27,000 | 9,000 units | €3.00 per unit |
| | | | | (€1.50 per hour) |

**Variable overheads (absorbed at €6 per direct labour hour)**

| | Hours | € | | Hours | € |
|---|---|---|---|---|---|
| Input | 17,200 | 108,500 | Finished | | |
| | | | 8,500 units | 17,000 | 102,000 |
| | | | Efficiency Var. | 200 | 1,200 |
| | | | Rate Var. | N/A | 5,300 |
| | | | Balance | Nil | Nil |
| | 17,200 | 108,500 | | 17,200 | 108,500 |

**Fixed overheads (absorbed at €1.50 per direct labour hour)**

| | Hours | € | | Hours | € |
|---|---|---|---|---|---|
| Input | 18,000 * | 28,000 | Finished | | |
| | | | 8,500 units | 17,000 | 25,500 |
| | | | Volume Var. | 1,000 | 1,500 |
| | | | Spending Var. | N/A | 1,000 |
| | | | Balance | Nil | Nil |
| | 18,000 | 28,000 | | 18,000 | 28,000 |

\* **Note:** budgeted hours

### 2. Responsibility for fixed production overhead volume variance

The fixed production overhead volume variance is calculated as the difference between **standard** hours for the actual output and **budgeted** hours multiplied by the fixed production overhead rate per hour. The above calculation of the fixed production overhead volume variance does not mean that costs were €1,500 more than anticipated. Rather, it means that actual production was not available to absorb all the fixed overheads that were expected to occur. Simply, this results in an under-absorption of fixed production overheads. (The volume variance can also be favourable – this will occur when actual production volume is greater than expected.)

The inevitable question is: who is responsible for the fixed overhead volume variance? It is not the production manager since it can be argued that he does not establish his production schedule in isolation. Rather the volume of production is determined by a group of managers on the basis of anticipated customer orders and other factors. This being so, the fixed overhead volume variance is not really controllable by the production manager and should not be attributed to him. It is simply a variance which can help explain the total overhead variance to top management, where a company operates a standard absorption costing system. This variance will not be computed under standard variable (direct) costing systems.

The more important question is why was capacity NOT utilised as anticipated? Clearly sales forecasts are always uncertain and such variances can be expected to occur. Another possible explanation is that some machines malfunctioned during the period which curtailed production or there may have been an industrial dispute or restriction on the availability of direct materials. Therefore, it is important to understand the causes of variances before corrective action can be taken. Furthermore, managers may find it easier to react to non-financial data, e.g. machine running hours or units produced during the period under review and compared against agreed targets.

*Solution 15.2 (Profit Reconciliation under Standard Costing (Variable and Absorption))*

**1.**          **Comparison of static and flexed budgets and actual income summary for quarter ......**

|  | Static budget | Flexed budget | Actual | Operating variances |
|---|---|---|---|---|
| Sales units | 10,000 | 9,500 | 9,500 | |
| Sales revenue | 250,000 | 237,500 | 247,000 | 9,500 F |
| Direct materials | 60,000 | 57,000 | 61,000 | (4,000) A |
| Direct labour | 80,000 | 76,000 | 72,000 | 4,000 F |
| Variable production overhead | 40,000 | 38,000 | 40,000 | (2,000) A |
| Variable administration overhead | 20,000 | 19,000 | 24,000 | (5,000) A |
| Contribution | 50,000 | | | |
| Fixed production overhead | 30,000 | 30,000 | 18,000 | 12,000 F |
| Fixed administration overhead | 20,000 | 20,000 | 22,000 | (2,000)A |
| Net profit | Nil | (2,500) | 10,000 | 12,500 |

The difference between the static and flexed budget profits can be explained by the sales volume variance. There were 500 less units sold than expected and the adverse financial impact is:

Sales volume variance: $(10,000 - 9,500) \times €5$ contribution per unit $= (€2,500)$ Adverse

In addition, the operating variances can be divided between the sales price variance and the various cost variances, subdivided as appropriate.

The sales price variance is: $(€26 - €25) \times 9,500 = €9,500$ F

| | € |
|---|---|
| Static budget profit (given) | Nil |
| Less: sales volume variance | (2,500) A |
| $(9,500 - 10,000) \times €5$ per unit | |
| = Flexed budget LOSS for quarter | (2,500) |
| Sales price variance | 9,500 F |
| $(€26 - €25) \times 9,500$ units | |
| Materials price variance | (1,000) A |
| $(€0.61 - €0.60) \times 100,000$ feet | |
| Materials usage variance | (3,000) A |
| $(100,000 - 95,000) \times 0.60$ per foot | |
| Labour rate variance | 8,000 F |
| $(€1.80 - €2.00) \times 40,000$ hours | |
| Labour efficiency variance | (4,000) A |
| $(40,000 - 38,000) \times €2$ per hour | |
| Variable overhead rate variance | Nil |
| $(€1.00 - €1.00) \times 40,000$ hours | |
| Variable overhead efficiency variance | (2,000) A |
| $(40,000 - 38,000) \times €1$ per hour | |
| Variable administration overhead spending variance | (5,000) A |
| Fixed production overhead spending variance | 12,000 F |
| $(€18,000 - €12,000)$ | |
| Fixed administration overhead spending variance | (2,000) A |
| Actual profit for period | 10,000 |

## 2. Variable (direct) costing

### Profit reconciliation (variable costing)

The cost variances are calculated by way of 'T-account' although the formula method could also be used and would provide identical answers.

### Direct materials @ €0.60 per foot

|        | Feet    | €      |              | Feet    | €      |
|--------|---------|--------|--------------|---------|--------|
| Input  | 100,000 | 61,000 | Finished     |         |        |
|        |         |        | (9,500)      | 95,000  | 57,000 |
|        |         |        | Usage Var.   | 5,000   | 3,000  |
|        |         |        | Price Var.   | N/A     | 1,000  |
|        | 100,000 | 61,000 |              | 100,000 | 61,000 |

### Direct labour @ €5 per hour

|          | Hours  | €      |          | Hours  | €      |
|----------|--------|--------|----------|--------|--------|
| Input    | 40,000 | 72,000 | Finished |        |        |
|          |        |        | (9,500)  | 38,000 | 76,000 |
|          |        |        | Eff'y Var.| 2,000 | 4,000  |
| Rate Var.| N/A    | 8,000  |          |        |        |
|          | 40,000 | 80,000 |          | 40,000 | 80,000 |

### Variable overheads @ €1.00 per DLH(€40,000/40,000 DLH)

|          | Hours  | €      |          | Hours  | €      |
|----------|--------|--------|----------|--------|--------|
| Input    | 40,000 | 40,000 | Finished |        |        |
|          |        |        | (9,500)  | 38,000 | 38,000 |
|          |        |        | Eff' Var.| 2,000  | 2,000  |
| Rate Var.| N/A    | NIL    |          |        |        |
|          | 40,000 | 40,000 |          | 40,000 | 40,000 |

### Fixed cost variances

|                         | Actual  | Budget  | Cost variance |
|-------------------------|---------|---------|---------------|
| Production overheads    | €18,000 | €30,000 | 12,000 F      |
| Administration overheads| €22,000 | €20,000 | (2,000) A     |

### 3. Absorption costing

Under absorption costing, the profit reconciliation will contain two differences, namely a change in the sales volume variance and an additional variance – a fixed production volume variance. The calculations are as follows:

Sales volume variance (500 units at €2) = (€1,000) A

The profit margin of €2 per unit represents the existing unit contribution (€5) less fixed production overhead per unit (€3, i.e. €30,000/10,000) under absorption costing.

   Under absorption costing, a fixed production overhead volume variance is calculated. First, we need to calculate the fixed production overhead absorption rate, based on direct labour hours. The calculation for the quarter, based on a normal output of 10,000 units per quarter (40,000 units per annum) – each requiring 4 hours of labour – would be:

Fixed production overhead absorption rate = €120,000/4 quarters = $\dfrac{€120,000}{€160,000 \text{ hours}}$ = €0.75 per hour

The fixed production overhead volume variance represents the difference between budgeted fixed production overhead (€30,000) and fixed production overhead absorbed (9,500 units × 4 hours × €0.75 = €28,500).

These two variances combined will explain the profit difference between static and flexed budget. The static and flexed net profit figures are exactly the same under both variable and absorption costing. This is because the number of units produced equals the number of units sold, so that no additional fixed production overhead is being carried in closing stock valuation.

### Profit reconciliation (absorption costing)

|  | € |
|---|---|
| Static budget profit (given) | Nil |
| Less: sales volume variance | (1,000) A |
| fixed production overhead volume variance | (1,500) A |
| = Flexed budget profit | (2,500) |
| Sales price variance | 9,500 F |
| Materials price variance | (1,000) A |
| Materials usage variance | (3,000) A |
| Labour rate variance | 8,000 F |
| Labour efficiency variance | (4,000) A |
| Variable overhead rate variance | Nil |
| Variable overhead efficiency variance | (2,000) A |
| Fixed production overhead spending variance | 12,000 F |
| Variable administration overhead spending variance | (5,000) A |
| Fixed administration overhead spending variance | (2,000) A |
| Actual profit for period | 10,000 |

## Solution 16.1 (Multi-choice Questions on Responsibility Centres)

| Question | Answer | Question | Answer |
|---|---|---|---|
| 1 | D | 11 | C |
| 2 | A | 12 | B |
| 3 | C | 13 | A |
| 4 | A | 14 | D |
| 5 | D | 15 | C |
| 6 | C | 16 | A |
| 7 | D | 17 | B |
| 8 | B | 18 | D |
| 9 | D | 19 | D |
| 10 | C | 20 | C |

## Solution 16.2 (Measuring Performance in Responsibility Centres)

**1.** Measures of performance to evaluate responsibility centres are, traditionally, based on accounting numbers. For example, for an investment centre, most text books suggest the use of financial metrics such as Return on Investment (RoI) and Residual Income (RI) which take account of the level of investment in the division.

The limitations of these measures are many but can be summarised as follows, although not necessarily in order of importance:

RoI or RI measures encourage a short-term focus since they are based on the profit reported for the period – typically one year or less. Responsible managers, evaluated by these metrics, are encouraged to make decisions which improve the short-term profit of the division and thus they may sacrifice long-term profitability and growth to this end.

All of these measures being financial in orientation may encourage managers to prioritise financial issues over non-financial issues in the division. Today it is recognised that the critical success factors for many firms are non-financial factors such as customer satisfaction and loyalty, based on quality of product and customer service. The exclusive use of financial performance measures may divert a manager's attention away from the important things that matter – the critical success factors and related key performance indicators.

Traditional performance measures typically use profit measures generated by an absorption costing system, i.e. a portion of fixed production overhead is automatically included in closing inventory valuation. The use of such a system encourages excessive focus on increasing output but increasing output, for inventory purposes, may not be in the best interest of the firm.

There are particular problems associated with RoI. RoI measures divisional performance as the profit of the division divided by the funds invested in that division. Thus managers will be motivated to make decisions to improve the profit of the division as mentioned above, but they will also be motivated to contain or reduce the capital of the business. This may result in managers making inappropriate asset replacement decisions, i.e. preferring to hold on to assets which have low depreciation charges and reduced net book values at the expense of acquiring new modern assets. Another problem with RoI is that managers will not wish to accept a project which may decrease the anticipated RoI of their division, even though the project for the company as a whole may be beneficial. Equally another project, which has a low return, may be accepted by a manager whose division is posting low RoI. It is possible in some situations that projects, which should be otherwise rejected, may, in fact, be accepted as a device to increase a low RoI.

RI overcomes many of the problems of RoI. RI is defined as divisional contribution less a cost of capital charge for the capital or assets employed in the division. The difficulty with RI is that it is an absolute measure (RoI is a percentage calculation) and therefore does not facilitate comparison of the performance of different divisions.

## 2. Alternative divisional performance measures

**Non-financial performance measures:** As mentioned above it is essential that an organisation identifies its critical success factors. These key factors will be the drivers of future success and are important elements in the firm's strategy. It is essential that appropriate key performance indicators reflect these critical success factors. Thus, if an organisation identifies product quality, customer service, innovation or other qualitative factors as its critical success factors, then the firm should adopt appropriate key performance indicators. Therefore, the firm must design measures that are suitable to review quality, service or innovation performance. There is no 'generic' set of measures that an organisation can adopt or import. Rather each organisation must review its own key success factors and design suitable measures for its own purpose. For example, if customer satisfaction is identified as a key non-financial success factor, suitable performance measures concerning this issue might be:

No. of complaints received
Average length of time to respond to complaints
No. of new customers
Level of repeat orders
Customer ratings of service provided (perhaps gathered through survey)

**New financial measures:** Economic Value Added (EVA) is a financial measure of performance which aims to align management decision-making with the key objective of maximising shareholder wealth. It is similar to RI but it adjusts the profit used in the calculation for distortions caused by generally accepted accounting principles. Thus it is intended that the disclosure and conservative requirements of financial reporting will not distort management decision-making. Rather under EVA, it is argued that managers always have the incentive to create long-term value. (Actually, EVA is similar to the previously mentioned RI, with appropriate accounting adjustments included.)

**Combining financial and non-financial measures:** It is now recognised that the best set of performance measures with which to evaluate any responsibility centre is a combination of financial and non-financial measures. The Balanced Scorecard extensively described by Kaplan and Norton is designed to align a firm's set of performance measures with strategy. It reviews performance in four core areas or perspectives: financial, customer, internal activities, learning and growth. This requires management to identify key objectives in each area and design suitable measures to review performance. However, Kaplan and Norton argue that further perspectives can be added, of which the 'community or environmental perspective' is the most common. In simple terms, the Balance Scorecard and its many derivatives are based on the simple construct: you get what you measure.

# Glossary of Management Accounting Terms

## A

**Abnormal gain:** an amount of physical gain that occurs in a manufacturing process, over and above that which is normally expected.

**Abnormal spoilage:** an amount of physical loss that occurs in a manufacturing process, over and above that which is normally expected.

**Absorption costing:** a method of product costing that includes both fixed and variable production costs as product costs.

**Accounts classification:** a technique that involves the identification of each cost element and a subjective analysis of its partition between fixed or variable components.

**Activity:** a unit of work.

**Activity-based budgeting:** an approach to budgeting that uses an activity cost hierarchy to budget physical inputs and costs as a function of planned activity.

**Activity-based costing (ABC):** a costing system that absorbs/assigns overheads to products using activities which cause these overhead costs to be incurred. Some of these will be volume related. Also, non-production costs will be assigned to build up a more complete picture of product cost for decision-making.

**Activity-based cost management (ABCM):** the identification and selection of activities to maximise the value of the activities while minimising their cost from the perspective of the final consumer.

**Agency theory:** a theoretical framework that examines potential conflicts between owners (principals) and managers (agents) and suggests incentives that can be used to reduce agency costs.

**Annuity:** a series of equal cash flows received or paid over equal intervals of time.

**Appraisal costs:** quality costs incurred to identify non-conforming products or services before they are delivered to customers.

**Average cost:** a materials recording system, which divides the total value of purchases by the number of units purchased to provide an average cost figure.

**Average method:** in process costing, a method that records the cost of work completed based on average cost incurred.

## B

**Backflush accounting:** a simplified method for recording cost flows under a JIT system.

**Balance sheet:** a financial picture of the organisation at a specific point in time, showing the assets under the control of the organisation and how they have been financed through shareholders' funds and liabilities.

**Balanced scorecard:** a performance measurement system that includes financial and non-financial measures which are related to the organisation's strategy.

**Benchmarking:** a formal exercise that usually compares similar firms in the industry, with the objective of identifying best practice and, therefore, improving performance. However, an internal benchmarking exercise can also be undertaken within the organisation.

**Beta coefficient:** the rate of change between X (explanatory variable) and Y (dependent variable).

**Break-even point (BEP):** the number of units (or monetary value) where total revenue equals total costs and neither a profit nor loss is generated.

**Budget:** a formal financial plan for a defined, future period of time.

**Budgetary slack:** occurs when managers intentionally understate budget revenues or overstate budget expenses in order to produce favourable variances for the department relative to actual performance.

**Budgeted financial statements:** usually consist of an income statement, cash flow and balance sheet and reflect the financial consequences of all the operating targets for a forthcoming period of time.

**Budgeting:** a process of projecting all the operations of an organisation and their financial impact.

**By-product:** A joint product whose sales value is not material compared with the total market value of all the joint products.

## C

**Capital budgeting:** a process that involves the identification of potentially desirable projects for capital expenditures, the subsequent evaluation of capital expenditure proposals, and the selection of proposals that meet certain criteria.

**Capital expenditure:** long-term investments of significant financial resources in projects to develop or introduce new products or services, to expand current production or service capacity, or to change current production or service facilities.

**Cash budget:** a statement presenting all the cash receipts and cash payments anticipated during a forthcoming budget period.

**Cash cow:** a product that has a low growth rate but high relative market share, based on the BCG growth/market share matrix.

**Cash flow statement:** a summary of cash inflows and cash outflows for the accounting period under review.

**Clock cards:** a docket used by employees to record total hours worked during the accounting period which are often supplemented by job cards.

**Coefficient of determination ($R^2$):** a measure of the percentage variation in the dependent variable that is explained by variations in the independent variable when the ordinary least squares method is used.

**Common cost:** a cost incurred for the benefit of two or more cost objectives – an indirect cost.

**Confidence interval:** a range of values used to estimate a variable with a specific confidence level – usually 95%.

**Contribution income statement:** an income statement format in which variable costs are subtracted from revenues to highlight contribution margin, and fixed costs are then subtracted from contribution margin to calculate net profit.

**Contribution margin:** the difference between total revenues and total variable costs; this amount goes toward covering fixed costs and providing a profit.

**Contribution sales ratio:** a ratio between unit contribution and sales price and which should be less than 1.

**Control/controlling:** the process of monitoring results against targets and deciding on corrective action, if appropriate.

**Control action point:** a situation where there is a significant variance between budgeted targets and actual performance highlighting the need for corrective action to be taken.

**Control by comparison:** the process of monitoring actual results against original targets to reveal variances.

**Control decision point:** a phase when a decision must be taken regarding whether a variance between budgeted targets and actual performance is significant or not.

**Conversion cost:** the combined costs of direct labour and manufacturing overhead incurred to convert raw materials into finished goods.

**Cost:** the resources consumed and/or foregone in order to achieve a particular objective.

**Cost allocation:** the process of assigning a direct cost to a single cost objective.

**Cost apportionment:** the (arbitrary) process of assigning overhead (indirect) costs to two or more cost objectives.

**Cost behaviour:** an analysis of how different costs respond to changes in the level of a related cost driver, often assumed to be units of output.

**Cost centre:** a responsibility centre whose manager is responsible only for managing costs in order to provide specific outputs. It is also referred to as an expense centre.

**Cost classification:** grouping of costs according to their common characteristics.

**Cost driver:** any factor that affects costs in a significant way.

**Cost estimation:** the determination of a formal relationship between cost and related cost drivers.

**Cost leadership:** a strategy whereby a firm outperforms competitors by producing products or services at the lowest cost.

**Cost management:** a process of transforming a firm's cost base through the identification of activities that cause costs to be incurred.

**Cost objective:** a product, object or activity for which cost data is required.

**Cost of capital:** the average cost of obtaining the resources necessary to make capital expenditure decisions.

**Cost of Quality (CoQ) report:** A report that attempts to compute a single aggregate measure of all explicit costs attributable to preventing and correcting defective products.

**Cost pool:** an area within the organisation that performs a significant activity and for which costs can be accumulated.

**Cost prediction:** the forecasting of future costs using a cost prediction model.

**Cost plus pricing:** a method of pricing based on costs incurred together with a profit margin included.

**Cost reduction:** identifying methods to reduce the cost of an activity.

**Cost structure:** the various cost elements and related classification which comprise total cost for the accounting period.

**Cost volume profit (CVP) analysis:** a technique used to examine the relationships between total volume, some independent variables, total costs, total revenues, and profits during a time period (typically a month or a year).

**Cost volume profit graph:** an illustration of the relationships between volume, total revenues, total costs and profits.

**Critical success factor:** an area in which superior performance is required for the firm to be successful and which is often measured in non-financial terms.

**Customer profitability analysis:** a technique associated with activity-based costing, which attempts to identify the profitability or otherwise of different customer segments.

**D**

**Data:** facts that are gathered on an individual or phenomenon under study.

**Decentralisation:** the freedom given to managers of responsibility centres to make decisions.

**Decision tree:** a diagram that shows the various decisions which a decision-maker can take and the various outcomes or states of nature that can occur.

**Denominator:** The denominator is the lower portion of a fraction used to calculate a rate or ratio including OHARs.

**Dependent variable:** a term used when predicting the value of a variable which commonly is the level of future costs.

**Differentiation:** a strategy whereby a firm outperforms competitors by offering superior quality of its products or services.

**Direct cost:** a cost that can be identified specifically with, or traced to, a given cost objective in an economically feasible way.

**Direct costing:** see *variable costing.*

**Direct labour:** wages earned by production employees for working on the manufacturing process.

**Direct materials:** basic materials that are converted into finished goods.

**Direct method:** a method of assigning service department costs to production departments based on the amount of services provided to production departments only.

**Discount rate:** the minimum rate of return required for an investment to be acceptable.

**Dog:** a product that has a poor competitive position based on the BCG growth/share matrix.

**Dual price:** the contribution foregone for want of an extra unit of a specified scarce resource. It is also referred to as a shadow price.

**Dysfunctional behaviour:** behaviour in an organisation that is not intended and which has adverse consequences.


E

**Elasticity:** the responsiveness of demand to price changes. If small changes in price result in large demand changes, the product is described as being elastic.

**Equivalent units:** a number of finished units that is equal, in terms of production output, to a given number of partially completed units in a production process.

**Expected Monetary Value (EMV):** the weighted average pay-off of each decision alternative, where the monetary pay-off of each state of nature is multiplied by its respective probability.

**Expected value of perfect information (EVPI):** a monetary amount determined as the difference between expected monetary value, given perfect information and the expected monetary value of an alternative, given current information.

**Expenses centre:** a responsibility centre whose manager is responsible only for managing costs in order to provide specific outputs. Also, referred to as a cost centre.

**External failure costs:** costs incurred when non-conforming products or services are delivered to customers.


F

**Feedback:** providing information on actual performance compared with budget or targets.

**Financial accounting:** an information processing system that generates general-purpose reports such as the income and cash flow statements and balance sheet of the firm.

**Financial reporting:** the process of preparing the income and cash flow statements, balance sheet and accompanying notes in accordance with generally accepted accounting principles which, increasingly, are based on international financial reporting standards (IFRSs).

**Finished goods inventory:** the completely manufactured goods held for sale to customers.

**FIFO (First in, First out):** a materials recording system, which assumes that the first unit purchased is the first item to be issued to production.

**FIFO (First in, First out) method:** in process costing, a method that accounts for unit costs of opening inventory units separately from those started during the current period. The first costs incurred each period are assumed to have been used to complete the unfinished units from the previous period.

**Fixed cost:** a cost whose total is unaffected by changes in the cost driver level, often assumed to be units of output.

**Fixed production overhead:** all fixed costs associated with converting direct materials into finished goods.

**Fixed overhead spending (or budget) variance:** the difference between budgeted fixed overhead and actual fixed overhead incurred during the period.

**Fixed overhead volume variance:** the difference between total budgeted fixed overhead and total standard fixed overhead assigned to production.

**Flexible (flexed) budget:** a budget that is prepared at the end of the period, based on actual output and, therefore, reflects what costs should have been for an attained level of output.

**Focus strategy:** a strategy that focuses on market niches, in which competition is typically weakest.

**Full costs:** an approach to pricing whereby all costs (fixed and variable) are included in determining total cost.

**Future value:** the amount a current sum of money earning a stated rate of interest will accumulate to at the end of a future period.

## G

**Goal:** a definable, measurable objective, usually of a long-term nature.

**Goal congruence:** a situation where there is consistency between the goals of the organisation and the goals of its employees.

## H

**Heterogeneous products:** products that are considered to be dissimilar by customers.

**High–low method of cost estimation:** utilises data from two time periods, a *representative* high activity period and a *representative* low activity period, to estimate fixed and variable costs.

**Historical costs:** costs relating from past decisions that cannot be changed.

**Homogeneous products:** products that are considered to be similar by customers.

## I

**Imperfect information:** information that is less than 100 per cent reliable.

**Income statement:** a summary of economic events during a period of time, showing the revenues generated by operating activities, the expenses incurred in generating those revenues, and any gains or losses attributed to the period.

**Incremental budgeting:** an approach to budgeting where costs for the forthcoming accounting period are based on agreed percentage changes applied to the previous period's budget or actual expenditure.

**Incremental cash cost:** a cash outlay that results from choosing a particular alternative.

**Independent variable:** a term used to explain the behaviour in the dependent variable in prediction and, in cost prediction, can be referred to as a cost driver.

**Indirect costs:** costs that must be shared arbitrarily between two or more cost objectives.

**Information:** Data that has a surprise effect on the user and has decision relevance.

**Inspection time:** the amount of time it takes units of output to be inspected.

**Internal controls:** an internal system of operating and financial controls established by management so that transactions can be recorded in an orderly and accurate manner and the assets of the firm protected.

**Internal failure costs:** quality costs incurred when materials, components, products, or services are identified as defective before delivery to customers.

**Internal rate of return (IRR):** the discount rate at which the net present value of a proposal is zero.

**Investment centre:** a responsibility centre whose manager is responsible for revenues, costs and overall investment in fixed assets.

**Irrelevant costs:** costs that do not differ among competing decision alternatives.

## J

**Job card:** a work docket indicating the required activities to be performed on a particular job according to client specifications.

**Job costing:** the manufacture of products, or delivery of services, in single customised units (or in special batches).

**Job cost sheet:** a document used to accumulate the costs for a specific job in a cost system.

**Joint cost:** The various costs which are incurred in producing all the joint products simultaneously.

**Joint product:** A product that is produced simultaneously with other products in a production process.

**Just in Time System:** A system that arranges the purchase of raw materials when they are needed and also schedules the production of finished goods when required by customers.

## K

**Kaizen costing:** a commitment by Japanese management and workers to continuously evaluate products and their production processes in an attempt to do things better and reduce costs.

## L

**Labour efficiency variance:** the difference between the standard cost of actual labour inputs and the flexible budget cost of labour.

**Labour rate (spending) variance:** the difference between the actual cost and the standard cost of actual labour inputs.

**Least regret:** a decision criterion which minimises the differences between expected pay-off and the pay-off that would have been generated if the outcome was known in advance.

**LIFO (Last in, First out) method:** a material recording system, which assumes that the last unit purchased is the first item to be issued to production.

**Limiting factor:** a resource constraint, e.g. shortage of raw materials, which restricts the ability of a business to produce goods or services.

**Linear programming:** a mathematical technique designed to identify the optimal solution, in physical and monetary terms, given multiple products and multiple constraints. The model assumes a linear relationship between all the input variables.

## M

**Management accounting:** a discipline concerned with financial and related information used by managers and other persons inside organisations to make strategic, planning and control decisions.

**Management by exception:** an approach to performance evaluation which focuses only on those areas where differences between target and actual results are deemed to be significant or important.

**Manufacturing cost budget:** a budget detailing the direct materials, direct labour, and manufacturing overhead costs that should be incurred by manufacturing operations to produce the number of units required for the production budget.

**Manufacturing organisations:** organisations that process raw materials into finished products for sale to others.

**Manufacturing overhead:** all manufacturing costs incurred during a period other than direct materials and direct labour.

**Margin of safety:** the amount by which actual or planned sales exceed the break-even point.

**Marginal cost:** the change in total cost as a result of producing one additional unit and which can often be used in pricing decisions.

**Marginal revenue:** the varying increment in total revenue derived from the sale of an additional unit.

**Master budget:** the grouping together of all financial and operational activities into a cash budget, a budgeted income statement and a projected balance sheet.

**Materials price variance:** the difference between the actual materials cost and the standard cost of actual materials inputs.

**Materials usage variance:** the difference between the standard cost of actual materials inputs and the flexible budget cost for materials.

**Materials requisition docket:** a document required to release materials from the store room and which records the type and quantity of each raw material issued to the factory.

**Maximin:** a conservative or pessimistic decision criterion in which the 'best' of the worst possible outcomes is selected.

**Maximax:** an optimistic decision criterion in which the alternative, which offers the greatest pay-off, is selected.

**Mission:** the basic purpose toward which an organisation's activities are directed.

**Mixed cost:** a cost that contains both a fixed and a variable cost element.

**Model:** a simplified representation of some real-world phenomenon.

**Multinational entity (MNE):** an enterprise that owns and controls value-adding activities in more than one country.

N

**Net present value:** the present value of a project's net cash inflows from operations and end of period disinvestment less the amount of the initial investment.

**Net realizable value:** Sales value less further processing and non-processing costs.

**Normal costing:** a method of costing which uses actual direct material and actual direct labour costs in addition to an estimated amount of production overhead based on a predetermined or budgeted OHAR.

**Normal spoilage:** an amount of physical loss usually expected in a manufacturing process.

**Non-value added activity:** an activity that does not add value to a product or service from the viewpoint of the customer. Customers will not be prepared to pay for such activities if they know about them.

O

**Objective:** a specific target to be achieved in the future.

**Objective function:** the value to be maximised in linear programming, determined with reference to unit contributions and the physical mix. (The objective function value could be minimised in the case of cost-reduction projects.)

**OHAR (overhead absorption rate):** a method of assigning a particular amount of overhead costs to units of output using a predetermined calculation, established at the start of the year, dividing budgeted overheads by the predicted level of related cost driver.

**Operating activities:** normal profit-related activities performed in conducting the daily affairs of an organisation. These are the major concerns of management in preparing and monitoring operating budgets.

**Operating budget:** detailed plans to guide operations throughout the budget period.

**Operating department:** a department that provides goods or services to customers for which they are charged.

**Operating leverage:** a measure of the extent to which an organisation's costs are fixed in relation to changes in volume.

**Opportunity cost:** the net cash inflow that could be generated if the resources committed to one action were used in the most desirable alternative.

**Optimal solution:** in linear programming models, the feasible solution that maximises or minimises the value of the objective function, depending on the decision-maker's goal.

**Ordinary least-squares regression:** a mathematical technique which fits a cost estimating equation to the observed data in a manner that minimises the sum of the vertical squared estimating errors between the estimated and actual costs at each observation.

**Organisation structure:** the arrangement of lines of responsibility within the organisation.

**Outsourcing:** the external acquisition of services or products.

**Over-absorbed overhead:** this occurs when the amount of overhead absorbed by production is greater than the actual amount of overhead incurred during the accounting period.

**Overhead absorption:** the process of assigning overhead costs to units of output, often using a selected cost driver such as direct labour or machine hours.

**Overheads:** costs that must be shared arbitrarily between two or more cost objectives.

P

**Payback period:** the time required to recover the initial investment in a project from operating cash flows.

**Penetration pricing:** an aggressive pricing policy that results in low selling prices, aimed to generate large and immediate market share.

**Perfect information:** a decision situation in which the decision-maker has advance and totally reliable knowledge of what will happen in the future.

**Performance measurement:** an activity which gathers data on a range of both financial and non-financial measures of performance which are important for an enterprise's success and which include comparing budget with actual outcomes.

**Period costs:** costs not related to manufacturing operations and are written off to the income statement as and when incurred.

**Periodic inventory system:** An inventory system whereby the physical amount of inventory is determined at the end of the accounting period by way of a physical count. It is usually associated with businesses that sell products of relatively low unit cost.

**Perpetual inventory system:** An inventory system in which the physical amount of inventory is kept continuously up-to-date and is usually associated with high value products.

**Planning:** the process of deciding on goals and objectives and how to achieve them.

**Present value:** the current worth of a specified amount of money to be received at some future date at some interest rate.

**Prevention costs:** costs incurred to prevent non-conforming products from being produced or non-conforming services from being performed.

**Price skimming:** a pricing policy that results in high selling prices.

**Prior department costs:** a situation which occurs in process costing whereby work is transferred from one department to another for subsequent processing.

**Process:** a collection of related activities intended to achieve a common purpose.

**Process costing:** the manufacture of similar products (but could also be the provision of services) on a mass and continuous basis.

**Process re-engineering:** the fundamental redesign of a process to serve internal or external customers.

**Processing time:** the time spent working on units.

**Product costs:** all costs incurred in the manufacture of products and which are used to value closing inventory.

**Product level activity:** an activity performed to support the production of each different type of product.

**Production department:** a department that produces goods for customers.

**Productivity:** an economic measure of efficiency, based on what was produced during a period in relation to the resources consumed, i.e. outputs divided by inputs.

**Profitability analysis:** an examination of the relationships between revenues, costs, and profits.

**Profitability index:** the present value of a project's operating cash flow divided by the initial investment.

**Profit centre:** a responsibility centre whose manager is responsible for revenues and costs.

**Profit reconciliation:** a technique associated with standard costing whereby static budget and actual profit figures are reconciled by a series of variance calculations.

**Purchases budget:** indicates the merchandise or materials that must be acquired to meet current needs and ending inventory requirements.

## Q

**Quality:** conformance to customer expectations.

**Quality costs:** costs associated with implementing quality in all aspects of operations.

**Quality of conformance:** the degree of conformance between a product and its design specifications.

**Quantitative model:** a set of mathematical relationships.

## R

**Reciprocal method:** a method of assigning service department costs that fully recognises services provided to other service departments. This method uses simultaneous equations to assign service department costs between service departments and production departments.

**Recovery of non-production overhead:** assigning a particular amount of non-production overhead costs to units of output using a predetermined calculation, established at the start of the year.

**Regression analysis:** a statistical technique which allows an objective linear cost function to be identified from a given data set.

**Relative market share:** The market share enjoyed by a firm relative to its next largest competitor.

**Relevant costs:** future costs that differ between competing decision alternatives.

**Relevant information:** information which has the potential to influence decisions.

**Relevant range:** the range of activity within which the assumption about fixed and variable cost behaviour, with reference to volume changes, remains valid.

**Responsibility accounting:** the structuring of performance reports addressed to individual (or group) members of an organisation in a manner that emphasises the factors they are able to control. The focus is on specific units within the organisation that are responsible for the accomplishment of specific activities or objectives.

**Responsibility centre:** a responsibility centre is any unit within an organisation that is headed by a manager who is accountable for those activities over which he can exert significant influence.

**Retail organisations:** entities that buy and sell goods without performing manufacturing operations.

**Return on investment (ROI):** a measure of the profit related to investment. The return on investment of an investment centre is computed by dividing the income of the centre by its asset base (usually total assets).

**Revenues:** inflows of resources from the sale of goods and services.

**Risk:** a decision situation in which probabilities can be reasonably assigned to potential outcomes.

**Risk neutral:** an attitude of a decision-maker who neither likes risk (risk lover) nor is afraid of it (risk averse).

**Rolling budget:** a budget system which adds an identical time period to the budget as each subperiod elapses, thereby always maintaining an overall budget period of exactly the same duration.

S

**Sales budget:** a plan of unit sales volume and sales revenue for a future period. It may also contain a forecast of cash collections from sales.

**Sales mix:** the relative portion of unit or monetary sales generated from each product or service.

**Sales price variance:** the impact on revenues of a change in selling price, given the actual sales volume. It is computed as the change in selling price times the actual sales volume.

**Sales volume variance:** indicates the impact on profit of change in sales volume, assuming there is no change in selling price. It is computed as the difference between the actual and the budgeted sales volume times the budgeted unit contribution (under variable costing).

**Scatter diagram:** a graph of past activity and cost data with individual observations represented by dots.

**Scrap:** the amount realised from the sale of defective goods.

**Selling and distribution costs:** all costs associated with the sale and distribution of products. They are period rather than product costs.

**Sensitivity analysis:** the study of responsiveness of a model to change in one or more of its independent variables.

**Service department:** a department that provides support services to other departments in the organisation.

**Service department (cost) reapportionment:** the assigning of service department costs to other departments in the organisation.

**Service organisations:** non-manufacturing organisations that perform work for others, including banks, hospitals, and other service firms.

**Set-up time:** the time required to prepare equipment to produce a specific product.

**Sequential method:** a method of service department cost reapportionment which begins with the service department that provides the greatest amount of service to other service departments.

**Shadow price:** the contribution foregone for want of an extra unit of a specified scarce resource.

**Shareholder value:** an argument that the primary role for any commercial enterprise is to maximise the value of shareholders' investment.

**Short-termism:** a management approach which focuses on short-term performance, sometimes to the detriment of long-term performance.

**Specific costs:** The costs incurred after split-off point (in joint costing) and represents the end point in a joint production process.

**Split-off point:** A stage of production when joint products assume their separate identities for the first time.

**Spoilage:** the physical amount of defective goods produced by a manufacturing process during an accounting period. Some of these may be sold as 'scrap'.

**Spending variance:** the difference between actual and planned expenditure during an accounting period and which can be favourable or adverse.

**Standard cost/costing:** a product costing system, based on a budgeted cost per unit, under efficient operating conditions.

**Standard cost variance analysis:** a system for examining the difference between the actual cost and flexible budget cost of producing a given quantity of product or service.

**Standard deviation:** a measure of variation of values around the mean.

**Star:** a product that has a high growth rate and high market share based on the BCG growth/share matrix.

**Statement of cost of goods manufactured:** a report that summarises the cost of goods completed and transferred into finished goods inventory during the period.

**Static budget:** a budget based on a prior prediction of expected sales and production.

**Step costs:** costs that are constant within a narrow range of activity but shift to a higher level with an increased range of activity. Total costs increase in a step-like fashion as activity increases.

**Step down method:** a method of service department cost reapportionment which begins with the service department that provides the greatest amount of service to other service departments. This is also referred to as the sequential method.

**Stock record card:** a card maintained by the materials store keeper which records all issues and receipts of inventory of direct materials and, therefore, the amount on hand.

**Stop/go controls:** the range of procedures and policies intended to regulate organisational activities before they happen.

**Strategic analysis:** A management process that involves the identification of the current position of a firm by analysing the environment in which the firm operates (external/environment analysis) and also analysing the firm itself (internal analysis).

**Strategic choice:** A management process that decides on how the firm is going to compete and achieve its overall vision.

**Strategic cost management:** represents making decisions concerning specific cost drivers within the context of an organisation's business strategy, its internal value chain, and its place in a larger value chain stretching from the development and use of resources to the final customers.

**Strategic direction:** A management process that decides on where the firm should be at some time in the future. This involves the preparation of a vision statement.

**Strategic management accounting:** a discipline which focuses on providing information to managers on strategy formation and its effective implementation.

**Strategic plan:** a guideline or framework for making specific medium-range or short-run decisions.

**Strategy:** a shared understanding about how the vision is to be achieved given the organisational strengths and weaknesses, together with the environmental opportunities and threats.

**Sunk costs:** costs relating from past decisions that cannot be changed.

## T

**Target costing:** an approach to pricing which starts with a consideration of what customers are willing to pay for the product with given functions and then subtracting a desired profit margin on sales to give an estimate of the required cost.

**Target volume:** a level of activity (output), which generates a required (pretax) profit target.

**Theory of the firm:** An explanation of how firms choose their prices and quantities and which is based on the assumption that the firm's ultimate objective is to maximize profits.

**Total quality management:** The range of procedures and polices within the organisation in order to facilitate continuous improvement practices.

**Traditional cost accounting (TCA):** a cost accumulation system that absorbs/assigns production overheads to products using volume-based cost drivers, typically, direct labour hours.

**Time sheets:** see clock cards.

**Traceability (of costs):** the ability to assign costs in an economically feasible way to cost objectives.

**Transfer price:** the price at which goods or services are transferred between units of the same corporate family.

**T-statistic:** a statistical value used to determine the reliability of the Beta coefficient in regression analysis.

**T-value:** the Beta coefficient divided by its standard error in regression analysis and is compared with the T-statistic to indicate statistical significance.

## U

**Uncertainty:** a decision situation in which there is a possibility that a forecast event or amount will deviate from the actual outturn but the underlying probabilities are unknown.

**Under-absorbed overhead:** occurs when the amount of overhead absorbed by production is less than the actual amount of overhead incurred during the accounting period.

**Unit contribution:** the difference between the unit selling price and the unit variable costs.

V

**Value:** the worth or usefulness or importance of a product or service to the customer.

**Value chain:** the set of value-producing activities stretching from basic raw materials to the final customer.

**Value-added activity:** an activity that adds value to a product or service from the viewpoint of the customer, who is usually prepared to pay for this activity.

**Value-added tax:** A tax on spending, based on the value that is added to the product (service) at each stage of production. Registered firms act as unpaid tax collectors for the government since they levy VAT on their sales (outputs) but can deduct VAT charged to them on their inputs.

**Value-engineering:** the design of products or their production and distribution in a manner to reduce a given cost base.

**Variable cost:** a cost whose total changes in response to changes in the amount of the related cost driver, often assumed to be units of output. Thus, the average variable cost is constant per unit of output.

**Variable costing:** a method of product costing that includes only variable production costs as product costs and fixed production costs are written off to the income statement as and when incurred.

**Variable production overhead:** all variable costs, except direct labour and direct materials, associated with converting direct materials into finished goods.

**Variable overhead usage variance:** the difference between the standard variable overhead cost for the actual inputs and the flexible budget cost for variable overhead based on outputs.

**Variable overhead spending variance:** the difference between the actual variable overhead cost and the standard variable overhead cost multiplied by the actual inputs.

**Variance:** a comparison of actual and budgeted performance, calculated in financial or non-financial terms.

**VAT:** a tax which firms must charge to their customers and pay to the tax authorities less VAT paid on the firm's inputs.

**Vision:** a formal description of what the organisation could become in the future.

**Volume variance:** the difference between actual and planned activity during an accounting period, which can be favourable or adverse. It can be expressed in physical or monetary terms and can be calculated in different ways.

W

**Weighted average cost of capital:** an average of the after-tax cost of all long-term debt and the cost of equity, based on relative proportions.

**Weighted average method:** in process costing, a costing method that spreads the combined opening inventory cost and current manufacturing costs (for materials, labour, and overhead) over the units completed and closing on an average basis.

**Work-in-progress:** partially completed goods that are in the process of being converted into a finished product.

**World Class Manufacturing (WCM):** the manufacture of high quality products reaching customers quickly (or delivery of a prompt and quality service) at a low cost to provide high customer satisfaction and loyalty.

Z

**Zero-based budgeting:** a method of budgeting in which managers are required to justify all costs as if the proposals involved were being considered for the first time.

# Index